AMAZON FRONTIER

JOHN HEMMING

AMAZON
FRONTIER

The Defeat of the Brazilian Indians

HARVARD UNIVERSITY PRESS
CAMBRIDGE, MASSACHUSETTS
1987

First published in the United Kingdom 1987 by
Macmillan London Limited

Library of Congress Catalog Card Number: 87-35
ISBN 0-674-01725-0

FOR HENRY AND BEATRICE

Contents

List of Illustrations

A Guaikurú chief using stirrups and a jaguar-skin saddle cloth, 1825.

Kayapó women carrying palm leaves.

The author among Txukarramãe, Jarina river, 1971.

Between pages 360–361

A canoe penetrating flooded forest.

Indians cut a passage for the explorer Henri Coudreau.

Fort São Gabriel guarded important rapids on the Rio Negro.

A construction crew on the ill-fated Madeira–Mamoré railway.

Karl von den Steinen descending a rapid on the Xingu.

Railway engineers meeting Karipuna on the Madeira river in the 1870s.

The professional Indian-hunter Martius with his victims, captive Xokleng women and children.

Indians of the Rio Negro during the rubber boom.

Modern Tukuna, living in poverty.

Parintintin were formidable warriors.

The Makuxi village Pirara was disputed by missionaries from Brazil and British Guiana in the 1840s.

A Salesian missionary among Indians of the Uaupés river.

A formal welcome in the village of Carib-speaking Wayaná.

A Wayaná woman removing jiggers from Crevaux's foot.

Steinen's expedition camped among Xingu Indians, 1887.

Steinen's expedition made the first contact with Kalapalo of the upper Xingu in 1884.

Xingu Indians launching a bark canoe.

The tense moment of Steinen's first contact with the Suyá on the Xingu, 1884.

Karl von den Steinen watching Bakairi flute players during his first exploration of the upper Xingu in 1884.

Acknowledgements

This is an opportunity to thank some of the organisations and individuals who helped me on my visits to Brazil. My first contact with Indians, the Iriri River Expedition, was supported by the Royal Geographical Society and by the Blue Star Line, Frigorífico Anglo, Shell and other firms. My next journey to Brazil was made possible by a Miranda Scholarship, awarded by Celso da Rocha Miranda through the Anglo-Brazilian Society. In the field I was encouraged by the greatest Indianists, Orlando and Cláudio Villas Boas, and travelled with Dr Roberto Baruzzi and his splendid team of volunteer doctors from the Escola Paulista de Medicina who give so much devoted care to the Xingu Indians.

In 1972 I was fortunate to be included in the team sent to study Brazilian Indians by the Aborigines Protection Society (part of the Anti-Slavery Society). We wrote a report which augmented that made by my great friends Robin and Marika Hanbury-Tenison on behalf of Survival International. During this visit to all parts of Brazil we were often helped by the staff of Funai, the Fundação Nacional do Indio, and by various missionary orders. But all movement was made possible, on this and other trips to Amazonia, by the daring pilots of the transport wing, Correo Aéreo Nacional, of the Brazilian Air Force, FAB.

When it came to studying the history of Brazilian Indians, I spent many pleasant weeks working in the magnificent library of books about Brazilian Indians belonging to Carlos de Araujo Moreira Neto in Rio de Janeiro. I am also very grateful to the staffs of various libraries: the Biblioteca Municipal in São Paulo, Museu do Indio and Museu Nacional in Rio de Janeiro, Funai in Brasília, the Biblioteca Nacional in Rio, Lisbon and Mexico City, the Instituto Indigenista Interamericano in Mexico, and the Royal Geographical Society, Canning House, London Library, British Library and Institute of Historical Research in London.

JOHN HEMMING

Maps

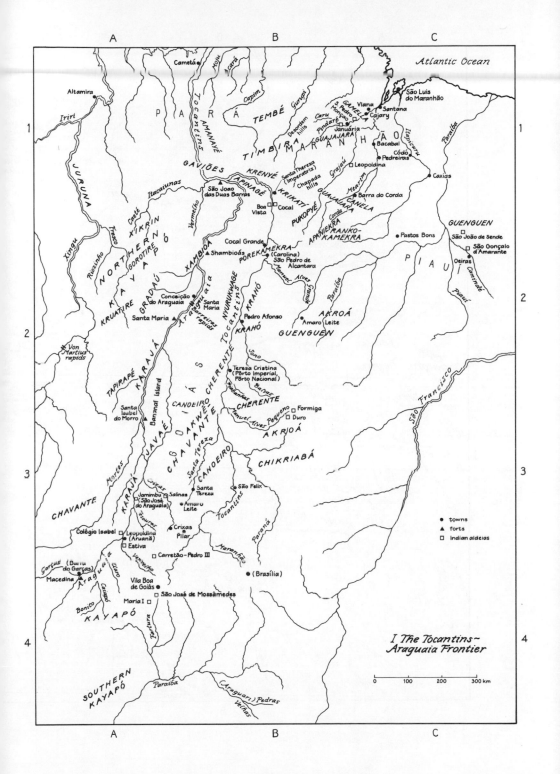

I The Tocantins~
Araguaia Frontier

● towns
▲ forts
☐ Indian aldeias

0   100   200   300 km

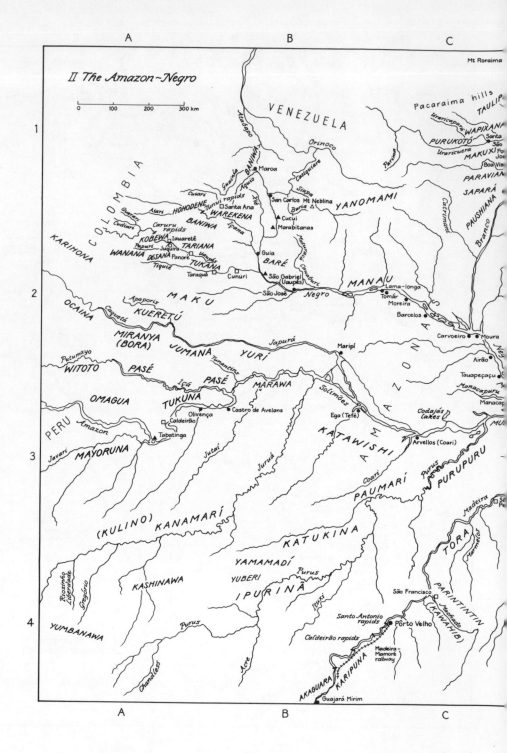

II The Amazon~Negro

0   100   200   300 km

Mt Roraima

VENEZUELA

Pacaraima hills

TAULIP

Urraricapara   WAPIXANA

PURUKOTÓ   Santa

MAKUXI   São   For   Joe

Orinoco

Boa Vis

PARAVIAN

SAPARÁ

Casiquiare

YANOMAMI

PAUSHIANA

Cauaburi

Branco

COLOMBIA

Guainia   BANIWA   Maroa

Atabapo

Cuiari   Tunui rapids

Aiari   HOHODENE

BANIWA   Santa Ana   San Carlos   Mt Neblina

WAREKENA   Cucui

Guaviare   Cuduiari   Caruru rapids   Marabitanas

KARIHONA   KOBEWA   Iauaretê   TARIANA   Guia

Papuri   Jiquira   Panore   Uaupés

WANANA   DESANA   São Gabriel   Uaupés   MANAU

Tiquié   TUKANA   Cunuri   Lama-Ionga

Taraquá   São José   Negro   Tomár

MAKU   Moreira

Apaporis   KUERETÚ   Barcelos

OCAINA   Caquetá   Carvoeiro   Moura

MIRANYA   JUMANA   YURI   Japurá   Airão

(BORA)   Maripí

Putumayo   Tumantini   Tauapeçaçu

WITOTO   PASÉ   Manacapuru

Içá   PASÉ   MARAWA   Manacar

OMAGUA   Solimões

TUKANA   Castro de Avelans   Codajás lakes

PERU   Amazon   Olivença   Ega (Tefé)   MU

Caldeirão   KATAWISHI

Tabatinga   Arvellos (Coari)

Javari   Jutaí   Purus   PURUPURU

MAYORUNA   PAUMARÍ

Juruá   Coari

(KULINO)   KANAMARÍ   Madeira   Sã   Pe

Tamões

KATUKINA   TORA

Roainho Liberdade   YAMAMADÍ   PARINTINTIN

Gregório   YUBERI   Purus   São Francisco   (KAWAHÍB)

KASHINAWA   IPURINÃ   Santo Antonio rapids   Porto Velho

Caldeirão rapids   Madeira-Mamoré railway

YUMBANAWA   Purus

Chandless   Acre   AKAGUARA   KARIPUNA   Guajará Mirim

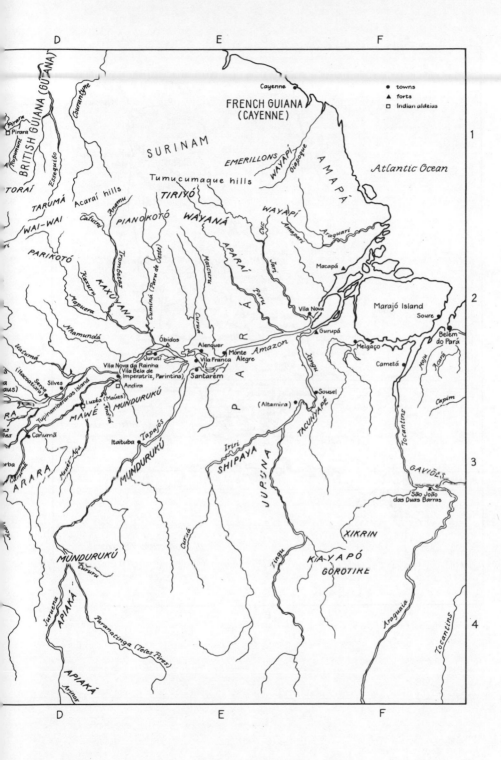

D   E   F

Cayenne

FRENCH GUIANA
(CAYENNE)

● towns
▲ forts
□ Indian aldeias

1

SURINAM

EMERILLONS

Atlantic Ocean

Tumucumaque hills

TIRIYÓ

WAYAPÍ

WAYANÁ

APARAÍ

A M A P Á

BRITISH GUIANA (GUYANA)

Pirara

Pirara

TORAÍ

TARUMÁ   Acaraí hills

WAI–WAI

PARIKOTÓ

PIANOKOTÓ

KAXÚYANA

Cuminá (Paru de Oeste)

Trombetas

Curuá

Maicuru

Paru

Jari

WAYAPÍ

Oyapoque

Oiapoque

Amapari

Araguari

Macapá ▲

Vila Nova

Gurupá

Amazon

P A R Á

2

Marajó Island

Soure

Melgaço

Belém
do Pará

Cametá

Óbidos

Alenquer

Monte
Alegre

Vila Franca

Vila Nova da Rainha
(Vila Bela de
Imperatriz, Parintins)

Santarém

Andira

Jurutí

Silves

Tupinambaranas Island

Luzéa (Maúes)

MAWÉ

MUNDURUKÚ

ARARA

Canumã

Itaituba

Tapajós

MUNDURUKÚ

Iriri

SHIPAYA

JURUNA

Xingu

TACUNYAPÉ

(Altamira)

Sousel

São João
das Duas Barras

3

GAVIÕES

Tocantins

Moju

Capim

XIKRIN

KA·YAPÓ

GOROTIRE

MUNDURUKÚ

APIAKÁ

Juruena

Paranatinga (Teles Pires)

APIAKÁ

Arinos

Curuá

Xingu

Araguaia

Tocantins

4

D   E   F

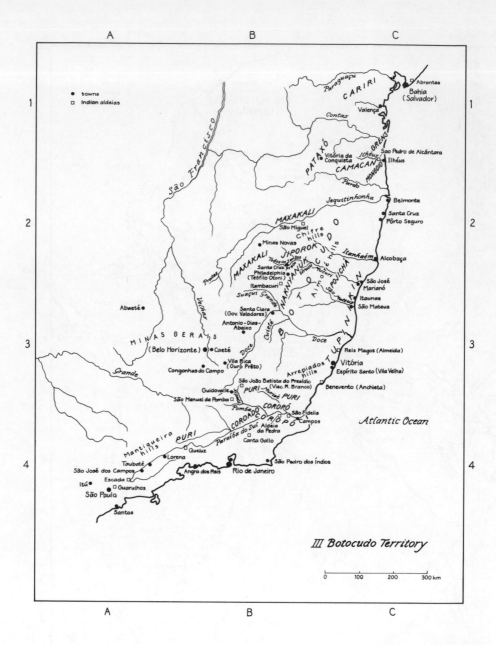

III Botocudo Territory

0   100   200   300 km

Map labels:

towns (●)
Indian aldeias (□)

Paraguaçu
CARIRI
Abrantes
Bahia (Salvador)
Valença
Contas
GRENS
São Pedro de Alcántara
PATAXÓ
Ilhéus
Vitória da Conquista
CAMACAN
MONGOIO
Pardo
Jequitinhonha
Belmonte
Santa Cruz
MAXAKALI
Pôrto Seguro
São Miguel
Chifre hills
Minas Novas
IHPOROK
Itanhaém
Alcobaça
MAXAKALI
Todos os Santos
Santa Cruz
Philadelphia (Teófilo Otoni)
São José Marianó
Itambacuri
Itaunas
Suaçuí Grande
São Mateus
Abaeté
Santa Clara (Gov. Valadares)
Antonio-Dias-Abaixo
MINAS GERAIS
(Belo Horizonte)
Caeté
Doce
Reis Magos (Almeida)
Vila Rica (Ouro Prêto)
Vitória
Congonhas do Campo
Arrepiados hills
Espírito Santo (Vila Velha)
São João Batista do Presídio (Visc. R. Branco)
Benevento (Anchieta)
Guidovalle
PURI
Venda Nova PURI
São Manuel da Pomba
Pomba
CORORÓ
São Fidelis
Grande
CORORÓ
Campos
CORORÓ
COROADO
Aldeia da Pedra
Mantiqueira hills
PURI
Paraíba do Sul
Canta Gallo
Queluz
Lorena
São Pedro dos Índios
Taubaté
São José dos Campos
Angra dos Reis
Rio de Janeiro
Escada
Itú
Guarulhos
São Paula
Santos

Atlantic Ocean

São Francisco
Pretas
Velhas
Doce
Grande

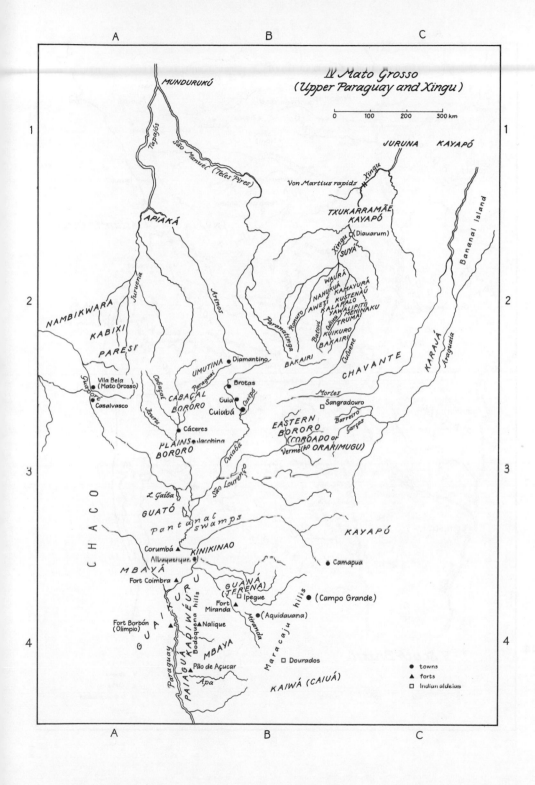

IV Mato Grosso
(Upper Paraguay and Xingu)

0   100   200   300 km

MUNDURUKÚ

JURUNA   KAYAPÓ

Von Martius rapids

TXUKARRAMÃE
KAYAPÓ

APIAKÁ

□ (Diauarum)

SUYÁ

WAURA
NAHUKUÁ   KAMAYURÁ
AWETI   KUSTENAÚ
KALAPALO   YAWALLPITI
YAWALLPITI   MEHINAKU
TRUMAI
KUIKURO
BAKAIRI

NAMBIKWARA

KABIXI

PARESI

UMUTINA   ● Diamantino

BAKAIRI

CHAVANTE

KARAJÁ

Vila Bela
(Mato Grosso)
● Casalvasco

CABAÇAL
BORORO

● Brotas

Guia ●
Coxipó
Cuiabá

Mortes
Sangradouro □
Barreiro
EASTERN
BORORO
(COROADO or
Vermelho ORARIMUGU)
Gargas

● Cáceres

PLAINS   ● Jacobina
BORORO

CHACO

L. Gaíba

GUATÓ

Pantanal
swamps

KAYAPÓ

Corumbá ▲
Albuquerque ●
KINIKINAO

● Camapua

MBAYÁ

Fort Coimbra ▲

GUANÁ
(TERENA)
□ Ipegue
Fort
Miranda

● (Campo Grande)

Fort Borbón
(Olímpio) ▲

▲Nalique

● (Aquidauana)

□ Dourados

Pão de Açúcar

Apa

MBAYA

KAIWÁ (CAIUÁ)

● towns
▲ forts
□ Indian aldeias

Bananal Island

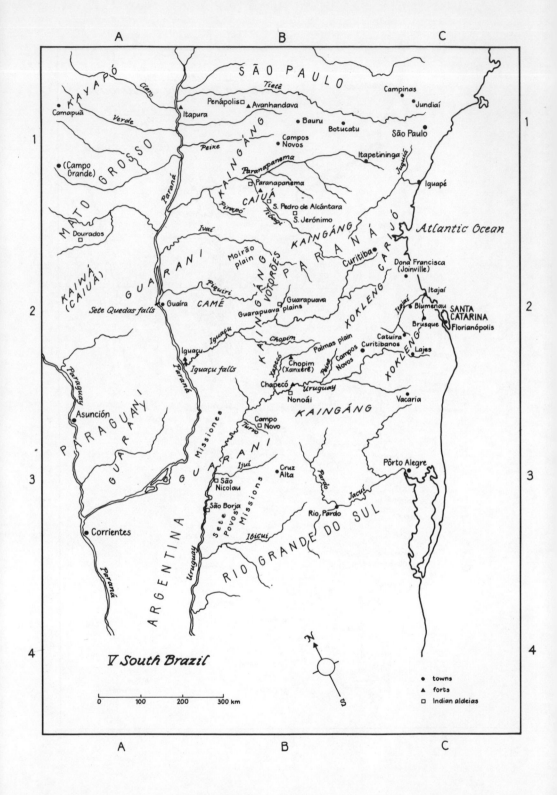

SÃO PAULO

KAYAPÓ

Camapuã

Tietê

Itapura

Penápolis □ ▲ Avanhandava

Campinas

Jundiaí

Bauru

Botucatu

São Paulo

Campos
Novos

Peixe

Itapetininga

Paranapanema

Paranapanema □

S. Pedro de Alcántara □

S. Jerónimo □

Iguapé

Atlantic Ocean

Dona Francisca
(Joinville)

Itajaí

Blumenau

SANTA
CATARINA

Brusque

Florianópolis

Curitiba

KAINGÁNG

PARANÁ

CARIJÓ

Moirão
plain

Ivaí

Tibají

Pirapó

KAINGÁNG CAIUÁ

KAINGÁNG

VOTORÕES

Piquiri

Guarapuava □
plains

XOKLENG

Catuira

Curitibanos

Lajes

(Campo
Grande)

MATO GROSSO

Dourados □

KAIWÁ
(CAIUÁ)

GUARANI

Sete Quedas falls

Guaíra

CAMÉ

Guarapuava

Iguaçu

Iguaçu

Iguaçu falls

Palmas plain

Chopim

Chopim
(Xanxeré) □

Chapecó ▲

Nonoái □

Campos
Novos

XOKLENG

Vacaria

Paraguay

Asunción

PARAGUAY

GUARANI

PARANÁ

Uruguay

KAINGÁNG

Campo □
Novo

Pôrto Alegre

ARGENTINA

GUARANI

Missiones

Turvo

Ijuí

Cruz
Alta

São
Nicolau □

São Borja

Sete
Povos
Missions

Pardo

Jacuí

Rio Pardo

RIO GRANDE DO SUL

Corrientes

Ibicuí

Paraná

N

S

V South Brazil

0   100   200   300 km

• towns
▲ forts
□ Indian aldeias

PART 1

The Directorate

1

False Freedom

The Indians of Brazil entered a new era in 1755. The Crown of Portugal issued a law on 6 June that 'restored to the Indians of [the Amazon basin] the liberty of their persons, goods and commerce'. This famous law was expressed in magnificent language; a ringing declaration of Indian freedom and an admission of past abuse by Portuguese settlers. It confessed that 'many thousands of Indians have been descended [i.e. brought downriver into Portuguese control] but are being extinguished, so that the number of surviving villages and their inhabitants is very small; and these few live in great misery.'

Indians were henceforth to enjoy all the rights and privileges of ordinary free citizens. Indian slaves were freed. No colonist was to control Indians: for the law admitted that Indians subjected to such forced labour had rapidly 'either died from sheer hunger and excessive work, or fled inland [back to their forests]'.

Along with their new freedom from slavery, the Indians of Amazonia were granted political self-government. In his law of 1755, King José I ordered that 'they are to be masters of their estates, just as they are in the wilds. These lands may not be removed from them, and they are not to be molested on them.' As free citizens, Indians would be at liberty to work wherever they wished and for anyone they chose. The colonial governor would fix rates of pay that amply covered the needs of native labourers.

Brazilian Indians were also to enjoy social equality. An edict issued a few weeks before the Law of Liberty of 6 June 1755 tried to end racial discrimination against Indians, the original inhabitants of Brazil. It was forbidden to describe people with Indian blood by the insulting word caboclo (peasant). Intermarriage between whites and

---

* References for all quotations will be found in the Notes and References, pages 545–621, indicated by the page numbers of the text and the last words of the quotation. Notes to other passages are indicated by an asterisk in the text and are likewise printed at the end of the book.

Indians was to be encouraged, all stigma was removed from half-caste children of such alliances. 'Their children and descendants will be left with no infamy whatever, but will rather become more worthy of royal attention. They will be preferred . . . for posts and occupations . . . and will be eligible for any employment, honour or dignity.'

On the day after the Law of Liberty, the King issued another law that ended two centuries of missionary control of native affairs. The edict of 7 June 1755 stripped missionaries of all temporal or civil control of Indian villages. In future, missionaries were to confine themselves to evangelical work, particularly to attracting and converting new tribes. Political power now lay with the royal governor and his officials, and at local level with the Indians' own chiefs and secular justices. Any European settler might have access to Indian villages. Trade was seen as a means of attracting natives to European civilisation and was therefore encouraged, 'for the more that Indians amass wealth through agriculture and commerce, the more benefit will follow for them.'

This spate of humanitarian legislation seemed a revolutionary approach to the treatment of Indians. No other colonial power had ever given so much freedom to its native subjects. It seemed remarkable that such a devoutly Catholic country as Portugal should free its colonial subjects from stultifying rule by missionaries. What lay behind such eloquent new laws and such a radical shift in royal policy?

The legislation was the work of one man, Portugal's chief minister Sebastião José de Carvalho e Mello, known to history by the title he was later awarded: the Marquis of Pombal. He had been in effective control of the Portuguese government since 1750, and in November 1755 he consolidated his power by his resolute response to the devastating earthquake and subsequent fire and tidal wave that annihilated Lisbon. Tall and strikingly handsome, Pombal was also tough, ambitious and ruthless. His self-assurance and pragmatism won him an ascendancy over King José I which made him virtual dictator of Portugal until the King's death in 1777. Soon after gaining power, Pombal sent his brother Francisco Xavier de Mendonça Furtado to be governor of the northern part of Brazil: the Amazon basin, then known as the state of Maranhão and Pará. The brothers maintained a regular correspondence, and Mendonça Furtado's reports from the Amazon confirmed Pombal's suspicions of the causes of decay of that colonial backwater.

For two centuries, ever since the Portuguese first planted permanent colonies in Brazil in the 1540s, missionaries had been in

charge of the native Indian inhabitants. The most disciplined, ener-
getic and intellectual of the missionary orders was the Society of
Jesus, which had come to dominate Indian affairs. The Jesuits were
particularly successful at the northern and southern extremities of
Brazil: Spanish Jesuits had created a theocratic state among the
Guarani tribe of what is now Paraguay and the Brazilian state of Rio
Grande do Sul; and Portuguese Jesuits had established mission
villages or aldeias along the lower Amazon and its tributaries. The
Jesuits reinforced their hold on the Brazilian missions by political
influence at the Portuguese Court: various monarchs had been
impressed by the eloquent pro-Indian arguments of their Jesuit
confessors or preachers.

The Jesuits failed with most tribes, either because their charges
succumbed to epidemics of newly imported diseases, or because the
Indians resented the missionaries' attempt to change their society
and beliefs. Only a few tribes responded to the Jesuits' missionary
regime, which consisted of a strict daily discipline of religious observance and agricultural labour, and total spiritual and temporal control from cradle to grave. The Guarani of Paraguay were a notably
spiritual people and were efficient farmers: they therefore respected
the Jesuits' religious magic and worked contentedly on plantations
or tending their missions' vast herds of cattle.

The formula was less successful on the Amazon, but the Jesuits
did manage to develop over sixty aldeias along the river's banks.
They possessed huge cattle ranches on the island of Marajó at the
mouth of the Amazon. They developed a thriving trade in hides,
agricultural produce such as cotton, tobacco or rice, and drugs and
dyes extracted from forest plants. This wealth contrasted with the
failures and poverty of ordinary Portuguese colonists, who were
defeated by the insects, parasites, suffocating vegetation, weak soil,
tropical rains, equatorial sun and immense distances of Amazonia.
The result had been a running battle between settlers and missionaries. The colonists were desperate for labour and wanted to enslave
native tribespeople or to employ mission Indians for derisory wages.
The Jesuits opposed slavery of Indians on religious grounds; but the
colonists accused them of wanting to monopolise native labour to
enrich their own mission plantations. There had twice been rebellions in which the colonists expelled all Jesuits from the Amazon.
The Court in Lisbon had been bombarded both with increasingly
strident attacks on the missionaries and with impassioned sermons
in their defence.

This dispute impressed Pombal. He came to share the colonists' conviction that the Jesuit Company had amassed great wealth. The black-robed Jesuit Fathers were arrogant, secretive and successful — an easily identifiable minority against which to direct popular discontent. When Mendonça Furtado left to become governor of Maranhão and Pará, he was secretly instructed to investigate 'the excessive power which the ecclesiastics have in that State, principally in the temporal estates of the missions . . . and the excessive power and great wealth of the regular missionary orders'. Mendonça Furtado's reports confirmed his brother's suspicions: he took a violent dislike to the Jesuits. He was soon writing that they ran their missions 'with pride and ambition' and that their initial religious zeal had long since turned to avarice. Mission Indians were 'condemned to the hard yoke of perpetual captivity' and there were twelve thousand of them working on the mission farms and ranches.

The Governor set off up the Amazon on a tour of inspection. A zealous, energetic man, he was easily frustrated when things went wrong. He tended to blame the Jesuits whenever his Indian paddlers deserted or a riverine mission village did not organise a big welcome for his convoy. He was gullible in believing all the settlers' most exaggerated slurs on the Jesuits, and suspicious of any contact with the Fathers.

A new bishop reached Pará at the same time as the Governor, and this prelate was a Dominican, whose order were the traditional rivals of the Jesuits. His despatches confirmed the anti-Jesuit bias of Mendonça Furtado. Pombal's dislike of the Jesuit Company grew steadily into a hatred that verged on paranoia. The 'freedom' bestowed on the Indians in the law of 1755 was therefore freedom from missionary control: it was as much a blow at the Jesuits as an act of disinterested humanity.

There was also an economic reason behind Pombal's Indian legislation. Portugal's colony on the Amazon was in miserable decline by mid-eighteenth century. When the first Spaniards had descended the mighty river in 1542, they found the banks densely peopled with a succession of prosperous tribes. The Portuguese did not begin to make permanent settlements on the Amazon until the 1620s, but their few hundred settlers soon wrought devastation on its inhabitants. Both settlers and missionaries were desperate for Indians to work their farms and fill their missions. They therefore organised expeditions to lure or coerce tribes down from the Amazon and its tributaries to the Portuguese towns near its mouth. Countless armed expeditions went up the rivers to seize slaves; military campaigns slaughtered tribes who resisted; and missionaries seduced tribes downriver with presents and promises of worldly comfort and spiritual magic.

All these movements of people were frustrated by an appalling decline in the number of Indians. One of the last Jesuits on the Amazon, Father João Daniel, wrote that there had once been so many Indians there that 'arithmetic would be exhausted in trying to count such an innumerable multitude.... The Indians were as numerous as swarms of mosquitoes, the settlements without number, and the diversity of tribes and languages beyond count.' By mid-eighteenth century there were between 1 and 1.5 million native peoples left in Brazil. When the first Europeans reached the shores of Brazil in 1500 there had been 2.5 million or more.

There were various reasons for this demographic catastrophe: cultural shock, a demoralisation that caused social disintegration and a collapse of the birth rate; deaths from battles, massacres and sheer overwork; but the biggest killer by far was disease. Otherwise healthy Indians had no genetic defence against new diseases imported from across the Atlantic. They died in their tens of thousands from epidemics of smallpox, measles, tuberculosis or influenza. Soon after his arrival in Brazil, Governor Mendonça Furtado wrote to his brother lamenting 'the terrible epidemic that ruined this state'. Charles Marie de la Condamine, a French savant who descended the Amazon in the 1740s, described hundreds of miles of river banks with no sign of human life and once-thriving villages that were devastated and empty. José Gonçalves da Fonseca wrote of the strategic town of Macapá in 1749: 'There used to be ample Indians in it, but successive epidemics of smallpox and measles have left it destitute of inhabitants of either sex or any age.' The great naturalist Alexandre Rodrigues Ferreira, who went to the Amazon in the 1780s, lamented that 'one sees places on that river that were once inhabited by innumerable heathen but that now show no signs of life beyond the bones of bodies of the dead. And those who escaped the contagion did not escape captivity' as slaves of the colonists.

Faced with such decline in the labour force and decay in the province, Pombal may have reasoned that bold initiatives were justified. The existing system was manifestly failing. A radical change to free enterprise, with Indian labour freed from missionary protection, might succeed in reviving this potentially rich region. At the same time as he granted liberty to the Indians, Pombal set up a trading company, the General Company of Commerce of Greater Pará and Maranhão. He granted many monopolistic privileges to this new enterprise, encouraged private investment in it, provided warships to protect its fleets and built a fort at Bissau in West Africa to ensure a good supply of black slaves.

African slave labour was seen as the necessary alternative to native Brazilian Indian slaves. Africans had inherited genetic defences against many of the diseases which decimated Indians — and which had often reached the New World in slave ships from Africa. Black Africans were mentally more robust and less liable to fatal depression when enslaved: they accepted the need to labour for other masters, a concept abhorrent to Indians. It was also more difficult for Africans to flee into the unfamiliar jungles of Amazonia. By a curious hypocrisy, no one — not even the most eloquent Jesuit champions of Indian freedom — questioned the illogicality of enslaving Africans in order to free American Indians. In an age of extreme racial prejudice, the Indians' pale coppery colour was evidently thought to be superior to black skin.

Pombal also had geopolitical reasons for granting liberty to the Indians of Amazonia. In 1750, the year in which he achieved power, the Kings of Spain and Portugal had signed the Treaty of Madrid to define the boundaries between their colonial empires in South America. The idea of two European powers carving up a continent — much of which was unpenetrated by whites — was morally outrageous. But the diplomats who drafted the Treaty of Madrid did an excellent job by colonial standards. They based the new boundaries on two sensible principles: they would respect de facto European occupation wherever it existed; and they would follow geographical features such as rivers or watersheds whenever possible. The new treaty recognised that the Portuguese had penetrated thousands of kilometres to the west of the Line of Tordesillas — the papal division of the world between the two Catholic monarchs effected immediately after Columbus' discovery of the Americas. Much of the boundary agreed at Madrid in 1750 is still the frontier between Brazil and her Spanish-speaking neighbours today.

The Treaty of Madrid had awarded Portuguese Brazil a gigantic territory larger than all Europe; the new frontier between Brazil and Peru was over two thousand kilometres up the Amazon river. Pombal wanted to assert Portuguese sovereignty over these vast dominions, which had been largely denuded by 150 years of Portuguese slave raids and oppression, but he was aware that tiny Portugal was too small to people these lands with its own colonists. He therefore repeated the dream of all his predecessors that the native tribes should be persuaded to become loyal subjects of the Portuguese Crown. He wrote to his brother Mendonça Furtado that the solution lay in a civil union of conquerors and conquered living freely under the same laws without distinction of origin. He pointed out that the Romans had successfully incorporated barbarous Portuguese into their empire by such means and hoped that benevolent treatment of Brazilian Indians might achieve similar success for the Portuguese empire. Miscegenation between whites and Indians would accelerate this fusion, producing a useful class of half-caste mestizos. This was the political explanation for the decree that sought to encourage intermarriage and to abolish racial prejudice against people of mixed blood.

A final motive behind Pombal's legislation may have been philosophical. His opposition to the Jesuits derived partly from a wish to assert the power of the royal government. Although Voltaire ridiculed eighteenth-century Portugal as a priest-ridden backwater, Pombal himself had travelled throughout Europe and absorbed more modern ideas. He wanted to break the traditional medieval balance of church and state as 'equal swords'. He also favoured the physiocratic notion that a virtuous man was a productive worker with a family rather than a reclusive, celibate ecclesiastic. There was a wild hope that Indians freed from allegiance to devout but impractical missionaries would blossom into hard-working and useful royal subjects.

The word 'Indian' is a misnomer, deriving from the mistaken belief of Christopher Columbus that he had reached India when he discovered the Americas. The indigenous peoples of the New World are sometimes called Amerindians to distinguish them from inhabitants of India; but the word commonly used in both Spanish and Portuguese is indios, and it is therefore simpler to translate this as Indians.

All American Indians reached the ancient land masses of North and South America by migration from Central Asia. Most arrived during the Ice Ages, when for thousands of years the lowering of the world's oceans exposed a land bridge where the Bering Strait now separates Alaska and Siberia. During the millennia after the end of the last Ice Age some twelve thousand years ago, the Asiatics who had reached the Americas migrated southwards, multiplied, settled and fragmented. Successive waves of migrants reached the part of South America that is now Brazil. They can be classified linguistically into four main language trunks and many lesser or isolated languages. The four principal groups were the Gê-speakers, who occupied the central Brazilian plateau, the watershed between the Amazon and Paraná—Paraguay basins and the rivers flowing into the Atlantic Ocean; the Tupi, who occupied a heartland in what is now Paraguay and were settled in populous tribes along the Atlantic seaboard, with some groups on the Amazon and its tributaries; the Aruak (or Arawak), largest of all the linguistic groups, who were found throughout the Caribbean and Central America and who had entered the Amazon basin probably from the north-west; and the Carib, traditional enemies of the Aruak in the Caribbean, who occupied much of the Guianas and entered the Amazon from the north or from its mouth. Indian tribes can be highly mobile, for they have few possessions, are self-sufficient in making all that they need, and can live off the land by hunting and fishing. Some of the linguistic families were thus widely dispersed. Small groups broke away to form separate tribes, and in a few generations these might migrate hundreds or even thousands of kilometres to distant plains or rivers. The Brazilian Indians were therefore scattered in a complex kaleidoscope over the vast lowlands of central and eastern South America. In parts of Brazil, linguistic groups occupied homogeneous territories as large as European countries; but in other places clusters of tribes speaking different languages lived in close and generally peaceful proximity to one another.

Among so many hundreds of tribes there was an infinite variety of social custom. Anthropologists record differences in rules and rituals of marriage, puberty, death, medicine and spiritual beliefs. Each tribe had distinct details of artefacts, personal ornament, architecture and even hair styles or body painting. Tribes evolved their own variations of legends and oral history and, after generations of isolation, would acquire a recognisable facial appearance or shade of skin colour.

Despite these many differences, some generalisations applied to most tribes of Brazilian Indians. Their lands contain no animals that can be domesticated, so tribes must hunt and fish. The great pre-columbian American civilisations – Incas in Peru, Aztecs in Mexico and Muisca in Colombia – could flourish because they had ample protein from domesticated guinea pigs and llamas, and such basic crops as maize and potatoes. The tribes of Amazonia had no similar staples. They therefore had to remain in small tribal units. They could not allow their populations to exceed the available game and fish or the fruits and nuts that could be gathered from widely scattered trees of the forests. Their farming had to be shifting cultivation in slash-and-burn clearings.

Brazilian Indians lived in tribal groups in which chiefs had little authority. Tribal rule was at once conservative, with little change in customs from generation to generation, and communistic, with day-to-day decisions made by meetings of the tribal elders. Each family unit was self-sufficient for its food and all small artefacts. People voluntarily helped one another in communal tasks such as building huts or clearing forest; there was no question of one man working for another. Early observers were all amazed by Indians' indifference to possessions; there were no rich and poor in Indian tribes.

In common with other native Americans, Brazilian Indians had not made certain discoveries that Europeans and Asians regarded as fundamental to civilised life: writing, the wheel, the arch. The lack of writing was compensated to some extent by vivid verbal traditions and legends: oratory around the camp fires, in the tradition of Homeric Greece. Wheels were unnecessary in the difficult environment of Brazil's forests and rivers — much of the country is being penetrated by roads only in the late twentieth century. Brazilian Indians also lacked metal and only a few tribes used stone. They suffered from the lack of metal: steel and iron tools were almost the only true benefit brought by European colonists. Stone was less important; Brazil had such a wealth of tropical timbers, lianas, leaves for thatch and vegetable gums that its natives never lacked building materials. Indians are highly artistic and dextrous. Each individual learns how to make superb ornaments of feather and bone, arrows, canoes, hammocks, combs and all other utensils. Beautiful thatched huts or malocas involved a high degree of architectural skill. The trouble was that the materials so readily available to Brazilian natives were all perishable. Fungi, termites and humidity soon destroy most things in the tropics. There are thus no lasting monuments to the creative ingenuity of the Indians, apart from collections of feather and wood artefacts in a few museums.

By mid-eighteenth century, many Brazilian tribes still lived in the traditional manner evolved over centuries of adaptation to the tropical environment. But most tribes had already suffered the impact of colonial invasion and, as we have seen, hundreds of thousands of Indians had died. Pombal's legislation of 1755 was aimed at the few tens of thousands of Indians who lived under Portuguese rule, in mission villages, in colonial towns or on settlers' farms.

Although Governor Mendonça Furtado had helped to inspire the new legislation, he hesitated to enforce it. This was partly because in October 1754 he embarked on a tour of inspection up the Amazon and Negro rivers. It was four years since Portugal had achieved its diplomatic triumph in the Treaty of Madrid. Now, having won almost half South America on paper, the Portuguese had to assert their claim in practice. Mendonça Furtado was named as boundary commissioner to fix the new frontiers between Portuguese and Spanish America.

Before setting off on his tour of inspection, Mendonça Furtado spent a year recruiting Indian crewmen while fourteen boats and twenty-three large canoes were built for his flotilla. His own vessel was 'equipped like a yacht' with a cabin lined in damask. He had the King write to the heads of the missionary orders to say that 'he would need a great quantity of Indians to propel the canoes and perform all the other services that may be necessary on the expedition.' If these Indians were not readily available, 'he may remove them by force.' As the Governor progressed past Marajó island and up the Amazon, hundreds of Indians ran off to the forests to escape the thankless task of paddling. Canoes were therefore sent to riverine mission villages to press more Indians into service.

Mendonça Furtado was most impressed when he reached the Rio Negro and saw the prosperity of its Carmelite missions. The friars had twenty-five flourishing villages on the Negro and a further five on its tributary the Rio Branco. In these and some other missions on the Amazon—Solimões, they had congregated a hundred thousand people. The Carmelites organised welcomes of hymn-singing Indians and arches of flowers and branches. The Governor was visibly gratified, and contrasted the affability of the Carmelites with the hostility of the Jesuits lower down on the Amazon.

Mendonça Furtado decided to establish the capital of a new captaincy of São José do Rio Negro (roughly the modern state of Amazonas) at a mission called Mariúa, 430 kilometres up the Negro from its confluence with the Amazon. This village was renamed Barcelos, as part of Pombal's campaign to replace native names with those of towns in Portugal. Indian labourers were set to work building imposing administrative offices, barracks and factories along its river front.

It was the intention of Governor Mendonça Furtado to meet his Spanish opposite number at Barcelos. In 1744 the Portuguese slaver Francisco Xavier de Moraes had discovered that there was a natural river link between the waters of the Negro and Orinoco. This link was the Casiquiare Canal, a sizable forested river that generally flows from the upper Orinoco south-westwards into the Negro — although the flow of its current occasionally reverses. The Spanish boundary commissioner was therefore to travel through the Casiquiare on to Portuguese waters of the Negro, to meet Mendonça

Furtado at Barcelos. When the Spaniard failed to come, Mendonça Furtado had his Indians paddle him back to Belém at the mouth of the Amazon.

His months on the Amazon and Negro rivers convinced the Governor of various things: that the freeing of Indians from mission control must be done with great caution; that the Jesuits would obstruct any threat to their authority and might even attempt to organise their Indians in armed resistance; that colonial settlers and the royal government could not dispense with Indian labour; and above all that if the Indians were genuinely free and in charge of their own administration, they would refuse to work for others.

Mendonça Furtado waited until February 1757 before publishing the decree freeing Indian villages from missionary control. He then announced that he had determined on a six-year transitional period before granting the Indians their freedom. That liberty was never achieved; the bold experiment of treating Indians as free citizens and giving them control of their own village government was nullified. For in May 1757 Mendonça Furtado issued a long decree by which white 'directors' were put in charge of Indian aldeias. This new system was known as the Diretório (Directorate), and it governed the sixty-one Indian villages of Maranhão and the Amazon for forty years. It was soon to be extended to the rest of Brazil.

The Directorate legislation denied Indians their freedom. In an edict of 21 May 1757, Mendonça Furtado openly admitted that he was emasculating the royal decree about Indian liberty. He declared: 'I am supposed to execute the two laws of 6 and 7 June 1755 in which His Majesty saw fit to declare the liberty of all Indians of this State. . . . However, having been in continuous contact with them and lived in their villages for over two years, I realised that the most pious instructions of His Majesty would be frustrated if these miserable rustic ignoramuses were given absolute control of the many villages that constitute this State.'

Pombal's brother thus quashed the radical and imaginative idea of giving Indians self-government under Portuguese rule. He wrote that 'it occurred to me . . . to place a [white] man in each settlement with the title of director.' He justified this disastrous policy 'because it is impossible for [the Indians] to pass from one extreme to the other'. The new officials would have no powers of coercion. 'They would have a directive only to teach [the Indians], not so much how to govern themselves in a civilised way, but rather how to trade and cultivate their lands. From such fruitful and beneficial labours, [the

Indians] themselves will derive profits that they will doubtless produce. Those profits will make these hitherto wretched people into Christians, rich and civilised.'

The Directorate legislation was a curious mixture of wishful thinking about Indians, instructions for the conduct of the new lay officials and moral justification for removing the missionaries. The clauses about Indian conduct were ludicrously misguided. They could have been written by any pragmatic Brazilian administrator right up to the present day; but they utterly failed to grasp the nature of Indian society or the terrible cultural shock of adjusting to alien European values.

The new system stressed rapid integration of Indians into Portuguese society. It was assumed that the missionaries had been wrong to isolate and protect Indians, or to allow them to continue certain traditional tribal practices while moving gradually towards Christian conversion. Mendonça Furtado was an arrogant, irascible man, convinced that he knew best. He was unwilling to admit that the Jesuits could have learned anything during two centuries of trial and error in their administration of Brazilian Indians. He accepted the settlers' conviction that the Jesuits isolated their Indians in order to exploit them. He wrote to his brother Pombal that 'all Indians on the mission villages, of either sex and of all ages, are the absolute slaves of the monastic orders.' Therefore, instead of conserving Indians as a separate race, his own legislation would end their isolation and abruptly turn them into 'civilised' Christians.

The Jesuits had used Tupi-Guarani, the language of the coastal tribes, as the lingua geral (general language) of all their Brazilian and Paraguayan missions. This was now to be forbidden and replaced by the Portuguese tongue. Mission villages were to lose their melodious native names and to be called after towns in the mother country, Portugal. The Portuguese language and culture were to be transmitted by primary schools, with Indian boys and girls segregated if possible. This provision was particularly absurd: colonists on the Amazon had little enough schooling for their own children and had always relied on ecclesiastics as tutors. The idea of finding any lay schoolteachers to work in Indian villages was wholly unrealistic – it is extremely difficult even in the late twentieth century.

Clause 11 of the Directorate legislation decreed that Indians should adopt surnames, preferably European ones. The next clause said that they must live in separate houses, to prevent the 'indecency' of families occupying sections of large huts or malocas. This provision struck at the root of Indian tribal society, which was based on a remarkably harmonious communal way of life. European observers had always been impressed by the innocence and honesty of South American Indians – hence the philosophical ideal of the noble savage. Marriage and sexual rules differed between tribes, but Indians conformed absolutely to established codes of conduct. The colonists had an abysmal record of sexually abusing Indians. Colonial legislation against immorality among Indians was thus the height of hypocrisy and ignorance.

Clause 15 of the Directorate ordered that Indians should wear modest clothing but not ornate decorations. Most tribes of the Amazon basin wore minimal or no clothing in its equatorial climate, relying on a variety of vegetable skin dyes as protection against insects. Clothes were a liability for isolated tribes: they created new needs – for cloth, thread, needles and soap; they tore easily in the forests; and they actually increased the risk of infection for Indians who, when soaked by tropical rains or by bathing in the rivers, then allowed their clothes to dry on them. Nevertheless, clothing for the natives had always been an obsession among colonial administrators, and it was necessary for Indians exposed to the prurient curiosity of settlers. Governor Mendonça Furtado admitted that the Jesuits kept their Indians fully clothed, but he was shocked by the conduct of other missionary orders. He encountered canoes containing solitary missionaries being paddled by crews of Indian girls. He wrote to Pombal that 'in the convent [the women] go about with no covering beyond a poor rag they call a skirt, which does not go below mid-leg, and all the rest of their bodies naked in scandalous indecency . . . I was in the Carmelite monastery . . . when I saw from the Vice-Provincial's window two scandalous figures of women bathing naked by the well. I told the Fathers that this was indecent, but they replied that it was the custom of Indian women.'

A more valid concern was to combat Indian drunkenness. Many tribes had their own alcoholic drinks, but nothing comparable in potency to the colonists' sugar-based spirit, cachaça. Indians who were demoralised by the cultural shock of invasion by an alien race sought relief in drink. For them, cachaça was a natural extension of their love of intoxicants and hallucinogens as a means of spiritual release. There may even be a genetic reason why all American Indians seem to have weaker heads and less resistance to alcohol than whites. Some tribes used no alcohol in their celebrations or culture: such Indians were indifferent to settlers' drink and have continued to shun alcohol to the present day. But other tribes became hopelessly addicted. The Directorate legislation urged the new officials to combat drunkenness, and specifically prohibited the use of cachaça in Indian villages.

The Directorate instructions reiterated the government's wish to merge the white and Indian races. Indian villages were thrown open to colonists for trade, and individual settlers of good character were permitted to reside among the Indians. It was hoped that this would expose the Indians to 'civilised behaviour' which they would emulate. Mendonça Furtado wisely prohibited the transfer of land titles from Indians to Europeans – it would have been too easy for cunning and legally experienced settlers to cheat Indians of their land. The colonists were encouraged to work manually. Most white immigrants shunned agricultural labour in the tropics, imagining that when they crossed the Atlantic their 'superior' racial status would be demeaned if they were seen to work on the soil. The new directors were urged to persuade their fellow colonists that the natives were not racially inferior, and to encourage interracial marriages. It was hoped that this would produce a 'solidly based and happy society'. It was all part of Pombal's overriding wish to fill the vacuum of the Amazon, depopulated by 140 years of colonial pillage, with loyal Portuguese subjects.

Having set out his pious and unrealistic hopes to transform Indians into worthy Portuguese, Mendonça Furtado turned to the real meat of the Directorate legislation: the mobilisation of Indian labour. Indians were considered to be naturally lazy. Clause 20 admitted that they had previously been employed for the private gain of their missionary or lay administrators instead of being available to 'help' any individual colonist. They were to be taught to be 'useful to themselves, to the settlers, and to the State'.

There were three ways in which the Indians of Amazonia were to produce food and export crops. They were to farm and fish for local consumption – growing manioc, beans, rice and other vegetables and raising cattle or catching fish to feed São Luis, Belém and the other towns. They were to work in plantations to grow crops for export – the equatorial sun and rain of Amazonia seemed ideal for plantations of cotton, rice, tobacco, cacao for drinking chocolate, and coffee. Above all, Indians were to plunge into the forests to collect their riches. Scattered among the thousands of species of trees and plants in the rainforests were a few that were prized in the eighteenth century. These were called drogas do sertão (drugs of the wilds) and included wild cacao,* sarsaparilla for medicinal tea, aromatic clove-like cravo, Brazil nuts, oil from turtle eggs, and dried fish.

It was hoped that the Indians could somehow fulfil all these different types of agricultural labour. Their subsistence farming was supposed to feed their own families and also to provide a flow of food to the markets of the colonial towns. The new directors were told to organise this trade in surplus produce; it was intended to correct serious food shortages that had occurred in the colonial towns just before the new governor reached Brazil.

In addition to these formidable agricultural tasks, the few thousand Indians of the Amazon villages were also expected to work for the state. Colonial governors had ambitious plans for public works: a shipyard to build ships with the splendid woods and rope fibres of the Amazon forests; great stone forts to protect the Amazon against foreign invasion; handsome public buildings for the state capital Belém do Pará; and expeditions of discovery, demarcation and trade paddled by Indians up tens of thousands of kilometres of rivers.

What of the profit from so much backbreaking work? Clause 64 of the new legislation proclaimed that 'in view of the rusticity and ignorance of the Indians it would be an offence against the laws of justice, and a failure of charity, to pay them *all* the profit earned by their labour. . . .'

The director himself, who was depicted elsewhere in the legislation as a disinterested philanthropic adviser, was to be encouraged by a commission of one-sixth of the value of everything produced or gathered communally by his villagers. He received no fixed salary from the government. The new system was thus to be financed directly by the labour of the Indians themselves. Of course, the director was supposed to be a Portuguese-speaking white gentleman of good moral standing. He could not be expected to participate directly in the labour of the plantations or to go on the tough collecting expeditions that plunged for months on end into the dark and dangerous jungles. Someone had to accompany these expeditions, to make the Indians work and ensure that they did not slip off into their forests. This expedition leader was the cabo or boss, and the Directorate rewarded him with a share – later fixed at one-fifth – of the profit of the venture. The director and the cabo were both public officials answerable to the colonial governor, even if their payment came entirely from the work of their charges.

It was a fundamental principle of the new freedom of the Indians that they should govern themselves. The legislation therefore tried to reward or bribe the newly appointed village chiefs. These lesser Indian officials were allowed to send a few of their own men to gather on their behalf on the collecting expeditions. Lastly, there was the interest of the church, which had to collect its tithe, or tenth, of all produce. At village level, the directors and local officials were told to assess the potential yield of each Indian's plot and to make an assessment that took account of his poverty. At the collective level, all the produce exported by Indian villages was to be shipped to a General Treasury of the Indians in Belém or São Luis. This central-ised marketing was supposed to obtain the best prices for the produce, and to prevent the confusion of allowing each director to do his own trading. It meant that the royal treasurer could remove the tithe before commissions were deducted or the Indians themselves were paid. It also meant that the royal treasury could fix low prices and reap profits on the export trade to Portugal.

There remained the problem of labour needs of colonial settlers who were not village directors. Portugal naturally wanted to per-suade as many as possible of its own people to settle in Brazil. Those who crossed the Atlantic thought themselves too important to labour alongside despised Indians and black slaves in the enervating humidity of the tropics. The few thousand colonists who had caused such devastation on the Amazon therefore clamoured for Indian labour as they were too poor to afford African slaves. The Directorate decreed that half the able-bodied Indians in each village should be made available for hire by settlers. Any Indian could be obliged to work for up to six months at a time in this way. It was determined that payment in full should be deposited in advance with the village director, to ensure that the Indian was paid at the end of his period of labour – and to prevent his running off before it was over. The Governor laid down a fixed scale of wages for ordinary labourers, for boatmen, and for skilled craftsmen. Payment was supposed to be in currency (which was just being introduced into Maranhão and Pará) or in trade goods. The royal authorities issued licences to settlers fixing the quota of Indians they could hire.

Such was Governor Mendonça Furtado's interpretation of the new Indian 'freedom'. He was sure that it would yield benefits to all, but most particularly to the government. It would ensure 'the spread of the faith, elimination of barbarism, propagation of the gospel, civil-ising of the Indians for the common good of the King's subjects, growth of agriculture, introduction of commerce, and finally the establishment of an opulent and completely happy state'.

Meanwhile, the Marquis of Pombal, Prime Minister and absolute ruler of Portugal under a compliant King, had developed a pas-sionate hatred of the black-robed Jesuit Fathers. He was encouraged by his brother's reports of Jesuit misbehaviour in Amazonia. He was also convinced that the Jesuit Company had great wealth that could save the flagging Portuguese economy, Pombal organised a propaganda campaign that grew increasingly hysterical, culminating in the law of 3 September 1759 in which King José proscribed the Jesuits and expelled them from Portugal and all her dominions. The law denounced them as 'corrupt, deplorably alienated from their saintly vocation, and manifestly unsuitable because of their many, abominable, inveterate and incorrigible vices. . . . Notorious rebels, traitors, adversaries and aggressors . . . by this law they are de-naturalised, proscribed and exterminated. . . . They are to be effectively expelled from all my Kingdom and Dominions, never to return.'

The new law was enforced quickly and ruthlessly. By 1760 six hundred Jesuit Fathers had been forced to evacuate their colleges and mission villages and leave Brazil. Their departure was a mortal blow to many mission Indians. The Jesuits had been bigoted and authoritarian; their missions were highly regimented, requiring total suppression of tribal customs. But the missionary Fathers were at least intelligent, and they had championed Indians against the worst excesses of the colonial settlers. In its heyday the Jesuit Company had wielded great power in Portugal and it had used its influence to persuade successive monarchs to enact pro-Indian legislation.

It is remarkable how quickly the once-mighty Jesuits fell. In 1767 the King of Spain, inspired by Pombal's success, likewise expelled the black-robes from his empire. Six years later, Pope Clement XIV declared the Society of Jesus extinguished; and it was many decades before it was revived in its modern form. Other missionary orders were removed from Brazil later in the eighteenth century, and the Indians were at the mercy of the new directors.

Opening Amazonia

During the oppressive decades of the Directorate, the banks of the mighty Amazon were empty. The world's largest river – through whose mouth flows a fifth of the fresh water that enters the oceans – had been denuded by almost two centuries of colonial oppression and the ravages of imported diseases.

The Amazon may be pictured as a great funnel. It is a Y-shaped system in which headwaters converge and then cut their way through the geologically ancient Guiana and Brazilian shields. The arms of this Y are the two largest tributaries, the Negro–Branco that flows in from the north-west, and the Madeira entering from the south-west. Above this junction, the Amazon is fed by a fan of silt-laden or 'white' rivers that carry sediment from the geologically young and unstable Andes mountains.

Below the junction, the two banks of the Amazon differ. To the north, 'black-water' tributaries drain off the Guiana highlands. These northern rivers are relatively short and steep, and their many rapids have discouraged settlement or exploration of their upper reaches. Their black colour is caused by a lack of sediment from the heavily weathered sandstones of the Guianas, and from the tannin content of vegetation grown on those soils. Some early explorers thought that the legendary kingdom of the Amazons lay near the source of these northern rivers; others were convinced that the rich Lake Parima and the treasures of El Dorado were hidden behind the cliffs of the sandstone table mountains. The problems of penetrating those northern rivers made such mysteries difficult to resolve.

Exploratory activity was therefore concentrated on the mighty southern tributaries, all of them as large as any river in Europe. Although each of these was cut by formidable barriers of rapids, they also had many hundreds of kilometres of broad, calm waters on which navigation was easy. From the east, these southern tributaries were: the Tocantins–Araguaia, whose mouth was close to the city of Belém do Pará; the Xingu–Iriri, whose lower reaches were settled in the seventeenth century but whose headwaters were not explored until the late nineteenth and twentieth centuries; the Tapajós; and the Madeira itself, which was seen as a potential trade route between the Amazon and Portuguese settlements far away to the south in Mato Grosso.

During the Directorate period in the late eighteenth century, there was a struggle between two Indian peoples for control of the southern shores of the middle Amazon. These two tribes, the Mura and Mundurukú, entered the vacuum left by many once-strong tribes that had been annihilated during the first century of European invasion. When the Portuguese first penetrated the Madeira, they waged fierce battles against the Tora tribe. A few decades later, when the Jesuits started to establish missions on the lower Madeira in the 1720s, they found themselves opposed by the newly contacted Mura. Mura hostility had a legitimate origin: a Portuguese trader had treacherously seized some Mura and sold them as slaves. In 1749 an expedition under José Gonçalves da Fonseca sent by the Portuguese to ascend the Madeira and try to open a riverine route to Mato Grosso had several engagements against the Mura, who were then living on a lake on the right bank of the Madeira upstream of the Jesuit mission Trocano (later renamed Borba). Gonçalves da Fonseca's men, using firearms, defeated the Mura in pitched battles. The Mura learned a valuable lesson from their losses: they never again offered open battle, but resorted to ambush and surprise attacks in the labyrinth of lakes and swamps near the mouth of the Madeira and along the main stream of the Amazon itself.

The Jesuit João Daniel described how missions had to defend themselves with stockades against frequent attack by Mura. These Indians waged 'continuous war against the whites, a war of revenge and undying hatred for which they had good reason' from past treachery. Their favourite tactic was to fire at boats, particularly when these were making their way through rapids. They used very long bows and arrows, and by holding the tips of their bows to the ground with their toes, achieved enough velocity in their shots to drive arrows clean through an ox or a man. They posted lookouts in the foliage of tall ceiba trees, which tower above the riverside forests. The English poet Robert Southey, who wrote a fine history of Brazil in the early nineteenth century, described how 'their ambuscades were usually placed near those points of land where the current was strongest, and boats had most difficulty in passing: there they were ready with grappling hooks, and a shower of arrows, which often times proved fatal before resistance could be offered. . . . No other nation impeded the progress of the Pará-men so much, nor inflicted such losses upon them.' Attempts to farm turtles near Barra do Rio Negro (modern Manaus) and in Codajás and other lakes between the Solimões (the main Amazon above the mouth of the Negro) and Negro had to be abandoned because of Mura attack.

The Portuguese were baffled by the new guerrilla tactics of this nomadic tribe. For many years fledgling towns along the rivers Amazon, Solimões and Negro lived in terror of Mura attack. 'They would kill our best Indian fishermen and white labourers with great skill and lightning speed. . . . No one was free to go to his place of work without an escort armed with shotguns. Far less could he go to the river to fish or hunt turtles to eat, without being assaulted.'

The authorities did their utmost to crush the Mura. Governors of Pará ordered annual attacks on their villages whenever these could be found. 'They suffered unheard-of slaughter and all other forms of hostility; but they did not desist from their animosity.' Elusive and highly mobile, brave and pitiless in war, the Mura rapidly expanded northwards and westwards from the lower Madeira. They harassed river traffic and occupied denuded stretches of the Amazon and Negro. When Francisco Xavier Ribeiro de Sampaio, the chief magistrate of the Portuguese Amazon, inspected the Solimões and Negro in 1774 he found everyone terrified of Mura ambush, for the warlike tribe's expansion was then at its height. The magistrate reported on the 'cruel and irreconcilable enmity' of the Mura and demanded 'the most furious war . . . to profligate and entirely destroy this nation'. Otherwise the colonies of the Amazon, Negro, Madeira and Japurá would be 'reduced to nothing'.

In 1775 the provincial government stationed a garrison at Borba on the lower Madeira as protection against the Mura. But, according to Robert Southey, 'the Muras were nevertheless so bold and so dreadful that they kept the place in perpetual alarm and deterred people from settling there.'

At the same time, another formidable tribe was moving north-westwards from a homeland on the upper Tapajós. This new aggressor was the Mundurukú. These great warriors were a match for both white settlers and other Indians – including the Mura, who became their avowed enemies. Bishop Caetano Brandão of Pará described the Mundurukú as 'a supremely pitiless and cruel heathen who kill everyone, sparing neither sex nor age'.

In 1778, Governor João Pereira Caldas organised a troop for a defensive war against both the Mura and Mundurukú of the Tapajós, although he cautioned the commander of this force to avoid 'practising on these barbarians the inhumanities that are usually perpetrated on similar occasions, with our men killing them with just as much cruelty as *they* do His Majesty's subjects'. Alexandre Rodrigues Ferreira, the first great naturalist to study the Amazon, felt that this instruction had been too mild. He wrote to the next governor in March 1784 recommending revival of legalised enslavement of any Mura or Mundurukú captured in battle. He argued that such a reward was the only hope of enlisting men to crush these bold warriors.

Fortunately, a war of extermination was not necessary against the elusive Mura. In 1785 the tribe unexpectedly decided to surrender. A large horde of Mura suddenly appeared at the settlement of Maripi on the Japurá, a tributary flowing into the north bank of the Solimões–Amazon. They obviously trusted the commander of this place, Mathias José Fernandes – although one popular tradition was that their unexpected and seemingly miraculous change of heart was due to the kindness of Bishop Brandão. Equally surprisingly, other groups of Mura surrendered simultaneously on the Madeira and Negro rivers, hundreds of kilometres from Maripi. Lourenço da Silva Araújo e Amazonas, the best chronicler of this period of history of the upper Amazon, noted that 'there was surprise at the speed with which their canoes appeared on different rivers, which seemed too far for them to have had time to take the news and give the agreed password "Comrade Mathias" as their means of recognition.' The Mura clearly knew fast routes through lakes and flooded forests, to move across country from the Solimões to the lower Negro and Madeira. Rodrigues Ferreira watched canoe loads of Mura men, women and children arrive at Moura on the Negro, to the amazement of its director and the other settlers and acculturated Indians. They explained that they had decided to accept 'reciprocal friendship that was promised to them in our settlements'.

Other Mura appeared at Borba on the Madeira, the town which had been garrisoned against them. Robert Southey explained why: 'The Mura were glad to seek the protection of this very town which had suffered so much from their hostility. . . . The Mundurukú, a tribe even more ferocious than themselves, had put them to flight.'

When Bishop Brandão visited Borba in 1788, he found a thousand Mura living there in rough shelters alongside its uneasy settlers.

The authorities had been uncertain how to treat the ferocious Mura when they tried to make peace. There was suspicion of their intentions. When one group presented itself spontaneously at Maripi on the Juruá in 1785, the garrison was promptly reinforced against them, 'for one may doubt that their attempt . . . to surrender peacefully to our friendship was sincere'. They were, however, given presents and told to return to the forests to persuade the rest of the tribe to follow their example. Governor João Pereira Caldas was naturally delighted by their unexpected surrender. He gave his personal word that the peace with them would be honoured, but, curiously, he suggested that they should be kept scattered in small groups rather than subjected to the usual practice of herding tribes into settlements. It had been their nomadic way of life that made them such formidable and elusive opponents; Governor Caldas nevertheless argued that 'it would never be advisable for them all to remain together, or their villages close to one another. This [dispersal] would make a future uprising more difficult. The best solution would be to try to remove them to more remote locations of the captaincy of Pará; but it will probably be impossible to persuade them to do this.'

There were half-hearted attempts to improve the lot of the Mura. When Governor Caldas returned to Lisbon, he urged that large quantities of dry goods be sent as aid for them, 'but the situation changed and opinions were different; so nothing was given to the Mura.'

The Mura had decided to come to terms with the colonists for three reasons: debilitation from disease, settler reprisals, and above all attack by the Mundurukú.

The Mundurukú had scarcely been known before the 1770s, when they suddenly burst in great hordes upon the settlements of the Tapajós. Annual reports by directors of villages on the lower Tapajós complained that Mundurukú attacks made it impossible for their charges to plant crops or go on expeditions to gather forest products. The German scientists Carl von Martius and Johann Baptist von Spix, who visited Brazil in the early nineteenth century, described the Mundurukú as 'the Spartans among the wild Indians of northern Brazil. . . . They zealously maintain their supremacy over their allies . . . and persecute various tribes with such inexorable fury that . . . some, being weak, will soon be completely exterminated.' The

Germans reckoned that there were then between eighteen and forty thousand Mundurukú, living on both sides of the Tapajós, partly on unforested plains.

The Mundurukú attacked by day, in long lines of warriors. They calmly awaited the arrows of their enemies, which the men avoided and the women dexterously caught in flight and handed to their men. During a campaign, all Mundurukú men slept together in common huts guarded by sentry patrols. During battle, they were marshalled by signals from a turé reed trumpet. To keep physically fit, the Mundurukú did not eat manioc porridge or inhale hallucinogenic paricá snuff, as did the neighbouring Mura and Mawé. Warriors' skins were covered in skilful tattoos of fine geometric lines.

When victorious, the Mundurukú spared no enemy men. They collected and kept as trophies the heads of their victims, which they sliced off with sharp bamboo knives. Eyes, tongues and muscles were removed and each head was then dried over a fire, washed in water and urucum oil, and dried in the sun. Once mummified, it was stuffed with cotton, given eyes and teeth of resin, and decorated with a feather headdress. This grisly trophy was kept constantly by the warrior who won it, hanging beside his hammock at night or from his body when hunting or fighting. (Examples of Mundurukú trophy heads can be seen in ethnographic museums in Rio de Janeiro, Belém and Vienna.)

In the 1780s a force of two thousand Mundurukú thrust eastwards and threatened Maranhão. This invasion was checked by the Gê-speaking Apinagé, who lived at the junction of the Tocantins and Araguaia rivers. But one group of Mundurukú pressed on and attacked Portuguese settlers on the Moju and Capim rivers close to Belém itself. This was too serious. The Governor sent a force of three hundred soldiers far up the Tapajós. The punitive expedition found a large Mundurukú village, perhaps near the tribe's heartland on the Cururu. The soldiers were in turn surrounded by vast numbers of Indians and had to fight their way back to the river. A thousand Mundurukú were killed in the battle, in which clubs and arrows proved to be no match for firearms.

Having failed with direct attack, Governor Manoel da Gama Lobo d'Almada tried more gentle methods. In 1795 he ordered a squadron to ascend the Tapajós to try to capture a few Mundurukú. After a battle, two young men were taken, slightly wounded by gunshot. The Governor ordered that they be healed and treated well. Five months later the two were taken back upstream and left close to their homes, loaded with gifts for the tribe. This conciliatory action made a deep impression. Over 150 years later, Mundurukú elders told the modern American anthropologist Robert Murphy what had happened in 1795: 'In the old days, our grandfathers were still wild and fought against the white men. The whites used to come up our rivers in their canoes, and we always battled. One day a group of them came up, and there was a fight and our men were driven off. Two of our young men were wounded and were left behind. They were captured and taken away.

'The next time the white men came we were about to attack when the two men who were captured stood up in the canoe and told us not to do anything as these people were our friends. They then came forward and showed us clothes, knives, axes, and many other good things that the whites gave them. They said that if we gave rubber and [manioc] farinha to the whites, we too would receive these things. The elders decided to do this and ever since we have been friends of the white men.'

In the year after their decision to make peace with the whites, masses of Mundurukú descended the Tapajós. They were settled in former Jesuit missions on the lower Tapajós – places that had once housed the populous Tapajós tribe, now vanished through disease and exploitation. They also filled new missions: Canumã near the mouth of the Madeira, and Maués and Jurutí on smaller rivers flowing into the south bank of the Amazon. One of these new villages was the personal initiative of a civilised Indian called Mathias, 'a master smith and captain of Light Infantry. Immediately after the Mundurukú tribe made peace with us . . . he went in person to the homes of these heathen and won them over with presents. He brought them to form the mission of Canumã, composed [in 1820] of eighteen hundred souls, to whom have been added a fair number of white families.'

The Portuguese were delighted by the unexpected pacifications, first of the Mura in 1785 and then a decade later of their enemies the Mundurukú, whom the explorer and army engineer Ricardo Franco de Almeida Serra described as 'one of the most valiant and feared nations in all the forests of the Amazon'.

During the four decades of the Directorate, the Portuguese had trouble with other tribes, although none opposed them as fiercely as the Mura and Mundurukú had done. During those same years, the Portuguese were pushing their rule into the far reaches of Amazonia, attempting to consolidate the territories awarded them by the Treaty of Madrid in 1750. When Governor Mendonça Furtado was on the

Rio Negro, he tried to make friends with native chiefs of the upper river, who lived on the new boundary; if they could be shown to be pro-Portuguese, their lands would be added to Brazil. Chiefs Manacaçari and Joá of the Aruak-speaking Warekena and Cucui of the Baré were brought down to Barcelos, to be loaded with presents and dazzled by the splendour of this riverside town. An expedition of fifty soldiers and 'tame' Indians went back up the Negro with the chiefs in September 1755, but when the Portuguese tried to claim the territories of these tribes, Chief Manacaçari massacred their native auxiliaries after a festival in his village. The whites on the expedition fled downriver. All the chiefs of the upper Negro rose against the would-be invaders. The furious Governor wrote to Portugal for permission to send a large force up the river, to defeat and enslave for ten years these 'rebel' Indians.

Nothing came of this fierce plan. Instead, as soon as the Governor left Barcelos in March 1757, 120 soldiers of its garrison mutinied. They had been unpaid for a year and lived in wretched conditions, subject to ferocious punishment by their officers. The mutineers looted the (largely empty) treasury, took the weapons from the arsenal, and fled down the Rio Negro and up the Solimões to seek asylum in Spanish Peru.

Later that year there was a genuine rebellion by mission Indians. The trouble started in the tiny mission village of Lama-Longa (formerly Dari) on the right bank of the upper Rio Negro. This had been the territory of the Manau tribe, but, as its numbers declined, the Carmelites had added Baniwa and Baré Indians to swell Lama-Longa's population. The spark that caused the rising was an attempt by a missionary to punish an Indian woman and separate her from her lover. The man, Domingos, formed an alliance with other chiefs and on 1 June 1757 attacked the missionary's house. The rebels destroyed and robbed everything in the settlement. By September, 'demoralised by the new "liberty" and by continued abuse' they rallied other Indians to their cause and advanced on Moreira (former Caboquena). There, on 24 September, they killed the Carmelite Friar Raymundo de Santo Eliseo together with a Caboquena chief and others who were collaborating with the authorities. The rebels advanced on Tomar (Bararoá), which was abandoned by its garrison of twenty soldiers. The village was burned and the church looted. The Indians defied their missionaries by fixing a statue of Santa Rosa of Lima to the prow of their canoe. They advanced on Barcelos itself, which was undefended after the mutiny of its soldiers. This 'formidable insurrection . . . had well nigh brought about the destruction of all the establishments upon the Rio Negro', but it was checked by the timely arrival of 120 troops sent upriver from Belém by the provincial governor. The force reached Barcelos just in time to defend it, for the Indians attacked next day. There was a bloody battle, with many Indians and some soldiers killed, but the rebellion was crushed and its leaders captured.

Governor Mendonça Furtado went up to the Rio Negro again in 1758 and found that most of the Manau tribe had fled to the forests. The Governor blamed a Mercedarian missionary for persuading them to flee. This missionary had 'told them to escape to the bush, because their villages would no longer be under [monastic orders]: they were to be administered by secular directors and parish clergy, under whose rule they would suffer infinite injustice and violence and would ultimately be slaves to the whites.' This was the first protest against the new Directorate. It was a terribly prophetic warning.

It was the Indians, not their missionaries, who were punished for what the Governor called 'atrocious crimes'. Two Manau chiefs were arrested near the rapids on the upper Negro and they and another rebel leader were hanged at Moreira. 'Their heads were left on the gallows, in order that their relatives would not quickly forget this most necessary and indispensable punishment.' Despite these executions, Mendonça Furtado admitted that the real leaders of the rising had not been captured. Many mission Indians were shipped downriver to prison in Belém do Pará. When the next governor, Manuel de Melo e Castro, reached Belém in August 1759 he found its jails full of Indians from the Rio Negro. Soon after his arrival, Captain Miguel Chaves arrived with many of Chief Manacaçari's Warekena. 'With this the jail became far fuller. [Indian prisoners] were dying of deprivation and hunger. No one whatever helped them with food for survival nor remedies for the illnesses they were suffering. They were being buried daily, to the great scandal of all these people. They went to their labour tied to a pole, naked, through the streets of the town, as if they were filthy animals and not baptised men as many of them were.'

Hostilities between the Iberian kingdoms intensified with the Seven Years' War of 1756–63, which found Portugal allied to England, and Spain to France. Portuguese and Spaniards manoeuvred for possession of the distant jungle rivers of the upper Amazon. Local Indian tribes were seen as potential allies in this game of geopolitics.

The Portuguese extended their influence with the help of an

unscrupulous chief called Yavita. He raided other tribes from the Japurá–Caquetá river northwards to the Uaupés, Xié and head-waters of the Negro, and then sold his captives to Portuguese slavers.

The Spaniards' second boundary commissioner, Don José de Iturriaga, came to Barcelos in 1759 with a team of surveyors, engin-eers and troops: he had a brief meeting with his Portuguese opposite number, Mendonça Furtado. When travelling south through the Casiquiare Canal from the Orinoco on to the upper Rio Negro, the Spaniards 'penetrated the country, explored it, insinuated them-selves and gained the friendship of the Indians in whose villages they erected palisades – on the pretext of protecting their party but with which they planned to justify later possession of the territory. This was in fact their claim for occupying territory on [the Negro] side of the Casiquiare, where they founded the military post of San Carlos.' Their moves were successful: for Spanish-speaking Venezuela now occupies the entire Casiquiare, and Colombia and Venezuela have the Rio Negro above the prominent landmark of the rock of Cucui.

In 1762 the next governor of the new Brazilian captaincy of Rio Negro, Joaquim Tinoco Valente, sent a large force up the river to drive the Spaniards out of the villages of the Marabitana Indians. As the Spaniards retreated, they burned the Indians' thatched malocas and took any natives they could upstream to San Carlos and Santo Agustino. The Portuguese set their Indians to work building forts to defend their Rio Negro frontier. One of these was at São Gabriel overlooking an important set of rapids; another was an earth pal-isade at Marabitana, far up the Negro near the new boundary. As always, local Indians were commandeered to build these forts and to carry the cannon, supplies and garrisons upriver to man them.*

A new treaty signed at San Ildefonso in 1777 both confirmed and modified the frontiers of the Treaty of Madrid. North of the Negro and Branco rivers, the frontier was defined as the watershed between the Amazon and Orinoco basins. Most of this watershed was un-explored, and its wild forested hills are scarcely penetrated to this day. But, founded on a sensible geographical definition, this boun-dary between the Portuguese and Spanish empires has survived without conflict for over two centuries. Farther west, the frontier was more difficult to determine. The headwaters of the Rio Negro and of the great white-water rivers that flowed off the Andes had all been explored by Spanish-speaking colonists or explorers. It was there-fore necessary to negotiate and establish which points on these rivers marked the divide between the two Iberian empires. The result was a fresh burst of frontier demarcation that lasted almost until the end of the century. All this activity had an important effect on the European exploration of Amazonia. It also had a strong impact on the Indian population.

Faced with the almost impossible task of demarcating thousands of kilometres of frontiers in the unexplored heart of South America, the Portuguese authorities divided the work into four. Each frontier division had its own commissioner and a team of surveyors (known as 'astronomers'), engineers and scientists. The first two divisions were in the south, surveying the boundaries between Brazil and what are now Uruguay, Argentina, Paraguay and Bolivia. The third division, based on Mato Grosso, was responsible for what are now the frontiers with Bolivia and Peru: the Guaporé, Mamoré and Madeira rivers, and the line from the Madeira westwards to the source of the Javari. The fourth division dealt with the Solimões (upper Amazon), Negro and Branco rivers, and was based on two towns: Barcelos on the Negro, and Ega (former Tefé) on the south bank of the Solimões six hundred kilometres upstream of the confluence with the Negro.

The sudden advent of these boundary commissions brought European engineers and scientists to the Amazon for the first time. The French academician Charles Marie de la Condamine, who had descended the Amazon in the 1740s, had been working on the measurement of the equator near Quito (a measurement that was to form the entire basis of the metric system of weights and measures), and his voyage down the river had taken the authorities by surprise. Apart from Condamine's unauthorised descent, all Brazil and the Amazon were rigorously closed to foreigners. When Captain James Cook called at Rio de Janeiro in 1768 on his first voyage, the authorities would not allow his men to land except for resupply. His frustrated naturalist Joseph Banks complained that 'no one even tolerably curious has been here since [the Dutch scientists] Marcgrave and Piso in about the year 1640, so it is easy to guess the state in which the nat. hist. of such a country must be.' Even at the end of the century, the great Alexander von Humboldt and his companion Aimé Bompland were refused entry when they tried to come down the Rio Negro from Venezuela.

The boundary commission on the Amazon and Negro (the fourth division) brought a fine team of engineers and scientists to that scientific vacuum. The team included Teodosio Constantino de Chermont and Henrique João Wilkens, both of whom had scientific leanings, and a good cartographer in José Vitorio da Costa. But its most distinguished members were to make reputations as some of Brazil's greatest explorers: Captain Ricardo Franco de Almeida

Serra, Manoel da Gama Lobo d'Almada and Francisco José de Lacerda e Almeida.

In 1784 the Portuguese even sent the first expedition of naturalists to the Amazon, under Alexandre Rodrigues Ferreira. He had with him two artists and a botanist, but Araújo e Amazonas complained that, instead of examining some of the world's richest wildlife which was all around them, the team 'wasted its time during its stay [on the Solimões] in sending back to the capital [Belém] to ask what it was supposed to do'. This judgement was unduly harsh. Rodrigues Ferreira did write a number of reports on such topics as what to do with the newly pacified Mura, and on the agricultural potential of the upper Amazon. He also wrote a classic account of his travels on the Amazon, Negro and Madeira: *Diary of a Philosophical Journey through the Captaincy of Rio Negro*.

The Amazonian boundary commissioners of both countries lived for almost a decade at Ega on the Solimões and Barcelos on the Negro. Such an increase in colonial masters, together with the many exploratory voyages they made, took a fearful toll on the Indians. Bishop Caetano Brandão said that the Solimões was being depopulated by the constant labour demanded of its Indians. Francisco de Sousa Coutinho, who governed the area at the end of the eighteenth century, complained of an excessive number of convoys 'for the apparent motive of the demarcation expedition': if these continued, 'the Indians will be totally extinct, or will have fled from the villages.' The governments of Mato Grosso and Pará were trying to establish a riverine trade route between their provinces. Sousa Coutinho deplored 'the extraordinary mortality among Indians', who would spend a year on the journey – four months upriver to the Madeira rapids, four months to overcome the hundred kilometres of rapids, and a further four months to reach Mato Grosso. The Indians 'are justifiably repelled' by such work, in which 'many have been consumed or sacrificed, so that the settlements are exhausted.' And Bishop Brandão saw the result: 'Very horrified and disgusted, they bury themselves in the forests and never reappear. The name Portuguese thus became odious to the heathen because of the disagreeable news it conveyed to them of our inhumanity.' He specifically blamed the naturalists' expedition of Rodrigues Ferreira for causing many native families to flee to the forests. 'Such navigation is fatal to the Indians, most of whom generally die or are incapacitated for life. They are so horrified by it that they choose to desert their villages rather than expose themselves to such a danger.' Robert Southey commented on the effect on Barcelos of being the headquarters of the demarcation team. 'They brought with them here, as everywhere else, a temporary increase of inhabitants; but this benefit was more than counterbalanced by the immorality which their people introduced, and by the effects of the compulsory service.'

The largest tributary of the Rio Negro is the Branco, so named because its waters are whiter than the black, tannic waters of the Negro. The Branco rises in the ancient sandstone rocks of the Guiana plateau, with one headwater flowing from Conan Doyle's 'Lost World' of Mount Roraima. It flows southwards, first over savannah plains and light woods and then down rapids into the rainforests of the Negro. The Portuguese had been exploring and raiding for Indian slaves on the Branco since the beginning of the eighteenth century. The greatest of these slaving expeditions was in 1740, when Lourenço Belforte (an Irish-born plantation owner Laurence Belfort) led an elite troop of soldiers and numerous Indians with their chiefs up to the rapids on the Branco's main headwater, the Uraricuera. The expedition spent two months exploring the surrounding plains and rivers – and seizing their unsuspecting Indians. The last official 'ransom troop' (a euphemism for a slaving raid) went up the Branco in 1748, after which Pombal's 1755 Law of Liberty forbad this traffic. A lull followed.

The Treaty of Madrid had defined the boundary between Portuguese and Spanish possessions in this unexplored region as the watershed between the Orinoco and other Caribbean rivers and the Negro–Amazon basin. Governor Mendonça Furtado worried that the Branco, which fell to Portuguese Brazil by this definition, was dangerously unoccupied. A result of his concern was an expedition of 1766 led by Lieutenant José Agostinho Diniz, which explored the Uraricuera and went on to the eastern headwaters, towards the Rupununi plains and the rivers of Dutch Guiana.*

Portuguese fears were realised in 1774, when a small force of Spaniards penetrated the Uraricuera. By pure chance, a Flemish deserter from the Dutch entered the upper Branco, heard about the Spanish force, and went to spend ten days in their camp before escaping with the help of Paraviana Indians. He made his way across the savannah and down the Branco, to report his alarming discovery to the Portuguese authorities early in 1775. The magistrate Francisco Xavier Ribeiro de Sampaio wrote that 'the accidental arrival of this stranger must be considered as a piece of extraordinary good fortune for us. The presence of Spaniards on the Rio Branco is as astounding as it is dangerous.'

This was a bad year for the Rio Negro: there had been a severe drought in 1774, then torrential rain the following year, described by the governor as 'indescribable winter weather which prevented the land being burned for a single plantation'. The colonists' Indians were exhausted by too many expeditions of exploration, and by having to defend themselves against constant persecution by the still unpacified Mura. Despite these problems, the Spanish threat was too serious to ignore. Soldiers were sent up the Amazon from Belém do Pará to join local troops and Indians on the Negro. In October 1775 a force of a hundred Portuguese soldiers and hundreds of native auxiliaries paddled up the Branco, under the command of an artillery officer of German origin, Captain Philip Sturm.

The Portuguese had no difficulty in surprising and capturing the two Spanish camps on the Uraricuera as well as an exploratory party that the intruders had sent eastwards up the Tacutu. In all, they captured forty Spaniards. The prisoners told of their long voyage up the Caroni and their march over forested hills on to the headwaters of the Uraricuera through a pass between the uppermost Caroni and Uraricaá rivers – an expedition that would daunt explorers to this day. The Portuguese authorities were disappointed to learn that the adventurers had been sent on 'the wearisome discovery of the Lake of El Dorado'.

El Dorado was the legend of the kingdom of a fabulously rich native ruler, the Gilded Man, who was thought to anoint himself with gold dust. In the sixteenth and seventeenth centuries countless expeditions had searched for this chimera; one of the last to do so was the English seaman Sir Walter Ralegh, but the failure of his attempt cost him his life – he was beheaded by King James I in 1618. Because the expeditions had failed to find this fabulous empire elsewhere in northern South America, a few romantics still thought that it might lie in the remaining unexplored region of the upper Rio Branco. Ever since the seventeenth century, maps had shown El Dorado on a lake called Parima in the Rupununi plains between the upper Branco and the Essequibo.

The explorers of 1774 were sent off to search for the legendary domain by the Spanish governor of the Orinoco, Don Manuel Centurión, who had been seized by the excitement of this mystery. An Indian had described El Dorado to him as 'a high hill, bare except for a little grass, its surface covered in every direction with cones and pyramids of gold . . . so that when struck by the sun, its brilliance is such that it is impossible to look upon it without dazzling the eyesight.' Even though the Spanish incursion was in pursuit of a fantasy, the Portuguese decided that they must urgently occupy the Rio Branco. Captain Sturm immediately started building a fort of earth ramparts and a wooden palisade near where the Uraricuera and Tacutu join to form the Branco. This fort, called São Joaquim, was later defended by stone walls and was manned for years by a small garrison.

Having established their fort, the Portuguese sought to attract Indians to settle in villages near it. They arrived on the upper Branco with plenty of presents and soon beguiled over a thousand Indians to move to six villages on the main river banks. Most of these were Carib-speaking Paraviana and Purukotó, but there were also some Makuxi and Aruak-speaking Wapixana. There were a few Ataraí (or Atruahi), and strenuous efforts were made to persuade chiefs of the Yanomami (then known as Waiká) to bring their people down from the forested hills of the Branco–Orinoco watershed. Although a few chiefs and family heads from these last two tribes accepted the blandishments of the white men, most refused to move: as a result the Atoraí and Yanomami have both survived relatively undamaged to the present day. The magistrate Ribeiro de Sampaio boasted of the ease with which the other tribes were won over by trade goods: 'This undertaking cost us very little effort. These Indians appear to have been eager to come under our rule. They made us understand how much they depended upon us [for tools and trade goods]. For, although the Dutch had helped them with many things, it was in exchange for slaves. Under Portuguese rule, they obtained what they desired without such violent means. . . . As for religion, they readily accepted ours since they themselves professed none at all. They offered their children for holy baptism with much joy and readiness, and the parents showed no less desire to receive it.'

The honeymoon between Indians and Portuguese did not last long. As so often in Brazilian history, the Indians quickly realised that they had been duped by promises of a comfortable life alongside the invading settlers. Their desire for tools was soon satisfied, and they rapidly learned that the colonists wanted them as labourers. Captain Sturm admitted that the Indians were treated badly, 'forced to do too much work, both outside and within their villages'. They were outraged by attempts to change their way of life: 'We try, gently enough, to forbid the abominable customs that they have always had – such as burning the bodies of the dead in the houses in which they died, or each man having as many wives as he pleases. . . . They are also very astonished to be forbidden to anoint themselves with [red] urucum body paint, and to be forbidden many other perverse and abusive customs that they are very loath to abandon.' It was, of course, easy for Indian hunter–gatherers with few material possessions to desert the artificial new villages: 'They can flee with ease, for they are in their own territory with the trails open before them.'

In February 1780, the Indians of two villages – one on the Tacutu and one on the Uraricuera – simultaneously deserted their settlements. A few months later they conspired to kill three Portuguese soldiers in the village of Conceição on the Uraricuera. The Commandant of Fort São Joaquim decided to seize the chiefs of another village and to send them in chains downriver to Barcelos. He made the mistake, however, of sending them in canoes paddled by members of their own Sapará tribe. The Indians managed to surprise and kill their seven-man military escort when it was camped one night on a river bank. They returned to the upper Branco and persuaded all but one of its newly settled villages to desert back to the forests.

The Governor of Pará, João Pereira Caldas, wanted to exact harsh reprisals. He wrote to his superior in Lisbon for permission to wage war on the tribes of the Branco: 'I consider it indispensable and very necessary to punish those barbarians: namely to chastise them by fire and sword.' But the answer from Lisbon was conciliatory. The Secretary of State was sure that Portuguese settlers had provoked the Indians: 'You will find that as a rule disturbances originate either in acts of violence by our side or from our demanding of the Indians more labour than they can perform.' The Portuguese minister recommended gentle treatment, and pointed out how often this had succeeded in winning over other Brazilian tribes. Governor Pereira Caldas followed this advice. On 28 February 1784 he issued a general pardon for the Rio Branco Indians, and replaced the belligerent commandant of Fort São Joaquim. He also sent a famous former Indian slaver, Miguel Archanjo de Bittencourt, upriver to try to lure the tribes back from their forests. Throughout 1784 and the ensuing years, this remarkable woodsman plunged into the forests and plains of the upper Branco to contact the Indians and convince them of the sincerity of the royal pardon. Gradually, groups of Paraviana, Karipuna and even uncontacted Makuxi and Wapixana visited the fort to negotiate, or brought their families back to the deserted villages.

Some years of uneasy calm followed. Indians in the Branco villages trusted the royal pardon and were impressed by the friendly commandant of the small fort.

The 1780s witnessed a magnificent spate of exploration. The Portuguese wanted to learn about the most distant frontiers of their empire. In quick succession, the upper Rio Branco was visited by the most famous contemporary explorers.

In December 1780 Governor Pereira Caldas sent two distinguished surveyors to investigate the river's headwaters – the army engineer Captain Ricardo Franco de Almeida Serra and the surveyor–cartographer Dr Antonio Pires da Silva Pontes. They reached Fort São Joaquim in January 1781 and had their Indians paddle and guide them eastwards to the upper Tacutu. They then had a tough march across the swamps and shallow lakes of the Rupununi plateau to verify the link between the waters of the Branco and those of the Rupununi and Essequibo. They reported that 'this interval between the Pirara and Rupununi rivers consists of plains and swamps which are transformed during the rains into a continuous lake.' It was this seasonal flooding that had given rise to the notion of the great lake called Parima, on which lay the legendary but non-existent golden cities of Manoa and El Dorado. The explorers made contact with many Makuxi, who inhabited all these plains and hills and whom they described as 'the most numerous and perhaps the least warlike tribe of the Rio Branco'. Turning back, Almeida Serra and Silva Pontes explored westwards, up the Uraricuera beyond the two destroyed Spanish camps and on to its northern tributaries. They saw the portage trail between the Branco and Orinoco basins 'by which the Purukotó tribe, who frequent these rivers in great numbers, drag their bark canoes'.

Five years later, in 1786, the naturalist Alexandre Rodrigues Ferreira made roughly the same expedition as his two colleagues from the boundary commission. He had been sent by the government of Portugal on the first scientific mission to investigate the natural wonders of Amazonia. Rodrigues Ferreira was therefore particularly interested in the source of some crystals that the Wapixana had brought to Fort São Joaquim. There had been much talk about a 'mountain of crystals'. Rodrigues Ferreira started up the Tacutu, but then explored northwards up the Surumú, towards the ancient sandstone table mountain Roraima. Leaving the river, his party went across the plain, often in chest-high swamps and with no shelter from sun or rain. 'With unspeakable hardship we ascended the first ridge, all of which consists of precipices of solid rock without any path or track to follow.'

The hills were indeed full of vast quantities of crystals. The travellers returned safely, thanks to the hospitality of the Wapixana. These Indians, whose great thatched huts were seen on all sides, were most friendly to the strangers, whom they fed with beiju manioc bread. Rodrigues Ferreira brought back from his journey a herbarium collection of plants, as well as drawings of wildlife and Indians.

His two artists were accurate but not very accomplished: their drawings of Rio Branco Indians were correct in detail, but stiff and naive in style. Back on the Branco, Rodrigues Ferreira noted that some seven hundred Indians had returned to the villages around São Joaquim. This relative success was the result of the policy of 'caressing and rewarding the natives who are now so familiar with us that they continue to descend [to the villages] of their own accord and motion'.

Hard on the heels of Rodrigues Ferreira, an energetic army engineer, Colonel Manoel da Gama Lobo d'Almada, visited the upper Rio Branco. He took with him an expedition of four officers, eight soldiers, and forty Indians from Portuguese-controlled towns of the Rio Negro. As always, much of the credit for this exploration goes to the Indians who paddled the canoes and hunted and fished to feed the men, their skills as woodsmen and boatmen overcoming any physical hazards. This future governor explored up the Uraricuera and Uraricaá, beyond the destroyed Spanish camps and further than any previous Portuguese expedition had ventured. He pushed upstream without any guide. At length he met some Indians, possibly Yanomami, and wrote in his journal: 'I have now finally come upon some natives, who are accompanying me on the journey, and this gives me more confidence. We are pushing ahead between mountains and over them.' His team crossed into the Orinoco watershed. One night his camp was hit by a flash flood – a familiar hazard on rivers rising in the heavily weathered rocks of the Guiana shield: rainwater pours off the cliffs, unchecked by sediment or vegetation. Lobo d'Almada lost two canoes, one of which contained most of his papers. Later, as he returned down the thunderous rapids of the Uraricuera, another boat sank with all his maps, clothes, hammocks and stores, and the leader himself was injured. Nothing daunted, Lobo d'Almada took only a short rest at Fort São Joaquim before pushing up the Tacutu, across to the Rupununi and up to the source of the latter in what is now southern Guyana. He also explored north, ascending twenty-one sets of rapids on the Surumú and Cotingo and climbing into the Pacaraima hills. Uncontacted Indians, presumably Wapixana or Makuxi, explained that the river rose on Mount Roraima.

Gama Lobo d'Almada had a vision of a prosperous colony on the plains of the upper Rio Branco. The problem was to persuade the hill tribes of the advantage of living among the Portuguese. He admitted that 'in their own manner, these Indians live more agreeably than among us.' It was therefore necessary to prepare manioc plantations

to lure them down. Those who came to Portuguese villages must be
fed and clothed and given time to build their houses and farm plots.
'They must not be burdened by demands for more labour than they
can furnish. They must be paid quickly and without usury whatever
they have been promised and are owed: they have earned this by the
sweat of their brows and sometimes at risk of their lives. . . . Fathers
should not be torn from their wives and children. They should be left
to enjoy the tranquillity that is their due under the humanitarian law
of liberty!'

Lobo d'Almada wrote a brilliant description of the topography of
each tributary of the Rio Branco, and mentioned all the tribes of the
region. The natural resources excited him: abundant cacao, medicinal sarsaparilla, monguba fruit, copaíba oil, many woods, dyes and
resins, and nuts such as cashews. He appreciated various fruits that
are still not exploited to this day: 'many are of excellent taste and
smell which, if cultivated, would be held in great esteem.' Above all,
Lobo d'Almada saw the potential for cattle ranching. 'Those fertile
plains are covered in excellent pastures for cattle, studded with
clumps of bush that would afford shade for the animals during the
fiercest heat, irrigated by creeks which render them fertile, and with
innumerable lakes from which is drawn a quantity of mountain salt.'
Lobo d'Almada had the first cattle transported upriver to these
fertile plains; two centuries later his prophetic vision has been
realised, for the Brazilian territory of Roraima (former Rio Branco)
is now a major cattle producer. The explorer also took bundles of
wild indigo and planted them successfully near Fort São Joaquim,
and discussed the possibilities of introducing cotton.

In 1788, the year after his expedition and his far-sighted report
about the future of the Rio Branco, Colonel Gama Lobo d'Almada
was made Governor of the captaincy of São José do Rio Negro. But
his attempt to revive the Rio Branco settlements was wrecked by
seemingly inevitable misunderstandings between natives and colonists. In 1790 some Makuxi living opposite the fort 'rebelled'. Indians
forced to work in the fishery went on strike and threatened their
administrators with knives in their hands; a chief fired a musket at
Portuguese soldiers; and a precious horse and mare from the
Governor's stud were killed. The tribe fled. An expedition sent in
pursuit caught the fugitives four days' march across the plains and
brought most of them back, but a Makuxi chief and other Indians
were killed in the skirmish.

Governor Lobo d'Almada decided on a drastic solution. Most of
the Branco villages had trusted the colonial administrators and did

not flee but, despite this, the Governor ordered that all but one of them be sent into remote exile. Sixteen chiefs were taken as hostages to Barcelos. Their people were uprooted and banished to new locations thousands of kilometres away from their homes and far distant from one another. One village was relocated at Arvellos on the Solimões, another at Borba on the Madeira, and the rest at Vila Nova da Rainha (modern Parintins) far down the main Amazon. The Governor wrote to the directors of places receiving these exiles, explaining that, if left near their homes, 'they were all ready to commit their habitual cruelties.' He hoped, however, that they would make good settlers and have no cause for complaint, now that they had lost all hope of ever regaining their original lands. 'Therefore treat them with pity and do them all possible good, to please them and keep them contented. The cruelties they have committed should inspire in you only caution and careful surveillance of these people; but do not hate them.' As a corollary to this grotesque experiment, other newly contacted Indians from the Rio Negro went as 'volunteers' to occupy the lands and villages from which the tribes of the upper Branco had been expelled.

The brutal exile of Indians from the Rio Branco in 1790 was not the end of the story of repression in that northern extremity of Brazil. In 1798 Paraviana and Wapixana Indians rebelled, killing their director, a squadron of soldiers and some settlers. A punitive expedition under Lieutenant Leonardo Ferreira was sent against them. The Indians were defeated and slaughtered at a place that became known as Praia do Sangue, the Beach of Blood. Seventy Indians who survived the massacre were transported for thousands of kilometres to join the earlier exiles at Borba and Parintintin, on or near the Madeira river. Indians from the Madeira were, in turn, transported north to fill the villages on the Branco* – even though they had committed no 'crime' in colonial terms.

While boundary commissioners were exploring the upper Rio Branco, more teams were penetrating and mapping other remote rivers. The surveyor Dr Francisco José de Lacerda e Almeida had the Indians paddle him up the fan of rivers that feed the upper Rio Negro. In 1785 and 1787 Manoel da Gama Lobo d'Almada was also active on the Negro's northern tributaries. He explored the Cauaburi and Maturacá, and discovered another natural riverine link between the waters of the Negro and Orinoco. The land here is flat, and during the rainy season meandering rivers flood and join others on the opposite side of the watershed. The Maturacá joins the Baria, which flows towards the Casiquiare Canal (another connection between the two river basins) from a vast forested canyon at the foot of Mount Neblina, the highest peak in the Amazon basin outside the Andes. These were formidable discoveries, in virtually un-explored regions still considered to be uninhabited. According to Araújo e Amazonas, these explorations were recorded on maps that were not preserved: they may have been stolen in Belém or sent to Lisbon and lost there.*

The boundary commissioners also had to fix the frontier farther south. The Treaties of Madrid and San Ildefonso agreed that the territories of Brazil and Peru should join at Tabatinga on the main Amazon–Solimões, in the lands of the Omagua and Tukuna tribes. But it was necessary to decide where the jurisdiction of the European powers met on unexplored rivers flowing into the Solimões from the north. This was the task of the boundary commissioners stationed at Ega. After some months of haggling and procrastination, the two teams set off in 1782 in a flotilla of boats and canoes to explore the Japurá–Caquetá river, led by Lieutenant-Colonel Teodosio Con-stantino de Chermont on the Portuguese side and Colonel Francisco Requena y Herrera for the Spaniards. It proved to be a tough jour-ney, with many dangerous rapids on the tributaries that the expedi-tion investigated. Fortunately for us, Colonel Requena kept a journal, and he is thought to be the artist of a charming set of watercolours that survive in two American libraries, showing the commissioners in three-cornered hats, pig-tailed hair queues, long-waisted frock coats and high boots. They are busy with telescopes and astronomical observations, or watching their Indians haul the boats through rapids or over watershed portages.

The expedition went up the Japurá to the Apaporis river (now the boundary between Brazil and Colombia), but it was terribly devas-tated by malaria. Requena sent 117 sick men back downriver at this point, and the Portuguese contingent was equally decimated. They continued up the Apaporis, but in June 1782 the remaining Indian paddlers were struck by some other epidemic. The two teams were reduced to only seventeen and thirteen Indians respectively with the result that the commissioners themselves had to tend the many sick. Requena described the ordeal: 'In this labour of mercy the Portu-guese commissioner treated his sick; and I, since necessity is the mother of invention, brought myself to prescribe capital remedies of emetics and bloodletting for those who most needed them, to the best of my ability, and quinine for those with fever. With good luck, I did not lose a single patient.'

The sick explorers had sheltered among Kueretú (Coretú)

Indians, and Araújo e Amazonas praised this tribe's hospitality: 'All honour to the Coretú Indians, in whose malocas the Europeans fell ill. These Indians treated them with great diligence: this can be explained only by the Indians' instinctive goodness of heart – for they are too ignorant to understand what our society calls philanthropy or the Church calls charity.'

The Directorate

The Directorate legislation of 1757, originally written for the mission Indians of the Amazon basin, was soon extended to cover the rest of Brazil. The Portuguese Secretary of State for Overseas Territories wrote to a newly appointed governor of Goiás in central Brazil, setting out official hopes for what might take place: 'The wilds of that vast continent are covered in Indians. It is *they* who should be the principal inhabitants of the settlements, towns and cities that are being founded.' He saw the civilising of the Indians as a 'far more important objective' than all the gold and diamonds that had been extracted from Brazil. All that was needed was kindness. 'This is not the method used by the Portuguese and the missionaries who accompanied them on the pretext of propagating the gospel. They entered the wilds of Brazil armed, to hunt Indians as if they were beasts . . . to massacre all who resisted, and to reduce to hard and cruel slavery those who escaped death but fell into their hands. The result was that the Indians buried themselves deeper in their forests, and from there wage a continuous, embarrassing and disadvantageous war against us, in their just and natural defence. His Majesty thus has the centre of his colonies covered in implacable enemies of Portugal instead of useful subjects who could fertilise, farm and enrich the lands of those colonies.'

Such was the official optimism from Lisbon. Gentleness and kindness were to transform noble savages into productive subjects. There was much talk of civilising Indians and bringing them into the bosom of the church. But in practice demands for Indian labour overrode any humanitarian considerations.

Settled agriculture was seen as the best means of civilising forest Indians. Clause 17 of the Directorate legislation insisted that

Indians should be persuaded of the benefits of agriculture. No one faced up to three problems that militated against the use of Indians in agriculture. One was the clash of interests in the employment of Indians. Settled agriculture demanded constant attention, particularly at planting and harvesting times; this could not be reconciled with forest collecting expeditions or work as paddlers on royal or private trading voyages, which could last for many months. A second problem was the difficulty of converting the soils beneath tropical rainforests for large-scale agriculture. The combination of tropical rains and sun, of weak laterite soils beneath cleared forest, and particularly of the teeming and voracious mass of parasites, weeds and predators, all tended to destroy European-style agriculture. Lastly, there was the cultural problem of changing Indian attitudes to agricultural labour.

In the late eighteenth century there was no attempt to understand Indian society. At the start of European discovery of Brazil and Amazonia there had been some curiosity about the inhabitants of the New World. Vaz Caminha, Vespucci and other explorers had marvelled at the harmonious, egalitarian way of life of the American Indians. Some of their awe had evolved among European intellectuals into the theory of the noble savage – the subversive philosophy that played a part in inspiring the French Revolution. But none of this intellectual esteem for the natives found its way to the shabby colonial backwater of the Amazon. The academic study of anthropology had not yet begun. With the Jesuits and other missionaries expelled, there were not even many champions of the Indians interested in converting them to Christianity and saving their souls.

In most tribal societies agriculture was women's work. Men did the hard labour of cutting and burning forests to produce the clearings that were the basis of slash-and-burn agriculture. Once the clearings (roças) were made, women (the fertile sex) tended the growing plants and harvested them. Men used their skills in hunting and fishing. Indian men therefore deeply resented the demeaning drudgery of farm labour. Just as repugnant to them was the system of working for someone else – in communistic tribal society each family unit was self-sufficient, and larger tasks such as hut building were done collectively. Indians also found the concept of overproduction for export and profit incomprehensible and alien.

Directorate villages were encouraged to grow basic crops such as manioc, rice, corn and cotton. Black beans, which are now a ubiquitous source of protein in Brazil, were planted only rarely, as was tobacco. Every Indian family was to feed itself from an individual plot, but patchy statistics based on tithe returns indicate that people lived close to famine, with an average of only about one alqueire (eight litres) of manioc flour to feed a household for a month. Most farming took place on each village's communal plot, which might be anything from five to twenty hectares in area. Directors decided what would be planted on this common land, but the produce was not for local consumption: it went to feed collecting expeditions, or for men employed in state service in dockyards or garrisons, or to supply the markets in Belém and other growing towns. The director of course deducted his commission of one-sixth, and the communal output also suffered payment of tithe.

Indians employed in such farming were virtual slaves. The native division of labour between the sexes suited the colonial directors: it meant that women could be drafted while their men were away on expeditions. Thus, although men did the heavy clearing and burning, women often did the planting and harvesting. The American historian Robin Anderson analysed reports from thirty-four Directorate villages, and found that women accounted for 61 per cent of the labour on community plots. One detailed return from Alenquer (the former mission of Surubiú, on the Amazon opposite the mouth of the Tapajós) showed precisely which sex worked on this labour on which days: this revealed that it took 72 man-days to clear the plot, and 248 woman-days to plant and tend it.*

Plantations belonging to settlers or to the state governments likewise used Indian labour. When Pombal removed Indians from missionary control and granted them illusory freedom, he launched a trading company for Maranhão and Pará. His plan was based on increased use of slave labour from Africa. For a time, black slaves were brought in larger quantities to the Amazonian part of Brazil and the new company was successful. Settler plantations consisted of long frontages along the innumerable Amazonian waterways, and it was up to the planter to penetrate into the forests behind. These plantations tended to concentrate on monoculture of crops for export, generally cacao, coffee, rice and sugar. They thus differed from the more haphazard farming of Directorate Indian villages, which grew manioc and rice for local consumption.

Much of the prosperity of the lower Amazon in the late eighteenth century came from rice. Laurence Belfort,* the wealthy Irish planter, introduced Carolina rice into his plantations in Maranhão in the 1760s – a lighter, smaller-grained strain than that used hitherto by Amazonian settlers. In 1772 the government instructed the Governor of Pará to introduce Carolina rice into his province, which he did with the help of the French-born engineer, Teodosio Constantino de Chermont. By the 1780s, rice exports from Maranhão and Pará greatly exceeded those from the rest of Brazil, and Portugal had become self-sufficient in rice from its American colony.

Cacao was another lucrative crop. Mexicans first discovered how to make chocolate from the seeds of the *theobroma cacao* tree, and drinking chocolate or cocoa had become a popular fashion in Europe. Plantations of cacao trees did well in the Amazon, where the tree anyway grew wild. Cacao became the Amazon's dominant export by the 1730s, but the trade was disrupted by a drastic decline in Indian gatherers caused by terrible smallpox and measles epidemics in the 1740s and 1750s. The use of African slave labour revived the plantations, and during the latter part of the eighteenth century Pará was exporting 715 to 850 tons a year, which was 90 per cent of the Brazilian total.* Indians played little part in this cacao boom – possibly because the crop required constant weeding and attention, for which there were too few men available in Directorate villages. Or it may have been because the cacao plantations were concentrated on the furos, the maze of channels that linked Belém with the Amazon to the west of Marajó island, an area which was relatively denuded of Indians by the late eighteenth century.*

The other new crop in Amazonia was coffee, which was grown on uplands between rivers, and generally under shade trees in the Central American manner. It provided steady exports throughout the late eighteenth century, but the annual quantity was usually less than a hundred tons, small in comparison with cacao or rice. Coffee was fairly easy to grow, and a number of Directorate Indian villages tried this new crop. Most of those who did so planted only a few hundred bushes; but at Vila Franca (the former Jesuit mission Cumaru on the Tapajós) the Director made his Indians plant almost sixteen thousand trees.

Two commodities which were of almost no concern to Indians were sugar and cattle hides. Sugar was grown only in plantations, generally worked by black slave labour, and it was not allowed to develop sufficiently to compete with sugar from Bahia and the Brazilian north-east. Cattle were raised in large ranches, chiefly on Marajó island. Most of the cattle ranches were former Jesuit properties, but they employed almost no Indians.

Although Indians escaped much of the toil in plantations, they were heavily involved in forest collecting expeditions, a task at which they excelled. Tribes have a fine knowledge of forest fruits and generally organise their year to gather plants at the appropriate seasons and locations. Agile and highly practised woodsmen, they can move through forests and recognise individual plants with skills that no whites or blacks ever seem able to match.

Collecting is also the most sensible method of exploiting rainforest. The forest ecosystem is so complex and the parasites are so infinitely numerous and voracious that rainforest trees scatter themselves to survive. Plantations are vulnerable to pests, and cleared forest yields pitifully little from agriculture. Therefore, ever since the advent of European colonists in the Amazon, Indians had been sent off to gather the drogas do sertão. The Directorate legislation sought to organise Indian labour from each village into yearly collecting expeditions. These tough journeys could last for many months; it did not strike the authorities as illogical to try to encourage both collecting and agriculture by the same labour force.

The plant products sought by these arduous expeditions were a curious mixture, and the function of many of them must have been incomprehensible to the Indians. There was sarsaparilla, the root of a small tree of the *Labiatae* family or of *Smilax*, a genus of climbers of the lily family with toothed, heart-shaped leaves. Dried sarsaparilla roots were shipped off to make medicinal teas and restoratives for European ladies or hypochondriacs. Another forest 'drug' was cravo. The word cravo means clove in Portuguese; but in Brazil, cravo was the name for aromatic barks of trees such as *Dicypellium caryophyllatum* or *Ambrosia polystachya* (ragweed) whose barks tasted like cloves. These were in demand as spices, to hide the taste of rotting meat in the days before refrigeration. During the Directorate, cravo accounted for 11 per cent of the exports of Greater Pará or Amazonia. A product of the forest that continues to be in demand as a luxury to the present day is Brazil nuts (castanhas do Pará); Indians had been collecting these delicious nuts for centuries, in forests near the lower Tocantins and from the Jari north of the Amazon. Then there were various products used in shipbuilding: caulking materials from barks, tar from resins, and ropes from liana fibres. Plants also yielded oils for cooking, soap or lamps – notably saps from the andiroba, copaíba and sumaúma trees. Outside Amazonia, in central Brazil, Indians collected the ipecacuanha or ipecac root – a substitute for quinine as a palliative for malarial fevers.

Yet even forest collecting had its destructive side. With Brazil nuts and some of the resins or oils, forest trees yielded annual crops; collecting was therefore consistent and relatively easy. But with sarsaparilla, collectors destroyed trees to rip up their roots. Collect-

ing expeditions therefore had to plunge ever deeper into the forests
to find new stocks of these medicines.

The Indians suffered too. In his official report of 1788, the judge
Antonio José Pestana da Silva inveighed against the cruelty of these
expeditions. He blamed the directors for sending off too many collecting expeditions, encouraged by their one-sixth share of the yield.
Each expedition was run by an armed cabo. These bosses were
generally soldiers and they tended to be violent and abusive: 'These
men generally reward Indians who bring or extract too little produce
with a beating, for they hate to disappoint their hopes and greed.'

Beatings in Amazonia at that time were vicious. The Jesuit João
Daniel acknowledged that 'experience has shown that thrashing is
the most convenient and appropriate punishment for Indians. All
who live and deal with them know that a punishment of only forty
strokes is recommended – this is what missionaries customarily
give.' Some white settlers were, however, far crueller: 'They kill some
with the violence of their blows, and place others at the gates of
death. If they themselves felt how agonising are the pains of a good
thrashing, they might perhaps be less inhuman to their poor
[Indians].' Daniel knew one settler who was accidentally hit on the
back by a whip in the dark. The pain was so intense that this man
vowed never again to beat Indians. Pestana da Silva pointed out that
settlers who had Indians working for them under temporary licence
would have no such scruples: 'a settler armed with his licence does
not want an Indian to sleep or rest, but gives him cruel beatings and
even throws pepper into his eyes to prevent him falling asleep.'
Soldiers were even worse than colonists. Pestana da Silva described
them as lazy, debauched, licentious and violent. 'For the Indians
there could be no men more odious than the military.'

In this brutal system, Indians spent many months in the forests,
after which they manned large canoes to take the produce downriver,
first to their Directorate village and then on to the capital, where,
after disposing of the cargo, they were promptly sent off on other
long paddling journeys. Ribeiro de Sampaio published tables to
show how little the Indians earned from tough forest collecting
expeditions. He asked the Governor to 'consider the great and dangerous work involved in the journey to the forests and to [Belém do]
Pará and the time spent in the forests themselves. Then recall how
little payment is given to compensate for such great hardships. The
canoes leave for the forests at the beginning of January and return at
the end of June. The voyage to Pará takes a month; another month is

spent waiting in that city; and two [months] on the return journey. The entire task thus takes ten months. Now average out the profit of this business . . . and observe how little an Indian earns per month!'

Since they were legally free men, the Indians were supposed to be paid for all this work, whether in forest collecting, on plantations or in farming. Their reward was a division of the profit from a collecting trip or from a village's sale of produce – but only after the director, cabo, state, church and other middle men had removed their shares. Payment was made in coarse homespun cotton cloth. In their natural state almost all Indian tribes went naked. Clothes were not necessary in the tropical climate of Amazonia. They were an impediment for people moving through forests or subject to sudden rain storms. And clothing created new wants: for needles, buttons, thread and soap. Nevertheless, Christian morality demanded that Indians must be clothed. Thus, ironically, payment for long and backbreaking work for the colonial masters was in cloth for which Indians had no need except to satisfy the prudery of those same masters. Directorate legislation argued that Indians were not yet capable of receiving payment in money, and eighteenth-century Amazonia generally functioned without currency. Settlers were urged to pay for Indian labour in goods other than cloth; but cotton cloth remained the normal means of payment. The rate of pay for Indian labour was fixed in 1751 and remained in force for over twenty years. Although expressed in money terms, directors, settlers and government officials converted the sums involved into lengths of cloth, at unfavourable rates of exchange.

An analysis of types of service by Indian men, based on an average of returns from Directorate villages during the forty years from 1758 to 1798, showed that collecting expeditions occupied 28 per cent of the men's time, miscellaneous and agricultural work 26 per cent, royal service 21 per cent, work for settlers 15 per cent, fishing 6 per cent and work for village officials 4 per cent.*

Of these various types of work, royal service was probably the worst. Indians were employed for the state in the shipyards at Belém, on expeditions to cut timber, in sawmills and other enterprises, and in the construction of a stone fortress at Macapá to guard the mouth of the Amazon. Men employed in these public works were badly treated, meanly paid or not paid at all, overworked, not released at the end of their contract terms, undernourished and vulnerable to diseases that ravaged their camps. Governor Pereira Caldas wrote in 1773 that 'the work at Macapá and other infinite and heavy services

. . . and the repeated expeditions to Mato Grosso have completely ruined the villages.'

The directors naturally tried to avoid sending their village Indians to royal service. In the early nineteenth century Spix and Martius observed that 'the directors are tyrants, absolute masters of the villages and of the native population of every age and sex. Far from having them taught or instructed, they carefully avoid any contact between them and the whites, claiming that the latter are a bad influence on the Indians. . . . Instead of encouraging them to make clearings or gather forest produce [for themselves], instead of placing the Indians at the disposal of the government or of the resident settlers, they employ the greatest possible number of them solely for their private ends. Even the most moderate directors would for appearance's sake send only a few Indians – generally those of least use to themselves – to work for the government in the forests or on some work ordered by the [authorities] in Belém. Apart from these, they used to lie and claim that they had no Indians available. They deliberately sought to lessen their Indians' respect for government officials or other whites.'

The royal shipyard at Belém was a formidable enterprise. During the fifty years of its existence the yard completed three brigantines, six frigates, seventeen other ocean-going vessels and many river boats. All the timber naturally came from the forests of the Amazon, as did the rope and pitch. Many of the work force were Indians or mestizos who had left the Directorate village system and who now formed the working class of Belém and nearby towns. There were smaller factories making a range of local manufactures in other Amazon towns. Thousands of kilometres from Belém, Governor Mendonça Furtado decided to develop the former mission of Barcelos, far up the Rio Negro, into a capital for the captaincy he had created on the Negro and upper Amazon. Rodrigues Ferreira described the two potteries in Barcelos in 1786. One was built on the site of a large thatched hut where the Indians formerly held dances and ceremonies taking the hallucinogenic snuff paricá. The other pottery was a royal business, making roof tiles for the barracks, grandiose government buildings and other local settlers' houses. It turned in a good profit for the treasury from the labour of its Indians. Demand for Indians in royal service was so great at Barcelos that its directors could not 'freely practise the activities they fancied. For the first interest of the town is the royal service, which incessantly requires Indians.'

The most demanding of all state activities was movement along the vast network of Amazon rivers. Although the larger river boats had small sails for use with a following wind, the main motive power of all the expeditions was paddling by Indians. Native boatmen were the only people capable of hauling boats up the innumerable rapids or steering them down their swirling waters.

Paddling and boating were tasks at which Indians excelled. Bishop João de São José, who visited his diocese on the Amazon in 1762–3, described Indians generally as 'weak, lazy and unaccustomed to work – if we except rowing, in which they are the best men in the world and tireless'. Later travellers continued to marvel at the skill and endurance of Indian paddlers. The British naval Lieutenant William Smyth, who descended the Amazon in 1835, wrote that 'the length of time that these men will continue to pull, with short intermissions, is quite incredible. . . . Their manner of paddling deserves notice: their stroke was regular, and for the first three-quarters of an hour slow, after which it gradually quickened, till at the end of an hour and a half they were striking as fast as the paddles could be moved, and the canoe seemed to fly through the water.' At a signal from the leader, the Indian paddlers changed sides, pair by pair, with such skill that the boat never lost momentum.

An American called Edwards, who went up the Amazon in 1846, described the galiota boat in which he travelled as some thirty feet long and seven wide, with a small cabin at the stern and a canvas-covered tolda or curved awning over the baggage hold. 'On either side of this tolda was a space a foot in width, and level. Here, in most awkward positions, were to sit the paddlers. These were Indians, mostly of the Mura tribe, heretofore spoken of as the worst upon the river.' Edwards was distressed by the sultry weather. 'But no matter how severe the heat, the Indians seemed not to mind it, although their heads were uncovered and their bodies naked. Every day, about noon, they would pull up to the bank for the purpose of bathing, of which they were extravagantly fond.' Not surprisingly, Indians would often run off in the midst of one of these arduous voyages. It was difficult to prevent this, for 'the detention of their little baggage or the wages accruing to them is a matter of perfect indifference.' They were equally unconcerned by a term of imprisonment: 'A detention in the calaboose [jail] would in itself be slight; but when it involves at least three hundred lashes from the cat, a most detestable animal to the Indian, it becomes something to be considered. Desertion is so common and so annoying, that it receives no mercy from the authorities.'

Edwards' men 'pulled steadily and contentedly from four in the morning until eight at night, frequently cheering their labour by songs. . . . We could never catch these wild tunes, but they were as natural to every Indian as his bow and arrow.' Prince Adalbert of Prussia, who was also on the Amazon in the 1840s, noticed how a shower of rain made them 'brisk and good-humoured: they instantly pulled off their shirts, to enjoy the refreshing coolness of the rain upon their backs, and set to work paddling with might and main, bantering jokes or accompanying the stroke of the paddles with their songs, which they improvised, and which, although the burden did not change, had a certain sweet and melancholy melody. At first only one sang, riming all the words that came into his thoughts: another would then take up the strain, and at the end of each stroke the chorus joined in.'

It was in rapids that Indian boatmen excelled. As movement along the network of Amazon rivers increased, groups of Indians would live near rapids to guide travellers through them or to haul their boats upstream in return for trade goods. The problem continues to this day. Anyone who has travelled or explored on tributaries of the Amazon will have had adventures in rapids, with vivid memories of the dangers and the exhaustion, the risk of sting-rays, and the swarms of pium blackflies that breed in them. An exciting description of his ascent of one set of rapids has been left by the Brazilian Indianist and explorer João Barbosa Rodrigues. Two crews of Indians toiled to haul a large boat and a canoe up a waterfall 'which appeared to me to be insurmountable. . . . The two crews worked together, part of them jumping into the water and the others going ahead with long lines of sipó [liana] attached to the canoe. Accustomed to this kind of work, the Indians paid little heed to the currents, bathing and diving now and then, and evidently enjoying themselves. The lines were secured to rocks above; my pilot took the helm, and the men in the water lifted the canoe with all their might, some with their backs, others with their hands, while others still were pulling on the line. After two hours of terribly hard work, they managed to get the boat off the rocks, and it would have been washed down at once but for the line. The men jumped aboard and the line was cast off; they shot down with incredible velocity, but obedient to the helm which my pilot handled most dexterously. Crossing the river, they sought a passage on the other side of the rapids where, although the current was heavier, there were no rocks in the way. Here, as before, long lines were thrown out ahead and attached to rocks. The men, working over their waists in the current, dragged and lifted the canoe and so pushed it along slowly. Thus in half an hour they had passed the first fall to a little pool above. Shouts of joy crowned the passage. Then, dragging on a line, they passed the rapids beyond without much difficulty and the canoe was brought to anchor by the sand beach to which the cargo had been carried.'

While one team of Indians hauled boats upstream, others had to manhandle the cargoes over the rocks of the rapids. A German engineer was impressed by huge loads that were moved up rivers in this way. 'Of the misery and annoyance of repeated unloading and carrying of heavy chests over glowing bare rocks, under the burning rays of the sun, against which the stunted growth on the stony soil offers no shelter worth mentioning to the poor Indians, only he can form an idea who has seen this kind of "navigation" with his own eyes.'

Indians were equally impressive when shooting down rapids. The American William Farabee, who led an expedition from the University of Pennsylvania to the Tapajós in 1914, had a canoeman with 'that quiet self-command common in the Indian'. In the navigation of rapids 'to the Indian there are no dangers, because he steers his bark easily and safely without accident. He never loses his self-possession, is never nervous, and always does the right thing at the right time. His canoe shoots by within an inch of the rock which might have dashed it to pieces, but he knew the inch was all the room he needed and had his canoe and men in such perfect control that there was no danger. . . . The traveller with such companions soon develops a confidence which allows him to enjoy the thrills of the passage.'

Such river work was the constant task of Indians, for month after month, up and down thousands of kilometres of Amazonian rivers. They worked as paddlers for their village directors, for private settlers, and above all for the government.

One of the best accounts of the working of the Directorate system came in a report to the King by Antonio José Pestana da Silva, the magistrate and general superintendent of the Indians of the upper Amazon. He wrote in 1788, after the Directorate had been functioning for thirty years, and his accounts are the fruit of first-hand experience. He roundly condemned the men chosen to be directors of Indian villages: 'They determine everything absolutely. They do not inform native judges or chiefs of their obligations, but make themselves superintendents and odious lords of all government and all business.'

Pestana da Silva was a royal official, and he recognised that the

Amazon provinces needed Indian labour. But he protested eloquently against the appalling distortion of the so-called Law of
Liberty: 'It is quite clear that the laws do nothing to protect the
Indians in their freedom. How could oppression and enslavement of
these wretches be worse? How could they possibly love the Portuguese nation or have any loyalty to the government? This is no way
for us to entice the heathen from the forests to join our empire . . . or
increase the number of faithful for the bosom of the church!' When
Indians were forced to work by violence it amounted to slavery. 'The
methods of recruitment recommended in the Directorate legislation
are altered in practice and are not just: they are violent. Is it not
violence to force an Indian who is working on his own farm to leave it
and go against his will to serve a settler, because the Governor has
given that settler a licence? Is it not violence for an Indian to leave the
shelter of his poor home, the comfort of his wife and children, and
the protection of his family, to go to navigate arduous rivers, to fish,
to build depots, to plunge into the forests, all to benefit a settler to
whom a licence has been granted? Is it not violence when a settler
obtains a licence to have two, three or more Indians, and believes
that he has a right to abuse their humanity, to beat them cruelly, to
leave them to suffer hunger without relief, to burden them with
excessive work throughout the day and a great part of the night –
certain that the Indian cannot leave because he is imprisoned by the
bars of the licence?'

These licences, issued by provincial governors to favoured or
influential settlers, prevented Indians from working freely for whom
they wished at the most competitive rates of pay. Anyone armed with
such a licence overworked the Indians assigned to him unmercifully,
beating them to keep them working day and night. If the Indians fled,
they were hunted down by overseers known as bariquaras; and if a
group of escapers formed a quilombo or runaway settlement, the
authorities sent troops to recapture them. 'If found, they suffer
punishment of hard labour in shackles and unpaid work on royal
projects.' Settlers, on the other hand, were never punished for mistreating Indians. The Indians rarely knew how to complain, and, if
they did, the settlers used their influence to quash the complaint. 'If
this system is not slavery, there can be nothing more destructive to
the roots of liberty. The wise and Christian provisions of the laws in
favour of the persons, property and conduct of the wretched Indians
are valueless.' Pestana da Silva urged the King to abolish the system
of distributing Indians to work for colonists. He cited many
examples of the horrors he described; and he reminded the King that

'all these facts are truly taking place. . . . I know them from my own experience, and to my own distress.'

This same inspector condemned the system of directors of Indian villages. 'These directors go to a village and set themselves up just like little lords, giving beatings and mistreating Indians at their whim and without cause. They do not care for the common interests of those wretches. By virtue of their office they are authorised transgressors, having a merry time obeyed as minor potentates.' They usurp the authority of the King, the governor and the church, and they do nothing in return. 'Their only task is to stay in the midst of their tyrannical and harmful command. They reward themselves from the work of the Indians, whom they send violently and in large numbers to labour in the remote wilderness, in order to get their sixth of all the produce extracted by the Indians at the expense of their blood, lives and sweat.'

Many other authors confirmed that the directors were generally cruel, greedy and wholly unqualified for their positions of trust. The Bishop of Belém, Caetano Brandão, made several tours to inspect his vast riverine diocese, occasionally visiting villages that impressed him by their good order and piety. But, more often, he found shocking anarchy. At the former mission of Souzel on the lower Xingu the Indians were quite sober and well behaved, but their director was 'drunken, licentious, rapacious, indifferent to religion, and treating the wretched Indians with the greatest inhumanity.' Not long before the Bishop's arrival, an old man had been removed half dead from a spell in the tronco – a stocks of a tree trunk in which victims were left for days on end. He had been punished for no offence, at the whim of the director. The Indians were powerless to protest. 'They were all sad and deplored his misfortune; but they tolerated it, I know not why.'

Upriver, at Barra, the Bishop found the Commandant of the small fort to be 'rapacious, licentious to an extreme with the greatest immorality one could imagine, and on top of this addicted to drink.' Sexual excess was an obvious result of installing petty tyrants in isolated villages of Indians from which most men were absent on expeditions of forced labour. Another bishop, the Benedictine João de São José, met a Director (a soldier of mixed blood) who had 'persuaded himself that the first fruits of the purity of virgins about to marry were his due. He punished any honourable resistance with nefarious punishments. He smashed the heads of some girls and broke the arms of others with furious blows, from which there were tragic and fatal results. . . . The frequency of his dissolution, incests, violences and punishments brought great consternation to the village.' Even during the Bishop's visit, 'he again proved his power on a young Indian girl. She emerged from his door covered in tears and blood, crying and lamenting injuries that were evident from her pain and innocence.' The Bishop vowed to bring this 'wolf among my sheep' to justice, but there is no record of his being punished.

The fallacy in Pombal's legislation soon became obvious: if Jesuit missionaries could not be trusted as altruistic guardians of the Indians, laymen could never be found for this difficult work. The French naturalist Auguste de Saint-Hilaire summed up the problem: 'Pombal wanted directors who were reasonable beings. Those who were given to the Indians were immoral, greedy men, often even fugitives from justice, and they became horrible despots. The Portuguese who mingled with the Indians tyrannised and corrupted them. The mission villages soon fell into ruin and the natives of Brazil relapsed into barbarism.' Other commentators complained that the directors were incapable of teaching their charges civilised manners or religion, and the English poet Robert Southey pondered Pombal's criminal naivety in establishing such a system: 'The directors were usually a set of brutal fellows, who solicited the appointment for the sake of extorting what they could from the miserable Indians. The law intended to intrust them with only a directive power; but how little must Pombal have reflected upon the nature of brute man, and the tendency of power to corrupt . . . if he supposed that such men would confine themselves within these limits.'

The problem was to find worthy and disinterested directors. As early as 1755, Bento da Fonseca warned that it would be impossible. The directors would be drawn from colonists and army officers. Did the authorities seriously imagine that soldiers, who were usually the worst persecutors of Indians, would now incur the odium of other colonists by defending Indian rights? Governor Ataide Teive admitted in 1768 that 'it is difficult to find men of honourable conduct for a job of such circumspection.' A later governor, Sousa Coutinho, was less restrained. He considered that a poor settler was too rustic and uneducated for the job of director, whereas a newly arrived Portuguese was worse than 'a blood-thirsty leech . . . more like a jaguar or a ferocious tiger!'

The directors' main abuse was to overwork their Indians. The Portuguese naturalist Rodrigues Ferreira was appalled to see Indians return to their villages after many months of arduous expeditions, and then be taken off again for another six months' service after a rest of only a few days. This meant that they had no time in which to prepare clearings or to hunt and fish to feed their families. During his travels along many Amazon rivers he saw one director making a good profit from a brickyard worked by Indian women, and other directors forcing their Indians into the hard labour of tobacco plantations.

Prolonged absence by Indian men had disastrous effects on the social fabric of village life. The shrewd judge Pestana da Silva noted that 'because of this disorder . . . the Indians are starving and in need and are not well fed or nourished, for the men are always on the move. Married men cannot sustain the upkeep of their marriages and bachelors have no homes or hope of them.' Women who conceived took irritant fruits in order to abort. 'They also sacrifice their lives with these excesses.'

Faced with such cruel oppression, a few Indian groups tried to rebel but were easily crushed by the guns of Portuguese troops. An easier alternative was flight. Bishop João de São José explained that 'they instinctively tend to return to the forest, as to a homeland where they were raised. . . . If they suddenly find themselves doing work of which they have no experience, they lose heart and flee. . . . They spend most of the year collecting cacao, oil or forest gums, when they would like to rest among their wives, children and relatives and to make small plantations. They greatly resent being put to continuous work by their directors.' Pestana da Silva saw that the attempt to impose an alien culture contributed to these flights: 'Severity and force are far from obliging Indians to become civilised in our manner and at our convenience. It is because of this that they flee from us and retire to the forests and the rites of their idolatry. One after another they have sought the jungles to escape our tyrannies. They lose temporal and spiritual benefits of which they once had high hopes.'

But Bishop João de São José fulminated against the insult to Christianity: 'I am certain that this type of heathen cannot be tamed without force. Those who return to the forests should be given severe and exemplary punishment. These flights are generally relapses into ancient errors – a return to their vomit, using many superstitions. . . . Those who have had ten or twelve years of Catholicism should not be pardoned lightly!'

Indians who fled and were recaptured were forced to labour on royal projects wearing foot shackles. Women and children were punished by repeated blows on their hands with a palmatoria, a perforated wooden paddle that raised painful welts. Governor

Francisco de Sousa Coutinho accused the directors of being cruel men who used excessive punishments for minor offences. They left Indians in troncos for days without food, or chained over nests of fire ants – the most toxic of all ants, a single bite from which causes agonising pain and fever. This Governor concluded that 'the Indians' sole recourse is to flee, and they do so indiscriminately . . . to preserve themselves . . . from the vices of the administrators. All is violence, and what is founded on violence cannot endure nor prosper.'

Apart from overwork, abuse, savage punishments and dissatisfaction with an alien way of life, a common cause for flight was disease. As we have seen, Directorate villages were particularly vulnerable to epidemics. The Indians were crowded together in unsanitary huts and were undernourished. They were in close contact with white colonists and prey to unknown diseases brought across the Atlantic in cargo and slave ships. Bishop São José wrote that 'almost sixty thousand died of measles and smallpox. Many fled, abusing the liberty that had very justly been proclaimed for them.' Village directors were required to write annual reports. Desertions inspired by fear of disease were described in such reports – from Soure in 1759, from Óbidos in 1761, Melgaço in 1772 and Santana de Cajary in 1794.* Ribeiro de Sampaio often saw villages that had been denuded by disease, and wrote in 1775 that 'the contagion of smallpox has increased continuously.' The tragedy was that those who fled often carried the epidemic to forest tribes beyond the settlers' control. Long before, in the early days of the colonisation of Brazil, a Jesuit had described the appalling toll from imported disease on his mission, and had written that 'the Indians say that this was nothing in comparison with the mortality raging through the forests.'

Runaways grouped together in forest clearings and their communities were known to the colonial authorities by the African names mucambo or quilombo, since many of the fugitives were black slaves. Close to Belém, there were mucambos in the centre of Marajó island, south-east and east of Bragança and beyond Santarém; other mucambos were high up the northern tributaries of the Amazon, in the Tumucumaque hills and the watershed of the Guianas. Deeper in Amazonia, it was even easier for Indians to escape. 'They fled from their directors to live in the headwaters of rivers, on lakes or elsewhere that would protect them from some order such as work in a [royal] pottery or fishery.'

Once a mucambo had been located, there would be an attempt to subdue it and recapture the fugitive labour, particularly if its members were raiding village crops. Directors occasionally asked for troops to mount such raids, or they rewarded chiefs who could persuade their followers to return to 'civilisation'. In 1760 an Indian brought sixty-two people back from a mucambo near Sintra, and Governor Mello e Castro gave him 'the title of chief as reward for his loyalty . . . and I also clothed him at my expense.' If the mucambo were extinguished by force its members were brought back 'fastened to tree trunks, because this is the only means whereby one can get them to come.'

There was an attempt to make good these losses by bringing uncontacted Indian tribes down to colonial settlements. Because the victims were lured or seized from refuges high up the Amazon tributaries, such raids were known as 'descents'. During the seventeenth and early eighteenth centuries, Jesuits and other missionaries had 'descended' many thousands of Indians. By the time of the Directorate, this was becoming more difficult. The directors' agents did not look as altruistic or benign as the missionaries; the more accessible rivers had long since been denuded; and many uncontacted tribes had heard of the settlers' unsavoury reputation and were consequently less gullible.

Now that slavery was not officially permitted, expeditions to descend uncontacted Indians were not financially rewarding. When Bishop São José reached Monte Alegre (former Gurupatuba) on the north shore of the lower Amazon in 1762 an army officer 'told us that he was ready to make descents if His Majesty would help him financially, and that he would bring back plenty of heathen. But the Director was more pessimistic. He said that he had made descents to a place called Nogueira, but to this day had not managed to reimburse himself from the royal treasury. He appreciated that it was a worthy task; but he reckoned that the obligation to support his wife and children was greater.'

Far away on the Içana tributary of the upper Negro, Canon André Fernandes de Sousa reported that a sergeant had in 1787 'gone up this river to catch heathen with thirty soldiers armed with powder and shot and a similar number of Indians with ropes. They surprised a village of heathen. Its men escaped, but they tied up the women and took them with them on the return journey. But they were attacked by the heathen in various assaults and ambushes, so that they lost not only their captives, but also their weapons and food, and would even have lost their lives had they not been sufficiently agile.'

Nevertheless, descents did take place. Directors' reports record the arrival of small groups of a few families or as many as a hundred forest Indians. A report of 1781 recorded 266 'wild Indians' descended in the captaincy of Rio Negro and 431 in Pará during the previous few years.* Government officials encouraged descents. Francisco Xavier Ribeiro de Sampaio, inspecting the Solimões and Negro in 1774, constantly urged directors to make more descents. He reported that the upper Amazon rivers were being rapidly de-populated since the expulsion of the missionaries. This, he felt, was because missionaries had had a strong motive for luring Indians down to their aldeias. He noted with approval that a few directors were replenishing their villages by bringing down more Indians. On the Solimões, the director of Alvaray near the mouth of the Tefé river had descended Indians from the Japurá in 1758; in 1768 Pariana Indians from the Tocantins streams had been settled in a new town at the mouth of the Içá; at Castro de Avelans, the Director was guilty of 'serious financial irregularities. . . . He should treat the Indians of that new village with much kindness, to make them believe that we descended them for their own good.'

Ribeiro de Sampaio ended his report to the Governor: 'I can tell Your Excellency that descents to the settlements on the Solimões have been continuous because of the proximity of rivers inhabited by innumerable tribes. With a minimum of additional effort in this respect, they could multiply far more.' There was similar potential on the Negro. The directors of Moura, Airão and Carvoeiro were urged to make more descents, particularly from the Rio Branco, which had for a long time 'been used only as a source of descended Indians'. An American researcher, Robin Wright, scoured Sampaio and other manuscript sources to compile a list of descents on the Rio Negro and its tributaries during the years 1760–90. He recorded thirty instances where he could identify the tribes and numbers of victims and their destinations. Several thousand Indians were involved in these recorded descents in one part of Amazonia: a chilling record of human misery.*

Although descents of forest tribes did something to replace the losses from Directorate villages, contemporary observers were con-vinced that the natives 'are daily diminishing appallingly'. During the forty years of the Directorate, the number of Indians administer-ed in Pará and Amazonia fell by over a third, from thirty thousand in 1757 to nineteen thousand in 1798. The figures emerge from general censuses in 1773, 1783 and 1797, and also from data in directors' reports. Analysis of these statistics shows that the most precipitous decline in the Indian population was before 1770, with a much slower rate of decline during the next decades.* In 1775 Ribeiro de Sampaio cited the town of Tomar (former Bararoá) on the Negro as an example of the decline. 'This town consisted of 1200 warriors; today it would have 140. Such is the proportion [of depopulation] in other villages of this river.'

Some of the vacuum in the villages along the banks of the Negro and other rivers was filled by white immigrants. Ribeiro de Sampaio in 1775 divided these into three classes. There were the offspring of slave raiders who had remained in Amazonia after their nefarious trade was outlawed. Then there were the descendants of men who had arrived with the teams of boundary commissioners and had chosen to stay and intermarry with Indians. Lastly, there were garrison soldiers, most of whom also married local women. Ribeiro de Sampaio commented that this settler population 'has thus been created almost unintentionally, without the introduction of married couples as was done elsewhere'. But the numbers of colonists were tiny: the villages of the upper Amazon rivers were nothing more than clusters of thatched huts on river-bank clearings, separated from one another by thousands of kilometres of unbroken forests. Most of the tributaries of these upper rivers were still scarcely penetrated, and their Indians were as yet unmolested.

The Rio Negro had been full of populous and thriving Carmelite missions in the first half of the eighteenth century. This prosperity was gone. During the 1720s there had been a fierce war against a rebellion by the Manoa of the middle Negro under their gallant chief Ajuricaba. In 1749 there was an unusually terrible epidemic of measles on the Negro and Solimões: contemporary missionary reports recorded some 2400 deaths among Indian converts. Governor Mendonça Furtado was still impressed by the Carmelite missions when he visited the Negro in 1755, but they declined soon after. Although Pombal's legislation of 1755 was aimed at the Jesuits, it also removed the other missionary orders from direct administration of Indian villages. Henceforth, missionaries were supposed to concentrate only on contacting and converting wild tribes.

After the expulsion of the Jesuits in 1759 the other orders rapidly lost any grip on the Indians. The Mercedarians, richest of the remaining monastic orders on the Amazon, were summarily recalled to Portugal and their Brazilian estates confiscated in the mid-1760s. In 1765 there were still eighty-nine Carmelites in five convents in Amazonia, but of these only eight were active as 'vicars of the Negro and Solimões rivers'. By 1781 there were only twenty elderly Carmelites left in three houses in Maranhão; a decade later the

Carmelite monastery in Belém had only five friars, all aged over sixty. At that same time the Franciscans in Pará were reduced to a mere twelve old friars in all their five missions and one convent.

In 1777 King José I of Portugal died and was succeeded by his daughter, Queen Maria I. The Marquis of Pombal fell from power with the death of the King he had dominated for a quarter-century. The Directorate system for the Brazilian Indians began to be challenged after the fall of Pombal, whose brother had instituted this inefficient and oppressive regime. In 1788 the Queen sent Antonio José Pestana da Silva to investigate. His report and recommendations on the treatment of Indians were a ringing condemnation of the Directorate. Similar criticism was reaching the Portuguese government from its colonial administrators and ecclesiastics in all parts of Brazil.

In 1790 Francisco de Sousa Coutinho became Governor-General of Pará, a position he held for thirteen years. During the last decade of the eighteenth century there was a shift in the official emphasis concerning Indian labour. Before that date, directors' correspondence with the provincial government was full of references to the recruitment of expeditions to gather exotic forest 'drugs'. Under Sousa Coutinho, more attention was given to agriculture. Directors were encouraged to have their Indians diversify their crops and try to plant coffee, cacao, rice, corn and cotton. This change may have been prompted by the steady decline in the population of Indian villages under colonial rule. There were too few Indians to man the long forest expeditions; and the forest products themselves were increasingly remote and difficult to find. The new governor curtailed a regular trade route up the Madeira and Guaporé rivers between the Amazon and Mato Grosso because it consumed too much manpower. He forbad the merchants operating this route from taking Amazon Indians upriver beyond their native province.

Finally, in August 1797, Governor Sousa Coutinho himself wrote a report of fundamental importance about the government of the Indians. His 'Plan for Civilising the Indians of the Captaincy of Pará' is in the archive of the Brazilian Historical and Geographical Institute of Rio de Janeiro and has, surprisingly, never been published. In it Sousa Coutinho described many ways in which directors cheated and overworked their Indians. He explained why disease and flight had denuded the Directorate villages. Had it worked according to the original plans, the Directorate might conceivably have been a practical, even idealistic, means of introducing the Indians to self-government and self-sufficiency under Portuguese colonial rule. It was, instead, a miserable failure. The blame lay squarely with the directors, whom the Governor felt wanted to perpetuate their own power by keeping the Indians in a state of subjugation. He gave examples of violations of almost every important article in the Directorate legislation. It could never succeed, for it depended on men who, on crossing the Atlantic, turned into 'ferocious jaguars. . . . When a European is overcome by a voracious hunger for gold, he respects nothing in order to satisfy his greed.' The Directorate should therefore be abolished.

Sousa Coutinho's advice was followed. On 12 May 1798 the Prince Regent Dom João abolished all clauses of Pombal's Directorate legislation. Indian freedom was reiterated. The royal decree claimed that it made Indians equal to other subjects. But it was another sham. It recognised Indians as legal minors 'as a guarantee of their rights and interests'. The decree in fact destroyed the Indian patrimony by disbanding Indian villages and selling off communal land. Any Indian who did not have a house and a 'fixed occupation' could be compelled to work for the state or for private colonists. Any outsider was free to exploit natural resources on Indian land.

The 1798 decree forbad 'offensive war' against Indian tribes; but it permitted 'defensive war' – which amounted to the same thing. Rewards were promised to anyone who 'descended' a new tribe. Such adventurers were urged to penetrate remote forests, taking presents as bribes to lure Indians to descend to a life of 'comfort' near the whites.

The most iniquitous aspect of the new law was its transfer of Indians into militia corps. They had to serve in military discipline, under non-commissioned officers chosen from their own chiefs or from local settlers. The great historian of the Jesuits, João Lúcio de Azevedo, commented: 'Under such an order, the change of the primitive system could not have been more radical. . . . Savage groups passed from the theocratic regime [of the pre-Directorate Jesuits] to the military – the captain replaced the religious, the soldier substituted the catechist. It does not require deep insight to realise that such an organisation could not favour liberty. The Queen's decree changed the legal statutes, but did not alter the situation of the Indians. The military regime, by its very nature tyrannical, facilitated oppression against which the primitiveness, timidity, and the habit of humble obedience of the natives made it impossible for them to react.'

Some great tribes that had recently made peace with the Portuguese – the Mura, Mundurukú and Karajá – were mentioned by name in the decree. Indians from these tribes could freely be used as labourers – provided they could be shown to have been educated and baptised! It was also permitted for anyone to trade with Indians, provided only that the trader did not supply them with guns or swords. This clause was the start of a century of sharp practice and debt-bondage by itinerant traders, who easily exploited Indians' ignorance and gullibility.

As with the Directorate legislation of forty years previously, the 1798 decree was really concerned with the supply of Indian labour. Its text spoke about 'masters' and 'servants'. Governor Sousa Coutinho ensured that there would be no doubt on this score. On 9 January 1799 he issued a circular that required outgoing directors to compile lists of all able-bodied Indians who could work for the state or for private persons. These were then to be removed from their villages and concentrated near the Amazon towns, so that they could be redistributed for labour. Thus any Indians who sought to escape forced labour by returning to their aldeias were sent back downriver to work under military discipline. The Governor's letter even gave precise instructions about the towns to which Indians from villages of each district were to be sent. 'I order the commandants of [the assembly towns of] Santarém, Gurupá and Portel to seek to handle them . . . so that none should be missing in the levies coming from those districts.'

Model Villages

The Amazon basin was physically separated from the rest of Brazil. There was no overland communication between Brazil in the south and the Amazon provinces of Maranhão, Pará and Rio Negro. Adverse currents and winds made it very difficult to sail along the Atlantic coast from north-east Brazil to the mouth of the Amazon – it was easier to cross the Atlantic back to the mother country, Portugal.

The colonial frontier of central Brazil lay eleven hundred kilometres west of the city of Salvador da Bahia. Two mighty rivers flow north towards the Amazon: the Tocantins and Araguaia, which run parallel to one another for hundreds of kilometres before joining and flowing over fierce rapids to emerge near Belém do Pará. Although there is some thick forest near their banks, the land around the Tocantins–Araguaia is fairly open – savannah, low dry woods called caatinga, or campo (which is sandy coarse grassland studded with thorny undergrowth, gnarled stunted trees, stands of buriti palms, and concrete-hard termite hills). This central Brazilian plateau lies on a very ancient geological shield. It was and is the home of Gê-speaking plains Indians. To the south, towards the headwaters of the two great rivers, were the Chavante with the related Cherente to their north; to the south of them the southern Kayapó (or Caiapó) and the northern Kayapó in forests beyond the Araguaia and Xingu to the north-west; groups of Timbira along the Tocantins; and near its junction with the Araguaia, Krahó, Apinagé, Gaviões, Canela (Rankokamekra) and other groups.

The first of these central Gê to suffer the impact of the advancing frontier were the Akroá and related Guenguen, who lived in the arid plains and low hills east of the Tocantins, in what are now the states of Goiás and Piauí. There were campaigns against the Akroá,

Guenguen and Timbira in the dry and bare interior of Piauí in the 1760s. It was a savage, tragic fight. The King of Portugal had permitted the war, but ordered that only adult men might be held as 'captives' – a euphemism for slaves, for slavery of Indians was now officially forbidden. The naturalist Rodrigues Ferreira quoted a number of letters from Governor João Pereira Caldas about this campaign. His first big expedition in 1764 killed only four Indians. Later that year another expedition led by Colonel João de Rego Castello took 171 prisoners and killed a similar number of Indians. The savagery of the fighting was revealed in the Governor's remark: 'I do not doubt that the number of prisoners would have been greater if the fury of the soldiers could be controlled in such combats; but they remember only to satisfy their passion.' Three weeks later, the Governor wrote to the King that he was disappointed that most of the captives were women and children. Few Indian men had allowed themselves to be taken alive.

A year later, he wrote that the war had yielded 337 captives and over 400 killed. The Governor dispersed young Indians as virtual household slaves: 'I had them distributed among the citizens on condition that these educate, clothe and feed them throughout the time that they keep them in their houses.' He sent the older Indian women to distant Indian villages in Maranhão; but many deserted, despite the distance, and tried to return to their families. By July 1765, Governor Caldas reported that one entire tribe of 558 Guenguen had surrendered. He ordered that they be 'descended' from their territory to settle near Oeiras, the capital of Piauí, where they would be available to work for colonists. 'However, this "descent" reached here greatly diminished . . . because of a considerable epidemic that overtook it on the road.'

The nineteenth-century German travellers Spix and Martius described how such campaigns in Piauí were typical of similar raids elsewhere on the long Brazilian frontier. 'Bandeiras [military expeditions] of regular soldiers and volunteers are organised. The government supplies them with weapons and ammunition, and the settlers bring the provisions that must be taken for long expeditions that may last for many months. Meanwhile herds of oxen are delivered to the military column. The men who undertake the raid seldom expect to fight a pitched battle. They try to make surprise attacks on the Indians in their remote and scattered villages.'

The defeated Guenguen and Akroá tribes of Piauí were settled in an Indian colony called São Gonçalo d'Amarante on the Canindé river near Oeiras. Another group of four hundred Guenguen were

sent to the village of São João de Sende some eighty kilometres north
of the frontier town. The defeated tribe was rapidly demoralised. By
1772 a local magistrate reported that they still clung to their tribal
beliefs – and were even converting other people in Piauí to their
spirit world. He described all Indians as 'inseparable from robbery
and drunkenness and generally, whatever their tribe, terribly stupid,
lazy and gluttonous. They are extremely wedded to their rites and
superstitions: they inflict them like a contagion on other inhabitants
of this captaincy.'

Spix and Martius visited these Indian colonies half a century after
their formation. They were dismayed by what they saw. By 1818
there were only 120 people in São Gonçalo and not all of these were
pure Indian. It was a feeble relic of what had once been an important
colony, now no more than a quadrangle of dilapidated huts and a
ruined chapel. Many of the original Indians had died of disease,
particularly smallpox, and others had managed to run away to their
homelands. The survivors were sad and dirty. They received no
guidance from a few drunken soldiers. Such an evident failure led the
two Germans to question the entire policy of forcing newly conquered tribes into aldeias; they became convinced that it was very
rare to succeed in colonising indigenous peoples. Such a view contradicted accepted wisdom in the age of enlightenment, and Spix
and Martius admitted that it would upset philanthropists convinced
of the benefits of European civilisation.

The reason for the Germans' pessimistic view of the settlement
policy was that it almost always followed a military defeat of the
Indians. The vanquished tribe was forced to leave its homeland and
accept settlement – though settlement was alien to its usual pattern
of semi-nomadic hunting and shifting farming. It was administered
in this new village by a government-appointed director and was
supposed to be instructed in Christianity by a priest. 'The Indians
are thus required to undergo an abrupt surrender of their natural
inclinations, homes and customs. Further, they must surrender to a
law and a religion that they do not understand. The inevitable result
is that the more resolute among them seek as soon as possible to
escape this intolerable coercion by flight. The remainder stay behind
among the Brazilians, but only as unassimilated strangers. They
decay morally and physically in the most pitiful hybrid way of life.'
Many fell victim to European diseases or to alcoholism; others were
not even left among their tribal kin but were dispersed to work on
farms and ranches. The Germans saw many members of these tribes
working as forced labourers in colonists' houses in Oeiras. Those

who had been recently captured – in 'countless raids' against their peoples – struck the Germans as being strong and skilful, and with 'a certain freedom and self-assurance in their facial expressions and speech that we sought in vain among the Indians long settled in the village of São Gonçalo d'Amarante.' They met the aged paramount chief of this new group, still vigorous and rather Ethiopian-looking.

Another group of Akroá had been defeated a few years earlier than their compatriots in Piauí. Portuguese moving down the Tocantins from Goiás had clashed with Akroá and related Chikriabá living west of the Piauí Akroá. A military force was sent against them under a Colonel Wenceslao Gomes da Silva, and there was considerable slaughter during campaigns in 1757–9 before these western Akroá made peace.* 'The mission aldeias of Duro and Formiga ["Ant"] were created for them, and enormous sums were spent on these with His Majesty's approval.' The expensive new settlements did not succeed for long. They were initially administered by Jesuits; but when these were expelled from Portuguese dominions, lay directors took charge. The conqueror, Colonel Gomes da Silva, was allowed to rule the people he had defeated. A document has survived, setting out the daily discipline for the soldiers stationed in these new villages of Duro and Formiga. Drums were to sound at daybreak and again at eight in the morning, at which time all Indians and soldiers were to parade. Punishments were prescribed for any who missed this roll-call, and for soldiers who went anywhere without their weapons, who molested missionaries or Indian women, or who allowed the Indians to use guns. Any soldier caught with an Indian woman in his quarters was to get eight days in prison, plus six hours in the neck stocks and six hours in an iron collar. Pereira de Alencastre, the chronicler of Goiás, described Colonel Gomes da Silva as unscrupulous, and the regime of these missions as military rule 'that produced the worst possible results'.

The Jesuit missionaries in these villages protested against the barbarous regime. The two villages were ravaged by epidemics in 1756, shortly after the introduction of the military garrison. The Indians 'claimed that up to then they had been governed by ministers of the church, but they had passed to being governed by dragoons. . . . They rebelled and entered the wilds, attacking travellers with the same firearms that our people had taught them to use. This rebellion was imputed to the Jesuit missionaries. . . .' Those who remained in the villages were 'calmed down after the uprising, whose barbarian leaders suffered the death penalty after sentencing'.

But the days of the Jesuits themselves were numbered, for Pombal was by then working towards their expulsion. The missionaries of Duro and Formiga were thus accused of fomenting rebellion among their Indians; and in 1758 came the royal order removing all Jesuits from missions and confining them to their convents.

The Glaswegian traveller George Gardner visited Duro in 1838. He reported that the village contained about twenty houses, 'all of which are of the most miserable description . . . many of them so much decayed from the united effects of time and weather that they no longer form a barrier against either wind or rain.' Although the village was in a fertile location 'with an abundance of excellent water' from the Manuel Alves tributary of the Tocantins, its surviving inhabitants were demoralised and indolent, with scarcely any food, so that 'they are generally in a state of starvation.' Even after eighty years of exposure to 'civilisation', these Indians preferred hunting and gathering wild fruits and nuts to the drudgery of settled agriculture. They were also prepared to work for pay on traders' boats plying the Tocantins. 'Very frequently some of the young men belonging to Duro hire themselves to work the canoes, and with the money which they receive for their services, purchase at [Belém do] Pará axes and other iron tools.'

The Brazilian frontier was now starting to push farther westwards. A number of expeditions had penetrated as far as the Araguaia river in the seventeenth and early eighteenth centuries, but this expansion became more intensive in the 1770s. It brought the Portuguese into contact with the distinctive Karajá, the great river tribe of the middle Araguaia.

Roughly halfway down its course, the broad waters of the Araguaia divide, not to rejoin for 340 kilometres. The river thus encloses what is probably the world's largest riverine island, Bananal ('Banana grove'), an enormous expanse of savannah, low forests, campo scrubland, and swamps and lakes. The great island of Bananal is the home of the Karajá, but these brilliant canoers range far upstream and down the Araguaia. Some of their villages are hundreds of kilometres north of Bananal, down the Araguaia towards its confluence with the Tocantins. They also make temporary camps in long barrel-vaulted thatch huts on the wide stretches of sand banks that are exposed when the river falls during the dry season.

The Karajá people – who also include the Javaé living on the southern part of Bananal, and the Xambioá living to the north near the Araguaia rapids – speak an isolated language unrelated to the four main linguistic groups of Brazilian Indians. They are distinct in many other ways too. Supremely skilled as boatmen and fishermen, the Karajá also excel in the delicacy and brilliance of their feather-work, combining the pink and white feathers of ibis and egrets with the dark blues and reds of macaw and the greens and yellows of other parrots into confections like delicate jewellery or into flamboyant radiating diadems. The Karajá are also accomplished potters, famous for clay dolls with rounded bodies and tapering limbs reminiscent of ancient sculptures from the Greek Cyclades. Another major art of the Karajá is music. The tribe has a large repertory of dances and complex songs, sung in a variety of vocal styles but without musical instruments other than gourd rattles. For religious dances, Karajá shamans dress in conical straw robes that cover them completely, with tall wood and feather crowns bobbing high above their concealed heads.

Portuguese explorers had discovered gold deposits between the headwaters of the Tocantins and Araguaia early in the eighteenth century. The gold-miners' camp grew into the colonial town of Goiás. During the early years of the Goiás gold-rush, there was fierce fighting between the tough miners and the Gê-speaking Kayapó. For a time the Kayapó threatened to destroy the Goiás settlement or to sever its communications with the Atlantic seaboard. The miners retaliated by enlisting a brutal Indian-fighter called Antonio Pires de Campos. He used a force of Bororo Indians – traditional enemies of the Kayapó – to wage a war of annihilation against them, plunging deep into the forests to track down and destroy the Kayapó villages. 'It is recorded that he did appalling barbarities and made a great slaughter.'

The Kayapó managed to kill Pires de Campos in 1751. His successor as military commander of Goiás was one João de Godois Pinto da Silveira, a man more interested in taking slaves from less bellicose tribes than in fighting the Kayapó. He struck north-westwards from Goiás in 1755, down the Araguaia past the Karajá's homeland on Bananal, attacking the relatively peaceful Tapirapé (a Tupi-speaking tribe living on a river named after them that flows into the Araguaia west of Bananal island). Father Luiz da Silva e Sousa commented that 'the only useful result of his expeditions was the capture of a hundred Tapirapé, all of whom died, perhaps from starvation in this town [Goiás].'

During his slaving expedition, Pinto da Silveira also clashed with the Karajá. It was the tribe's first experience of hostile whites – their previous contacts had been with Jesuits coming upriver from Pará or with one or two small expeditions making perilous descents of the Araguaia. Such expeditions had behaved well, anxious not to offend the large tribe on which they depended for hospitality. As a result, the Karajá were unprepared for European treachery and firearms. Another Portuguese learned twenty years later what the Karajá had suffered: the leader of the 1755 expedition 'dealt with these people in peace and friendship for some days, at the end of which he made a surprise attack on their principal village. He did not even spare the lives of the innocent. The echoes of their cries are still heard to this day by these wretched people: they cannot relate these just accusations without tears that bear witness to their pain. Having done this slaughter he took many prisoners, leading them off in chains to be his captives. . . . This man's cruelty went so far as to order these prisoners to be tied to trees along the trail. For his amusement, he ordered that they be given many lashes, saying that this was so that they would understand what was meant by captivity.' He traded Indian prisoners for cattle in farms near Goiás. Some of these slaves managed to escape back to their homelands, to tell of white men's cruelty.

Twenty years later, in 1775, a governor of Goiás decided to attempt a peaceful contact with the Karajá. He needed the tribe's friendship in order to open the Araguaia as a route for river traffic between Goiás and Pará, and so he sent an intelligent young ensign, José Pinto da Fonseca, to them with a hundred soldiers. After a month's hard journey, the expedition reached the Araguaia and the territory of the Karajá. Pinto da Fonseca treated the Indians with tact, using as his interpreter a Karajá woman who had been captured in the 1755 raid. He brought plenty of metal tools as presents. He was also armed with a letter from the Governor of Goiás to the chief of the Karajá, promising to send many men to help fight the tribe's enemies, the formidable warlike Chavante. He used music as an instrument of acculturation: 'Since the Karajá were very fond of music José Pinto used to go every day to an earthwork with the musicians he had taken with him. There he played and sang, to the delight of the savages. During these revels, which were frequent, the Indians neglected to eat or sleep, such was the delight that overcame them.'

Pinto da Fonseca was also aware of the importance of gaining the approval of the Karajá women. He said that he had presents for the women, but that he could give these only if they came in person. The chief finally brought two daughters and his aged sister. 'This old lady was still unconsolably lamenting the loss of her only son, killed in the attack twenty years before. The commander sought to console the venerable old lady. He told her that, just as she had no son, he had no mother. For this reason, she adopted him as her son from then onwards.' The chief was delighted by this, and by the dresses and combs that were given to his daughters.

The process of friendship culminated in a celebration of mass, which the Indians presumably enjoyed despite their incomprehension, and the island of Bananal was named after a Portuguese saint. The Javaé group of Karajá heard about all the festivities and suddenly appeared, in their plumed finery, in a flotilla of canoes. The Karajá and Javaé celebrated the meeting with friendly wrestling contests, and their respective chiefs then came to Pinto da Fonseca and performed what the Portuguese took to be an act of submission. Letters were dictated in their name to the Governor of Goiás, in one of which, dated 3 August 1775, chief Aboe-nona of the Karajá explained his view of the new friendship pact:

'Your people arrived in my land, sir, and gave us things that we value greatly, for which may God repay you. Also a paper that speaks good things for us. Your "son" said to us that you are of good heart, and that the great father of the whites, who lives on the far side of the great lake, [wishes] to take care of people of our skin. This therefore seems good to us, since your people do us no harm. I want your promise on their behalf that it will always remain so, and that you will deliver us from the Chavante. I and our people will remain your comrades for all time. When your son returns to your land, I am sending my son to visit your house. I hope that you will send him back again, so that my heart does not fall ill.'

A few weeks later, the chief put his mark to a document, written by the Portuguese, in which he declared that 'Aboe-nona, chief of the Karajá nation, in the name of all my subjects and descendants, I promise God and the King of Portugal to be henceforth, as I now am, a loyal vassal of Your Majesty and to keep perpetual peace with the Portuguese.'

The Karajá doubtless saw this ceremony as a pact between tribes of equal importance. They knew little of the origin, size or intentions of the strange tribe of white men that had irrupted into their world. The Portuguese viewed the matter quite differently. For them it was the first step in subjecting another tribe to their expanding colonial empire. Pinto da Fonseca returned to the Karajá the following year, accompanied by an ouvidor (judge), Antonio José Cabral. They tried to assemble the Karajá and Javaé in a village called Nova Beira and left a small garrisoned fort on Bananal. Both settlements soon failed when they were struck by illness and deaths. The chronicler Pizarro e Araújo lamented that Nova Beira was abandoned so soon, after twelve thousand cruzados had been spent on it.*

A greater prize for the Portuguese authorities was to subdue the fierce Gê-speaking tribes: the Kayapó who had threatened Goiás and had suffered such persecution in the 1740s; and the ferocious Chavante, the most warlike of all tribes of the Tocantins–Araguaia basin. A new governor called Luis da Cunha Menezes reached Vila Boa de Goiás in 1778. The gold that had brought a rush of prospectors to Goiás earlier in the century was now almost exhausted, and the remaining settlers were turning to cattle ranching and subsistence farming.

The colonists were still terrified of attack by the Kayapó, and the new governor determined to try to win over these formidable enemies. He chose the classic method of wooing by presents rather than by armed attack, and sent to them a former Kayapó-fighter, José Luiz Pereira, leading fifty men but armed with presents and instructed to behave peacefully. As so often in Brazilian history, the tactic succeeded. The Kayapó wanted friendship with the whites and were easily seduced by the metal tools and other gifts. The expedition returned in September 1780 after five months, bringing thirty-six Kayapó under an old chief called Romexi. These envoys were greeted with artillery and musket salutes in the town of Goiás, with the Governor and his staff arrayed in full-dress uniforms. He promised the Kayapó the full protection of the Portuguese Queen Maria I.

The Indians were then taken to see a model village, São José de Mossâmedes, which the previous governor had built as 'a regular, permanent establishment . . . that would be the envy of all the forest Indians . . . and would serve as a university for those who wished to settle in villages.' The Governor had chosen a good site, well watered and surrounded by forests and plains, at the foot of the Dourada hills some thirty-five kilometres south of Goiás. He built permanent buildings and workshops, a cattle ranch, and clearings for farming. Although he worried about the expense of all this, he argued that it might soon become self-financing from its own produce.

A thanksgiving mass was sung in the church of Mossâmedes, and the aged Romexi was so delighted by what he saw that he sent men back to fetch the rest of his people. He said that they would return in eight months and, to the surprise of the colonists, 236 Kayapó entered Goiás on 29 May 1781 led by their great chief Angraí-oxá.

Governor Cunha Menezes welcomed them with all the pomp at his command. The Indians camped near his residence. In July there was a mass baptism of over a hundred Kayapó children, and the Governor himself acted as godfather to the two chiefs. Meanwhile, another aldeia was prepared for the Kayapó on the Rio da Fartura, the River of Plenty, some eighty kilometres south-west of the town. Soon, other Kayapó had emerged from the forests to settle in this aldeia, which was named Maria I after the Queen of Portugal. Father Luiz da Silva e Sousa commented that the expedition to attract the Kayapó had 'had least equipment and most success'.

The ceremonial of mass baptism was important to both Indians and Portuguese. It seemed as if a new era of peace had come between the traditional enemies. The Kayapó were only too pleased to stop fighting an enemy whose firearms had destroyed so many of their people. The model village Maria I looked attractive, and they had not yet appreciated that they were now supposed to settle permanently and try to survive without shifting cultivation or nomadic hunting. Tribal feuds among them were normally resolved amid ceremonies, so they doubtless loved all the singing and parades, and the chance for both sides to wear their finest ornaments. Above all, they now had ready access to the Europeans' metal tools, knives and firearms. The Governor welcomed them with presents, and it seemed as if the white men had finally learned the generosity over material possessions that was usual among Indians.

To the Portuguese, the settlement of a dangerous tribe meant an end to fears of attack and ambush. Kayapó lands could now be opened to invasion and colonial settlement. The ceremony of mass baptism satisfied the original pretext that the colonisation of Brazil was done to bring Christianity to its peoples. The Governor could also boast that he had brought another subject nation into the control of the Portuguese Queen. The hope was that the Kayapó would respond to settled village life and become loyal subjects. The Governor was pleased by his apparent triumph. He boasted to the Queen that 'the system of kindness and humanity that Your Majesty ordered to be practised with the Indian tribes in these dominions is the most potent weapon with which to conquer people who are naturally receptive to the full range of our benefits. . . . From the day on which I started this process of civilisation, I have experienced none of the assaults and killings that these Kayapó used to perpetrate every year.' The Queen wrote back to say how pleased she was, and to order that the Indians settled in the new villages should always be treated benevolently.

Emboldened by this success, the next Governor of Goiás, Tristão da Cunha, determined to try to pacify an even more formidable tribe: the Chavante. These tall, tough plains Indians run so fast that they can hunt game on foot, killing it with arrows or clubs. They often round up game with circles of fire on the dry savannahs. Like the Timbira, these fellow Gê-speaking tribes keep exceptionally fit by running log-races. The two halves of each village race against one another, starting far from the village and ending with a run around its circle of huts. The race is a relay, each team carrying a massive and very heavy section of buriti palm trunk which is borne on one Indian runner's shoulder until he rolls it on to that of a team-mate. The race ends as the two packs of runners come pounding into the village, their bare feet kicking up a thin cloud of dust. As the teams finish, they drop the log and walk away with feigned indifference, scarcely out of breath from the fast and punishing race.

The Chavante were fine archers, but their favourite weapon was a long hardwood club, a blow from which could smash the skull of game animals or human enemies. With such weapons, the Chavante had terrorised colonists who attempted to settle in their territories north of Goiás. In 1786 they killed twelve people in a camp on the Crixás river two hundred kilometres north of the mining town. The Governor sent eighty-five under Ensign Miguel de Arruda e Sá to protect Crixás and punish 'this insult by that ferocious and bloody heathen'. He took with him some Kayapó, Portugal's new allies and traditional enemies of the Chavante. In 1787, on the Governor's instructions, the Kayapó managed to capture a Chavante warrior with four women and some children, who were taken back to Goiás and given the most attractive possible welcome. It was a classic tactic of pacification: the captives were returned to their tribe loaded with presents and able to report on the kindness of the whites. After some hesitation, the Chavante acquiesced. They sent to tell the Governor that they accepted peace and were prepared to surrender.

The Portuguese authorities quickly prepared a clearing and built a village to house the Chavante. The chosen site was at Carretão ('Carter'), 130 kilometres north of Goiás: tidy rows of huts were built around a square and the aldeia was named Pedro III after the Queen's consort. A team of Chavante warriors came to Goiás to meet the Governor and were taken to inspect the new village; they approved the location, and the tribe started to migrate towards it.

This great exodus of over two thousand Chavante took six months. The tribe moved slowly, for it was bringing its old people and a mass of children, with infants carried on their parents' shoulders. The colonial settlers of Goiás were terrified by the approach of their enemies. 'Some began to hide their families, others to lock their shops. But it was extraordinary how, after [the Indians] had stayed for a few days at [a camp near the town], the settlers' attitude changed from one extreme to the other. All their fear and horror changed to love and affection when they recognised the good faith and affability of the heathen. Soon they were all busy giving the Indians more than they could afford from their meagre possessions.'

The Chavante finally moved on and entered Pedro III (or Carretão) on 7 January 1788. 'They made their entry to the sound of their disagreeable instruments, shouts and dances.' They were welcomed by José Pinto da Fonseca, the man whose gentle treatment had won over the Karajá. ' "Our great captain [Queen Maria]", he declared, "pitied your miseries and sent us to your lands to invite you to leave the nomadic life in which you lived like untamed beasts, and to come among us to enjoy the comforts of civilised society." '
He presented the aldeia and its extensive lands to the Chavante in the name of the Queen. But when the Queen's consort later heard about the award, he suggested that all the settlers should pay a tax towards the cost of building the village. For, although the peaceful settlement and conversion of the Chavante coincided with the monarch's 'most catholic and religious intentions', it was the settlers who gained by occupying lands formerly 'infested by those barbarians'. Everyone was delighted that a captaincy 'devastated and reduced to the ultimate state of misery by those enemies' had achieved tranquillity through their settlement. Important Chavante chiefs were invited to Goiás, where the Governor 'received them with sufficient pomp to impose respect and to give them a different impression of our forces'.

It was decreed that the Chavante in Carretão aldeia should live under the Directorate regime, even though most administrators were aware of its failings. The same Overseas Council that made this order had received repeated complaints about oppression of Indians by directors. It had recorded a typical indictment of the system: 'The violence, injustice and disorder, the despotism and tyranny and illegal enslavement of Indians have depopulated Portuguese America and have meant that, instead of an extensive and opulent dominion full of useful and obedient subjects, Your Majesty possesses extremely vast plains and deserts of no value.'

A further error was to mix the Chavante with their enemies. Over a thousand of the Javaé branch of the Karajá were also brought down to Carretão. The Gê-speaking Chavante from the plains had nothing in common with riverine Karajá. In the early days of the new village, there was the usual mass baptism of Indians. This was a necessary part of the Queen's divine mission to convert the heathen, but it was done by a vicar after the most cursory instruction. The Chavante and Javaé had even less idea of the faith they were nominally espousing than they would have had twenty years earlier in the days of Jesuit missions.

Tragically and ironically, this introduction to Christianity coincided with the first impact of the lethal diseases imported unwittingly from the far side of the Atlantic. Despite their superb physical fitness, powerful Chavante warriors were struck down by such epidemics. The priest who went to convert 'this great multitude of innocents' found Carretão ravaged by disease. 'This vicar administered the sacrament to 412 [Indians], even though many of the families were absent from the aldeia. They had plunged into the woods to flee from an epidemic [of measles] that attacked them there immediately after their arrival. About a hundred died from it, but all received baptism at their final transition.'

Two factors always compound the effect of sudden depopulation by disease. Such decimation inevitably heightens the impact of the cultural shock brought by first contact with an alien and powerful colonial society. The coincidence of these two devastating processes demoralises the victims. They must suspect that death by disease is another manifestation of white men's power – for the colonists are visibly immune to diseases that wipe out far more athletic and physically perfect Indians. Some tribes therefore lose the will to survive or to raise children into frontier society, where Indians become humiliated marginals. This death wish is no fantasy. Jesuit missionaries documented examples of Indians committing suicide or simply giving up the ghost. In recent times, I myself have been told by two Bororo chiefs that their group of adults had no children because they saw no future for them.

Quite apart from this collective despair, most tribes have social systems that keep their populations small and stable. Hunter-gatherers cannot allow their numbers to exceed the game, fish and other food resources available on their territory. Tribes therefore evolve customs such as late marriage, unions across tribal moieties, years of infant breast-feeding (which inhibits conception), contraceptive plant medicines, abortion, and infanticide of any deformed or inauspicious infants. When these tribes suddenly see their numbers halved by disease, they cannot quickly abandon their regulatory customs and so they fail to restore their populations by the necessary rapid breeding.

The five Goiás aldeias – Duro and Formiga in the north of the province, and the three near Goiás – São José de Mossâmedes, Maria I, and Pedro III or Carretao – were the most important official attempt to settle Indians anywhere in Brazil during the Directorate period. The authorities lavished expenditure to make these model villages: they wanted to show that they could be as successful in acculturating Indians as the expelled Jesuits had been. It is therefore worth seeing what became of their attempts.

Once the Chavante had survived the first epidemic, they settled down and tried to provide for their families. They worked hard at agriculture, impressing the authorities by their vitality. José Rodrigues Ferreira wrote that they 'do more in a few hours than negroes in many days', and they remain an energetic tribe to this day. For a time, the Kayapó in the two villages south of Goiás also flourished. They particularly liked the aldeia of Maria I, and other Kayapó groups settled there, bringing its population to seven hundred people in four hamlets. Aldeia Maria consisted of two large tiled adobe houses for the Director and his soldiers, surrounded by a circle of thatched Indian huts. There was a church and opposite it a covered hall where the Indians could perform their dances. The chief of each tribe was given the title of colonel and other leading Indians were called captain and ensign, all with appropriate uniforms or badges of rank. During processions in the town of Vila Boa de Goiás, the chief of São José de Mossâmedes wore short breeches, a cotton shirt, three-cornered hat and gilt buckles, and carried a gun. It was decreed that every Indian man should be issued with trousers and a shirt, and the women with a skirt and blouse. But in practice most went naked, in the comfort to which they were accustomed. They also preferred to build themselves straw thatch huts with low entrances, which were warmer and more welcoming than the plain rectangular huts provided by the authorities.

After the initial enthusiasm by Indians and provincial governors, the Goiás experiment started to fail. The villages were ravaged by disease. The more vigorous Indians decided to return to their 'primitive' way of life, where they enjoyed more plentiful hunting and fishing, freedom from working for others, and their traditional society was unmolested by soldiers or ecclesiastics. The riverine Karajá and Javaé were probably the first to leave, slipping away from Maria I and São José de Mossâmedes to return to the islands and sand banks of the Araguaia. Some Kayapó also chose to move south, back to the forests of Mato Grosso. Most of the fiercer and more independent Chavante left Carretão, aware that the promised benefits of village life in Portuguese society were a fraud. The colonial authorities became equally disillusioned. The aldeias had become neither self-sufficient nor the hoped-for source of cheap labour and tax revenue. By 1809 a governor admitted that almost nothing was spent on the aldeias and that the popular view was that they should be abolished. This particular governor nonetheless still saw them as a source of potential rowers for river traffic on the Araguaia. In 1812 the southernmost aldeia, Maria I, was so reduced by disease and desertion that its few surviving Indians were forcibly moved to São José de Mossâmedes, nearer to Goiás. By that date the combined population of the two villages was only 267.

In 1819 the Goiás aldeias were visited separately by two European scientists, the Austrian Johann Emanuel Pohl and the Frenchman Auguste de Saint-Hilaire. From them we have the first clear picture of what had gone wrong. The Brazilian priest and historian Ayres do Casal had written in 1817 that the villages were failing 'because of the repugnance of white men to ally themselves with Indian women'. He saw the villages as a means of breaking down Indian society by intermarriage with white settlers – and naturally adopted the racist view that unions between white men and native women were acceptable, while the reverse was unthinkable. The European observers blamed white men for more obvious abuse. They found São José run by a Corporal Commandant, 'a vulgar cavalryman, crude, ignorant and cruel. He feared the Indians so much that he never left his house without drawing his sabre. During religious services on Sundays and holy days, his [sixteen] soldiers have to remain on guard with loaded muskets.' The Indian men were obliged to work for five days a week in communal farming under armed supervision. Their women had to spin and weave cloth, instructed by a mulatto woman. The product of all this work was distributed among the Indians by the Commandant, but he kept a large part to be sent to Goiás or to reward himself. In return, the provincial government sent salt, tobacco, cotton cloth and tools, and provided a smith to repair the tools and a carpenter to build the village's huts.

It is hardly surprising that Pohl reported that 'the aldeia is very close to decadence. . . . The Kayapó lead a life that is repugnant to them. Discontent with their administrators, punishments that often cause them to starve to death, and heavy labour to which they are subjected in the plantations are the reasons for their diminution and loathing of the system.' There was no scope for hunting or fishing at São José de Mossâmedes, and its few Indians longed for their former independence. The cruel Commandant had the right to inflict punishments: the tronco for men and palmatoria hand beatings for women and children.

Saint-Hilaire approved of settling Indians in villages, for he regarded them as devoid of foresight and therefore incapable of governing themselves – even though their tribal societies had functioned smoothly for many millennia. But Saint-Hilaire admitted the absurdity of using soldiers to govern Indians: 'What can one hope of men like the footsoldiers who, drawn from the lowest class of society and all mulattoes, are accustomed only to abuse?' They were too isolated to be controlled by military discipline. 'Badly paid, they have no objective other than to exploit the Kayapó for their own interests. . . . One solitary missionary of the Jesuit Company often used to lead a thousand Indians. Yet with seventeen soldiers it is difficult to retain two hundred Kayapó, who are assembled to no advantage for the State and without great utility for themselves.'

Disease, of course, was a constant problem for the settled Indians. Many died from a form of pox similar to European smallpox combined with high fever. They tried to combat this with native herbal remedies, generally disdaining Portuguese medicines – and, according to Pohl, were right to do so.

The Kayapó found consolation in many traditional ceremonies. Like the Chavante, they still performed the log-race. Their funeral rituals followed tribal practice. They continued to be brilliant archers. Pohl tested the remarkable Kayapó system of shooting high in the air to hit a distant target. With the women standing behind their men to hand them arrows, the Kayapó hit a chicken five times out of six at a distance of eighty yards (seventy-three metres). They kept the hunter's instinct to take food only when it was needed. This apparent improvidence infuriated Saint-Hilaire, as it did many other European observers. He complained that 'they give no thought to the morrow, never accumulate, live only for the present and are sublimely happy when they can satisfy their taste for meat, cachaça rum, and chewing tobacco.'

One person who tried to stop the decline in the Goiás aldeias was a remarkable Kayapó lady called Dona Damiana da Cunha. She was the granddaughter of the chief who had led his people into the villages in 1781. She was baptised, with Governor da Cunha as her godfather, and was then educated in successive governors' households in Goiás itself. The authorities concentrated on the education of Damiana and her brother, in order to use them in the 'civilising' of their people. They succeeded with Damiana. She spoke Portuguese well and was a devout Christian. Saint-Hilaire found her 'with a cheerful manner, open and spiritual'. Her Christianity was surprising. Pohl found that, although baptised, most Indians had not the slightest idea of the Christian religion and none could recite any prayer. Their curate contented himself with saying mass on Sundays and spent the rest of his time on his private sugar mill. He 'could have turned these gentle and docile child-men into Christians . . . and civilised them, becoming for them a second providence; but instead he makes sugar!'

Undeterred by this spiritual neglect, Dona Damiana wanted to bring more of her people into the aldeia system. She told Saint-Hilaire in 1819 that she was planning to go on a three-month expedition to seek uncontacted Kayapó. She had made such a venture into the forests in 1808, luring out seventy people. The French traveller expressed doubts about her project. But she was convinced that her status as granddaughter of the paramount chief would make all Kayapó obey her. She was equally convinced of the rectitude of what she was doing, sure that life in the dusty aldeia was better than that of hunter–gatherers in the wilds. She was obviously the dominant person in her aldeia and, having once been married to a soldier of the Goiás guards, was an intermediary between frontier society and her tribe. She doubtless deplored the decline in São José de Mossâmedes and determined to restock her village. The Governor shrewdly enlisted Dona Damiana to lead an expedition of armed men and authorised her to be absent for three months. She was gone for far longer, but returned with a further seventy Kayapó. Many of them, however, soon fled back to the freedom of their forests.

In 1821 Damiana set off again at the head of a third expedition. A Brazilian who was in Goiás a few years later said that Dona Damiana 'arbitrarily governs the Kayapó Indians. When it is necessary, she goes naked, paints herself, and sets off for the interior, leading the Indians just as she wishes.' She brought back a great quantity of Kayapó from her third expedition. But these were troubled times on the Goiás frontier, with ugly fighting. For a time the hostile, uncontacted Kayapó were joined by fugitive black slaves and they harassed the road to Goiás. In brutal retaliation, the government mounted attacks on Kayapó villages and slaughtered their inhabitants indiscriminately.

Despite the new recruits introduced by Dona Damiana, the village of São José de Mossâmedes was visibly dying. By 1824 it had only 128 Indian inhabitants. The houses once built for the Kayapó were entirely occupied by squatters, poor mulattoes whom the Governor permitted to take up free lodging there and to farm on Indian land.

The Indians themselves preferred to live in thatch huts at some distance from the aldeia centre. In 1827 a new Governor was worried that he might be blamed for the extinction of this remaining aldeia. He turned to the formidable Dona Damiana, now in her late forties. She set off on yet another pacification, travelling across the parched campos and thick, low forests of southern Goiás and Mato Grosso, south-westwards to the Camapuã river on a journey of at least sixteen hundred kilometres. She brought back a hundred Kayapó, including two chiefs. They were embraced by the Governor and baptised amid the usual short-lived pomp of an official welcome.

Two years later, fighting flared up again on the upper Araguaia and Claro rivers. There was the familiar round of Indian attacks on invading settlers followed by exaggerated reprisals. The colonists were frightened by sightings of Indian camp fires and appealed to the Governor for help. He in turn begged Damiana to go to attract these Kayapó, promising that they would be treated as free men, as 'our brothers, sons of Brazil', and rewarded with metal tools if they would lay down their arms and come to Goiás. Damiana plunged into the forests yet again, on her fifth expedition. She was accompanied by her second husband, another soldier, and by a faithful team of woodsmen. The expedition was long and arduous, but it failed to lure back any Indians and Damiana fell ill from exhaustion, hunger and fever. Early in 1831, she died. She was buried at São José (now called simply Mossâmedes) as a Brazilian heroine, and with her died the last chance of peaceful attraction of the southern Kayapó.

Emanuel Pohl went north from Goiás in 1819 to visit Pedro III or Carretão, the village built for the Chavante thirty years previously. The aldeia was on two hills, with a large sugar mill, a corn mill and the houses of the administrator and soldiers on one hill, and some thirty mud and thatch huts of the Indians across the small Carretão river on the other. In its heyday Carretão had housed 3500 Indians, but it now had only 227 of all ages. The few who remained were becoming thoroughly assimilated: they had abandoned all their tribal customs and wanted to speak only Portuguese; most wore some clothes and preferred guns to bows and arrows.

Although the Carretão Indians had to do much work 'for the King' and to enrich their administrators, they could also sell any surplus to buy guns, powder, shot, machetes, cows and blankets. It was through a desire for such goods that they had been drawn into a monetary economy. Such a transition was the hope and plan of the colonial authorities. As usual, however, peaceful change was frustrated by corrupt officials. Pohl wrote that 'the Chief, talking confidentially to me, often complained of the bad treatment endured by the Indians here, of heavy labour imposed on them, and above all of frauds permitted against them. For example, when an Indian sent his corn to be ground at the mill [the administrators] generally kept half of it.' The Indians were forced to work for the authorities for the first three days of each week, the men labouring in plantations of corn, manioc and cotton, and the women spinning or weaving.

The vast majority of Chavante had long since abandoned this regime of semi-servitude. 'Terrorised by the rough, imprudent and bad treatment of the administrators of that aldeia, and convinced by repeated proofs that there was no intention of fulfilling the promises that had been made to them, they returned to their former nomadic life in the wilds.' Angry and disillusioned, the Chavante reverted to a bitter hostility that was to last for 150 years. 'From that time on-wards, they no longer confided in any white man but fled whenever possible. They are impetuous, vengeful, and with an excellent memory for insults and humiliations. . . . These abused people have therefore changed from compatriots into the most dangerous and determined enemies. They generally kill anyone they can easily catch; but it is also admitted that, in cruel reprisal, if they meet whites they can expect only death. A form of war of extermination is being waged, and it offers a truly sad spectacle.'

Pohl described the bravery and audacity of the Chavante. Settlers along the upper Tocantins lived in fear of their attack. They felt safer in tiled houses, for the Indians would set fire to thatch with flaming arrows. Their huts on fire, the colonists would have to choose between being burned alive or running out to face Chavante arrows and clubs. But Pohl apportioned blame for this frontier warfare: 'There can be no doubt that the greater blame for these clashes lies with the settlers. They frequently make overtures of attraction or conciliation. But if the savages accept, the result is to have their children seized and carried off.' Chavante women were goodlooking, with lithe figures and pale skin. 'One of the principal causes for the bloody conflicts between the descendants of the Portuguese and the Indians is the former's desire for Indian women. . . . [The Chavante] cleverly instruct their women and girls to pretend to submit to the will of the Portuguese and to clasp them until hidden Indian men can run up and kill them with their clubs.'

The Central Coast

At the beginning of the eighteenth century, the centre of gravity of Brazil shifted dramatically to the south. The stimulus for this move was gold. Fabulous deposits of gold were discovered at Ouro Prêto ('Black Gold') in 1701 and later at other sites in what was to be called Minas Gerais ('General Mines'). The nearest port from which this treasure could be shipped to Portugal was Rio de Janeiro. This town with its superb natural harbour had grown steadily ever since the Portuguese evicted a French attempt to colonise it in the 1560s, and with the advent of gold it now flourished into a fine baroque city. In 1719 gold was discovered near Cuiabá in the remote interior of Brazil, and in 1725 at Goiás. It took months of arduous travel to reach these new gold-mines, but the point of departure was the town of São Paulo and its port of São Vicente or Santos, two of the oldest Portuguese settlements in Brazil.

These great gold-rushes transformed Brazil into one of the richest colonies of any European power. The discoveries of gold coincided with a boom in cattle ranching. Later came the discovery that coffee – a new passion in eighteenth-century Europe – grew well in the temperate climate of south-central Brazil. In 1763 the Portuguese government formally recognised the economic shift away from the hot, tropical north-eastern bulge of Brazil, whose sugar had once been the colony's most profitable enterprise. Portugal therefore transferred Brazil's capital from Salvador (Bahia) 1300 kilometres south to Rio de Janeiro.

There were few Indians left along the immense Atlantic coastline of Brazil. Large and belligerent Tupi tribes that had once occupied those coasts and plied their islands and inlets in great flotillas of canoes had succumbed to European colonisation and disease. By

mid-eighteenth century, most Portuguese settlement was still concentrated on the coast, for communication with the mother country
and within the American colony was easiest by ship. But the coastal
Indians were gone. The only exceptions were clusters of acculturated Indians in a few aldeias that had once been flourishing missions.
Indian blood of course survived in many ordinary Brazilians, in
mixtures with black African slaves or white Europeans.

The Directorate legislation was extended from Amazonia to the
rest of Brazil on 8 May 1758. There were the same clauses about
supplanting native languages with Portuguese, about destroying
communal tribal huts to force families into separate dwellings, about
making Indians dress and 'not permitting them to go naked,
especially the women – as one sees in almost all villages, to the
scandal of reason and horror of morality!' There was the same
admission that the true purpose of the legislation was to obtain
Indian labour. All Indians between the ages of thirteen and sixty
were eligible to work for the settlers. 'To animate the Indians to
[work] cheerfully . . . the Directors should explain to them the utility
that would result to them from their work.' Should any Indians who
were sent to work for settlers run off before the end of their period of
forced labour, they 'will lose two-thirds of their payment, which will
at once be handed over to the same settlers'. As in Amazonia,
payment under this unjust system was expressed in lengths of cotton
cloth.

The majority of the men who became village directors in the rest of
Brazil were as disgracefully unsuitable as those in Amazonia. A
report complained about the sixteen directors appointed in 1769 to
run the former mission villages of Bahia: 'It is obvious that persons
of probity should have been chosen: men capable of teaching [the
Indians] civilised manners and religion. Instead, men were sent who
did not even command the first rudiments of reading, writing and
arithmetic. . . . The directors were concerned only to establish
estates in places best suited to their ambitions, using the Indians for
labour in their fields. All the directors who have been named are
generally indigent' and intent only on self-enrichment. Indians were
forced to beg for food from neighbouring settlers because they were
too busy working for their director to grow their own. 'These
wretched Indians continue in this unhappy state of misery and
poverty knowing no law or reason. . . . They find themselves fatigued
and exhausted by the work which every one of their missionaries,
parish priests and directors heaps upon them every day. . . . In short,
they watch the degeneration of their race, scandalously contrived by

those same people who are supposed to be promoting their temporal and spiritual welfare.'

By the mid-eighteenth century, the largest surviving concentrations of Indians in north-east Brazil were around Bahia and along the São Francisco river. Some of the São Francisco valley missions had been Jesuit, but the majority were run by Franciscan Capuchins. There had been a move by the Franciscans to import European friars, from France in the seventeenth century and from Italy in the eighteenth. The Italians were not a success. A report written in 1761 made ugly accusations of 'tyrannies, cruelties and insolences by Italian bearded Capuchin fathers' on the São Francisco river in the interior of Pernambuco. The friars were accused of beating, castrating and killing men and flogging women as punishment for trivial offences. The report, by a senior army officer, gave precise details of these atrocities and was clearly more than mere xenophobia or anti-clericalism.

Other reports from the Directorate period gave a picture of tranquillity and regimented poverty in the Indian villages, of which there were some eighty along the São Francisco and thirty in the state of Bahia. In 1758 the Portuguese Crown sent two members of its new Overseas Council to supervise the reform of Indian villages following the Law of Liberty and the abolition of temporal control by missionaries. These inspectors chose to concentrate on a large village near Salvador da Bahia, which had been run for two centuries by the Jesuits as the mission of Espírito Santo and was now renamed Abrantes. Their report offers a vivid portrayal of this village. It housed seventy families in fifty-three simple huts arranged in rows around a large central square. The huts had rush flooring and hardly any furniture beyond beds and clothes pegs in the walls; almost none had tables or chairs. A fire burned in the middle of each hut, with the smoke escaping through the thatch. All the Indians spoke the lingua geral; many men and a few women spoke Portuguese; and a few men could read. The men wore only cotton trousers – no hats and generally no shirts. Women usually wore a long wrap called coruta or tocó hanging from their neck to their feet, although a few were changing to skirts and blouses. The women complained to an inspector in 1761 that the modest long wrap had been replaced by a very short dress. 'Modern economy found that [the long] fashion was wasteful and an impediment for work. Today, therefore, they use the same dress, but so short that it does not cover above the waist or much below the knees.'

Work was the main theme of various reports from the Directorate period. A judge wrote from Pôrto Seguro, on the coast south of Bahia, that he had been trying to improve his Indians' villages by replacing thatches with tiled roofs. 'Many of the Indians are now clothed and shod from what they earn by their daily labour and from farming land or fishing in the sea. I apply them to such work, to dissipate the vagrancy and idleness that are such a common vice in these lands, even among the whites.' This same judge, José Xavier Machado Monteiro, had broken up Indian families and 'distributed about four hundred of both sexes in salaried jobs in the houses of the whites', a forced labour that he claimed was rapidly making them more civilised. In 1777 Judge Monteiro issued additional instructions to augment the Directorate legislation for his captaincy of Pôrto Seguro. His clauses were concerned with schooling, apprenticeship, baptism and marriage, segregated rectangular houses for each family, agriculture, and of course availability of Indians to work for settlers. 'There are Indians in whom the abominable sin of laziness is engrained. . . . These should be the first that Directors should distribute for daily labour for whites and mestizos who ask for them, on land or sea.'

Two factors that undermined the Directorate system were admitted in correspondence from north-east Brazil at this time. One was the failure to honour wage payments to Indians. Official hopes that Indians could be drawn into a competitive economy were always frustrated by Indian indifference – or 'idleness' – and colonists' exploitation. It was all too easy to defraud Indians. The Pôrto Seguro legislation of 1777 admitted that 'since Indians are extremely rustic, many whites and coloureds easily succeed in cheating them, selling them goods for exorbitant prices and paying extremely little for what they buy from them.' Unsuitable old clothes or alcohol were used to pay for Indian labour.

Another perennial and tragic problem was disease. In 1779 there was yet another 'terrible epidemic of smallpox suffered by this city of Bahia'. The Governor was impotent to help: he could only write that he 'witnessed with horror the devastation caused by this pernicious evil'. Hospitals and disused convents were crammed with the dying, and the disease did not spare the fittest young people. As usual, most of the victims were Indians.

This same Governor dealt leniently with a rebellion by Curema Indians in the Piancó district far up the São Francisco river. These Indians had fled from their villages and were attacking ranches. But a local official reported that the rebellion was largely justified, since the Crown was wrongly claiming land that had been usurped from this peaceful tribe. Thus, when the dispute was resolved in 1789 after a decade of strife, the rebels were pardoned because they had been 'moved solely by your rusticity and misery' and had been provoked beyond endurance by the 'tyrannies and excesses' of their Director.* On this occasion, the guilty Director was removed.

There were a few places where difficult terrain enabled tribes to survive, isolated, uncontacted and hostile, near the Atlantic coast. One such area was the long stretch of coast running southwards from Bahia. The coastal plain here had seemed promising to the first colonists and for a time settlements and sugar plantations flourished in the captaincies of Ilhéus, Pôrto Seguro and Espírito Santo. But expansion into the interior was blocked by a range of hills and dense forests that ran parallel with the coast a few kilometres inland. Worse than the geographical barrier was the existence of warlike and indomitable Indians in these forests.

The tribes that inhabited the forests of the upper Jequitinhonha, Mucuri and Doce river valleys were natural guerrilla fighters. They shunned open battle, and thus avoided the fate of the populous and warlike Tupi tribes of the coastal plains. The Portuguese could use their horses, armour and firearms to defeat the Tupi; but these weapons were almost useless in the shadowy world of dense forest. The first European settlers called the Gê of these forests by the derogatory Tupi word Aimoré; but by the eighteenth century they were called Botocudo because they wore discs (botoques) in their ear lobes and lower lips. Ayres do Casal dismissed this as 'the extravagant and ridiculous custom of piercing their ears and lips and considerably expanding them with wooden discs, because they believe that they thus appear more savage and fearsome'.

One of the earliest English visitors to Brazil, Maria Graham (Lady Calcott) admired the Botocudos' looks: 'Some of the young women are really pretty, of a light copper-colour which glows all over when they blush; and two of the young men were decidedly handsome, with very dark eyes . . . and aquiline noses.' But she strongly disapproved of the lip and ear discs. 'The rest were so disfigured by the holes cut in their lower lips and their ears to receive their barbarous ornaments, that we could scarcely tell what they were like. [Lip discs] are extremely frightful, especially when they are eating. It gives the mouth the appearance of an ape's; and the peculiar mumping it occasions is hideously unnatural. . . . The mouth is still more ugly without the lip-piece, the teeth appearing, and saliva running through.' Various northern Kayapó tribes still wear these discs, in order to make their warriors more frightening to an enemy. Having myself seen many of these, I can sympathise with Maria Graham's reaction.

The Botocudo were tall, handsome people. A Jesuit wrote that they were as 'lusty as Germans, and with some females as pale-skinned as any other nation'. The Portuguese could do nothing against these formidable warriors. They were nomadic, moving about their forests with speed and unerring trackers' skills. It was thus impossible to locate their villages and slaughter them in sur-prise attacks. 'They are excessively strong and carry very long bows . . . with arrows to match.' They chose to fight in 'treacherous assaults and ambushes without any battle order, and they easily hide themselves under the little leaves [of the forest floor].' If attacked, they instantly scattered and fell upon their enemies from the rear. Another Jesuit complained that the Botocudo moved about in small bands and 'without being seen, they shoot arrows at people and kill them. They run away agilely and disappear into the woods like wild goats, often running on hands and feet with their bows and arrows on their backs. . . . Our men cannot see them – until they feel them-selves hit by arrows.'

They compounded these devastating tactics by being utterly fear-less. Small groups of Botocudo would attack Portuguese stockades with reckless bravery. The Englishman Anthony Knivet, who was a captive in seventeenth-century Brazil, described them as very resolute and desperate, and as swift as any horse. The colonists were terrified of them. Most of the early plantations and settlements of this coast were soon abandoned and no traveller dared move about without a powerful escort.

By the early eighteenth century, the Botocudo had been driven from the coast but still had full control of their forests. A smallpox epidemic ravaged the coast and was believed to have raged in the interior. The Botocudo were decimated by this disease – which could penetrate beyond the reach of Portuguese arms – and it was thought that they were almost extinguished. But they survived and recover-ed. Within a few generations they were once again 'absolutely dominant in those extensive forests'. As an anonymous author admitted in 1781, 'experience has not yet revealed any means of civilising them. Only with excessive effort can they be extinguished, but not tamed.'

A local vicar lamented that no one was strong enough to oppose these tribes, who 'pass victoriously through these forests as if behind walls. One fears a wild Indian behind every tree: for when one least expects it, an arrow comes.' A decade later, it was admitted that the captaincy's inland road was abandoned for fear of these tribes and was becoming overgrown with vegetation.

The Botocudo terrified not only white settlers, but also neighbouring tribes of Indians. They were constantly at war with the equally formidable Puri, who lived south of them in forests along the Paraíba river. They raided and skirmished against the Tupi tribes of the coastal plain, who had been populous and settled in large villages before their destruction by the Europeans, but were now diminished and partly acculturated into colonial society. The Botocudo were also at war with tribes to the west of their forested hills. The Maxakali (pronounced Mashacali), Panhame and other tribes who lived on the plateau of Minas Gerais towards the gold-mining towns gladly helped the Portuguese in campaigns against the Botocudo.

Because of this inter-tribal fighting, the Portuguese had more success in pacifying the Botocudos' neighbours: Puri to the south-west, Maxakali to the west and north, and Pataxó, Mongoio and Camacan to the north.

In the 1780s there was a rumour of gold in the forested hills of the Puri and Botocudo, north of Rio de Janeiro. The Governor had sent a priest, Father Manuel Luis Branco, to attract the Puri living in the Arrepiados ('Bristling' or 'Unkempt') forests beyond the Paraíba river. It was this priest who reported potential gold and rich pastures in that region. The result was a large expedition of eager prospectors or land claimants, led by General Francisco Antonio Rebelo. In August 1781 his men cut their way up the steep and densely forested hills of Arrepiados. After a tough march they reached the top and saw broad plains inhabited only by Indians. 'On the day after this examination, 373 claimants for mineral lands assembled to demand them. The general acceded to their demands, and ordered that the lands be divided among them. . . .' They then pushed on northwards into the forests of the Cuieté river, which runs northwards into the Doce. The expedition had to have a military escort, for fear of the Botocudo, and skilled woodsmen to open paths. The prospectors and settlers finally reached the stockade or presídio where the Cuieté joined the Doce, and were welcomed by its village of pacified Indians seeking refuge from the Botocudo in the lee of the fort.

Back in Rio de Janeiro a few months later, Rebelo resorted to a drastic method to press-gang settlers for his new colony. 'He ordered the commanders of each district of the captaincy to arrest all vagabonds and insignificant persons and send them to the prisons of [Rio de Janeiro]. From there most of them were sent to Cuieté, assisted with food, clothing and tools needed for mineral working, and under the control of a lieutenant.' The new arrivals were set to work clearing forest and cutting trails. They found no gold, but some remained on the Doce to try to develop farms. By the early nineteenth century, colonists were starting to push eastwards into this same frontier region from the gold-mining districts of Minas Gerais. They were protected by a few stockaded forts garrisoned by handfuls of soldiers. Possibly because of this pressure from the west, the Botocudo intensified their raids on to the lower Doce and Jequitinhonha rivers and the coastal plain between them. The backward captaincy of Espírito Santo was largely denuded as a result.

The northernmost group of Botocudo was a tribe living between the Pardo and Contas rivers in southern Bahia or Ilhéus. These were known by a Tupi word Camacan (meaning 'twisted hair') but they were also called Menians or Aimoré by the Portuguese. Reckoned at about two thousand, they inhabited densely forested hills and had all the characteristics of an agile Gê-speaking tribe: they ran the traditional log-race, slept on platform beds rather than hammocks, wore straw penis sheaths and let their hair hang long over their shoulders. From what we know of them they may have been culturally and linguistically related to the Chavante and the many other Gê tribes of the central Brazilian plateau. On the lower Pardo river, between the Camacans and the ocean, lived their enemies, the Mongoio.

A seventy-six-year-old conquistador or Indian-hunter from Portugal called João Gonçalves da Costa had pushed up the Pardo in 1806 to subdue these tribes. He and his son, Captain-Major João da Silva, led a typical raiding party of 'soldiers, settlers and tame Indians' and soon surrounded a village of peaceful Mongoio. The docile Indians readily surrendered, and their five or six villages were placed under Portuguese protection.

Gonçalves da Costa's troop moved on into the interior, determined to avenge one of its men killed by a Botocudo or Camacan arrow. After four days' march they found an Indian village and attempted the customary murderous surprise attack on it. They hid in the forests 'in order to besiege it at dawn next day – which is the appropriate hour at which [the Indians] are all gathered in their huts.' The Portuguese commander described how his attack failed to achieve the intended slaughter. The Indians resisted valiantly 'without fearing the booming of the guns or our warlike drum'. They fired arrows from behind trees, with the women feeding arrows to their men. They fearlessly shot at guns at point-blank range. The Portuguese drew their swords and charged; but the Camacan retreated, abandoning the village. The soldiers gathered up eight Indian children and one mother with a baby at her breast. (This battle inspired a dramatic drawing by Johann Moritz Rugendas (*plate 2*).) To console themselves for this meagre haul of captives, the raiders went on to subdue four more peaceful villages of Mongoio.

A decade later, the sympathetic and perceptive German traveller Prince Maximilian zu Wied-Neuwied visited the area and reported that some Camacan had accepted life under Portuguese rule. Gonçalves da Costa had established a palisaded settlement with the boastful name Conquista on the hills between the Contas and Pardo rivers. His soldiers were disappearing and he suspected that the Indians were luring them into the forests one by one to kill them. Costa therefore determined on a treacherous reprisal. 'He ordered his men to have their guns ready. He then invited all the savages to a festival and, while they confidently abandoned themselves to its enjoyment, they were surrounded on all sides and almost all killed. After that, the savages buried themselves in the forests and the camp achieved calm and security.'

Wied-Neuwied met Colonel Gonçalves da Costa when he was an old man of eighty-six. He told how he had reached Brazil in 1746, aged sixteen, and had penetrated great areas of forest, fighting Pataxó, Camacan and Botocudo. He boasted that he had been the first European to navigate the Pardo, Contas and Ilhéus rivers. In 1806 a formal peace treaty had been signed with the Camacan after their defeat by the Captain-Major João da Silva. The Camacan were then settled in half a dozen villages near the Pardo river.

The German traveller described the Camacan as 'a nomadic people, freedom-loving and warlike, who defended their territory foot by foot against the Portuguese. . . . They visit regions cultivated by Europeans only with repugnance. Like all Indians, they prefer to return to their dark forests. They have become circumspect and suspicious because of frequent examples of tyrannical methods adopted by the whites. When we visited them, they hid their children and young men in the forest.'

Despite this understandable shyness, the Camacan were valuable allies of the Portuguese settlers. They had suffered from other groups of Botocudo and were therefore willing to help fight their fellow tribesmen. The Camacan thus defended the Pardo against Botocudo attack, and their warriors guided expeditions against uncontacted Botocudo. Wied-Neuwied wrote that 'this tribe's skill in all manual tasks makes it very useful to the Portuguese. . . . They employ these Indians in clearing land, for they fell trees with great speed and use axes with dexterity. They are experienced hunters. They are excellent archers, as I myself witnessed on various occasions, and some of them shoot very well with shotguns.' The Camacan traded weapons and handicrafts with the Europeans. They also sold wax torches made of leaves artistically wrapped around cords of wild beeswax, which gave an aromatic smell when burned.

Unlike the Camacan, the Mongoio settled near colonial towns and took to farming corn, cotton and bananas. They accepted Portuguese rule willingly enough, because it protected them against the Botocudo. They were skilled potters and bartered their ceramics. They also produced much wild honey. Some of it was boiled – along with the bees who created it – to make a strong fermented liquor. This gave the Mongoio alcoholic release from its woes, for the tribe had suffered after submitting to colonial rule.

According to Wied-Neuwied, 'the government placed Portuguese directors in these aldeias to civilise the savages. But this process is proceeding very slowly and with little effect, because the directors themselves are uncultured men, often soldiers or sailors, and hardly likely to gain their confidence. The poor Indians are tyrannised, treated like slaves, ordered to work on the roads or at felling the forests, ordered to take messages for long distances, and recruited to fight against enemy tribes. Since they do this without or almost without receiving any payment whatever, it is not surprising that, being naturally inclined to freedom, they have no goodwill towards their oppressors.'

Another tough Indian fighter called João Domingues Monteiro, in repeated campaigns, forced the Maxakali (northern neighbours of the Pataxó and Camacan) to move inland. The Maxakali were restrained by fear of firearms. 'During his ambushes and attacks he captured many, who were added to the fraternity of the Church and died Catholics.' Then, in 1786, one group of Maxakali emerged from the forests to make peace with the Portuguese. They did this to obtain 'cutting tools to make weapons with which to defend their tribe against their Pataxó and Botocudo enemies, with whom they maintain a most implacable war, in which they have no recourse but flight because of the superior forces of these two ferocious tribes.'

In 1794, a further two hundred Maxakali laid down their weapons and asked for religious instruction. They particularly wanted tools and cloth. A priest who helped in their submission was surprised that these Maxakali were not interested in the gold-mines and jewels thought to lie in their territory. Instead, 'all their zeal and interest consist only of not being deprived of their land which was given them by God (they point to the sky), nor of their women.'

In 1808 there was a decisive change in the government of Brazil. Napoleon's revolutionary French troops had invaded Portugal the previous year and declared the House of Bragança to be deposed. Although Wellington's Lines of Torres Vedras prevented a French occupation of Lisbon, the Portuguese royal family sailed for Brazil – partly to escape from their invaded country and partly to affirm their control of the vast American empire. By then, power was in the hands of the Prince Regent Dom João, whose mother Queen Maria I had been mentally incapacitated since 1792.

Immediately after his arrival in Brazil, the Prince Regent Dom João was assailed with complaints about the Botocudo. The warrior tribe was defending its territories too aggressively against colonial settlement, and was harassing isolated farms in Minas Gerais and on the coasts of Espírito Santo and Ilhéus in southern Bahia. The Prince Regent sent Luis Thomas Navarro de Campos to make the difficult journey overland from Bahia to Rio de Janeiro. His instructions were to report 'which are the nations of heathen [tribes of Indians] that most persecute the inhabitants of the area between the capital of Pôrto Seguro, Vitória, and the Rio Doce?' and 'What measures are necessary to protect their lives and agriculture?' Campos was a rigid official with no understanding of Indians. He reported that the Botocudo were the most ferocious and feared of tribes, and were 'certainly anthropophagic'. He told the Prince Regent that the settlers were clamouring for government action because of Indian attacks.

All Indians were regarded as potentially 'sinister and tumultuous'. 'Ever since these lands were colonised by the Portuguese, these barbarians have always raided the settlers, destroying their plantations, smashing their factories, killing their slaves and servants and even the settlers themselves.'

It never occurred to Navarro de Campos that the Indians had a right to defend themselves against invasion and oppression. He was thoroughly influenced by the hatred of Indians that has always been characteristic of the Brazilian frontier. However liberal and distant urban legislators might be, the colonists on the frontier itself waged constant war on their Indian neighbours. A mixture of fear, greed, vengeance and occasionally guilt impelled them to want the Indians destroyed or driven off. Campos therefore recommended to the Prince Regent that 'violence is the most effective means to make the lands raided by these barbarians tranquil and once again fit for settlement.' Experience had shown that 'love, suffering and beneficence' had failed to attract the Indians to 'civil society and the bosom of the church'. These objectives 'would be achieved more easily by ambushing them, opposing them with force of arms, and bringing them violently to settle in the towns. Once there, they ought not to remain free, for they would certainly relapse, as some have already done.' The royal inspector thus advocated a drastic return to violence: to legalised war against Indians and a return to slavery for prisoners captured in battle.

Dom João, a young autocrat freshly arrived from Europe, listened to this terrible advice and to the anti-Indian hysteria of the most reactionary colonists. On 13 May 1808 he issued a decree against the Botocudo, particularly those of the Rio Doce. The text of his edict said that this tribe had refused all peaceful overtures and was constantly attacking settlers' farms. 'They have forced many proprietors to abandon their fazendas. . . . They have practised the most horrible and atrocious scenes of the most barbarous anthropophagy, killing both Portuguese and tame Indians. [They kill] with wounds from which they later suck blood, or dismember the bodies and eat their sad remains.' Auguste de Saint-Hilaire, who visited some peaceful Botocudo a few years later, said that the local settlers hated Indians and had fabricated the accusation of eating human flesh. Maria Graham blamed missionaries keen to enhance their own achievements for the gross exaggerations about Botocudo savagery.

After repeating these wild and false accusations, the royal decree proclaimed an 'offensive war' against the Botocudo. Local governors were ordered to deploy troops in garrisons along the Doce. 'You will continue the war in the dry season of each year, and will cease only when you have the pleasure of dominating all their habitations and demonstrating to them the superiority of my royal arms in such a way that, moved by justified terror, they beg for peace and submit to the gentle yoke of the law and promise to live in our society.'

In addition to declaring the last official war against Indians in Brazilian history, this savage decree restored legalised slavery of Indians. The Prince Regent ordered that 'all Botocudo Indians captured with weapons in their hands will be considered as prisoners of war and may be delivered into enslavement to the respective commander for ten years. . . . He should keep them with appropriate security, in irons if they give no sign of having abandoned their atrocities and anthropophagy.'

Such a decree was tantamount to declaring an open season on any Indians. Its dire consequences were soon felt. Saint-Hilaire witnessed how it 'has given rise to the most horrible abuses. Mulattoes and even whites buy [Indian] children from their parents for trinkets, or carry them off by force, and then sell them in the villages of the interior of Minas Novas. When I was on the banks of the Jequitinhonha there were already no children left in those tribes that communicate most with the Portuguese; and in order to be able to sell more children those tribes make war on others farther distant.'

Far away to the north, the German ethnologists Spix and Martius reported that 'in the provinces of Goiás, Piauí and Maranhão countless manhunts were launched against hostile tribes of the Tocantins and Mearim rivers. Such tribes were designated by the general name "Botocudo" and were brought back as slaves just as if they were.' The Germans saw many Pimenteiras, captured in this way, being used as slaves in Oeiras, the capital of Piauí. That was thousands of kilometres away from the homelands of the Botocudo.

A persistent problem was to find secular clergy to replace the intelligent and well-organised Jesuits. The Jesuit Company had been less active in north-eastern Brazil than on the Amazon or in Paraguay. It had only seven missions in the bulge of Brazil (in the captaincies of Pernambuco, Paraíba and Ceará) and nine in Bahia. The authorities tried to persuade ordinary clergy to fill the Jesuits' shoes by promising them the Jesuits' fine houses and possessions, and by allowing them to charge fees for religious services for births, christenings, marriages and deaths. Despite these inducements, there were few applicants. Robert Southey said that the Indians regarded the successors to the Jesuits as mercenary interlopers. 'The poor Clergy themselves were little pleased with the society into which they were banished, and the privations which they had to endure. Some gave up their situations in despair; others fled to save their lives. Insurrections against the system took place; some Indians were cast into prison; others took to the woods.' As elsewhere, the immediate effect of sudden transition from missionary to secular control 'was to thin the villages and corrupt the remaining inhabitants'.

A few foreign missionaries were active along this coast of Brazil, although not remotely to the same extent as the expelled Jesuits. The authorities permitted Italian Capuchins to establish themselves in Bahia and operate among the most acculturated Indians. In 1808 the Prince Regent's investigator reported that a missionary called Antonio Lomba was in a decaying Indian village at the mouth of the Pardo river; he had lured some Maxakali down from the forests to receive baptism and restock his aldeia. Spix and Martius met a venerable old Capuchin called Friar Ludovico from Livorno at a village of Camacan on the Pardo in 1818. The Germans, freshly arrived from Europe and convinced of the virtues of Christian civilisation, were enormously impressed by this missionary. 'If anyone were capable of converting these restless and primitive savages to sentiments of peace and obedience to the voice of religion, it could only be that worthy old man. Serenity and good humour radiate from the face of this man, whose hair and beard were turning white in the worthy office of pastor of souls. His noble bearing imposed itself, as a member of a more elevated race, on the timid natives. These were likely to receive the first impressions of religious sentiment through the confidence they placed in him.' Friar Ludovico was having most success with the women. These were dressed in cotton skirts, although they preferred their own small aprons of palm leaves. They worked willingly as household servants for the colonists, and were planting manioc and maize for their tribe. Not content with the acculturated Indians in his parish, Friar Ludovico also penetrated the forests 'to unite more scattered Camacan Indians at his altar'. The Germans approved of this, as they did the man's evident calm and humanity. 'His deeds reconciled us to the harmful influence of Europe on this new continent, where our civilisation has sown seeds of destruction.'

It was half a century since Pombal had expelled the black-robed Jesuits. With the departure of the wealthy and regimented Fathers, as we have seen, their extensive missions rapidly disintegrated. Many of the aldeias were plundered. A viceroy of Brazil complained in 1789 that the Jesuit mission of Santo Antonio dos Guarulhos, north of Rio de Janeiro, was 'entirely abandoned . . . with the greater part of its lands totally dispersed through the negligence of the ministers who were supposed to care for its output but instead made themselves arbiters to dispose of them as they saw fit'. At that same time, another royal official complained of the 'unhappy state of misery and poverty' of the former mission Indians of Bahia. Their religious instruction was inadequate. 'They find themselves fatigued and exhausted by the work which every one of their missionaries, parish priests and directors heaps upon them every day. . . . Those same people who should be promoting their temporal and spiritual welfare scandalously contrive the degeneration of their race.' A few years later, another official complained to a bishop about the venal conduct of a parish priest who was charging Indians far too much for religious services: 'a great dishonesty and fatal ambition reign in the person of Father José Carlos Barata!'

Maria Graham felt that the Jesuit system had failed because it was too egalitarian. 'The rock on which the education of the Indians split was the community of goods. When a man has no property, but depends for the supply of his daily wants upon the providence of others, he has no incitement to particular exertion. The stimulus to industry cannot exist where a man has no hope of growing richer, no fear of becoming poorer, no anxiety about the provision of his family.' But she deplored the chaos that followed the expulsion of the Jesuits in 1759. 'The history of Brazil for the next thirty years is composed of the mismanagement and decay of the Jesuit establishments.'

Far inland on the lawless frontier, matters were much worse. In the Tocantins valley, 'the newly discovered regions are battlefields on which gangs try to exterminate one another for a few fathoms of land if they suspect a vein of ore. The new settlers commit deeds so inhuman that the cruelty of the savages cannot compare to it. Never was a clerical pastureland administered by more degenerate priests, nor have missionaries of worse character ever been seen in any apostolic capacity.' The English traveller Henry Koster, who was in north-east Brazil at the beginning of the nineteenth century, commented: 'There are now no enthusiastic missionaries; the Jesuits no longer exist in that country, and the other orders of friars have become lazy and worse than useless.' In his powerful memorandum addressed to Queen Maria I about the failings of the Directorate system, Antonio José Pestana da Silva wrote in 1788 that missionaries should stop trying to bring fresh Indians down to their villages, but should go to live among them in their tribal homelands. This was, of course, a forlorn hope: if zealous and disciplined religious orders could not persuade their missionaries to work in the forests, there was no incentive for lay priests to risk the isolation, discomfort and danger involved in such activity.*

Although some commentators blamed evil or incompetent priests for the obvious failures to attract Indians to the church, others agonised over the seemingly intractable intellectual problem of such conversion. Ever since the start of Portuguese colonisation in the sixteenth century, it had proved almost impossible to turn Indians into lasting Christians. Most tribes stubbornly clung to their native customs and beliefs. This infuriated and baffled Europeans convinced of the superiority of their culture and religion. Spix and Martius noted that Indians enjoyed the ceremonial of Christian mass without being interested in its alien and irrelevant spiritual message. When the Germans visited a new mission among the

Coroado ('Crowned' Indians because of their tonsured hairstyle) and Coropó of Minas Gerais, they noted that 'the clergy and the Portuguese in general take great pains to propagate Christianity among them; but even the better-informed [Indians] have so far acquired no notion of the essence of Christianity. . . . They are merely induced [to church] by the ceremony at which they gaze with astonishment, without betraying any emotion of mind, or reflection.' Other more self-assured tribes such as the Botocudo 'spurned the Christian religion with determination'. The German artist Johann Moritz Rugendas saw that most Indians living among the Portuguese were baptised, 'but it is evident that this is the extent of their Christianity. They go to mass when they know that they will have food and drink after it; but they consider this obligation as a task done to please the whites.'

There were a few secular clergy who tried to fulfil a disinterested mission among Indians. Today, we would question the desirability of their attempted conversions. By imposing Christianity they undermined and destroyed indigenous cultures. Few tribes could survive such a threat to their self-esteem. But these few genuine missionaries at least had the welfare of their congregations at heart, even if their methods and objectives were misguided.

Spix and Martius praised the benign old priest Ludovico, whom they met at his mission of São Pedro de Alcantara on the Ilhéus coast of southern Bahia. Another priest who was praised in his day was the Brazilian-born Manuel de Jesus Maria, who in 1767 penetrated the forests of the Pomba river, a tributary of the Paraíba in south-eastern Minas Gerais. He established himself as chaplain of the Coroado and related Coropó, and spent forty-three years among them, dying there in 1811. He settled his tribes in villages, to which he built trails – thus opening their territory to colonial invasion. He himself taught in his village schools, and the high point of his ministry was when one Indian boy was ordained as a priest in Mariana in 1790.

Other priests were active with nearby groups of Puri. Some members of this tribe had been settled at an aldeia called Guarulhos near Rio de Janeiro. With its territory overrun by settlers, the remnants of the tribe dispersed to the valley of the Paraíba. In the 1770s the Viceroy, the Marquis of Lavradio, ordered that some of these Puri be invited to Rio 'in order to lose their horror of civilised customs and to become domesticated so that they would be of greater use to church and state. The project took place. The proselytes returned to their land loaded with axes, scythes and other similar tools that the Marquis had given them.' A later viceroy followed up this seduction by sending two Italian Capuchins and financing them from rents of the abandoned village of Guarulhos. These friars, Angelo Maria from Lucca and Vitório from Cambiasca, 'satisfactorily tended the Indians' spiritual welfare'. They founded a mission called Camboa on the banks of the Paraíba and in 1799 built a handsome church dedicated to St Fidelis. Prince Maximilian of Wied-Neuwied visited the place in 1815 and met Friar Angelo; old Friar Vitório, who had just died, had been greatly respected by the Indians; but they disliked the surviving priest: 'In fact, they once expelled him, alleging that he had no right to instruct them since he was worse than they were.' The German traveller left a drawing of São Fidelis. It was a tall, tile-roofed church, looking very Italian and standing in isolation on a meadow by the river bank. Nearby was a row of tidy mission huts and a banana plantation; but just beyond were banks of steep hills densely wooded with virgin jungle.

Only parts of the Puri and related Coroado accepted permanent contact with the whites. Groups of Coroado who lived beyond the Serra dos Orgãos (the aptly named Organ-Pipe mountains) raided plantations that were spreading into this rich frontier region. In 1789 the Viceroy sent a Captain Inacio de Sousa Wernek to 'attack them in their own villages', and his savage reprisals checked their raids. A royal order of 7 March 1800 recommended that the Coroado be civilised, and this task was entrusted to a rich local rancher called José Rodrigues da Cruz, who was already on good terms with the tribe, which he helped with food and tools. The combination of the Indian-fighter Wernek and the bountiful farmer Cruz succeeded in 'drawing to the bosom of the church many lost souls, adding to the State a numerous people, and taking possession of the lands that they occupied without farming them in any way.'

The church followed, to complete the triumvirate of Indian exploiters: in 1801 Father Manuel Gomes Leal went as missionary priest of the Coroado, whom he had fought on various earlier campaigns. He founded an aldeia called Cobras ('Snakes'), later known as Nossa Senhora da Glória de Valença. But the colonial frontier was exploding into this fertile region and Valença rapidly became a magnet for land-hungry settlers. By 1814 it contained seven hundred non-Indians, and by 1820 over a thousand European settlers. A royal order of 1819 sought in vain to stem the tide. This decree accused a settler of 'notorious oppression' in trying to evict the Indians and claim that the land was devoluta or unoccupied. The Crown declared that 'a territory marked as an Indian aldeia should not be considered as unoccupied, especially when its church is already built and some [Indian] inhabitants live in the aldeia itself.' The speculator who had tried to seize the land of Valença was ordered to leave the aldeia. But when Saint-Hilaire visited it at that time, he found it entirely populated by settlers and the Indians gone.

The Puri and Coroado were not left in peace on the Paraíba. Gold was discovered on the Pomba tributary of the Paraíba, a mere 200 kilometres from Rio de Janeiro, and prospectors poured in. The centre of this lawless community of prospectors was a wooded hilly country called Canta Gallo (Cock's Crow). John Mawe, the first British traveller allowed into the interior of Brazil, visited the place in 1809 and found it full of settlers. He wrote that the government had 'issued many injudicious regulations, oppressed the natives beyond example, built registers [forts] in various parts to prevent contraband, and filled the whole neighbourhood with guards.'

Mawe went to see the half-acculturated Indians. He found them living in the forests in thatched frame houses. They farmed little, but made a scanty living gathering ipecacuanha bark (a fever palliative) for a settler whom they regarded as a 'kind of chief'. The men wore a waistcoat and trousers, and the women 'a chemise and petticoat, with a handkerchief tied round the head after the fashion of the Portuguese females. . . . They are loathsome in their persons, and in their habits but one remove from the anthropophagi; for they will devour almost any animals in the coarsest manner, for instance a bird unplucked, half-roasted, with the entrails remaining. They are not of a shy or morose character, but have a great aversion to labour, and cannot be brought to submit to any regular employment.'

The only thing that impressed Mawe about these Puri and Coroado was their skill as archers. He saw them all hit an orange at thirty yards and a thin banana at forty: 'Not a single arrow missed its aim, though they all shot at an elevated range.' He watched them stalk birds in the forest. 'Cautiously creeping along until they were within bow-shot, they never failed to bring down their game. The stillness and expedition with which they penetrated the thickets, and passed through the brush-wood, were truly surprising.'

When Prince Wied-Neuwied visited São Fidelis on the Paraíba in 1815, he found the Indians at different stages of acculturation. Those who had lived there for years were 'still fairly pure', although they lived in mud-and-wattle huts and had adopted hammocks for sleeping. All could speak Portuguese, although they naturally used their own language among themselves. On weekdays the men went barefoot and wore only trousers and a white cotton shirt. 'On Sundays, however, they dress better and cannot be distinguished from the lower class of Portuguese. . . . The women are more elegant than the men, sometimes using a veil and liking ornaments.'

Across the Paraiba river were newly contacted Puri. This was Wied-Neuwied's first encounter with uncontaminated Indians. He was enchanted to find that 'these strange people received us in a most amicable manner. . . . That group of dark, naked people constituted the most interesting and singular spectacle. Men, women and children were intermingled, and observed us with a curious but timid look. They had all adorned themselves as best they could: only a few women used a cloth around their waist or breast, most were completely unclothed.' Many were painted with red urucum or black genipap vegetable dyes. The Puri had been hunting monkeys and tried to offer the Germans some smoke-blackened meat, with the heads and fur still on the animals. Some trading ensued, with the Indians wanting knives and anything red, and their women 'avid for mirrors'.

The German Prince witnessed the settlers' racist hatred of Indians, born of arrogance, fear and guilt. Some Puri were accused of having killed a black slave and cut off his limbs, allegedly with a view to eating him. 'The colonists, from an erroneous attitude of considering them to be animals, menaced the Indians with horsewhips, which naturally excited their anger and led to ill-will, hatred and violence. Because of this, they were all enchanted with us strangers because we treated them with gentleness and courtesy.' At a ranch lower down the river, the Germans met the manager, who 'declared his profound hatred of [Indians], repeatedly declaring that he would happily kill our young Puri. He added: "It is inconceivable that the government has not yet adopted effective measures to exterminate those brutes. If we advance any distance up river, we inevitably encounter their huts." '

The government was in fact taking the extreme measures demanded by such colonists. In the wake of the Prince Regent's order of 1808 declaring war on the Botocudo, a line of eight forts was established between the upper Doce and Paraíba rivers against them and the neighbouring Puri. Wied-Neuwied reported that 'a sufficient number of soldiers has now been brought down from Minas Gerais. They are well armed and provided with a defensive cuirasse called *gibão d'armas*. Everybody has some of these cuirasses, which are an indispensable protection against arrows, which the savages fire with great force. They are broad, made of cotton cloth and heavily padded with several layers of cotton kapok. They have a high, hard collar to protect the neck and short sleeves that protect the upper arms. They descend to the knees, and are uncomfortable because of their weight, especially during the hot season. . . . The most powerful arrow does not easily penetrate this coat of mail, even when fired at close range.' The settlers placed great faith in such protection. Even the most experienced woodsmen were frightened of the Indians. 'They all confess that the Botocudo are far more skilful hunters and more experienced in the forest than they. Hence they have to be very cautious on their expeditions into the jungles.'

The German artist Moritz Rugendas visited some of these military outposts and was unimpressed by what he saw. They were simple stockades manned by a few soldiers under a junior officer. 'Such outposts are generally nothing more than miserable huts. The soldiers' guns are in appalling condition and their main defence is a padded protective jerkin. . . . Some civilised Indians sometimes form part of the garrison; and they do not lack good dogs.'

From time to time the garrison would venture out on a punitive campaign. Men would assemble from the various posts and frontier farms. 'They hunt the Indians, attacking them wherever they find them. They seek if possible to surprise them in their villages. When discovered, they are surrounded during the night and at daybreak the still-sleeping Indians are fired upon from all sides. Surprised in this way, the savages attempt to flee. The soldiers generally massacre all who fall into their hands. Only very rarely do they spare women and children, even when all resistance has ceased – although resistance is often stubborn. The Indians are sometimes warned of the approach of the soldiers by their dogs and pigs, and then all of them – women, children and the men themselves – flee.'

The Indians were equally capable of mounting ambushes. When they attacked in the forests, guns were of little use: only those wearing padded armour escaped Indian arrows. When Indian wars flared up, outlying farms were abandoned and both soldiers and settlers retreated into the larger towns. Rugendas concluded that 'no army, however numerous, could remain in the forests for more than a few days. The use of artillery or cavalry is absolutely impossible. Even firearms give the soldiers little advantage, for in the forests it is rare to have sufficient distance to take aim without an arrow hitting the man who is shooting. Also, humidity makes the guns misfire, leaving the Indians with the use of their bows.'

The constant, common belief among most officials and observers was that the Indians must be won over from their nomadic freedom. They must be settled in fixed communities and be persuaded to farm rather than hunt. Only if they were civilised in this way would they 'be transformed into a source of public prosperity'.

The southern Paraíba river rises close to São Paulo and runs north-eastwards, parallel to the coast and inland of Rio de Janeiro. Although most Puri were on the lower reaches of the Paraíba, north of the Brazilian capital, some were farther upriver, in the hills midway between São Paulo and Rio. There were campaigns against these Puri, who lived in forests between the upper Paraíba and the Mantiqueira hills. A provincial governor in 1771 issued powder and shot for an expedition to crush these Indians, although other documents spoke of them as timid and unwarlike. At the end of the century, the settlers of a village called Lorena mounted further attacks into nearby forests that were 'full of wild heathen'. One such expedition captured seven Puri, and a second captured ten, including an old man called Vuti. This tribal elder promised to bring out the rest of his people on condition that they were well treated. He did this, bringing eighty-six men, women and children down to the Paraíba where they 'laid down their arms and surrendered peacefully'. The Governor of São Paulo was delighted. He allocated to the new arrivals a stretch of the left bank of the Paraíba and land extending inland to the Mantiqueira hills. This became the Puris' village of São João de Queluz.

In 1800 the Governor chose a worthy priest called Father Francisco das Chagas Lima to be the resident vicar of Queluz since he was 'one of the very few' to possess the necessary education, gentleness and other virtues. But any good that this missionary might do was nullified by the appointment of an unscrupulous old Indian-fighter called Januário Nunes da Silva as the village's Director. Father Lima wrote a journal of the early days of this mission. He described the Puris' ethnography and their peaceful manner. Although they regarded all whites as their enemies, they had not molested or robbed those who penetrated their forests in search of the medicinal root poaia. The Father also reported that the old Indian Vuti, who had persuaded the others to surrender, wisely refused to do so himself. 'After bringing down the others, he withdrew and could not be caught. After a long time he returned to the aldeia, but stayed in it for only fifteen or twenty days. He fled again, taking with him another old man, with whom he is presumed to be wandering in the forests.'

Soon after settlement at São João de Queluz, the Puri were struck by disease. 'When they saw some of their people die of a plague which attacked them in this place, they fled off to the forests on various occasions', but their ferocious Director 'forced them to return'. A church inspector who visited Queluz in 1803 wrote a glowing report of Father Lima's 'untiring zeal, excessive devotion and ardent charity'. Father Lima was gone within a few months, sent south by the government to work with another newly contacted tribe. Greedy settlers coveted the land that had been granted to the Indians. Their unscrupulous Director Nunes da Silva persuaded the Puri to leave Queluz, destroyed their huts, and proceeded to sell off their land. All this was countermanded by the Provincial Governor, who ordered that unless the huts were all rebuilt and the Indians returned to them, the Director would be brought to São Paulo under arrest. They did return for a time, but the decline of the aldeia was inexorable.

When Spix and Martius passed by Queluz in 1817, they commented on 'an insignificant aldeia of Indians from numerous tribes. . . . These Indians are now either extinct or mixed with negroes and mulattoes, and live in a state of half-civilisation among the colonists.' The Indians were apathetic and demoralised: they shunned contact with the settlers as much as possible, and fled from the ministrations of a priest, who complained to the German travellers that the government had been too lenient to the Indians. Four years later, there were only thirty-three Indians left in Queluz: far too few to farm its huge territory. The settlers petitioned for the lands, and the Indian reserve was quickly divided into plots and extinguished. The last word came in 1831. A local officer reported that only six Indians remained alive out of 'many more who were removed from the forests many years ago'.

The story of the rise and fall of the Indian village of Queluz was typical of similar minor tragedies taking place throughout Brazil at this time. The abolition of the Directorate system in 1798 meant that Indians who had accepted Portuguese rule lost tyrannical masters. But they also lost their land.

There was similar demoralisation in Indian aldeias near São Paulo. This city was one of the oldest in Brazil, originating in a settlement that grew alongside a Jesuit mission in the 1550s. Some of the Indians living in the aldeias that survived into the eighteenth century were thus the remnants of tribes which had been in contact with the conquerors for over two centuries. São Paulo was the home of the toughest frontiersmen and Indian-fighters – hardly a place where one would expect to find good treatment of Indians. Jesuit control of the missions near São Paulo had been interrupted for a long period during the seventeenth century, after the Fathers had been evicted by the settlers. Since then, Jesuit rule had been weak and the remaining aldeias were in a state of decadence and abandon.

Most Indians of the plateau around the city of São Paulo were either long-since extinct, or were working as slaves or vassals of the great fazendeiros or farming barons. In 1767 a Governor of São Paulo held a meeting of the various Indian directors, whose financial frauds in the aldeias of acculturated Indians he was concerned to stop. There were nomadic and unacculturated Indians in the forests of the coastal hills south of São Paulo, and the Governor wanted to settle these in a village so that their labour could be of use to the state. He sent public funds to buy tools, seed, powder and shot for this operation, and urged his local administrators 'not to vex them. . . . Everything that vexes them will be severely punished at my pleasure, if someone denounces it to me.'

By the end of the century the inevitable collapse had occurred. In 1798 an army colonel called José Arouche de Toledo Rendon wrote a powerful report on the appalling condition of the remaining São Paulo aldeias. Although well intentioned, Rendon's solution was one with dire consequences for the Indians: he proposed to 'end the isolation from the whites in which they have lived for over two centuries'. He argued that under the Jesuits Indians on isolated missions had 'had an imaginary liberty. They were separated from contact with whites and were intermarried with male and female black slaves.' The aldeia of Guarulhos had become a parish full of settlers and Rendon hoped to turn the former Jesuit fazenda of São José into a similar parish. It would be removed from the control of a rapacious Director, a man 'who governed by the law of his own free will'. If the aldeia were abolished, the Indians would soon inter-marry, lose all vestige of tribal identity, and merge with the mestizo population. 'The memory of the aldeia would be lost, and it would soon not be known who were the [original] Indians, as happened at Guarulhos. The wretches in São José live in great poverty. They started as slaves of the first settlers; and today they still live in the aldeias more or less in a state of subjection, despite the royal laws prohibiting slavery. They have no notion of morality, work, or the ambition that animates man to progress. All this is not solely the fault of their laziness and smallness of spirit. It is also the fault of the whites, who neither teach nor stimulate them.'

The attempt to replace Jesuit missionaries was a failure here as elsewhere. Under Directorate law, a director received one-sixth of the output of his Indians. But in 1790 one governor, Luis Antonio de

Sousa Mourão, who wanted to attract priests to work in Indian villages, ordered that *all* Indian produce go to the director, who was then to give the Indians one-third of the profit, take his own sixth, and keep the remaining half 'in a chest for the church and priest'. By the end of the century, three of the São Paulo aldeias were run by Franciscan Capuchins. At one of them, Escadas, the Indians were obliged to work for three days a week for the Superior: 'these wretches were thus in worse condition than slaves, for the latter were at least supposed to be fed and clothed by their masters.' The Capuchins imposed harsh discipline, with punishments in the stocks for ecclesiastical misdemeanours. At São João de Peroíbe the Capuchins demanded from each Indian 480 reis and a pound of rough thread every month 'which is a very heavy burden and the principal cause of the [aldeia's] depopulation'.

The Provincial Governor was impressed by Rendon's arguments. He wanted the remaining Indians to merge with the rest of the population and lose their separate identity. He also wanted the lands of the Indian aldeias to be dispersed among the settlers. Therefore, in July 1803, he recommended to the Prince Regent that the directors of all but one aldeia be sacked, and that the words 'aldeia' and 'Indian' be suppressed. His advice was followed. The only aldeia which continued to function was São João de Queluz, because its Puri Indians were newly contacted. But, as we have seen, its days were also numbered.

The Jesuits had run a large mission called Reritiba on the coast north of Rio. In the days of the Jesuits that aldeia had twelve thousand Indians; after the Jesuits' expulsion, the place was renamed Benevento and entrusted to a curate, but its population fell to nine thousand; by 1820 Pizarro e Araújo reported that it had only 2500 people, many of whom were non-Indian. The rest had all dispersed or died. The coast farther north was equally deserted for fear of Botocudo attack. The French traveller Auguste de Saint-Hilaire told the story of Benevento's decline, which was typical of so many former missions along the coast of Brazil. The Tupinikin of Benevento were given inalienable title to a vast square of land measuring six leagues by six leagues (130,000 hectares) when the Jesuits were expelled. 'But since the land was fertile, governors soon gave portions of it to their friends without troubling themselves about the rights of the Indians, who sought in vain to make their complaints heard.' Some Indians sold their land for cachaça rum; others left, and their land was invaded by settlers. By the time of Saint-Hilaire's visit in 1817, virtually all the land was gone and the few remaining Indians worked for hire for the new owners. They were also being forced to work in three-month shifts of 'illegal corvée' building a new road for the provincial government. Many had run off to avoid this conscription, and more settlers were moving in. Saint-Hilaire explained how helpless the Indians were: 'When an Indian demands justice against a Portuguese, how can he obtain it? He has to address his complaint to the friends and compatriots of his adversary, since the ordinary magistrates of Benevento are all Portuguese.' There was no hope of appeal to higher judges, since these were remote and 'often deaf to any who presents himself empty-handed'. Benevento is now a town called Anchieta in memory of an early Jesuit missionary; but it has no Indians.

There was similar oppression and decline farther north at the once-thriving Jesuit mission of Reis Magos, renamed Almeida or Vila Nova. Because its land was infertile and infested with ants and because it was exposed to Botocudo attack, there was little danger of invasion by settlers. But the place was falling into ruin by 1817, with its buildings in disrepair. Its Indian population was down to 1200. Every month the provincial government removed Indians to work on the road being pushed inland towards Minas Gerais and on public buildings in the provincial capital Vitória. These victims were taken off in shackles and were badly fed and ill paid. Saint-Hilaire found acculturated Indians to be intelligent, industrious and quick to learn. They were excellent fishermen and hard-working wood-cutters. But in common with most observers, he was dismayed by their apparent improvidence. 'Whatever they earn, they spend the same instant. They drink, make love, and when they have nothing left they suffer hunger without any complaint. They are as patient and gentle as they are carefree.'

Southern Brazil

The most intense field of rivalry between the Spanish and Portuguese empires was in southern Brazil, between what are now the republic of Uruguay and the southernmost Brazilian state of Rio Grande do Sul, and between Paraguay and the adjacent Brazilian states. It had always been a Portuguese dream that their Brazilian colony might stretch from the Amazon to the Plate. To establish the southern boundary, they had for years clung to a fortified town called Colônia do Sacramento, on the north shore of the Plate estuary roughly opposite Buenos Aires.

Portuguese southward expansion was threatened by Spanish Jesuits, who had created a successful theocracy in their missions among the Guarani Indians of Paraguay. This tribe was by nature highly spiritual. It also practised agriculture on a large scale and lived in populous and well-ordered villages. For all these reasons, the Guarani – almost alone of South American Indians – responded to the religion and discipline offered by the Jesuits. With the Jesuit missions or reductions flourishing in Paraguay, the Fathers spread eastwards to the Guarani-speaking tribes of Rio Grande do Sul and towards the Atlantic Ocean. Throughout the seventeenth century this eastward drive had been checked by Portuguese Paulistas, the people of São Paulo. Paulista bandeirantes opposed the Paraguayan Jesuits and colonists partly from nationalistic opposition to Spain. But their true motive was baser: the easy capture of slaves from among Christian converts in the mission villages. As a result of the savage depredations of the bandeirantes, a vast expanse of territory south and west of São Paulo was virtually denuded of Indians.

The Treaty of Madrid of 1750, which made the Uruguay river the boundary between the lands of the two Iberian kingdoms, meant that

seven prosperous Spanish Jesuit missions of Guarani were stranded
to the east of the new frontier. Their lands, villages and churches
were transferred to Portuguese jurisdiction. These devout Indians
had always been told by their priests that the Portuguese Paulistas
were devils incarnate, enemies who threatened to destroy their
missions and take them off into slavery. The peoples of the seven
missions therefore refused to accept the change of sovereignty or to
leave their homelands for exile in Spanish territory west of the
Uruguay. All attempts to bully or cajole these Indians failed. In the
end, they had to be subdued by a joint Spanish–Portuguese army. In
February 1756 this army attacked a force of Christian Guarani, who
marched into battle at Caibaté with their holy images and banners
aloft, trusting in the faith that the Jesuits had taught them. They
were slaughtered, by grapeshot, gunfire and cavalry sabres. Fourteen
hundred pacific Guarani were killed. Voltaire ridiculed the horrible
spectacle of the two Catholic monarchies destroying the only tribe
of lowland South America that had wholeheartedly accepted the
Christian faith – the religion whose propagation had been the
original excuse for European colonial invasion. By June 1756, all
seven missions had surrendered.

Only three years later came the expulsion of the Jesuits from
Portugal and all its dominions. Then in 1767 the once-powerful
Jesuit Company was also proscribed and banished from the Spanish
empire. The departure of the black-robed Fathers exposed their rich
missions to pillage by any adventurers, and the plight of the mission
Indians of Paraguay and southern Brazil was worsened by a series of
wars between the two European powers for control of this fertile
cattle country.

With rival armies on the march, the Indians suffered terribly. In
the lawless and impoverished world of the colonial frontiers, the
Guarani missions were rumoured to be fantastically rich and ripe for
plunder. Indians were evicted from their lands, pressed into service
in the armies' baggage trains or forced to labour on ranches that
usurped former Jesuit mission lands.With the collapse of government in the war zone, many Indians died of starvation. The missions'
plantations ceased to function. Any Indians who managed to grow
food had it commandeered by passing armies.

The plains and pampas of southern Brazil, Uruguay, northern
Argentina and eastern Paraguay were perfect cattle country. Cattle
introduced in the seventeenth century had multiplied into immense
herds of tens of thousands of head. In the wars between Spanish and
Portuguese 'the conquerors were convinced that so much cattle

could never come to an end. They started to destroy it like tigers or starving wolves on corrals of sheep. The entire war was against veal.' Soldiers would kill a cow just to eat its tongue; or kill one animal for lunch and another for dinner, rather than carry meat with them.

When the Jesuits were still in power, they managed thirty missions with a population of over a hundred thousand people. Included in this total were the seven missions, Sete Povos or the 'seven peoples' east of the Uruguay river, in the territory that had passed into Portuguese control. At the time of the transfer in 1756 those seven reductions had some twenty-two thousand people, or a fifth of the total. By the turn of the century the populations had been halved. A Portuguese military commander of the Sete Povos described the abandon of his province: 'It reached the disgraceful condition of having many of its inhabitants die of hunger. Those same people who had previously had ranches full of cattle and storehouses full of food, passed to the misery of eating leather harnesses. The sudden desolation of these people is terribly evident.'

The seven missions soon fell into ruin. Each had had a great baroque church capable of holding congregations of up to five thousand. Alongside were the priests' houses, refectory, school and other administrative buildings. The Indians lived in tidy rows of small thatched huts surrounding a large rectangular parade-ground plaza. Each hut had a veranda and a single room in which the family cooked, ate and slept in hammocks. The Jesuits had totally destroyed the native Indian culture and replaced it with daily regimentation and strict social control. After their expulsion, the Indians continued to work hard – but they were forced to work for alien masters, unable to enjoy their own produce.

A witness of 1802 described them as 'generally depressed and dirty, because of their [cramped living conditions] and the poverty to which they are reduced. They are scarcely civilised and all go barefoot, with little stimulus to virtue or sentiment against vice. They are allowed no property, neither hereditary nor temporary. The men are used for any task or purpose, without regard to the damage to their own farming or resulting shortages for their families.' Women were given no days for rest. They were occupied in agriculture, and every week were given three bundles of cotton which they had to spin into thread. 'Any lack in these is punished with a beating.'

The Sete Povos reverted to Spain in the Treaty of San Ildefonso of 1777. But this did not mean a return to missionary security. The great theocratic Jesuit empire of Paraguay had passed into secular control when Spain expelled the Jesuits a decade earlier. Thus the

Guarani of the seven missions did not prosper during the quarter century of Spanish rule after 1777.

In 1801 they changed sides yet again. Napoleon Bonaparte incited a brief war between Spain and Portugal, in an attempt to win Portugal away from its alliance to Great Britain. During this war a small force of Portuguese troops surprisingly recaptured the shattered seven missions. They were helped by the Indians, who hoped that they could improve their fortunes and 'free themselves from the slavery in which they lived'. Instead, their lot worsened. 'The missions were conquered by undisciplined men whose first objective was to plunder.'

When Portuguese troops regained possession, they promised to respect Indian property. 'But', according to a later Portuguese military governor, 'nothing escaped the greed and ambition of those conquerors. . . . Many [Guarani] deserted. Many more died, of hunger or from lack of treatment of their diseases – owing to lack of compassion by their administrators and the contempt felt for that class of people. All [colonists] wanted to make their fortunes at the expense of the Guarani people.' Indian lands were sold cheaply to a horde of carpet-baggers. 'Ruined traders, banished men of evil reputation, inundated this province. . . . Egotism, ambition and lack of humanity were evident in almost all who were entrusted with the well-being of those people.'

When the Portuguese first acquired the mission of San Nicolás, in 1756, it had fourteen thousand cattle, a thousand tame oxen and seven hundred horses. By the end of the century it had lost all this livestock as well as all its communal lands. One Portuguese administrator tried to revive the collective method of working Indian lands. He wisely saw that this system was essential to the Guarani. 'During the five months of my command I sought to examine ways of bringing these wretches out of the misery in which they lived. . . . I had the satisfaction of seeing the natives begin to raise their heads, although in so short a time there was no chance for my ideas to develop.'

During the years after 1801 there was frequent raiding and plundering of that wretched frontier region. After winning independence from Spain, Paraguay broke away from the United Provinces of the River Plate. There was a succession of revolutions, with each pretender to power relying on the help of the mission Indians. One such caudillo, José Artigas, sent his adopted son Andresito at the head of a Guarani Indian army in a raid on the Portuguese missions beyond the Uruguay river. Andresito besieged the mission of São Borja in 1816, but was driven back after defeat by the Portuguese commanders Abreu and Chagas. In 1817 the Portuguese crossed the Uruguay into what is now Argentine Missiones. They sacked and plundered, robbing church ornaments, killing over three thousand people and removing others as prisoners, together with thousands of head of cattle and horses. Andresito was back in 1818 with an army of seven hundred Guarani bent on revenge. Bitter fighting led to many deaths and the total destruction and burning of the missions of São Carlos, Apostolos and São Xavier. No stone was left standing of the great Jesuit churches – symbols of the only example of successful conversion to Christianity of American Indians in eastern South America. In the following year, Andresito crossed the Uruguay again with two thousand men. After initial victories, he was defeated, captured and taken to imprisonment and death in Rio de Janeiro. But the real victims of this anarchy were the Guarani Indians and their once prosperous plantations.

The French artist Jean-Baptiste Debret visited the region and described how by 1820 some Indians had come to terms with colonial rule. The erva maté aromatic tea industry was flourishing – although the Indians did most of the work without reaping much profit. The Guarani of one village near Rio Pardo were famous for making black soap; those of another made a wine similar to dry madeira which was exported to North America. The only legacy of Jesuit rule was a love of music. The Indians made their own violins, rebecks, cellos and flutes, and were employed by churches to play and sing psalms which they had learned from the missionaries. At Christmas, families of nomadic Guarani came into the town of Rio Pardo, 'where their children dance in grotesque fantasy costumes to music played by old people, and beg for alms'.

A more dismal picture was painted by other French travellers. Auguste de Saint-Hilaire in 1821 noted that 'the Guarani were abandoned to men who saw in them only instruments of a quick fortune. The country soon grew poor, and finished by falling into total decadence. The Portuguese treated the Guarani even more badly than the Spaniards had done.' Saint-Hilaire reckoned that the Sete Povos missions had had a population of 30,000 when the Jesuits left, that by 1801 they had only 14,000 and that by 1814 they were down to 6400; and he observed a census in 1821 that revealed a total Indian population of only 3000 – a decline of 90 per cent in sixty-five years!

Another Frenchman, Alcide Desalines d'Orbigny, who travelled across the region in 1827, noted that after Argentina became independent in 1810 the Brazilians 'had again ravaged these rich provinces of the Jesuits, had set fire everywhere and entirely destroyed this province where, since then, a pile of ruins replaced those fine buildings . . . wounds that were still fresh, still bleeding.' Not that Argentine independence helped. At the time of d'Orbigny's visit, the Paraguayan mission Indians were at war with the people of Corrientes to the south, who had been raiding their cattle. Any Indian captured in that war with the Argentines was immediately killed.

Mid-way between São Paulo and the Paraguayan capital Asunción are the forested hills of Guarapuava, at the headwaters of the Iguaçu river. In the early days of the Paraguayan missions, Spanish Jesuits had established missions here and on other rivers flowing westwards into the Paraná. The Jesuits knew this area as Guairá. It received the first brunt of Paulista slave raids, and in 1631 the Jesuits abandoned it, taking their Indian congregations down the Paraná in a great fleet of canoes. The tribes that remained were harassed by bandeirante raids, until by the end of the seventeenth century such slaving diminished. For some decades, the Indians of Guarapuava were left unmolested in their forests and pine woods in the western highlands of what is now the state of Paraná. Most of them were Gê-speaking Indians, distant relatives of the Kayapó who were being settled near Goiás far to the north across the central Brazilian plateau.

In 1767, almost a century and a half after the exodus by the Spanish missionaries and their congregations, the Captain-General of São Paulo, Luiz de Sousa, sent three expeditions into Guairá (which the Portuguese called Guaíra). This was a military enterprise, part of the consolidation of frontiers after the Treaty of Madrid of 1750 and before the adjustments of the Treaty of San Ildefonso of 1777. One team explored for a year but found only forests; another was captured by the Spaniards; but the third discovered the rich plains of Guarapuava in 1770, before withdrawing after seven soldiers were killed by local Indians. The Governor was angry about this reverse. He wrote to his superior in Portugal that the defence of southern Brazil depended on the occupation and fortification of the Tibagi hills between Curitiba (capital of modern Paraná state) and the Guarapuava plains. Luiz de Sousa wrote that 'one of the main obstacles to the discovery of Tibagi was the ferocity of its Indians, who were treacherous, rancorous and violent. They did not subordinate themselves easily to the gentle and peaceful methods ordered by the King.' The Governor asked permission to use force 'to oblige them to emerge from their forests to live in Christian order and urbanity'.

The tribe that had dared to resist Portuguese blandishments
was the Coroado ('Crowned' Indians), who knew themselves as
Kaingáng and Xokleng, and the survivors of the tribe are called by
these names today. They owe their survival to their bellicosity and
their shrewd suspicion of white men – even when these were bearing
gifts. The Kaingáng fought back even more vigorously after the
bandeirantes stopped molesting them. As Robert Southey wrote,
'Their audacity increased as the Paulistas became more regularly
industrious, more commercial, more opulent, and therefore less
enterprising: and the line of road to Curitiba, which used to be safe,
was depopulated by their murderous incursions, and became so
perilous that travellers did not venture upon the journey, unless they
were collected in large bodies. Even from São Paulo to Minas Gerais,
it was usual to travel in troops of twenty to thirty laden mules, with
five or six men, well armed with swords, guns, and pistols, and two or
three very large and fierce dogs.'

The salvation and protection of the Kaingáng lay in the forests
they inhabited. They had once lived on open plains of savannah
but were forced into the forests by their enemies – other tribes and
slave-raiding whites. Jules Henry, who made a brilliant anthropological study of the Kaingáng in the 1930s, described their forests
as 'vast and mighty; they are rich and well watered, tall and gloomy.
Saplings and trees six feet in diameter crowd close upon one another.
Bushes cluster about the trees, and the whole is woven into one solid
mass by the vines that hang from trees, twine about bushes, and
creep along the ground. The forest everywhere grows right down to
the edges of the rivers and looms on both sides like the walls of a
great corridor, silent and lovely, impenetrable except with knife or
club.' In winter these woods were cold and wet, and the naked
Kaingáng huddled miserably around their fires.

Another protection for the Kaingáng was their indifference to
European trade goods. They had successfully resisted the attractions of the Jesuits' great plantations and regimented mission reductions. Now, as Ayres do Casal complained, 'It seems that, of all that
the Paulistas possess, these barbarians value nothing except iron.
Their ferocity has impeded those Paulistas from extending towards
the west.'

The Kaingáng were brutally repressed for daring to resist. On 5
November 1808 the Prince Regent Dom João issued a declaration of
war against the Indians of São Paulo, which then embraced Paraná.
The edict was similar to the repressive legislation against the
Botocudo earlier that year, and declared that 'there is no means of

civilising barbaric peoples except to bind them in a harsh schooling. . . . I am moved by these and other just motives to suspend
immediately any humane measures that have been ordered regard-
ing them [in the past] . . . and to launch a war against these barbarian
Indians.'

But they were not merely subjected to war. Enslavement of captured Indians was reintroduced, half a century after it had been
outlawed by Pombal. The government was not prepared to pay for
the campaign against the Kaingáng: as in the past, it was to be
financed by the sale of captured Indians. 'Any militiaman or settler
who catches any of these Indians may consider him as a prisoner of
war [or slave] for fifteen years.' This fierce law permitted slavery only
of Indians caught bearing arms, even though all Indians used bows
and arrows daily for hunting. Needless to say, raiders used this as a
pretext to enter the forests in search of Indians. According to the
missionary Father Francisco das Chagas Lima (who had previously
been with the Puri of Queluz), they fought a 'brutal war' against the
forest tribes, 'imprisoning many'.

A royal order of April 1809 made a last attempt to pacify the
Kaingáng of Guarapuava. Woodsmen started cutting a trail through
the forests in August of that year, and by June 1810 it was ready for
an expedition. This consisted of two hundred armed men and two
missionary priests, one of whom was the well-meaning Father Lima.
The expedition reached Guarapuava and was delighted by the sight
of its rich plain. It made contact with a group of Kaingáng, offering
the usual presents. 'Despite their simplicity, when the Indians saw
themselves well treated and regaled with pieces of cotton cloth, some
tools and hardware, they immediately showed themselves to be
docile; but it was difficult to deal with them, since we had no knowledge of their language.'

A number of Indians, of the Votoröes and Camé sub-groups,
surrendered to the expedition in 1812 and agreed to settle in aldeia
villages. Father Lima noted the same problems that had frustrated
every would-be proselytiser of Brazilians ever since the first missionaries arrived in the sixteenth century: the onslaught of imported
diseases, and the Indians' reluctance to abandon their beliefs and
accept permanent conversion to Christianity. The Kaingáng's initial
enthusiasm for Christianity soon evaporated. 'They always lacked
persistence. After the first five months of domicile a large part of
them entered the forests and fled. Despite this, they would return
almost every year to spend some months in the aldeia. They had me
teach them Christian doctrine and asked that their children be

baptised . . . but after that they would secretly escape. . . . I considered them semi-barbaric and difficult to instruct.' Finally in 1823
all the Votorões sub-tribe departed simultaneously for distant
forests where they could not be contacted. They reappeared four
years later. Father Lima was dismayed to find that the men had
changed wives or married additional wives and had abandoned the
'morality' he had tried to inflict on them. 'They had pursued an
erring course, even though they knew full well the instructions they
had received from their missionary who had exhorted them so much.
Their occupations were dancing and fishing.' There was fighting
between the Kaingáng settled in aldeias and the wild Dorins
Kaingáng who wanted their tools. A number were killed in these
vendettas, for which the missionary largely blamed his settled
Indians.

Father Lima tried to contact the Xokleng living between the upper
Iguaçu and Uruguay rivers, but he complained that, like the related
Kaingáng, they were 'generally debauched, occupying themselves in
fishing, hunting and dancing. It is difficult to uproot their ancient
vices and the debauches in which they are engulfed. They are cruel,
vindictive, avid to shed human blood, have no chiefs, and show no
signs of religion.' He objected to the tribe's custom of killing decrepit
old people 'on the pretext of compassion' or deformed infants in
order to ensure the survival of the small tribe in its hostile surroundings.

The missionary described his frustration, in a passage which
reveals his own doctrinaire inflexibility. He was evidently arrogant
and stubborn, in a manner sadly typical of successive missionaries to
this day. 'I sought to banish all the errors of their beliefs and barbarities. [I wanted] to make catechumens of them and exhorted them
after they were baptised, seeking to suppress their physical
needs. . . . But the village Indians were like some wet substance that
is difficult to ignite and then burns very slowly. They were distracted
by warlike actions and the resulting calamities. They were preoccupied with indulging their ancient barbarous vices. They responded little to the labour and diligence of their spiritual director
and their faith was generally very weak. They were never prepared to
abstain from obscene dances, which they frequented to excess amid
intoxicating drink. These entertainments always ended in brutish
licentiousness. When I reproved them, they would go off to huts in
the forests, both men and women, and would spend days and weeks
in these obscenities!'

Such was the missionary's fury that he almost rejoiced in the deaths of Indians who shunned his teaching. He was helped by one Indian zealot called Pahy, 'a person of moral virtues, eager in conversion: he moved the others to their duty . . . and admonished them with his exhortations.' Despite this, some Kaingáng continued to practise polygamy and 'would not yield to the laws of the Church. These abandoned themselves in the forests, where they perished miserably at the hands of their enemies.' When some Votorões Kaingáng returned to the mission village in 1827, Father Lima was helped in a terrible way. 'An event occurred which, although calamitous, did at least profit their instruction. There was an epidemic that lasted nine months. During that time I, the missionary, was the nurse who was most assiduous in seeking their health and spiritual welfare. I treated and instructed both the sick and healthy at that time. Experience shows that the most edifying and useful lessons for this type of people are exhortations made to the dying, when the sick are being disposed for baptism and final sacraments.'

After the epidemic had abated, the missionary tried to bribe the Indians to continue religious instruction. He offered 'rosaries, veronicas, prints of saints, beads, ribbons, mirrors and other trifles; and if these failed, sugar and brown sugar'. Over four thousand responded. But within a few years most of the converts were gone. 'Plague, fighting, and other diseases and desertions have consumed many people.'

The missionary effort was also hampered by the royal edict of 1808 which permitted enslavement of Coroados (Kaingáng) found carrying weapons. 'Many were deluded and deprived of their liberty, despite their voluntary surrender, and despite the laws that declared that they should not be forced to move from their homelands.' As a result of all this, 'the fruits of the mission of catechism were less abundant than should have been expected.' The missionary admitted that he had failed to change the Indians' beliefs. 'They rejected the entire notion of the Creator as preserver of the universe and He who rewards the good and punishes the evil in the after life. They believed in the free satisfaction of their passions. They were convinced that their souls went to heaven without any difference from merit or blame: this can be noted in their burial ceremonial. . . . In this way they acquired a great facility for killing and, in short, for allowing themselves all the debauches of this life.' It was their 'facility for killing' that saved the Kaingáng. Their bellicosity and rejection of missionary teaching ensured their survival throughout the ensuing century in the forests of western São Paulo, Paraná and Santa Catarina.

The authorities made another attempt to invade the Guarapuava plains. A town was formed in 1819 beside the stockade of Atalaia. In the instructions for its foundation, the Indians were to be settled in the nearby aldeia of Malaia. There was an attempt to prevent soldiers from entering this aldeia or Indian women from wandering into the settlement except to work or learn a craft. 'This separation is essential, because the mixing that has occurred up to now has been one of the greatest obstacles to the perfect conversion of these people.'

A decade later, the provincial council of São Paulo launched another armed attack on the Kaingáng of Guarapuava. The instructions for this campaign admitted that Indians could be successfully settled only if a good man were 'chosen to rule, lead and help the Indians. Abuses by such administrators or directors have caused many aldeias, created at great expense, to disappear.' The same instruction condemned aggressive missionary efforts. 'It is an intolerable folly to try to claim that the Indians should immediately become pious observers of divine precepts. This has produced great harm rather than benefits.'

To the west of São Paulo, the ground slopes gently towards the gigantic basin of the Paraná and Paraguay rivers. This is the central Brazilian plateau, an ancient geological formation covered for thousands of kilometres in low forests. The mighty Paraná and Paraguay rivers run southwards parallel to one another, until they join to flow into the Plate estuary. The flat land between them was known as Mato Grosso (Dense Forest) because it was covered in trees to the horizon in every direction. Westwards, towards the Paraguay, the forest often opens into campo. The Paraguay river rises during each annual rainy season to flood one of the world's largest swamps, the Pantanal. For thousands of square kilometres the Pantanal is covered in clumps of floating vegetation and occasional islands with stands of trees. As the waters recede, there are lakes and marshes full of piranha, alligators, frogs and water snakes. At the height of the dry season, in September, expanses of sandy riverbed are exposed, but the higher ground is covered in matted vegetation, the home of jaguars, tapirs, peccary and many rodents. The entire swamp and the barren Chaco beyond the Paraguay are a paradise for aquatic birds, notably brilliant white egrets and pink ibis.

The Chaco (which is now largely in Paraguay), the plains of eastern Bolivia and the low hills and campo alongside the Paraguay river were the home of the Guaikurú, perhaps the most remarkable or eccentric of all Brazilian tribes. The Guaikurú infuriated the Christian invaders in various ways. They were an aristocratic warrior people who regarded white men with as much disdain as they did other tribes. They practised sexual activities, abortion and infanticide which drove the missionaries to despair. They were nomadic and resolutely refused to settle in mission aldeias or reductions. Above all, they adopted the Europeans' horses and became invincible horsemen.

The Guaikurú had their first contact with white men when the Spaniards explored up the Paraguay river in the early sixteenth century. They fought well then; but they were far more formidable in the seventeenth and eighteenth centuries after they had acquired horses. In the Chaco and some of the campo country of Mato Grosso, the Guaikurú had the open spaces necessary to take full advantage of horses. They took to riding with the skill and passion of North American plains Indians or Chilean Araucanians. When the Paulista bandeirantes penetrated this far west in the mid-seventeenth century, they found the Guaikurú 'already masters of great herds of cattle, horses and sheep'. The explorer and army engineer Colonel Ricardo Franco de Almeida Serra reported in the 1790s that 'their most interesting riches, which they prize most and about which all Guaikurú care most, consist of their six or eight thousand horses.' The entire tribe moved across the plains, living in hide tents, in order to find good pasture for their beloved steeds.

The Guaikurú looked after their animals extremely well. 'They know their horses' diseases better than their own. According to their knowledge, they bleed them and remove their tumours or deworm them with such skill that they generally recover. If one has an accident, the Indians visit it frequently, and bring it into shelter to cure it.'

'They use neither saddles nor stirrups on their horses. They ride bareback and mount them in a single leap. Even when they are walking or playing, one can see the suppleness of their bodies. They run after the horses to catch them or tie them with almost as much agility as the beasts themselves. They use no lassoes or lariats to catch them, or corrals to subdue them. . . . If the horses break and scatter . . . they use their agility to bring them back as before, running to regroup them.' During the rainy season, the hard ground of the Chaco is covered by a metre of water. The Guaikurú made use of this. 'They tame horses in water that comes almost up to their bellies, so that the horse cannot throw them and any fall will hurt less. Their war horses are used for no other purpose.' 'The Guaikurú pride themselves on being a mounted nation, on the light and strong horses they always choose for war.'

Men and women rode equally well. Most rode bareback, mounted on the horse's rump or croup. But for long journeys they placed two bundles of grass in the hollow of the horse's back and covered this with a hide, a blanket or a mat of palm leaves. This formed a saddle, a bed at night, or a raft for swimming across rivers. The Guaikurú bred and trained their horses to be very fast, but some observers criticised their riding techniques. Ayres do Casal wrote that 'they all ride, as a result of which they are bow-legged. But they are bad horsemen, for they only know how to gallop. They use no saddle or stirrups . . . and their reins are two cords . . . held in the horse's mouth like a halter.' The Franciscan friar Francisco Mendes complained that they exhausted their mounts 'by chasing deer and ostriches – [a sport] from which they derive all their glory'.

When the Paulista bandeirantes pushed their slave raids westwards to the Paraguay, they had the nasty shock of encountering mounted and bellicose Guaikurú. For once, there were battles in which Indian horsemen charged and trampled white men on foot. The Jesuits of Paraguay had to retreat to their docile Guarani near Asunción, having failed to subdue or convert the Guaikurú. In the eighteenth century, when gold was discovered at Cuiabá at the headwaters of the Paraguay river and deep in Mato Grosso, the only way for the Portuguese to bring it to the Atlantic coast was by a very long and tortuous river route, first down the Paraguay, then by tributaries and portages across to the Paraná, and thence up rapid-infested rivers to São Paulo. There were hostile tribes along most of this route: Bororo near Cuiabá; Paiaguá in canoes on the Paraguay river, allied to the mounted Guaikurú on its banks; Kayapó in the forests between the Paraguay and Paraná; and Kaingáng (Coroados) between there and São Paulo. During the early decades of the century there was fierce fighting between these tribes and the convoys of canoes carrying men and gold. Many Portuguese were killed and entire convoys were annihilated. By mid-eighteenth century, heavily armed counter-attacks had destroyed many Paiaguá and had tamed the Guaikurú.

With their splendid horses and personal bravery, the Guaikurú terrorised other Indian tribes as well as the whites. 'As soon as the Guaikurú saw [their enemy] they would join their horses, covering their flanks with oxhide, and attacked in such a way that [the enemy] broke. They trampled their foes with the violence of their charge and killed with their lances any they caught in their path.' As they charged, each warrior crouched along the flank of his horse, hanging on to the mane, so that the horse protected him from enemy arrows. The French artist Jean-Baptiste Debret did a magnificent painting of Guaikurú charging into battle. The flying manes and galloping hooves of Debret's horses were worthy of his friend Delacroix, and he showed the Indians lying along the flanks of their horses like circus performers.

The Guaikurú had the advantage of possessing no false sense of honour. They preferred to attack by surprise when their enemy was weak or unprepared. 'They pursue [the enemy] in hiding, watching until some carelessness gives them an opportunity to kill as many as they can without risk or pity, and to capture women and children.' But their weakness was to have no overall strategy or plan. They made devastating attacks on isolated farms or outposts, but chiefly to steal cattle and horses. They were too proud to acknowledge single command in battle. When a chief organised a raid, those who felt like going would follow him; but there was no organised chain of command or concerted campaign. Rodrigues do Prado, who commanded a Portuguese fort on the Paraguay river, said that over the years the Guaikurú killed some four thousand Portuguese. Felix de Azara, a Spanish geographer and boundary commissioner, reckoned that had the Guaikurú had proper military discipline 'there would not now [in 1800] remain a single Spaniard in Paraguay or Portuguese in Cuiabá.'

If the colonial powers' military men were thwarted by Guaikurú fighting skill, the missionaries were baffled by the tribe's practice of abortion and infanticide. Guaikurú women tried to abort every child until they were about to enter their menopause. Ricardo Franco de Almeida Serra wrote: 'When they feel themselves pregnant they immediately abort the foetus with violent little injuries which they practise once or twice a year. This operation soon makes them look older than they are. It normally leaves them sterile from the age of thirty onwards, which is when they would like to rear children and want to conceive – something they rarely succeed in doing.' Felix de Azara reproached the Guaikurú men about this, but they merely smiled and said that it was the women's affair. He then harangued the women about it. They were not interested. One finally explained: 'When we give birth at the end of a pregnancy it mutilates, deforms and ages us. You men do not want us in that state. Besides, there is nothing more tedious for us than to raise children and take them on our various journeys, during which we are often short of food. This is why we decide to arrange an abortion as soon as we feel pregnant, for our foetus is smaller then and emerges more easily.' Other observers agreed that this was done out of excessive zeal to please the men. Francisco Mendes said that it was partly to avoid the effort of rearing children in their nomadic existence, but also 'I think that this perverse custom was introduced to leave the women freer to divorce.' The censorious Jesuit José Sánchez Labrador believed that 'the misery in which they wander from place to place, and the licence with which they loose the reins of brutal passion have obliged them to exterminate even their own loved ones.'

Such violent birth control naturally threatened the aristocratic Guaikurú with depopulation. Very few of the highest caste of Guaikurú had children in their tents. Rodrigues do Prado recalled: 'I know twenty-two nobles, each aged about forty and all married, but only one has a daughter. For this reason I expect that this tribe will soon cease.' The Guaikurú's answer to the threat of extinction was to steal children from other tribes. This became one of the chief motives for their raids. When they overran an enemy camp or village they ruthlessly killed adult men, but seized children, women and horses.

The Guaikurú were a handsome race. The naturalist Alexandre Rodrigues Ferreira described them as 'all broad-shouldered and robust, with broad chests, flat stomachs and muscular backs and arms.' The men are 'tall, so that many among them are 6½ feet in height. They are well built, well muscled and with an almost indescribable capacity for enduring hunger, thirst and sustained effort.' The men went naked, apart from a blanket made of jaguar skin or of wool in broad red, white and black stripes. Both sexes painted their bodies in geometric designs, in red and black vegetable dyes. This body painting evolved over the years. Designs came to be tattooed rather than painted, and the geometric designs became increasingly elaborate, developing into a complicated arabesque of curves and spirals over faces, chests and legs. A fashion grew for asymmetrical decoration, with the two halves of the body tattooed with contrasting patterns. All body hair was plucked, including eyebrows and eyelashes. Men wore their hair short, coated in wax and brilliant red urucum dye. Sometimes they fastened birds' wings to their ears. Both sexes wore plenty of ornament: necklaces, rings, bracelets and girdles made of silver or beads.

Handsome young Guaikurú men did no work apart from tending their horses. 'Among those Indians . . . only the aged work. The young men say that their age is suited only to amusing themselves.

They in fact spend most of the day in the arms of their wives. They are so inseparable that they do nothing – even corporal necessities, walking about or other actions – unless wife and husband do it together.' All observers noted how tenderly Guaikurú men loved their wives. But they branded their women on a breast or leg with the same mark they branded on to their horses; and Rodrigues Ferreira said that they mounted them from behind like animals.

Guaikurú women struck the Franciscan Mendes as 'generally pale-skinned and very good-looking – although they immediately lose their [pale] colour because they go about naked from the waist up, and from the abuse of painting their faces and arms. . . . In speech they are very eloquent and of a happy and joyful nature: amiable, but not very docile.' This brash disposition and their body tattooing did not conform to everyone's ideal of eighteenth-century feminine beauty. To Rodrigues do Prado, 'The women have none of the innocent grace of Milton's Eve. Their broad faces and the harsh tints with which they paint themselves make them disagreeable to our eyes. They have their foreheads pricked with thorns, to form [tattoo] lines that start at the roots of their hair and end at their eyelids, cheeks and chins, where they form a grid like a chess board. They then stain it with genipapo dye and remain throughout their lives painted with greyish colour. The ladies also paint squares on their arms. They suffer cruel pain in all these operations.'

Unlike their men, Guaikurú women were rarely idle. They wove the fine rugs used by both sexes and the smaller cloths that the women used as breeches to cover themselves from waists to knees. It was the women who set up the tents, cutting and carrying the supports and weaving the sleeping mats. Older men and women did the more servile domestic tasks such as fetching water and firewood, gathering nuts or palm-hearts, and tending small allotments. A French observer, Amedée Moure, wrote that both sexes had a 'holy horror' of manual work in farming the earth. What the men really enjoyed was 'eating and sleeping, sleeping and eating'. The old people did the cooking, but it was not brilliant. Dr Moure blamed it for the Guaikurú's sleepy disposition: 'Their digestion is necessarily painful, since they generally eat a gluey stew as thick as mastic, of animal tripes and offal. One can easily understand why, when they are ill, they resort to a total diet to recover.'

The sexual behaviour of the noble caste of Guaikurú was equally surprising to the Europeans. On the one hand, couples were faithful and the women 'are very careful to preserve their chastity and honour until someone of equal rank solicits them as wives. Otherwise they do not lose these – except in very illicit ways during some drinking bout or festival.' Events worth celebrating included the first menstruation of important girls, marriages, the return of victorious war-parties, or the annual rising of the Pleiades in August. Everyone drank a form of mead made from wild honey – 'a terrible wine for their continuous carousing and festivities'. For these revels, 'they paint, mask and ornament themselves extraordinarily. The festival ends only when they are all so drunk that they fall. . . . [Such parties] always end with everyone going and seeking a companion, with a man forgetting his wife and she her husband. They follow only their inclinations. None refuses the first request, in the hidden places they seek out for these bacchanalian encounters in the forest or by the river.'

During these great drinking bouts, the Guaikurú imitated the nearby Paiaguá in self-mortification akin to that of fakirs or dervishes. Robert Southey wrote that 'in the state of ferocious drunkenness which the drams produce, one operates upon another by pinching up the flesh of his arms, legs and thighs, as largely as his fingers can command, and running skewers through at inch distances, from the ankle to the fork and from the wrist to the shoulder. This is a public spectacle.' Spanish women used to watch this in Asunción, but ceased looking 'when the savages in like manner pierce their tongues and genitals. The Indian women behold it with composure; and the men who endure these torments betray not the slightest emotion, either by look or gesture. The blood from the tongue is received in the hand, and they rub their bodies with it; but that from the genitals they let fall into a hole in the ground, dug with their fingers.' The resulting wounds could disable men for long periods and leave permanent scars. 'The only reason which they assign to this tremendous custom is that they may show themselves to be brave men.'

Along with their casual, drunken promiscuity, the Guaikurú could easily divorce a partner if the marriage failed. Aristocratic ladies had male admirers. 'Every woman, especially the ladies, has one or two eager boy-friends who constantly go about with her and sleep at her side. Husbands are not jealous of these, saying that they are there to guard and protect her. One of these suitors generally sleeps with her when the husband is doing the same with some other woman.'

Equally vexing to the Europeans was a Guaikurú custom of having male transvestites or female surrogates. These 'act as their women, especially on long journeys. These cudinhos are nefarious demons who dress and adorn themselves like women, speak like them, do women's work, wear jalatas [female knickers] and urinate squatting. They have a "husband" who looks after them and constantly keeps them in his arms, and are very keen to be wooed by the men. Once a month they affect the ridiculous pretence that they are menstruating: they go to the river as the women do each day with a gourd in the pretended hollow of their jalatas.'

Another remarkable characteristic of the Guaikurú was their self-assurance and pride. Francisco Mendes wrote that 'they greatly presume to be noble and valiant; being well built and as tall as they are helps them in this.' This was confirmed by Almeida Serra, who knew the Guaikurú intimately. 'They consider all other tribes as their captives, and do not even judge themselves inferior to the Spanish and Portuguese.'

Their pride and indolence were bolstered by a symbiotic relationship with the Guaná, a large and passive tribe which attached itself voluntarily to the bellicose Guaikurú and worked for them as household slaves and farmers. 'It is in practice a very gentle slavery, for a Guaná submits voluntarily and abandons it whenever he pleases. Furthermore, his masters give very few orders, never use an imperative or demanding tone, and share everything with the Guaná – even carnal pleasures.' The nomadic Guaikurú descended periodically on Guaná (Terena) villages and expected to be given quantities of food: for the Guaná were excellent farmers, and the Guaikurú despised manual labour. In return, the Guaná received military protection. Almeida Serra said that the Guaná 'allow themselves to be called their slaves and voluntarily give them part of their harvests, in order to spare the rest [of their food] and the deaths they regularly used to suffer.' All observers noted how kind the Guaikurú were to their slaves. 'They treat them like their children. They rarely reprimand or mistreat them and . . . are affectionate and affable in their speech although they always speak with emphasis and arrogance.' Rodrigues Ferreira felt that this was because the Guaikurú were devoid of material ambition and did not use their slaves to enrich themselves. They ate with their Guaná slaves and had no odious class distinctions against them.

For their part, the Guaná were 'extremely docile'. They exasperated Francisco Mendes by the ease with which they adopted and then abandoned Christianity. 'They are very sensual, base and thieving, and look equally well upon good and evil.' Guaná women were 'very facile and amorous, with excellent bodies and appearance. They are generally brown, although some are whiter and many are half-breeds. They are crazy about singing. This is why they are so prone to become healers and soothsayers, a ministry in which they have more opportunity to practise singing – if one can use that word for the din they make with a gourd full of shells and pebbles like that of the [Guaikurú] shamans.' At least the Guaná did not imitate the Guaikurú practice of abortion. 'They do not have the diabolical custom of killing their children in the womb. This is the reason why these heathen are so abundant.'

The alliance between the Guaikurú horsemen and the Paiaguá in their fast canoes proved invincible during the early years of the eighteenth century. After initial successes that annihilated Portuguese convoys, the Paiaguá were defeated and many of their finest warriors were killed. In 1768 the remnant of the Paiaguá decided to throw in its lot with the Spanish and went downriver to Asunción.

The Portuguese decided to build a fort on the west bank of the Paraguay to protect Mato Grosso against Spanish attack from Asunción and to assert a Portuguese presence in the Chaco. This Fort Coimbra, a simple palisade like a stockade in the American wild west a century later, was the southernmost Portuguese outpost on the river. It was in a terrible location – in the midst of the Pantanal swamps, isolated by floods for seven months a year and useless for agriculture or ranching. It was started in May 1775 in response to an attack by twenty canoes full of Indians, thought to have been Guaikurú, on an outpost near Vila Maria far up the Paraguay. That raid left sixteen dead colonists; and an attack by Paiaguá shortly afterwards killed a further twenty-eight. The Indians were said to have burned houses and put their victims' heads on lances. The government's response was to create in 1778 another outpost, Albuquerque, a short distance north of Coimbra and also on the west bank of the Paraguay.

The last great Guaikurú aggression against the Portuguese occurred on 1 January 1778. A large band of Guaikurú rode up and camped near the new Fort Coimbra, bringing sheep, turkeys and deer skins to trade with the garrison. The fort's Commander ordered them to remain three hundred yards from his outpost and suggested that the trading be supervised by twelve armed soldiers. But the Guaikurú said that they themselves were unarmed. They asked the soldiers to remove their guns as these frightened the Indian women, and the officers agreed. There were the usual celebrations, with Guaikurú chiefs being entertained in the fort and Indian women offered to the lonely men of the garrison. The Guaikurú chief then ordered a treacherous attack. A few Indian women are said to have protested, but most – 'veritable Delilahs' – held the European soldiers while their men killed them. The commander, Antonio de Medreiros, fought hard with his sword, but was eventually tackled round the legs, thrown to the ground and killed. The Guaikuru rode off with their spoils, leaving forty-five dead Portuguese.

There was talk of a joint Portuguese–Spanish action to punish the Guaikurú. But rivalry between the two Iberian kingdoms was too great and nothing happened. In the end it was the Guaikurú who took the initiative. In 1791 they 'spontaneously sought the friend-ship of the Portuguese'. Ricardo Franco de Almeida Serra thought that this change of heart was inspired by fear of the Spaniards: the Guaikurú had been raiding Spanish farms and feared reprisals from Paraguay into their territory. They therefore sought the protection of Fort Coimbra, which they also welcomed as a source of trade goods.

Alexandre Rodrigues Ferreira gave some credit for the pacifica-tion to a new Commander, Joachim Joseph Ferreira, who reached Fort Coimbra in 1790. He sent a contingent to parley with the Guaikurú, fearing that the Spaniards were courting the tribe. The Portuguese troops were well received. Finally the paramount Guaikurú chief Queimá agreed to visit the stockade. He arrived with three warriors and two Guaná slaves. 'Led into the presence of the commandant, he seemed too frightened to speak. However, his spirit was calmed by fair words and by presents he was given. Raising the chief to his feet and embracing him warmly, [Commandant Ferreira] said to him in a proud voice: "My friend Queimá." '

During the ensuing months there were frequent embassies to the Guaikurú camp. The culmination of the diplomacy was a state visit to Vila Bela de Mato Grosso by the two powerful chiefs Emavidi Channé and Queimá. They arrived with seventeen of their men and a black creole girl captive called Victoria as interpreter. 'They were received with great pomp. The Governor went to meet them with a large concourse of nobility and ordinary people.' Chief Queimá was then dressed in a scarlet uniform, and his beautiful Tapuiá Indian wife and the rest of his party were also given fine European clothing. The two chiefs accepted baptism, taking the Christian names, res-pectively, of the Governor and Commander of Fort Coimbra. On 30 July 1791, before a large assembly of military and notables, the Guaikurú chiefs put their marks on a treaty of peace. They agreed to 'subject themselves and give blind obedience to the laws of Her Majesty'.

The alliance between the Guaikurú and the Portuguese remained reasonably secure, but during the 1790s the Guaikurú continued their annual attacks on Spanish settlers. The Spaniards accused them of destroying a hundred farms and stealing twenty thousand head of horses and cattle, and retaliated with campaigns against the tribe. That of 1796 killed 310 Guaikurú, including Chief Queimá. His fellow chief Emavidi Channé went to meet the next Governor of Mato Grosso at Cuiabá. He said that he and his people were fleeing from persecution by the Spaniards. In the name of the Guaikurú and Guaná, he asked to be settled in the lands they had always occupied between Coimbra and Albuquerque, 'showing repugnance at being located anywhere else'. The Governor finally agreed, and four hundred Guaikurú and six hundred Guaná settled in the disputed territory.

In 1797 it was learned that a thousand Spaniards under Colonel José Espindola were marching to attack the Guaikurú on the Mondego (Miranda) river, an eastern tributary of the Paraguay. Almeida Serra, who had recently arrived from his explorations in Amazonia, was sent to establish a stockade and to try to stop the Spaniards. He built a fort and named it Miranda after the new provincial governor. Although Serra had only eighty troops, he gathered the Kadiwéu Guaikurú and Guaná in the lee of his fort and saved them. The Spanish expedition departed with six thousand recaptured animals but no captives. Three years later, to the disgust of Colonel Serra, many Guaikurú decided to go off to join the Spaniards who had been wooing them. They left without compunction, despite nine years' friendship with the Portuguese. But they were back in 1802, disillusioned by Spanish brutality. They lost many people and hundreds of animals crossing flooded rivers during this exodus. They appeared at Albuquerque 'in the greatest misery, thin and in consternation'. The royal treasury paid to feed them, and the Guaikurú were resettled along the Miranda river.

Throughout these turbulent years, in which the Guaikurú were caught between the colonial ambitions of Spain and Portugal, the tribe managed to preserve its dignity. One Governor of Mato Grosso suggested that they should settle down, build houses, plant crops, raise pigs and marry Portuguese wives. They held a meeting and decided that all this sounded good, but they sent to ask 'How many slaves His Excellency was going to send to make those plantations, for they themselves were not slaves. They said the same about the houses: the wood for them was very hard and hurt their shoulders. They wanted them very much; but the Portuguese should come and build them for them. As for the marriages, they all said that they wanted Portuguese wives. But they found it unacceptable to impose the condition that they might not part from these until death.' When Almeida Serra invited Chief Queimá's daughter Dona Catarina to go to Cuiabá to meet the Governor, she declined because, being single, she feared that the Governor would want to marry her and 'being an important lady and daughter of the great Queimá she could not contemplate this.'

PART 2

Independence

Attitudes to Indians

The Portuguese Court's move to Brazil in 1808 to escape Napoleon's army had important political effects. The arrival of the Prince Regent Dom João and his incapacitated mother Queen Maria I transformed Brazil from a colony into the seat of an ancient monarchy. Brazil's independence was confirmed fourteen years later. In 1822, after King João VI had returned to rule in Portugal, his heir Dom Pedro proclaimed himself Emperor of Brazil. Brazil became an independent empire and severed its links with the mother country Portugal. It was an almost bloodless declaration of independence.

Such political changes had little effect on the Indians. As we have seen, the Prince Regent had abolished the Directorate in 1798, ten years before he moved to Brazil. Yet almost immediately after his arrival in the New World, he was persuaded by colonist hardliners to declare war on the Botocudo and Kaingáng. Slavery of Indians, which had been abolished by Pombal over half a century previously, was reintroduced for captives of these two tribes. By moving from the distant court of Lisbon to Brazil itself, Dom João's attitude had hardened. He was closer to the frontier and therefore more influenced by reactionary settlers and landowners.

Among non-colonists a more romantic view had been propagated, a view which started with admiration for Indian self-sufficiency. As hunters in the luxuriant tropics, Brazilian Indians never doubted that there were plenty of fish, game and wild plants to be found in the forests, plains and rivers around their villages. They knew precisely where and when such food would be available. They also had little means of storing perishable food in their humid and pest-ridden world; they therefore tended to hunt or fish daily, and to consume their catch immediately with no thought for the morrow. They had no severe winters to fear.

The Indians' lack of possessions, ambition or material greed had impressed and delighted the first discoverers of Brazil. One sixteenth-century Portuguese observed that 'Each man is able to provide for himself, without expecting any legacy in order to be rich, other than the growth which Nature universally bestows on all creatures. . . . they have no property and do not try to acquire it as other men do. So they live free from the greed and inordinate desire for riches that are so prevalent among other nations.' No Indian tribe had any notion of private ownership of land. As hunters and shifting cultivators, they regarded the land and water as resources to be used communally and as freely as the air they breathed.

One old Indian asked the French missionary Jean de Léry why his countrymen crossed the ocean to acquire Brazilian wood and other riches. When it was explained that a trader did this to amass wealth for his descendants, the Indian answered with devastating logic: 'I now see that you French are great madmen. You cross the sea and suffer great inconvenience . . . and work so hard to accumulate riches for your children and those who survive you. Is the land that nourished *you* not sufficient to feed them too? We have fathers, mothers and children whom we love. But we are certain that after our death the land that nourished us will also feed them. We therefore rest, without further cares.'

Along with this admirable lack of possessions or greed, the Indians lived in egalitarian and communal harmony. Pero de Magalhães Gandavo wrote in 1576: 'They have no class distinctions or notions of dignity or ceremonial. And they do not need them. For all are equal in every respect, and so in harmony with their surroundings that they all live in justice and in conformity with the laws of nature.'

The notion of Indians living effortlessly in a terrestrial paradise had a powerful appeal to sixteenth-century thinkers such as Montaigne, Rabelais, Ronsard and to a lesser extent More and Erasmus. The Indians' classless and unmaterialistic society evolved into the theory of the noble savage. Montesquieu, in *The Spirit of Laws* (1748), stressed the freedom and equality of American tribes. Diderot repeated these qualities in the entry 'Savages' in his famous *Encyclopaedia* of 1761. In his essay on the character of savage man, Diderot also praised the Indians' love of liberty and reluctance to leave their forests for the 'civilisation' of colonial towns. But the man who argued most strongly for man's inherent goodness was Jean Jacques Rousseau. He also believed passionately that infants should be breast-fed (Rousseau gave presents of ribbon bows to any women he knew who fed their babies themselves) and free from the constraints of swaddling clothes – both ideas which he learned from reports of Brazilian Indians. Early, somewhat romantic, ideas about Brazilian Indians thus had an influence on the philosophers and political thinkers who inspired the French Revolution.

Although Brazilian Indians thus gave unwitting stimulus to European political progress, they themselves gained almost nothing in return. Lofty ideals about the rights of man did not take hold among the colonial rulers of Brazil. This was a country whose plantations depended on slave labour and whose frontiers were gradually pushing inland to conquer Indian territories. The age of enlightenment produced some pious platitudes about Indians in Brazilian legislation. But these laws were hardly more benevolent than the Jesuit-inspired rulings of colonial monarchs; and they tended to be ignored with impunity in the harsh world of the frontier.

The political changes of the early nineteenth century did, however, improve our understanding of contemporary Brazilian Indians. When the Portuguese court moved to Brazil, it became less frightened of the designs of other European powers on a colony that had been the jewel in the Portuguese crown. Tiny Portugal had successfully repelled French, Dutch, English, Irish and Spanish attempts to establish colonies in what is now Brazil. It had therefore been understandably secretive about what lay within this immense land. During the eighteenth century, foreign travellers and scientists were rigorously excluded. As we have seen, Captain Cook in 1768 and Alexander von Humboldt in 1800 were both denied entry by suspicious officials. Humboldt and the French naturalist Aimé Bonpland went up the Orinoco in southern Venezuela and passed through the Casiquiare Canal on to the waters of the upper Rio Negro. When they tried to move downriver from San Carlos de Río Negro to the Brazilian fort at Marabitanas, Humboldt was arrested as a spy and his notes and instruments were confiscated. All this was done on orders from the Portuguese Crown to the Governor of Pará. As the official *Gazeta da Colónia* put it: 'A certain Baron von Humboldt from Berlin has been travelling through the interior of America, making astronomical observations in order to rectify certain errors in the existing maps, and collecting plants. . . . Under this pretext, this stranger may hide plans for propagating new ideas and new religious principles among the loyal subjects of this realm.' After much discussion, Humboldt and Bonpland were released and their possessions returned to them; but they were refused entry to Brazil.

This paranoid xenophobia changed with the arrival of the Portuguese Court in 1808. European travellers started coming soon after. Most wrote books about their adventures in this exciting new world; and almost all managed to visit one or two tribes of Indians. There was the German mining engineer Wilhelm Ludwig, Baron von Eschwege, who was in charge of the mines in Minas Gerais between 1809 and 1815, and so had a chance to observe the Coroado of Xapotó and some groups of Botocudo on the road between Rio de Janeiro and Ouro Prêto. The Englishman John Mawe also penetrated Minas Gerais, the source of Brazil's fabulous wealth of gold and diamonds. Another Englishman, the sugar trader Henry Koster from Liverpool, travelled in north-east Brazil in 1811 and described the Cariri and other Gê-speaking tribes. But the greatest of these early travellers was the German Prince Maximilian zu Wied-Neuwied. This aristocrat was a delightful travel writer, a keen observer, fond of Indians and of natural history, and with a fluent literary style. Wied-Neuwied travelled up the coast from Rio de Janeiro to Bahia in 1815 with the naturalists Friedrich Sellow and Georg Freyreiss, visiting Puri and Botocudo inland and a series of tribes along the coast. With his narrative, Wied-Neuwied published fine engravings of dances and village scenes – the first pictures of Brazilian Indians to be readily available to European readers. These handsome engravings became a model for later artists.

The influx of inquisitive and literate foreigners became a torrent as a result of events in 1816 and 1817. In June 1816 a French frigate reached Rio de Janeiro with the Duc de Luxembourg, ambassador of the restored King Louis XVIII. He brought with him a French artistic mission led by the Secretary of the Institut des Beaux Arts of Paris. This included such luminaries as the artists Nicolas Antoine Taunay and Jean-Baptiste Debret; the sculptor Auguste Taunay; distinguished architects, engravers and cabinetmakers; and particularly Auguste de Saint-Hilaire and other naturalists.

In the following year Dom Pedro, heir to the throne of Portugal and future Emperor of Brazil, became engaged to the Austrian Archduchess Leopoldine Caroline (Leopoldina in Portuguese), daughter of the Habsburg Emperor of Austria, Friedrich I. Thanks to the Austrian Chancellor, Prince von Metternich, the young Princess brought with her to Brazil another formidable scientific mission. There were botanists, entomologists, artists and other naturalists. But the men who became most passionately interested in Indians were the zoologist Johann Natterer, the mineralogist and botanist Johann Emmanuel Pohl, and above all two Bavarians whom King Maximilian Joseph I of Bavaria had asked to be included in the team

– the zoologist Johann Baptist von Spix and the botanist Carl Friedrich Philip von Martius. Most of these scientists made useful observations about one or two Indian groups, but Spix and Martius travelled for five years deep into the interior of Brazil visiting dozens of tribes, and they have been hailed as the fathers of modern Brazilian ethnography.

With the exception of the French artist Debret, who was forty-eight when he reached Brazil, all the other travellers were young men in their twenties or early thirties. They were generally intelligent and curious observers. They spoke no Indian languages and had no anthropological training. Their visits were very brief. They thus missed many of the finer points in tribal society, and the best that can be said was that they were good reporters, reasonably unbiased, sympathetic but not over-romantic.

Some of the ideas of these Europeans became established as commonplaces and were repeated by later writers. They liked Indian simplicity and nakedness. Wied-Neuwied spoke of the Coroados at the mission of São Fidelis on the Paraíba as being 'still fairly pure'; and newly contacted Puri nearby 'observed us with a curious but timid look' and were easily delighted in their childlike innocence. Henry Koster, meanwhile, wrote that 'Indians are in general a quiet and inoffensive people. . . . [An Indian's] favourite pursuits are fishing and hunting; a lake or rivulet will alone induce him to be stationary for any length of time.'

Europeans who visited Brazil in the early nineteenth century all believed in progress and the perfectibility of man. They were convinced that their European civilisation was the acme of human achievement. They tended to look down on the rustic New World society of Portuguese Brazil; and many were sure that tribal Indians were from a lower human order. They reported characteristics among the Indians similar to those observed by their predecessors in earlier centuries, but the conclusions they drew were less favourable. They saw no charm in the Indians' freedom from cares or ambition. Most regarded this as laziness and improvidence. Henry Koster wrote that, although some Indians were brave and resolute, 'the general character is usually supposed to be cowardly, inconstant, devoid of acute feelings, as forgetful of favours as of injuries, obstinate in trifles, regardless of matters of importance. . . . The Indian seems to be without energy or exertion; devoid of great good or great evil.' He acknowledged that the Indians lived wretchedly under the eye of a director 'by whom they are imperiously treated' and from whom they naturally tried to escape. 'They have been unjustly dealt with, they have been trampled upon, and afterwards treated as children; they have been always subjected to those who consider themselves their superiors.' But this did not excuse their demoralisation and apparent apathy. 'If they are a race of acute beings, capable of energy, of being deeply interested upon any subject, they would do more than they have done. The priesthood is open to them; but they do not take advantage of it. I never saw an Indian mechanic in any of the towns; there is no instance of a wealthy Indian.'

Indian 'laziness' was a theme taken up by most European travellers. Ever since the first colonists and missionaries reached Brazil, Europeans had been baffled by Indians' self-sufficiency. It was impossible to bribe such people with promises of payment or material success, when they were so irritatingly unimpressed by the supposed benefits of civilisation. Ayres do Casal, in his magnificent survey of Brazil in 1817, echoed this gloomy view: 'It is not yet possible to change the natural indolence [of the Indians] nor inspire them with noble sentiments of glory, honour or self-interest. They are not found in higher education, and it is rare for any to learn liberal arts. If they have a shirt and trousers of coarse cotton and a straw hat they are generally satisfied. Almost nothing arouses their appetite.'

Spix and Martius, who were travelling deep into the interior of Brazil at that time, were even more scathing about the Indian character as they saw it. They repeated the settlers' distorted, uncomprehending view: 'An Indian is born, as the colonists commonly say, only to be commanded. Neither thieving nor deceitful, but with no enthusiasm for anything that does not relate to the wants of his stomach, he always remains isolated and separate with his family. However carefully attended by the colonists in sickness, or in general loaded with benefits, he feels . . . almost incapable of gratitude, and flees . . . back to his gloomy forests. . . . By no means inclined to conversation, he sleeps during part of the day; plays with his domestic animals, when not occupied with hunting; or sits gazing intently, without thought, sometimes frightened by dreamlike fanciful images. Chained to the present, he hardly ever raises his eyes to the starry firmament.' The Germans recorded a Brazilian colonist's hatred of the Botocudo, among whom he had lived after being captured in a raid: 'Wicked and deceitful by nature, fearful by habit, indolent from laziness, greedy from boredom, false from a knowledge of their own weakness, inconstant and careless from their childish folly.' Yet Spix and Martius went on to note the determina-

tion with which the Botocudo rejected Christianity, and the generous manner in which they traded for the European goods – alcohol
and metal tools – which they wanted.

Their reputation as the founders of modern ethnographic observation of Brazilian Indian tribes and their languages should not
obscure the failure of these two Germans to comprehend Indian
character. Nothing they saw fitted their ideas of human progress.
Such prejudice made them unsympathetic to the achievements of
native society or to the magnitude of the cultural shock that resulted
from defeat by an alien race. The baffled Germans felt that 'the entire
life of these people is a dull dream from which they almost never
awake'. They came to despair of the 'perfectibility' of Brazilian
Indians in European terms. They dismissed Indians as 'a race that
detests any duties of civilisation whose benefits lie beyond their
narrow comprehension. This hatred is not based on pride, but on
indifference and dreamlike indolence. Here we touch on a situation
that contradicts the philanthropy of our agitated and experienced
century. It pains us to say it: but our conviction, based on some years
of observation of Brazilian natives, disputes the common view of the
perfectability of the race of red-skins.' The travellers noted that
attempts to make Indians equal to other settlers had failed, and that
depopulation had robbed Indians of their power or wealth. 'We must
therefore incline to the conclusion that the Indians cannot endure
the higher culture that Europe wishes to implant in them. Progres-
sive civilisation is the vital element of flourishing human society; but
it irritates them like a destructive poison. They therefore seem to us
destined to disappear, like many other species in the history of
nature. They will leave the ranks of the living before they have
achieved the highest level of progress whose seed is implanted in
them. We thus think of the red man as a stunted branch of the trunk
of humanity . . . incapable of producing the highest flowers and
fruits of humanity.'

Martius curiously combined fine scientific observation of Indians
with theories and conclusions that now seem hopelessly wrong and
naive. His writings contain a mass of highly important ethnographic
and linguistic information – all the more important because some of
the tribes visited by him and Spix are now extinct. But he also had
strange ideas about the origin of American Indians. Some authors
thought that they were a lost tribe of Israel or an offshoot of a
European nation. Martius believed the theory that Plato's sub-
merged civilisation of Atlantis lay beyond the Pillars of Hercules or

Straits of Gibraltar. He wondered whether Atlantis had been near
South America. Other observers guessed correctly that the Indians
had come from central Asia – although it was many years before the
theory of a migration across a natural land bridge between Siberia
and Alaska became accepted.

Martius did not subscribe to the ideal of a noble savage. He
regarded Indians as degenerate survivors of a once-flourishing civilisation, correctly seeing the hundreds of tribal dialects as a sign of
centuries of linguistic fragmentation. But he assumed that the
Indians' social structures and notions of priesthood, chiefs, divinity
and marriage were vestiges of a former advanced society rather than
autochthonous creations. Allowing his imagination to run riot,
Martius wondered whether some calamity such as an earthquake or
an eruption of deadly gases had doomed the Indians. This might
have filled their descendants with such horror that their spirits were
darkened and their hearts hardened. Perhaps a flood or drought had
driven them to constant inter-tribal warfare. (It never occurred to
these Germans to contrast the savage fighting in European history
with the relative calm of Brazilian tribes.) Martius even pondered
whether the aloofness that he mistook for dimness of intellect was a
sign of some organic disorder that doomed Indians to eventual
extinction. All these doubts and suppositions were aired at a special
meeting of German scientists at Freiburg in 1838.

One problem was that Spix and Martius visited only tribes that
were already in contact with white settlers. They could not speak
Indian languages and rarely remained with a tribe long enough to
gain its friendship. They formed an impression that some Indians
were physically unattractive. They accused the Indian race of
'gloomy stupidity and reserve, which is manifested in the dark un-
steady look and shy behaviour of the American.' But they admitted
that 'the constraint of civilisation to which he is wholly unaccustomed, and intercourse with negroes, mestizos and Portuguese increase
the melancholy image of internal discontent and abasement. The
manner in which they are treated by many of the new landowners
contributes to this moral and physical degeneracy.'

Unable to talk to the Indians, the Germans failed to appreciate
their spirituality. They thought that the Indians lacked the nobler
ideals that were prized by German romantics. 'The Indian temperament is almost wholly undeveloped and appears phlegmatic. All
powers of the soul, and even the more refined pleasures of the senses
seem to be in a state of lethargy. They do not reflect on the whole
of creation . . . but live with their faculties directed only to self-

preservation. They scarcely distinguish past and future and therefore never provide for the following day. Strangers to complaisance,
gratitude, friendship, humility, ambition, and to all delicate and
noble emotions which adorn human society, obtuse, reserved, sunk
in indifference to all things, the Indians use nothing but their
naturally acute senses, their cunning and retentive memory, and
then only in war or hunting, their chief occupations.'

These errors of observation led the Germans to their prejudice
about Indian intelligence. Although they found some tribes 'noble'
and handsome, others they condemned as brutish. They wrote a
savage attack on a group of Botocudo they met in Minas Gerais: 'The
appearance of these people, who had scarcely any trace of humanity
in their wild exteriors, caused a terrible impression. Indolence,
stupidity and animal brutality showed in their square, flat faces and
their small, timid, staring eyes. Greed, laziness and grossness were
expressed by their protruding lips, paunches, and in all their
grotesque bodies and tripping gait.' The Botocudo's ferocity was
exemplified to Spix and Martius by one woman who had been beaten
and shot with arrows by her husband as punishment for marital
infidelity. 'She was slowly following the horde, covered with bloody
and swollen wounds on her arms, legs and breasts.'

Martius sensationalised these distorted images of Indians in a
folio of engravings which accompanied the account of his travels.
One drawing showed a moonlit dance by apelike Puris. The Indians'
bodies are deformed, with square heads sunken into their shoulders
and long arms hanging down their flanks. Such distortion was too
much for Prince Maximilian of Wied-Neuwied. He had seen the
same Indians shortly before Spix and Martius and expostulated in
his private diary: 'In some recent descriptions of journeys in Brazil,
portraits of Puris were published that are all very bad. This is
especially true of the dance of the Puris by moonlight, inserted in the
Atlas of Spix and Martius. It has no single element that conforms to
reality and is a horrible engraving. All its grotesque figures have
uniformly ugly faces and toad-like bodies – of which not the remotest
resemblance is found in any tribe of Brazilian Indians. This engraving should immediately be eliminated from the *Atlas*, which is otherwise beautiful.'

Farther north, in Piauí in north-eastern Brazil, the Germans were
impressed by the toughness and self-assurance of a group of unacculturated Timbira who entered the frontier town of Caxias.
These Indians had magnificent bodies and were as tall as the European visitors. But Spix and Martius failed to appreciate the men's

dance. 'One of them invited the others to dance by blowing on a boré, a large cane trumpet that gave out a rattling sound, with a monotonous howling that the entire horde repeated endlessly in horrible unison. They kept up this fearful din through the streets of the silent town, and surprised a crowd of bats from neighbouring roofs. The disorganised leaping and turning, the warlike and menacing swing of their weapons, the hatefully distorted expressions of this unbridled band, and the frightful unharmonious howling accompanied by the throb of their maracá rattles, could have passed for a scene in hell.'

In contrast to his compatriots, Prince Wied-Neuwied was delighted by a dance of the Camacan tribe. He lovingly described the tribe's preparation of cauim maize beer, its body painting and delicate personal ornament, and the symmetrical movements of lines of dancers. At one point 'the women enter the dance and remain in pairs with the left hand of one on another's back; then men and women alternately girate without stopping around the urn that contains the desired drink, to the sound of their enchanting music. They dance thus in the heat of the day at the hottest season of the year, with sweat running all down their bodies. . . . The women accompany the song in subdued voices but with no form of modulation. They perform the dance with heads and upper bodies inclined forward. These savages dance thus throughout the night without growing tired, until the vessel is empty.'

Auguste de Saint-Hilaire was as appalled as Spix and Martius by the Puri-speaking Coroados of the Rio Bonito north-west of Rio de Janeiro. He described this nomadic people as 'the ugliest and most disagreeable of all the Indians I have encountered. . . . Their expression has something ignoble. . . . They are at once nonchalant, sad, indifferent and stupid. They pay attention only to someone who woos them or gives them presents.' Saint-Hilaire revealed traces of racial prejudice by commenting that these Indians were dark-skinned, small, and with large heads flattened on top and sunk into their shoulders. But he blamed the settlers for their ill-treatment. 'They are at the mercy of mulattoes and men of lower class among whom they live. No one thinks to give them any notion of morality or to raise them to the feeble degree of civilisation of which they would be capable.'

Farther afield, Saint-Hilaire was shocked by frontiersmen's loathing of Indians. At Viana on the coast of Espírito Santo, 'people often talked about savage Indians. This was an inexhaustible topic of conversation in that country. It was never raised without showing a hatred approaching delirium against those unfortunates. I tried in vain to make these good men understand that such sentiments were not in accord with the religion they claimed to profess. In their eyes the "heathen" do not belong to the human species but are ferocious beasts.'

The French traveller reasoned that Indians needed official protection since they could not adjust to competitive European society. He observed the Waitaká of the former Jesuit mission of São Pedro dos Indios on the coast not far north of Rio de Janeiro. These were survivors of one of the first tribes to be struck by European conquest. Now largely acculturated, they wore clothing and spoke Portuguese. They appeared to be demoralised, extremely lazy, fond of alcohol and improvident for the future. Saint-Hilaire confessed that 'two hundred years of civilisation under two entirely different regimes [of missionaries and directors] have modified the character of these Indians as little as their social organisation or physical appearance. They have remained as rootless and improvident as they once were in the depths of the forests and swamps. Or, if you prefer, they have remained children despite all the trouble taken to make men of them. . . . The Indians need to live under protective tutelage. If, as is probable, they cannot be allowed to enjoy this advantage, they will soon have disappeared from the face of Brazil and other parts of America.' There was some justification in this harsh prophecy. The call for disinterested tutelage is common to many Indian well-wishers to this day. Saint-Hilaire was right to assume that the Waitaká would never enjoy it. Despite its stubborn attempt to survive, this coastal tribe is now extinct.

Indian improvidence exasperated foreigners throughout the nineteenth century. Observers convinced of the virtue of the work ethic and the idea of human progress could not tolerate people who thrived without undue effort, and who preferred enjoying time with their families to labouring as a working class. The Scottish botanist George Gardner, who was in Brazil in the late 1830s, observed this among the Krahó and Akroá living in the decaying mission of Duro near the Goiás–Piauí border. 'Although both the soil and climate of the mission are well adapted for the cultivation of the various productions of the tropics, the inhabitants are so indolent that they are generally in a state of starvation.' But Gardner did at least acknowledge that the Indians were efficient hunter–gatherers. He noted that they ate a wide range of wild fruits at different times of year. When he was with them, they were working hard gathering nuts of the shodó palm and cracking their tough husks with heavy stones. He also saw that young Indians much preferred hunting to labouring in a plantation. They were generous with their catch: 'On their return to the aldeia, this spoil was divided among their friends; it was all immediately devoured without salt or any kind of vegetable, except a few small capsicums. On the following day, scarcely an Indian was to be seen stirring abroad; like the boa constrictor, they were sleeping away the effects of their overdose of food.'

Gustav von Koenigswald said of the Kaingáng of Paraná in southern Brazil: 'These Indians . . . are always serene and contented when they have little work to do and can play or converse at home, preferably with their children and the various household pets (especially parrots) that are found in large numbers in every hut.'

There were only two exceptions to this infuriating indifference to material possessions. Brazilian Indians were and always have been thrilled by metal cutting tools. In their stone-age existence and with their great manual skills, they could make marvellous use of metal knives, machetes and axes. Unlike the pre-conquest natives of the Andes, lowland forest Indians never learned to mine or work metals.

Karl von den Steinen, the great German anthropologist and explorer who first contacted the tribes of the upper Xingu in the 1880s, wrote a famous account of the contrast between stone and metal axes. A Bakairi from the Arinos river acted the problem for him in mime: 'What exhaustion a Bakairi endured to cut down a tree! Early in the morning, when the sun [*tchishi*] is rising over there in the east, he starts to wield his stone axe. *Tchishi* rises in the firmament while the Bakairi continues to chop: "sock, sock, sock." His arms become steadily wearier. The Bakairi rubs them, letting them hang down loose. He lets out a great breath to fan his face. He continues to chop but no longer strikes with a clean "sock"; now he does it with deep groans. The sun reaches its zenith. His stomach is empty – he rubs it and bends double: how hungry the Bakairi is! His face takes on an unhappy expression. Finally when *tchishi* is well down on the horizon the tree falls: "*tokale* [one]", and he holds up his little finger. But the *caraíba*, the "civilized" man – everything about the actor changes to life and vigour – the *caraíba* takes his metal axe, raises it with strength, lets it fall violently chop, chop, boom – Ah! . . . and the tree (he stamps down hard) is already on the ground. Here, there, everywhere one sees trees fall. Conclusion for the Indian: give us your metal axes!'

Steinen saw this same mime acted for him by successive tribes. 'It described the contrast between the stone axe and the metal axe. There was something impressive and moving about it. . . . It was like the stammering protest of a people who do not know metal against the blows that were destroying their culture.' Other explorers making first contacts with Brazilian tribes discovered the overwhelming impact of the metal cutting edge. An uncontacted Indian would handle his first machete with curiosity. Hesitantly at first, he would slice through a sapling. Then with increasing wonder and delight, he would move through the undergrowth, chopping, slicing and cutting to right and left with new-found power, freedom and joy.

Colonists and missionaries soon learned that their metal tools were the most potent influence on the Indians. An official who wrote a plan for civilising Brazilian Indians in 1788 recommended that missionaries go to them armed with cheap presents. 'The cost would be trivial, for these wretches are content with anything. Their natural preference is for beads, bells, mirrors, brightly coloured ribbons, knives, axes, machetes and similar ridiculous things.' Metal tools were and still are the standard means of winning the friendship of hostile or uncontacted tribes. Tools and clothing were used to win over some Kayapó in Goiás in 1780, Pataxó in Espírito Santo in 1802, Baniwa on the Içá river on the upper Negro in 1807, and Botocudo on the Doce in Minas Gerais in 1819. With the start of the independent Brazilian empire in 1822, Jean-Baptiste Debret said that many Brazilians joined in efforts to 'civilise' Indians. 'At that time frequent delegations of wild Indians were brought for the first time to Rio de Janeiro. They came to beg from the Sovereign tools to work as farmers or weapons to serve as auxiliary soldiers.'

Tools were also used as one of the few methods of payment that appealed to Indians. The Cherente of Goiás were said to be willing to sell even their children for tools and firearms. George Gardner reported that the related Akroá of Duro aldeia in northern Goiás would work as paddlers on the Tocantins for payment in axes and other tools. Various officials saw the attraction of tools as the only means of turning Indians into a wage-earning proletariat.

Francisco Rodrigues do Prado, who commanded Fort Coimbra on the Paraguay at the end of the eighteenth century, wrote about the problem of getting the Guaikurú accustomed to work when they had been born free and lived lives of ease and plenty. It was a transition that must be accomplished gradually. 'Over a period of time we will form a new character in them, making them dependent on work. Changing the tools that they can obtain in the wilds for knives, axes, beads and trinkets would be a very gentle method of making them inadvertently lose their ferocity and natural suspicion, and adding them to the working population. . . .'

Many years later, a Capuchin missionary, Friar Luiz de Cemetille, had to admit that one Indian remained at his mission only because 'he could no longer do without our tools. [This chief said] that it was too late for him to accept a new religion for he was an old man. He was so old that he could not learn to make the sign of the cross. [Once he had his tools], he left with a guffaw of laughter, slapping me on the back and saying a sarcastic farewell. . . . In my view, the easiest way to inculcate in them a love of work is the ambition to gain and possess things. These should not be given as presents . . . but earned by their efforts.'

Dr José Viera Couto de Magalhães (a lawyer who was successively president of various Brazilian provinces in the later nineteenth century and who had contact with many tribes during a series of impressive expeditions) took an even tougher line. He recommended forced labour, which would be paid for in hardware. Rather than give many presents, 'it would be better to force them to work as paddlers, at which they excel, in return for a small stipend. Do not say that this idea is barbarous. Do we not force our fellow citizens to be soldiers and sailors? . . . Should Indians have more rights than other Brazilian citizens? Of course not. This measure, used with discretion, would rapidly attract them to true civilisation: namely love of work, love of family and of order!'

Much of this was wishful thinking. Indians were intelligent enough to acquire the few tools they needed and then cease to be interested in working for more. They could resist the temptation even of things they wanted badly. An Italian traveller, Bartolomeo Rossi, described his attempt to seduce the chief of some semi-acculturated Paresi in western Mato Grosso in 1862. Rossi wanted the chief's son. 'I asked the chief of the tribe for his son in exchange for my shotgun (which he spent hours examining), powder, shot, axes, knives and various other objects that he greatly admired. The Indian's hesitation was understandable, given the powerful influence of my seduction. . . . Finally nature triumphed. That savage father answered me: "No, great captain! If my son goes, he cries, I cry. . . . My son dies, I die!" '

The other thing that Indians wanted from the colonists was more dangerous and addictive than metal tools. Most were excited by sugar-cane alcohol, the cachaça rum that is Brazil's national drink. Many tribes themselves brewed mildly intoxicating manioc or maize beer and used it in their festivals. They responded to the far more powerful spirits distilled by the settlers: getting drunk on rum gave them spiritual stimulus and temporary release from despair at the cultural shock of conquest by an alien power.

Articles 13, 14 and 41 of the Directorate legislation of 1757 urged directors to discourage the use of alcohol in their villages and try to prevent its entry. These clauses were in vain. Some directors exploited alcohol as a means of dominating and profiting from their charges. Bishop João de São José saw that 'both Indians and whites in [Amazonia] die for sugar-cane alcohol. They call it the divine or enchanting drink.' When Bishop Caetano Brandão went up the Amazon in the 1780s, he found the former mission aldeias decayed and their Indians degraded. 'Nothing could be more lamentable than their morals; drunkenness and incontinence were their incorrigible vices.'

A report of 1802 on the acculturated Indians of the Ilhéus coast of Bahia noted of the Pataxó that 'rum is their joy and their ruin, and they are becoming accustomed to insubordination.' Johann Moritz Rugendas observed that drink released Indians' inner passions. 'Their hatred against whites is revealed whenever they imagine that they can express it without danger of punishment. The ill-treatment they receive so frequently makes too strong an impression to be appeased by isolated favours from some individuals. Their true feelings toward the whites are usually revealed when they are inflamed by alcohol. They then utter violent imprecations, even against those who do them only good.'

The missionary Francisco das Chagas Lima fulminated against the Kaingáng's 'obscene dances held amid intoxicating drink.' But Henry Koster saw no such orgies among the Cariri of north-east Brazil in 1811. 'They are much addicted to liquor,' he wrote, 'and will dance in a ring, singing some of their monotonous ditties and drink for nights and days without ceasing. Their dances are not indecent, as those of Africa.' The French artist Hércules Florence observed similar dances among the Bororo of Mato Grosso a few years later. The Bororo used to come to a ranch near Cuiabá, where the farmer's wife gave them food and cachaça, to which they were already addicted. Then, almost drunk, they would perform their traditional dance, forming a great circle, singing, clapping their hands and stamping a steady rhythm with their feet. They alternately raised their faces to the sky and then bowed down, repeating these monotonous movements to enact the slow advance of a sloth or a cautious jaguar hunt. The fazendeiro gave them the alcohol as protection against their raids and to buy their labour or produce.

Many Europeans who visited Indians in the early nineteenth century noted their weakness for alcohol. Wied-Neuwied saw that the newly contacted Puri would raid sugar plantations and remove large quantities of cane. They enjoyed chewing it, but they had also learned to distil it.* Saint-Hilaire commented that the Kayapó of the Goiás aldeias used to make a strong drink from peppers, but had abandoned this since knowing more potent cachaça.

Unscrupulous colonists used alcohol addiction as a weapon against Indians. Guy Marlière, a former French officer who devoted many years to helping Botocudo and other tribes of Minas Gerais, named cachaça as one of the five ways in which white men destroyed native Brazilians – the others were slaughter in battle, tuberculosis, syphilis and smallpox. He tried to help his Indians by organising trade for their produce. But, as Rugendas commented, 'for them such trading becomes a source of abuse and deception, for they cannot resist their addiction to alcoholic drinks. The same often happens to those who hire themselves out as labourers for the colonists.' Marlière himself described two frontier trading posts as 'Sodoms which live from robberies committed on the Indians. To satisfy the requirements of religion, [the Indians] come well dressed on feast days. They emerge naked, evicted by bar-keepers. There is a man in every tavern who throws them out on to the street when they are drunk, where they die, apoplectic or crushed by carts and horses. . . . [Cachaça is] the plague of the aldeias, an infallible way to incite Indians to every sort of excess. There are glaring examples of the deadly effects of this pernicious drug. In exchange for it Indians give their wives and children to evil contractors. . . . It kills more of these wretches than does the plague. The main business of inn-keepers is to evict them when drunk after robbing them of all they have earned by their work, leaving them naked in the street.' The Bishop of Mariana confirmed this. He was appalled to see Indians at São João Batista do Presídio lying dead drunk or being carried off as inert as corpses, while their women drank cachaça as they suckled their babies.* Far inland on the Tocantins, another Frenchman, the Count of Castelnau, witnessed similar degradation of the Krahó: 'this tribe seemed to us completely demoralised and abandoned to drunkenness.'

Drink was almost the only way to press-gang Indians into paddling boats along the Amazon's thousands of miles of rivers. The York-shire botanist Richard Spruce wrote that traders who plied the rivers 'have a very bad habit of stealing Indians from one another, going themselves or sending emissaries with cachaça by night, and making the Indians dead drunk, then tumbling them into the canoe like so many logs and setting sail immediately. When the Indian wakes up from his drunken sleep he finds himself far from port and embarked on a voyage he dreamt not of undertaking; little, however, cares he for this. . . .' One of Spruce's own paddlers on the Rio Negro sold everything for drink. 'One old fellow made it his first business to dispose of the whole of his earthly goods (leaving himself only a pair of trousers), namely his hammock, shirt, knife and tinder-box, with the proceeds of which he got so gloriously drunk as to be in a state of utter helplessness for a couple of days. Yet this man, when removed beyond the scent of cachaça, proved the very best fellow in the lot – always in good humour, always ready for work.'

What Should Be Done About Indians?

Many theorists anguished over the problem of what to do about the Indians. Government officials, politicians, ecclesiastics and foreign visitors all had their personal analyses of Indian character and solutions for the problem of 'civilising' this baffling race.

The trouble was that the Brazilian Indians were morally in the right. They were resisting colonial invasion by a totally alien culture. Outside observers were reluctant to admit that the spread of their own supposedly superior society was wrong. Many appreciated that the Indians had a radically different social outlook; but almost none could accept that tribal society was as good as their own European model.

To the embarrassment of Brazilians and Europeans, all Indians had a fierce love of freedom. They preferred escape to the forests to life among 'civilised' settlers. Tribe after tribe voted with its feet to flee from the colonial frontier. The great explorer Ricardo Franco de Almeida Serra laid the blame squarely on his fellow colonists. In 1797 he wrote: 'Tribes fled the scourge that was devastating them and emigrated to lands ... more distant from the greed of the Portuguese. The latter abandoned themselves to brutal laziness and sought the labour of others to feed and enrich themselves. By right of force, they stole from the ancient and tranquil lords of America their uncultivated lands, their children, wives, and even their beloved freedom. Now the remnants of those terrorised tribes have concentrated in the most isolated parts of this vast land.' Robert Southey saw that the choice facing the Indians was 'to remain and be treated like slaves, or fly to the woods and take their chance as savages.'

The Portuguese naturalist Rodrigues Ferreira discussed in 1786 the problem of attracting Indians to live among the colonists. 'They are not enticed by liberty, for they are absolutely free in every sense in their forests; nor to our customs, for ours are far more restrictive than theirs; and as for food and clothing, it is provided by nature. . . . [For those living among the whites,] all their passion and wellbeing is for the forests they left. . . . An aversion to and horror of white men has taken such a grip of them all, that its memory alone causes them to bury themselves deep in the forests.'

The French artist Debret described how the Camacan of Espírito Santo 'retreated into the dark forests, to hide their shame and despair after a brave and tenacious but futile defence of their territory from Portuguese invasion. Although now dispersed, they continue to be jealous of the delights of freedom.' The Camacan had a horror of colonial society and equated white men with tyranny. 'Thus isolated in their rustic huts, they still tremble at the memory of the European invasions. This tradition of mistrust and hatred has been transmitted from generation to generation and seems to have strengthened over the centuries.' When Spix and Martius wanted to study some Botocudo at a settlement in Minas Gerais, a few came very reluctantly. 'They were all very sullen, silent and distrustful. . . . They were not to be diverted either by friendly treatment, presents, or music. They thought only of means to escape into their forests: in fact, all of them successively disappeared.'

Those who had most experience of trying to acculturate Indians admitted that they were usually better fed before contact and conquest. Chief Aropquimbe of the Kaingáng told an Italian missionary that 'he was happier in the virgin forests, where the game, fish and fruit were more abundant, and where sufficient food for him and his numerous family never failed.' José Viera Couto de Magalhães was aware that Indians who were brilliant as hunters and gatherers could not succeed as sedentary farmers of weak Brazilian soils. After settlement, 'they are subjected to farming land to obtain food that is inferior to that which they obtained with less effort by hunting and fishing, when they were freely able to do so in the semi-nomadic life to which they were accustomed. From this stem the disgust, laziness, and inertia that inevitably corrupt them all and create prostitution, drunkenness and other vices.' It was impossible not to admire tribes like the handsome Guató who hid themselves in the swamps and lakes of the upper Paraguay. 'Love of independence keeps them in these solitudes, where no one disturbs them. In this sense they are happier than some sedentary tribes to whom civilisation has revealed only its aspects that are least attractive to simple men.'

Despite such evidence, many theorists clung to the belief that

Indians must be settled in supervised villages if they were ever to form
part of the 'civilised' labour force. During the two centuries in which
the Jesuits largely controlled Brazilian Indians, they had relied
heavily on the aldeia system of highly regimented mission villages.

Other administrators still looked to aldeias as a weapon for
taming hostile tribes. It was hoped that the Pataxó of southern Bahia
could be reduced to aldeias – by persuasion and presents if possible,
by military force if not. Once reduced, they should be divided in
small groups and housed alongside villages of 'tame' Indians, to
whom they would be subjected. 'Dispersed in this way, it would be
difficult for them to unite again. They might even turn docile, learning from the others to know us better and to live in peace.'

The former French officer Guy Marlière was one of the very few
people who tried to help Indians in the early nineteenth century, but
even he relied on aldeias for the Botocudo whom he contacted along
the Doce river in Minas Gerais. He saw these supervised villages as a
necessary prelude to the religious conversion of Indians and their
instruction in the better aspects of European society. He insisted
that the aldeias be on traditional Indian territory, so that the tribal
people would not be relocated. The settled Indians should be given a
pretence of self-government. 'Each chief . . . may be decorated with
the pompous title of Captain and his deputy with that of Ensign. The
choice of sergeants, corporals and soldiers can be left to them. These
ranks are of no consequence to the state.' Meanwhile, other
Botocudo near the mouth of the Doce were being settled in new
aldeias. Three such aldeias were created in 1824, each with a fron-
tage of a league along the river and a depth of three leagues. Once
again, directors were appointed to run these settlements, even
though the Directorate system had been such a disastrous failure. As
always, the objective behind the villages was to get Indians to work;
and their director had eighty soldiers to help him assert this authority. The director's role was to 'direct the Indians' work, arouse their
interests and apply them to farming the land and paddling on the
river. He is to supervise transactions between the Indians and farmers who employ them on their plantations. He is to keep the peace
between Indians and settlers. . . .'

It was extraordinary that the government should still be creating
Indian aldeias a quarter century after the abolition of the hated
Directorate. Observers everywhere reported that Indian aldeias were
in decline and their inhabitants demoralised. Sargento-Mór
Francisco José Rodrigues Barata said, as early as 1799, that the
Goiás aldeias – which had been founded with so much enthusiasm

and public expenditure only a few decades before – 'had begun to experience decadence. . . . Some aldeias are deserted and others almost deserted . . . although all the settlements once had large populations.' An official who travelled into the interior of Pernambuco noted that an Indian settlement founded on an island in the São Francisco river in 1761 with 270 families was by 1805 'in great decadence . . . with under twelve families'. He blamed the depopulation on the lawless state of this cattle country. There was near-anarchy in the wild interior, with marauding gangs of cowboys murdering respectable ranchers, with prisoners released from jails, and with laws unenforced. Docile, semi-acculturated Indians suffered most from such chaos.

When foreign visitors began to reach Brazil, they confirmed such reports. In 1818 the Austrian botanist Johann Pohl wrote that the aldeias in Goiás were 'very close to decadence'. The historian Pizarro e Araújo described these villages as in their final agonies at that time; and George Gardner saw the final collapse of the aldeias of northern Goiás a few years later. By contrast, observers such as Prince Maximilian of Wied-Neuwied found that the coastal aldeias in Espírito Santo and southern Bahia were managing to survive. Although their men were often subjected to forced-labour levies, they subsisted from fishing and from pottery and baskets made by the Indian women.

Well-intentioned administrators despaired at the failure of efforts to civilise Indians. The more honest among them had to admit that tribes degenerated after contact or conquest by the whites. Captain Francisco de Paula Ribeiro was a remarkably enlightened officer sent to open a route between the interior of Maranhão and the Tocantins valley in northern Goiás. In 1815 he described the handsome Amanajó Timbira who had taken refuge from inter-tribal wars among the settlers of Pastos Bons. After fifty years of coexistence, 'they are today destroyed . . . and mixed with blacks and mulattoes. This small remnant now numbers less than twenty people and is totally degenerate. The savage chief Tembé of the Kapiekran Timbira recently asked me (before he himself was killed by smallpox in Caxias): what was the reason why among so many numerous tribes of his race, whom he knew by tradition had lived for many years among us Portuguese (as he was now proposing to live with his people), he had not met a single tribe that had multiplied in proportion to that period of time? Instead, they had all evaporated and the memory of them was about to expire. Naturally no one told him the truth. Had they done so, this barbarian would have been scandalised and fled back to the forests where he was born rather than experience – as he in fact did – tragic proof of the reasons he wanted to know.'

Robert Southey was saddened that exposure to European civilisation did not make Indians more affectionate towards one another. Any indifference could, however, 'be explained by the effects of habitual misery and a feeling . . . that early death is a lot far more desirable than a life of hopeless labour'. Johann Moritz Rugendas admitted that 'one cannot deny that up to now contact with Europeans has had only disastrous results.' He saw 'civilised' Indians sunk in lethargy and regarded them as insensitive and vengeful. He even thought uncontacted Indians such as the Botocudo handsomer than the oppressed and acculturated coastal Tupi. 'Civilisation, in the early stages [of acculturation], does not seem to have a favourable effect on their character. Far from making them lose the sombre ferocity of their previous existence, imposed constraint makes them even more melancholy and less sociable, and their hatred of the whites is revealed whenever they imagine that they can express it without danger of punishment.'

The scientists who saw most tribes and were most appalled by the decline of aldeia Indians were Spix and Martius. They wrote of the Guayaná settled in the Aldeia da Escada near São Paulo: 'It is difficult to imagine that this warlike and enterprising tribe could have been reduced in a short period to such small numbers and to such a state of decline and insignificance. It is an object of pity rather than of historical interest.' The Germans correctly blamed imported diseases for the disastrous and irreversible decline in Indian population. Great numbers of natives had, of course, been killed by epidemics in the sixteenth century. 'Soon after this, famine, the system of slavery practised with increasing cruelty, the periodic return of similar contagious diseases, and destructive germs of other disorders that came in the wake of the foreign settlers, were all powerful causes to extirpate this population, which was never considerable.' Spix and Martius were both medical doctors as well as naturalists. 'As physicians, we were particularly struck by the incredible extent of syphilis and its incalculable fatal consequences on the health and morals of the inhabitants of [Goiás]. . . . The unblushing openness with which it is discussed destroys all moral feeling and particularly violates the rights of the female sex.'

In Minas Gerais Spix and Martius noted that contacted Indians declined because all their lands were stolen by settlers. When they saw the bedraggled aldeias of Piauí, they became convinced that successful assimilation of Indians was almost impossible: conquered tribes would always resent their subjection. In Maranhão, tribes that were still free impressed the travellers as visibly more self-assured and resilient than those under Brazilian rule, who were diseased and drunken, decaying 'morally and physically in a most pitiful hybrid existence'. Many others noted similar decline among acculturated tribes. Friar Francisco dos Prazeres said in 1820 that the christianised Indians of Maranhão were becoming indolent mestizos; Wied-Neuwied noted that the Camacan of southern Bahia were still completely rustic and hated their colonial oppressors; the French artist Hércules Florence visited the former Jesuit mission of Guimarães near the Bolivian frontier west of Ciuabá and wrote that its Indians 'live in misery and possess almost nothing'. The Count of Castelnau was shocked by the demoralisation and drunkenness of the Krahó on the Tocantins in 1844; the American Methodist missionary Daniel Kidder found the Indians of Ceará degraded and pitiable and 'of no service to themselves or to anyone else'. Some years later, Vicente Ferreira Gomes was saddened by the miserable state of the Karajá on the Araguaia. Things were no better by the end of the nineteenth century. Oscar Leal wrote of the Apinagé (whose goodness had enchanted Vicente Gomes and other earlier travellers) that acculturation transformed them from being 'unpretentious and healthy to becoming jealous and bad. Little by little, many of them lost their former innocence and good faith.' The French explorer Henri Coudreau said that the once-proud Mundurukú were 'in total decadence from the social, moral and economic points of view'.

During the forty years of the Directorate, a number of optimists had argued that the Indians could be turned into good citizens if properly educated and nurtured. At the turn of the nineteenth century, well-intentioned men such as Rendon and Ricardo Franco de Almeida Serra hoped for successful assimilation if Indians were dispersed among white society. Almeida Serra wrote: 'I do not despair of the civilisation of the Guaikurú and Guaná. . . . I believe that they would learn our customs more quickly if they were intermingled with us.' Moritz Rugendas thought that Indians could be 'transformed into a source of public prosperity' if acculturated gradually.

The Directorate legislation had hoped to merge Indians into colonial society as ordinary hard-working peasants. Portugal was such a small country and its colonial empire so vast that its rulers always relied on conquered peoples as potential subjects. Whereas the British and French in North America wanted land free of its Indian inhabitants, the Portuguese had hoped to enlist the Indians to swell its population. The Directorate encouraged mixed unions to produce mestizos – although there was a distinct racist bias in this: it was assumed that white men would take native women, but never the reverse; and it was assumed that such unions would be concubinage rather than marriage. Half-caste mestizos were presumed to be illegitimate and, despite some pronouncements in the 1757 legislation, higher government posts were denied them.

The Viceroy of Brazil, Luiz de Vasconcellos e Souza, wrote to the Queen in 1784, spelling out his tough views about dispersing Indians for labour and about mixed marriages. The Indians must 'gradually lose their discredited customs. The unemployed should be added to settlers' fazendas to labour on agriculture. . . . Above all, dowries must be provided for Indian women to marry white men. These will lower themselves to receive such [women] only for financial reward. This policy is intended to extinguish the [Indian] race, forming a new creation of different men. It might implant a new form of shame and desire which could attract other Indians, who now live in despair and idleness.'

A contemporary official boasted that he had set the Indians of Pôrto Seguro to work 'to dissipate the common vice of vagrancy and idleness'. Four hundred of both sexes had been 'distributed in paid jobs in the houses of whites'. This close contact was making them 'civilised'. 'Without such familiarity with white people it would be almost impossible . . . to destroy their almost congenital vices which are repeated from father to son.' Jean-Baptiste Debret was impressed by Indians and mestizos whom he saw in the capital. He thought that prisoners captured from warlike tribes should 'immediately be interned in the cities of the interior to disorientate them. Nevertheless, it is almost always only the children who can be civilised.' Some families in Rio de Janeiro kept Indian servants and these were dedicated and capable. 'Beneath their apathetic appearance they devote themselves generously to the interests of their masters. Their sons, raised in civilisation, become excellent servants at the age of twelve: lively and intelligent, and fearless horsemen, hunters and swimmers – valuable qualities when accompanying their masters on journeys.' Debret believed that the Indian race would improve as it gradually merged with Brazilians of European origin. He cited mestizo families of São Paulo and Minas Gerais which combined the best qualities of both races. Their men were graceful and muscular with remarkable stamina. He particularly admired mestizo women, who enjoyed 'the noble features of [white] Paulistas, to which are allied the delicate eyes and curvaceous figures of caboclas, to

produce a gracious and exciting beauty.' Guy Marlière, having contacted a series of Botocudo groups in northern Minas Gerais,
encouraged his soldiers to help and instruct Indians. He opened
large tracts of Indian land to invasion by settlers and believed in
intermarriage. Meanwhile, dispersal of newly contacted Indians was
being used elsewhere as a pretext for enslavement.

Explorations of the western hinterland of São Paulo and Paraná
in 1815 were to be financed by captured Indians. The leader made
his nefarious plans sound almost philanthropic: 'For the expenses
of this expedition, he would form a company whose object would be
to divide the Indians he brings back among the shareholders.
These would adopt Indians and consider them as their children or
pupils. In this way they will be reduced more easily to the com-
munion of the church and become useful citizens.' This covert slave
raid was duly licensed. In the event it brought back only twenty-three
Indians, most of whom were children. These were duly distributed
among those who had financed the venture. In theory, the Indians
were to work for their masters until 'ready to leave their tutelage' and
fend for themselves.

Twenty years later, a similar experiment was carried out with
Kaingáng from the same part of Brazil. The President of the province
of São Paulo took seven Kaingáng families from the plains of Itapetininga (where their presence disturbed the frontier colonists) and
gave them to a judge in Iguape to be distributed among settlers. The
judge was to find citizens 'capable of treating the Indians well, to
support and clothe them and at the same time to try to employ them
in useful pursuits. For this [the settlers] would be reimbursed for any
expenses they might incur. It would accustom the Indians to work
and also to learn to live in society without suffering hardship.'
Eighteen years later, most of these were either dead from measles or
had fled back to their homeland and were opposing the frontiersmen.

Auguste de Saint-Hilaire favoured intermarriage, but he believed
strongly that Indians should be left to govern themselves. He visited
a series of aldeias on the Rio das Pedras (now the Araguari in western
Minas Gerais). Here, on the trail between São Paulo and Goiás, a
group of Bororo had been settled in the 1740s to help subdue the
Kayapó who were attacking the Goiás gold-fields. These Bororo had
intermarried with black slaves by the time Saint-Hilaire saw them in
1819. He found the resulting mestizos ugly, but well built, docile and
intelligent. These mestizos and Indians were some of the happiest he
had seen, largely because they were their own masters. 'No one
vexed them, no one troubled their repose. They did not even pay a

tithe. They had few needs and few temptations. Their lands were excellent and light work sufficed to assure their subsistence. . . . They lived in profound peace and were in harmony – as are all Indians generally. They knew most of the true advantages of our civilisation but ignored the evils. They were devoid of luxury, greed, ambition or that foresight which plagues men of our race and poisons their present for an uncertain future.'

An essential element of successful integration was for Indians to clothe themselves if they were ever to be transformed into 'useful citizens'. Clothing was in fact unnecessary for Indians in the Brazilian tropics: far from being a benefit, it damaged both their health and their economy.

Jesuits and other missionaries had been obsessed with the need to cover Indians' 'indecent' nakedness, and the importance of clothing had also been stressed in the Directorate legislation. With the ending of the Directorate system, many aldeia Indians abandoned their clothing. Johann Pohl described the Kayapó of the Goiás villages as 'untidy and dirty. The women are very ugly and their flaccid and pendant breasts deform them even more. . . . The law states that the village should give these Indians some light clothing: trousers and shirts for the men and a skirt and blouse for the women. Despite this they are mostly naked.' But the Indians probably hid their more attractive women for fear that the strangers would molest them. Another German, Dr Kupfer, who visited a Kayapó reservation near Santa Anna de Paraíba some years later, said that when he arrived the women ran into their huts and then reappeared wearing dirty rags on their hips. But Kupfer noted approvingly that 'the young women had firm, small, somewhat pointed nipples and outward-tapering breasts, while the mature women showed full but attractive breasts.'

Some observers regarded clothing as one of the great benefits of civilisation. John Henry Elliott, a young American seaman who explored the interior of Paraná in 1845, wrote that the settled Indians near Curitiba (presumably Carijó Guarani or Kaingáng) greatly loved his patron, the Baron of Antonina. 'As part of his prodigious philanthropy, he banished at his own expense hunger from their families and preserved them from the rigours of nudity. The noble Baron greeted them with affection, and distributed among them rum, tobacco, brown sugar, salt, clothing, beads, etc.' Vicente Gomes urged the government to give or trade clothing with the Indians of the Araguaia river: 'I say that, once the Indians have experienced the advantages of clothing they will always wish to be clothed. They will work to harvest the produce they must trade in exchange for clothing. And they will thus become more active and industrious.' The Karajá did not succumb to this pious hope that they would work to acquire clothing. At the end of the century, the prejudiced Henri Coudreau observed that the Karajá still lived among white settlers completely naked. 'These nudes, of little aesthetic merit, circulate amid the daily lives of the civilised families. Little [white] boys and girls are in constant contact with these animated anatomies, who speak Portuguese and are sufficiently civilised to be crafty and vicious.'

The German ethnologist Gustav von Koenigswald was one of the first to appreciate how clothing and other imported goods undermined tribal culture. He saw the Kaingáng of western São Paulo lose their natural ways and develop a false modesty when forced to wear clothes. He felt that clothing weakened Indians' resistance to disease. 'Also, the artistic sense and dexterity that they demonstrate in their artefacts . . . weapons and household utensils suffer greatly from civilisation, which brings them firearms, cloth and cheap trade goods.'

Just before Brazil became independent of Portugal in 1822, a number of proposals concerning Indians were addressed to the Cortes Gerais, the Assembly of the United Kingdom of Portugal and Brazil. Some of these made no mention of missionaries. But the Bahian delegate Domingos Borges de Barros presented a draft law in March 1822 which called for a director of gentle character and good morals for each Indian aldeia. Surprisingly, he suggested that the best people for this purpose would be Protestant Moravian Brethren, who were active at that time among Indians of the United States. Francisco Moniz Tavares, a priest and deputy from Pernambuco, wanted protection for Indian lands and greater religious activity. He recommended the example of William Penn in North America and wanted each province of Brazil to choose friars and priests 'who possess the greatest talents and virtues to go with the gentle weapons used by the Holy Church to convert and assemble Indians who are nomadic.' Nothing came of this: almost no priests were interested in the difficult and unremunerative task of converting reluctant Indians.

Henry Koster commented that there were no enthusiastic missionaries in Maranhão in 1811. With the expulsion of the Jesuits 'the other orders of friars have become lazy and worse than useless.' Francisco de Paula Ribeiro was deeply shocked by the activity of a priest at that time, who was organising slave raids on Indians of the lower Tocantins. Saint-Hilaire deplored the behaviour of a curate among the Kayapó in the Goiás aldeia of São José de Mossâmedes in 1819: he was too busy running a sugar mill to attend to his flock.

By contrast, there were a few zealous priests who were admired by their European contemporaries. We have already learned of Father Lima, of the Italian Capuchins of Camboa and of Friar Ludovico from Livorno. An Italian Franciscan, Friar Vital de Frescarolo, was employed in pacification of hostile tribes in the interior of Pernambuco and Ceará in 1804. Using kindness and charity, he contacted the Indians, who had fled from coastal aldeias. 'The Indians themselves claimed that the motive for their rebellion was ill-treatment they had received from the settlers, who had even assembled them in a courtyard on the pretext of religious instruction and put them to the sword.'

The call for more missionary priests gathered momentum in the 1830s. The President of Mato Grosso said in a speech in 1837 that only ten of the fifty-three known tribes in his province were 'domesticated'. He wanted missionaries to convert them, in order to open up more territories for mining and colonisation, employing the Indians themselves as guides in these conquests. A President of Goiás urged gentle methods in the acculturation of Indians. 'Missionaries of good life and zealous for the public good are the only people who can keep the Indians settled in aldeias and in a civilised state. Directors interested in making their fortune, clerics who seek only to make money, or soldiers who do everything by the rules of military discipline will never convert or keep Indians in our society.'

The government responded to these pleas with a series of orders to import more Italian Capuchin missionaries. The first contingent came in 1840, with the Brazilian government paying their passages and wages on arrival. The change back to a missionary solution for the Indians was confirmed in Imperial decree no. 426 of 24 July 1845.

But the overwhelming impression from the first decades of the nineteenth century was of abuse and hatred of the native Brazilians. Foreign visitors were generally shocked by the settlers' loathing of Indians. Wied-Neuwied heard colonists refer to the Puri as animals and saw them threaten them with whips. Saint-Hilaire found that the settlers of Espírito Santo detested Indians and claimed that they were flesh-eating. Throughout northern Goiás, colonists and 'even educated priests' told Johann Pohl that the Indians were beasts who should be exterminated. 'They are a plague on humanity: only by annihilating the Indians can the King please and enrich his subjects.' In Maranhão, Henry Koster witnessed cruel indifference to

Indians brought to die in the jail of São Luis, while in the interior Spix and Martius saw the settlers' fear and fury against the Gamella Indians. 'You can appreciate this deadly enmity when you know that some of their Christian neighbours murderously gave the Indians pieces of clothing infected with smallpox. The epidemic spread among the wretches with unheard-of fury, so that in the end they had no alternative but to kill off their sick with arrows!'

In this atmosphere, most settlers were interested only in the labour of settled Indians and the extermination of hostile tribes on the frontiers. Then as now, the situation was worst in the most distant parts of the country. Frontiersmen hated the natives whose land they were invading and whose arrows they feared. Pious hopes of attracting Indians and legislation for their welfare were the prerogative of city-dwellers living far from the frontier forests. Moritz Rugendas explained: 'In order fully to understand the situation, I should add that the settlers with whom the Indians are in contact are little more than brutes or often outright criminals seeking to flee from the rule of law to the remotest regions of the colony.'

Settled Indians who had survived the Directorate were still forced to work for the state and for the settlers after its abolition. Brazil was so vast, imported black slaves so expensive, and the farming, ranching and mining so labour-intensive that Indians had to be pressed into service. In 1803 the Governor of São Paulo wrote about the wretchedly poor Indians of the ten aldeias in his province: 'I pondered all the ways of making them useful to the state. I summoned them to labour on public works and religiously paid their salaries.' When this failed, the Governor followed Rendon's advice and abolished the protected Indian aldeias, releasing their Indians into Brazilian society.

On the Paraguay frontier at that time Colonel Almeida Serra was trying to attract the Guaikurú to useful work, while the Guarani in the far south of Brazil saw their women forced to spin cotton and the men 'employed for any use or purpose without attention to the damage to their own work or the resulting shortages for their families'. Wied-Neuwied and Saint-Hilaire were both shocked to see the way in which Indians of Espírito Santo were forced to clear forests, build roads and carry messages. Many had fled to avoid this unpaid 'illegal corvée'. They were shackled and badly fed while labouring for the state. Debret saw Indians working in the naval yards of Rio de Janeiro and as paddlers of the Emperor's launch. At that same time, Pohl noted that Indians in the Goiás aldeias were forced to work for the first three days of each week 'for the King'.

When the Indians had done their government service, they might
also work for the settlers. Robert Southey wrote that during the
Directorate 'the white inhabitants regarded the improvement of the
natives whom they employed with perfect indifference: provided
they worked like beasts, like beasts they might live and die.' Since it
was illegal to enslave Indians and they were reluctant to work for
wages, settlers tried to trap them in debt bondage. At the end of the
Directorate, a governor of Pará wrote that those who employed
Indians sought to pay them as little as possible. 'And what they do
come to pay them, they try to remove with poor-quality goods sold at
enormous prices. . . . They want to be served, and to treat [Indians]
as they treat slaves – or worse, for once Indians reach an age when
they can no longer work, it is of little concern whether they live or
die.' Some coastal tribes managed to trade successfully for their
simple needs, often selling pottery or baskets which they had made.
But tribes with no experience of a monetary economy were easily
duped. They would sell surplus food or forest produce such as the
ipecac root (a palliative for malarial fever) and receive in return
derisory amounts of cheap trade goods or, worse, alcohol. The
German artist Rugendas commented that 'for them such trading
becomes a source of abuse and deception, for they cannot resist their
weakness for alcohol. The same often happens to those who hire
themselves out as labourers for the colonists.'

The cheating of unsophisticated Indians included robbing them of
their land as well as of their labour and produce. When Baron
Eschwege was in the remote western part of Minas Gerais, a local
boss submitted to him 'a plan that aimed at nothing less than the
gradual expulsion of the Indians from their district, in order to
divide their lands among the Portuguese.' Eschwege indignantly
refused to countenance the fraud; but government troops were withdrawn from the area and by 1821 the Indians of the Velhas and
Grande rivers were trying to protest to the authorities that they were
being evicted from their lands. Meanwhile, in the coastal aldeia of
São Pedro dos Indios, Saint-Hilaire observed that the extensive
lands belonging to the settlement were being rented to whites at
peppercorn rents. The Indians there were running their own local
government and seemed contented. But the cheap rentals were
attracting swarms of colonists and the Indians' lands were rapidly
being lost to them.*

Loss of land was as devastating to a tribe's survival as the most
virulent epidemic. Without sufficient land, a tribe could not feed
itself by hunting, fishing, gathering or shifting agriculture. But land

meant far more than a mere source of food. It was the basis of all tribal tradition, ancestral burials and patriotic fervour. It also provided the essential buffer to protect a tribe from violent cultural shock: behind the shelter of its familiar forests, rivers and plains a tribe could keep its identity and adapt to change at its own speed. Without such land a tribe was quickly dispersed, demoralised and destroyed.

Idealists' Solutions

Amid all the incomprehension and hostility between settlers and Indians, there were a few idealists who tried to help the conquered native race. In the two centuries during which they controlled Brazilian Indians, the Jesuits had acted as their champions against colonists, slavers and harsh royal laws. But the Jesuits were not disinterested. They were fanatical missionaries intent on replacing native society and beliefs with their own Christian model. Any good they did in arguing the Indians' cause was nullified by the damage of their regimented and destructive theocratic regime. After their expulsion, there had followed the forty-year vacuum of the Directorate. As we have seen, Indians under Portuguese control were freed from slavery but were subjected to terrible rule by greedy lay directors. When the Directorate was finally abolished in 1798, most of the former mission aldeias were in decay. There was in prospect no obvious improvement on the discredited system of rule by directors. In this climate, it was remarkable to find anyone devoting his life to the Indian cause.

Many foreign visitors went to see the work of Guy (known to the Brazilians as Guido) Marlière, and they were unanimous in praise of this altruistic man. Marlière's origins are obscure, and both he and his widow refused to discuss them. He was born in France in about 1769 and was an officer in the French army. He evidently rose fairly high, for among his papers was found a letter from Napoleon to the administrators in Versailles, dated 1797. For some reason, Marlière deserted and joined the Portuguese army: he became an alferes (lieutenant) in 1802 and married a Portuguese girl. He was a member of the military force that accompanied the Prince Regent Dom João to sanctuary in Brazil in 1808. He went to Vila Rica (Ouro Prêto) in Minas Gerais in 1811, but was arrested on suspicion of being a French spy; after being taken to Rio de Janeiro, he was released when no disloyalty was proved against him.

The turning-point for Guido Marlière came in 1813, when he was sent to investigate disputes between Indians, missionaries and frontiersmen in northern Minas Gerais. He went to the remote forested parish of São João Baptista do Presidio (now Visconde do Rio Branco). There was friction between Coroado, Coropó and Puri Indians, missionaries who had recently converted these tribes, fazendeiros who were opening farms on the frontier, and gatherers of the medicinal root ipecacuanha. The Count of Palma, Governor of Minas Gerais, issued humane orders to Marlière: he was to hear the Indians' complaints and 'without the use of violence, to ensure that the lands unlawfully occupied by Portuguese intruders be restored to them.' 'Any who persecute, upset or mistreat Indians or destroy their plantations or livestock are to be expelled from the aldeias even if they have title deeds to land there. Any Portuguese declared to be criminals or who traffic in Indian land are to be brought to me under arrest, for me to decide their fate.'

When Marlière fulfilled this mission satisfactorily, he was appointed Director-General of the Indians of the parishes of São Manuel da Pomba and São João Baptista. He started work among the peaceful Coroado and Coropó tribes of the upper Paraíba river. With their help he subdued the hostile Puri. At that time, official policy reflected the hard line laid down in the Prince Regent's decree of 1808. Marlière recalled years later: 'I remember ordering two bandeiras into the forest in 1814 or '15 against the Puri, who were then hostile. The first . . . was composed of Portuguese of the Forest Squadron and Coroado Indians; the second consisted only of Coroado.' Both raids were reprisals for killings of aldeia Indians by the Puri. Marlière soon learned the folly of such aggression, and tried promises of gentle treatment and presents of trade goods; with these he won over the Puri. Peace was made with them, and by 1819 they were settled in two aldeias.

Marlière's obvious affection for Indians and his success in their pacification gained him promotion. In 1818 he was appointed inspector of two divisions of Indians on the Rio Doce; in 1819 inspector of two more divisions; and in 1820 inspector of all divisions of Minas Gerais which contained Indians. By 1824 he was able to report that he controlled seven villages and 4300 settled Indians.

These included Coroado and Coropó, but most were Puri.* In that year, Guido Marlière became Director-General of all Indians of Minas Gerais.

The most serious threat on this frontier came from the Botocudo, the brave and elusive tribes that had been resisting Portuguese expansion for almost three centuries. The generic term Botocudo embraced a number of sub-tribes, notably the Naknyanuk and Jiporok. They spoke their own linguistically isolated language Borun and occupied densely wooded hills that run parallel to the Atlantic coast. They lived between a series of turbulent eastward-flowing rivers – the Doce, São Mateus, Mucuri and Jequitinhonha. Interspersed among them were their enemies the Maxakali and the Pataxó to the north-east.

The tough law of 1808 had damaged many tribes but had had little effect on the Botocudo themselves. A Governor of Minas Gerais declared that 'experience has shown that the Botocudo are savages who cannot be civilised. They are the enemies of other Indians whom they devour. . . . Nor do the Portuguese escape this voracity. The only course to follow is to make them retreat by force of arms into the heart of the virgin forests.' Maria Graham reported that 'several well appointed detachments were sent into different parts of the country for the purpose of repelling Indians, whose inroads had destroyed several Portuguese settlements. . . . Strict orders were given the commanders to proceed peaceably, especially among the friendly Indians; but such as were refractory were to be pursued even to extermination. . . . The party that was sent up the Rio Doce discovered one hundred and forty-four farms that had been ruined by the Indians, and which they restored: they formed a friendly treaty with several tribes of Puri Indians, whom they found already settled in villages, to the number of nearly a thousand.'

In 1819 Guido Marlière took charge of the line of dispirited stockades along the Doce frontier. He decided to end the policy of aggression against the Botocudo. A canoe full of food and tools was sent down the Doce, commanded by a brave sergeant with an interpreter. It soon met a large group of Botocudo, armed and ready to fire their arrows. The canoe approached the bank, making signs of friendship. Hesitant at first, the Botocudo allowed the canoe to land and took its presents; a few warriors accepted an invitation to return to visit Marlière himself. The French inspector of Indians received them with joy and more presents, and it was clear that the Botocudo were eager to end the fighting against Brazilian firearms.

One of the Botocudo envoys was a sixteen-year-old called

Pocrane. Marlière won his allegiance and came to rely on Pocrane as the main emissary and interpreter in contacts with his people. The young Indian was baptised with Marlière as his godfather, and took the name Guido Pocrane. His reward for helping the Brazilians was to become highly civilised. He eventually owned a farm with cattle and wore European clothes. But he also took four wives and could not resist making occasional raids against his tribe's Puri enemies. Guido Pocrane died in 1843, aged forty, a soldier in the Second Division of troops manning this frontier.

Marlière was determined to persuade the authorities to change their policy on the Doce frontier. He succeeded. When in November 1820 the King appointed him inspector of the divisions of soldiers fighting the Botocudo, he was told to try peaceful methods, 'after long experience of failure of methods used to try to conquer and reduce the heathen'. Eighteen months later, Marlière boasted to the King that 'total pacification reigns . . . throughout the Province of Minas Gerais, which obtains a vast income from trade in ipeca-cuanha with the Indians.' In 1824 Marlière sent Guido Pocrane down the Doce to seek out the Naknyanuk Botocudo. He contacted a group of these relatives but had no presents to give them beyond his own knife. He managed to part on amicable terms, and Marlière wrote that 'the civilisation of the Botocudo will no longer be a problem.'

During these years, Marlière rid his command of the most incorrigible Indian-fighters. He managed, instead, to attract a group of dedicated subordinates. One was Captain Gonçalo Gomes Barreto, a fazendeiro who farmed a few kilometres from the main presídio, São João Baptista. This man had a genuine affection for Indians and blacks, and Marlière therefore made him Director of the fort's Indians. But Marlière had to reprimand him for being too lenient to oppressors of his charges: 'you never find occasion to prevent nor punish crimes.' Another helper was Captain Lizardo José da Fonseca, former commander of a military post on the Doce. Fonseca had once been a zealous campaigner against the Botocudo, but he changed completely and became dedicated to peaceful contact. His family wanted to return to the city, but Fonseca was determined to continue his work among the Indians. He built a road down the Doce to a place called Antonio-Dias-Abaixo – which, of course, opened more territory to invasion by colonists.

Marlière wanted missionaries – preferably foreigners – for the Botocudo he was contacting. He relied on them more for their moral influence on both settlers and Indians than for their actual spiritual teaching. He insisted that missionaries learn Indian languages, and hoped to educate young Indians to become missionary priests. Missionaries who could not converse with their charges were 'like a statue in a square which cannot hear and which the people admire but do not understand. . . . The former Jesuits, our masters and models in civilising Indians, were well aware of this essential role – hence their success. But the Jesuit body perished, and with its death the Indians of Brazil reverted to a condition worse than the primitive.'

Marlière's admiration for missionary priests arose from the example of two who had preceded him in contacting the warlike tribes of northern Minas Gerais. The Brazilian mulatto Father Manuel de Jesus Maria had spent forty-four years, from 1767 to 1811 contacting the Coroado and Coropó of the Pomba river. He converted many to Christianity and had them build roads and villages. The other missionary, Father José Pereira Lidoro, was still active when Marlière arrived, working on the conversion of the Maxakali of the Jequitinhonha river. Marlière named him Director of the Indians of that river, and his Maxakali converts were herded into an aldeia of wooden, tile-roofed houses. Marlière encouraged Lidoro, sending him a consignment of '50 men's shirts, 50 women's, 50 pairs of trousers, 50 skirts, 12 ponchos, 12 pairs of scissors, 12 bags of beads, 200 fish-hooks, 12 mirrors, 12 metal necklaces and 200 needles – all taken from the barracks' stores – 50 axes, 500 hoes and 200 knives.' When the settlers, resentful of Lidoro's missionary work, accused him of stealing quantities of supplies destined for the Indians, Marlière wrote strongly in his defence.

Marlière believed in catechism of Indians. He relied heavily on missionaries to pacify them 'by the evangile, the cross and food; but not by guns'. By modern criteria, this was an error. But there were few well-intentioned people other than priests to help him.

Marlière himself was a liberal, almost a free-thinker: he antagonised many by his outspoken criticism of the church. In other respects, too, he was ahead of his time, developing his thought along the lines of the twentieth-century champions of Indians Cândido Rondon or even the Villas Boas brothers. He was totally opposed to attempts to move Indians from their homelands. 'We must renounce absolutely any project to establish settlements composed entirely of Indians unless these are in their native forests. . . . They loathe the plains. Removing them from the forest means removing their lives. Entire bands of Botocudo have died on leaving that habitat.' He did favour settled villages of Indians in their tribal territories, feeling that agricultural training was a necessary prelude to incorporation into Brazilian society. 'Their lives should be made agreeable by means of plantations and other philanthropic benefits.' Once they had learned to feed themselves – through agriculture of the ecologically sound slash-and-burn type – 'teachers of technical trades should be distributed as rapidly as possible among the sons of Indians of all tribes, to teach them carpentry, weaving, metalwork, shoemaking and tailoring'. Marlière persuaded the government to issue large quantities of agricultural tools to the Indians; these were marked with the letter 'I' to denote Imperial service and to prevent colonists from acquiring them. But this was largely in vain, for the settlers did get the tools, stealing or buying them from the Indians for trifling sums or for alcohol.

Marlière developed a fazenda for himself. He called it Guidovalle (Guido's Valley) and employed many Indians on his cotton plantation; but he at least paid them correct wages. After leaving government service in 1829, Marlière retired to Guidovalle, where he remained until his death in 1836. Before that, he had always had Indians living near him at his frontier headquarters. He was sometimes exasperated by them, but knew better than to shut his door or to refuse to share his belongings in the communal tribal manner. In 1824 he wrote in French to the visiting scientist Auguste de Saint-Hilaire: 'I can write very little for I am continually surrounded by Botocudos. If I shut the door they enter through the window. In short, they sometimes irritate me. There are agents to administer what they need but those here want to receive even their food from my own hands! Their impertinence is excessive. They ask me for horses to go to the river port; and at the port for canoes to carry them across the river and from place to place. They have already lost two canoes for which I will have to compensate the owners. But in time, with patience, we will have canoers and farmers: for they are starting to enjoy work.'

When it was necessary to protect Indians, Marlière was determined and outspoken. When a fazendeiro wanted armed guards against Indian attack, Marlière wrote: 'If I were your enemy, I would send you these blood-thirsty guards that you request to kill Indians. Because, for every Indian that dies, a century of revenge will descend on your house. . . . I follow a different course with the Indians. I give them food, some instruction and a paternal kiss. In this way, without deserving it, I see my works blessed by the Indians' god. If you treat them well and do them no harm, you will see how they come to you. As for the use of firearms against them, I would never do this until I had exhausted my philanthropies.' He wrote to the sergeant commanding one of the aldeias, who had been buying ipecacuanha from the Indians at derisory prices: 'You are a shameless thief to swindle poor people to whom you are sent by His Majesty and paid to protect.' On another occasion, Marlière was furious because 'some diabolical Brazilians' had attacked the large Botocudo aldeia Cachoeirinha, killing two Indians. The Botocudo retaliated, shooting two Brazilians with arrows, 'but unfortunately these did not die. If these villains appear here they will be arrested by the Commander of the Seventh Division, and I sincerely hope that they will be punished as murderers and disturbers of the public peace.'

There were many bitter disappointments in the attempt to help Indians in the hostile era of the early nineteenth century. Lethal imported diseases were always a problem. Marlière used to write pro-Indian articles in the local magazine *Abelha* (Bee), in one of which he gave a terrible account of contact with a group of Botocudo: 'In December 1823, Chief Jacú came up the unhealthy shores of the Rio Doce guided by his son Kijame, whom I had sent from this barracks to the Cuieté. He reached Onça Pequena [Small Jaguar] at the height of the rains. His men brought in their bosoms the deadly germ that causes premature death to so many young people! Scarcely had they arrived than all fell ill. The floors of the houses were covered in poor Indians. The store ran out of cloth to cover them, and the surrounding fazendas ran out of chickens to feed them. It was no use.' Chief Jacú, his beloved wife Punang and a young daughter all died. Their son Kijame held his father's body on his knees and intoned the tribal funeral dirge. The chief was buried in a grave dug by soldiers. 'When this sad ceremony was over, Kijame aroused the others from the gloomy lethargy into which they had fallen. He cried to them: "Let us flee!" A thousand arguments could not persuade him to remain. "No," he said, "This place is very bad," and they all left, marching towards Petersdorff. The division commander followed, with animals loaded with food to sustain them, but in vain. The first dead body appeared after a few yards, and it was that of the terrible Kijame with his face turned towards the tomb of his parents. The rest travelled no more than two leagues before they also died.'

Marlière's letters are full of the problems that beset him. The Botocudo were ravaged by smallpox and malaria. His faithful interpreter Norberto, who had done wonders working for him, suddenly took forty pacified Indians from the post of Ramalhete and returned to live in the forests. His troops deserted. There was a lack of doctors and missionaries; failure of supplies; jungle hardships; and constant crimes against the Indians and their families. Alcohol was a constant

1. *Eighteenth-century frontier propaganda: Botocudo massacring settlers and their black slaves.*

2. *Indians resist guns and bayonets with bows and arrows.*

3.   *A family of Botocudo, once the most feared of Brazilian Indians.*

4.   *Spix and Martius watching the Puri dance by moonlight. Prince Wied condemned their inaccuracy describing the Indians' 'ape-like' appearance.*

5. *Indians helping a European traveller.*

10. *The great Paraguayan missions were destroyed during fighting between Spaniards and Portuguese afte expulsion of the Jesuits.*

11. *Spanish and Portuguese troops march into a Paraguayan Guarani mission after the expulsion of the Jesu*

12. *Partly acculturated Apiaká on the Tapajós, 1895.*

Xokleng warriors with the weapons they used to fight frontier expansion in Santa Catarina – a nineteenth-century studio photograph.

14. *Indian domestic servants and washerwomen in Rio de Janeiro in the 1820s.*

15. *A Guaikurú chief using stirrups and a jaguar-skin saddle cloth, 1825.*

worry too. Marlière inveighed against bar-keepers in the frontier towns who made Indians drunk and robbed them. He complained that the chief accountant of Mariana sold liquor licences to all fazendeiros and ipecacuanha-collectors. These then openly sold cachaça in the Indian villages and claimed that Marlière could not stop them.

Parish registers of the period leave no doubt that there was a fearful death rate on this frontier from tuberculosis, smallpox and syphilis. The ravages of disease were heightened by undernourishment. There was little that the authorities could do. They used quinine to lower fevers, applied capivara grease in a futile attempt to build up victims' strength, and burned the clothing of the dead. Syphilis was rampant in the many prostitutes who accompanied Marlière's troops. He mentioned two who were found by a doctor 'with enough syphilis in them to infect any army'.

When Marlière moved on from directing the Coroado, Coropó and Puri aldeias to work with the Botocudo, there was no one to defend those Indians. Marlière wrote to the King: 'As soon as I left that command, there were deaths of Puri Indians and of Portuguese who were their unjust aggressors. . . . There should be a judicial enquiry and the aggressors punished so that a cruel war will not begin again. The Indians once had a tribunal to protect them, but this tribunal ceased. The Indians are unprotected, dead, persecuted, and some are despoiled of their lands. The aggressors excuse themselves by saying that [the Indians] were not baptised – this in the nineteenth century!' Two years later, he protested to the Provincial President that colonists had seized the lands of the Puri, who had fled after they were thrashed. At Marlière's insistence, a judge had ordered an enquiry. 'But what happened? What normally happens in a case involving Indians! These, seeing their plantations devoured by the usurpers' cattle, return to the forest. The robbers then come and claim that there are no more Indians. . . . If Indian property is not respected, what is the use of the promises in the Constitution?' In another letter, he eloquently demonstrated the injustice of all this. 'The Constitution describes a freed slave as a citizen. But it does not yet give such a title to Indians, the owners and natives of the immense land we inhabit! Such is your equity. Brazilians, why do you still continue to kill them like jaguars? All they ask of you is love and liberty.'

Spix and Martius visited Marlière's aldeias and his estate Guido-valle in 1819. They approved of his system of administering Indians, using large landowners as their directors under his supervision. Such directors were supposed to persuade the Indians to settle, to get them to farm the land allocated to them, and to give 'advice and assistance in the state of society which is new to them'. The directors were to protect Indians against 'frequent hateful encroachments of the neighbouring colonists; and in general to take care that they enjoy the protection of the law as free citizens'. In return, the directors received no pay; but they could use Indian labour to clear and work their fazendas. The system was an invitation to abuse. The German visitors found the Coroado living near the presídio (fort) of São João Baptista to be 'very sullen, silent and distrustful, probably because they were afraid that we should take them away for military service'. The Indians hid their women and disappeared into their huts. When Spix and Martius entered, 'the men lay silent, motionless, and with their backs turned to us, in their hammocks. . . . On our asking for a draught of water, one of them turned his head, and pouting out his mouth, and with gestures indicating impatience, pointed to the neighbouring stream.'

Marlière himself was often disillusioned by his difficult task. He wrote to the Provincial President in 1825: 'For thirteen years I have been complaining to successive governments against the killers, oppressors and invaders of Indian lands. I have had nothing but commissions of enquiry which were not verified, and orders that remained unexecuted. Not one single killer of Indians has been hanged!' Three years later, he wrote to Saint-Hilaire: 'I am now 58, have received two wounds, and done forty years of campaigns. . . . I really need some respite, but I seek a successor in vain. I will have to die for these poor people, in their midst.' Marlière was finally pensioned off in 1829 with the rank of colonel, aged sixty and seriously ill from malaria. As soon as he was gone, settlers poured into the valley of the Doce river. He had once listed thirteen villages of Botocudo under his care. Within three years, by 1832, there was not a single Botocudo village left on the banks of the Doce.

Marlière suffered the dilemma that has always confronted any who contact and pacify hostile Indians. The Indianist is well intentioned: he sees a need for the first contact to come from a sympathiser rather than a volley of gunfire. But by winning the friendship of Indians and persuading them to cease fighting, this would-be benefactor merely exposes their territory to invasion. The pressure of the frontier is inexorable. The land-hunger and greed of the pioneers is constant; and colonists breed far faster than Indians.

Saint-Hilaire wrote a sadly prophetic epitaph on Marlière's

efforts: 'He will have obtained a few years of peace for the Indians. But the traces of his noble work will soon be effaced. In the long run it will have produced no result other than accelerated destruction of those whose happiness he wanted to ensure.'

Guido Marlière performed his work throughout the period of Brazil's transition from a Portuguese colony to an independent empire, and he was impressed by the thinking of the man described as the Patriarch of Independence. Marlière wrote: 'I recommend . . . the excellent memorial about the civilising of Indians by . . . José Bonifácio d'Andrada. I have never seen or met him, but I offer him my thanks for his well-directed work, which entirely conforms to my own ideas. For in it he proved that he loved the Indians.'

José Bonifácio (as he is always known affectionately to Brazilians) was born in 1763 to a rich family in the port city of Santos. He was sent to Europe for many years of study as a mineralogist, and found himself in Paris during the heady early years of the Revolution. He became Professor of Geology at Coimbra University in Portugal and a senior official in the Portuguese ministry of mines. It was not until 1819 that, at the age of fifty-six, he finally obtained permission to return to Brazil with his family – after an absence of thirty-six years. He rapidly became influential and, after independence, was the principal figure in the Brazilian government with decisive influence over the Emperor Dom Pedro I.

Soon after his return to Brazil, José Bonifácio travelled into the interior of São Paulo on a journey to examine its mineral potential. It was here that the Europeanised liberal had his first sight of the treatment of Indians. At Itú he saw an expedition being prepared to go and 'buy' Kayapó from the banks of the Paraná. José Bonifácio was shocked. He wrote: 'The fate of those Indians, as well as that of the Guarapuavas [Kaingáng] near Curitiba, deserves our full attention. We must not add to the shameful and inhuman traffic in the sons of Africa an even more horrible trade in unfortunate Indians – whose lands we are usurping and who are [legally] free.'

In the following year, he wrote the first version of the famous essay that so impressed Guido Marlière. *Notes on the Civilisation of the Wild Indians of the Empire of Brazil* was written in October 1821 and submitted to the Cortes Gerais of Portugal in March 1822. José Bonifácio made slight alterations to it, and then submitted the essay to the Constituent Assembly of Brazil in 1823. His was a romantic vision of Indians as noble savages. 'The Indians have few wants. To feed themselves, they find lands that abound in game and fish. They do not need houses, comfortable clothes or the pruderies of our civilisation. In short, they have no idea of property or desire for social distinctions or vanities that are the powerful incentives driving civilised men into activity.'

Sadly, the Patriarch of Independence never saw real Indians or experienced the strength and cohesion of a tribal society. He therefore shared the prejudices of most of his European contemporaries. He blamed Indians for lack of foresight: 'Anything that does not immediately concern their physical survival and few crude pleasures escapes their attention and is of no interest to them. Lacking refined reason, lacking foresight, they are like their companions the wild animals.'

José Bonifácio openly admired the Jesuit missionary system, and urged that Jesuit methods be adapted and perfected. He recommended 'gentleness, constancy and suffering on our part, as behoves us as usurpers and Christians'. He even praised the governors of Goiás for their policy of settling Akroá, Karajá, Kayapó and Chavante in aldeias – apparently unaware of the utter failure of that system – noting that those tribes had been settled 'by freeing prisoners, clothing them, inspiring them, and persuading them to come and live under the holy laws of Christianity.' Like Marlière he believed that missionaries should be given training in Indian language and customs before being sent as parish priests of new aldeias. Because it would be difficult to find candidates for such work, they should be well paid and given the necessary privileges. In attracting new tribes, they should accompany armed but peaceful bandeiras, for the Indians were to be won over with 'presents, promises and good conduct'. Missionaries might also dazzle Indians with displays of electric machines, phosphorus and inflammable gas. Once subdued and settled, the Indians were to be introduced to Christianity only gradually. Missionaries were to instruct them in agriculture and supervise their dealings with the whites to prevent their being cheated. Alcohol was to be prohibited; roads and commerce opened to neighbouring towns; and unsuitable native customs to be replaced by choral singing and gymnastics. José Bonifácio's ideas were thus a mixture of enlightened and conservative thinking, with much that was hopelessly impractical and irrelevant.

José Bonifácio's plan was only one of several about Indians that were submitted to the Portuguese Cortes in 1822. Perhaps because this plan came from a man who, later that year, became one of the architects of Brazilian independence, it was ignored. The Cortes was disbanded in the counter-revolution of 1823. When the same plan was placed before the Brazilian Constituent Assembly (over which José Bonifácio was presiding as its elected President) in that same year, it was received with respect. The Assembly had created a committee to deal with problems of immigration and of the absorption of Indians into Brazilian society. This committee recommended that the plan be published in full 'for presentation to this august Assembly and for the instruction of the nation'. The pamphlet was duly published in a twelve-page edition. But the Assembly could take no action about Indians because it was abruptly dissolved by Dom Pedro in November 1823, when the new Emperor of Brazil asserted his autocratic rule. José Bonifácio and other liberals were driven into exile in France. When the new Brazilian Constitution appeared in 1824, it contained none of these pro-Indian proposals. Indeed, there was no mention of Indians, for the large landowners had won the day.

The Brazilian politician João Severiano Maciel da Costa, later Marquis of Queluz, served Dom Pedro in various cabinet posts and, where Indians were concerned, his influence was reactionary. On 28 January 1824 the Imperial government ordered the provincial authorities of Espírito Santo to grant land to any settlers who wanted it along the Rio Doce. This meant that the Botocudo Indians whom Marlière had pacified were to be swamped by frontier invasion. The same decree called for land to be designated for aldeias for the Botocudo. It justified the removal of their territories with the old hypocrisy: 'Great benefit for civilising the savages will result from the proximity of and dealings and communication with civilised colonists.' This negated Marlière's achievements. Because the Botocudo had ceased to resist, they were to be defrauded of their homelands. Marlière's protests led the Imperial government to issue another resolution telling the provincial authorities to ask the settlers to treat Indians generously. The frontiersmen were to avoid 'any acts of barbarism or vengeance . . . which are totally contrary to the progress and civilisation of the Indians which we are making such efforts to achieve'.

In 1826 Dom Pedro asked the civil and ecclesiastical authorities in each province to send information and proposals for a 'General Plan for Civilising Indians'. Each report was to deal with the character, customs and inclinations of the Indians, as well as lands available for aldeias. The authorities were to try to explain why all efforts to integrate Indians had failed, despite considerable expenditure from the royal treasury.

All the respondents to this enquiry criticised the methods used in instructing and converting Indians. Most approved of the system of Jesuit missionaries. In other respects, the reports differed widely. Some were hostile to the Indians. From the interior of Minas Gerais, the Baron of Congonhas do Campo wrote that the shortage of labour was so acute that it was necessary to seize (enslave) Indians from Goiás. 'Having in mind the pure intentions of His Majesty the Emperor and in fulfilment of his imperial orders, I authorised the magistrate of the district of Itú to carry out this innocent commerce whenever possible. From it we can achieve the civilisation of those green peoples and at the same time acquire labourers for agriculture.' Slaving has been called many things in Brazilian history; but never before 'innocent commerce'.

Most replies were more sympathetic to the Indians, but few were optimistic about their acculturation. From Goiás, Caetano Lopes Gama described past horrors: the cruelty of the first bandeirantes, the venality and incompetence of chaplains, and the disastrous effects of the Directorate. 'The system of trying to subjugate Indians and bring them into our society by bandeira raids should be totally forbidden.' He recommended instead the sending of 'missionaries of probity, prudence and true fervour to propagate the light of the evangel'. The Bishop of Olinda wrote from Pernambuco that the blame for disasters in contacting Indians lay with subalterns rather than with governors. The so-called directors had been men devoid of patience, kindness or charity. The Bishop also called for peaceful and disinterested priests to catechise the Indians. Under a new system based on 'gentleness, prudent liberty, and protection, Brazil would happily see the unfortunate remnant of its tribes emerge from their ancient woods.' From nearby Piauí, Colonel José da Cunha Lustosa wrote that the Cherente would respond according to whether they received truly humane or cruel treatment. 'In my opinion, the reasons that have obstructed their civilization up to now are the ideas they have formed of oppression and enslavement, from the violent invasion of their country, and the bad faith and cruelty with which their various conquerors have treated them.'

Some respondents correctly identified land rights as critically important. The Bishop of Mariana wrote about Marlière's old parish São João Baptista do Presídio: 'On the question of land for aldeias . . . I say only that sufficient lands must be demarcated for their plantations, and these must be forbidden to others who want to settle within them. If aldeias are not established and defended in this way . . . they will soon be deserted and we can never count on peace and harmony.' From Uberaba in western Minas Gerais, a respondent reported that a thousand once-hostile Kayapó were now very quiet and contented. They had been pacified in the classic way, with presents of clothing, tools and trinkets. This official wrote sarcastically: 'A square league [3600 hectares] of land was given to a great family of Indians. Another neighbouring square league was given to one Brazilian from a great family. They are thus being intermingled and civilised without further cost to the nation – although a parish priest should be provided to serve both the Indians and Brazilians.'

Guido Marlière also replied to this questionnaire. He analysed fifty-nine subjects that affected the wellbeing of the Indians – from rum, smallpox, land and missionaries to fishhooks, bananas and native dances. He looked a century into the future and called for a single service to assist Indians, which would enjoy uniform jurisdiction from Minas to the Atlantic Ocean. He insisted that murderers of Indians must be punished. 'What greater enemies does the Empire have than its own subjects who kill or order the killing of peaceful Indians without manifest and prior provocation?' All this advice did little to affect the attitudes of the new empire.

At last, in 1831, after the Emperor Dom Pedro I had abdicated in favour of his six-year-old son, the Regency totally revoked the infamous law of 1808 which had permitted war and enslavement against the Botocudo and the Kaingáng of Paraná. Any Indians who were prisoners or slaves were set free. Indians generally were placed under the protection of justices of the peace and were given the legal status of orphans.*

None of these provisions solved the dilemma of what to do about the Indians. Ever since the first Europeans reached Brazil in 1500 and the first colonies were established there in the 1530s, there had been an insoluble contradiction in official thinking. On the one hand, the Portuguese and later the Brazilian government wanted possession of a country that would be opened up on European lines. They were thus invading the homelands of Brazil's native population. This colonial conquest required immigration by Portuguese or other settlers. On the other hand, Christian and liberal thinking wanted to be kind to the Indians, who were occasionally admitted to be the original and rightful owners of the land of Brazil. But the Indians refused to co-operate with the colonial design. They clung stubbornly to their culture and language and rejected the supposedly superior and desirable European civilisation (which in fact was never really offered to them). They also refused to labour voluntarily as peasants and artisans. And they were pathetically vulnerable to disease, so that their numbers declined catastrophically. They could not change their social systems in order to breed quickly. Those within the Brazilian Empire were thus insignificant: too few and too unsuccessful even to deserve special mention in the Constitution.

When the Portuguese Court reached Brazil in 1808 there were well over two million inhabitants in the colony. By the time of Independence this had probably risen to some two and a half million. Almost two-thirds of this number were blacks and coloureds, of whom the majority were slaves. Over a quarter of the population was white. There were thus less than a hundred thousand pure Indians – under 5 per cent of the people of the new Brazilian Empire. Uncontacted tribes may have had populations of several hundred thousand. But there had clearly been catastrophic depopulation of the native race, which probably amounted to almost two and a half million when the first Europeans sighted Brazil in 1500.*

In 1840 the new young Emperor ended his regency and mounted the throne as Dom Pedro II. He reigned for almost fifty years more and was well loved by his Brazilian subjects. He had a benign affection for Indians, and on paper the legislation during his reign was more liberal than that of the preceding period. But in the rural areas, where it mattered most, all the old mechanisms of domination continued to operate.

The only hope for the Indians seemed to be to return to a missionary regime. In October 1840 the provincial government of Pará sought to create more missions; but no priests could be found to man them. An inspector of missions was appointed and the first and only incumbent was a worthy ecclesiastic called Antonio Manoel Sanches de Brito. He was Vicar-General of Upper Amazonas and priest of the parish of Maués (home of the Mawé Indians). Although known to be zealously pro-Indian he proved to be too busy to make any inspections, and the post was abolished.

It was hopeless trying to find Brazilian priests prepared to abandon themselves among the Indians. The solution seemed to be to import dedicated missionaries from Europe. In May 1840 the Regent had required the government to pay the passages and daily allowances of Italian Franciscan Capuchins. The first six of these missionaries reached Rio de Janeiro in September 1840 led by Frei Fidélis de Montesanto. Twelve more came in 1842, and by 1870 there were forty-five working among Indians and in frontier settlements. Law no. 317 of October 1843 regulated the arrival and distribution of the missionaries throughout Brazil. This policy culminated in Decree no. 426 of 24 July 1845, the main Indian legislation of the Brazilian Empire, often known as the new Regimento das Missões.*

The Indian legislation of 1845 was well intentioned by the standards of its day. It had some positive features. Tribes were to have their territories demarcated in aldeias (reserves) which they would enjoy collectively. Warfare and bandeiras against Indians were forbidden, as was slavery of captives. There was no provision for Indians to be forced to work for private farmers or settlers. Indians were protected in their various activities: there was to be no use of force in their acculturation.

Acculturation was, however, the main objective of this law. It repeated the often stated hope that Indians could be induced to enter Brazilian society as loyal and labouring subjects of the Emperor. This was to be achieved by religious instruction, primary education, and training in agriculture and trades. Commerce with aldeia Indians was permitted only by licensed traders, and any who cheated Indians or corrupted them with alcohol were to be expelled. Individual Indians were to be encouraged to turn to private enterprise. Any who showed themselves particularly industrious could be rewarded with plots of private property within the reserve lands. All Indians were to be given tools, clothes and medicine to stimulate wants and a desire to work.

Despite its liberal veneer, the new Regimento das Missões of 1845 was less benign than it appeared. It tried to bring back two different and potentially contradictory management systems: lay directors with military ranks, and missionaries. Each province was to have a director-general of Indians with the rank of brigadier, appointed by the Emperor. Beneath him, each aldeia was run by a director with the rank of lieutenant-colonel. Large aldeias would also have a treasurer with the rank of captain, a storekeeper, a doctor and a missionary. Conversion to Christianity (and the consequent ethnocide: destruction of native cultures) was a prime objective. This was to be achieved by importing more foreign missionaries, since these were available and seemed more disinterested than their Brazilian counterparts.

The good aspects of the new law were obliterated by various highly damaging clauses. There was provision for forced labour. Indians were forced to work for the state, for pay; for their aldeia, also for pay; and liable to military conscription, provided this did not clash with tribal custom. The director (now known as a *diretor parcial*) could punish aldeia Indians at his sole discretion, with up to six days' imprisonment. Needless to say, the provision for forced labour on 'public works' was open to almost any interpretation and was highly damaging.

Most serious of all were clauses about disposal of Indian land. The provincial director-general of Indians was empowered to suggest moving aldeias or merging them. He could then propose uses for the land 'spontaneously abandoned by the Indians' or from which he had evicted them. He could also decide how much of the aldeia's land the Indians needed. If he judged their population to be too small to use it all, he could rent out other areas for three years at a time. The potential for self-enrichment by the directors and for invasion of Indian lands by settlers is obvious. 'Superfluous' land let out in this way would gradually pass into the permanent possession of the fazendeiros who rented it.

The thinking behind this clause was based on a European fallacy that tropical soils could be used constantly. Unlike rich temperate soils, much land in Brazil is too weak to sustain constant farming. Indian tribes had learned from centuries of experience the virtue of slash-and-burn (or swidden) farming, whereby patches of forest were cleared and then allowed to revert to forest cover after they had been farmed for two or three years. It is also now known how skilfully Indians exploit the woods and forests surrounding their villages. They alter the forest to suit themselves by planting preferred species along their hunting trails. And they gather food, fruits, resins and other materials from the forest without destroying it. This intelligent 'conservation for sustained human development' (the modern objective of the International Union for Conservation of Nature) demanded extensive territories for future use. But such land would be judged to be superfluous and could be leased off by the new directors.

Another assumption underlying these provisions was that Indian populations were shrinking. It was true that, as we have seen, exposure to imported disease, malnutrition caused by removal of hunting and fishing grounds, and forced labour on public or military service did denude tribes under Brazilian Imperial control. But the Indians themselves had no wish to disappear; and some tribes remained reasonably stable in population once they had settled down in the aldeia regime. Regardless of a tribe's size, its lands were usually removed to satisfy a single colonial landowner. As the official from Uberaba wrote in 1826, a great family of Indians was equated with just one Brazilian from a great family when it came to land distribution.

Any merit in the 1845 law was further frustrated by lack of public funds to implement it, and by the usual dearth of good men to administer it. Educating Indians, providing tools and medicine and demarcating reserve lands were all expensive. Such pious hopes failed without financial support. The necessary officials, teachers and tools were never supplied.

The new directors were little better than their Pombaline predecessors in the eighteenth century. The President of Mato Grosso wrote in response to this new law that 'I have been unable to find in this province any person who combines all the desirable attributes for director-general of the Indians. This is because the men of greatest esteem and probity dedicate themselves assiduously to business or live on their estates far from the capital.' Despite this, he nominated two fazendeiros and a colonel of the National Guard for the sensitive job.

The fundamental injustice in nineteenth-century Brazil was that Indians were robbed of their land. Unlike the governments of the United States and of some Spanish-speaking American countries, the Brazilian government did not respect tribes as sovereign peoples. There were no treaties with Indian tribes that acknowledged their possession of substantial homelands; no tribe survived the nineteenth century with large territorial reserves comparable to some in the American middle west. The official attitude to Brazilian Indians was paternalistic and patronising. Carlos Moreira Neto, the modern Brazilian historian of the treatment of nineteenth-century Indians, wrote that Imperial legislation denied the Indians their 'right to aspire to either cultural or political autonomy or to own the lands they had traditionally occupied'.

Just two years after the Indian Law of 1845, the Minister of the Empire (who controlled internal Brazilian affairs) reported that Indian aldeias throughout Brazil were being invaded and despoiled of their land. 'These usurpations are widespread and frequent. They are causing the total abandonment and annihilation of many aldeias.' The loss of territory was irreversible. Should Indians try to recover their land, 'it will be too late, and will bring little or no benefit to Indians currently living in the aldeias.'

The assault on Indian land was effectively codified in the Law of Lands of 18 September 1850. This was the basic property legislation of the Brazilian Empire. It defined private lands as those that were *purchased*, legally owned and occupied. This principle, which guaranteed colonists' rights, 'was of dire consequence for the natives. Indians were generally unable to take the necessary legal steps to consolidate their territorial rights. As a result, many of them came to lose their rights over such land, either from ignorance or inertia, or as a result of the astuteness or wicked initiatives of their neighbours.' This same law awarded unoccupied lands (terras devolutas) to the state. Article 12 empowered the government to use unoccupied lands to create Indian aldeias; and clause 72 of a decree of 1854 went into great detail about how such aldeias should be formed. All this was negated by article 14 of the 1850 law, which authorised the government to sell off unoccupied land.

The result was accelerated selling-off of aldeia lands, especially in the north-east. Only a month after the 1850 law, the Minister of the Empire ordered that Indian lands in Ceará should cease to enjoy reserve status if the Indians themselves had merged with the local population. 'It is judged that [such lands] cannot be applied to the purpose for which they were originally intended . . . since hordes of savage Indians no longer exist there, but only their descendants who have melted into the mass of the civilised population.' By 1856 the Minister wrote in a report that: 'In all regions for a long time, Indian lands have been invaded by powerful persons. . . . All of these now call themselves owners of the lands they have been occupying. . . . Today it would be extremely difficult to ventilate all the issues involved in this business or to resolve them judicially.' This minister's report described the condition of aldeias in many provinces, with countless examples of usurpation. For instance, the largest aldeia in Alagoas, Atalaia, once occupied four square leagues (57,600 hectares); it still contained 1214 Indians, but 'could be considered extinct, with its population intermingled with the other inhabitants'.

The Tocantins–Araguaia Frontier

It was on the remote frontiers that rivalry between settlers and Indians was fiercest. Henry Koster wrote that in the wild interior of Brazil – the sertão – 'the administration of justice . . . is most wretchedly bad: every crime obtains impunity by the payment of a sum of money. An innocent person is sometimes punished through the interest of a great man, whom he may have offended; and the murderer escapes who has the good fortune to be under the protection of a powerful patron.'

The rule of law was even weaker on the frontier itself. There was no legal authority to enforce pro-Indian legislation. The few magistrates were drawn from the colonists and therefore shared their fear and hatred of Indians. But even if a judge had wished to punish crimes against Indians, it was almost impossible to learn about them in the vast, empty interior and there would be no witnesses or police to help the legal process.

The 'frontier' was the limit of settlement and political control by colonists descended from European immigrants, their African slaves, and the acculturated tribes whose territories they had conquered. Beyond lay unexplored forests, campo undergrowth or savannahs. These were the lands of uncontacted or hostile tribes, Indians whose way of life had not yet suffered the impact of alien invasion. Paradoxically, the greater civilisation often lay beyond the frontier, among Indians who were artistically accomplished, skilled woodsmen, and who lived in harmonious societies with long traditions. They had nothing to gain from the tough and uncouth colonial frontiersmen.

At the end of the Directorate, the western frontier ran roughly along the Tocantins, with some penetration to the parallel Araguaia.

From Goiás a road was being opened to Cuiabá, to replace the complicated river route from São Paulo to the Paraná and thence to the Paraguay. There was colonised territory around Cuiabá and Vila Bela, but not far to the north or north-west of them to the Parecis hills. There were a few forts but very little settlement along the Paraguay river and almost no clearings in the vast expanse of dry forests between there and the Paraná. The interiors of what are now the states of São Paulo, Paraná and Santa Catarina, which had been ransacked for Indian slaves by Paulista bandeirantes in the seventeenth century, were covered in forests, which no settlers now penetrated. The extensive dry plains of Brazil's north-eastern sertão – the dusty hinterland of Bahia, Pernambuco, Ceará and Piauí – were occupied by thinly populated cattle ranches. North-west of them, the forested rivers flowing into Maranhão were scarcely penetrated, although a trail was being opened from Maranhão to northern Goiás and the Tocantins valley.

There was thus a main western frontier that roughly followed the edge of the Amazon rainforests from Cuiabá and the Guaporé north-eastwards to Maranhão, although there were large pockets of forests and Indian territory – and hence other frontiers – between that line and the Atlantic coast.

Much of the fighting between Indians and frontiersmen went unrecorded. We know about a few raids and battles only because a literate observer happened to see and write about them. On the northern frontier in Maranhão, the colonists were weak and scattered. Most were poor and culturally backward. They owned a handful of livestock and grew pathetically little on the tracts of land they claimed. Disorganised and lacking social cohesion, they presented little threat to large warrior tribes – the Gamella, Guajajara, and eastern Timbira groups such as the Chakamekra or Pukopye (now generally known as Gaviões).

The normal pattern of warfare in Maranhão would start with an attack or imagined threat by Indians on an isolated farmstead. The colonists would retaliate by organising a bandeira, a posse to launch a raid or surprise attack on the natives. This would take a month or two to assemble and rarely consisted of more than two hundred men, poorly armed and with little stomach for a fight or experience in woodsmanship. They rarely succeeded in inflicting a serious defeat on the Indians, but would eventually resort to treachery, cajoling a tribe with presents and false promises until they could enslave or slaughter it. Otherwise, having failed against powerful and warlike tribes, the bandeira might turn on weaker and peaceful settled Indians in order to reap some spoils.

During the last decade of the eighteenth century, there were a number of bandeira attacks on the Kapiekran (Canela) Timbira, a handsome tribe that lived on the cerrado plateau of western Maranhão. In 1794 there was a raid on the Gamella of Codó, forest Indians living near the lower Itapicurú. This raiding party from Caxias managed to surround the most northerly Gamella village, but the Indians parleyed for long enough to be reinforced by men from another village and the bandeira was forced to withdraw.

The Pukopye Timbira (now generally known as Gavioes) successfully resisted invasion of their lands until the mid-nineteenth century. In 1804 they routed a bandeira under Francisco Alves dos Santos and compelled it to release some Indians it had captured. Ten years later they destroyed Manoel da Assumpção's bandeira: only one wounded man escaped from a contingent variously described as forty or eighty-six. The Indians caught the raiders in a defile when they were trying to storm a fortified village in the Serra da Desordem (Confusion Hills).

An explorer called Antonio dos Reis was the first to descend the Grajaú river in 1811. From hides in the forest the Timbira frequently tried to ambush his boat: he saved himself and his family from their arrows by stuffing the awning of the boat with an armour of thick ox skins. Reis charted over eighteen hundred bends, rapids and straight stretches along the unexplored parts of the river. He then attracted forty settlers to a new village called Porto da Chapada, on the site of the modern town of Grajaú. The Indians were determined to destroy this threat. They managed to kill some local farmers who were defending the area, then they attacked the new settlement, catching its inhabitants off guard and burning them alive in their huts. They also set fire to the boats on the river bank, after removing any salt and food they could carry off and throwing the rest into the flames or into the river. 'This carnage took place in 1814. The only survivors were a girl whom the barbarians took captive and five or six people who were fortunately outside the village at the time of the disaster.'

The men of Pastos Bons (Good Pastures) and of São Pedro de Alcantara (now Carolina) on the Tocantins assembled a punitive expedition, but were ignominiously repelled. Captain Francisco de Paula Ribeiro witnessed the behaviour of this reprisal expedition of 1815 after it had 'shamefully retreated' from the Gaviões and he left the most harrowing and authentic account of frontier bloodshed. He saw the bandeira return to the plains near São Pedro, hoping to imprison some docile Indians. Its victims were the Porekamekra Timbira – a tribe that, only two months earlier, on 30 May 1815, Captain Ribeiro had watched perform a ceremony of alliance with the Portuguese on the banks of the Tocantins. The men and women had formed two columns and paraded before the whites, unarmed and carrying branches as a sign of friendship. 'They were led by their chief Cucrite, a man of medium height, some fifty years old, and whose conduct was not that of a barbarian. They performed their dances and embraced us with much pleasure. They went to rest two hundred yards from our lodging, in an open plain, and stayed there that entire day in the sun, very satisfied and content even though we had nothing to give them other than an ample dinner. They danced all through that night and repeated the same ceremony next day.'

When this tribe heard that there were soldiers of the returning bandeira in the vicinity, it prudently hid its families in the forests. The expedition had some Krahó Indian auxiliaries who could speak Gê to the hidden Porekamekra. The Krahó were ordered 'to shout to them from the hill tops that they should emerge from the thickets in which they were hidden, for the [whites] wanted only peace and friendship and to fill them with good fortune, as they had done the Krahó themselves. The wretched Indians were convinced by the persuasion of their own people, who seemed contented. The less suspicious therefore began to appear and to deliver themselves and their families, a total of 364 souls, to the good faith of this expedition. Imagine their horror, grief and belated regret when they found themselves seized and robbed by the Krahó, their maidens deflowered, and their sons dragged off to be distributed among our men. Some Indians were revoltingly killed on the plain so that their better-looking wives could be raped – and this with the full consent of [our officers] who could have prevented it! Those who could, fled. But they left 164 shackled captives. I saw these enter this town on the 27 July 1815, as sad and downcast as can be imagined at the miserable state to which they were reduced by that horrible treachery – for these were people who had voluntarily sought to become subjects of our august Sovereign. At four o'clock that afternoon, 130 of them were branded with hot metal on their right wrists, just like slaves bought for trade goods on the coast of Africa. The brand was a large O. Naturally, the youngest were destined for sale in the usual manner: they were taken to Pará a few days later in two boats by João Apollinario. The older and unsaleable were condemned to work in private service in the town. I saw that parents could only [bear to] gaze at their children for a moment, when they contemplated the slavery to which their credulity had reduced them. But the tenderness with which they observed them at that moment was so intense that I have retained a very vivid memory of it. I can never easily forget this affair.'

Captain Ribeiro blamed the royal laws of 1808 which permitted enslavement of captured Botocudo. 'Similar events . . . are proof of the appalling abuse that has been made of [these laws], the cruelties practised in their shadow, the greed and evil provoked by them, and the perverse interpretation given to the most pious intentions of the best of monarchs.'

One month earlier, Captain Ribeiro had seen similar treachery on the Mateiro ('Forest') Timbira. This warlike tribe harassed farms and travellers along the road from Caxias to Pastos Bons, west of the Itapicurú in central Maranhão. A strong force from Caxias moved against these Mateiros, but they retreated into impenetrable forests. They were offered 'in the name of our lord the King, our protestations of friendship and promises of good protection for their families, of tools for their farming, of being honoured and considered as free men among us in an egalitarian society, and lastly of an inviolable alliance'.

Some of them accepted these promises, solemnly proclaimed by royal emissaries, which repeated what had been written in many royal edicts about treatment of Indians. 'But, what evil, most abominable evil! The welcome they received was very different from that promised. They were immediately and treacherously put in irons. Lives were taken in cold blood and without cause. Their children, families and they themselves were divided up as perpetual slaves, even being auctioned off in a public sale in that same town of Caxias. They were taken to the cotton gins of local fazendeiros where, tied like galley slaves to their bench and oar, their bodies were roughly lashed to speed up the tasks assigned to them and they suffered appalling hunger.' Much of the tribe escaped. Its survivors took with them a knowledge of the barbaric perfidy of the settlers, and 'have sworn a perpetual and irreconcilable hatred of us'.

The frontiersmen managed to exploit inter-tribal rivalries. The Canela (Apanieka and Rankokamekra or Kapiekran) were another Timbira tribe bitterly opposed to the Mateiros. The Canela had been defeated by the Mateiros and therefore co-operated eagerly in the colonists' expedition of 1815. They then dispersed into roving bands. Some took to killing cattle or raiding plantations: no one had told them not to, and the cattle were very tempting to a hunting tribe. Ribeiro told a terrible tragedy that befell some Canela. In order to stop their depredations, 'they were wickedly summoned to Caxias, which was then aflame with an epidemic of smallpox. They were deceived into thinking they were to be allies in a fictitious war against other Indians. They enlisted promptly, proud to be loyal allies. Once there, they were not given enough food to support their multitude. Instead, they were made to experience a terrible subjection. Some were put in the stocks and they or their wives were beaten, as happened to their chief Tembé. Some even lost their lives. They protested against these outrages and the treachery done to them.'

The Canela 'fled to find safety, but it was too late: for they took their ruin with them in the epidemic of smallpox. . . . In their consternation, these defenceless fugitives were attacked by a force sent against them in their retreat, near a place called São José. Many were left dead on those plains and later served as food for wild beasts and vultures. The disease they carried with them was not fatal to them alone. It spread to all other savage communities of the province and even to our people. . . . But it was principally among the Indians that it caused such horrifying slaughter. It raged for so long that it was still active in October 1817 among those living in the wilds beyond the Tocantins, according to reports that reached us from São Pedro de Alcantara: seven Apinagé appeared near there afflicted by that contagion. It is impossible to give an exact idea of how many thousands perished from it – particularly if you know the extravagant methods by which these brute men attempt to cure themselves: by lying in rivers to cool themselves so that they hardly notice the heat of their fever, or immediately taking the lives of any who show clear symptoms of the disease.'

Ribeiro mentioned two other tribes living near the Itapicurú: 'the Karekateye, today mostly dispersed by the unjust war waged against them in 1814. They had previously asked for peace, but this was denied them in order to enslave them and sell them in the captaincy of Pará. Many were indeed sold there! At the same time the unfortunate Nyurukwaye, a tribe settled to the west of the Tocantins, suffered the same fate.' Ribeiro also told how the Augutge tribe was duped by a bandeira in 1816. Its members were enslaved, some being sold in Pará, others sold to itinerant traders who disposed of them in Piauí. Its chief was hacked to death when he protested against this treachery.

The Brazilian authorities protected their frontiers with occasional forts or stockades. This was the obvious way of asserting colonial authority in distant and sparsely settled areas near the territories of unconquered tribal nations. The Spaniards had such forts on their frontiers, in Mexico, Argentina and Bolivia; the United States had them in its wild west; the British in Canada and on the north-west frontier of India. In 1797 the Portuguese built one such fort or registro, São João das Duas Barras (St John of the Two Bars) at the junction of the two great rivers Araguaia and Tocantins.

A populous Timbira tribe, the Apinagé (or Apinayé) lived nearby in the triangle of land, the mesopotamia between the Araguaia and Tocantins. Although various raiders and missionaries had penetrated the lower Tocantins in the seventeenth and early eighteenth centuries, the first recorded contact with the Apinagé was not until 1774. A traveller called Antonio Luiz Tavares Lisboa found himself surrounded by a crowd of Apinagé. 'In addition to these, there were so many downstream on the beach on the left bank that they looked like regiments in battle order.' Canoe-loads of Apinagé moved across the Tocantins to reinforce those surrounding the Portuguese. There was a skirmish with arrow shots answered by gunfire. In 1780 the authorities built a six-cannon fort called Alcobaça to protect this stretch of the river. The Apinagé were said to be raiding settlers as far downstream as Cametá – for, unlike most Gê-speaking Timbira tribes, they used canoes and could move on rivers. Thomaz de Sousa Villa Real, who descended the Araguaia in 1793, described the Apinagé as powerful and industrious. He recommended alliance with this tribe because its great manioc plantations could be valuable. He thought that they could be won over by kindness and by gifts of metal tools that they coveted. The fort of São João was built in 1797 with a triple purpose: 'to stop gold smuggling, to prevent slaves escaping [upriver] from Cametá to Goiás, and to check the aggressions of the Timbira, Karajá and Apinagé.' For a time, there were friendly contacts between the fort's garrison and the Apinagé. The Indians even travelled down to Belém in Pará to trade their produce for metal tools. But relations then turned sour. Francisco de Paula Ribeiro blamed the soldiers: 'Cruel and unjust violence was done to [the Indians] when they passed through the garrisons of São João and Santa Maria do Araguaia. This turned them into irreconcilable enemies of ours.'

The Apinagé, in common with other Timbira tribes, were and still are strikingly handsome. Many travellers were impressed by their slim, graceful bodies, pale colour, and the perfect figures and beautiful faces of their women. Johann Pohl found these good looks enchanting. 'They are particularly distinguished from descendants of whites by their firm, turgid breasts.' He wanted to take away one girl and her mother. 'This young Indian girl was graced with the most distinctive beauty ... which would have aroused attention in Europe.' Some years later, the magistrate Vicente Ferreira Gomes visited the Apinagé and was romantically charmed by them. 'The ease with which these people generally greet strangers, the goodness with which they treat visitors, their simplicity, ingenuousness, that same state in which the Creator placed them on earth – all this produced a feeling of love, friendship, compassion and interest. . . . One observes nature in all its simplicity: one sees no adornments concealing natural defects, nor artifice or caprice hiding beauty. . . . These people are by nature peaceful, laborious and hospitable. . . . They live in perfect tranquillity and harmony, obeying their chiefs. And yet they all live completely naked!'

In their struggle with the fort of São João, the Apinagé exploited the beauty of their women. The Indians themselves were strictly monogamous once they had married. 'The desire for Indian women by descendants of the Portuguese is one of the main causes for the bloody conflicts between them and the Indians. . . . [The Apinagé] cleverly instruct their women and girls to pretend to submit to the will of the Portuguese and to entangle them until hidden Indians run up and kill them with their clubs. Almost all the men killed by the Apinagé were caught in this way, especially in their attacks on the registro of São João das Duas Barras.'

Father Luiz da Silva e Sousa wrote in 1812 that the Apinagé had been at peace 'but they encountered some men from the garrison of the presídio who were destroying their plantations; so they killed them. As a result, their aldeias were surrounded by the military garrison which even brought up artillery for the purpose, and they were devastated.'

A royal decree of 1811 had ordered that the tribes of the Araguaia–Tocantins should if possible be won over peacefully. This edict admitted that the Karajá, Apinagé, Chavante, Cherente and Canoeiro tribes were hostile because of 'the rancour they preserve from ill-treatment suffered at the hands of some commandants of aldeias. Nevertheless, there is now no alternative but to intimidate them and destroy them if necessary, to prevent the damage they are causing.'

Two years later, the founder of Carolina, Francisco José Pinto de Magalhães, described the Apinagé as a fierce and populous tribe with so many warriors that they had sixteen war chiefs. 'They are in revolt, instigated by Christian deserters from Pará, and we can dominate and exploit these Indians only through war.' Despite such threats and the belligerent royal decree, the Indians won an important victory. On 11 February 1813 an alliance of Karajá, Chavante and perhaps Apinagé managed to storm and destroy the stockade of Santa Maria which had just been built at the head of the main rapids on the Araguaia.* The small garrison of this presídio soon abandoned it. Thirty-eight men, women and children fled down the Araguaia. Some drowned, others died trying to escape across country, and only a few reached the other fort of São João.

In 1817 the Apinagé were struck by smallpox – the same epidemic that had spread westwards from Caxias in Maranhão, destroying countless Timbira Indians. This catastrophe sapped the Apinagé's will to fight. By the following year they were reported to be at peace and helping travellers pass the rapids.

In 1823 the Apinagé lent 250 warriors to a force of frontiersmen and prospectors who were attacking the last outpost of Portuguese royal authority on this frontier. After the proclamation of Brazilian independence in 1822, the Portuguese royalists sent a force of seventy-eight well-armed soldiers to try to stop rebels moving down-river from Goiás to Pará. The commanding officer of this force was Francisco de Paula Ribeiro. His men put up a stiff fight on Botica island in the Tocantins; but they were overwhelmed by the rebel settlers and their Apinagé and Krahó allies. Major Ribeiro tried to escape through the forests. But he was caught, taken to Carolina, and executed by the insurgents whose leader was a rancher from Pastos Bons, José Dias de Mattos, the self-proclaimed 'Captain–President of Independence'. The Indians thus, ironically, helped destroy one of their very few champions.*

The Apinagé were described at that time by Brigadier Raymundo da Cunha Mattos as a powerful tribe with over 4200 people in four villages, two of which were not far north of Carolina.* They continued to be at peace with white neo-Brazilians from that time onwards, and in 1840 were subjected to the ministrations of an Italian missionary. Ignacio Accioli de Cerqueira visited the Apinagé and watched them perform their traditional log-races. One squadron of warriors in the village near Carolina was commanded by a runaway black slave, originally from Angola and with a disc in his lower lip in the Indian manner. This African, Joaquim, 'had fled from Cametá ten years before, and had succeeded in being elevated to that position through his courage, fighting for the Apinagé against the Kamekran'. The Indians admired a man for what he was, rather than for his birth or privilege.

The southernmost group of Timbira were the Krahó, living up-stream of Carolina on the east or right bank of the Tocantins. This tribe had probably once lived farther east on the plains towards the Maranhão–Goiás border. Cattlemen had pushed the Krahó west-wards towards the Tocantins; but the Indians retaliated against ranches being formed along the Balsas tributary of the Sono. Ribeiro described the Krahó as the strongest Timbira tribe, with three large villages. 'In former times, their warfare was felt along the banks [of the Balsas]. Because of it, entire estates were abandoned with many of their inhabitants losing their lives.' In 1809 Captain Ribeiro had taken part in a bandeira organised by a rancher from the Balsas. The raid consisted of 150 colonists and twenty soldiers. It surprised one Krahó village, taking seventy prisoners who were sent into slavery at São Luis do Maranhão. This made the Krahó sue for peace and stop their defence of that frontier. From then onwards they were allies of the Portuguese.

The man who won over the Krahó was Francisco José Pinto de Magalhães, a mining prospector who founded the settlement that became Carolina. He had previously formed an alliance with the Porekamekra group of Timbira on the west bank of the Tocantins. 'There was a mutual understanding, a form of agreement whereby the Indians obeyed [Magalhães] unconditionally and he guaranteed them protection against enemy attack.' In return the Indians helped Magalhães avoid paying royal tax on his mineral finds. But in 1813, after some years of this peace, Magalhães went to Pará for two years and, during his absence, the Porekamekra fell victim to slaughter by 'Ensign Antonio Moreira da Silva, a [mulatto] of some fifty years, tough, active, violent and brave. He was the terror of the Indians of this region because of his toughness, rigour and cruelty. He was constantly fighting Indians, killing hundreds of them on his expeditions without losing a single one of his men.' When Magalhães returned from Pará he found the Porekamekra shattered, frightened and angry with him.

Magalhães brought with him one of the few disinterested Indian-lovers of that period: Placido Moreira de Carvalho. This educated and well-travelled Portuguese had spent some years in England and in 1810 had been captured by Napoleon's troops in Portugal and taken to Paris. Carvalho now devoted his life to helping Indians. Johann Pohl met him at the village of Cocal Grande on the Tocantins in 1818 and was deeply impressed by his goodness. Carvalho's simple house was always full of Indians, whom he treated with a blend of firmness and affection. His fame spread and other tribes wanted to make peace with him. The Apinagé, for instance, sent a delegation to ask Carvalho to move down the river to live with them.

It was after his return from Pará that Magalhaes made an alliance with the Krahó. He had a Krahó girl as his mistress and she helped in the negotiation. Magalhães and other miners settled among the tribe, which fed and looked after them, and the Krahó became Magalhães' willing allies in attacks on other tribes. He naturally claimed that his raids were defensive measures to protect his new colony; but we know from Ribeiro that the motive was to capture slaves for sale in Pará and Piauí. The Krahó chief Apuicrit helped in this. According to Magalhães, 'he magnanimously turned over all his own captives' to him. This evil chief was later poisoned by his own people. Magalhães himself eventually sold even his Krahó concubine in his greed for slaves.

The Krahó were still a strong tribe, estimated at over three thousand in 1815. Captain Ribeiro recalled that his camp was visited by over four hundred of them. 'Since we were few we were not very pleased by this. It was made worse because we had no tobacco to give them, nor salt – something of which they are delighted to receive a handful.' On a later occasion, the Krahó fled into the forests when Ribeiro approached: he had to persuade them that he was friendly. In 1815 Ribeiro found that, after eight years of contact with whites, the tribe had changed very little in its customs, or its 'immodest nudity and inactivity. They want cotton, tobacco and wheat but have not learned to grow any of these. . . . Far removed from anything that could bring true civilisation to them, they continue in the same barbarism with no hope of improvement, hardened in sloth and disorder. . . . The only lesson I have seen them taught was devastation and inhumanity: orders to rob and imprison their innocent compatriots, [so that these could] be sent as slaves to São Pedro de Alcantara [Carolina] and sold for the profit of the seducers!' The provincial government of Goiás sent a priest to convert the Krahó, but he was a disaster. 'The miserable tribes he came to catechise found in him their most formidable adversary. For he was the first to organise illegal expeditions against those wretches, in order to acquire slaves. Finally, after having done no single act of piety appropriate to his calling, he fled to Pará on 12 July 1815, taking some Indians to sell.' Eight years later, in 1823, the Krahó and Apinagé helped their frontiersmen friends defeat Major Ribeiro's contingent of royalist troops. After the execution of their sympathiser Ribeiro, the Krahó moved steadily southwards away from the cattle ranches of Carolina.

   The related Porekamekra were also decimated, soon after settling
in an aldeia with the good Placido Carvalho. 'These poor Indians
were attacked by terrible smallpox: hundreds of them died and many
were left disfigured.' Pohl reported that they also suffered much
syphilis introduced by the miners and cattlemen. Their remnant
seems to have merged with the Krahó. In 1825 Cunha Mattos said
that the latter tribe could muster two hundred warriors from their
three villages. A Brazilian director was sent to live among them in
1830 and was still there when the French scientist the Count of
Castelnau visited them in 1844.

The name Chavante struck terror on the Brazilian frontier from the
1750s to the 1950s. There were originally three main groups of Gê-
speaking Chavante: the Akwê, divided into what are now the
Chavante and the extinct Chikriabá, the Cherente, and the Akroá.
We have seen how the Chikriabá and Akroá accepted settlement in
eighteenth-century aldeias. These two groups vanished long ago as a
result of their accommodation with the whites. The Cherente
occupied the right or east bank of the Tocantins, upstream of the
Krahó. And the Akwê–Chavante, who had briefly accepted settlement
in the Goiás aldeias in 1788, separated from the Cherente in the early
nineteenth century and began a westwards migration. By keeping
west of the colonial frontier and by remaining fiercely warlike, these
Akwê–Chavante survived intact until the mid-twentieth century.
   The split between Chavante and Cherente seems to have occurred
between 1800 and 1820. Disillusioned by their experience of a Portuguese aldeia, the Chavante crossed the Tocantins and thus escaped
colonial pressure. The Cherente stayed on the east bank. Because
the Tocantins was an artery for colonisation, the Cherente were soon
hemmed in by settlers and had to accommodate themselves to white
rule. The Chavante, by contrast, moved westwards and by the 1860s
were far away beyond the Araguaia in eastern Mato Grosso. When
the anthropologist David Maybury-Lewis was with the modern
Cherente in 1955 they told him that they regretted their decision to
remain on the Tocantins. 'Perhaps if we too had fought the whites
and refused to accept them . . . perhaps then we would now be strong
like the Chavante. We would have our own lands and the white men
would fear and respect us. But we made peace, and look at us now.'
   Johann Pohl told how the Akwê–Chavante had been abused and
brutalised in the aldeia of Carretão or Pedro III. Realising that the
promises made to them in 1788 were a sham, they escaped and
returned to their former nomadic life in the wilds – but with bitter

memories of their experiences in the Goiás aldeia. In 1856 a missionary accompanied by a few acculturated Chavante made contact with a hostile group on the Rio das Mortes, west of the Araguaia. The missionary explained through interpreters that he desired peace, but an old Indian 'replied that Christians are very bad. When [the Chavante] were at Carretão they had suffered torments, with ferules, stocks, chains, whips and collar shackles.' These outrages had taken place seventy years previously; but their memory still rankled. Because of them, the Chavante became avowed enemies of all whites. They destroyed many frontier farms and struck terror into the settlers.

There was even greater fear of another tribe which was thought to live east of the Tocantins, near the Chavante and Cherente and close to the settlements of Goiás. This fierce and elusive tribe was called Canoeiro ('Canoers') because it moved swiftly along the rivers – unlike the Timbira, Chavante, Cherente and Krahó, who were superb runners but unskilled and ill at ease on the water. One theory was that the Canoeiro were Tupi-speaking Carijó who had been brought from São Paulo as forced labourers by seventeenth-century bandeirantes, and had escaped and settled on this frontier. They were particularly dangerous because of their knowledge of European fighting methods and their implacable hatred of their former oppressors.

The Canoeiro were blamed for having destroyed early ranches along the Tocantins. A fourteen-boat expedition against them in 1789 caused great slaughter, but 'this tribe resisted with distinction: even the women and a great mob of wild dogs they brought with them joined in the fighting.' They fought with bows and arrows and long pointed lances and were 'a most cruel and bellicose tribe which does not know how to flee, resisting until death in combats'. Being so resolute themselves, the Canoeiro never spared or pardoned their enemies. They also enjoyed raiding cattle and had a taste for horse meat. Their warlike reputation earned the Canoeiro a mention in the Prince Regent's royal order of 5 September 1811. They were one of the tribes of whom he wrote: 'There is at present no alternative but to intimidate and if necessary destroy them, to prevent the damage they are causing.'

Johann Pohl witnessed a bandeira against the Canoeiro when he was on the Tocantins in 1819. There had been extensive preparations for this reprisal expedition, which the Governor of Goiás had authorised only reluctantly: 'in his opinion, the murdered settlers had provoked their horrible fate by their rash conduct, which irritated the Indians and led to fighting.' Each frontier district provided food, money and men for the campaign. 'But when it came to seriously forming the troop, the courage with which the fighting youth had once appeared to be inflamed disappeared completely.' Many young men fled into the forests to avoid fighting the dreaded Canoeiro. The expedition was led by a sickly old man with a reputation for being timid, and for three months his men wandered aimlessly through the forests, suffering hunger. On the return journey, they saw a trail and followed it to an Indian village, which they surrounded. But its chief – a proud old man who had once lived among the colonists of São Paulo and had been baptised – refused to consider negotiations. 'To this the commander of the bandeira, Major Joaquim Pereira said: "Then you will all die!" To which this Indian shouted, "And you, too!" Scarcely had he spoken these words than he was hit by a shotgun. The bandeira then opened fire on the palm-thatch huts and set them alight. It killed all the Indians who tried to flee from the huts, by sword or shot, without compassion, so that only two escaped. Six children and one old woman were taken prisoner. . . . This victory, shamefully achieved, in no way exterminated the Canoeiro tribe, for most of its men were away from the village raiding. They will certainly avenge themselves for this business in the future.'

The Imperial legislation of 1831 put a stop to the enslavement of Indians captured in punitive raids. There was thus even less incentive for colonists to risk their lives on these dangerous and brutal expeditions. But in practice, the law was often flouted on the remote frontier. In January 1830 the Cherente had attacked the edge of Pôrto Imperial (now Pôrto Nacional), killing a young man and destroying cattle and other goods. They then attacked Pontal, killing the justice of the peace and some of his household. A punitive raid caught the Indians, releasing thirteen of their captives and capturing nineteen Indian children. The Judge of Orphans of Pôrto Imperial did nothing for the welfare or education of these children: he simply distributed them as servants in colonists' households. There were more raids by the Cherente and fruitless counter-attacks by the settlers. Similar actions took place against the fiercer Canoeiro around Amaro Leite and São Felix.

In 1836 the provincial government of Goiás (since 1834 run by an assembly and annually elected president) sent a force of 271 soldiers to attack the Chavante, Cherente and Canoeiro – there was evidently confusion about the whereabouts and identity of the three tribes. The campaign was a fiasco. As the President complained, 'The disunity of its commanders, the insubordination of the troops, and principally the lack of interest of each man in the success of the expedition, caused the frustration of such a sumptuous and expensive bandeira. All it did was to burden this province with fruitless expense, and give the savages a very unfavourable idea of our courage.'

Two years later, the President of Goiás spoke of the 'terrible aspect' of the three tribes along the Tocantins. 'Instead of abating them, the campaign of 1836 only encouraged them in their hostilities. Twenty-two people have been killed, cruelly tortured by those inhuman barbarians and fourteen have been carried off as prisoners, possibly to be victims of greater atrocities. It causes grief: one cannot hear such horrible events without trembling. These three tribes seem to have planned to finish off the inhabitants of Carolina, Pôrto Imperial, Natividade and Amaro Leite [along the Tocantins]. There is no security and almost no hope for these unfortunate settlers – who are themselves partly to blame for the evils they suffer.'

By the 1830s the Krahó, Apinagé and Timbira had ceased to be a military threat and as a result their lands were being invaded by cattle ranchers. Although all three tribes still exist, they have never succeeded in regaining territories lost to them at that time. The Cherente were soon to surrender and be engulfed in the same way. The Chavante and Canoeiro alone continued to fight. They were wise to do so. As Johann Pohl wrote: 'Had the Canoeiro not been so cruel (for they never spare a Christian) they would long ago have been exterminated, dispossessed or enslaved.'

In 1842 a number of travellers on the road near Pilar were killed in Indian attacks. The Canoeiro were blamed, and the authorities sent guns and ammunition to a local major to organise yet another reprisal raid. The Vice-President of Goiás declared in a speech: 'I am convinced that the greatest benefit that could be done for the province of Goiás, which was once so flourishing, would be to disinfest it of the savage Indians who annually commit the cruellest hostilities. These Indians are *irreconcilable*. . . . I must speak clearly, gentlemen. It is necessary to strike hard against all Indians who attack us, but to give assistance to those who live at peace with us.' This represented a return to the hard policy of frontier war.

When the Count of Castelnau wanted to travel down the Araguaia in 1844, the President of Goiás consulted military commanders who had led expeditions against Indians. It was decided that he might attempt the descent, which had been interrupted for many years because of attacks by Chavante and Canoeiro. Castelnau first visited the old aldeia of São José de Mossâmedes and found it totally abandoned. Its lands were overgrown by forest and the barracks roof had collapsed. Farther north, prettily situated above a stream, was Carretão. The place built for the Chavante in the eighteenth century now contained only a few Christian members of the tribe, wearing white cotton trousers and loose shirts, led by a powerful and respected old lady, Dona Potencia, and by a chief whom the French described as 'a sort of old monkey wearing the uniform of a Portuguese officer: he dragged behind him an immense rapier.' It took three Indians to draw this rusty sword to show the visitors. The Indians of Carretão performed a spirited dance around a fire that night, but the atmosphere was 'extremely lazy' and demoralised. Castelnau blamed the mission's decline on disease, the employment of Indians as muleteers for passing caravans, and dispersal of the inhabitants in disgust at the absence of missionaries.

Farther down the Araguaia, the new aldeia of Salinas on the Crixás–Mirim was still quite flourishing, with 180 pure Chavante who were largely unacculturated and therefore most hospitable. Descending the great river, the French expedition had many agreeable encounters with the Karajá. There was much trading between the visitors and this large riverine tribe; and Karajá helped guide Castelnau's men through the rapids. The Frenchmen were impressed by the villages they saw – the largest with fifteen hundred inhabitants – and by the fine plantations that surrounded them. The Karajá grew cotton for their women to make into hammocks. Although one chief had a uniform and gun taken from Brazilian army deserters, there was almost no evidence of trade with frontiersmen. The French reckoned that they were the first white men to visit the capital village, where they were entertained by magnificent dances. Some Karajá wore the famous conical straw masks that covered the dancer from above his head to the ground. Castelnau praised the 'gentleness and even timidity of these Indians: the mere sight of firearms made them tremble.'

The atmosphere on the Tocantins was very different to that on the uncontaminated Araguaia. The fort of São João das Duas Barras at the junction of the two rivers was manned by thirty soldiers under a brutish old lieutenant, who struck the expedition as cruel, base and arrogant.

The French were shocked by what they saw farther up the Tocantins. The frontier town of Carolina was abandoned to nights of orgies, with lascivious dances to guitar music and the entire population corrupted by a handsome young army captain who commanded its garrison. The people of Carolina spent their days in drunken sleep. This debauchery had affected the nearby Krahó; Castelnau wrote that 'apart from some good qualities, this tribe seemed to us completely demoralised and abandoned to drunkenness.' Four years after the visit by the French expedition, an Italian missionary, Friar Rafael of Taggia, moved the Krahó up the Tocantins to the mouth of the Rio do Sono – where they are still located. The move was intended to rid Carolina of the Krahó, whose land was wanted by ranchers. It was also to place them as a buffer against the powerful Chavante and Cherente living to the south.

At the mouth of the Manuel Alves, Castelnau met a fazendeiro called Colonel Ladislao who claimed an immense ranch of thousands of square kilometres of former Indian territory. Not surprisingly, the Indians had been killing his cattle and attacking his retainers. He had organised a reprisal raid. 'The government does not get involved in such matters, so that frontier settlers have to organise their own bandeiras or else perish to the savages' clubs.' His thirty men had surprised a Chavante village, taking fifty-one captives and leaving many dead. The prisoners had been divided among local farmers as slave labour – in flagrant violation of imperial law.

As the French expedition moved southwards up the Tocantins, they found the settlers in constant fear of Indian attack. The frontier population was everywhere declining and colonists were moving into towns to avoid massacre. There were particularly lurid stories about the Canoeiro, who were most feared. It was said that, unlike other tribes, the Canoeiro tortured their victims, by tying women in front of canoes, forcing them to eat their children, and other fantasies. Even in the presidential address, there were references to Canoeiros' imagined cunning, their fluency in Portuguese, and even ability to mimic Christian prayers. It was said that when a bandeira was massacring a group of Canoeiro on 8 September, one old Indian woman shouted at her attackers: 'Ah, you Jews, killing people on the day of Our Lady!' Closer to Goiás itself, the French saw fine orange plantations full of unpicked fruit, frequent blackened remains of farms, and some ruins still containing skeletons of their occupants.

The next President of Goiás, J. Ignacio Ramalho, was unusually intelligent about Indian affairs, recognising the futility of retaliatory raids. The destruction of frontier towns was due not solely to Indian attacks, but also to 'the ineffectual methods by which we attempted to domesticate [the Indians]. Far from achieving their intended purposes, these have made them irreconcilable enemies of the civil-

ised classes.' He opposed movements of Indians from their traditional homelands to distant aldeias. He also realised the futility of
rapid integration. 'One cannot obtain a sudden change in their
customs or subject them to work, when their customs are different.'
He wanted gradual, imperceptible change in aldeias created inside
tribal territories. Therefore in 1846 he founded Santa Maria do
Araguaia and other aldeias along the Araguaia, hoping that the
Karajá and Chavante would be attracted to such places peacefully.
'They will gradually convince themselves that our civilised race does
not want their destruction but rather their wellbeing. They will
readily develop needs that will oblige them to adopt a social life in
order to satisfy these needs.' Although the aim was still to undermine tribal culture, the methods were at least more benign. President Ramalho declared: 'I do not attribute the ferocity of the Indians
to their nature or to the barbaric customs seen among them. It is due
to bandeiras and other acts of violence whose sole purpose was to
bring them to our society by terror.'

The new gentler policy had some success from the authorities'
point of view. Newly introduced Italian Capuchin missionaries
founded missions on the Tocantins and Araguaia. But the frontier
was not entirely peaceful. There were occasional skirmishes with the
Chavante near the Araguaia, and with Indians thought to be
Canoeiro on the Tocantins. As usual, the tribes were acting largely in
self-defence – to protect their lands from invasion. A more bellicose
president of Goiás declared in 1861 that the peaceful Karajá 'may
appear domesticated . . . but they are profoundly deceitful: they lose
no opportunity to destroy any establishments that are founded in the
territory they inhabit.'

In the following year a future president of Mato Grosso, Dr José
Viera Couto de Magalhães, travelled down the Araguaia. He visited
Leopoldina, a town of thirty houses that had been founded in 1850,
destroyed by Indians three years later, and refounded on another site
in 1856. Farther downriver and to the east along the Tocantins,
frontier pioneers were still terrified of the mysterious Canoeiro.
'When the Canoeiro strike, destruction is certain, for they do so only
after choosing an opportune occasion. . . . These savages seem to be
dominated by some profound hatred against the white race: they
persecute it incessantly and give no quarter.' The Canoeiro were said
to be highly disciplined, preferring death to surrender or settlement
among the whites. They used effective weapons: metal-tipped
arrows, captured swords, daggers and bayonets, and their own heavy
wooden clubs hurled at the end of cords. All northern Goiás was in
ruins from Canoeiro attack. Couto de Magalhães saw the extinct

camp of Tesouras, whose inhabitants had been killed and their town burned. The sertão of Amaro Leite, which had once had three thousand settlers, had been deserted for years. Once-rich cattle lands of São Felix, Cocal, Agua Quente and Amaro Leite were 'all reduced to ashes by them, besides Crixás and the town of Pilar, which were decimated'.

Mystery surrounded the tribe which was preventing Brazilian expansion so successfully. Couto de Magalhães thought that they were descendants of runaway Carijó, but others wondered whether attacks by the elusive Canoeiro were not in fact done by the Chavante or riverine Karajá. The German anthropologist Paul Ehrenreich, who wrote an authoritative summary of Brazilian tribes in 1891, dismissed the notion that the Canoeiro were Tupi or even Bororo. Nothing had been heard of the Canoeiro for twenty years, and Ehrenreich therefore assumed that they were a group of Akwê–Chavante.*

And yet, as recently as 1974, there were contacts with an isolated Tupi-speaking group known to modern Brazilian Indian authorities as Avá–Canoeiro. These live on the watershed between the Araguaia and Tocantins, east of the southern tip of Bananal island. The tribe that fought so brilliantly from the 1780s to the 1860s may thus have survived, hidden in this remote mesopotamia.

11

The Bororo

From Goiás, the nineteenth-century frontier swung westwards to Cuiabá in Mato Grosso. It roughly followed the arc of the central Brazilian shield, an ancient geological formation that is the watershed between the Amazon and Plate–Paraná basins. To the northwest stretched the mighty Amazonian rainforests, which formed a natural barrier to European expansion and a sanctuary for forest tribes. The lands of the central plateau were less densely forested, usually covered in campo or cerrado undergrowth on sandy soils, or dry mato woods as opposed to mata rainforest, and were thus suitable for cattle ranching. There was desultory pressure to open this ranching frontier in the nineteenth century, but its great distance from the cities of the Atlantic seaboard and Brazil's small population meant that only a few hardy pioneers braved Indian hostility in this part of Brazil's wild west.

There was a more active frontier around Cuiabá, because this remote place had been the focus of a gold-rush in the 1720s and a small but prosperous town had existed there ever since. During the Directorate there was an attempt to open a riverine route between Cuiabá in Mato Grosso and the towns of the Amazon and Pará. One such route was along the Guaporé–Mamoré–Madeira rivers, and the stone fort of the Príncipe da Beira was built on the banks of the Guaporé to defend this remote river against Spanish invasion. The fort still stands, a white elephant in the midst of endless forests. Near the source of the Guaporé, there was a short-lived gold-rush at Vila Bela, now the dusty frontier town of Mato Grosso City.

The dominant tribe around Cuiabá and Vila Bela was the Bororo, with its own Bororo language unconnected to the main linguistic trunks of Brazil – Tupi, Gê, Aruak and Carib. The Bororo were divided into two groups, living west and east of the Paraguay–Cuiabá river line. To the west were the Campanha (Plains) Bororo and the Cabaçal Bororo – the former on the plains near the Jauru headwater of the Paraguay and the upper Guaporé river, the latter north of the Jauru along the Cabaçal (Gourd-tree) river. To the east lived the Bororo who called themselves Orarimugu-dogue (Speckled-fish eaters) but whom the Brazilians knew as Coroado, because they piled their hair in crowns on top of their heads. These eastern Bororo lived on a forested plateau between the São Lourenço and Vermelho (Red) tributaries of the upper Paraguay and the Garças (Herons) source of the Araguaia. Their territory thus straddled the land route that was being opened between Goiás and Cuiabá.

By the early nineteenth century, the descendants of those Bororo mercenaries who in the early eighteenth century had attached themselves to the discoverer of the Cuiabá gold-field, the handsome and dashing bandeirante Antonio Pires de Campos, were still living in southern Minas Gerais. They were contented enough in their aldeias, but were heavily intermarried with black slaves by the time that Baron Eschwege and Saint-Hilaire visited them.

Other Bororo were less friendly to white colonists. Towards the end of the eighteenth century, we read in the annals of Mato Grosso about a dismal series of punitive raids against Bororo. In 1779 a bandeira of eighty men marched against the eastern Bororo near Cuiabá. It captured two hundred Indians, but most of these managed to escape after killing some of their captors: the raiders returned with a haul of only five men, eight women and eight children. Similar expeditions marched against the Cabaçal Bororo near Cuiabá and Jauru in 1780, 1781 and 1796.

These punitive raids had the desired effect. In 1797 four emissaries of the Aravira Bororo who lived along the Cabaçal river appeared at Vila Bela to seek friendship. The Governor of Mato Grosso had invited them, 'but they came full of fear despite his presents.' The ensuing peace lasted for twenty years, but in 1815 and again in 1818 we read of bandeiras against the Cabaçal Bororo because of their disruption of the Cuiabá–Vila Bela road near Jauru. By now the southernmost Bororo, the Campanha group, were on peaceful terms with the Portuguese, and the Cabaçal group were generally docile. Only the warlike eastern Bororo remained implacably hostile.

In January 1827 one of the most distinguished and eccentric expeditions to central Brazil reached Cuiabá. This was a grandiose Imperial Russian scientific expedition, led by Baron Georg Heinrich

Langsdorff, a German medical doctor and naturalist who had been in the service of the Russians for some twenty-five years. The young Langsdorff had been a naturalist on the Russian voyage of circumnavigation in 1803–6. After working in the St Petersburg Academy of Sciences, he was sent by Tsar Alexander I to be the first Russian Consul-General in Rio de Janeiro, at the time when the Portuguese court was in Brazil, and Russia and Portugal were allied against Napoleon. For seven years from 1813 to 1820 Langsdorff was a popular diplomat in Rio de Janeiro: he was host to every visiting scientist and frequently made collecting excursions with them. He then formed the idea of a great scientific expedition into the interior and persuaded the Tsar to back it. Langsdorff gradually assembled a talented team of Brazilian, German, Russian and French naturalists and artists.

After years of preparation, the expedition finally left São Paulo in 1826, sailing in a flotilla of seven boats and canoes flying Imperial Russian flags. Langsdorff chose the old river route to Cuiabá – a difficult voyage full of wild rapids and infested with mosquitoes. It took seven months to cover this journey of over three thousand kilometres and 114 rapids. Most of the scientists and artists were in their twenties, and some disliked their elderly leader, now aged fifty-two. Some of the young scientists accused him of being preoccupied with a blonde German girl he had taken with him. The French artist Hércules Florence accused Langsdorff of abandoning himself to sensual pleasures in the free-wheeling frontier town of Cuiabá. These debauches were said to have aggravated incipient madness.

A year spent at Cuiabá gave the expedition's members time to make excursions and visit Indians in the vicinity. Hércules Florence and Adrien Taunay went on one such trip to the huge Jacobina fazenda, the richest in the province with two hundred adult and sixty child slaves. During their visit, the owner invited a group of Bororo to a meal. The two young French artists eagerly painted these scarcely contacted Indians. Their delicate paintings of Bororo and other tribes encountered by the Langsdorff expedition are the finest paintings ever done of Brazilian Indians. Since neither artist had had academic training, their work was wonderfully vivid and highly accurate. They faithfully portrayed Indian bodies, with their tapering limbs and stout chests, and even the Indian manner of standing with feet sometimes turned inwards. The accuracy of their ethnographic observation surprised later observers: their paintings of artefacts, ornaments and huts were so precise that they form an important record of the society of this lost western branch of the Bororo.

The Jacobina fazenda had been carved out of Bororo territory. Ten years before the expedition's visit, the Plains Bororo had been raiding Jacobina and had killed eleven black slaves. In 1816 the fazendeiro Lieutenant-Colonel João Pereira Leite asked King João VI for permission to repel the Bororo by force, and this was granted. During a six-year war, Leite's men killed 450 Indians and 'he seized fifty prisoners who were more or less enslaved for work on the fazenda, mainly tending cattle.' The fighting ended only in 1822 when Leite's men captured the Bororo chief. Leite won the friendship of his prisoner, had him baptised with his own name, and acted as his godfather. The Indians explained that they attacked only blacks, whom they considered evil and unlike ordinary men. The chief promised to return with his tribe after two moons, and he did. The group had remained friendly ever since.

Colonel Pereira Leite 'personally undertook their civilisation. He succeeded to such an extent that he employed the men and boys in field labour, and he practised the *jus primae noctis* with the feminine sex.' The parents of Bororo virgins were rewarded with presents by the colonel. 'They rapidly became accustomed to this fatality and kept their daughters in order to deliver them to that minotaur of the region. For they were punished if they permitted their daughters to sleep with any man before Colonel Pereira Leite had taken his tribute.' Whenever these Bororo visited his fazenda they were given food and particularly cachaça rum to which they became addicted. Bororo women responded to fazenda work better than the men: for in the tribe it was women who tended the crops after their men had felled the forest. The women seemed pleased to undergo a form of Christian conversion and to wear dresses.

Florence and Taunay were impressed by the appearance of the Bororo, a tribe famous for the beauty of its feather ornaments and the handsome stature of its men. A file of Bororo appeared at the fazenda, blowing a cow-horn trumpet. The naked men were tall and robust, with ferocious expressions. Their long black hair hung far down their backs, or was piled in a thick spiral on top of their heads with a plume of hair hanging from this topknot. They wore superbly artistic headdresses of feather diadems and bright feather vizors with friezes of jaguar claws and teeth around the brims. The men had only penis sheaths, with their prepuces tied to a cord belt; but the women wore broad bark girdles so tight that their flesh bulged above and below these belts and their bodies seemed deformed by them. One old woman's arm was wounded by gunshot from the years of fighting. The chief alone was dressed, in badly torn trousers, shirt and uniform jacket. The group of Indians was plied with cachaça, after which they formed a circle to perform a drunken dance. These western Bororo are now extinct, apart from the isolated Umutina contacted in recent years, whose women still wear the tight bark girdles.

At the end of 1827 the Russian expedition finally marched north from Cuiabá to the frontier town of Diamantino, the scene of a diamond-rush. Malarial fevers were raging at Diamantino, and Langsdorff and other members of his team were soon infected. In April 1828 the expedition embarked on the Arinos river and reached a village of peaceful Tupi-speaking Apiaká Indians. Langsdorff decided to impress the natives when he saw that the Apiaká chief had a Brazilian army uniform and helmet. Florence wrote that 'this caused Mr Langsdorff to put on his uniform of Consul-General of Russia, with a plumed hat, sword at his side, and decorations.' The amiable Apiaká shouted with delight, to welcome the travellers and at the sight of the Russian diplomat in all his finery. Langsdorff noted in his diary that he gave presents to the chief. 'In order to flatter his self-esteem, since he appeared before us in full uniform, I ordered the hoisting of the Russian state flag and put on my full-dress coat, cocked hat and small sword. All these made a strong impression on the people.' This was a perfectly normal gesture in such a contact between two alien cultures. But Langsdorff's detractors mocked it. Alfredo d'Escragnolle Taunay, a distinguished Brazilian historian and nephew of the artist Adrien Taunay (who drowned on the Langsdorff expedition), wrote that an Apiaká girl borrowed the Russian diplomat's magnificent consular jacket and ran off with it into the forest. 'The victim began to run like a desperado after his dress coat, in the utmost and grotesque fury.' The expedition spent two days at the Apiaká village trying to recover its leader's uniform.

The Apiaká made a very favourable impression on the visitors. The men had good physiques and bearing, with their bodies embellished in black and red painting, and clan figures of animals, fish and people tattooed on their faces and limbs. The women were pale and pretty: Florence thought that 'some of the younger ones almost resemble women from southern Europe.' The Apiaká paddled fast and dextrously in their bark canoes. Near the village was a fish trap from which the Indians dived each day and brought up enough fish to feed the community. They were skilled potters, and vessels made by the Apiaká were so fine that they weighed half the European equivalent. Their basketry and hammocks were likewise excellent.

When the Portuguese first descended the Arinos–Tapajós in the 1740s, settlement was prevented by the 'valiant and terrible Apiaká tribe'. But this hostility changed. When a group of explorers was sent to open a navigable route down these rivers in 1812, the Apiaká 'received us with pleasure mingled with fear. They at once lost this fear when they saw the kindness we did them; we gave them axes, machetes, knives, mirrors, beads, fishhooks, tobacco and some clothes. They accepted it all very happily, and responded with pieces of forest pig (peccary), manioc flour and some bows and arrows.' These travellers praised the courtesy, intelligence and cleanliness of the Apiaká. The tribe remained firm friends and allies of the Portuguese; its territory was a safe haven in forests occupied by hostile tribes, and its brilliant paddlers guided many travellers down the rapids of the Arinos and Juruena. The Apiaká also gathered large quantities of medicinal sarsaparilla for the Brazilians.

Hércules Florence was enchanted by his sight of Apiaká society. He reacted in the same way as the Portuguese on first seeing Brazilian Indians in the sixteenth century. He marvelled at the virtue of this uncontaminated people, comparing these noble savages unfavourably with his own sophisticated civilisation. 'One can say the same of their society as of their nakedness, food, etc., when comparing it to that of our people. Everything among them is simple; but nothing is repellent. They are naked; but they never wear frills or dirty or ragged clothing. Their bodies are always clean. . . . They do not know the great principle of property. There are no robbers or murderers among them, no poisoners, or cheats or pilferers – none of the moral evils that afflict civilised men.' But the French artist noticed one ugly legacy of contact with passing neo-Brazilians. He observed that Apiaká women were well treated and that married couples were very faithful. 'As among civilised peoples, there are however women who belong to no man. But there is this difference: since these women have no clothes or artifices they leave visible to all the tragic presence of syphilis with which strangers have infected them.'

Langsdorff's expedition suffered terribly when it went on downstream in 1828. There were losses of canoes and men in the rapids of Salto Augusto. Langsdorff's malaria began to affect his sanity. He wrote pathetic entries in his diary: 'As to what happened on the 18th, I know nothing. I fell into a delirium. I was not conscious of what I did.' And two days later: 'Again a two-day attack. Two days passed unhappily! . . . I did not think that I would endure yesterday.' On 13 May he wrote, 'I was without memory and did not and do not know what took place.' On the 16th: 'Weak in body and soul, I sit here and the only thing that can be said is that I live.' Four days later, Langsdorff became totally deranged and ceased to lead the expedition.

The scientists reached the Amazon without further misadventures and eventually returned to Europe. Langsdorff lived on in Germany until 1861 and may have regained his sanity. Unfortunately, members of the expedition had undertaken to publish nothing until their leader's notes had been edited. As the American missionary Daniel Kidder wrote in 1845, the world was deprived 'of the benefit of investigations made at so much expense and labor . . . [because] Baron Von Langsdorff returned to Europe in a state of mental alienation, the result of sickness and exposure in the regions through which he had passed. In that state he has long survived, and thus a lamentable silence was imposed upon the whole corps of his associates.' Most of the expedition's papers and pictures are now in the Academy of Sciences in Leningrad, still unpublished.

It is worth noting another European scientist who was at Cuiabá just before and after the flamboyant Russian expedition – Johann Natterer, one of the galaxy of scientists and artists who accompanied the Austrian Archduchess Leopoldina when she sailed to Brazil in 1817 to marry the future Emperor Dom Pedro I. Natterer was a zoologist, but he made a brilliant collection of Indian artefacts in addition to his huge collections of natural history. He had reached Cuiabá by the overland route from Goiás in 1824, but was travelling on the Paraguay and upper Guaporé when the Russian expedition arrived. Natterer was also stricken by violent attacks of malaria, but he survived and in 1829 went down the Guaporé–Madeira river route to the Amazon. He visited many tribes on the Rio Negro and its tributaries and on the upper Branco: he was probably in contact with more Indians than any other European visitor. Alfred Russell Wallace met a beautiful mestiza on the Içana tributary of the upper Negro some years later, and was assured that she was Natterer's daughter by a Baniwa Indian woman. Natterer's superb ethnographic collection is in the Museum für Völkerkunde in Vienna. Sadly for us, he wrote no popular account of his travels and his notebooks were all lost in a fire in 1848.

The Apiaká helped a number of Brazilian expeditions during these years. The provincial government appointed inspectors to supervise this friendly tribe. One of these officials proposed that the Apiaká be settled in a village near the Salto Augusto rapids on the Arinos river. The Indians could be conveniently enlisted to steer travellers' canoes down these rapids or haul their boats up them. This outpost was finally founded in 1842 with a few settlers, soldiers and slaves. But the soldiers and men soon mutinied. The inspector had to seek refuge among the Apiaká, and when he died in 1845 the establishment was abandoned. It was an unhealthy place, and the colonists could not adapt to local conditions as successfully as the Apiaká.* The authorities lost interest in the Arinos–Tapajós route between Mato Grosso and Pará. The Apiaká were thus left in relative peace until wild rubber trees were discovered in their territory.

Although the Plains Bororo were coexisting peacefully with frontier settlers (and are consequently extinct), the eastern or Coroado Bororo resented the invasion of their territories. There was the usual sad litany of skirmishes. An expedition in 1829 attacked Bororo who had resisted exploration towards Camapuã in southern Mato Grosso: three Indian children were brought back as prisoners. The Indians killed some settlers in the following year and a force of eighty men was sent against them. This expedition returned with only two small Indians, but its Guaná (Terena) auxiliaries 'made much slaughter among the [Bororo] women and children against the commander's orders'. In 1839 the Coroado Bororo attacked fazendas on their São Lourenço river and on the Goiás–Cuiabá road. There were also 'the most horrific scenes' along a new road that was being built from Cuiabá south-eastwards towards Rio de Janeiro. This road aroused the fury of the Bororo, for it cut into the heart of their territory. 'Attending to public outcry, the government felt itself obliged to send fairly numerous bandeiras into the forests to punish them. It did this even though it was aware, from more than a century's experience, that similar expeditions involved great expense and occasionally committed acts of barbarity. The sole result of these expeditions was the deaths of many adults and the capture of some children. Nevertheless they continued this practice – which had been adopted since the first foundation of the province – for the tranquillity of its settlers.' The President of Mato Grosso tried to establish forts on the Piquiri river (a tributary of the São Lourenço 250 kilometres south-east of Cuiabá) and at the Sangradouro (Outlet) tributary of the Mortes east of Cuiabá on the Goiás road. These outposts were intended to lead to peaceful parleys between the soldiers and Indians. 'However, far from having the desired result

. . . they succeeded only in infuriating them: for the [Piquiri] road had to pass through one of their villages.' The Bororo made daring reprisals, to the very gates of Cuiabá. Farmers everywhere were terrified: they abandoned farms to take refuge in the towns.

In 1849 the eastern Bororo struck at the new road from Rio de Janeiro to Cuiabá. A new president, Colonel Pimentel, was travelling along it to take up office in Cuiabá. He himself rode ahead, leaving his son Lieutenant Pimentel following with his carriage and baggage. The Bororo attacked at night near the Itiquira river. They shot the sleeping lieutenant: he died ten hours later from painful arrow wounds. The furious President ordered bandeiras to march out from Cuiabá and from Miranda on the Paraguay; but the Bororo eluded these reprisal raids.

A permanent military outpost on the São Lourenço river failed to tame these eastern Bororo. They burned and destroyed farms and mills near their territory. By 1862 the President of Mato Grosso admitted that 'they continue to fight us ferociously . . . and it has not even been possible to call them to parley.' Ten years later, another president was still complaining that these Bororo 'lose no occasion to persecute us, killing the persons and animals of both travellers and settlers'. Such ferocity saved the eastern Bororo. They are the only significant groups of the tribe to survive to the present day.

The western Bororo were less fortunate. There was some renewed fighting against them. In 1837 bandeiras were sent to attack them: forty or fifty Indians were killed in the fighting and four adults and twenty-four children captured into slavery. A later president of Mato Grosso deplored 'the distasteful task of resorting to the methods used in 1837 to punish and repel the barbarities of the Campanha Bororo'. In 1840 the Cabaçal Bororo frightened the settlers of Vila Maria by boldly marching through their village. A French traveller, Dr Amédée Moure, wrote that these Indians 'pillage, steal and kill without pity or mercy'. The stockade of Jauru, which had once had six hundred Brazilian inhabitants, was reduced to seventy 'thanks to repeated attacks by the Cabaçal Bororo'.

Then, in 1842, a parish priest from Mato Grosso City called José da Silva Fraga went 'alone armed only with a cross into the midst of this barbaric horde, which respected the missionary'. As so often, the Indians wanted peace and responded readily to a kind overture. Some Cabaçal Bororo agreed to settle near the bar of the Jauru. A mission was established for them at a beautiful location overlooking the left bank of the river. When the Count of Castelnau visited the place in 1845 he saw 110 Indians settled in twenty small straw huts arranged in a square and surrounded by banana plantations. He described these Bororo as fine men but excessively dirty. 'They are covered in scabs and disgusting maladies, and they paint their bodies red with urucum [anatto] dye.' To Dr Moure, 'their barbarity has softened and they have become human and sociable. [If another good missionary could be found] these savage Bororo might become useful labourers.'

The Cabaçal Bororo were doomed because their territory contained open savannahs that made good cattle country. Castelnau was struck by the wealth of the fazendas on the road between Cuiabá and Vila Bela. The town of Pocone, south-west of Cuiabá, had immense herds of tens of thousand head of cattle.

The Cabaçal Bororo soon paid the penalty for their submission. Their peaceful village changed dramatically. The cause was an epidemic of a disease to which the powerful Bororo had no immunity. Castelnau's companion, the English botanist Hugh Weddell, returned to the Jauru mission later in 1845. He was shattered by what he saw. The scabs noticed by Castelnau a few months earlier were signs of deadly sickness: the Indians were dying of disease and starvation. Weddell wrote a heart-rending account of one emaciated young mother lying on a mat in her hut, begging for scraps of food. Her husband and children were dead; beside her lay a bloated dying baby. 'Her hideous state of misery made one shudder. . . . She was reduced to a state of emaciation difficult to imagine. Her body was all covered in horrible dirtiness. She raised her head but her legs no longer moved. . . . In a short time, perhaps a few days, the aldeia of the Cabaçal [Bororo] will exist in name only.'

Some Cabaçal Bororo had not accepted settlement. A report of 1863 said that these Bororo 'were still very numerous until a short time ago'. Then a passing rancher fired at a Cabaçal and the Indian responded by killing him. 'The result of this killing was that the victim's mother ordered that the greater part of them be killed.' An official report admitted that because the Cabaçal Bororo 'infested' the Cuiabá–Mato Grosso road, 'some raids have been launched against them. Great slaughter was caused by this rather unchristian measure – for the bandeiras did not seek to take prisoners, but only to exterminate all whom they were fated to encounter, without respect for sex or age.' The few surviving Cabaçal Bororo surrendered and were put in a settlement called Caeté on the Cuiabá–Mato Grosso road near the Jauru river. Rodolpho Waehneldt said in 1863 that these were 'generally of good disposition. Almost all are clothed, but they always maintain a profound melancholy.'

To the south, a few pacified Plains Bororo survived near the border between Brazil and Bolivia. Waehneldt visited a village of 140 of them, surrounded by the vast Cambara ranch with thirty thousand head of cattle. He found these isolated Indians scarcely acculturated. The traditional Bororo rituals were fully practised, particularly faith healing by five or six elderly shamans. Known as 'padres or doctors', these pagés practised their art amid unintelligible chants, puffs of smoke and strange noises with their instruments. Waehneldt thought that this was done 'to torment and delude the poor laity as much as possible, in order to obtain the resulting advantages [of the best food]. It is just like other religious systems today, even among more civilised nations.' The tribe went naked apart from the men's penis strings and the women's tapir-hide girdles; and they had superb ornaments of feathers and animal skins. The Bororo women worked very hard. Their men did less: hunting, fishing and occasionally hiring themselves out as cowhands for very minimal pay. All this contrasted with the anti-Indian prejudice of the frontiersmen. Waehneldt admitted: 'I received an impression of the Indians which was different from what we had heard from the inhabitants of that province. They are not bad by nature. They enjoy work, provided it is not too much and they are given a mediocre reward and good treatment. If the opposite occurs, they immediately disperse into the forests, from which they sometimes take just revenge.'

Beyond Mato Grosso and the lands of the Bororo stretched the vast unexplored heart of South America. Most of the tribes of the endless forests, rivers, table mountains, plateaux, savannahs and campos of what is now Rondônia were uncontacted and unknown. At the eastern edge of this wilderness was the land of the large Paresi tribe. This peaceful and industrious people had been badly mauled by Paulista slavers in the eighteenth century. Amédée Moure said that by the mid-nineteenth century, the Paresi had retreated into the gorges of the hills named after them. They disliked civilisation, partly because they had often been cheated. Despite this, they sometimes hired themselves out to gather ipecac roots. They would appear in the towns to trade their crops and manufactures – particularly tobacco, cotton and beautiful hammocks – for metal tools. They eluded occasional raids sent against them. The English explorer William Chandless described the Paresi as 'an indolent, inoffensive tribe'. They represented the westernmost frontier in central Brazil.

The Cabanagem Rebellion

Brazilian expansion has almost always been commercially motivated. The frontier has lurched inland in response to a series of economic booms or rushes inspired by the discovery of a new product. Uncontacted Indians gained respites between these bursts of activity.

When Pombal and his brother expelled the Jesuits and introduced the Directorate system in Amazonia, they also tried to revive commerce in this difficult part of Brazil. Their vehicle for this revival was the General Company of Commerce of Greater-Pará and Maranhão, which lasted for twenty-three years from 1755 to 1778. Accelerated imports of black African slaves were supposed to replace the need for Indian slave labour. With Portuguese government subsidies and monopoly protection the new company prospered. In Maranhão at the mouth of the Amazon river, that prosperity was based on cotton and rice. In Amazonia the main crop was cacao, which accounted for over 60 per cent of exports during that period. There was a determined attempt to grow cacao in plantations, but local Indians resisted work in the plantations and responded better to collecting expeditions into the forests.

The relative prosperity of Amazonia continued for a time after Pombal's fall from power in 1777 helped bring about the closure of the General Company in 1778. The American War of Independence (1776–83) interrupted cotton exports from North and South Carolina, so that exports from Maranhão increased dramatically. Cotton sales benefited from the start of the industrial revolution in England. Cacao gained from the craze for drinking chocolate in Europe; and when the Napoleonic Wars cut England off from Spanish Venezuelan cacao, Amazonia increased its exports. In economic terms, there was some vitality in the upper Amazon (then called the Captaincy of Rio Negro) in the late eighteenth century during the governments of Manoel da Gama Lobo d'Almada in Rio Negro (1786–99) and of Francisco de Sousa Coutinho in Pará. The province was stimulated by improvements in its river communications, by the encouragement of agriculture, fishing, shipbuilding and other basic manufactures, by the introduction of cotton and cattle into the upper Rio Branco, and by the explorations of the boundary commissioners following the Treaty of San Ildefonso. One contemporary historian wrote that Lobo d'Almada's 'capability and patriotism led him to plan the aggrandisement of the region very surely'.

All this activity was at the expense of pacified Indians. Once-thriving mission villages along the Rio Negro and Solimões declined and collapsed from a combination of overwork of their men, decimation by disease, attacks by the Mura before their surrender, the labour requirements of boundary expeditions, and flight back to the forests by oppressed Indians.

We have an insight into working conditions in a report by Governor Lobo d'Almada about the cotton factory he had established on the Rio Negro. The factory employed ninety-six Indians in preparing the cotton for spinning. Sixteen men and women operated eighteen looms – with the men and women carefully segregated so that they would concentrate on their work. The working day was from five in the morning to six in the afternoon, with a half-hour break at eight o'clock and two hours at midday. The Indians were paid either in wages or, for spinners, by productivity. The Governor insisted that no coercion or punishment were used: recalcitrant workers were simply returned to their villages. In 1797 this factory produced 407 rolls of cotton cloth, and half its profits went to the royal treasury.*

Other government projects that took a heavy toll of Indian labour were woodcutting, shipbuilding, construction of forts and colonisation settlements, fisheries, and commercial paddling and navigation. At the height of the Directorate in 1772 there were only 19,000 Indians under Portuguese control in Pará, of whom 4000 were in Directorate villages. By the close of the eighteenth century there was an acute labour shortage in Pará. Several hundred Indians were brought to Belém to defend the town from possible French attack launched from Cayenne (French Guiana). But, when they arrived, there was such a shortage of food that in 1796 these Indians were distributed to nearby farmers. In 1797 any Indian, black or mestizo who agreed to work as a fisherman was released from the light infantry corps. By this time there were only about four thousand Indians available for labour, the majority of whom were working in the Directorate villages, largely on collecting expeditions. Thus only a thousand men were available to meet the government's many labour demands and, as we have seen, this desperate shortage of manpower was the real reason for the abolition of the Directorate.

The system that replaced the Directorate was based on a labour corps of Indians, to whom were added as many blacks and mestizos as possible. Governor Sousa Coutinho organised this corps along military lines. As we have seen, he ordered the outgoing directors to compile lists of Indians available for government service. These were then assembled at the four main towns of Pará, in order to make them available for work. The labour corps had officers and uniforms and its members were subject to military discipline. There was also provision for private employers to compete for Indian labour by offering attractive pay. It was assumed that Indians would respond to this market system. In the event, they preferred to live in 'idleness' – fishing or farming enough to feed their families but unimpressed by the rewards for backbreaking labour for private farmers. The answer was coercion. Although Indian labourers were free to seek the best possible pay and type of work, they could not withhold their labour altogether. Local judges were to 'assign' involuntary labourers. Indians could exempt themselves from this forced labour only if they were paying tithes equal to a daily salary. To some extent, the new system and the abolition of the Directorate villages solved the government's labour shortages.

A growing number of Indians had drifted towards Belém, many living on the mudflats and várzea floodplains near the city and on the island of Marajó. These formed a body of free Indians, protected by nature from harassment by tyrannical directors. Such Indians came to the city when they paddled canoe-loads of merchandise from their villages to the provincial capital. As more and more of them chose to remain at Belém, their villages were correspondingly denuded. In 1815 the government made a last futile effort to reverse this trend. It ordered all Indians in Belém to return to their places of birth within two weeks; but the order was ignored.

Contemporary observers were depressed and pessimistic about Amazonia. According to one Brazilian historian, the region 'passed through a continuous and uninterrupted crisis' during the first decades of the nineteenth century. The world price of cacao fell during these years. American cotton recaptured the European mar-

kets, so that Maranhão suffered. Coffee never flourished in equatorial Amazonia – its later boom occurred when the crop was grown in
the more temperate climate of São Paulo. And sugar-growing was
restricted in Amazonia in favour of Pernambuco and Bahia. Rubber
had not yet become the wonder crop that was to transform the
Amazonian economy.

Lourenço da Silva Araújo e Amazonas, the shrewd contemporary
writer, noted that the natives were in varying stages of acculturation.
After the abolition of the Directorate, 'they were released to live as
they chose, which is how they live today. Some are isolated and
practise all their savage customs in territories that are still unexplored (such as part of Guiana between the Branco and Nhamundá
rivers, all Mundurucania, and the lands of the Solimões). Others,
exposed by ancient persecutions, live near our towns in complete
contact with civilisation. Such people have chosen "civilisation", but
are retarded only because of the indifference in which they are
abandoned, which is nothing less than a formal rejection. Then there
are those who were born in our towns, who now form a very important part of our society.' This urban proletariat worked at extracting
forest drugs such as cravo and ipecac, fishing, gathering turtle eggs
for their oil, making tobacco, cotton and coffee, and in trades as
carpenters, smiths or leather-workers.

Araújo e Amazonas noted the hypocritical contradiction in attitudes to these Indian workers. 'They are accused of being lazy; and
yet where this is said they are the only ones who work. They are
accused of being insincere; yet an Indian is lucky if among ten
employers he finds one who pays him. . . . Throughout the province
there is still an excessive tendency if not for slavery, then undoubtedly for a system of using indigenous labour that seems to differ from
slavery in name alone.'

The situation of the Indians of Rio Negro (the upper Amazon,
corresponding to the modern state of Amazonas) was made worse by
bad governors. During the interim government of Colonel José
Antonio Salgado, 'who was already very decrepit . . . the hateful
system of shackling aldeia Indians for government service was instituted. This was later made more odious by being executed by
soldiers of the 1st Line Regiment. . . . It is an appalling and insufferable burden to press-gang a married Indian from the bosom of his
family for various public works, without wages or pay for many
months or a year of work. His poor hut is surrounded by soldiers,
who tie him up and shackle him to carry him off for this labour. What
inhumanity! His wife is left with no manioc plantation to support

their little children, with no one to protect the house, without food or sustenance, finding help only from God and public charity.' Canon André Fernandes de Sousa, who witnessed this injustice, was vicar of the upper Rio Negro at this time. He expostulated: 'From my observation, Portuguese governors seem to regard Indian tribes as belonging to some other species, mere accessories from which they should derive profit.'

There was a respite under the Count of Arcos, who in 1804 again moved the capital of Rio Negro down from Barcelos to Barra (Manaus) at the mouth of the river. His successor, José Joaquim Victorio da Costa, was a rapacious exploiter. He prohibited Indian men and women from working for settlers, claiming that this prohibition would help the royal factories. It was in fact a device to use their labour himself, particularly on some plantations near Manaus owned by the governor and his brothers-in-law. 'A third of the Indians of Rio Negro were occupied on these plantations. They were changed every six months. They were forced to make the journey down from their villages; but allowed to make their own way back, increasingly without payment for their work.' Araújo e Amazonas wrote that 'the oppression of Indians increased markedly during this governorship. Five hundred Indians worked for some years in a plantation [Victorio da Costa] founded at Tarumá. And in Manaus natives were seen working in chains like convicts. There was excessive depopulation of Indians at this time, as a result of such oppression and from interminable work in the fisheries of the Rio Branco and Manacapurú, in rope-making, cloth mills, etc.' Lesser officials imitated the Governor. Canon Fernandes de Sousa accused successive commandants of the fort of Ega (Tefé) on the Solimões of being especially harsh, with imprisonment and extraordinary punishments for any who resisted. Desperate Indians fled to the forests.

When the Governor saw the province being depopulated in this way, he permitted uncontacted tribes to be seized by force and sold to any who wanted them. This was a flagrant violation of laws prohibiting Indian slavery. Governor Victorio da Costa was described as 'a dishonest and avaricious man' who encouraged 'terrible and infamous raiding parties to enslave the heathen and creole Indians of the Rio Negro. The result is and will continue to be the desolation in which [the province] currently languishes.'

Victorio da Costa was succeeded in 1818 by an even worse governor, Manoel Joaquim do Paço. 'It was as if the government wanted to give the final blow to this province, already almost inanimate.' Indians were now forced to pay a third of their manioc harvest to the state. 'The miserable and wretched Indians are scattered from one another. They are oppressed not only in manioc levies . . . but also in continual labour, victims condemned to work throughout their lives until they are carried off on the wings of eternity. In Rio Negro Europeans regard Indians as animals of another species.'

Needless to say, the few landowners on the Amazon saw the situation differently. They desperately needed native labour to make their enterprises function. Captain Francisco Ricardo Zany was a settler of Italian origin and a brother-in-law of the rapacious governor Victorio da Costa. After Brazilian independence he wrote a memorandum to the Emperor complaining about the situation since the abolition of the Directorate. He looked back nostalgically to the good times when royal factories worked by Indian labour had earned enough profit to pay the salary of the Governor, of all the civil servants, of a two-hundred-man military contingent, of vicars, and for the running of the Royal Military Hospital. In those days, settlers had Indians to work for them and so had merchants. With the abolition of the Directorate (and of the covert Directorate system that continued for some years thereafter), the Indians had been filled with ill-conceived notions of liberty. Since independence, Indians had been considered citizens and no longer obliged to work for the state. 'Work in the factories slackened, as did farming and commerce. For Indians lost their subjection and respect for the government. They no longer feared being called to work in the factories or on the rivers. Most therefore ceased to do agricultural labour and refused to work for private persons. They buried themselves in the forests, where they live in their customary idleness.'

The Bavarian zoologists Carl von Martius and Johann Baptist von Spix visited the large plantation of this same Francisco Ricardo Zany at Manacapurú just north of Manaus. The enterprise had twenty thousand coffee bushes and as many cacao trees. In front of the main house were huts for spinning cotton; and the quarters of the slaves and Indians were on either side. The Germans were favourably impressed by Zany. 'Mr Zany has mainly Pasé, Yurí and Makuna working for him. He orders them brought here from the forests of the Japurá [six hundred kilometres to the west]. The first two tribes . . . are distinguished by their activity, skill and loyalty to their masters. All these tame Indians have happy and animated expressions, the result of their present condition – so favourable in comparison with the cares and uncertainties of life in the forests.' The Germans were hopelessly wrong. The disaffection and desertion of these supposedly loyal and happy workers led Zany to submit to the Constituent

Assembly a plan for converting more tribes, as well as the memorandum of complaint to the Emperor a few years later.

Near Zany's plantation was a camp of sixty nomadic Mura, one of the roving bands of this tribe who managed to trade successfully on the fringe of frontier society: they kept their independence, selling quantities of turtle eggs and fish to the settlers. Zany took his German visitors to see this group. The Mura welcomed him, hoping that he had brought cachaça. They had even dressed in some clothing to please him, although they looked uneasy in clothes and their hair was tangled, their faces dyed red with urucum. They danced in the moonlight, stamping and singing in unison, in a large circle with the men on one side and the women on the other.

Spix and Martius had first seen a group of Mura a few weeks earlier and were appalled by their primitive way of life. The Mura were on a sandbank roasting turtles. They were naked, although some men wore wooden plugs in their lower lips and had their bodies painted with black and red dyes. Some girls had their bodies caked in river mud as protection against mosquitoes. But, to the Germans, the Mura women had expressions of 'ferocity, indecision and baseness', and 'the raw misery of the American savages nowhere seemed so horrible and sad. Everything indicated that even the most simple necessities of life were satisfied here in an almost bestial manner.' What the Germans would not accept was that the Mura had survived precisely because of their nomadic existence: large sedentary tribes with efficient villages had fallen easy prey to the colonial power. The Mura attempt to make peace with the settlers had failed. The tribe was again accused of harassing river traffic. 'Because of this, European colonists were persecuting the Mura as wild Indians more implacably than any other tribe.'

In 1814 the Mura had been struck by an epidemic of malarial fevers. No one at that time knew that malaria was caused by bacteria carried by mosquitoes. One theory was that the fevers came from humid or bad air – hence the name 'mal aria'. The Rio Negro flooded in 1814 and this was blamed for the epidemic. It made the ground 'exhale a cold humidity, which caused a general contagion of fevers from which many Indians died, not only children but also adults. This mortality was caused largely by lack of treatment or of warm houses – for they were accustomed to living in healthy country and did not bother to build themselves good houses.' Despite this tragedy, there were still thought to be six or seven thousand Mura warriors in 1819, which would indicate a total population of some thirty thousand. But the Mura had been driven from the lower

Madeira by the Mundurukú, and they were now scattered in bands
along the Solimões, Negro and Amazon rivers.

When the French traveller Paul Marcoy visited the Mura on their
lakes near the mouth of the Madeira many years later, he found them
morally crushed but defiant. 'Among these Indians, a mournful
apathy, a fierce melancholy have replaced the warlike and ferocious
spirit of their ancestors. Of all the tribes civilised or brutalised by the
conquerors' regime, none seemed to us to exceed the Mura in their
disgust and fatigue of the whites. The solitude of the great lakes is
not sufficiently profound for them. The mere sight of a pale face is
enough to put them to flight. In the Muras' haste to avoid all contact
with white men, one senses hatred rather than fear.'

The Mundurukú – the other great warrior tribe that had made
peace in the late eighteenth century – reacted quite differently,
remaining surprisingly faithful to the colonial government. Spix and
Martius met one tough old man who had been a Mundurukú executioner and had decapitated many enemies. Such ferocity was valued
by the Portuguese. On the Tapajós, 'with their courage and large
numbers, they protect immigrant settlers against abuse by other
natives.' From 1800 onwards the Mundurukú, bribed by presents of
trade goods, helped the Portuguese crush the Mura, 'who were
wandering in small bands and had become dangerous, robbing and
raiding navigation on the river and settlements. This campaign by
the Mundurukú helped by Portuguese arms continued for twenty
years with unparalleled cruelty.'

The Mundurukú were slow to change their way of life. When an
expedition was sent to open a trade route down the Tapajós in 1812,
it found the Mundurukú 'more barbaric and even poorer' than the
less contacted Apiaká farther upriver. Men and women were still
naked and stained with black genipapo body dye. The only signs of
contact with settlers were small paring knives among the men and
red and white beads among the women; but they still made their
hammocks of liana fibres without using cotton. The process of assimilation then accelerated. By 1817 Ayres do Casal noted that 'almost
all hordes of Mundurukú are our allies, and some already Christians.' They were moving down towards the Amazon, to be nearer
their new friends and to take over territories of extinct tribes. At one
village on the Tapajós, the Mundurukú had started planting vegetable gardens, with some of their men wearing trousers and some
women cotton skirts.

Spix and Martius visited various Mundurukú groups in 1819.
They saw a large village of them on the Canumã river – a mission

founded in 1811 by a Carmelite friar José Alves das Chagas, but now run by a secular priest Antonio Jesuino Gonçalves. The Germans admired this priest's courage, surrounded by a thousand Mundurukú who had only recently ceased to live in complete freedom in the forests. The priest was trying to break down the tribal culture by bringing acculturated Indian girls from other tribes to marry its men. The Germans found Mundurukú women hospitable and the men amiable. But they were dismayed by the tribe's 'backwardness': 'It appeared that the tribe was no more aware of such concepts as "state", "law", "king", "modesty" and so forth than they had been in their free condition.' The priest complained that his Indians 'rejected everything that might have directed them towards further studies in civilised community life.' Although tall and sturdy, the Mundurukú seemed to the Germans surprisingly dirty, with insufficient bathing areas for such a large community.

Some months later Zany took Martius far up the Japurá river. This remote and difficult northern tributary of the Solimões had been explored in 1782 by the Spanish and Portuguese boundary commissioners Requena and Chermont. One astrónomo or surveyor on that ill-fated expedition was José Joaquim Victorio da Costa, the man who later became the evil governor of Rio Negro. Martius reported that in 1808 Victorio da Costa had founded a settlement of Yurí, Kueretú and Jama Indians far up the Japurá at a place he called São João do Príncipe. Any good intentions that the Governor may have had were frustrated by a white 'judge' who was placed in charge of the settlement. When Zany and his German friend arrived, the few remaining Indians fled to their forest clearings. 'These poor people feared the approach of any white man because of the forced labour to which they were subjected, ostensibly for "public works" but exclusively for the benefit of the judge. They begged me [Martius] to expose to the government their helpless condition and the oppression by their enemy. There had already been complaints against this man, both for stealing tithes and for his cruel and lustful behaviour towards his charges.'

After a while, Chief Pachicu of the Kueretú arrived to welcome Zany and Martius. The chief wore cotton breeches, a blue frock coat and a silver-topped staff – symbols of office given him by the boundary commissioners. Chief Pachicu was bold and astute: he portrayed himself as a loyal vassal of the King of Portugal, but made sure that his tribe was far away in the forests. He had developed a lucrative trade, raiding rival tribes to capture prisoners for sale to Portuguese settlers. Martius commented: 'Thus, for the first time in the interior of America, there was brought into our presence a complete replica of an African chieftain who made his business from slave trafficking. By endorsing such a chief, the government harmed the Indians just as much as by appointing the white judge.' Slave raiding was still rampant on these remote rivers – many decades after enslavement of Indians had been prohibited by law. Martius reported that all the Japurá tribes were tragically reduced in numbers because of 'descents' to the Solimões and Negro. The survivors had a pallid colour, swollen bellies and hardened livers, the legacy of constant malarial fevers. 'Because of this, and because of their idleness, white settlers do not buy them.'

Upstream of the Kueretú, Martius visited the village of Chief Miguel of the Yurí and was impressed by the spacious huts, good plantations of banana, urucum, cotton and manioc, and the abundance of fish and game. He watched the village's peaceful daily round. The day began with everyone bathing in the river, then a period for resting and chatting, during which the naked women painted their children or played with pet monkeys and birds. The men went off to hunt and fish; the women did their many household chores, bathing often through the day. In the evening there were moonlit dances in extravagantly painted masks, and a frightening display by warriors brandishing round tapir-hide shields.

Every three months, the chief of these Yurí sent a relay of four men down to Ega to work for pay in the boatyard. He also traded prisoners, captured on long expeditions into the forests. Farther upriver another Yurí chief was off with all his warriors on such a raid, escorted by a mestizo slaver from Ega. The Yurí had once been one of the three powerful tribes controlling the lands between the Içá and Japurá. Now they were reduced to less than two thousand, 'because they were carried off more than any others to the white men's settlements, and have therefore been extinguished in racial mixing'.

Far up the Japurá–Caquetá, Martius was enchanted by the unspoiled Miranya (Witoto-speaking Bora). Their vivacious welcome contrasted with the 'sad gravity' of acculturated Indians. 'We rightly ascribed this innocence, this warm interest in everything concerning us, to their freedom and natural condition. Far removed from the whites, they were free from fear of forced labour that is such a horror for all other Indians.' Martius was particularly impressed by Miranya women who, although completely naked, were always clean and well combed and who worked constantly. They made fine palm-fibre hammocks and other artefacts that were sold throughout the

Rio Negro. They struck the German visitor as far more sensitive and civilised than their lazy menfolk.

Amid this edenic simplicity, two things appalled the European scientist: the Miranya ate human flesh, and they were active slave-raiders. When Martius interrogated a Miranya chief about his eating human meat, the Indian gave a reasoned answer: 'Whites do not like to eat crocodiles or monkeys even though these are tasty. But if they had fewer turtles and pigs they certainly *would* eat them – for hunger hurts. All this is merely a question of habit. When I kill an enemy, it is better to eat him than to let him rot: for big game is rare, since it does not lay eggs as turtles do. Death itself is worse than being eaten. If I am killed, it would be of no concern to me whether or not [my enemies] the Omagua ate me. In fact, I know no game that tastes better than [human flesh] – although you whites are too sour.' Despite the good taste of human meat, the Miranya chief said that he would always prefer to sell a captive to the whites than eat him, 'for cachaça rum tastes even better than blood'.

One day, the Miranya's log drums sounded and a flotilla of canoes appeared. Chief João Manuel was returning with thirty warriors and a number of prisoners. Martius was shocked to see the Indians triumphantly painted in red and black geometric designs. They were proud of their booty of fellow Miranya captured after a two-day march through the forest. The warriors pushed their captives ahead of them, loaded with sacks of food. One large man who had tried to escape had his feet locked into log stocks; but the others wandered freely about the village. Martius had been trading tools and weapons for native artefacts. The chief now gave him five young men, two girls and three boys. 'I accepted these wretched creatures from the hands of this fiend all the more readily because all were ill from malarial fever and would certainly have died without attention.' The chief was angry because Martius and Zany would not buy all his captives.

The Miranya celebrated their successful raid that night. Hundreds of warriors arrived from the forests, summoned by log drums. Martius and Zany were trembling from malaria and shattered by the noise of the dancing. In their weakened state they feared for their own safety, but managed to hide most of the Miranya's poisoned arrowheads and blow-gun darts on their canoes in the river. Despite his lofty disapproval of slaving, Martius took his captives down the Japurá. Two died during the journey 'of cirrhosis of the liver and dropsy', but he gave seven to the military commander of Ega and the magistrate of Belém. He himself took the older girl back to Munich, along with a Yurí boy he had also acquired. He planned some social experiment with these native curiosities but 'unfortunately both paid with their lives, because of the change of climate and other circumstances.'

Canon Fernandes de Sousa accused Governor Lobo d'Almada of starting the policy of encouraging tribes to seize their neighbours for sale to the whites. That was in 1785; and all succeeding governors had pursued this 'odious plan of facilitating the seizure of heathen [uncontacted] Indians and their sale as slaves. . . . Born free and independent, they are reduced to slavery in their own country! What cruelty! What ingratitude! I have observed that . . . from "descents" made with such seized captives – claimed to be peaceful descents – only a third or a quarter survive. This is because they are torn violently from their homes and are despoiled of their children and wives after having their few possessions sacked. Young and old die constantly, either from eating earth [to commit suicide] or struck down by disease.'

Fernandes de Sousa described the slave traffic. 'Anyone who can obtain a roll of coarse cloth, some knives and a flask of gunpowder, goes up the Japurá river. He engages Indians in one of its settlements and takes them inland to surround the huts of the heathen by night and tie them up. His men fire guns to terrify them and kill most in this way for the [slavers'] opinion of them is nil. These barbaric Indian accomplices of the whites are rewarded, in addition to their pay, by the spoils of the heathen: their blow-guns, bows and arrows, curare poisons, feather ornaments, gourds, murucu lances, and other things that they usually own.' Sousa accused Spix and Martius' friend Zany of being a leader in this traffic. 'In 1815 the Italian Francisco Ricardo Zany went to Ega to organise the trade in Japurá Indians with Ega's military commander Captain Francisco Videira Zuzarte. This trade resulted in the seizure of many hundreds who were then sold in Manaus for from ten to forty milreis. The traffickers will say that this is my fabrication; and the buyers in Manaus claim that such sales continued for only three years. But I maintain that this traffic lasted until Governor Manoel Joaquim do Paço succeeded Governor Victorio. . . . Some of these traffickers still go up the Negro showing off more and more servants. Others have already retired, replete with money earned from heathen Indians of Amazonas. Why do they not seize Mura, Arequena (Warekena), Mundurukú or other warlike tribes, but only peaceful and hard-working Indians? Cruel and immoral men!'

Sousa said that these seizures started with Captain Marcelino José

Cordeiro on the Negro during the governorship of Lobo d'Almada: hundreds of Indians were brought out of the forest by armed soldiers to work in the factories. The surveyor Lieutenant-Colonel Henrique Wilkens protested but was overruled. Then Sergeant Miguel Archanjo operated the traffic on the Japurá until his death. Captured Indians were put to work hauling carts of clay in brickyards or as fishermen; their women were made to comb cotton in the mills. In those times, directors claimed that everything was done in the royal service. This was the standard excuse. As Canon Fernandes de Sousa said, 'whatever its nature, it was always "public service". Because of it, Indians are constantly put to work away from their homes. This abuse cries out for remedy.' Similar protests had led to the abolition of the Directorate: Indians were made 'equal to other subjects and controlled by the same laws that govern everyone. I must report with regret that none of this has been observed, particularly not in Rio Negro. The remoteness of that captaincy, and the lack of literate people to protest about the oppressions, both combine to allow the abuses to continue unheard.'

The trouble was that Amazonia attracted the worst immigrants. Some of the pioneers who pushed the frontiers forward in central Brazil were hard-working farmers. But those who went to the remote waters of the Amazon tended to be young adventurers. 'Devoid of education or the fear of God, they are monsters of evil who infect everything with their pestiferous and poisonous breath. . . . They are generally from the very lowest class that exists in Portugal; but on landing they assume all manner of airs. They are immediately seized by the general contagion of this country: a spirit of dissolution, laziness and negligence that ruins everything. . . . Their preferred occupation is to run a tavern or ribbon shop, or to travel from town to town selling trinkets. From this they sink into the abyss of vices – vices that undermine their health and finally render them odious in the eyes of God and men.' There were traders who plied the Indians with cachaça. To the puritanical Fernandes de Sousa, these were 'the most scandalous, both in their business dealings and in their base obscenities. They spend their lives contentedly, laughing, enjoying themselves in deep sleep.'

All this was confirmed by Henry Lister Mawe, a British naval officer who travelled down the Amazon in 1828. He agreed that the Amazon settlers were ignorant and boorish. 'But whether convicts or settlers, their station on getting up the [Amazon] was immediately changed from the lowest class of society to be lords and masters of the country; and as in the latter capacity, to use their own expression,

they have "no hands", to remedy this deficiency they deem it necessary to make use of Indians.' They blithely ignored any pro-Indian
legislation. Lister Mawe noted that the Japurá was still the most
favoured region for illegal slave-raiding. People who wanted Indians
obtained a 'licence' to go raiding, and then armed themselves with
an Indian guide, guns, and some trade goods to buy prisoners from
chiefs who had some to sell. Leaving their canoes, they 'proceed
silently and cautiously through the woods, looking out for anything
like an Indian's rancho. Should they find one, they hide themselves,
watch the motions of the unfortunate inmates, and take a favourable
opportunity to rush upon them. . . . After being captured, they are
chained to logs, and taken down to the boats or canoes.'

At Manaus, Lister Mawe was entertained by the ubiquitous Francisco Zany, and commented that he 'had many Indians at work' on
his fazenda. The English officer was appalled by the colonists' prejudice and hatred of Indians. 'Anger, or ignorance, or selfishness, or
perhaps all three combined', inspired the settlers. 'The fact is that in
the remote parts of the province of Pará, "might makes right", and
power and interest rather than justice form the practical administration of the law. The Emperor may send forth edicts and the President
orders, but the isolated branco is himself an emperor, and much
more absolute than Dom Pedro at Rio de Janeiro. The Emperor has
declared all his Indian subjects *free*; the brancos still hunt and
enslave them. Where then is the power? Where is the absolute
authority?'

The English observer noted a contradiction in the settlers' attitude to Indians. It was argued that Indians were lazy because they
did not maintain permanent farms in their forest homelands (an
argument utterly flawed by the usual failure to appreciate that weak
tropical soils cannot stand constant farming). Because Indians did
not farm intensively they should be brought down to work on settlers' fazendas. But, as Lister Mawe pointed out, 'We were told that
every means was taken to hunt out their retreats and enslave them.
The consequence therefore of making regular chacras [fields] would
be that they could more easily be found and captured.'

There was nothing paternalistic about slavery in Amazonia. 'The
effects of the slave system are that Indians obtained by injustice, but
without much expense, are regarded only for their physical force and
labour. When they die, which they not uncommonly do in numbers
after their capture, the owner considers that he has lost so much
property of a description that was rather disliked for its trouble and
uncertainty than cherished with feelings of esteem or humanity.' To

prevent Indians from fleeing to the forests, owners tried to make their slaves addicted to cachaça and therefore dependent on remaining to obtain it. One Indian declared that Pará was 'fit for whites but uninhabitable for Indians'.

By the 1820s the situation had become explosive. The province had been in economic decline for twenty years. There was a growing proletariat of semi-acculturated and discontented free Indians and caboclos around Belém. Once-prosperous mission villages along the main rivers had been shattered by the Directorate and were now in utter decay. And far away on the western rivers of Rio Negro, uncontacted tribes were being seized and enslaved.

There were other factors contributing to the unease. During the Napoleonic Wars, at the end of 1808, a force of soldiers from Pará was taken by Portuguese and British warships to occupy French Guiana (Cayenne) adjacent to Brazilian Amapá. The occupation was a success. Brazilian soldiers held Cayenne for eight years until it was handed back at the Convention of Paris in 1817. When the men returned to Pará, they found the province in economic decline. They themselves had had a taste of military success and had been exposed to revolutionary thinking.

Disease was another problem. The great smallpox epidemics that decimated Pará and Amazonia periodically during the eighteenth century had subsided. But in their place, malaria had been introduced to the Amazon and was on the rampage. Early travellers' reports of Amazonia praised its healthy climate and never mentioned fevers. But by mid-eighteenth century this was changing. By the nineteenth century, every visitor suffered from fever and countless natives died from it.

Brazilian independence was the cause of the first disturbances in Belém. When Dom Pedro I proclaimed Brazil's independence in distant Rio de Janeiro in 1822, Pará remained loyal to Portugal for a few months. A military rising in favour of independence was quelled bloodlessly in April, but the new imperial government sent Lord Cochrane with the Brazilian navy to take Maranhão. Cochrane was an amazing figure: one of Nelson's most brilliant captains, he had been Member of Parliament for Westminster but was disgraced for involvement in a Stock Exchange fraud. Cochrane protested his innocence and, in disgust, accepted an invitation to command the navy of Chile during its struggle for independence from Spain. He reached Brazil in 1822, fresh from dazzling naval triumphs in the Pacific during José de San Martín's campaign to liberate Chile and

Peru. Cochrane sent Captain John Grenfell with the brig *Maranhão* to Belém. Grenfell pretended that he had a fleet. His deception succeeded 'so well that the provincial junta immediately gave its adhesion to the Emperor, and Grenfell was welcomed in the city.'

Soon after Pará had declared allegiance to the independent Brazilian empire, there was a revolt by the liberal faction against the conservative junta ruling the province. The junta sent for Captain Grenfell to quell this mutiny by some of its troops. Grenfell's marines did so with undue ferocity. Five soldiers were chosen at random and summarily executed. Another 253 soldiers were imprisoned in the hold of the galley *Palhoço* on the night of 16 October 1823. They were crushed into a 'black hole' far too small for their numbers and were left without water on a humid tropical night. In the words of Prince Adalbert of Prussia, who visited the Amazon some years later: 'The prisoners made an attempt to escape and the sentinels fired on them through the hatchways, when the miserable men, excited to desperation by the stifling heat and confinement of their prison, fell to attacking and tearing one another in the most inhuman manner. This scene was accompanied with all the horrors of death by suffocation, and the next morning out of the 253 only four survived, who had concealed themselves behind a water-cask. Many similar scenes of horror occurred during the insurrections which ensued, when thousands of prisoners languished in the forts, until death released them. It is said that, on board the prison-ship *Xin-Xin,* above three thousand persons perished in the course of five or six years.'

Most of the victims of this repression were ignorant soldiers, largely mestizos, mulattoes and Indians. The American geologist Herbert Smith laid much of the blame for the massacre on Captain Grenfell, who had provided the prison-ship. 'Certainly, he did not show by his subsequent acts that he was at all just or merciful. The junta declared that the prisoners, actuated by the same spirit that led them to revolt, had killed each other in a mad frenzy. Of course the liberals magnified the crime and made the most of it. There was no peace for the province. Even after the empire was fully acknowledged, the division of parties continued as strong as ever; on the one side an invincible hatred of the Portuguese and a general running to anarchy; on the other hand an equal hatred for the liberals and all sorts of oppressions. The prisons and prison-ships were crowded with rebels and "suspects" who died there by hundreds; for years the city [of Belém] and country were full of tumults.'

The newly independent province was rent by dispute between

conservative and liberal factions. The imperial government printed money to finance its Cisplatine War in Uruguay and this fuelled growing inflation. Falling world prices for Pará's raw material exports aggravated distress in that province. 'Brazilian' settlers in Pará blamed rich and more conservative 'Portuguese' merchants for their economic problems.

The years of bitter and cruel skirmishing between factions of the ruling class in Pará finally exploded into the most revolutionary of all rebellions in nineteenth-century Brazil. At long last, the oppressed Indians and coloureds of Pará united in a revolt that hoped for radical social change. This revolt was the Cabanagem, named after the cabanos – the homeless or migrants who lived in cabano huts on the floodplains near Belém or the forested banks of the Amazon. General Francisco Soares d'Andrea, who commanded the province during the latter part of the rebellion, wrote that 'all coloured men born here are linked in a secret pact to put an end to anything white.'

The main Cabanagem revolt lasted for sixteen months, from January 1835 to May 1836; and fighting continued elsewhere in Amazonia until the end of 1839. There had, however, been earlier outbreaks of popular fury. Savage sentences on those involved in a rising of 1831 led bands of fugitive blacks and caboclos to wreak havoc on isolated farms near Santarém, on the Moju river near Belém, and on the island of Marajó in the mouth of the Amazon. The most bloody fighting occurred during an attack on Cametá on the lower Tocantins. In April 1832 the garrison of Manaus mutinied under a soldier called Joaquim Pedro. It killed the aged Commandant, freed prisoners, and ran amok in the arsenal. On 22 June the settlers of Rio Negro declared that province independent of Pará – as it had been under Portuguese rule and is now as the state of Amazonas. The provincial government sent a force from Belém which managed to reach Manaus in August after initial defeats during its ascent of the Amazon and quelled the mutiny.

In June 1833 there was a rebel attack on the settlement on Tupinambaranas island in the Amazon downstream of Manaus. The local justice of the peace sent a frenzied appeal for help from Pará. 'On that calamitous day, 24 June at 6.30 in the evening, a terrible and fearful anarchic volcano erupted. . . . Its prime movers were the Indians of this parish, led by the so-called Chief Crispim de Leão. He attacked our property, decorum and political existence, and then moved towards this capital [Manaus]. . . . He is, sir, a turbulent individual who never ceases to seek ways to hurl us into a deep and bottomless abyss of revolts!' This revolutionary force of tapuios (the contemporary name for part-Indian caboclos of Amazonia) and blacks was too much for the garrison of Manaus, and help had to be sent from Pará.

In December 1833 Bernardo Lobo de Souza became President of Pará. He was an energetic man, but too opinionated and agitated to be a suitable leader at that time of crisis. He ordered an amnesty for the rebels, but he also relied on strengthened military activity to enforce his control of Amazonia. Hundreds of reluctant tapuios were conscripted into the infantry. White settlers were mobilised into a national guard and, in the end, the warring factions of the elite united against the proletarian rebels.

A number of leaders emerged among the revolutionary cabanos. There was Canon João Batista Gonçalves Campos, a brave and adventurous priest and a fine journalist. Canon Campos was editor of the newspaper *O Paraense*. He had been a reluctant leader of the revolt crushed by Grenfell's marines in 1823 and now exercised a unifying influence over an otherwise disorganised revolutionary rabble. There were three young Vinagre brothers, led by the oldest Francisco Pedro. The Vinagres were rubber workers from the Itapicuru river in Maranhão. They were uncultured, but tough and intelligent. As a military leader, Francisco Vinagre was energetic, astute and very brave: he excelled in guerrilla activities in the forests and swamps near Belém. But he was blamed for inciting the masses in violent terrorist activities. Felix Antonio Clemente Malcher was a former infantry officer. Sombre, impetuous and irascible, Malcher was a political intriguer who became the first cabano president. He was very different from Eduardo Nogueira 'Angelim', an ardent young revolutionary, dedicated to the cause of reform and the third of the cabano presidents. Angelim was also notable as a military leader in irregular actions within Belém. He adopted the nickname Angelim after one of the hardest trees in the Brazilian forests.

Matters came to a head with the publication in October 1834 of a pastoral letter by the Bishop of Belém condemning freemasonry. President Lobo de Souza forbad it as too subversive; but Canon Campos published it in *O Paraense*. Campos fled to Malcher's fazenda on the Acará river south of Belém. The Vinagre brothers and Angelim joined them there, and proclamations were issued against the government. The rebels destroyed the first expedition sent against them; but Malcher was captured when President Lobo de Souza sent a river expedition of three hundred soldiers. The militia and soldiery were, however, increasingly disaffected. In December, the sensible Canon Campos died (from a cut when shaving with a cut-throat razor) and the cabanos lost his calming influence.

A few weeks later, rebel forces gathered around Belém and entered the city on 7 January 1835. They attacked the barracks, and many soldiers and officers changed sides to join them. Another column attacked the presidential palace. Lobo de Souza bravely left a hiding place to return to the palace but was shot and killed by an Indian called Domingos Onça (Jaguar). Prisoners were freed from jail and the crowd ran amok. There was an orgy of looting and vengeance against the former elite. The American consul, Charles Jenks Smith, wrote that 'about fifty prisoners were set at liberty, who, in a body, proceeded to a part of the city called Porto do Sol and commenced an indiscriminate massacre of all the Portuguese they could find in that neighbourhood. In this manner about twenty respectable shop-keepers and others lost their lives.' Felix Malcher had himself proclaimed President, but promised to remain loyal to the Brazilian Empire. Naval ships therefore joined the rebellion rather than attempting to quell it.

The revolutionary leaders soon disagreed among themselves. Malcher tried to arrest Francisco Vinagre on 19 February. There was sharp fighting in the streets of Belém between the two factions, and a bombardment by ships under Malcher. But by 21 February, the tough Vinagre was in control and was proclaimed president; Malcher was betrayed and killed. The imperial government in Rio de Janeiro now sent a new president, Marshal Manoel Jorge Rodrigues, and after further internecine fighting Vinagre handed over the province to Rodrigues on 21 May.

Marshal Rodrigues tried to reassert armed authority. Francisco Vinagre was arrested with two hundred supporters, but most rebels escaped to the Acará. Eduardo Angelim led them back to attack Belém on 14 August 1835. There was a week of heavy street fighting, during which Antonio Vinagre was killed, but the rebels took most of their objectives. Throughout 16 August there were rebel attacks on the arsenal; marines from English and French warships intervened briefly to help the government side, but by the 22nd Marshal Rodrigues abandoned the last four buildings under his control and fled to the ships. On the 23rd the cabanos were in control of Belém again. They elected the fiery young Eduardo Angelim as president.

Modern historians have hailed the Cabanagem as the most pro-found rebellion against the injustices of nineteenth-century Brazil. Gustavo Moraes Rego Reis has identified four remarkable aspects of the Cabanagem: 'the effective and dominant participation of the masses; the rise of leaders from the lowest strata of society; the unbridled violence of the rebellion; and the scale achieved by this insurrection, which managed to seize power and hold it for a considerable length of time.' Prince Adalbert of Prussia condemned the rebellion as 'a reign of horror and anarchy'. But he knew why it had happened: 'These disturbances were the fruits of the ceaseless oppression which the white population had, from the very first, exercised on the poor natives, and in no part of Brazil more than here.' Brazil's leading historians have echoed this view. Capistrano de Abreu saw the cruel Directorate of the late eighteenth century as the root of the Cabanagem. Basílio de Magalhães blamed the medieval behaviour of the big landowners, who illegally treated Indians as slaves and exploited forced labour on so-called 'national factories' or 'common plantations'. Sérgio Buarque de Holanda saw it as 'the explosion of the mestizo and Indian masses against the lives and property of those who enjoyed political power, wealth and social superiority. . . . The men who took part in the Cabanagem and led it . . . were all – leaders and soldiers – men of the people from the humble classes of society.'

The cabano rebels never devised a government or formulated a set of aims or demands. Although it was a popular rising inspired by the downtrodden masses' hatred of the rich, the successful cabanos never abolished slavery. They simply shouted slogans against the Portuguese and other foreigners and masons. They remained in favour of Catholicism, Brazil, Pará, liberty and the Emperor Dom Pedro. Liberals in Rio de Janeiro had no sympathy with the Cabanagem and referred contemptuously to its perpetrators as rabble from the brutish masses.

Contemporary travellers were understandably frightened. The German botanist Professor Eduard Poeppig was caught in the disorders. Foreign residents helped him escape from Belém to a nearby village, where he waited three months for transport to Europe. Professor Poeppig saw the Cabanagem as 'hordes of robbing and bloodthirsty mestizos, mulattoes and negroes who had united in the neighbourhood of Pará. Although regarded as anarchists, they broke out in countless sorties on the Amazon after part of the soldiers sent against them had joined them. They pushed on from place to place sparing only the largest towns, killing whites with indescribable cruelty and plundering and burning settlements or passing ships. Everywhere, their arrival was a signal for revolt by the coloured rabble who formed the majority of the blind workforce of the superior white Brazilians.'

General Francisco Soares d'Andrea described the Cabanagem in 1838 as 'a ghastly revolution in which barbarism seemed about to devour all existing civilisation in one single gulp. . . . With the exception of the town of Cametá, the parish of Abaeté, the fort of Macapá and the small towns and settlements on the Xingu, I know of no other part of this vast province that escaped the fury of the ruffians. Most sugar mills and fazendas were destroyed and their slaves killed or dispersed. Cattle were consumed and even crops of foods most essential for daily nourishment were extinguished. There are districts in which they left no single white man alive.'

The American lawyer and naturalist William Edwards, who was on the Amazon ten years after the Cabanagem, confirmed how frightened the ruling class had been. 'The president of the province was assassinated as were very many private individuals of respectability, and the city was in possession of the insurgent troops assisted by designing whites and Indians. All the citizens who could, fled for their lives. . . . Everywhere the towns were sacked, cities despoiled, cattle destroyed, and slaves carried away. . . . The disastrous effect of these disturbances is still felt, and a feeling of present insecurity is very general.' The writer Francisco Bernardino de Souza was told by an old lady what it had been like to live through the cabanagem in the Amazon town of Óbidos: 'How we all suffered, because of men who wanted something that no one knew, not even they themselves! The Cabanagem was a scourge sent by God to punish us. It was a plague that ravaged the land where I was born. Everyone suffered from it.' The English botanist Richard Spruce observed that 'in the rebellion of 1835, to be unable to speak *lingua geral* and to have any beard were crimes punished with death by the Cabanos, who carefully extirpated any vestiges of hair from their own faces.' American Indians naturally grow little facial hair; this is why South American men now grow moustaches to prove their European blood.

Two British naval officers, Lieutenants William Smyth and Frederick Lowe, went down the Amazon from Peru to the Atlantic in early 1835, just as the Cabanagem was breaking out. On the Solimões they were warned that in Pará 'the Indians were murdering all the Europeans'. Despite this warning, Smyth and Lowe continued downriver. On the island of Marajó they met 'a Portuguese creole called Jacco who infested the lower part of the river and who had murdered great numbers of Portuguese'. But Jacco welcomed the visitors and said that he had great respect for the English. In Belém itself, the naval officers found that almost all prosperous Brazilians and Portuguese had fled. Others had taken refuge in the houses of American or British residents.

In October 1835 the English ship *Clio* approached Belém with a cargo of arms ordered by President Lobo de Souza before his death, but the rebels boarded the ship near the city, killed its crew and captured the cargo. In March 1836 an English naval force under Captain B. Strong reached Pará and demanded compensation for the lost crew and cargo and punishment of the guilty. The cabano president Eduardo Angelim met Strong, and the English captain suggested that Greater Pará should secede from the Brazilian Empire, which had failed to respond to its grievances. Britain would support an independent Pará. Angelim angrily rejected this proposal. He declared that the fight was between Brazilians and of no concern to foreigners. The British flotilla was ordered to leave immediately or be fired on by the guns of the fort.*

The Cabanagem revolt spread far up the vast network of Amazon rivers. Boatmen told about the extraordinary events in Belém, and oppressed natives and mestizos everywhere joined the movement. The rebels fortified themselves at Icuipiranga near Óbidos on the middle Amazon. From there they attacked the riverine villages of Luzéia (now Maués), Parintins, Silves and Itacoatiara – all on or near the huge riverine island of Tupinambaranas downstream of Manaus. Each settlement resisted for a time, capitulated, and then eagerly joined the rebels. The attack on Luzéia was launched by Mawé Indians. Everywhere the cabanos had the advantage of being superb boatmen who knew every Amazonian backwater; and they had the fervent support of the lower class in each town.

Finally, on 6 March 1836, a thousand cabanos under Bernardo de Sena laid siege to Manaus. The town council had protested loudly in favour of the government and had tried to organise resistance against the Cabanagem. But the town capitulated without a fight. On the day after its fall, the town council declared its support for the rebels. The Vicar João Pedro Pacheco celebrated a Te deum laudamus. Bernardo de Sena was a magnanimous victor and there were no persecutions of former masters. With the arrival of Apolinário Maparajuba, another famous rebel, there was generally enthusiastic approval of the new regime by the people of Manaus. As in Belém, however, the rebels lapsed into internecine quarrelling:

Sena was killed in a barracks mutiny and the cabano hold on the upper Amazon began to weaken.

Despite its military successes and the genuine rising of the oppressed masses of Amazonia, the Cabanagem revolt lacked direction or cohesion. The American Methodist missionary Daniel Kidder, who was in Belém just after the rebellion, described the period of cabano rule as 'a reign of terror. But it was not long a quiet reign. Disorders broke out among the rebels, and mutual assassinations became common. Business was effectually broken up, and the city was as fast as possible reverting back to a wilderness. Tall grass grew up in the streets, and the houses rapidly decayed. The state of the entire province became similar. Anarchy prevailed throughout its vast domains. Lawlessness and violence became the order of the day.'

The government in Rio de Janeiro sent a powerful force of 2500 troops, well armed with guns and powder, under Francisco Soares d'Andrea. This fleet reached Belém in April 1836. Andrea started to destroy Cabanagem units on islands near the city in a series of efficient actions. His ships blockaded Belém. President Angelim was faced with growing anarchy among the rebels and felt his authority weakening. He asked for amnesty but Andrea refused and would not let the rebels leave Belém for the upper Amazon. Angelim tried to fight his way out with the rebel forces, but they were badly beaten. Although Angelim himself escaped, the abandoned city fell to government forces on 14 May 1836. The cabanos left Belém in shambles, with piles of refuse in the streets, gutters clogged, weeds everywhere, houses stripped of doors and window frames that had been burned for firewood, and much damage from the naval bombardment and fighting.

The imperial government appointed Andrea as President of Pará. He now started to subdue the rebellion with his disciplined troops divided into nine commands. A rebel force was routed at the fazenda on the Acará and Eduardo Angelim was captured. Government soldiers went on to destroy rebels throughout Amazonia with brutal repression. As Andrea himself declared with chilling candour: 'The state of war required that the enemy be attacked by all methods until annihilated by force. To make this effective it was necessary to suspend the formalities by which the law shields criminals. Any man accused of any crime was certain to be sought out and arrested before he had time to escape. Any revolutionaries who appeared were arrested, despite existing laws and against all rules of individual liberty. . . . We used as a norm the attainment of just ends by sure methods!'

Daniel Kidder confirmed that Andrea 'proclaimed martial law, and by means of great firmness and severity succeeded in restoring order to the province. It was, however, at the cost of much blood and many lives. He was accused of tyranny and inhumanity in his course towards the rebels and prisoners; but the exigencies of the case were great, and furnished apologies. One of the most disgraceful things charged upon him and his officers, was the abuse made of their authority in plundering innocent citizens, and also in voluntarily protracting the war so that their selfish ends might be advanced. Certain it is, that the waste of life, the ruin of property, and the declension of morals were all combined and lamentably continued; and yet in this state of things we see nothing but the fruits of that violence and injury which, from the first colonisation of Pará by the Portuguese, had been practised against the despised Indians.'

Andrea's task was helped by the activities of pro-government forces on the Negro and upper Amazon. The military Governor of remote Rio Branco, Ambrosio Pedro Ayres, resisted the cabanos at Bararoá (now Tomar) on the middle Negro river, and took the name of the town as his nom de guerre. This 'Bararoá' led a company of loyalist settlers in a series of campaigns against the rebels on the Negro, Amazon, Tapajós and Maués rivers. Bararoá's force managed to recapture Manaus in late 1836 and held the town against a cabano counter-attack. He then led his men in the capture of the cabano stronghold at Icuipiranga. A later President of Amazonas wrote that Bararoá and his fellow caudillo Manuel Taqueirinha 'practised with impunity, in the name of legality, the most barbarous, inhuman and cannibalistic crimes for the mere satisfaction of their bestial instincts'. Bararoá massacred prisoners systematically and ravaged towns suspected of helping the rebels. He was particularly brutal to Indians, and the Mura and Mawé suffered terribly from him.

Long after the conflict was over, Herbert Smith wrote about it: 'A more frightful civil war has never been recorded. . . . It was a struggle of parties, neighbour against neighbour, a massacre in the streets, a chasing through the forests and swamps. To this day old men will tell you brave stories of the great rebellion; how they fought hard with this or that party; how brothers were killed and families driven away; how men were shot down by scores because they would not renounce their partisan tenets. . . . Even now one hears of the extreme republicans or communists. . . . Hatred to the Portuguese is still a part of their creed; the overturning of both church and state power seems to be their ultimate object. . . . The people are hot-headed; in the excitement of political strife they were carried to deeds which they would not have dreamed of in sober moments; as for the Indians and blacks, they followed in the wake of their leaders and, being ignorant, often went beyond them in cruelty.'

The suppression of the Cabanagem rebellion continued throughout 1837 and much of 1838. Pockets of rebel resistance continued in many rivers, forests and isolated villages of the vast province. In August 1838 the ruthless Bararoá led 130 troops and many of the able-bodied men of Manaus, with nine cannon, to the lakes of Autazes, a swampy labyrinth of forested lakes between the junctions of the Madeira and Amazon rivers. This was the homeland of the riverine and highly mobile Mura, and it had become a sanctuary of the cabanos. Bararoá decided to return to Manaus with his personal armed gang, abandoning the men of Manaus to their fate in the Autazes waterways. Lourenço Araújo e Amazonas wrote in 1852 that 'his motives for this are still given a horrifying interpretation.' But Bararoá never achieved his dubious purpose. As President Andrea reported, 'on the afternoon of 6 [August 1838], when he was passing between two islands, he was attacked by seven rebel canoes, mostly manned by Mura Indians. He defended himself until nightfall and attempted to escape overland; but he was caught and cruelly killed. This was a very serious loss. It will be difficult to find another man with the valour, skill and intelligence of this victim.' Bernardino de Souza wrote that the Mura tortured their oppressor to death.

As the shattered province was reconquered, there were devastating epidemics. President Andrea wrote to the government in November 1836 begging for smallpox vaccine. 'We do not yet have a plague of cholera. But we do have frightening malaria that may recur, and an epidemic of confluent smallpox that devours everything.'

These epidemics did not deter the President of Pará from introducing a new system of Workers Corps. He improved the province's militia, filling it with 'well-educated people of noble sentiments'. But he decreed that 'all coloured men who appear in any district without any known motive will immediately be arrested and sent for the government to dispose of them unless they are guilty of some crime. Any individual living in a district who is not regularly employed in useful work will be sent to government factories or hired out to any private individual who needs him. If he still neglects his work despite this measure, he will be remitted to the Naval Arsenal to work for rations alone for a term judged necessary by his conduct.' If there were no work to be done, the military commander was to choose a piece of empty land and force 'those who deserve it' to work under armed guard.

Matters improved somewhat with the installation of a new President, Bernardo de Souza Franco, in April 1839. He was appalled by his predecessor's repression and exploitation of native labour. In a report of December 1839, Souza Franco wrote that 'the province was subjected to three years of strong and rigorous administration . . . in which obedience was commanded by terror.' Although apparently subdued and crushed, Pará was seething with 'suffocated passions. The underprivileged and wronged understand one another. They communicate their grievances and rancour to a large number of others. It is easy to find reasons [for such grievances] in the forced labour, exigencies, constraint and oppression that always accompany such dissensions and civil wars.'

In November 1839 President Bernardo de Souza Franco obtained from the Emperor an amnesty and general pardon for the remaining cabano rebels. The town council of Manaus issued a similar edict of clemency for those still resisting on the Maués river. The government's military commander of Luzéia backed this up with force and, on 25 March 1840, 980 cabanos surrendered there under their commander Gonçalo Jorge de Magalhães. They came 'with their arms assembled, bows and arrows . . . and this example was imitated successively by others at other places, when they recognised the good faith with which the government beckoned and received them.'

The warlike Mundurukú tribe helped government forces suppress the last hideouts of rebellion. Ever since this tribe's surrender to the Portuguese in the previous century, most Mundurukú prided themselves on being loyal allies of the Europeans. When the French engineer Alphonse Maugin de Lincourt went up the Tapajós in the 1840s, he noted among the Mundurukú a deadly hatred of blacks but sympathy for white men. The aged Chief Joaquim told him about his exploits against the cabanos: 'I am Chief Joaquim. I love the whites and have never betrayed them. I left my friends, my cacao plantations and my house on the banks of the Madeira to defend them. How many cabanos insurgents have I not killed when I showed my war canoe that never fled?' Mundurukú warriors helped government forces recapture Santarém on the lower Amazon. Because of this, Herbert Smith noted, 'through the city you will hear only good words of the Mundurukús, and if a tattooed chief visits the place, he is received with all hospitality, as befits his position.'

The passionate Cabanagem rebellion was said to have caused the deaths of thirty thousand people – a fifth of the total population of the province. Roughly equal numbers were killed on either side. The city of Belém suffered much damage and countless farms were abandoned and cattle destroyed. The economy of Brazilian Amazonia was devastated.

Treatment of Indians in Amazonia

The furious explosion of the Cabanagem was a watershed in Amazon history. Once the rebellion had subsided, the vast expanses of the world's largest river basin settled into a new pattern of social exis- tence. Some Indians and mestizos were now established as accultu- rated and detribalised members of Amazonian society. They lived as free men in Belém and other riverine towns and settlements. Although these caboclos were clearly at the bottom of the class structure they were slightly less oppressed and molested than their forebears had been.

The great English naturalist Henry Walter Bates, who was collect- ing on the Amazon for eleven years from 1848 to 1859, noted that 'the original Indian tribes of the [lower Amazon] are now either civilised or have amalgamated with the white and negro immigrants.' These acculturated, detribalised Indians were known throughout Amazonia as tapuios; less contacted tribal Indians of the upper rivers were known as indios or gentios (gentiles or heathen). Bates described the Asiatic features and skin colour of Amerindians: 'Their features exhibit scarcely any mobility of expression; this is connected with the excessively apathetic and undemonstrative character of the race. They never betray, in fact they do not feel keenly, the emotions of joy, grief, wonder, fear, and so forth. They can never be excited to enthusiasm; but they have strong affections, especially those connected with the family.'

Bates repeated the common canard that Indians were ungrateful. 'Brazilian mistresses of households, who have much experience of Indians, have always a long list of instances to relate to the stranger showing their base ingratitude.' But the English observer under- stood the reason for this: 'they did not require and do not value such benefits as their would-be masters confer upon them. . . . All the actions of the Indian show that his ruling desire is to be left alone; he is attached to his home, his quiet monotonous forest and river life; he likes to go to towns occasionally, to see the wonders introduced by the white man, but he has a great repugnance to living in the midst of the crowd; he prefers handicraft to field labour, and especially dislikes binding himself to regular labour for hire. He is shy and uneasy before strangers, but if they visit his abode, he treats them well, for he has a rooted appreciation of the duty of hospitality; and there is a pride about him, and being naturally formal and polite, he acts the host with great dignity.'

Some foreigners recorded the quiet daily life of riverine villages. The Italian traveller Gaetano Osculati, who was on the Amazon in 1848, wrote that 'women, men, children, chickens, monkeys, birds, etc. are huddled together' and the people 'spend the greater part of the time stretched in their hammocks in the most complete immobility'.

The German doctor Robert Avé-Lallement was at Vila Bela da Imperatriz (now Itacoatiara) on the Amazon a few years later. He arrived during a holiday when the atmosphere was 'entirely tapuio in its perfect quiet and unshakeable peace. Normally Indians are not allowed to be lazy; on the day of St John, however, it is permitted for them. . . . I did not see a single Indian occupied with any form of work.' He was struck by the openness of the houses. Windows and doors were wide open, and the split-palm walls were a mere grid that hid nothing inside. 'Some tucumã palms near the house, some hens and pigs and big slices of pirarucu fish drying in the sun, as well as naked children: these are the attributes of a tapuio house in Vila Bela.'

Some observers shared the view of the great Baron Alexander von Humboldt that life on the Amazon was too easy. Maize, manioc and especially bananas grew so readily that the people could survive without exertion. Humboldt argued that civilisation could never flourish without some hardship. If the Amazon were to develop, banana groves should be abolished by decree – they were far too easy to grow!* The Swiss professor Louis Agassiz blamed the uniform temperature of Amazonia for the indolence of its people – although he himself liked that constant warmth combined with humidity and regular easterly breezes.*

There were mixed views about miscegenation. The Brazilian Tavares Bastos, who knew Amazonia in mid-nineteenth century, approved of intermarriage. 'It produces those mestizos who are so vigorous, intelligent and adept at rough labour in that climate. . . . Pure, primitive Indians are disappearing, leaving behind them more docile, more lively descendants who are more receptive to the influx of civilisation. The half-caste population is always increasing: it forms the industry that produces and exports, and the consumer that attracts imports.' Henry Bates was impressed by the mixed population of Cametá on the lower Tocantins. In the course of two centuries Portuguese settlers had intermarried with beautiful Cametá Indian women. 'The result has been a complete blending of the two races. . . . The people have a reputation all over the province for energy and perseverence. . . . The lower classes are as indolent and sensual here as in other parts of the province, a moral condition not to be wondered at in a country where perpetual summer reigns. . . . But they are light-hearted, quick-witted, communicative and hospitable. . . . It is interesting to find the mamelucos displaying a talent and enterprise, for it shows that degeneracy does not necessarily result from the mixture of white and Indian blood.'

But Bates' contemporary, the English botanist Richard Spruce, preferred to employ pure Indians, 'for the least streak of white blood in an Indian's veins increases tenfold his insolence and insubordination'. Professor Jean Louis Rodolphe Agassiz – who led an expedition to the Amazon in 1865 in a vain attempt to refute Darwin's theory of evolution and to examine whether the Amazon valley was caused by glaciation* – made damning racist generalisations about the mixed races. He found that mamelucos (the product of unions between Indians and whites) were 'pale and effeminate, feeble, lazy, and rather obstinate. It seems that the Indian influence has been just powerful enough to eradicate the higher attributes of the white without imparting any of the Indian energy.' By contrast, cafuzos or carafuz (of mixed Indian and black parentage) were by temperament 'a happy combination of the playful humour of the black with the rustic energy of the Indian'. And mulattoes (of mixed black and white blood) were 'full of self-confidence but very indolent'.

Despite such views, the Swiss professor and his American wife were much impressed by the Indians they met along the main rivers. 'The open character of the houses and the personal cleanliness of the Indians make the atmosphere fresher and purer in their houses than in those of our poor. However untidy they may be in other respects, they always bathe once or twice a day if not oftener, and wash their clothes frequently. We have never yet entered an Indian house where there was any disagreeable odor.'

Lourenço da Silva Araújo e Amazonas described Indians as docile,

generous and compassionate to their friends. He was aware that they
could be equally cruel and pitiless to their enemies. 'Oppressed and
insulted, Indians appear to be suspicious and resentful.' This impression was misleading. If a stranger spoke Tupi and was affable, Indians immediately responded with relaxed smiles. Acculturated
Indians were modest and grave in bearing, even during their festivals. They worked hard as fishermen, collectors or artisans, but they
were indifferent to wealth. They did not strive to get rich. Ingenuous
in business and legal matters, which they found incomprehensible,
they hated and despised 'a society of whose vices they are the angry
victims and in which they are assigned the social standing of slaves'.

This intelligent and experienced observer knew whom to blame
for this depressing situation. It was aggravated by abuses of the
provincial authorities. 'To the shame and disgrace of our civilisation, this situation was made more infamous by the provincial
Assembly of Pará which, in a relic of a barbarous instinct . . .
demanded so-called "descents" and enslavement of Indians. It
promulgated the law of 1837 that created the so-called Workers
Corps. This monopolised in favour of certain privileged speculators
the slavery of almost two-thirds of the population of the region.'

Foreigners who could not communicate with Indians mistook
their reticence for apathy or mental backwardness. The American
Herbert Smith unfavourably compared white and Indian children.
'An Indian is content to see or hear a thing, without troubling
himself about the whys and wherefores; even such incomprehensible
pursuits as fossil-collecting or butterfly-catching or sketching pro-
voke hardly any curiosity. The people look on quietly, sometimes
asking a question or two, but soon dismissing the subject from their
minds as something they are incapable of understanding. . . . So,
too, babies are unambitious; they do not cry after pretty colours, or
stretch out their hands to a candle. And the men have no apparent
desire to better their lot. They go on just as their fathers did; submit
to the impositions of the whites, a little sullenly, but without a
thought of rebellion unless there is a white or a half-breed to lead
them. . . . As an Indian will paddle steadily all day, while his wife at
home hardly ceases her monotonous cotton-beating, so the little
ones have an inexhaustible gift of patience.' Such passivity irritated
foreign observers who were convinced of the virtues of work and the
inevitability of human material progress.

Some authors imagined a dazzling future for the Amazon. As early
as 1820, Spix and Martius indulged in such a fantasy: 'What marvellous perspectives are opened, when the banks of the majestic stream

will one day be occupied by populous cities, when the nations to the west cross the natural barrier of the Andes, and highways link the capital of Peru with the Marañon, the Pacific Ocean to the Atlantic, when the empty melancholy forests of the Casiquiare echo to the cries of sailors travelling from the Orinoco to the Amazon, when the rapids of the Madeira have been made navigable, the watersheds of Aguapei and Camapuan have been pierced, and when the same sails move from the still waters of the Negro to the majestic Amazon and far to the south emerge safely on to the busy Plate! A philanthropist happily contemplates this vision of a fine future, when civilisation and nature will have created in the world's richest land . . . a nation of fortunate people, whose industry and wellbeing are mutually rewarded.' Humboldt had had this same vision when he travelled through the Casiquiare Canal at the beginning of the century. He compared the Casiquiare to the Rhine and imagined boats sailing from Peru to the Caribbean by this route. 'A country nine or ten times larger than Spain, and enriched with the most varied productions, is navigable in every direction by the medium of the natural canal of the Casiquiare and the bifurcation of the rivers. This phenomenon . . . deserves to be carefully examined.'

In the middle of the century, the American government sent two naval officers, William Lewis Herndon and Lardner Gibbon, to investigate the potential of the Amazon. They reported enthusiastically, adding a list of all the forest gums (including of course india-rubber), fruits, rare woods, fish, game, exotic birds and 'insects of the strangest forms and gayest colours. . . . We have here a continent whose shores produce, or may be made to produce, all that the earth gives for the maintenance of more people than the earth now holds. We have here also a fluvial navigation for large vessels, by the Amazon and its great tributaries. . . . Let us now suppose the banks of these streams settled by an active and industrious population, desirous to exchange the rich products of their lands for the commodities and luxuries of foreign countries; let us suppose introduced into such a country the railroad and the steamboat, the plough, the axe, and the hoe; let us suppose the land divided into large estates and cultivated by slave labour so as to produce all that they are capable of producing; and with these considerations we shall have no difficulty in coming to the conclusion that no territory on the face of the globe is so favourably situated, and that, if trade there is once awakened, the power, wealth and grandeur of ancient Babylon and modern London must yield to that of the . . . Orinoco, Amazon and La Plata.'

Many other optimists echoed such visions. The French geographer Abbé Durand described the banks of the Madeira as fertile and suitable for every form of agriculture. The river and its tributaries were also full of gold. 'Therefore let men of all nations soon come to the shores of these river highways. Agriculture, commerce, industry, and the exploitation of gold-mines all promise them an incalculable prosperity.' Richard Spruce wrote that 'some of the mighty rivers might seem to have been made by nature's hand expressly for steam navigation, being so wide and deep, and flowing with so gentle and equable a descent, as to allow vessels of considerable size to reach the very foot of the mountains whence they take their rise.' The American naval lieutenant Mathew Maury became excited by the potential of the Amazon as a second Eden. He insisted that the prosperity of the United States depended on the opening of the Amazon to foreign shipping, 'peacefully if we can, by force if we must'. His British counterpart, Lieutenant Henry Lister Mawe, predicted that ten years after the introduction of steam navigation 'the country will be no more recognisable.' British and American pressure to have the great Amazon river opened to international shipping finally triumphed in 1866, with the internationalisation of the main Amazon and many of its tributaries.

The prophets of an industrialised Amazon saw no role for native Indians in their utopia. Spix and Martius argued that 'the Indians cannot endure the higher culture that Europe wishes to implant among them. A progressing civilisation, which is the vital element of flourishing mankind, irritates them like a destructive poison. They therefore seem to us destined to disappear, like many other species in the history of nature.' Henry Bates felt that 'the inflexibility of character of the Indian, and his total inability to accommodate himself to new arrangements, will infallibly lead to his extinction, as immigrants endowed with more supple organisations increase, and civilisation advances in the Amazon region.'

Later in the century, observers noted how devastating contact could be to isolated tribes. Franz Keller, an engineer sent in the 1860s to investigate the possibility of making the rapids on the Madeira river navigable, saw decadent remnants of the once-powerful Mundurukú tribe. The nearby Mura were despised by whites and blacks, and treated as pariahs. Keller was pleased that this tribe might soon die out; its loss, he felt, would not be 'to the detriment of the country, which can well spare a stubborn element, incapable of adapting itself to the new order of things fast approaching'. Soon, 'easier communications and the all-levelling influence of trade will have erased the last traces of real Indian life from these regions.'

Notions of a European master race pervaded the writings of the boastful French explorer, Henri Coudreau, who had himself propelled by Indians up many Amazon tributaries at the end of the century. He predicted that European immigrants would soon create a great city on the banks of the Amazon. This would 'prove with legitimate pride to the astonished rest of the world the achievement of this new labour of Hercules. The Aryans will have tamed the equator; but the Indians will have contributed almost nothing to this result.' Coudreau gloated that the Mawé, like other tribes, 'melt into the civilised element or are extinguished'. Coudreau argued that when an 'inferior' race confronts a 'superior' one, 'despite the dubious results of intermarriage, the inferior variety suddenly fades and does not take long to disappear forever. . . . Here comes the civilised race setting out from the east. . . . The Brazilians and their European friends will come to sow peace and concord in places where savage Black-faces left nothing but their grotesque and odious souvenirs of attempted sorcery and of murders committed on defenceless women and on men fallen during their sleep or some repast of friendship.' José Verissimo, a contemporary Amazonian intellectual, agreed that tribes could not withstand the crushing pressure 'of a great immigration by a vigorous race which will, in the struggle for survival of which Darwin speaks, annihilate them by assimilation'.

Such were the ravings of colonialists at the height of European imperialistic expansion. Coudreau conjured up visions of Indians killing white men and women when he knew that the vast weight of evidence was of whites annihilating and oppressing Indians. He was echoing frontier settlers, who wanted Indian land and would extinguish tribes to get it. Coudreau imagined that 'it will not be long before nothing remains of all these wandering hordes but their lands, now widowed. But these lands will always be there, beautiful, rich and only awaiting men of goodwill.'

In the late twentieth century, some of these predictions have been realised. Most Indian tribes are gone, although their remnants cling stubbornly to vestiges of their tribal culture. While most of the world has been decolonised, Brazil and Amazonia remain the only place in the tropics where Europeans are permanently established. Roads and colonisation schemes are finally penetrating Amazonia from the east and south, and across the Peruvian and Ecuadorean Andes. But the region could hardly be seen as an industrial miracle. The complex rainforest ecosystem has defeated colonial visions. New roads have opened parts of Amazonia to deforestation and devastation. But Humboldt's dreams (and those of later visionaries) of teeming riverine waterways have not materialised. There are probably smaller riverine populations and less river traffic in Amazonia now than there were a century ago.

While the jingoists applauded what they saw as the march of civilisation, more sensitive observers deplored what was happening. At the beginning of this century, Antonio Domingos Raiol, a distinguished Brazilian historian and politician, attacked those who thought that the extermination of Indians was an inevitable consequence of civilisation. 'Some claim that inferior races tend to disappear in the face of superior races. This principle of sociology is invoked to justify the gradual disappearance of settled Indians. But it fails to demonstrate the fundamental cause of such a phenomenon – which is contrary to the law of nature that implies growth and multiplication for all creatures. The reason is undoubtedly found in the abuse, violence and assaults by the stronger against the weaker.'

Raiol urged that the surviving tribal Indians be left in peace in their forests. It was unnecessary to introduce them to the world of material wants and social pretensions. 'They fear and detest the civilisation that we want to "give" them – at the cost of their own sweat, blood, lives, dignity, wives and children. . . . No one has the right to change other peoples' customs by arbitrary and violent means. Let us stop molesting these unfortunates. Leave them in peace, scattered and uncontacted in their wilds, absolutely ignorant of the marvels of the much-vaunted progress that has been so fatal to them.' José Viera Couto de Magalhães, the Brazilian statesman and explorer, agreed that tribes should be left in isolation: 'Each tribe that we settle in aldeias is a tribe that we degrade and eventually destroy – albeit with the best intentions and a waste of our money.'

By the beginning of the twentieth century, acute observers realised that Indian decline was due to disease and physical factors more than to some Darwinian law of natural selection. Theodor Koch-Grünberg, a sensitive German anthropologist who worked among the tribes of the upper Rio Negro and Uaupés, watched Indians crushed by toil as boatmen and rubber gatherers. 'This drudgery for capitalism – the god of modern culture – leaves them no time to till their fields. Fever and diseases of civilisation to which their weakened bodies can raise no opposition, account for the remainder. . . . They still call themselves "Barés", because the name sounds well in the region around. The majority also still speak, in addition to Spanish [or Portuguese], their soft, tuneful speech. But as a tribe they have ceased to exist.' Kenneth Grubb, a missionary with wide experience of Brazilian Indians, saw that tribes were more likely to disappear from disease and low birth-rate than to merge with the advancing civilisation. He wrote a sad requiem about the denuded Amazon. A traveller could travel from Belém to Peru 'without seeing a distinctively tribal Indian. Many, of course, have become civilised and have married with the caboclo breed. The tribal life over the Brazilian interior is in its last stages of dissolution. . . . These rivers are silent today, except for the lap of the waters along some deserted beach, the hoarse cry of the parrots or the call of the inambu [tinamou bird]. The past has gone, with its peoples, in central Amazonia, leaving only that bitter sense of impotence, as of being present before a consuming conflagration and at the same time being powerless to assist.'

Amid all the criticism of and despair about Indian men, some travellers commented favourably about Indian women, who were constantly busy about the village, cooking, spinning and weaving, raising their families and growing crops. (Visitors tended not to see the men when they were at their most impressive: tracking, hunting, fishing or clearing forest.) Europeans who managed to visit remote tribes were struck by the beauty of the women. Carl von Martius admired the Pasé women of the Japurá river. 'The wife of Chief Albano had such regular features, such brilliant black eyes, and such a perfectly formed body that, with her blue-black tattooed lower face, she would have caused a sensation even in Europe.'

Farther upstream, Martius noticed the beautiful figures of the Aruak-speaking Yumana women – indeed, it was for their figures that the Yumana and nearby Marawá were eagerly sought as slaves by settlers. Martius observed that Indian women wore clothes only when strangers were present. The Italian traveller Ermanno Stradelli found that this practice had not changed seventy years later; even tribes that had been subjected to missionary teaching dressed only when whites arrived. 'Their clothing is nothing more than an ornament, of which they are proud in front of those who teach them to wear it, but which they abandon once the whites have passed.' Stradelli observed that the Tukano (Tukana) women of the Uaupés wore tiny tanga fringed girdles when dancing, but were otherwise completely naked, 'with their labia major tucked in and the mons veneris completely devoid of hair, which they pluck with pincers of split pieces of uambé liana.'

Acculturated Indian women could be equally delightful. The English explorer William Chandless admired the pleasing manners of the Mundurukú women on the Jutaí river. 'Their brightness and vivacity were unconscious and quite distinct from forwardness. It seemed to me to be the elasticity in the first freedom from woman's bondage of tribe-life, and probably may pass away; for those on the Maué-assú had nothing of it: indeed they were dull and shy.' Araújo e Amazonas said that civilised Indian women held their long black hair with semicircular high-fronted gold combs. A white kerchief was worn on either the hand or the shoulder. These women used perfumes from forest plants and wore small bouquets of flowers. 'The lady's good taste and coquetry is shown by where she places this garland on her head, at one side or as a pendant.' Amazon Indian women were modest and pious, observing all church festivals and dancing less voluptuously and more monotonously than in other parts of Brazil.

But the feature that most excited onlookers was the acculturated women's blouses. These had wide sleeves, held near the wrists by large gold buttons. They left the wearer's elegant neck fully exposed, and they were made 'of lacework or muslin so fine that it shades rather than covers the breast'. Robert Avé-Lallement could not take his eyes off these bright transparent shirts. 'At every step, the fine cloth of the blouses buttoned at the neck quivered over firm and elastic breasts, whose exuberance needed no corset to support them.' This doctor had a medical explanation for these fine figures: 'Constant baths in the river maintain the tension of the skin, and the swelling of the cellular tissues matures rapidly with age.'

Araújo e Amazonas was even more lyrical about the charms of mameluco women. He found them near perfection in character: happy, frank, generous, patient and resigned in work. Their natural talent compensated for lack of education: they quickly learned new skills. Angelic mothers and dedicated wives, they were morally as good as they were physically beautiful. 'Small hands and feet, ample black tresses, the proverbial necks of Indian women, figures of the most perfect proportions, added to a tanned colour: all these were enhanced by an original facial expression, and by vivacity and grace infinitely superior to what one would have expected for a race isolated in that wilderness.'

Indian women obtained their ornaments and trinkets from itinerant traders. In the thousands of kilometres of empty Amazon rivers, enterprising traders became the main means of contact between 'civilisation' and isolated riverside farms or settlements. Such a roving merchant was called regatão or haggler – because he negotiated mercilessly and drove a hard bargain. Many were unscrupulous rascals. They gained a terrible reputation and aroused the furious condemnation of Amazonian politicians and writers. As early as the 1830s, Ignácio Accioli de Cerqueira e Silva wrote that the regatão traders perpetrated with impunity many indignities and crimes on their gullible customers. They travelled in fleets of montarias, river boats paddled by Indians and mestizos. Their crews, called cani-curus, would often get drunk and behave disgracefully during their masters' commerce and the wild festivities that accompanied them.

William Edwards, an American lawyer and naturalist who was on the Amazon in 1846, described the trade. 'Coarse German and English dry goods, Lowell shirtings, a few descriptions of hardware, Salem soap, beads, needles, and a few other fancy articles, constitute a trader's stock. In return are brought down balsam, gums, wax, drugs, turtle-oil, tobacco, fish and hammocks.' Knives and guns were prized possessions for Indians, who had no idea of their true market value. Edwards observed that 'cheap German guns are abundant throughout the country, and it is wonderful that accidents do not frequently occur with their use. Unless a gun recoils smartly, an Indian thinks it is worth nothing to shoot with; and we knew of an instance where a gun was taken to the smith's and bored in the breech to produce the desirable effect.'

The traders wanted a wide range of native produce. Edwards saw prodigious quantities of aromatic balsam from the copaíba tree: it was floated down to Manaus in hollowed logs, each of which contained up to 2500 gallons of the precious oil. The emetic sarsaparilla was still a popular medicine, and quinine, which grew 'pretty universally', was needed to reduce malarial fevers. Vanilla 'grows everywhere and might by cultivation be elevated into a valuable product'; indigo was used for dyes; tonga beans were picked in the forest near Manaus; beautiful fabrics could be made from the down-like silky cotton of the sumaúma tree; and the pixiri fruit was an admirable substitute for nutmeg or sassafras. Edwards and his fellow American Lardner Gibbon liked the popular brownish drink made from guaraná, a nut that was roasted and ground by the Mawé Indians. 'A teaspoonful grated into a tumbler of water forms a pleasant beverage; but when drunk to excess, as is generally the case, its narcotic effects greatly injure the system.' The French traveller Paul Marcoy said that guaraná was popular throughout Pará both among Indians and among settlers. But, to his sophisticated palate, guaraná was too bitter and it smelled of old rhubarb. The Jesuit priest João Betendorf described guaraná in the late seventeenth century as giving the Indians great stamina during their hunting trips. It allowed them to travel for a day without hunger; and they also used it to treat fevers, headaches and cramps. Humboldt collected it on the Orinoco in 1800 and gave it its scientific name *Paullinia cupana.* Today, some 300 tons of guaraná are produced annually in Brazilian Amazonas, either in sticks, powder or liquid extract; but demand for the nut far exceeds supply.

William Edwards also noted that rubber trees abounded in Amazonia. But in 1846 rubber had not yet become the product that was to transform the region. Edwards commented that there was little demand for rubber in Manaus, where it was used only medicinally as a dressing for inflammations. He remarked prophetically: 'But when it is wanted, enough can be forthcoming to coat the civilised world.'

The waters of the Amazon once teemed with turtles. The naturalist Alexandre Rodrigues Ferreira noted fifteen species in the late eighteenth century, of which the most common was the podocnemis. These magnificent reptiles grew to weigh seventy kilos and yielded a marvellous range of produce for the natives. Turtle meat was appreciated, particularly during the long rainy season when fishing was more difficult. The large shells were found as basins or bowls in every kitchen, as buckets for carrying mud to building sites, or even as stepping stones for crossing muddy streets in Amazon villages. Turtle shells were cut into combs and turtle skins were made into tobacco pouches or stretched over frames as tambourines. The first explorers to descend the Amazon in the sixteenth century had found Omagua Indian villages surrounded by tanks full of thousands of turtles, and as late as the 1850s Henry Bates noted that every house in Tefé on the Solimões 'has a little pond in the backyard to hold a stock of these animals through the season of dearth – the wet months.'

Indians had become highly skilled at fishing for turtles. They would wait patiently in canoes near the reptiles' favourite feeding places or would lure them to the surface with bait of fruit or manioc. The Paumarí of the Purus and Mura of the Madeira could dive to nine metres to catch swimming turtles. Many travellers described great round-ups, with swarms of Indians beating the water and driving a churning mass of podocnemis into nets or shallow ponds. The easiest way to hunt turtles was to lance or harpoon them when they were sleeping near the surface. The Mura and the Conibo (Kunibo) of the Ucayali in Peru had both perfected a method of shooting arrows high into the air so that they would fall and pierce the thin top of a turtle's shell. The arrow-head would be detachable, tied to the shaft by cord, so that if a wounded turtle dived the arrow shaft would still be bobbing on the surface and the reptile could be hauled up by the embedded head. Turtles have limited vision and cannot see arrows falling from above, but William Edwards wrote that 'even long practice can scarcely make perfect; and fifty arrows may be shot at the unconscious sleeper before he is secured.'

Amazon Indians had fished and farmed turtles for thousands of years without destroying this rich resource. Such restraint ceased with the European penetration of Amazonia. The settlers found the fat and oil from turtle eggs more valuable even than the meat and shells of the adults, and turtle-egg oil was used for cooking and for lighting lamps.

In October each year, a female turtle would lay over a hundred eggs in a nest on a sandy beach. Egg hunters soon became adept at probing to find these nests and would take every egg they discovered. Thousands would be crushed in canoes. Whites and yolks were mixed with water and left in the sun to bring the yolk fat to the surface; this was then skimmed off and boiled in kettles to be purified and reduced. The Jesuits had imposed some form of conservation in this traffic: they insisted that a third of each turtle-hatching beach be left undisturbed. A few intelligent officials had called for protection of turtles in the late eighteenth century. Rodrigues Ferreira wrote two essays on the turtle trade and his contemporary Gama Lobo d'Almada demanded that 'the inordinate slaughter of turtles must be stopped at once. Turtles are a source of wealth because of the prodigious amount of butter that is made from their eggs and fat. . . . It is necessary to estimate carefully the quantity of butter that could be produced from the banks of the Rio Branco, and then permit the manufacture of only a third or half that amount. Such a policy would ensure the continuation of the trade and maintain the price of the product.'

Such pleas went unheeded. Adult turtles were slaughtered with reckless abandon and their eggs were destroyed in their millions. Rodrigues Ferreira noted that the finest oil came from mature turtles; but after it had been extracted from hundreds of reptiles, their meat was thrown into the rivers 'to feed buzzards, caymans and fishes such as piranha'. It took eleven nests containing about a thousand eggs to produce one pot or jar of oil. According to Rodrigues Ferreira, one canoe of hunters on the Rio Negro would collect a thousand such jars of oil a year. During the Directorate period, fifteen beaches most frequented by egg-laying turtles were designated as royal factories. Humboldt said that five thousand barrels of turtle oil were produced on the Orinoco in 1800; he calculated that it needed thirty-three million eggs laid by 330,000 females to produce this quantity. Twenty years later, Spix and Martius watched Indians, blacks and mulattoes joining to dig up hundreds of thousands of newly laid eggs on the Solimões. The German scientists wrote that the Solimões produced eight thousand large barrels of oil a year, out of a Brazilian total of fifteen thousand.

In 1851 Lardner Gibbon met a hundred turtle-egg hunters on the Madeira. They told him that the oil was used for cooking but particularly as lamp oil. 'Turtles are now said to be scarce. We see millions of eggs destroyed by the oil-hunters, who search all the islands and drive the turtles from one to the other.' A few years later, William Chandless found that traders on the Purus were employing local Paumarí to hunt the great reptiles. A village of these Indians would often bring in two or three hundred turtles a day. Chandless recalled: 'I have counted more than sixty canoes floating down river together in chase of turtle, each with a woman steering and an Indian standing like a statue in the bow of the canoe watching for turtle rising.' They were paid one barbed iron arrow head for each turtle. Far upriver Chandless also came upon three hundred rotting turtles that had been flipped on to their backs by Ipurinã Indians and left in the sun to die. By the end of the century there were some half-hearted attempts at protection. But, as Coudreau observed of the Nhamundá river, 'the very officials entrusted with conserving turtles were the first to work at devastating the sandbanks where turtles deposited their eggs.'

This profligate slaughter continued every year throughout the nineteenth century. Despite it, there were still so many podocnemis on the Madeira in the 1850s that they impeded river traffic near their nesting beaches. J. Coutinho, a zoologist who wrote about turtles in 1868, said that when they mated the clashing of their shells could be heard for great distances. As late as 1872, the railway engineer Edward Mathews saw a remarkable spectacle on the Madeira: 'For miles as far as the eye can see, which hereabouts runs straight for some six or seven miles, were continuous rows of turtle at the water's edge: the rows being eight or ten deep, many thousands must have collected together.' We have records of the quantity of turtle oil traded in Brazilian Amazonia during the last quarter of the nineteenth century. It represented the destruction of between one and five million eggs every year. No species could survive such a massacre. The Amazon turtle podocnemis is now endangered. Modern man does not seem to have the modicum of restraint and discipline needed to farm this magnificent source of food, as was done by the Omagua Indians in the sixteenth century.

Such were the forest products sought by the regatão traders. Successive presidents of Amazonas attacked these wicked merchants, who exploited Indians through debt bondage. In 1849, President Jerónimo Francisco Coelho reported that 'The bosses always have fraudulent open accounts with the Indians. They give them scraps of trade goods for quadruple their worth; and at the same time pay minimal amounts for their labour. The Indian is thus always in debt. . . . The main corrupters of Indians are squadrons of canoes of regatão pedlars or river vendors, who ply the rivers and penetrate everywhere. They fill the Indians' minds with false ideas, delude them with trickery, excite unfounded terrors in them, and give them bad advice to remove them from regular settlement and obedience. They portray themselves as their friends. But they do so with the cunning, perverse object of keeping an exclusive monopoly of their commerce, so that they can cheat them with impunity. For the Indians have no clear understanding of the value of the goods they exchange.'

In 1852 the Americans Lewis Herndon and Lardner Gibbon saw traders paying Indians in cachaça rum, hatchets, knives, fish hooks and beads. Henry Bates wrote that the Mundurukú of the upper Tapajós sold thousands of baskets of manioc and large quantities of sarsaparilla, rubber and tonka beans to traders who sailed up the river during the rainy season. Robert Avé-Lallement consoled a chief on the upper Rio Negro, who had paid a formidable price in forest produce for two baskets of salt. He described the traders as 'cancers who infest the margins of the Rio Negro and cause the backwardness of the Indians'.

The Brazilian authorities grew increasingly alarmed by this problem. The Bishop of Pará wrote to the imperial Minister of the Interior in 1865: 'It is difficult to imagine the extortions and injustices that most of these traders commit, abusing the weakness and ignorance of those unfortunate Indians. They sell them the most inferior objects at fabulous prices, and take their produce by force or deceit; at the very least they buy from them at minimal prices. They often make fathers of households drunk so that they can dishonour their women more easily. In short, there is no immorality that the greedy adventurers do not commit.'

President Araújo Brusque told how Indians were being driven deep into the forests to escape 'civilised' deceit and abuse. He portrayed Indians as docile and welcoming to strangers. 'There is no lack of adventurers who seek them out. These travel enormous distances, penetrate to their lodgings, and soon gain command over the tribe by means of supplying some object to which the Indians give an exaggerated value. They govern the tribe as they see fit. From then on, no one else enters there, and the wishes of the regatão are law. . . . The poor Indians obey him blindly! . . . He at once employs them extracting oil, nuts, sarsaparilla and other natural products. When they return to their homes in the village after three or four months of arduous work, he makes an account with them in such a way that the miserable Indians are still in debt to him.'

President Brusque quoted a series of examples of exploitation – a pair of cheap cotton trousers being traded for a barrel of copaíba oil worth twenty times as much; a gun for three barrels of oil worth twelve times as much; a barrel of gunpowder for eight drums, a ninefold mark-up. He told the Pará Assembly that the entire population of Turi Indians of the Capim river were at that moment 'trailing off into the forests of Candirú to extract oil and hunt for land tortoises for a certain regatão who imperiously sends them off on his service.' The prolonged absence of these men meant that their manioc plantations were abandoned and the huts of their village were decaying. Worse even than the financial cheating was abuse of Indian families. 'Even if the wife has not been seduced and the daughter raped, tender children are almost always torn from their families: on his return to the city, the regatão divides these among his accomplices.'

This president of Pará told of a village of Tembé Indians on the upper Purus river south of Belém. In October 1861, seven young men of the tribe rebelled against the depredations of a group of regatão pedlars. They finally killed them and their families, nine people in all. The police chief of Termo went and thrashed the Indians until they revealed the authors of the attack. He also burned their village and carried off nine children. President Brusque had restored these children to their mothers and expelled the police chief and other traders from the area. But innumerable similar incidents throughout Amazonia went unrecorded and unpunished. Araújo e Amazonas deplored the total lack of justice: it was because the country was so abandoned that the regatão was sure of impunity – thus he enforced his barter using 'the most revolting methods, including even intoxication, intimidation to excess, [and] horrible iniquities.'

Provincial governments imposed crushing taxes on the hated regatão traders, although this levy may not have been entirely disinterested. Araújo e Amazonas and Tavares Bastos both commented that the regatão traders were small businessmen interfering with the monopolies of the large trading companies. The latter carried electoral clout and political power. For all their exploitation, the pedlars did perform a useful function. A president of Amazonas revealed that in 1864 there was not a single missionary in Amazonia. 'Today no one goes to meet the Indians – except for the regatão.' These enterprising adventurers did at least bring the Indians the trade goods they wanted. Indians judge value by the utility of an object and by the effort involved in making it. They could not possibly know outside market values of such items as guns, powder, axes or knives. As far as they were concerned, such objects were beyond their ability to manufacture; whereas copaíba oil, rubber and other forest products were freely available to anyone prepared to go and get them. The directors of Indian villages (political appointees who rarely went near their charges) naturally resented the activities of the traders. A President of Maranhão noted that the colónias or aldeias of São Pedro and Januária on the Pindaré and Caru rivers 'are disturbed by the regatão traders, who plunge into the forests and there . . . traffic with the Indians. They delude them, and extract from them their harvest of copaíba oil in exchange for goods of little value – harvests that were awaited by the Directors, who thus had their designs upset.'

We have seen how, half a century after the abolition of the hated Directorate system, Amazon Indians were once again subjected to lay, or partial, directors. Antonio Domingos Raiol described the 1845 law as a total failure. It simply 'spread some more dragons through the country or satisfied the vanity of some local worthies. With a few honourable exceptions, the Partial Directors considered themselves authorised to practise all forms of arbitrariness and menaces against the Indians, forcing them to work for nothing, robbing their time, profaning their women, and seizing their children to give as gifts to their relatives or friends as rare objects of curiosity.'

By mid-century, there were few pure Indians under government control in the vast reaches of Amazonia. In his report of 1849, President Francisco Coelho listed only five active missions, thousands of kilometres from one another on the upper Rio Branco, the Japurá and Solimões, the middle Amazon, upper Tapajós and upper Tocantins. Apart from these there were various aldeias nominally controlled by lay directors. In practice, none was truly functioning. By 1855 there were theoretically fifteen directors in the province, but only five Indian villages were actively managed. 'The rest are in complete abandon by their respective directors, who make use of their office only when they want to derive some profit from the work of their Indians.'

Various travellers saw these new directors in action. Avé-Lallement in 1859 met the director of a thousand Mura and Ota Indians at Serpa on the lower Madeira and a white inspector among demoralised Indians upriver at São José de Amatari. Henry Bates visited Chrysóstomo Monteiro, director of the Indians of the Japurá river, 'a thin wiry mameluco, the most enterprising person in the settlement. . . . At this time he had 200 of the Japurá Indians in his employ. He was half Indian himself, but was a far worse master to the redskins than the whites usually are.'

Four years later, the director-general of Indians of Pará, Baron Jaguarary, named ten prominent citizens who were partial directors in his province. He admitted that he had confidence in almost none of these because it was very rare for them to have any dedication or zeal for their task. In 1864 the President of Amazonas decided not to fill some vacant directorships. He declared: 'I consider that the Indians would at least gain some benefit if I deliver them from those official persecutors.'

By the mid-1860s, the provincial authorities were calling for the abolition of the system. José Couto de Magalhães, President of Pará in 1864, said that he received constant complaints about the directors, who subjected the Indians to true slavery. In the following year, the Bishop of Pará wrote to the Interior Minister in Rio de Janeiro about this problem. In the Bishop's view, the honours offered were insufficient to attract prudent and intelligent men to live among primitive Indians in the remote wilds. The only good partial directors were those who did nothing about their charges. 'The rest, Minister, should not be called directors but rather masters of the Indians. And what masters! I do not wish to sadden Your Excellency by telling you the atrocities, tyrannies and outrageous injustices practised by these officials in the name and under the aegis of the government. . . . The wretched Indians are put to flight, oppressed, despoiled and enslaved just as at the time of the conquest. In some places they are even clandestinely sold like contraband merchandise. I myself have witnessed these facts.'

The situation was no better in neighbouring Maranhão, south of the mouth of the Amazon. The province had prospered more than Pará during the Pombaline era of the late eighteenth century, and its southern and eastern regions were settled with fazendas and ranches

by mid-nineteenth century. Maranhão had three main groups of
Indians. The Gamella, living on the lower Pindaré, Mearim and
Grajaú rivers not far inland from the provincial capital São Luis,
were rapidly declining in numbers. The numerous, hard-working
and largely acculturated Tupi-speaking tribes of Guajajara, Tembé
and Amanayé, known collectively as Tenetehara, occupied the
middle Mearim, Grajaú and particularly the Pindaré and Gurupi
rivers towards Pará. Near them were many sub-tribes of Gê-speaking
Timbira, fierce and handsome plains Indians, enemies of the Tupi-
speaking tribes and more resistant to frontier influence. They lived
on the upper rivers in south-west Maranhão and formed the northern end of the great crescent of Gê-speaking tribes of the central
Brazilian plateau. The best-known Timbira tribes were Canela
(Rankokamekra), Apinagé, Krahó, Krikatí or Gavião ('Hawks') and
Pukopye.

We have seen how these tribes resisted the expanding frontier in
the early nineteenth century. There was a lull during the 1830s. In
1840 the President of Maranhão, the Marquis of Caxias, founded a
fortified colónia at São Pedro do Pindaré not far upstream of
Monção, to protect river traffic on the Pindaré. 'Many Indians visited
this centre of civilisation, and told their relatives of the humane and
charitable manner in which they were treated.' After the law of 1845
reintroduced Indian partial directors, a directorate was established
at Barra do Corda, where the Corda river joins the Mearim in
southern Maranhão. This has always been a centre of Indian population. The new directorate controlled seven Guajajara aldeias and
two villages of Mateiro (Forest) Timbira: a total of 2270 Indians.

In the years after 1850, Krenyé and Pobzé Timbira presented
themselves in growing numbers near Bacabal on the lower Mearim.
It is not clear why these Indians chose to migrate down to be near the
frontier settlements. They probably wanted the civilizados' trade
goods and food, and having successfully fought those settlements in
1818–19 were not frightened of them. After two thousand Timbira
had appeared near Bacabal, the local farmers grew alarmed. The
President of Maranhão noted that 'the mere presence of them is
uncomfortable, and the slightest imprudence could lead to serious
and disastrous conflict.' A contingent of troops was sent up the
Mearim, and a colónia called Leopoldina was re-established near
Bacabal. The provincial government sent a load of presents to
seduce the Indians. By 1854 the President reported that 'the ferocious Timbira, terror of the farmers of the Viana district, are – after
various attempts and constant effort [to attract them] – finally at

peace with us and ready to settle in aldeias. They are abandoning the life of violence and raiding to which they are accustomed.' In 1855 there was an order to found another colonia, Capivary, near Viana, to accommodate local Gamella and roving bands of Timbira.

As so often in Brazilian history, this move to settle Indians ended in disaster. In 1855 the Indians of Leopoldina were struck by a deadly epidemic of intermittent fevers. The disease baffled the authorities. President Olimpio Machado said that it was not 'the deadly plague of smallpox which has been raging more or less intensively since last November. . . . It has caused more ravages even than the yellow fever which raged here in 1851, which may God remove far from us. It is not possible to give a precise name to this scourge . . . nor is it possible to determine its origin.' The provincial government sent medicines and vaccinated fifteen thousand inhabitants, including many Indians, but this was too late and inappropriate to the new fevers.

By the 1850s, Maranhão was suffering a shortage of labour. Many men were starting to leave to join the growing Amazon rubber trade, and efforts to attract European settlers to Maranhão had failed. So local colonists began to look enviously at the athletic and robust Indians of the new colónias. Attempts to harness Indian labour, combined with the devastating epidemic, had the obvious result. By 1857 the Director of Leopoldina, Father Carlos Winckler, reported to the President that it was 'tending to become extinct'. An Indian called Henrique had rebelled against his chief Faustinho and persuaded many of his tribe to leave the disagreeable place. By 1862 there were only 336 Indians left at Leopoldina, from the Kukoe-kamekra, Krenyé and Pobzé tribes of Timbira. This was the last mention of the Pobzé: they were down to ninety-one people by 1862 and doomed to extinction.

The authorities had higher hopes for 'civilising' the more docile and industrious Guajajara. A report of 1855 said that there were eight villages of Guajajara on the upper Pindaré, whose inhabitants were employed in gathering and extracting copaíba balsam oil and were 'happily endowed for social life'. Another colónia was founded for the Pindaré Guajajara at Januária where the Caru river joins the Pindaré. Near Barra do Corda, 250 kilometres south of Januária, there were 2600 Guajajara. It was hoped that these could easily be converted to Christianity and put to 'useful' work. The President of Maranhão said that 'these Indians like peace and work: they are docile, hospitable and faithful.' If they were given plenty of tools and presents, it would inspire them with affection for the whites, and might also give them a taste for 'the necessities of a more cultivated life'. The hope was to lure them into dependence on manufactured goods. As a reward for their good behaviour, the Guajajara of Barra do Corda were formed into one of the notorious new Workers Corps by a decree of 25 July 1854.

Things did not progress as intended. In 1859 the President had to sack the directors of the two Pindaré colónias for mistreating their Indians, and by 1860 it was reported that, instead of progressing, the colónias of São Pedro and Januária on the Pindaré and Leopoldina on the Mearim were 'daily declining'. They contained, respectively, only 76, 100 and 100 Indians. Farther up the Pindaré, the Tupi-speaking Amanayé came under the influence of fugitives from the Cabanagem rebellion in nearby Pará. These fugitives told the Amanayé to trade their copaíba oil and cravo only with regatão traders, instead of delivering them to their official directors. The outsiders were accused of making the Amanayé dependent on alcohol, of exploiting them, and of inspiring the killing of a director called Oliveira.

The docile Guajajara of Barra do Corda finally rebelled in 1860 against the 'rather harsh behaviour' of their Director João da Cunha Alcanfôr. The Director himself escaped, but the Indians killed his brother-in-law and set fire to his farm. They also resisted a contingent of troops of the First Line Regiment and national guards sent against them from Barra do Corda. As a result of this rising, most Indians abandoned their aldeias and fled to the forests. Meanwhile, in villages on the Grajaú river, six hundred Guajajara and many Mateiro Timbira died of 'epidemics of flowing smallpox and malignant intermittent fevers that rage annually among the Indians'.

Successive provincial presidents criticised the inadequate partial directorate system, yet it continued in force. One of them, in 1866, deplored the fact that the Indian service had been totally neglected: no one could tell him anything about the numbers, state of integration, resources or potential of the province's Indians. There was no policy other than the long-discredited one of trying to settle Indians into colónias or aldeias. The Guajajara of the upper Grajaú were assembled in a new colónia called Palmeira Torta (Crooked Palm-tree). But in 1867 these Indians rebelled against the new regime; and their revolt spread rapidly among the Tupi tribes of the upper Pindaré. Troops were sent, who managed to contain Indian aggressions against small farmers in the region. But the Provincial President knew that these very farmers were to blame for the trouble. They and local regatão traders had obtained posts as partial directors and, being unpaid, both groups exploited their positions. The traders cheated the Indians in usurious deals, and the fazendeiros made them work without proper pay. 'Some have abused their position by despoiling the Indians of their children, using seduction or even violence for this. This was probably the main cause of the savages' recent attacks, and of the disgust that makes them distrust and avoid our civilised people.'

Nothing improved. In 1872 we hear of the partial director leading an armed attack by forty-seven men on one of the Leopoldina aldeias. Indians were killed and wounded, and the Provincial President sacked that Director. Eleven years later, another President made a damning contrast between settled and uncontacted tribes. After many decades of directorate tutelage, the Timbira still retained most of their tribal customs. Even the Guajajara, although deemed to be 'almost white and intelligent', would not imitate the colonists in every respect. 'Indians of the various directorates consider themselves in a state of subjection. They learn nothing because they are taught nothing. And they are objects of speculation to the many who abuse their simplicity. In contrast, the nomadic tribes are increasing in numbers and live contentedly . . . either isolated in the midst of their forests or attached to well-intentioned fazendeiros and farmers.'

In 1887 the authorities of Maranhão were still calling for the abolition of the partial directors. There were then six colónias in the province. Twenty-four partial directors theoretically attended to some twenty-five thousand Indians, mostly Timbira and Tenetehara. But none of them resided in his village or performed his obligations in the correct manner.

Possibly because they became acculturated more readily than almost any other tribe, the Guajajara population remained reasonably large. The Guajajara (who called themselves Tenetehara) had numbered some twelve thousand in 1830. They were spread over a vast region, with some five thousand on rivers south of Belém in the province of Pará and the majority on the upper Pindaré and Gurupi rivers in Maranhão. The Tembé group of Tenetehara migrated westwards in the 1850s to the upper Gurupi river on the boundary between Maranhão and Pará. We have seen how some fled further west to the Capim after killing nine regatão traders in 1862. A decade later Gustav Dodt reckoned that there were nine thousand Tembé, of whom six thousand were on the Gurupi living scattered in family communities. Because of this isolation, Barbosa Rodrigues wrote that the Tembé 'had little contact with whites and were considered primitive.' Although the Tenetehara in Pará have now declined in numbers, there are probably as many Tenetehara in Maranhão now as at the time of their first contact. The American anthropologist Charles Wagley attributes this to the tribe's long contact with settlers and missionaries: the latter encouraged large families and the Indians realised that children could be valuable collecting babassu nuts for trade with the settlers.

In 1901 relations between the docile Guajajara and the Brazilian authorities suddenly deteriorated. Italian Capuchins from Lombardy had installed themselves among the Guajajara at Alto Alegre near Barra do Corda in 1897. The newly arrived missionaries were too violent in imposing their faith on the Indians, using the classic tactic of removing young children for indoctrination in strict boarding schools. All Indians love their children passionately and will not tolerate any corporal punishment or abuse of their young.

Guajajara unease at the missionary regime reached despair and fury when in 1900 a measles epidemic killed thirty children in the school. On 13 March 1901 the Indians attacked the mission, killing all the missionaries – four friars, seven nuns and a novice – and all whites who worked on the mission or were staying there to have their children educated in the school. The Guajajara went on to attack local fazendas, travellers and itinerant traders. It was open war. For three months the Guajajara defended their territory with trenches and barricades. They were sufficiently acculturated to understand civilizado fighting methods and they had an armoury of old shotguns. At first their superior forest skills gave them an advantage, until the whites enlisted the Guajajara's traditional enemies, the Gê-speaking Rankokamekra (Canela). Chief Major Delfino Kikaipó sent a contingent of forty Canela warriors to help a heavily armed force of 140 police, militia and colonists. The Guajajara were defeated in battle in mid-June.

By August it was all over. The Guajajara had melted into the woods and been tracked down. Their traditions say that mothers smothered their infants to prevent them crying and betraying hiding places. Hundreds of Indians were killed in battle or died of starvation. Local folklore still tells terrible stories of brutality by both sides, and a church in Barra do Corda has a mosaic façade with portraits of the martyred missionaries.* Forty Guajajara leaders were imprisoned in Barra do Corda and their chief, João Caboré, died in prison.

*

One of the most odious tasks of the directors was to recruit Indians for military service. Ever since the first conquest of Brazil, some native tribes had fought with the Portuguese. Indians fought on both sides in the wars in which the Portuguese defeated French and Dutch attempts to colonise Brazil. During the Napoleonic Wars, troops from Pará had taken French Guiana, and most of the men involved in that campaign were Indians. Native soldiers had an obvious value in Amazonia because of their brilliance as woodsmen, trackers and boatmen. During much of the nineteenth century, however, Indians were drafted to swell the ranks of infantry regiments. Their skills were wasted in the drudgery of barracks life and drill.

We have seen how Mundurukú helped the authorities to suppress the Cabanagem revolt. After the rebellion was ended in 1839, the provincial government used military service as a means of stripping the region of potential future rebels. William Edwards was on the Amazon in 1846 and noted that 'during the last few years, the enrolment of Indians [into the army] has been carried to an unprecedented extent, through apprehension of renewed disturbances. Since 1836 ten thousand young men are said to have been carried to the south, to the incalculable injury of the agricultural interest. As might be supposed, all this enlistment has not been voluntary. The police are constantly upon the alert for recruits, and the instant that a poor fellow sets foot within the city he is spirited away unless some protesting white is there to intercede in his behalf.' Many huts near Belém were occupied only by women and children, and women paddled the market boats because their men dared not appear.

There was something tragically comic about the Indian recruits. Edwards was amused watching them 'during their early drillings . . . encumbered with oppressive clothes, high leathern stocks beneath their chins, and a wilderness of annoying straps about their bodies. Their countenances are models of resignation, or of apathetic indifference.' Thousands of kilometres away, in 1841, Richard Schomburgk watched men of the provincial militia at Fort São Joaquim on the upper Rio Branco. They wore white cotton pantaloons and jackets with black facings. Their weapons were 'old condemned English muskets, dating from the reign of one of the Georges. . . . Those weakly striplings of Mars, streaming with perspiration, were worrying themselves to do the honours with these blunderbusses.' These soldiers had not been paid for three years, and they desperately sought to sell to the visiting Germans some tobacco they had grown. Other Indians from the Rio Negro worked as labourers at the

Fort. 'There was something deeply affecting, infinitely disquieting, in the mute gestures with which these poor unfortunates contemplated and welcomed our free [Makuxi] companions, who in return cast a glance of pity upon these victims of some slave raid, and then one of rage and anger upon their drivers.'

A few years earlier, Richard Schomburgk's elder brother Robert was sent by the Royal Geographical Society to explore the rivers of southern British Guiana. He travelled down the Tacutu towards Fort São Joaquim on the Rio Branco in 1838. During this descent, he saw the canoes of a 'press-gang, a most villainous looking body, lately sent by the Brazilian authorities to press Indians for the navy'. It had come from the Rio Negro and was led by 'a man who is already famed for the successful descent upon unsuspecting Indians, "not for the conquest of souls", but for selling them as slaves to his allies'.

When he reached the Fort, Robert Schomburgk saw some of the victims of this press-gang. They told him 'that they had been surprised at night, had been fired at, two huts set on fire, and those who had not been able to make their escape had been led away with their hands tied to their back. The conduct of the ruffians towards their women and children incensed them most. They brought away little children of 5 and 6 years old, and showed us that even *they* had been tied with their hands to their backs.' One grandmother had given offence to the raiders and was treated particularly harshly. After securing the victims, the press-gang 'rifled the huts and carried away what they considered of value – parrots, spun cotton, dogs, &c. There being a number of children, the march towards the canoes proved slow, and their provisions failed; nevertheless, they were driven forward like a herd of cattle, flanked by these ruffians with their muskets loaded and primed.'

Without food, they were driven across the savannahs and arrived starving at the landing place on the Tacutu. There were forty Indians, of whom eighteen were children, thirteen women, and nine men, most of whom were aged over thirty. It was obvious that these were not being pressed for service in the navy. Schomburgk asked: 'Are sucking babies, women, boys of tender age, and men near the climacteric fit subjects for serving in the Brazilian navy? Nay, the whole expedition bears the stamp of the most barbarous kidnapping, only worthy of a government of the darker ages.' The explorer protested to Pedro Ayres, brother of the military commander of Upper Amazonas, Captain Ambrósio Ayres (the notorious cabano-fighter Bararoá). This man at first pretended not to believe the story of atrocities. Confronted by the evidence, he admitted that 'the inferior officers wished to use the pressing of Indians for the navy as an excuse to procure young and old, in order to sell those who were not fit for that purpose to their allies. . . . He expressed his persuasion that only those who could really serve in the navy would be selected, while the aged, women and children would be returned.'

Six months later, Schomburgk travelled down the upper Rio Negro. As he passed the mouth of the Içana, he heard that the numerous tribes of the upper Içana had recently been victims of 'an expedition sent under pretence of pressing them for the service of the Brazilian navy, but in fact to send them into the interior to the mines as slaves; and such was the terror caused by it, that many of the villages were tenantless or inhabited only by women.' Farther downriver, Schomburgk found the commander of the small fort of São Gabriel fearful of an Indian attack to avenge 'the barbarities of the slaving expedition'. And at another place, the traveller took into his canoe some Indians whom the government had ordered to be returned to their villages as unsuited for military service. 'They consisted of two old men, five women, and two children, who were left to themselves and almost starving. . . . Another party of seven were to follow on the next day.'

In 1852, the British botanist Richard Spruce saw the commandant of Fort São Gabriel seizing Indians of the Uaupés river for service on the postal canoes between there and Manaus. 'A detachment of soldiers is sent by night to enter the sitios [riverside settlements] and seize as many men as are wanted, who are forthwith clapped into prison and there kept until the day of sailing – in irons if they make any resistance. The voyage averages fifty days, and these poor fellows receive neither pay nor even food for the whole of this time. . . . Such treatment is a great disgrace to the Government, and it is not to be wondered at that the Indians hide themselves in the forests.'

That same year the American naval lieutenant Lewis Herndon said that the military force of Amazonas consisted of two battalions of Guarda Policial. These thirteen hundred men were divided among the province's villages. They were not paid and had to provide their own uniforms of white jacket and trousers. From time to time, groups of them had to go to the towns to do actual paid military service as soldiers of the line. 'This is a real grievance. I have heard individuals complain of it; and I doubt if the government would get very effective service from this body in the event of civil war.' Fifteen years later, the German engineer Franz Keller criticised the superior officers of the Guarda Nacional on the Madeira river. 'These have the privilege of selecting men for military service in the line; and they generally abuse this right in the grossest way, leaving unmolested those who will work for them without wages, and sending away those who show a disposition to resist.'

When Brazil fought a long and bloody war against Paraguay, the situation worsened. Professor Agassiz witnessed atrocities by press-gangs on the middle Amazon in 1865. At a riverside village near Manaus, 'the women said the forest was very sad now, because their men had all been taken as recruits, or were seeking safety in the woods. . . . They were taken wherever found, without regard to age or circumstances, women and children often being dependent upon them; and if they made resistance were carried off by force, and frequently handcuffed or had heavy weights attached to their feet. Such proceedings are entirely illegal; but these forest villages are so remote that the men employed to recruit may practise any cruelty without being called to account for it. If the recruits are brought in in good condition, no questions are asked.' At Manaus, the visiting professor and his wife saw a room of the jail packed with army recruits waiting for the steamer to take them to war. Acculturated, free Indians were being seized throughout Amazonas. 'The system of recruiting, or rather the utter want of a system, leads to the most terrible abuse of authority in raising men for the army. . . . The defencelessness of the Indians in the scattered settlements has made them especially victims.' Many Indians mutinied and fled to escape this conscription.

Paul Marcoy saw similar forced enlistment of tapuio Indians on the Solimões at that time: the Commandant of Tabatinga used them as his feudal serfs, sending them off to hunt or gather forest produce for him, and despatching some for sale in the towns for his personal profit. 'Such conscription is, with smallpox, the thing most dreaded by a Tapuyo Indian.' By 1870, the English traveller Henry Wickham found the towns of the Rio Negro neglected and deserted because their men had been drafted to serve in the Paraguay War 'where the mortality among them had been excessive, a mere fraction returning to the land of their birth'. Normally friendly and docile Indians 'have become hostile from the system of kidnapping the young men for service in the Brazilian army'. Even in 1873, long after the war was ended, the British surveyors Barrington Brown and William Lidstone had Indians of the middle Madeira river flee from them, fearing that they had come 'to search for deserters or get levies for the Paraguayan War'.

Forced labour for the state was closely linked to conscription into the armed forces. Arbitrary seizure of Indians for public works had

Chavante fiercely resisted the advancing frontier
for 150 years.

17.   Settlers admired the beauty of Apinagé women.

8.   Tukuna elder, near Tabatinga
on the Solimões.

19.   Canela (Rankokamekra), Eastern Timbira of Maranhão.

20. *The Marquis of Pombal.*

21. *The rubber baron Nicolás Suárez.*

22. *Karl von den Steinen* (centre).

23. *Johann Baptist von Spix.*

24. *Cândido Rondon in Bororo territory, 1895.*

The English naturalist Henry Bates, attacked by toucans.

26. *Baron Georg Langsdorff, leader of the ill-fated Russian expedition to central Brazil, 1827.*

27. *A Bororo warrior in macaw-feather headdress.*

28. *Yanomami.*

29. *The Kadiwéu Guaikurú of the Paraguay valley were brilliant horsemen.*

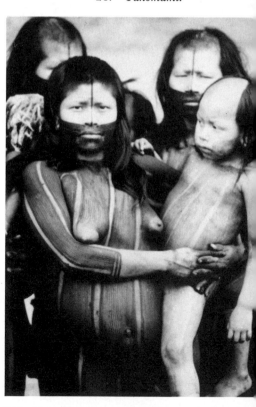

30. *Kayapó women and children with shaved he and body dye.*

31. *A Bororo couple after contact.*

32. *Tiriyó, Tumucumaque hills of Guiana.*

Bororo in full regalia of feather headdresses and labret in lower lip.

34. *Parintintin, fearless and skilful warriors.*

35.   *Wapixana warriors and a girl brewing paiwari.*

36.   *Guarani women in Rio de Janeiro wea*
      Empire dresses in the 1820s.

37.   *A Guarani artilleryman in the Brazilian army, Rio de Janeiro, 1825.*

38.   *A dance of Kayapó women, singing in unison.*

39.   *A Kayapó family, the father wearing a lip disc.*

40. *Kayapó women carrying palm leaves.*

41. *The author among Txukarramãe, Jarina river, 1971.*

been widely blamed as one of the causes of the Cabanagem revolt. Despite this, the practice continued after that rebellion was ended. At the height of the Cabanagem, General Andrea formed a new and tougher Workers Corps to which all Indians without regular means of support were enlisted. This meant that any Indian who did not own a plantation could be pressed into service. As Count Castelnau commented, it meant 'in a word, the entire Indian population'.

Such a law was a licence for oppression and covert slavery. When Robert Schomburgk sailed down the Rio Negro in 1839 he found 'a melancholy and utter picture of desolation . . . houses in ruins and without inhabitants; the plants clambering over the roofs and the high bushes and grass before the door'. During a journey of several weeks, descending eight hundred kilometres of river, the travellers saw only one native boat – and it fled at their approach. 'The desolation . . . is caused by the oppression which the Indians receive from those petty officers to whom the official duties are entrusted, and who compel the Indians to work with no other pay than a slender subsistence. This is sufficient to ruin commerce and agriculture, and cause the desertion of the Indians.' Three years later, Schomburgk's brother Richard met a Brazilian colonel on the headwaters of the Rio Branco. He asked him what goods he traded with the Indians to persuade them to work. 'The Colonel assured us that as this was unnecessary he had brought none: the Indians had to render him the help demanded without any recompense.'

The government's ambivalent attitude to this legislation emerged in the annual reports of successive provincial presidents. In 1849, President Coelho of Pará said that the Workers Corps had been created in 'a sentiment of morality and order . . . but abuse has converted it into a means of servitude and private gain.' The trouble was that Amazon Indians had abundant food and hence no *need* to work. They were therefore most reluctant to submit to compulsory toil, 'especially when the obligation to work, which is imposed by law, has so generally been converted into vexatious speculation by abuse!' What infuriated the authorities was their inability to force the 'free' coloured citizens of Amazonia to work. President Coelho claimed that the Workers Corps' 'principal object . . . was to give employment to an excessive number of tapuios, negroes and mestizos – people void of civilisation and education and who exceed in number the worthy, laborious and industrious part of the population by more than three-quarters'.

William Edwards was often frustrated by the difficulty of getting Indian crews to paddle him. He therefore defended the system of compulsion. He described how each local captain of workers could requisition men in his district to navigate a boat or for some other purpose. The captain sent an order to the Indians' chief or tuchaua, 'and the men must be forthcoming, no matter what may be their private engagements. This looks very like compulsion, but it is really no more so than jury duty. The men make a voyage to the city and back and are then discharged, perhaps not to be recalled for several months.' Edwards claimed that the boatmen were correctly paid and well treated. He also asserted that they were strongly protected by law – he himself had seen a white man imprisoned in Manaus 'for merely striking an Indian in his employ'. But anyone (even a lawyer like Edwards) who could equate jury service with weeks of paddling akin to the punishment of a galley slave can hardly be taken seriously. Edwards concluded: 'The government has been sometimes severely censured for its conduct towards the Indians, but it is difficult to see what more it could do for them than it has done.'

When Herndon and Gibbon investigated the Amazon in 1851, they reported that all Christian Indians were 'registered and compelled to serve the State' either as soldiers of the Guarda Policial or as labourers in the Workers Corps. The province of Pará had nine such corps, numbering 7444 labourers and 182 officers. Each regional section was under a fiscal-major who was supposed to protect the interests of both workers and employers. Each town had a company of workers commanded by a captain, sergeant and several corporals. 'The duration of engagement is unlimited and at the will of the contracting parties. The captains are always obliged to furnish workers for either public works or private persons, unless all are already employed. Payment is sixty centimes a day plus food which is fish and manioc flour.' All workers were obliged to appear before the fiscal-major once a month, so that he could inspect them and hear their complaints. He had the power to imprison them for eight days, and they could suffer longer sentences for serious offences in the public service.

Two years later, a Provincial President admitted the desperate need for labour in the immense expanses of Amazonia. He was also aware of the failure by the government to protect or educate this pathetic proletariat. Indians were 'the only labourers that exist in the province, apart from a small number of [black] slaves. But since they have not received the slightest glimmering of education, they generally present the same simplicity, ignorance, improvidence and habits as their grandfathers. They continually elude the hopes of anyone who counts on them for permanent or regular labour.'

Indians fled to the forests because their bosses abused and failed to pay them. The employers argued that they kept Indians without pay because, if they did pay them, they promptly deserted. Nevertheless, 'domesticated Indians form the greater part of the known population. They are the only labourers on whom one can count for navigation, agriculture, extraction of forest produce, and domestic service.'

Part 3

Amazonia: The Rubber Boom

The Rubber Boom

After the middle of the nineteenth century, a powerful new force emerged on the Amazon. The world was beginning to exploit the sap from a wild Amazonian tree – rubber. This new product developed steadily and came to dominate the Amazon economy, becoming a magnet for settlers and adventurers. The boom it engendered pushed the frontier into the remotest headwaters of the Amazon river system. It was thus the force that shattered the isolation of many Indian tribes.

Rubber had been known for a long time. On his second voyage of 1493–6 Christopher Columbus watched natives of Haiti playing with bouncing rubber balls. But the commercial possibilities of rubber were not noticed until the mid-eighteenth century. The French scientist, Charles-Marie de la Condamine, who descended the Amazon in 1743, was impressed by an elastic and waterproof material exploited by the Omagua of the Solimões, who used it to make unbreakable bottles, boots and hollow bouncing balls. At Omagua feasts, each guest was given drink in a rubber syringe.

The Omagua call this resin 'hevé', whence comes the botanical name for the tall rubber tree, *Hevea brasiliensis*. Because the Omagua used it for syringes, the Portuguese call rubber 'seringa'. Maynas Indians of the upper Amazon Napo river used the name 'cau-chu', meaning 'wood that gives milk', which led to the French word 'caoutchouc'. The English name was coined by Joseph Priestley, the discoverer of oxygen, who noted in 1770 that the dry gum was sold in London to rub out pencil marks – hence 'rubber' or 'India rubber' because of its origin among the Brazilian Indians.

When la Condamine returned to France he read a paper to the Academy of Sciences about this remarkable product. But the true pioneer of the rubber industry was Condamine's friend François Fresnau, Seigneur de la Gatandière, an engineer who was sent to rebuild the fort of Cayenne in French Guiana. He spent fourteen years studying rubber trees and identifying the true hevea. In a memorandum of 1747, Fresnau brilliantly foresaw the use of rubber for waterproof cloth, fire-fighting pumps, awnings, diving suits, pot handles, ammunition cases, boots and carriage harnesses. By the time of the boundary demarcation expeditions of the 1780s, Alexandre Rodrigues Ferreira was already referring to the 'famous gum or elastic resin commonly called seringa milk'. He gave full credit to the Omagua Indians for its discovery, and noted that it was being used in Pará to make 'syringes and also other articles such as boots, shoes, hats, jackets, etc., all of which are impermeable by water'. Two men's waterproof suits were sent to King José in Lisbon. Surgeon Francisco Xavier d'Oliveira was sent to Amazonia to investigate. He set up a small factory to export rubber goods, and advertised in the *Gazeta de Lisboa* in March 1800 to sell his fine rubber probes, rubber candles, and little bags to hold the urine of incontinent persons or 'even gonorrheal materials'. The first European rubber factory was founded in France in 1803, to make ladies' elastic garters.

When Spix and Martius visited the Amazon in 1819, they saw policemen in Belém wearing waterproof rubber capes. They described the work of rubber-tappers (seringueiros) in the forests near Belém, whom they observed placing the rubber sap into 'innumerable clay forms, whose modelling offers great scope to the inventive genius of the seringueiros. The most common shape is that of the pear, from which the syringe originated. However, they also adopt the shapes of native fruits (cashews, sugar apples, pineapples, mangoes, etc.) or animals (fish, jaguars, monkeys, manatees) and even figures of people or imaginary creatures, not always decent.' By the 1830s, Americans were using rubber for galoshes or overshoes. In 1842 Prince Adalbert of Prussia wrote that men of the villages of the lower Xingu worked from June to December each year gathering and preparing rubber. (During the wetter 'summer' they collected sarsaparilla, copaíba balsam, cravo 'cloves' and cacao.) In the early days, rubber gathering was largely done by unorganised private enterprise. Greedy seringueiros slashed trees all round the trunk to remove all the gum in one day. Thus, when Paul Marcoy descended the Amazon, he did not even list rubber among the many products exported from Manaus. He met some tapuio Indian seringueiros in the channels near Marajó island at the mouth of the Amazon, but they were very poor, and were having difficulty finding enough hevea sap to earn a living.

Yet there was a serious drawback: rubber reacted to temperature, freezing in the snow or melting stickily in heat. A series of inventions was needed before it could become a major industry. In 1820 Thomas Hancock, 'the father of the rubber industry', first started making rubber goods on a large scale in England. In 1823 Charles Macintosh of Glasgow found that naphtha from a local gas works could convert rubber into a pliable coating for fabric; he opened a factory making macintosh waterproofs. In 1839 Charles Goodyear, a sickly inventor in Massachusetts, discovered after years of experiment how to harden rubber. He accidentally touched a mixture of rubber gum and sulphur to a hot stove, and to his delight found that it hardened like leather, no longer froze or melted, but remained waterproof. He called his process vulcanisation, after Vulcan, god of fire. Rubber was soon used as a solid covering for wheels. In 1845 R. W. Thomson patented a pneumatic wheel in England. But the most spectacular modern use was invented only in 1888. John Boyd Dunlop, a veterinary surgeon in Belfast, made the first detachable pneumatic rubber tyre to help his ten-year-old son win a tricycle race. He patented 'a hollow tyre or tube made of India-rubber and cloth . . . said tube or tyre to contain air under pressure or otherwise and to be attached to the wheel in such method as may be found most suitable'. The French cyclist Michelin tried out such tyres on a run between Paris and Rouen. Bicycles developed explosively as a cheap form of transport for the masses. In 1894 there were 250,000 bicycles in France; twenty years later, there were almost five million. World demand for rubber grew insatiably.

In 1827, rubber exports from Amazonia were worth £1000. During the next five years exports averaged £5500 a year; from 1833 to 1840 they rose rapidly despite the Cabanagem revolt, but still averaged only £19,000. By 1840 rubber represented only 17 per cent of Amazon exports, and by 1848 this had risen to 24 per cent. In quantity, rubber production rose from 156 metric tons in 1830 to 388 tons in 1840, 1467 tons in 1850, 2673 tons in 1860, and 6591 tons in 1870.

It was Macintosh's and Goodyear's inventions that caused these changes. World demand for rubber increased enormously, and went on growing throughout the latter half of the nineteenth century. The English botanist Richard Spruce saw rubber gathering along the entire length of the Rio Negro. He explained that 'the extraordinary price reached by rubber in Pará in 1853 at length woke up the people from their lethargy. . . . Mechanics threw aside their tools, sugar-makers deserted their mills, and Indians their roças [farm clearings], so that sugar, rum, and even farinha [manioc flour] were not produced in sufficient quantity.'

With the rise in world demand for rubber, the price of the product grew steadily in real terms throughout the latter part of the nineteenth century. Output also increased to match demand. Seringueiros gradually explored westwards in search of forests containing the tall hevea trees with their smooth grey bark and precious white sap. At first rubber was found near Belém; by 1850 it was being tapped on the Xingu and Tapajós; then in 1850–70 the search went up the Madeira, Purus and Juruá rivers.

The economic historian Roberto Santos has tried to calculate the number of men employed in rubber extraction, basing his estimates on the known quantity of rubber exports. He reckoned that there were 5300 rubber men in 1850, and that this number rose to 15,400 by 1860, 31,000 by 1870, 47,300 by 1880, 82,800 by 1890, 124,300 by 1900, 175,800 by 1910, and a peak of over 190,000 men in 1912 when the rubber boom began to collapse. Many Indians were pressed into service. But such quantities of men went far beyond available numbers of local Indians. They involved internal migration within Amazonia, and later from other parts of Brazil. In the early years, Belém and Manaus were stripped of labour as rubber gatherers flocked westwards. The government tried to sponsor immigration from outside Brazil, but was largely unsuccessful. In 1854 a thousand Portuguese and some Chinese were settled at Colônia Mauá downstream of Manaus, and at Itacoatiara. In 1866–7 a few hundred American colonists were imported after the end of the American Civil War. They settled in a colony near Santarém; but most failed and went home.

The wealth generated by the 'black gold' rubber was spectacular. Rubber exports rose sharply in quantity, and even more dramatically in value. In 1880 Brazilian Amazonia exported 7000 tons; by 1887 this had risen to 17,000 tons; and during the first ten years of the twentieth century, annual exports averaged 34,500 tons. With demand for rubber increasing prodigiously throughout the industrialised world, the price of this black gold rose in real terms by 144 per cent between 1890 and 1910. The 21,000 tons exported in 1897 were worth £13.5 million; and by 1909 Brazilian Amazonia exported twice that quantity at three times the value.*

During these giddy decades, Amazonia enjoyed a monopoly of the world's finest rubber. All of this was wild rubber, tapped by seringueiros who milked trees in the depths of the forests. There was little attempt to create plantations of rubber trees. It may in fact be impossible to grow such plantations in Amazonia – there are so many insect predators and parasites in the teeming rainforests that each tree species must defend itself by scattering its seeds. Rows of trees in a plantation eventually fall victim to one of the myriad scourges. The increases in rubber output thus resulted from finding ever more trees in the most distant parts of the mighty Amazon river system. More and more rubber tappers infiltrated the uppermost tributaries and headwaters of Amazonia's eleven thousand rivers.

The great rubber monopoly was a pyramid, with thousands of seringueiros supplying hundreds of traders who in turn sold to the few powerful merchant houses of Manaus, Belém and Iquitos. Although individual rubber barons came to control immense stretches of river, the rubber millionaires tended to live in the new cities rather than on their steamy estates. Manaus became a boom city which put the Klondyke or the Rand to shame. British engineers were engaged to build a floating dock to cope with the annual rise and fall in river levels. There was electricity and the first tramway system in South America. Vast quantities of stone were imported to cobble the streets and build the tycoons' marble palaces. Robin Furneaux has written that these houses were 'furnished with the finest pieces from England and France, and festooned with crystal chandeliers. Their linen came from Ireland and unused grand pianos littered their salons. At their parties champagne at $50 a bottle flowed like latex off a virgin tree. No extravagance, however absurd, deterred them. If one rubber baron bought a vast yacht, another would install a tame lion in his villa, and a third would water his horse on champagne.' The crowning glories of Manaus were a massive customs building modelled on that of New Delhi, prefabricated in England and shipped out in pieces; and the famous opera house whose dome towers above the centre of the city. Both buildings have recently been restored to their pristine splendour; but there is no record of an opera ever being performed in this city fifteen hundred kilometres up the Amazon.

One of the richest and most powerful rubber barons was Nicolás Suárez. By the height of the rubber boom at the beginning of the twentieth century, Suárez controlled all trade along the upper Madeira and all rubber-gathering operations on the tributaries above its rapids. Henry Pearson, editor of the American trade magazine *The India Rubber World*, regarded Suárez as a most romantic figure. His life history was 'a very stirring one. He began as a trader for rubber, dealing with savages whom none other had dared to even communicate with. Soon he and his brothers began to acquire great concessions. They pushed further and further into the interior, trading with the Indians, practically ruling them, and avenging any insult or lack of faith most terribly. One of his brothers was murdered by savages, and it is said that Nicolás Suárez practically exterminated the [Karipuna] tribe to which his murderers belonged.' Suárez contacted the tribes of the Beni, Mamoré and Madre de Dios rivers, 'savages whom no white man had ever dared to approach. Soon this man and his brothers obtained concessions which were little short of countries with sovereign rights. He ruled the wild Indians with a firm hand, exacting terrible reparations for the slightest insult or treachery.' At the height of his power, Suárez monopolised transport down the Madeira river. He had over ten thousand employees on his payroll, with four hundred men engaged in portaging around the Madeira rapids. He controlled five million hectares of rubber lands, had ranches with 250,000 head of cattle, a sugar mill, a power plant, an ice factory and countless trading depots.

Henri Coudreau admired Paulo da Silva Leite, who had arrived on the upper Tapajós with nothing and had become a powerful rubber baron. Silva Leite was 'the boss and protector of the Apiaká. . . . A great rubber producer, he disposes of an Indian tribe.' The middle Madeira came to be dominated by three rubber barons, all of Spanish Bolivian origin and employing mainly docile Bolivian Indian labour. These potentates lived relatively luxuriously, with imported furniture, music-boxes from Switzerland, Hennessy brandy, silk umbrellas and Panama hats. They employed a few demoralised local Karipuna – remnants who stayed behind when most of their tribe left, 'driven out by the vanguard of civilisation engaged in the quest for rubber'. An American visitor watched the estate manager of one of the barons offer drink to these bedraggled, deculturated and impoverished Indians. They grimaced when they drank. It turned out to be kerosene or paraffin rather than cachaça. The manager 'assured us that kerosene would not hurt Indians'.

A railway engineer called Dalton described how the Karipuna and related Akaguara 'have freely given us yuca [manioc], plantains, bows, arrows and feather ornaments in exchange for shirts, machetes and fish-hooks. I am convinced that no danger or inconvenience will arise from their presence.' The Brazilian official Julio Pinkas said that Indians wanted shirts and trousers 'which they accept only when new – and never remove again until they fall to pieces'. Pinkas reported instances of Akaguara saving the lives of soldiers who were lost in the forests. He doubted the wisdom of trying to enlist Indians to work on railway building or even as hunters or gatherers. He regarded them as neither friends nor enemies: mere spectators of the extraordinary invasion of their territory.

Although the Karipuna and Akaguara were so docile, Pinkas wrote in 1884 that 'they always find English or American guns pointed at them when they show natural curiosity to see what these men have come to do in their forests. Only after they have experienced the cruelty of firearms do they use their legitimate right of self-defence, answering those unprovoked aggressions with arrows. It is said that the Americans made an expedition to an Akaguara maloca to intimidate them. They surrounded it and killed all they encountered, in revenge for one arrow shot at the contractor's brother when he was alone in the forest.'

The hard labour on the Madeira rubber concessions was done by acculturated Indians brought down from Bolivia. Julio Pinkas was appalled by the way in which these Bolivians were cheated and held in debt servitude. They worked hard to extract four or five kilos of rubber a day but were paid only a thirtieth of its true value. In return they had to pay ludicrous prices even for such basics as candles or boxes of matches. Bolivian Indian women wore long cotton gowns and were often made to work as hard as their men on the rubber trails. They freely offered themselves to men descending the river from Bolivia, and filled the bosses' harems. One old woman left her master, the deputy sheriff of Santo Antonio, and followed Pinkas' detachment of soldiers. When she refused to return, she was to be punished by being shot from a cannon. Pinkas was just able to stop this execution. The rubber bosses were amazed when he told them that enslaving Indians was illegal in Brazil.

Two events made a profound impact on the Brazilian rubber trade, although their effect on Indians was limited. These were the efforts to build a railway around the Madeira river rapids, and the annexation of the territory of Acre. Much of the best rubber was found in northern Bolivia, along the rivers draining into the upper Madeira. The trouble was that for 380 kilometres the Madeira was blocked by eighteen raging cataracts. It took local Indians weeks to haul boats and stores up and down this barrier. There was a portage trail through the forest alongside the river, but this hardly solved the problem of bringing Bolivian rubber down to the main Amazon.

A Bolivian general first suggested in 1861 that a railway should be built beside this difficult stretch of river. Six years later, the German engineer Franz Keller made a survey in which he gave estimates of the costs of various possible solutions: ramps for hauling boats, a paved road, a railroad, or canals with locks. The Bolivians then enlisted the dashing American engineer Colonel George Church. He registered the National Bolivian Navigation Company in 1870, which raised the necessary finance and engaged a British construction company to build the railway. Engineers were sent out, but by 1873 the work was abandoned. The company petitioned to be released from its contract, claiming that 'the country was a charnel house, their men dying off like flies; that the road ran through an inhospitable wilderness of swamp and porphyry ridges alternating; and that, with the command of all the capital in the world and half its population, it would be impossible to build the road.' Two British engineers reported on the problems in the same year. In their view, the insuperable obstacle lay in the unhealthiness of the region. It was 'the haunt of terrible fevers'. Spanish labourers imported by the English company died in droves.

Colonel Church tried again in 1879, this time with the American company P. & T. Collins. Over nine hundred Americans, including six women, were sent to help. Eighty of these drowned when their aged ship foundered. Of the remainder, 141 died during the eighteen-month concession as well as four hundred Brazilian labourers from Ceará and two hundred Bolivians. Only one of these victims was killed by local Karipuna Indians. But the epidemic of malaria that killed so many tough labourers undoubtedly also ravaged the tribal Indians. The American company gave up the hopeless attempt, and Colonel Church's concession was cancelled in 1881.

Towards the end of the nineteenth century, the rubber traffic penetrated the southernmost headwaters of the Purus and Juruá rivers. These remote forested rivers were first explored by the Brazilian mameluco Manuel Urbano da Encarnação and then by the English explorer William Chandless in the 1860s. In later decades, rubber men found that the area of the Acre river was richer than any other part of Amazonia in rubber trees. Eighteen thousand men poured into the Acre territory.

There was ambiguity about the location of the frontier between Bolivia and Brazil in that wild region. Under the old treaties of Madrid and San Ildefonso the Acre territory belonged to Spanish America (Bolivia), but these Brazilian seringueiros resented Bolivian attempts to tax and control them. They formed themselves into a near-independent republic and rebelled in 1899 and again in 1902. The dispute culminated in the Treaty of Petrópolis, 17 November 1903, by which Brazil bought Acre from Bolivia for £2 million and a promise to complete the Madeira railway far south into Bolivia. During these turbulent years, many uncontacted tribes clashed with rubber men. But both sides in these skirmishes and massacres were illiterate, so we know almost nothing of the history of the Indians of those distant forests.*

The key to the construction of the Madeira–Mamoré railway lay in the health of its workers. The ill-fated venture had gained a terrible reputation. It was said that a man died for every sleeper laid along its line; and the most deadly killer was malaria.

Malaria seems to have entered the Amazon basin in the eighteenth century. Reports by missionaries and explorers in the sixteenth and seventeenth centuries do not mention fevers – indeed some Jesuits went out of their way to praise the Amazon's healthy climate. By the nineteenth century this had changed radically. Spix and Martius reported in 1820 that 'malignant intermittent fevers' had arrived 'very recently' on the Solimões. Such malaria regularly decimated the population which succumbed more quickly with no medical help.

On the Japurá, the German travellers found a fertile region depopulated because of malarial fevers; its Indians had pallid colours and hardened livers from the disease. Martius and all his companions suffered terribly from fevers. Meanwhile his colleague Spix found that the middle Rio Negro was gripped by 'virulent fevers that kill in the space of three or four days. It is so bad that in a few years' time almost all settlements [on the Negro] will be depopulated. In Carvoeiro, Moura and Barcelos a great many people have died and are still dying of pernicious fever.' A few years later, the Russian scientific expedition led by Baron von Langsdorff found that the diamond prospectors' town Diamantino was riddled with malaria. Langsdorff never recovered from the disease, and all his companions, including the French artist Hércules Florence, suffered terribly from it.

The situation grew steadily worse. In 1840 the President of Pará listed places along the entire length of the Amazon that had suffered huge declines in population and numbers of households. 'All these places are of converted Indians and all are being extinguished by disease, etc.' William Edwards noted malaria on the Madeira in 1846, and his fellow American Lardner Gibbon was racked by fevers, 'with pains that forbade sleep at night', when he descended that river in 1851.

There were other diseases imported into the Amazon. Richard Spruce watched a panic in Belém when yellow fever appeared there for the first time in 1850. The population reacted by flocking to church, firing cannon in the streets, and burning lumps of odoriferous white pitch. Spruce wrote that in Santarém almost everybody, himself included, suffered attacks of influenza and 'slow fever'. Henry Bates blamed the same disease for great mortality among Indians brought as captives to Ega (Tefé) on the Solimões. The Yurí and Pasé tribes near there were almost extinct from 'a slow fever, accompanied by the symptoms of a common cold, "defluxo" as the Brazilians term it, ending probably in consumption'. This was probably tuberculosis, which remains a scourge of modern Indians.

But malaria was the greatest killer. In 1850 Richard Spruce said that 'in the villages up the Tapajoz ague of the worst kind was rife, and above four hundred people fell victims to it.' The Yorkshire botanist blamed malaria on an unprecedentedly fast rise of the rivers, with consequent flooding and stagnant waters. In 1851, Spruce received a letter from his friend Alfred Russell Wallace who was at São Gabriel (Uaupés) on the middle Negro. Wallace was 'almost at the point of death from a malignant fever, which has reduced him to such a state of weakness that he cannot rise from his hammock or even feed himself.' He was taking nothing but orange and cashew juice. Wallace described his ordeal: 'I was attacked with severe ague, which recurred every two days. I took quinine for some time without apparent effect, till, after nearly a fortnight, the fits ceased, and I only suffered from extreme emaciation and weakness. In a few days, however, the fits of ague returned, and now came every day. Their visits, thus frequent, were by no means agreeable; as, what with succeeding fever and perspiration, which lasted from before noon till night, I had little quiet repose.' Three years later in 1854, the tough Spruce himself was struck. He had crossed from the upper Negro on to the Atabapo in southern Venezuela. So bad was his malaria that he lay prostrate listening to local people discussing how to divide his belongings when he died. Henry Bates was lucky to survive for nine years on the Amazon without malaria. He finally caught it in 1858, however, and although he dosed himself liberally with quinine, his health deteriorated so badly that he decided to return to England.

The Swiss Professor Louis Agassiz noted in 1865 that the Indians suffered most from malaria. 'It is a curious thing that the natives seem more liable to the maladies of the country than strangers. They are very subject to intermittent fevers, and one often sees Indians worn to mere skin and bone by this terrible scourge.' In the previous year, William Chandless was forced back from the sources of the Purus because his men were stricken by malaria. 'In respect of ague the Ituxí has the worst name of all the affluents: the Pamanás, a tribe on it, are said to be always suffering, and consequently very indolent and unwilling to work, whatever price be offered.' This vulnerability of native Indians is further evidence that malaria had reached Amazonia only recently. Indigenous peoples had had no time to develop genetic immunities to the imported disease.

Many travellers noted that malaria was worse on the upper tributaries than on the main Amazon river. It was precisely in the distant forests of those tributaries that rubber men had to work. Conditions were bad enough in Manaus. Alongside the city's glittering opera house, cathedral and opulent taverns and shops of the rubber boom were hovels and open drains in which mosquitoes bred freely. In the year 1910, 2200 people died of disease in this opulent city. Malaria was by far the deadliest killer. An analysis of deaths in Manaus between 1897 and 1902 showed that malaria accounted for 50 per cent; digestive and intestinal complaints, 8.5 per cent; beriberi, 3.6 per cent; tuberculosis, 3.5 per cent; dysentery and other diseases for the remainder.*

As we have seen, the origin of malaria remained a mystery throughout the nineteenth century, most theories blaming it on humid or putrid air. It seemed to be worst during different months of the year on different Amazon rivers. William Chandless therefore tried to find whether it related to the rainy season when rivers were rising or to the dry months when they fell. But he obtained conflicting results from the Canumã, Acarí, Machado (or Jiparaná) and Maués-Açú rivers. Spruce linked malaria to flooding of the Tapajós. Others were convinced that malaria came from sweat-soaked clothing or from sudden changes in temperature. Still others blamed too much brandy, or such foods as sugar cane, pineapple or water melon – there was a saying: 'There's a shake in every melon.' The French geographer Elysée Reclus attributed the disease to bad hygiene. So did the Brazilian poet–explorer Antonio Gonçalves Dias and the English naturalist Henry Bates. Bates also suspected that it was foolish to bathe when fevered or to eat raw fruit. Professor Agassiz saw poor diet as a cause of disease: too much reliance on salted fish and manioc flour and not enough cow's milk. (It did not occur to Agassiz that Amazon riverine clearings were unsuited to cattle, unlike his native Swiss pastures; but Agassiz was often wrong.)

One theory was that malaria was caused by stagnant pools in river rapids 'in which vegetation decays and gives off miasma under the glare of the tropical sun'. During the attempt to build the Madeira railway in the 1870s, an energetic Englishman called Davis tried to drain all such pools. He dynamited some and pumped water out of others, but with the rise and fall of the rivers, this was a labour of Sisyphus. Davis eventually died – not of malaria but of sheer exhaustion.

The cause of malaria was finally discovered in a series of brilliant experiments towards the end of the century. Crawford in 1807, Notts in 1847 and King and Koch in 1883 had all guessed that mosquitoes might be to blame. But it was not until 1880 that a Dr Laveran of the French army in Algeria discovered minute amoebic parasites in the blood of malaria victims. Fourteen years later, both Laveran and Dr Patrick Manson in England suggested that these amoeba were transmitted by mosquitoes. Research in Italy, India and England pointed to this insect; and in 1900 Manson proved that mosquitoes that had bitten malaria victims could infect other volunteers. In 1905 Major Ronald Ross of the Indian Medical Service narrowed the search to mosquitoes of the anopheles group. It was known that such insects bred in still water and in the swamps that had always been blamed for the disease. It was thus possible for the contractors working in Amazonia to try to eliminate pools in which mosquitoes might breed, and to be especially careful with mosquito netting during the rainy season.

There has never been a fully effective cure for malaria. It was discovered in seventeenth-century Peru that quinine from the cinchona plant was a palliative which reduced the effect of fever. In 1854 Clements Markham, a young employee of the British India Office, made a daring dash across the snow-capped Andes to smuggle the cinchona plant out of Peru. Quinine was then grown successfully in plantations in India, and its cost fell dramatically.

Having acquired Acre in 1903, the Brazilians had to fulfil their part of the bargain: to build the infamous Madeira railway. The next contract to do this went to an American, Percival Farquar, who formed The Madeira–Mamoré Railway Company. Farquar employed the civil engineers May, Jekyll and Randolph, and this company landed men and materials on the Madeira in 1907. Work continued for five years. A total of twenty-two thousand men were signed on, most of them from southern Europe, India and the West Indies. At any given time there were four to five thousand men at the company's headquarters at Pôrto Velho. Of these about four hundred were Americans.

Now that it was known that mosquitoes transmitted malaria, there were vigorous efforts to fight the disease. Railway workers were forced to sleep under mosquito nets, and pools in which mosquito larvae hatched were drained. Great attention was paid to hygiene and sanitation. Drinking water was drawn from special wells, and there was a hospital staffed by up to ten doctors and eight male nurses. Despite all this, there was much suffering. The hospital was often filled with three hundred patients. In addition to malaria, 'the most troublesome diseases were beriberi, blackwater fever, and dysentery. Quinine, of course, was the remedy generally used and most potent. It was brought by the ton, and three laboratory men were kept busy from morning to night making it up into pills.'

These precautions succeeded. The first 92 kilometres from Pôrto Velho to Jaci–Paraná were opened to traffic in 1910 and 364 kilometres to Guajará–Mirim were finished by 1912. The full railway promised in the Treaty of Petrópolis was never built. As Kenneth Grubb wrote in 1930: 'Unfortunately, the opening of the line coincided with the crisis in the wild rubber trade, and today only one train a week is run.'

The railway construction company tried to avoid conflict with Indians. 'All the men were obliged to sign a contract to pay no court to the Karipuna Indian women, nor sell firearms to the men. If this contract was violated they were discharged without pay. The result of this wise policy was that the Indians were very friendly, and furnished the camp with many turtles and lots of fish.' When the railway opened, Karipuna Indians regularly supplied timber for its engines, bringing loads of logs to refuelling points along the line. But the tribes undoubtedly suffered from the range of diseases imported by the construction workers.

Ironically, it was detribalised tapuio Indians of the Tapajós who helped to kill the Amazon rubber monopoly. They took part in one of the world's most brazen and lucrative robberies. In 1870 Clements Markham of the India Office – the same explorer who had spirited cinchona plants from Peru – decided that rubber had become so important that it must be grown in plantations. The British already had an elastic gum from the wild fig *Ficus elasticus* that grew in Assam in north-east India. Other places had their own gum trees: manicoba in Brazilian Ceará, castilla in Mexico, or the sap of the landolphia vine in the Congo. But none of these could compete with the hard black Pará variety. Britain was already importing three thousand tons a year of this expensive Amazonian rubber, at a cost of £720,000.

In the same year, 1870, the young Englishman Henry Wickham visited the Rio Negro and, like so many other travellers, wrote a book about his adventure. He described the rubber trade and included drawings of the *Hevea brasiliensis* rubber tree. Wickham suggested that this valuable tree might grow elsewhere. He corresponded with Dr Joseph Hooker, Director of the Royal Botanic Gardens at Kew. Markham and Hooker were friends, and they developed together the idea of engaging Wickham and other botanists to try to smuggle rubber plants out of the Amazon. Wickham had by 1873 settled near Santarém, built a house and brought an English bride and his widowed mother to live in Brazil; but his attempts to start a plantation of sugar or tobacco had failed. When Hooker asked him to send hevea seeds, Wickham asked what he would be paid. It took Markham some months to persuade his masters at the India Office that there was much at stake, but in July 1874 he was able to write to Hooker: 'They have agreed to pay Mr. Wickham £10 for every 1,000 seeds.'

There was further correspondence. Wickham pointed out the huge difficulties involved in gathering the plants. In April 1875 Hooker told him that the India Office had authorised him to collect ten thousand seeds by any possible means. They wanted 'the tree which produced the true Pará rubber of commerce'. As Wickham commented, 'Fortunately, I was left quite unhampered by instructions as to way or means. A straight offer to do it; pay to follow result. Now with that opportunity, question came home to me, how on earth to bring it off?'

After Brazil had opened the Amazon to foreign shipping in 1866, steamers rapidly started to ply its vast network of waterways. One such vessel was a new English ocean-going liner, the SS *Amazonas* of the Inman Line, which sailed 'from Liverpool to the Alto-Amazonas direct'. In 1876 Henry Wickham attended a party to celebrate the arrival of this new ship. 'Then', in Wickham's words, 'occurred one of those chances, such as a man has to take at top-tide or lose for ever. The startling news came down the river that our fine ship, the *Amazonas* had been abandoned . . . without so much as a stick of cargo for the return voyage to Liverpool.' Brazilian traders had cheated the *Amazonas'* captain of his cargo of rubber. 'I determined to plunge for it. . . . It was true that I had no cash on hand out there. . . . The [rubber] seed was even then beginning to ripen on the trees in the high forest. I knew that Captain Murray must be in a fix, so I wrote to him, boldly chartering the ship on behalf of the Government of India; and I appointed to meet him at the junction of the Tapajós and Amazon rivers by a certain date.'

'There was no time to lose. Hurriedly getting an Indian canoe, posting up the right coast of the Tapajós and traversing the broad river – rather ticklish work in a small canoe at that season – I struck back from the left shore for deep woods, the *monte alto*, wherein I knew were to be found the big full-grown Hevea trees. . . . Working with as many Tapuio Indians as I could get together at short notice, I daily ranged the forest, and packed on our backs in Indian pannier baskets as heavy loads of seed as we could march under. I was working against time. . . . I got the Tapuio village maids to make up open-work baskets or crates of split *calamus* canes for receiving the seed, first, however, being careful to have them slowly but well dried on mats in the shade, before they were put away with layers of dried wild banana leaf betwixt each layer of seed; knowing how easily a seed so rich in a drying-oil becomes rancid or too dry, and so losing all power of germination. Also I had the crates slung up to the beams of the Indian lodges to insure ventilation.'

Wickham was racing against time, to collect as many hevea seeds as possible and get them to the rendezvous with the *Amazonas*. 'I had got to look upon the heavy oily seeds in their dappled skins as become very precious, after having backed them down so many long days tramping across the forest plateaux; and so lost no time in getting them carefully stowed under the *tolda* [awning] of the canoe, and starting away down stream, duly meeting the steamer as appointed at the mouth of the Tapajós.'

The next worry was to clear Brazilian customs at Belém do Pará, at the mouth of the Amazon. Had the authorities discovered a shipload of hevea seeds, they would either have confiscated the cargo or referred the matter to Rio de Janeiro – by which time the seeds would have died. Captain Murray kept steam up on the *Amazonas*. The British Consul at Pará, a Mr Green, helped Wickham's deception. 'He, quite entering into the spirit of the thing, went himself with me on a special call on the Barão do S—, chief of the Alfandega [Customs], and backed me up as I represented "to his Excellency my difficulty and anxiety, being in charge of, and having on board a ship anchored out in the stream, exceedingly delicate botanical specimens specially designated for delivery to Her Britannic Majesty's own Royal Gardens of Kew.". . . An interview most polite, full of mutual compliment in best Portuguese manner, enabled us to get under way as soon as Murray had got the dingey [*sic*] hauled aboard.' Neither British gentleman revealed that the 'botanical specimens' were all of one species – and an extremely valuable commercial plant at that.

There was good weather during the Atlantic crossing and Wickham kept the hatches off to ventilate his crates of seedlings. He himself landed at Le Havre and hurried to tell Hooker in the middle of the night in London. Hooker and Markham moved with characteristic vigour. They chartered a special night train to meet the *Amazonas* when she docked at Liverpool. The seedlings were rushed to Kew, where the orchid and propagating houses were unceremoniously emptied to make way for the precious new arrivals. Wickham was delighted. 'The Hevea did not fail to respond to the care I had bestowed on them. A fortnight afterwards the glass-house at Kew afforded (to me) a pretty sight – tier upon tier – rows of young Hevea plants – 7,000 and odd of them.' It was decided to send the rubber plants to Ceylon. 'Meanwhile the young seedlings were growing apace in the Kew glass-houses. . . . Being placed under charge of a Kew man, they were put up in wardian cases, and dispatched down the Thames by barge to British India liners at the river mouth.' Wardian cases were miniature glasshouses invented by a researcher called Nathaniel Ward: being hermetically sealed, these thirty-eight cases allowed the seedlings to absorb their own condensed moisture. They thus continued to grow during their passage to India.

The seedlings were mistakenly planted in swampy conditions in Sri Lanka and most died. But a few survived, and these formed the basis of the great rubber plantations of Malaya. The parasites and predators of Amazonia did not exist in South-east Asia, which also had a plentiful supply of labour to tap the trees, so hevea plantations at last proved practicable. It took twenty-four years for the Asian trees to grow. The first four tons of Asian rubber reached London in 1900. By 1912 this had risen to 8500 tons compared to Amazon production of over 38,000 tons. But by 1914 Asian rubber output at 71,400 tons far outstripped the wild rubber gathered in Amazonia. By 1923 the Amazon rubber boom was finished: oriental rubber had risen to 370,000 tons, whereas production on the Amazon had collapsed to under 18,000 tons. And the payment to Henry Wickham for this most spectacular theft was just £1505 4s 2d.

South-east Asian plantation rubber grew faster and yielded more than the wild hevea of Amazonia. Experimental breeding and grafting from trees known to have a high sap content increased the output still further. There was ample native labour in the Asian rubber countries. Men milking trees in plantations did not waste energy moving long distances between their trees. Malayan plantations were near the coast, so that their rubber did not have to be moved down thousands of kilometres of rivers. Plantation rubber was coagulated chemically and the end-product was far purer than a roll of rubber smoked over a fire in a primitive seringueiro's hut. The Brazilian government also exacted far higher taxes on exported rubber than its Malayan counterpart. The result of all this was that Malayan rubber rapidly came to be cheaper, of better quality and available in vastly greater quantity than its wild Amazonian rival.

The Amazon boom burst with frightening speed. The marble palaces of Manaus decayed and crumbled. The opera house that had never witnessed an opera was boarded up. The tycoons, speculators, traders and prostitutes departed and tropical weeds sprang up between the imported cobble stones. The ruin was even greater on the remote rivers, where bosses' depots and seringueiros' huts were abandoned to termites and vegetation. The only beneficiaries were the tribal Indians. For the next half century there was little incentive for strangers to penetrate Amazonia's distant rivers and forests. There was a respite for the Indians who had taken refuge in them.

Indians and Rubber

During the early years, the rubber trade was not too damaging to Amazon Indians. Some tribes came to terms with the new product. In 1852 Henry Bates observed the Mundurukú of the upper Tapajós gathering large quantities of rubber and other forest produce to barter with itinerant traders. The Mundurukú were a cohesive tribe on good terms with the whites, and they enjoyed an enviable reputation as warriors. Traders therefore treated them with respect, bringing their wares – cotton clothing, axes, knives and cachaça – and waiting for weeks or months to get rubber in exchange.

By 1860, however, this was changing. William Chandless noted that rubber gatherers now operated far upstream above the rapids on the Tapajós. He met a group of clothed Mundurukú working for two black runaway slaves on the Juruena, a headwater of the Tapajós. As well as selling their own rubber, the Mundurukú sold food to the seringueiros who operated in their territory. As always, the Indians were keen to obtain imported trade goods, but were hopelessly uncommercial. Their ideas of supply and demand placed an inflated value on manufactured goods that they themselves could not make. They had no knowledge of Brazilian writing, law or arithmetic. They were thus easily duped. Antonio Tocantins visited the rubber areas of the upper Tapajós in 1875 and published financial accounts of transactions between regatão traders and Mundurukú chiefs. The lists showed fourfold mark-ups on shoddy goods – including patent medicines and a fair quantity of cachaça. He commented: 'When one asks these Indians how much they owe, they always answer: "Who knows? Only the boss could know." '

Tocantins saw traders holding many Indians of both sexes by force in their houses. The men were sent off to tap rubber, and their families were kept as hostages for their return. He described the rise and fall of a mulatto boatman called Manoel Quirino Paes from Mato Grosso, who controlled long stretches of the Tapajós in the late 1860s and eventually had five thousand rubber trees in his domain. He started with one Mawé Indian tapper and increased the number until there were a hundred of both sexes working for him. Energetic and efficient, Paes sold large quantities of rubber and grew rich. But his Indians were virtual slaves, working long hours in the four large buildings of Paes' rubber factory.

Rubber traders – tough, ruthless and isolated on forested rivers – demanded the services of Indian women. One Mawé girl called Francisca refused to submit to Manoel Paes. She ran off twice but was recaptured and punished. In desperation, Francisca Mawé persuaded an Apiaká boy to help her kill their oppressor. They ambushed Paes one night near his house. José Apiaká hesitated, but the Mawé girl grabbed the gun and shot and killed the hated Manoel Paes. The couple were tried by jury in Santarém in 1871. 'Francisca Mawé declared herself the sole author of the crime. She raised her short skirt before the tribunal and showed marks on her legs from shackles, which she had suffered for a long time. Before a numerous and horror-stricken audience, the Indian girl reported scenes of barbarity and disgusting licentiousness that had taken place in the factory of that ferocious man, and of which she and her fellow captives had been victims. The jury absolved her' – but it condemned José Apiaká, 'a boy of sweet and attractive appearance', to exile and prison in Bahia.

The following year, an Italian Capuchin missionary was sent to the Mundurukú of the upper Tapajós. Frei Pelino de Castrovalva refounded the old mission of Bacabal with five hundred Mundurukú in February 1872, and tried to destroy and supplant the tribe's culture. He wrote in 1876 that his greatest endeavour 'has been to eliminate their inveterate superstitions from the heads of the Indians. What haven't I done or said to tear this pernicious witchcraft from their hearts?' He also declared war on the regatão traders. Within two years of Friar Pelino's appointment, the leading traders of Itaituba sent an hysterical complaint to the legislative assembly in Belém. 'The missionaries, ill-informed and imprudent, listened to jealous zoileans and adventurers and immediately declared cruel war on the traders. They called them all without exception thieves and perverts, and advised the Indians not to pay their debts because they did not owe them. They prevented the Indians from working in the canoes on dangerous journeys through the rapids – which led to very serious losses in 1872-73, such as the loss of twelve canoes with their cargoes and some lives!'

An impartial commentator on this quarrel was the American Herbert Smith. He reported that in 1876 some Mundurukú chiefs went down to Belém to complain about Friar Pelino. They received little satisfaction. On the return journey, one Mundurukú jumped under the steamer's paddle wheel rather than return to the missionary's tyranny. Smith said that the Mundurukú 'gather the [rubber] gum in immense quantities, and sell it to the traders or bring it to Itaituba. . . . Of course, the Indians are kept in debt to the merchant, and the merchant to the exporter; an inverted pyramid, all resting on the Indian workman.'

The missionary made a powerful defence. He wrote to the President of Pará that the traders had debauched his mission village during his absence. 'As is their usual custom, they first made the Indians drunk on cachaça and, when they were deprived of all reason, removed all that they could from them – manioc farinha, ducks, chickens, etc. – giving in exchange only the cachaça they were drinking. They practised public prostitution by day and night in the doors of the houses. Oh, Your Excellency, in this respect they were really excessive! There wasn't a family of the poor Indians whose honour and dearest decorum was not abused in a horrible manner. Such was the demoralisation that the Indians in their drunkenness forgot all my good instructions and imitated the regatão traders in their licentiousness. During those days the mission became a veritable den of vice.'

Friar Pelino's detractors accused him of profiting from his Indians' labour. He was said to have sold vast quantities of rubber, sarsaparilla and copaíba oil and to have sent the profits to Europe. A newspaper campaign was organised against him. There was a spirited debate in the legislature; the President of Pará visited Bacabal and was impressed; but the powerful traders won. In December 1876 the Minister of Agriculture sacked Friar Pelino. The mission of Bacabal soon collapsed – to the good of Mundurukú cultural survival – and was not revived until the twentieth century.

Similar exploitation of Indians was taking place on other rivers that contained rubber trees. In 1864 William Chandless observed that the Paumarí of the middle Purus 'now work to a great extent, though lazily, at collecting india-rubber, and well understand the value of it, and of what they receive for it'. In 1867 this same explorer found the Katawishí of the lower Juruá 'now all up-river, working at india-rubber for a trader'. A few years later, two British engineers saw dishevelled Paumarí cutting wood for rubber steamers on the Purus. On that same river, they passed an island with 'the terribly significant name of "the Island of the slaughtering of the Puru-Purus" '. Far up the muddy Juruá river, they saw Katawishí who were occasionally hired to gather rubber. At the mouth of the Jutaí, farther to the west, they visited a large plantation in which the owner had many Katukina from the upper Jutaí and a few Miranya working for him.

Although tribes such as the Mundurukú on the Tapajós or the Juruna on the Xingu were drawn into the rubber economy, many forest tribes retreated from the rubber frontier. They migrated to the headwaters of Amazon tributaries and buried themselves deep in the forests to escape this madness. The brunt of rubber tapping therefore fell on the acculturated Indians and mestizos of Amazonia.

It was relatively easy to seduce half-acculturated tapuio Indians away from their sleepy riverside villages. Rubber traders supplied these detribalised Indians with 'presents' of food, firearms and clothing on credit. 'This needless extravagance was often encouraged in order that they could run up huge bills, to be paid for in rubber by the unfortunate Indians later on. This they were unable to do, and were reduced to a state of peonage as a result.' Cachaça was also used as an instrument of seduction. Indian men were persuaded to go off to tap rubber. 'Thus these poor, simple children of nature were induced to abandon their cattle, their homes and cultivated grounds at the suggestion of the wily adventurer. . . . Without thought these Indians were soon victims of slavery and dishonour, and were lucky if their troubles ended quickly in death. In this way families and whole villages were completely extinguished.'

As early as 1854, a President of Pará was complaining that the province now had to import basic foods which had previously been grown there. Too much of the available labour force was occupied in rubber extraction. The black gold of rubber was inspiring a gold-rush. President Barros lamented that the new trade 'is leading into misery the great mass of those who abandon their homes, small businesses and even their families to follow it. They surrender themselves to lives of uncertainty and hardship, in which the profits of one evening evaporate the following day.'

To make matters worse, the 'vast profits of this [rubber] industry, which is absorbing and annihilating all others' were not evenly spread through small-scale private enterprise.

Most of the rubber wealth was accumulating in a few hands, and many of these were foreign. A later President tried to counteract this tendency. In 1861 President Silva Coutinho sought to establish private ownership of forests containing *Hevea brasiliensis*. A settler would be given such a seringal on condition that he did four things: cut four wide trails through the forest to delimit his territory; grew enough food for his own workforce during two months of the year; used the 'milking' system of tapping, so that trees were not destroyed; and planted new rubber trees to replace old ones.

In the following year, President Brusque deplored the way that a large part of the population of Pará had rushed into rubber work. 'From it they achieve, instead of the dreamed-for wealth – which is concentrated in a few hands – ruin and death. A society such as ours, of Christian morality, should not remain indifferent to the ruin, destruction and death of this inexperienced and blind class.'

Rubber tappers on remote river banks were kept in penury by a trading system known as aviamento. 'Aviar' in Amazonia meant 'to supply' trade goods on credit. The old network of regatão traders thus evolved into the aviamento, an economic system in which everyone was perpetually in debt to the next boss up the ladder. At the top of the pyramid were the large merchant houses of Belém and Manaus who outfitted itinerant traders or aviadores, who in turn filled the stores of the rubber bosses. The seringueiros who did the tapping and smoking of rubber had to come to these stores to feed and equip themselves.

Individual illiterate seringueiros always owed money on the ledgers of the rubber bosses. They traded the rubber they collected for imported goods, but the prices paid were grossly in favour of the bosses. Armed guards in the rubber workings ensured that 'indebted' seringueiros could not escape. Police in the cities and even other rubber bosses would send back such debtors. There was no outside check on the books of the bosses. Escape was made more difficult by the immense distances along the Amazon river system.

M. Pimenta Bueno, himself a rubber trader, wrote that 'the life of these extractors is surrounded by every sort of hardship. Under-nourished – for their food is reduced to dry pirarucu fish and farinha d'agua [fermented manioc flour] – they are exposed to recurring fevers and malarias that decimate them, sometimes killing entire families. They are obliged to undertake gruelling journeys. They earn in a day's work more money than they would achieve in many days of other rural labour. But they return home as poor as when they left. They thus assume the role of veritable machines, working for someone else's profit.' Euclides da Cunha, one of the best-loved authors of late-nineteenth-century Brazil, echoed this. He wrote that 'in the luxurious forests of heveas and castilloas, the most criminal organisation of labour ever devised by the most unbridled egotist awaits [the seringueiro]. He actually comes to embody a gigantic contradiction: he is a man working to enslave himself!'

We must treat the violent tirades against aviadores and regatão traders with some caution. The big trading companies resented these energetic and unscrupulous interlopers. The views of the city-based companies were reflected in speeches of provincial presidents and legislation by the Assembly in Belém. There was even a hint of xenophobia and anti-semitism in the outbursts against the traders, for many of them were Levantines or Sephardic Jews. The traders *did* fulfil a service to the isolated rubber tappers. By bringing their overpriced goods up thousands of kilometres of Amazonian water-ways, they gave seringueiros the supplies and companionship that they needed, and an outlet for their rubber. This meant that in the early decades of the rubber boom many rubber gatherers were inde-pendent. They could escape to remote forests to work rubber trails during the dry season.

At first, the rulers of Amazonia opposed rubber because it de-prived them of agricultural labourers. Caboclos invariably preferred the freedom of gathering forest produce to the drudgery of work in plantations. The iniquitous workers' brigades, the corpos de trabal-hadores, which were formed at the end of the Cabanagem revolt, were intended to prevent such erosion of the diminished workforce. Seven years after the end of the Cabanagem, one vice-president defined Pará's criminals as 'escaped prisoners, deserters, runaway slaves and other individuals who, even though they claim to be occupied in collecting rubber, live in complete independence'. The workers' brigades were a failure: they could not prevent caboclos drifting off to the lucrative rubber trails. By the 1850s the authorities began to realise the importance of rubber. The gum became Amazo-nia's largest export and the provincial government's main source of revenue. In the 1860s the workers' brigades were summarily abolished.

The shortage of labour was an advantage to individual rubber workers: it gave them leverage in resisting oppressive masters. In the early decades of the rubber boom, many seringueiros worked in a private capacity or migrated to remote rivers if conditions became intolerable. Thus, from about 1850 to 1880, rubber helped many tapuio Indians and mestizo caboclos to prosper through their own hard work. The British consul in Pará, James Drummond Hay, wrote a perceptive report about this in 1870. He noted that only about a tenth of the population of Pará and Amazonas was available for contract work. 'Labourers and workmen are clamoured for.' Tapuio Indians did most agricultural and domestic work and also met 'government demands for recruits in the national service'. Drummond Hay praised the Amazonian mestizos. He found them to be clever workmen, eminently capable, intelligent, sober and hard-working. 'Yet does this native workman require kind and encouraging treatment, and refuses to be driven or spoken to harshly at his work. For he then avails himself of the scarcity of workmen to resign his engagement and seek employment elsewhere.'

Consul Drummond Hay appreciated that rubber collecting was the perfect outlet for these industrious people. Rubber yielded a high return for relatively little labour. 'A family gang or a single man erect a temporary hut in the forest and, living frugally on the fruit and game which abound and their provision of dried fish and [manioc] farinha, realize in a few weeks such sums of money, in an ever-ready market, with which they are able to relapse into the much-coveted idleness and enjoy their easy gains until the dry season for tapping the rubber-tree . . . returns.' Thus, in the early decades of the boom, there was considerable freedom for the seringueiros. It was only later that the main rivers came to be controlled by rubber barons with armed henchmen.

From 1872 onwards came the ruinous attempts to build the railway past the rapids of the Madeira and Mamoré rivers. This involved successive immigrations by groups of Frenchmen, Azores islanders, Portuguese and Spaniards. But most of the workers in Amazon rubber came from other parts of Brazil, particularly the impoverished north-east. The 'bulge' of Brazil was overpopulated and had declined in prosperity with the eclipse of its sugar wealth. It was also struck by droughts, aggravated by the felling of its coastal forests and by the import of cattle – heavy and thirsty animals unsuited to fragile tropical soils. North-easterners had been moving to Amazonia throughout the nineteenth century; but their migration was swollen and accelerated by a terrible drought in Ceará in 1877. Many chose to try their luck as seringueiros. They preferred work in Amazonia to labour in the coffee plantations of south Brazil, which was considered slave work. They were attracted by the lure of rubber riches, and imagined that work as a seringueiro was independent. Transport from the north-east to Amazonia was plentiful and the journey was short. There were even government subsidies for immigrants to Amazonia. Most of those who went from the north-east came from local Indian or mestizo stock.

Such inexperienced immigrants were quickly drawn into debt bondage. Euclides da Cunha explained that 'the seringueiro begins to owe, from the very day that he leaves Ceará. He owes his steerage passage to Pará and the money he receives to equip himself. Then comes the cost of transport to the distant barracão [rubber depot] to which he is destined, in a gaiola [cage] launch.' A rubber tapper owned only a few possessions: 'a two-handled cooking pot, a pan, an iron hatchet, an axe, a machete, a Winchester carbine with two hundred bullets, two plates, two spoons, two cups, two blankets, a coffee pot, two reels of line and a case of needles. Nothing more.' He also obtained his basic foods on credit. He thus started his first season of rubber-gathering deeply in debt. And his boss ensured that he never emerged from that debt bondage.

Oswaldo Gonçalves Cruz was a great Brazilian doctor and public health official who tried to combat the diseases and malnutrition at the height of the rubber boom. He wrote: 'Addicted to alcohol, which they abuse to an incredible extent, the seringueiros have no proper food; and yet they pay fabulous prices for what they get. Their basic foods are dried meat and manioc farinha d'agua. The former almost always arrives rotting, which happens easily because of its appalling conservation and the humidity of the region.' Manioc flour and meat were infested with the insects that penetrate everything in Amazonia. Towards the end of the century, richer seringueiros ate tinned food. But there was danger of poisoning. 'These tins are sold without scruples and are mostly defective. Fraud is so extensive that importers of tinned goods have an employee called "tin solderer". His job is to pierce tins swollen by gases of putrefaction, in order to let these gases escape, and then resolder the hole he has made. They thus deceive buyers who are well aware of the danger of preserved food in tins deformed by fermenting gases (which are due to bacteria that cause infections and digestive poisoning). The seringueiro in remote regions . . . has to eat these rotten substances or die of hunger.'

The working routine of the seringueiros was monotonous and at times arduous. In opening up a new seringal, the key man was a matteiro or expert machete man. It was he who discovered the hevea trees among the bewilderingly rich biomass of the Amazon jungles. He had to recognise the smooth grey bark of the tall hevea amid many hundreds of competing species of forest tree. The matteiro then linked two or three hundred trees in a network of paths through the undergrowth. 'It is the matteiro's duty not only to place the seringueiros on these paths, but to supervise their work. In addition, he is always an expert on forest lore. . . . All the different species of the trees are known to him, the flooded ground and the dry ground. Every rivulet has its distinctive appearance, and he can tell at once where an almost stagnant igarapé or stream is going to flow out.'

The seringueiro then established his open-sided thatch hut at the end of one of these trails. During the six-month rubber season, he worked his path daily, rising very early to catch the rubber latex before it coagulated in the midday heat. He covered eight to ten kilometres of trail each day, emptying cups fastened to each tree. By the afternoon he would have carried back nine litres of latex. Back at his hut, he smoked this gum in dense white creosotic smoke from a fire of palm such as attalea. The rubber was hardened around a pole, condensing this spool until the ball of rubber weighed about fifty kilos. Kenneth Grubb described this dreary existence: 'Day after day he passes in identical circumstances and the same solitude. To the monotony and sadness of the forest around he adds the uniform burden of his task.'

'The life of the seringueiro is the most miserable that could be imagined. . . . He has no knowledge of sanitary precautions, is barely acquainted with the use of quinine, and the effect of the constant attacks of the intolerable *pium* [biting *simuliidae* black-fly] – a plague far worse than the mosquito by night – is seen in a body covered with ulcers for which he employs no treatment. Under-nourishment is always present, the peril of loss and starvation in the forest constantly threatening, and the rifle the only known remedy for abuses and wrongs.' The immense forest brings out 'the worst instincts of man, brutalizes the affections, hardens the emotions, and draws out with malign and terrible intention every evil and sordid lust.' Two British engineers met seringueiros when they were idling away the rainy season at one of the tiny river towns. 'We found the men as uninteresting a class as possible, with no thought beyond the India-rubber trade. Their one topic of conversation was about the [amount of money] they were making yearly.'

The novelist José Rivera knew how destructive the rubber trade could be. 'Labourers in rubber know full well that the vegetable gold enriches no one. The potentates of the forest have no credits beyond those in their books – against peons who never pay (unless with their lives), against Indians who waste away, against boatmen who rob what they transport. Slavery in these regions becomes life-long for both slave and owner. . . . The forest annihilates them, the forest entraps them, the forest beckons in order to swallow them up. Those who escape . . . carry the curse in body and soul. Worn out, grown old and deceived, they have only one desire: to return, to return to the forest – knowing that if they return they will perish.'

Women were another commodity in the meagre world of the rubber tappers. In the early decades of the rubber boom, seringueiros took their families with them. The women and children tended plantations on river-bank forest clearings while the men tapped their trees. Later, when the boom gathered momentum, aviadores imported only men. Single women who appeared on the rubber rivers were objects of envy and dispute. Some traders therefore installed prostitutes in their barracão depots: the girls' services were charged to the tapper's account like any other commodity. On one occasion the Governor of Amazonas ordered the Manaus police to round up women from the cabarets and a boatload of 150 women was sent to new rubber areas on the upper Juruá. Some caught malaria and died: others returned to Manaus; but the rest stayed, married rubber men and helped Brazil colonise the disputed area that became the state of Acre. With such an acute shortage of women, Indian tribes were harassed for their girls as much as for the labour of their men.

A few forest tribes had the wisdom to use the rubber boom to their advantage. They did not work for the rubber men, but prospered instead by trading their own artefacts or food with the seringueiros. Such tribes sold hammocks and manioc, or worked portaging canoes over rapids or cutting wood for steamers. Other tribes resisted the seringueiro invasion. For many isolated forest tribes, rubber gatherers were their first contact with the outside world. Such contact was rarely well-intentioned on the gatherers' part and often violent. The once-dreaded Mura waged their last battles against travellers on the Madeira in 1849 and 1852. They then retreated to their swampy lakes and sandbanks. James Orton visited their lagoons in 1867 and found them the most lazy and wretched tribe of Amazonia. He blamed missionary catechism for their degradation. A decade later, Princess Therese of Bavaria visited some Mura and described them as short, corpulent and uglier than most Indians: cruel, lazy and thieving, they were constantly on the move in their canoes and 'fled from civilisation.' They were hated and pursued by other tribes; but she reckoned that there were still twelve thousand Mura on the Amazon.

One tribe which fought successfully against the rubber frontier was the Parintintin of the middle Madeira river. This warlike Tupi-speaking tribe called itself Kawahib; but it was known by the Munduruku name Parintintin, meaning 'enemy'. The Parintintin originally lived near the Mundurukú in the forests west of the upper Tapajós and Juruena, but they seem to have been driven further west by the powerful and implacable Mundurukú. The tribe was shattered and dispersed during this fighting. But one group settled in a triangle of land between the east bank of the Madeira, its tributaries the Machado (or Jiparaná), and the Marmelos. This group came to dominate the Madeira opposite the present town of Humaitá.

In 1852 these Parintintin clashed with copaíba-oil extractors on the Marmelos; between 1858 and 1860 they attacked rubber gatherers on the Merari tributary of the Madeira, killing seven men; and in 1865 and 1869 on the Madeira itself. The authorities had tried to establish missions on this section of the Madeira: São Pedro existed from 1854 to 1876, with less than a hundred Mura Indians; Crato nearby had some Mura and a handful of Mundurukú, Tora and Karipuna; and in 1871 a mission called São Francisco was established for 135 Arara and Tora near the mouth of the Machado river. This was a provocation to the Parintintin. In 1874 they attacked São Francisco, killing its chief and trying to invade the mission. All the Parintintin attacks involved deaths, wounding and burning, so that the tribe gained a reputation for ferocity.

Such hostilities aroused the fear and fury of the seringueiros. We can grasp the hatreds of the wild rubber frontier from the writings of two foreign engineers who visited the Madeira at that time. The Englishman Edward Mathews was sent in 1872 to investigate the feasibility of building a railway past the rapids of the upper Madeira. He visited Humaitá, then a thriving place belonging to a Portuguese rubber baron called João Monteiro, 'who is the wealthiest settler on the Madeira River'. Upstream of Humaitá lay the territory of the Parintintin, the 'deadly enemies of any settlers, whether whites or mestizos. . . . They now have the reputation of being cannibals, and no settler dares to set up a hut on their territory, although it contains very rich growths of rubber trees. The Brazilian government does not allow the improvement of these savage races by the only practical method, namely extermination, but trusts to the efforts of a few missionary friars. . . . These efforts might doubtless be successful in partially civilising milder tribes (such as the Mundurucús of the Amazon, the Pamas [Paumarí] of the Purus, or the Caripunas of the Madeira) but they are perfectly unable to tame fierce tribes, such as the Parintintins of the Madeira, the Yçanga-Pirangas [Akaguara] of the Jamari, or the Sirionós of [the Mamoré in] Bolivia, tribes that refuse to hold any converse with the white faces, but attack suddenly with their arrows whenever they can come across an unprepared party. For these irreclaimable sons of the forest there is no taming method other than the rifle and bullet. It is no use trying to shirk the fact that they must be removed out of the way of the opening up to commerce of the Amazon and its tributaries.' Mathews advised any travellers to this region to take 'a Winchester sixteen-shot repeating rifle, for they make splendid shooting, are light, portable, and carry a good armament ready at hand in case of a brush with savages'. He also recommended presents of knives, beads, fish-hooks and flannel shirts 'in readiness for the chance of an amicable "pow-wow" with the "bárbaros" ', so that the traveller could obtain some native artefacts as souvenirs.

Both Mathews and Franz Keller, the German engineer, mentioned an episode when Parintintin attacked the house of a seringueiro and were said to have been caught roasting and eating their victim on a sandbank. A posse was formed, which found a Parintintin village and punished its inhabitants. The Parintintin 'have never again ventured out of the depths of their forests'. Two other English engineers who were on the Madeira in 1873 reported that people kept huge bloodhounds at their landing stages for fear of the Parintintin. The tribe attacked the settlement of Santo Antonio at the foot of the great rapids of that name. They were driven off by gunfire from engineers and labourers, but they took clothing from a sick man lying in an isolated hut. 'It proved to be a fatal memento, for the loathsome disease of small-pox spread rapidly among them, carrying off many victims.'

The Parintintins' resistance was remarkably effective. Settlers became too frightened to venture into the forests they controlled. As the American explorer Neville Craig reported, 'no effective defence was possible against savages, who realised the great advantage they had over us, both in facilities for stealthy approach and the superiority at close quarters of their noiseless weapons. Our one source of confidence was the fact that the Parintintins were ignorant of the use of firearms and regarded them with superstitious awe.'

Unable to fight the elusive Parintintin in their own forests, the rubber men tried to enlist other Indians to do so for them. The French geographer Auguste Plane spoke of a seringueiro on the upper Machado arming the Jarú to fight Parintintins. And when three traders on the Madeira were killed by Indians from the Machado in 1895, their neighbours determined to inflict heavy reprisals. They went across to enlist the Mundurukú of the Tapajós. 'They spread out the merchandise that they had brought as presents for the Mundurukú, and spoke of a fine harvest of heads to be reaped on the

Machado.' Sixty Mundurukú warriors accepted the offer and set out
westwards with forty women. They crossed the Tapajós and Sucun-
duri rivers but were then struck down by virulent malaria. So severe
was the disease that only four very sick Mundurukú returned home
after many months. By 1903, Plane described the Machado river as
being empty because of the Parintintin. There was pitiless warfare
between Indians and rubber men. Plane described the Parintintin as
'an intractable tribe, today almost completely destroyed'. He was
wrong; for it was twenty years later that the brilliant German anthropologist Curt Nimuendajú finally achieved a dangerous pacification
of this brave tribe. Nimuendajú (whose real name was Unkel, but
who adopted the name given to him by the Guarani) used what is
now the classic method of leaving presents of knives, axes and other
useful tools for the Parintintin. He survived a barrage of arrows, and
finally, by never retaliating, convinced the tribe of his peaceful
intentions.

The Indians of the Solimões were not seriously affected by the rubber
boom. This long stretch of the mighty Amazon had been denuded by
slavers during the seventeenth century. Rivalry between Spanish
and Portuguese missionaries and colonists caused most of its Tupi-
speaking Omagua and Yurimagua tribes to migrate deeper into
Peru. The resulting vacuum was occupied by a few Tukuna (related
to the Yurí and Miranya of the Içá river) on the north bank, and by
Panoan-speaking Mayoruna and Kulino on the south. But most of
the river remained empty.
    The Tukuna have long been famous for two things – their masks
and their ritual dances. Tukuna masks are wonderfully vivid: frightening, roaring heads of all the birds and animals of the forests or
grotesque human beings and deities. These masks are made of light
balsa woods, carved and painted with virtuosity, and backed by
hoods of bark-cloth (the cloth-like membrane between the wood and
bark of some Amazon trees). Tukuna men wore masks for various
ceremonies, of which the most famous was the initiation and hair-
plucking of girls at puberty. Many travellers described these dances,
at which masked Tukuna looked like a fantastic carnival of the
animals. To Spix, the initiation was a drunken bacchanal in which
masked dancers leaped about like goats, imitating the spirits. 'One
of these horrendous apparitions suddenly came up to me and tried to
pull the shiny buttons off my coat, since they seemed suitable as
earrings.'
    Some visitors regarded the Tukuna as incorrigibly lazy and

apathetic, and the Commander of the frontier garrison at Tabatinga treated them like personal serfs. They were forced to hunt and fish for him, to gather sarsaparilla for his profit, to collect turtle eggs and manatees, or were sold as slaves. Many Tukuna were conscripted to fight in the war against Paraguay in the 1860s. Curt Nimuendajú found that they still recalled the horrors of that service many decades later. They hated the recruiting officers, whom they called 'Varavayu' after the war for which they were seizing men, and took up arms to resist the military press-gangs. The few Tukuna conscripts who returned brought with them a lethal epidemic of smallpox.

Slavery continued on the Içá and Japurá, the two great rivers that flow into the Solimões from the north-west. The traffic had declined since 1820, when Spix and Martius visited the Japurá with their slaver friend Zany – but the decline was largely because there were fewer Indians to be caught on those rivers. When Henry Bates was at Ega (Tefé) on the Solimões in 1850, he found that all its domestic servants and much of its native population had been forcibly brought down from the neighbouring rivers, and commented that such captives had no desire to return to their tribes when they grew up. However, 'the boys generally run away and embark on the canoes of traders; and the girls are often badly treated by their mistresses, the jealous, passionate and ill-educated Brazilian women.'

When Jules Crevaux went up the Içá–Putumayo in 1879 he found its banks deserted. Indians had fled from the main river to find sanctuary on small tributary streams where hunting and fishing were easier, and 'they are not molested by whites who want to exploit their labour and violate their freedom. From time to time these children of nature accept relations with a sarsaparilla or cacao collecter, but this does not last for long. Once an Indian has exchanged his stone axe for a knife or machete, he finds the company of whites intolerable and returns to his forests.'

On the Caquetá (the Colombian name for the upper Japurá) Crevaux was amazed to find the Carib Karihona with a chest full of civilised trade goods, even though they lived a thousand kilometres from the main Amazon river. The Karihona chief had ten guns and as many cavalry sabres. This wealth came from a traffic in captives sold to Brazilian traders. 'A suckling infant is reckoned to be worth an American knife; a girl of six years is valued at a machete or sometimes an axe; an adult man or woman fetches the price of a gun. Thus armed, these Indians make raids on neighbouring rivers, attacking their peoples who have nothing but arrows with which to defend themselves. They kill any who resist and take the rest prisoner, to be transported downstream to the merchants of human flesh.'

The tribe that suffered most from this slave traffic was the Miranya of the Japurá – people closely related to the Bora and Witoto living in Colombia and the Tukuna on the Solimões. Tavares Bastos said in 1865 that Tefé and other towns were full of Miranya who had been slaves for many years. They reached these settlements weak and profoundly depressed from ill-treatment during the voyage down-river; hundreds of them died of disease, melancholy and ill-treatment. But it was impossible to obtain convictions in settlers' courts of those who enslaved and abused Indians.* The naturalist João Barbosa Rodrigues said that the Miranya were persecuted because of 'their docile, amenable, frank and open character, from their noble sentiments and good heart, which make them good friends and good workers. For these reasons everyone seeks them as slaves. . . . They suffer from homesickness more than any other Indians. Shortly after leaving their homes, they often grow sad, become thin and pale, and suffer obvious change: there are disorders in their digestive system which reduce hunger, upset the intestines and bring them to the grave. . . . It is always death that delivers them from the power of white men's civilisation. I have seen so many examples of it!'

South of the Solimões, the boundary between Brazil and Peru had been defined since 1750 as the Javari river. The upper reaches of the Javari had never been explored, and its banks were defended by Mayoruna. A boundary demarcation expedition was sent up the Javari in 1866. It progressed slowly, alert for signs that hostile Indians were watching its progress from the banks. The feared attack finally came when the expedition was near the headwaters, opposite the mouth of the Batã tributary. Indians, probably Kapanawa, killed a Brazilian with their arrows and wounded his companion. The explorers retreated downriver. Another Peruvian–Brazilian commission went up the Javari eight years later. Indians on the banks burned trees to send them crashing across the stream, and the surveyors were often frightened by strange noises, drumbeats or threatening markers. The men were exhausted, battling against the current. This expedition was also attacked. The silence had sudden-ly been broken by great shouting from a crowd of Mayoruna. The Indians appeared on a sandbank, brandishing their weapons, firing a cloud of arrows, shouting defiance, with their brilliant feather orna-ments sparkling in the sun. The warriors ran up to surround the expedition, which was hauling its boats up a rapid. The Brazilian commander, Captain Antonio von Hoonholdtz, immediately gave the order to fire. The beach full of Mayoruna was raked by gunfire, the chief and others killed and the rest put to flight. Von Hoonholdtz kept the chief's headdress as a souvenir and boasted: 'Without losing a single man, we asserted through today's victory our supremacy in this region of indomitable natives.'

There were battles between Indians and seringueiros in other isolated parts of Amazonia. Henri Coudreau said that the Asurini of the forests between the lower Xingu and Tocantins attacked rubber tappers with increasing success. The rubber men were terrified of forest Indians and, when attacked, immediately ran off, allowing the Indians to take their guns and boats. Higher up the Xingu, acculturated Juruna attacked a seringal, but pretended to be wild Suyá to avoid reprisals on their village.

Such fighting was generally one-sided. Indian tribes sought to defend their territories but were inevitably forced to yield and retreat. They pitted their skill as woodsmen against the firearms and ruthlessness of the rubber tappers. Ambushes and arrows were no match for carbines. Arthur Ferreira Reis, the great Brazilian historian of the Amazon, noted that most tribes chose to flee from contact with uncouth seringueiros. 'The brutality on either side reached a striking degree of intensity. The seringueiros regarded Indians as enemies who seemed to them elusive, treacherous, dangerous and people with whom there could be no compromise.'

The worst fighting between Indians and rubber men came in the later years of the rubber boom, and in the far west of Brazil. Alfredo Lustosa Cabral witnessed a raid on some Katukina of the upper Juruá. This tribe had raided a seringueiro's hut, killing three people. Twenty men were promptly organised into a reprisal raid. Each took a Winchester and three hundred cartridges. After three days' march, the attackers came upon a maloca, a beautiful circular thatched hut the size and shape of a circus tent. It was on a plateau, surrounded by clearings full of planted crops. The posse arrived at nightfall and slept some distance from the clearings. It moved forward before dawn, forming lines of fire outside each of the hut's two doors. 'With cries of alarm the Indians came running from the two doors, and at that moment the deadly shots of the attackers knocked them to the ground. There was great mortality, but many also ran off. Approaching the hut [the raiders] managed to catch some fifteen children aged from eight to ten years: they left the younger ones. On the return journey, the prisoners began to cry too much. It was necessary to abandon them, leaving them lost and tied in the rope.

Some [of our men] practised savagery, taking off the tops of the children's heads with bullets.'

James Wells said that the President of Amazonas went up the Purus as far as the Acre river in 1882 and was told of atrocities against natives. 'Conspicuous among these crimes are the barbarous persecutions by Leonel Antonio do Sacramento of the Indians of the upper Purus, which resulted in the destruction of more than five villages and the murder of over two hundred men, women and children.' The President promptly sent ten soldiers and a judge and prosecutor to punish the guilty seringueiro. Wells praised this action, but noted that it resulted from a chance journey by the Provincial President. 'There are scores of similar, or even worse, crimes that happen and pass away unheard of.'

Another Governor of Amazonas admitted in 1898 that fighting between Indians and 'civilised' rubber men was almost always the fault of the latter. Governor Pires Ferreira said that he had been filled with horror by an account by Engineer Almeida Braga of 'scenes of savagery and evil perpetrated against the Jauaperi Indians [Yuberi of the middle Purus]'. The rubber men had harassed this tribe to get its men to work for them. In return, the Indians 'declared a war of extermination on their persecutors' and a war of reprisals had resulted. The Governor concluded that 'exploitation of Indians is almost a second slavery. Only an almost iron will could put a stop to this abnormal situation.'

The English missionary and Indianist Kenneth Grubb told of similar murderous raids or correrias. Among the seringueiros, such a raid ' "comes out well" if they are able to annex the men without bloodshed and carry them off; but if much bloodshed takes place it is "an ugly thing", but apparently a necessary one. . . . The Indians are beasts and must be treated as such. Society . . . is divided into two strata, Christians and *bichos da matta*, or beasts of the forest. Christians are, of course, disciples of Christ, characterized by a boundless mercilessness. . . . *Bichos* comprehend the tribal Indians without exception.' Grubb liked the caboclos of Amazonia – simple, hospitable and hard-working people. But he recognised the lawlessness of their extremely remote forested frontiers. They told him: 'We do not respect the Constitution here; we have our own constitution and one article in it – Article 44 of the Winchester constitution.' The Winchester 44 rifle was the settlers' favourite weapon.

Father C. Tastevin saw a massacre perpetrated by Peruvian caucheros (latex gatherers) on the Panoan-speaking Yumbanawa of the Tarauacá headwater of the Jutaí. In this case some sixty Yumbanawa (known to the whites as Papavo) had been assembled amid acculturated Indians and were being used as slave labour. After a few months the Indians tried to escape back to their forests. The Yumbanawa were shut into a hut for some days under heavily armed guard. Eventually some 'civilised' Kashinawa Indians arrived. These were given carbines by the rubber men and encouraged to pick off the Yumbanawa as they tried to run the hundred metres from the prison hut to their canoes. 'Apart from the young women, who were kept for the so-called civilised Indians, only one man managed to escape.' Tastevin also described a massacre of the nearby Nehanawa by Peruvians who ambushed their hut. On the other side of this ugly fighting, Tastevin met the famous Kashinawa chief Teskon, 'who boasted of having personally killed twenty-two civilizados and having pillaged an incalculable number of rubber stores'.

On the Liberdade headwater of the Juruá, Tastevin found that most tribal Indians had been exterminated in pitiless raids. A well-intentioned white man made friendly overtures to the Kashinawa of the Liberdade. Their chief Tercum said that no white had ever spoken peacefully to them. 'The whites had killed many of his people and had carried off his wife and a suckling baby son. They had cut the corn in his clearing and set fire to it. His people no longer knew where to live. They had emigrated from the Riozinho da Liberdade to the Gregório river, but they now had nowhere to go. Their children were dying of hunger: they could neither hunt nor fish, for the "carius" [whites] shot bullets at them wherever they encountered them.' Similarly, the Kuriná of the Gregório were exhausted by continual flight. They had welcomed the first scringueiros with customary Indian hospitality. But they suffered such violence that they fled from any contact and became avowed enemies of the whites. They found themselves harassed and surrounded by caucheros. When one settler finally made peaceful contact with these Aruak-speaking Kuriná, he found them desperate to make peace and end their enforced retreat.

The situation in Acre improved somewhat after it was ceded to Brazil. Its Governor, General Gregorio Thaumaturgo de Azevedo, started a strict programme of Indian protection there in 1906. The first pro-Indian inspectors entered the lawless headwaters of the Juruá–Purus only in 1911. This remote frontier had suffered acutely by being on the borders of Brazil and Peru, exploited by rubber and latex tappers from both countries and far beyond the reach of any legal authorities of either nation. The reports are full of terrible episodes of cruelty to Indians. We must assume that these represent a fraction of similar skirmishes that went unrecorded during the previous decades of the rubber boom. On the Inauini headwater of the Purus, an inspector found a camp of Peruvian caucheros with sixty Yamamadí in their forced employ. These were surrounded by a ring of armed guards. 'They had been captured in their maloca, many leagues from there, and had been taken to the latex forest with every sort of violence. This included hunger, for they received no food whatever during the entire journey. Some died during the march, others when they reached the camp.'

There were ugly skirmishes with the nearby Ipurinã. Two seringueiros had tried to seize an Indian couple, but had killed the man after a fierce physical struggle; the woman fled. Two days later an expedition of nine seringueiros was driven off by the Ipurinã under Chief João Grande, leaving six dead. Ten days after that, a troop of fifty heavily armed seringueiros 'made a surprise attack on a maloca, wreaking a veritable slaughter. All the malocas then united and armed themselves. Terrified by the attitude of the Indians, the seringueiros fled precipitously from the banks of the Purus, often abandoning all their possessions.' Another seringueiro had taken two children from the Kanamarí of the upper Juruá. The tribe finally managed to free these boys. The seringueiro's revenge was the usual dawn attack on a maloca, in which four women were killed. 'Two children who failed to escape were thrown into a stream and there killed with rifle shots. Not satisfied with this, the attackers then sacked the maloca, destroying everything they found, from the plantations to the houses and utensils, leaving these people in complete misery.'

Henry Pearson wrote that rubber men were tormented by Indian attacks on the Pauini headwater of the Purus. But a policy of savage reprisals succeeded in forcing the Indians to retreat. 'The owners of the seringals exact a heavy penalty for massacres, and the reports of killing are becoming less and less frequent. . . . The remaining wild tribes, as a rule, live back in the forests above the limits of navigation.' There was a similar atmosphere in the distant north-west of Brazil, where the German anthropologist Theodor Koch-Grünberg reported bloody battles in 1904 between wild Tukana-speaking Kobewa of the upper Uaupés and Colombian rubber gatherers.

The vast majority of battles between seringueiros and Indians went unrecorded. In the few accounts of such fighting that exist, the observers were on the side of the rubber men. It is therefore exceptional to have an eyewitness description of such warfare from the

Indian side. But we do have one written by an American traveller called Algot Lange, though he may have somewhat exaggerated his story. Lange was with the Panoan-speaking Mayoruna (Mangeroma) on the Ituí, a tributary of the Javari near the boundary between Brazil and Peru. One day his Indians sighted a dozen Peruvian caucheros prowling up the Ituí in search of rubber or Mayoruna women. The chief sounded a signal drum, whose powerful xylophonic sounds vibrated through the forest to summon back the tribe's hunters.

Lange wrote: 'I now had a remarkable opportunity to watch the war preparations of these savage cannibal people, my friends the Mayoruna. Their army consisted of twelve able-bodied men, all fine muscular fellows about five feet ten in height and bearing an array of vicious-looking weapons such as few white men have seen.' The first three warriors carried very long, tough caripari-wood clubs, each with jaguar teeth projecting from its striking end. Then came three men armed with three-pronged poisoned spears, 'a horrible weapon which always proves fatal in the hands of these savages'. The third division was three teenage boys armed with bows of great length and a quiver full of five-foot arrows with sting-ray heads. Finally came three blow-gun men, 'the most effective and cunning of this deadly and imposing array'. All the warriors had their faces painted for battle with stripes of scarlet urucum and black genipap dyes. The chiefs wore brilliant plumages of macaw and egret feathers. All except the club men wore girdles decked with black plumes from the mutum curassow and multi-coloured fringes of squirrel tails. Lange filed off into the forest with this magnificent squadron. He himself carried a Luger automatic pistol and thirty-seven bullets.

After an hour's movement through the jungle, the Indians stopped in ambush. Scouts were sent forward. 'An anxious half hour passed before one of them returned with the report that the Peruvians were now coming towards us and would probably reach our position in a few minutes. I could almost hear my heart thump; my knees grew weak. . . . The Chief immediately directed certain strategic movements which, in ingenuity and foresight, would have been worthy of a Napoleon.' His warriors were posted in the dense woods to form a trap between two hills. 'After a pause that seemed an eternity to most of us . . . we heard the talking and shouting of the enemy as they advanced . . . cutting their way through the brush. . . . Before I could see any of the approaching foe, I heard great shouts of anger and pain from them. . . . The blow-gun men . . . had prudently waited until at least half a dozen Peruvians were visible before they fired a volley of poisoned arrows. The three arrows fired in this first volley all hit their mark. The blow-gun warriors then withdrew, taking their long cumbersome tubular guns.

'Now the conflict was at its height and it was a most remarkable one, on account of its swiftness and fierceness. The bow-and-arrow men charging with their sting-ray arrows poisoned with the wourali [curare] took the place of the cautiously retreating blow-gun men. At the same instant the spear-men rushed down, dashing through the underbrush at the foot of the hill, like breakers on a stormy night.

'The rear-guard of the Peruvians now came into action, having had a chance to view the situation. Several of them filed to the right and managed to fire their large-calibre bullets into the backs of our charging bow-and-arrow men, but, in their turn, they were picked off by the blow-gun men, who kept firing their poisoned darts from a safe distance. The fearful yells of our men, mingled with the cursing of the Peruvians, and the sharp reports of their heavy rifles, so plainly heard, proved that the centre of the battle was not many yards from the spot where I was standing.

'The club-men now broke into action; they could not be kept back any longer. . . . With fierce war-cries of "*YOB-HEE-HEE*" they launched themselves into the fight, swinging their strong clubs above their heads and crushing skulls from left to right. By this time the Peruvians had lost many men, but the slaughter went on. The huge black clubs of the Mayoruna fell again and again, with sickening thuds, piercing the heads and brains of the enemy with the pointed jaguar teeth.'

Suddenly two more Peruvians, including their moustachioed leader, appeared and took aim at Lange and his companions. 'But before he could pull the trigger, [a warrior called] Arara, with a mighty side-swing of his club, literally tore the Spaniard's head off.'

So far, Algot Lange had taken no part in the battle. He then felt several bullets whirr past him at close range. 'Now a caboclo, with a large, bloody machete in his hand, sprang from behind a tree and made straight for me. I dodged behind another tree and saw how the branches were swept aside as he rushed towards me. Then I fired point-blank, sending three bullets into his head. He fell on his face at my feet.' Another Peruvian had an arrow through his upper abdomen with the broken shaft projecting behind his back. Four Indians were killed by rifle bullets. But the dozen Mayoruna had wiped out the entire party of twenty caucheros. They thus prevented any enemy escaping to bring a reprisal raid against their maloca.

*

The most famous case of oppression of forest Indians by rubber barons occurred just outside Brazil, on the Putumayo river (which changes its name to Içá when it enters Brazil). At the height of the rubber boom, in the first decade of the twentieth century, the vast triangle of forests between the Putumayo and Caquetá rivers was a no man's land claimed by Ecuador but in practice occupied by a few Peruvians and Colombians.

A Peruvian called Júlio César Arana was a general trader on the upper Amazon in the 1880s and 1890s. After various business ventures, he established himself at a place called La Chorrera to trade in Putumayo rubber. This region yielded only an inferior type of rubber known as sernambi, and caucho from the *Castilloa elastica* tree. But it had the advantage of a reasonable number of docile forest Indians who could be coerced into rubber gathering. The tribes of the region were peaceful Witoto, Andoke and Ocaina and more warlike Bora (Miranya). As the rubber boom spread its tentacles up the most distant of Amazonia's thousands of rivers, rubber men established depots or colonies on the banks of the Putumayo and seduced or bullied its Indians into working for them. As Arana himself testified: 'I entered into business relations with the said colonies, exchanging merchandise for rubber, buying produce and making advances. [Hitherto] the Indians on [these rivers] had resisted the establishment of civilisation in their districts. . . . But from about the year 1900 onwards the Indians became more civilised, and a system of rubber collected by the Indians for European merchandise sprang up between the Indians and the said colonies. From that time my business in the Putumayo district gradually increased, but by slow degrees.'

Arana traded successfully and prospered. He steadily took over the various settlements along the Putumayo, monopolised steamer movement, and in 1906 paid £116,700 for an area of no less than twelve thousand square miles (thirty-one thousand square kilometres). The Peruvian government covertly supported Arana, seeing his company as a means of gaining possession of this disputed region. In 1907 Arana took the bold step of floating his business on the London stock market. It was a time of speculation in rubber, so his Peruvian Amazon Rubber Company had no difficulty in raising capital of a million pounds.

It was also in 1907 that the first reports of atrocities started to emerge from the Putumayo. A crusading editor called Benjamin Saldana Rocca published eyewitness reports in his news-sheet in the Peruvian Amazon town of Iquitos, until he was stopped by the authorities early in 1908. It was clear that conditions on the Putu-

mayo had gone beyond the illegal – but fairly commonplace – raiding
and enslavement of tribal Indians. Men on the Putumayo were
forced to work excessively, even by the standards of the day. To
intimidate and coerce them, Arana's company resorted to syste-
mised torture. This in turn degenerated into an orgy of sadism.
Testimonies from the rubber men themselves told of perverted mutilations of Indian men, women and children. The Colombian authorities made sure that these horrifying accounts (many of which
involved abuse of Colombians by the Peruvian company) reached
a wider audience, and leading newspapers of Manaus and Belém
published them in June 1908.

Late in 1907 two American railway engineers, Walter Hardenburg
and William Perkins, had sailed down the Putumayo to seek employment on the railway being built on the Madeira river. During this
descent they fell foul of the Peruvian Amazon Rubber Company,
which held them prisoner for a time and stole their luggage. They
witnessed a massacre by company employees and were sure that
they themselves were saved from murder only by their American
citizenship. When he reached Iquitos, Hardenburg obtained from
Saldana Rocca's son the original texts of the testimonies of the
Putumayo rubber gatherers. Hardenburg brought an action against
Arana's firm, now called simply Peruvian Amazon Company. He
tried in vain to get the American consul in Iquitos to involve the
United States government, then forwarded his terrible depositions
to the Anti-Slavery Society in London, and they were published in
1909 in a series of sensational articles in the English magazine *Truth*.
They were the subject of a question in Parliament on 29 September
1909. British interests were involved in those remote atrocities, not
only because Arana's company was registered in London, but also
because he had recruited almost two hundred British subjects from
Barbados to swell the ranks of its infamous overseers.

The article in *Truth* magazine was gruesome. Headed 'The Devil's
Paradise' and subtitled 'A British-owned Congo', it said that Arana's
men forced the Witoto Indians on the Putumayo to work day and
night without the slightest payment, and 'that they give them nothing to eat, that they rob them of their own crops, their women and
their children, to satisfy the voracity, lasciviousness and avarice of
themselves and their employees, for they live on the Indians' food,
keep harems of concubines, buy and sell these people wholesale and
retail in Iquitos; that they flog them inhumanly until their bones are
laid bare; that they do not give them any medical treatment but let

them linger, eaten by maggots till they die, to serve afterwards as food for the [overseer's] dogs; that they mutilate them, cut off their ears, fingers, arms and legs, that they torture them by means of fire and of water, and by tying them up, crucified head down; that they cut them to pieces with machetes; that they grasp children by the feet and dash out their brains against walls and trees; that they have their old folk killed when they can no longer work and finally that to amuse themselves, to practise shooting, or to celebrate the *sábado de gloria* . . . they discharge their weapons at men, women and children, or, in preterence to this, they souse them with kerosene and set fire to them, to enjoy their desperate agony.'

Faced with a barrage of criticism, the British directors of the Peruvian Amazon Company decided that they must send a commission of enquiry to the Putumayo. In addition to the four members of the commission supplied by the company, the Foreign Office sent a famous diplomat, the forty-six-year-old Roger Casement, who was British Consul-General in Rio de Janeiro and had previously been Consul in Belém do Pará. Casement thus knew his way in Amazonia and spoke some Portuguese, but his main qualification for the Putumayo job was a fine investigation he had done in 1903 into atrocities in the Belgian Congo; his revelations about massacres and mutilations in that African rainforest had won him fame.

The commission of enquiry went up the Amazon and reached Iquitos in August 1910. It immediately started hearing testimonies about the horrors on the Putumayo, many of them from Barbadians unafraid to incriminate themselves. Casement and the other commissioners then went for several months to the Putumayo itself. They saw plenty of evidence of torture, from ugly stocks to scars known locally as 'Arana's marks' on victims' bodies. They heard reports of lingering deaths from starvation, drowning or hanging, mutilations, burning alive, and fiendish variations of the cepo stocks. All the commissioners were convinced that the system on the Putumayo was hideously cruel and corrupt. Their report, written in 1911, said as much.

In his personal diaries, Roger Casement showed that he saw a similarity between the plight of the American Indians and his own Irish compatriots. Both colonised peoples were losing their language and culture to that of the dominant occupying power. Casement also brought back personal souvenirs from the trip: two Indian boys. He purchased one, Omarino, for a shirt and a pair of trousers; the other, Ricudo, was nineteen and married. He took them to England for experimental education; but after a period as social curiosities, during which William Rothenstein drew their portraits, they were returned to Peru.

Roger Casement was the main author of the *Blue Book on the Putumayo*, published in July 1912, and was knighted for it. A long, complicated House of Commons Select Committee enquired into the conduct of the Peruvian Amazon Company. Very little came of it all. The Peruvian government at first seemed appalled and set up its own enquiry, but in the event no one was convicted. Such was invariably the way in Amazonia. Even Júlio César Arana, although disgraced in Europe, continued to live in luxury in the upper Amazon. The Barbadians returned to the Caribbean.

Sir Roger Casement, for his part, soon declared himself for Irish independence. He was landed in Ireland by German U-boat, caught, and executed for treason in London in 1916. Júlio Arana sent him a long and ironic telegram when he was in the Tower of London awaiting trial, accusing him of fabricating evidence about the Putumayo. The telegram ended: 'You tried by all means to appear a humaniser in order to obtain titles and fortune, not caring for the consequences of your calumnies and defamation against Peru and myself, doing me enormous damage. I pardon you, but it is necessary that you should be just and declare now fully and truely [*sic*] all the true facts that nobody knows better than yourself.'

Conditions elsewhere in Amazonia were not as terrible as those on the Putumayo. This was partly because collection of the Putumayo caucho involved the destruction of trees: the company thus had no incentive to conserve its territory and workers, as was the case with rubber from *Hevea brasiliensis*, which was tapped and was thus a renewable resource. By the twentieth century, when the rubber trade had been established for many decades on the main Amazon tributaries, tribal Indians had either adapted to the traffic or fled from it.

One tribe that adapted fairly successfully was the Mundurukú of the upper Tapajós. We have seen how they gathered huge quantities of rubber and traded it with merchants and aviadores. By the height of the boom a ruthless and autocratic rubber baron called Raymundo Pereira Brazil controlled the upper Tapajós. And yet he himself wrote in 1914 that the Cururu tributary of that river was 'the exclusive domain of four hundred tame Mundurukú Indians' who tapped rubber and grew manioc on it. The French explorer Henri Coudreau also found 'a certain number of Mundurukú working rubber stands that belong to them'.

The reward to the Mundurukú for their co-operation with the

whites and participation in the rubber trade was to survive as a tribe. They still control the Cururu and still tap rubber successfully. But the price they paid was deculturation. By 1885 Charles Hartt was writing that the Mundurukú of the lower Tapajós were 'all civilised and so mixed with the general population that their nationality has in great part been lost'. William Chandless said that those of the Maués-Açú river were 'civilised and live in families, not as in tribe-life'.

William Farabee, leading an expedition from the University of Pennsylvania to the Tapajós in 1914, described the Mundurukú as 'honest, upright, good laborers and with careful treatment will become of inestimable value to the region'. He said that they were doing remarkably well at adapting themselves to the regular daily work needed to collect rubber, but that their hunting was threatened by competition from other rubber men. A new Franciscan mission was established on the Cururu in 1911 – and it is in operation there to this day. Thus, in 1914, 'their wants are increasing from their association with the whites.'

Henri Coudreau wrote that this dependence on outside goods had sapped the spirit of the once-warlike tribe. 'The Mundurukú are in total decadence, from the social, moral and economic points of view. They are no longer "the terrible Mundurukús". To the civilised people of the Tapajós, they are nothing more than "the people of campinas [savannahs]", "the black faces" or "the skinned heads". In its decline the horde is no longer an object of terror to anyone, not even small neighbouring tribes. . . . There remain only very vulgar bandits of the wilds, who travel in strong troops and . . . fall upon defenceless and inoffensive villages unexpectedly by night. . . . Their plains and forests would lend themselves perfectly to European colonisation, and even more so to local colonisation. I would offer a large bet that it will be only a few years before one sees the last Mundurukú sorcerer dry his last human head.'

The seventy years of the rubber boom were not as catastrophic to the native population as might have been expected. Although many tribes were affected, relatively few were directly involved in extracting rubber. The hard work was done by immigrants from other parts of Brazil or from Europe, by detribalised tapuio Indians, or by natives brought down from Bolivia. For Brazilian tribal Indians, the most serious ravages were from imported diseases and the intrusion of tough rubber men into hitherto unexplored areas. Ecologically, rubber-tapping caused almost no damage. Trails and clearings cut by seringueiros quickly reverted to forest when they left, and the hevea trees did not suffer from having their sap milked. The rubber boom thus did less lasting harm to the environment of Amazon Indians than the cattle ranches of central Brazil or the coffee plantations of São Paulo did to those frontiers.

Messianic Movements,
Upper Rio Negro

The Rio Negro was catastrophically depopulated and depressed by the mid-nineteenth century. Every traveller commented on the desolation he saw along its banks. The forts of Marabitanas and São Gabriel were almost deserted; once-flourishing missions consisted of a handful of wretched thatched huts or had reverted entirely to invading jungle; the only tiled houses along the entire two thousand kilometres of the Negro were at Barcelos, and those were in ruins. A Venezuelan official who descended the river in 1855 wrote that 'the Rio Negro presents a sad picture of ruined towns, even those that enjoyed some importance at the end of the last century. . . . The natives of the Rio Negro have almost disappeared. Although I noted many places along the river where they reside and have their huts, I do not think that they exceed six hundred persons in the entire 260 leagues [1560 kilometres]' from São Gabriel to Manaus. The Yorkshire botanist Richard Spruce wrote in 1851 that 'the Rio Negro might be called the Dead River – I never saw such a deserted region. In Sta. Isabel and Castanheiro there was not a soul as I came up, and three towns, marked on the most modern map, have altogether disappeared from the face of the earth.'

There were various reasons for this decline. One was lack of commercial incentives: forests near the Negro produced medicinal plants and turtle-egg oil, but the rubber boom had not yet penetrated this northern tributary of the Amazon. There was an acute lack of native labour; and there were periodic epidemics, following the succession of lethal diseases that destroyed the Indian population in the eighteenth century. A missionary wrote that in 1852 'this river was in a poisoned state: many died of malign fevers and measles. This will finish off the remaining people of the Rio Negro.' A few years later there was a terrible outbreak of yellow fever and cholera on the river.

In 1850 the province of Amazonas was separated from Pará. The new province covered the middle Amazon, the Solimões, Negro and Madeira valleys, with its capital at Barra, now renamed Manaus. Successive presidents of Amazonas felt that it could prosper only if its tribal Indians were subdued or 'catechised' and turned into labourers. With the Negro itself so badly denuded, attention focused on a cluster of rivers that flowed from Colombia into the upper Rio Negro: the Uaupés with its tributaries the Tiquié and Papurí; the Içana and Aiari; and the Xié. These rivers still had a considerable native population: Tukana-speaking Tukano (Tukana), Tariana, Desana, Kobewa and other sub-tribes on the Uaupés; and Aruak-speaking tribes known collectively as Baniwa on the Içana and Xié.

Since the great Carmelite and Mercedarian missions of the eighteenth century there had been a long lull in missionary activity on the upper Rio Negro. Schomburgk's old sparring partner Friar José dos Santos Inocentes was moved from the Rio Branco to be vicar of the upper Rio Negro in 1846. But this controversial missionary was too old and exhausted to do much proselytising. The English naturalist Alfred Russell Wallace met him in 1851 and found him 'thoroughly worn out by every kind of debauchery. . . . He told tales of his convent life just like what we read in Chaucer. . . . Don Juan was an innocent compared with Frei José; but he told us he had a great respect for his cloth and never did anything disreputable – *during the day*!' Although well versed in religion, Friar José was helping the commandant of Marabitanas obtain Baniwa Indians to collect sarsaparilla for his thriving trade in this medicinal plant.

There was a reaction in official policy towards Indians. The first President of the new province of Amazonas, J. B. F. Tenreiro Aranha, openly reverted to armed militia attacks against uncontacted or 'rebellious' Indians – a flagrant violation of the peaceful approach ordered in the legislation of 1845. It was aimed particularly against the Mura on the Madeira and the Maku (a word that embraced all nomadic tribes, including the Hohodene Baniwa) of the upper Rio Negro. He declared that 'to inhibit all these criminals, I issued circular orders to the police and military authorities and to all administrators of Indian aldeias and workers' camps. I will thus re-establish police action everywhere . . . with the citizens themselves always . . . ready to rally to preserve order, public tranquillity and private security.'

The new provincial government appointed an elderly Carmelite missionary, Friar Gregorio José Maria de Bene, to work on the upper Rio Negro. He was to be supported by directors of Indians: a police lieutenant Jesuino Cordeiro at São Gabriel and his deputy Lieutenant Felisberto at the frontier fort Marabitanas. Friar Gregorio reached the Uaupés in 1852 and soon chose three sites for his missions among the Tukana. Although ill and lacking transport, he vigorously baptised all the children and young adults he could find. The Indians responded eagerly enough to this undemanding and potentially useful magic. By 1854, Friar Gregorio had baptised a third of the estimated 2300 Indians in fifteen villages he visited along the Uaupés. He also had the natives cut a trail from the Caruru rapids on the Uaupés north to the Aiary tributary of the Içana. During eight months of 1853, Friar Gregorio was busy among the Baniwa: he baptised 165 people, which he reckoned was a fifth of their population. He was partly frustrated by Lieutenant Felisberto, who had been exploiting the Baniwa from his base at Marabitanas. The missionary wrote: 'I did not find a living soul in five places, because they had gone with their families to gather sarsaparilla, to pay their debts to the Director and Commandant of Marabitanas.' The friar gave up after only two years, overcome by ill health and, according to the German anthropologist Theodor Koch-Grünberg, unequal to the confrontation with Lieutenant Jesuino Cordeiro. According to the lieutenant, Friar Gregorio 'did not know the ropes, nor how to lead, nor show any kindness'.

Lieutenant Cordeiro 'knew the ropes' only too well. He was a native of the Rio Negro – his father had arrived with the great explorer–governor Manoel da Gama Lobo d'Almada – and he had served for years on the Cauaburi river, at São Gabriel and at Marabitanas and Cucui on the Venezuelan frontier. He spoke lingua geral, which was still a lingua franca among caboclos throughout Amazonia a century after the Jesuits' expulsion. He used his power as a police lieutenant and director of Indians to sell sarsaparilla collected by his natives, and occasionally to traffic in Indian children. After his appointment in 1852, Lieutenant Cordeiro tried to close the Uaupés to traders other than himself. He pushed up the river to explore its upper limits, where his policy was to favour the chiefs and persuade them to relocate their people in villages on the main river – so that he could easily reach their men. Some tribes complied. But Cordeiro himself admitted to the provincial president that one chief of the upper Uaupés 'advised his people not to leave the depths of the forest for the river banks. He told them that the white men and the Governor wanted them to leave for the river banks . . . so that they would be together and united, in order that the Governor and the whites could then come and capture them to take them downriver.'

Alfred Russell Wallace penetrated the Uaupés river at this time. He noted in 1852 that Kobewa and Wanana villages were empty. This was because a trader called Chagas and Lieutenant Jesuino Cordeiro 'have taken all men with them up the river to assist in an attack on an Indian tribe, the Carapanás [Hohodene Baniwa], where they hoped to get a lot of women, boys and children to take as presents to Barra [Manaus]'. The raiding party returned in a fleet of canoes with one man and nineteen women and children prisoners. They had also killed seven Hohodene men and one woman, for the loss of one of their own. 'The man was kept bound and the women and children well guarded, and every morning and evening they were all taken down to the river to bathe. At night there was abundance of caxiri [beer] and cachaça drunk in honour of the newcomers, and all the inhabitants assembled in the great house.' This was to celebrate the successful inter-tribal raid.

Unscrupulous traders had long been exploiting wars and feuds between tribes in order to acquire captives. (Inter-tribal raids were commonplace, usually launched to obtain women or prized ornaments.) When Wallace and Spruce were on the lower Uaupés in 1851 they saw a trader called Lima send a local Tariana Indian to the Apaporis river 'to procure some Indian boys and girls for him. . . . This procuring consists in making an attack on some maloca of another nation, and capturing all that do not escape or are not killed. . . . The negociantes [merchants] and authorities in Barra and Pará ask the traders among the Indians to procure a boy or girl for them, well knowing the only manner in which they can be obtained; in fact, the Government in some degree authorises the practice.' Wallace watched Lima give the Tariana powder and shot for his gun, and trade goods with which to buy such captives. The chief of police of Manaus and another prominent citizen had each asked Lima, who was 'an old hand at the business', to bring them an Indian girl.

The trader managed to convince Wallace that, had he not bought these young Indians, they might have been killed in inter-tribal wars; and once installed in houses of Amazonian citizens, they were somewhat civilised and 'though at times ill-treated' they were legally free since Indian slavery had long been abolished. They 'can leave their masters whenever they like, which, however, they seldom do when taken very young'. In 1853 Spruce saw and sketched two attractive and remarkably pale Maku girls 'taken in a marauding expedition at the head of the Içana, and recently purchased by the Commandant of Marabitanas. . . . The poor creatures were downcast, as might be expected of captives.' Spruce also sketched Uiaca or Callistro, chief of all the Tariana, who had his large maloca at the foot of the Iauaretê Falls on the Uaupés – now the frontier between Brazil and Colombia and the site of a large Salesian mission. This Callistro was 'a fine old man. The Brazilian traders did not much like him, but I could see no other reason for it except that he would not allow himself to be duped or outraged by them.' Spruce observed that, although the oppressive government fazendas had been abolished and the seizure of Indians outlawed, 'yet the practice still exists and is carried out. I speak of this with certainty, because since I came up the Rio Negro two such expeditions have been sent up a tributary of the Uaupés called the Rio Papury to make *pegas* [seizures] among the Carapaná [Hohodene Baniwa] Indians. I have also seen and conversed with two female children stolen from the Carapaná in these expeditions.' Friar Gregorio confirmed that 'the Directors of these rivers take advantage of their authority to fill their houses, by violence if necessary, with Indians to serve them almost gratuitously.'

Lieutenant Jesuino Cordeiro suffered Indian retaliation for his outrages. Early in the morning of 13 April 1853, when he was at Santa Cruz of the Kobewa far up the Uaupés, a flotilla of Hohodene and other tribes landed at the village. As Cordeiro told it: 'Judging that these nomadic people had come to meet me or speak to me about something, I did not prevent their disembarkation. When I reached the door of my house, these devils came armed with bows and poisoned arrows, poisoned spears, lances and clubs.' The attackers failed to harm the lieutenant, but they did club some of his Kobewa to death. Cordeiro ordered a shot to frighten off the attack, and two Indians were killed by this. Friar Gregorio judged that 'the only motive for this attack was the killings and seizures [of Indians] that took place last year.' Lieutenant Cordeiro sent to São Gabriel for reinforcements; fifteen soldiers came, but it took them two weeks to reach the territory of the Kobewa. There was then an ugly punitive reprisal expedition. The modern anthropologist Robin Wright obtained from the Hohodene an oral history of the tragic events that took place 120 years previously. His informant described the attack on the Kobewa village, then told about deaths of his people and how they were taken and tied up. 'They killed . . . Toowh! Oooh, that one! . . . Toowh! Oooh, that one! . . . Toowh! Everyone! Not one single one among them did they spare! That's all we are. So many of them, even to the smallest girl. . . . Then they are ready to burn the house. When done, they beat the drum: tuu-tuu-tuu.' Cordeiro's troops removed some Baniwa chiefs, who were taken down the Negro, together with the tribe's sacred ornaments. The chiefs were eventually granted Brazilian patents or commissions and uniforms of captains in the Brazilian army – standard practice for chiefs of docile tribes all over the country – and were then sent home; but the Hohodene chief found that he was the sole survivor of his entire tribal group.

The provincial government at Manaus tried ineffectually to stop its officials raiding Indians. Letters to directors of Indians urged them to use only peaceful methods in recruiting native labour. But the government decided in the late 1850s to build a new frontier fort at Cucui – a landmark chosen in the eighteenth century to demarcate Portuguese and Spanish colonial possessions on the upper Rio Negro, because Cucui is a famous brown granite sugarloaf outcrop towering above the river bank. The nearby town of Marabitanas had grown relatively large at this time, with over three hundred inhabitants. The decision to fortify Cucui contradicted official exhortations to treat Indians well – for local tribes were expected to provide the labourers to build the fort. A local trader, Francisco Gonçalves Pinto, was hired by the commander of Marabitanas to recruit Baniwa from the Içana river for this work; but most tribes refused to go.

The officer sent to supervise the construction of the new fort, Captain Joaquim Firmino Xavier, found when he reached the upper Rio Negro in late 1857 that 'all the Indians have fled: they have gone to the forests or fled into Venezuela because of bad treatment they have received and the minuscule daily wage they are paid. . . . In this place, where everything is very scarce and expensive, no Indian labourer wants to be subjected to work cutting timber and other tasks for a daily wage of 100 reis. They say that they would have to work for three months to buy clothes that do not last twenty days in public labour – which is what happens.' Captain Xavier was also appalled by the soldiers on the upper river: they had been there for ten or fifteen years, were intermarried with Indian women, undisciplined, insubordinate and wholly unaccustomed to military service. The captain found that most of Marabitanas' thirty-five huts were 'old and threatened with ruin' and many of its people – of Baré, Baniwa and Warekena Indian origin – gone to other settlements because of ill-treatment.

The Venezuelan Michelena y Rojas met only one priest on the entire Rio Negro in 1855, presumably Friar Manoel Salgado. He had with him a beautiful white woman who had left her husband in Barcelos. The two were travelling as man and wife and were openly engaged in commerce. Despite this unpromising pastor, an official report of 1855 recommended more priests and more conversions of Indians. Michelena y Rojas disagreed, arguing that it was hopeless to try to catechise Indians because they strongly resisted change in their beliefs and because there was almost none left on the Rio Negro. 'They have disappeared from persecutions and forced labour.'

Into this spiritual vacuum a messianic figure now emerged among the Baniwa of the Içana river. The Indians, disorientated and demoralised by the activities of military, missionaries and traders, turned eagerly to this self-proclaimed saviour. The messiah was a mestizo woodcutter from San Carlos (a few kilometres upriver from Cucui, but within Spanish-speaking Venezuela) called Venancio. This Venancio Christo, as he came to call himself, had been raised by a preacher called Don Arnaoud, an evangelist who made a deep impression on the people of San Carlos with his call for correct living, morality and strict Christian observance. Venancio had fallen into debt with the Commissioner of San Carlos and, possibly to avoid a sentence of prison and stocks, had gone farther up the Negro–Guainía to Maroa. There, his new employer sent Venancio up the Aquio river to trade with the Baniwa of the Brazilian Içana. The land here is very flat, with rivers meandering across a desolate landscape of low forests, scrub and stands of palm trees, swamps and outcrops of bare rock. During the rains, from May to October, the rivers flood and there are easy passages from one river system to another. Venancio stayed for some months in 1856 at Baniwa settlements on the Içana, but he fell badly into debt for some cloth he obtained from the regatão trader Pinto.

In 1857 Venancio started preaching on the Içana, imitating his mentor Don Arnaoud. He would hold a cross or stand near to one, teaching Christian doctrine or singing litanies. His prestige was enhanced because he suffered from the disease catalepsy, which was fairly common in this part of Amazonia. Victims of catalepsy became paralysed, with their jaws and teeth clenched together and their bodies racked with convulsions. Venancio began to claim that he had visions during these seizures. Captain Xavier reported that 'one day he started to say that he had gone to heaven, had spoken with God, and other similar idiocies. The Indians believed him, above all when he had attacks of epilepsy from which he suffered. He said that after he had "died", God had called him and told him to order that none should cut wood, that they should give him chickens, pigs, etc., and that he was empowered to pardon the debts of any who gave him what he asked for.' Venancio would announce when he felt the approach of an attack of catalepsy; and the Indians marvelled when he successfully emerged from the trance-like paralysis.

Venancio taught remission of Indians' debts, which had a strong appeal. He went on to predict the end of the world in a great conflagration on Saint John's Day, 24 June 1858. 'He gave as the reason for [this apocalypse] his descent there . . . as determined by God. From this general burning would be spared those on the Içana River who followed his teaching, which consisted of dancing in circles to the lugubrious and monotonous sounds of the words "Heron! Heron!" – words without any significance. They repeated it night and day with all veneration and continuity. . . . Some even sacrificed their lives because of the continuous motion and lack of food.' Venancio assured his followers that the more generously they gave to him, the more quickly would they escape the conflagration and ascend to heaven. He said that there was no need for crops or worldly goods in heaven – an irresponsible teaching which caused his followers to neglect their farm clearings. He himself assumed the title Christo and he appointed elderly men and women as his ministers, giving them the names of Christian saints.

All these teachings had a powerful effect. The idea of a final judgement was a blend of both Christian doctrine and Baniwa mythology. An important Baniwa legend has the world ending in a great fire while the hero, Kuai, ascends to a paradise free from sickness. Venancio Christo's reassuring messages about the absence of hunger in heaven and the cancellation of debts to traders both delighted a people worried about such threats. Bewildered and defeated tribal Indians had turned to messianic leaders ever since the start of European colonisation in the sixteenth century. Indeed, messianic movements have always been common on the Amazon – I witnessed one such preacher, who swept along the Solimões in 1971 in canoes loaded with gifts from devout followers, conducting pseudo-Christian ceremonies to large congregations – to the dismay of conventional missionaries. Venancio Christo was evidently a tribal shaman and a mesmerising preacher. His assemblies and dances attracted crowds at villages all along the Içana, and Tariana Indians of the Uaupés also came to learn from this famous messiah.

The first Brazilian official to hear about Venancio was Friar Manoel de Santa Ana Salgado, the vicar of São Gabriel and Marabitanas. He went to the Içana in September 1857 to deal with this 'foreign missionary', and summoned Venancio to meet him at the village of Santa Ana do Cuiari. The messiah, surprisingly, obeyed the summons, and Friar Manoel – a forceful and licentious priest, heavily involved in commercial activities – threatened him with punishment if he did not leave Brazil. In November, these threats were backed by military force. A detachment of soldiers from Marabitanas surprised a dance festival in progress on the Piraiuara tributary of the Içana. The troops sacked the Baniwa maloca. They also arrested and deported three old disciples of Venancio who called themselves Holy Father, Saint Lawrence and Saint Mary. 'They held public confessions, divorces and new marriages, and followed them with profane diversions of dances, feasting and drinking . . . according to the teaching of the doctrine and supposed miracles of the one called Christ.' The three old shamans were taken down the Rio Negro and imprisoned for their blasphemy.

A rumour spread that this military raid was to be followed by a more serious campaign that would kill everyone involved in the messianic movement. Venancio Christo himself fled back to Venezuela and most people of the Içana and Xié and many from the Uaupés joined him in the exodus. When Captain Xavier went up the Içana in late November 1857 he found almost no one whatever living in fifteen villages which had contained six hundred people two years previously. The largest village at the Tunui rapids had been 'reduced to ashes' by the Indians before they left. Captain Xavier was told that four hundred people had been seen paddling up the Cuiari river towards Venezuela. Others had hidden in the forests. Xavier made contact with these, but was told by one chief that 'his people still refuse to leave the woods, for they are afraid and do not believe promises. Many white men have already travelled there, among them a Captain Pinheiro and a Lieutenant Cordeiro, who deceived them with promises but then tied them up and killed many, taking their children as slaves.' Despite this, Captain Xavier persuaded two hundred Baniwa to return to their riverside villages – and then took twenty-five men downriver to work on the fort at Cucuí.

Damning reports about Captain Xavier himself were made next year. Canoes full of manioc flour, pitch, baskets (which the Baniwa make with consummate skill), and manioc graters, as well as labourers for the fort, were all going downstream to fulfil debts to the captain. A chief complained that after starting well Xavier had become tyrannical. He paid Indian labourers abominably: for two

months' work at Cucui, a man was paid only one pair of trousers in
heavy American denim and enough of the same cloth to make a shirt.
All merchants were barred from the Içana except Xavier's friend the
trader Pinto: as a result the Baniwa were short of tools, fish-hooks
and cloth. Pinto had raided and robbed Indian villages. His idea of
fair trading was to pay a cup of salt for an alqueire (13.8 litres) of
manioc flour or a yard of heavy cloth for two alqueires. 'In sum, Pinto
only wanted to deceive them.'

Throughout 1858 the normally docile Baniwa were in rebellion.
'Indians who had taken refuge in the forests could be made to emerge
and reassemble only by force. . . . They do not want to be governed
by anyone. . . . They do not want to build houses in the aldeias. . . .
Little can be hoped for from these people, thanks to their innate
laziness, weakness and indolence. . . . Scattered in small clearings
on remote creeks, they live in the most complete independence and
do not want to perform any work whatever nor to build [the barracks]
of Cucui. . . . Hidden on their creeks, they abandon themselves to
drinking, libertinage and savage dances.'

As for Venancio Christo, his reputation survived his wrong prediction of the end of the world and he continued to preach and flourish
on the Aquio river within Venezuela. The Brazilian poet and amateur
anthropologist Antonio Gonçalves Dias was sent to the upper Negro
in 1861 and reported that canoes were still going from the Uaupés to
the Aquio 'with boxes and presents to see the Christ Venancio'. Dias
brought back two carved wooden figures of the Christ, as well as
jaguar-tooth necklaces, quartz pendants and macaw-feather headdresses.

In 1858 Venancio Christo's movement spread from the Içana
south to the Uaupés and north-east to the Xié. In February of that
year, a man called Alexandre (who was probably a Tukano) imitated
Venancio by organising messianic dances at the village of Juquirá on
the Uaupés. Alexandre was a married man who had been living at
Marabitanas but had returned to his native river. The lower Uaupés
was in turmoil following a military expedition by a Captain Mathias,
which had removed many Indian goods as well as young men and
women to serve him. Many Indians had fled, fearing a fiercer military
incursion. So when Alexandre proclaimed himself a Christ and
started organising ceremonial dances, his message was well received. It was at his village of Juquirá that Alfred Russell Wallace
had watched a thrilling dance a few years earlier: 'The wild and
strange appearance of these handsome, naked, painted Indians, with
their curious ornaments and weapons, the stamp and song and rattle

which accompanies the dance, the hum of conversation in a strange language, the music of fifes and flutes and other instruments of reed, bone and turtles' shells, the large calabashes of caxiri constantly carried about, and the great smoke-blackened gloomy house, produced an effect to which no description can do justice.' The Tukano therefore responded eagerly to a return to their tribal dancing.

Alexandre Christo assembled hundreds of Tukano and performed baptisms, marriages and prophecies similar to those of Venancio on the Içana. Alexandre wore a large metal cross, which he ordered his followers to kiss. He promised that manioc would come from heaven on a certain day; but when that day came and went without the promised manna, he lost credibility. His teaching then became more radical and subversive. He now predicted that Indians and whites would change places, with Indians gaining control over their colonial oppressors. 'Indians would be transformed into whites . . . with the same power and riches, to compensate for the time during which the whites have governed them.' A missionary called Father Romualdo wrote that it was essential to capture this Alexandre Christo, 'for this sainthood business . . . seems to be a form of conspiracy against all civilised people'.

Friar Manoel Salgado went up the Uaupés at the end of March 1858 to investigate. He found 'multitudes' of men and women assembled at Juquirá but they denied knowledge of Alexandre Christo's whereabouts and rebuffed the friar's offers to preach to them. They also sullenly rejected his request for children to baptise. Friar Manoel finally had to force the chief and three others at gunpoint to help paddle his canoes. When the group disembarked at the Ipanoré rapids and was moving along its portage trail, the Tukano chief and his men vanished into the forest, from where there followed a volley of gunfire and arrows. Four of Friar Manoel's men were hit, but they returned the fire and fatally wounded two Tukano in a half-hour gun fight. The friar hurried downriver to summon military help from São Gabriel. Alexandre's rebellion spread for a time to the Xié under a local messiah, a former soldier called Bazilio Melgueira. There were dance festivals on the upper Xié.

By May 1858 alarming reports were pouring in to the provincial authorities. The President of Amazonas feared that the risings might be part of an international conspiracy to wrest the remote north-western corner of the country away from Brazilian control. President Furtado therefore sent the Municipal Justice and Police Chief of Manaus, Marcos Antonio Rodrigues de Sousa, to investigate and pacify the upper Rio Negro. Sousa was told to use gentle and persuasive methods in handling the Indians. He ordered the mutually antagonistic Captain Xavier and Friar Manoel out of the area. His mission was a success from the authorities' point of view. Sousa heard a mass of evidence and himself went up the Uaupés, where he behaved with tact and restraint. Indians who fled at the approach of the armed expedition were wooed back with presents, and their grievances were heard. None was punished. Alexandre himself vanished up the Tiquié river – a party sent in pursuit failed to catch him. Sousa managed to assemble six chiefs and a large number of Tukano and Tariana at the village of Urubaquara on the lower Uaupés. He made an important and conciliatory speech, saying that the President knew all about the messianic dances but pardoned the Indians for them. He traded with the tribes and provided materials for them to build a chapel, which was completed by sixty-six men in four days. Father Romualdo led a procession to consecrate it 'with all veneration and respect, apart from the naked ones whom I set aside and did not allow to enter the temple'. By August, all seemed calm on both the Uaupés and the Xié. One last follower of Alexandre Christo, a man named Caetano, sought to revive the messianic cult, but he was seized by the chief of the settlement at the Caruru rapids and handed over to the authorities. This messiah was taken prisoner to be judged at São Gabriel, but in a brave act of defiance 'Caetano . . . threw himself into the river above Santa Izabel at midnight on the eighth day of the voyage, bound hand and foot as he was, and his corpse did not reappear until the next day.'

The messiahs on the upper Rio Negro were soon forgotten. By 1859 the main complaint of the President of Amazonas was that too few Indians were presenting themselves for labour on public works. He therefore sent an army captain up the Negro to seek them, and was surprised when forty appeared 'in a few days without any violence'. After the captain's expedition, a further 155 Indians were enlisted. The President ceded some of these to private employers, on condition that they were paid the same paltry wage they would have earned from the government.

In that year the German doctor Robert Avé-Lallement was on the upper Rio Negro. He reported that Indian villages were forced to supply labourers to help build the fort of Cucui. This caused the Indians 'to flee and hide themselves at the headwaters of the creeks, where it is impossible to catch them without resorting to force. Indian men and women who remain in the villages hide themselves in the forests to escape the work of cutting wood, which is in fact arduous.' A chief of the Siusi on the Içana told Avé-Lallement that his people refused to build houses and settle at Santa Ana at the mouth of the Coari 'because they do not want to labour', while another nearby chief said that his tribe hid and refused to settle in government villages 'because they do not want to be governed by anyone'.

For over twenty years, during the 1860s and 1870s, the upper Rio Negro was relatively calm. The directors of Indians at São Gabriel were local men who opened the region to traders and rubber tappers. This process accelerated after 1866, when after much debate the position of director of Indians (which had been reinstituted in 1845) was finally abolished. Although the Indians of the Uaupés and Içana were cheated and exploited by regatão traders and rubber aviadores, they found markets for their manioc flour and did at least exchange their labour for trade goods. There was less attempt by the military to force Indians into virtually unpaid public service; and the lack of missionary activity left tribal cultures unmolested.

During these decades, rubber became king on the upper Amazon. Missionaries were sparse and generally ineffectual. One of the very few missions in mid-Amazonia had been among the acculturated Mawé of the Andirá river. The mission had been created in the 1820s by the Carmelite Friar José Alves das Chagas, whom Bernardino de Souza described as 'the true example of a Catholic missionary, a dedicated friend of the Indians, which earned him the genuine, profound and dedicated affection of the sons of the forest'. The Mawé joined in the Cabanagem rebellion and their villages were a focus of revolt. When peace was restored, an Italian missionary called Pedro de Ciriana was installed among the Mawé. This missionary saw his role as isolating and protecting his congregation from surrounding influences – that had been the policy of the Jesuits in the previous century, and it again aroused the wrath of laymen. Friar Pedro was accused of trying to make his Andirá mission into a miniature Paraguay (the Jesuit heartland) for his personal interest. He claimed a vast area of river and forest for his mission and refused to accept civil orders or inspections within this domain. He expelled all traders and insisted that commercial transactions should pass only through him. This may have been to protect the Mawé from being cheated, but it looked like personal profiteering. 'He started to trade on a large scale, establishing commercial relations with the firms of Crespo & Ferreira in Óbidos and José Pereira Pinto in Villa Bella. . . . Irascible and violent, he treated his Indians with the despotism of a tyrant.'

The Mawé were good workers and skilled woodsmen. The missionary and the lay authorities therefore vied to employ them collecting guaraná (whose seeds made the popular and stimulating drink) and cacao for drinking chocolate. By 1852, when Amazonas became a separate province, Andirá was almost its only active mission, with 570 Mawé intermingled with whites and black slaves. Henry Bates visited Andirá at that time and sided with the missionaries 'who take care that the Brazilian laws in favour of the aborigines shall be respected by the brutal and unprincipled traders who go amongst them'. The bickering between missionary and civil authorities was won by the latter: Friar Pedro was sent packing and in 1855 Andirá ceased to be a mission and became a lay vila.*

Evicted from the Mawé mission, Friar Pedro de Ciriana was sent in 1854 to create a new mission on the Purus. This great southern tributary of the upper Amazon – a long, meandering white-water river, full of sediment from the Andes – had recently been explored and, although slavers had denuded its lower reaches, the upper river was only now being discovered. But its pristine condition did not last long: for the Purus and the nearby Juruá proved to be the best of all Amazon rivers for rubber. Within a few years of their first exploration, the Purus and Juruá were flooded with seringueiros, and their Indians vanished into the forests. Friar Pedro's mission was therefore short-lived, and he himself returned to Italy frustrated and disillusioned.

A fresh wave of missionary activity came in 1870 with the arrival at Manaus of an eager group of Capuchins. Two of these, the Corsican Friar Mathieu Canioni and the Italian Giovanni Villa, went to try to revive the mission on the Purus; another went to create a mission called Calderão on the Solimões near the Peruvian frontier; and a third group was to revive missions on the Madeira. These Franciscans set out 'with the intention of civilising the Indians of the Madeira, Purus and Solimões and uniting them in villages'.

The Italian Capuchin Giuseppe Coppi, a veteran of missions in Bolivia, was sent in 1882 to run the mission of São Francisco on the Machado river, which had been established with Arara and Tora Indians. When Friar Giuseppe arrived, however, he found it in total decadence; there were very few inhabitants and, as he complained: 'The Indians were always drunk, lazy, rascally and insubordinate. Some white traders had turned almost all of them into slaves, on the pretext of demanding repayment of their debts. Since these bosses were arbiters of the lives and labour of their servants, it proved impossible for [me as] their missionary to have them for instruction in religious and moral precepts.' The friar managed to persuade the Provincial President of Amazonas to visit this mission in October 1882. The President cancelled the Indian congregation's debts, ordered the expulsion of any traders who held captives, and sent two soldiers to protect Friar Giuseppe. It was no use. The soldiers sided with the traders against the impetuous foreign missionary. The row between him and the traders grew so intense that he was attacked while saying mass and there was a defamatory campaign against him in the leading newspaper of Manaus. Coppi felt abandoned and asked to be recalled after less than a year at São Francisco. It was a victory for local traders (whom the Indians often liked, despite their excesses) against doctrinaire ecclesiastics. Similar quarrels caused the collapse of the Purus mission, of Calderão on the Solimões, and of São Pedro on the Madeira upstream of São Francisco.

The Italian missionaries who failed so rapidly on other Amazon rivers were moved, to try their luck on the Uaupés and upper Rio Negro in the 1880s. The Indians of these distant rivers had had a respite from missionary activity since the suppression of Venancio Christo and other messiahs in the late 1850s. Regatão traders and rubber gatherers had been active; but tribal culture and village life were little disturbed by soldiers and priests during the intervening decades.

In the 1870s, an aristocratic Spaniard, Don Germano Garrido y Otero, had acquired control of the trading activities of the upper Rio Negro. When he was in the area in 1903 Theodor Koch-Grünberg knew and liked Don Germano, who ran a thriving depot at the former mission of São Felipe near the mouth of the Uaupés, efficiently trading manufactured goods for rubber. The Indians of the Içana and some from the Uaupés 'live in a form of debt-servitude to the House of Garrido. This is imposed on natives of the entire Negro river by white landowners and traders. The whites deliver to the Indians as many goods as they want – on credit and reckoned at unbelievably high prices. The debtor must then work off the resulting very high sums, either by delivering manioc flour, sarsaparilla and other local produce, or by working in the rubber forests. Between these labours, he must also work for months on end in close attendance on the master as a hunter or fisherman.' Indians never escaped their debt bondage. To his credit, Don Germano tried to correct the worst of this system. He treated the Indians in a 'stern but fatherly' manner, and they saw him as a friend and protector. He flourished as a result. The American traveller Gordon MacCreigh described Don Germano as having 'the manners of the hidalgos of old Seville . . . the King of the Içana, he holds down an army of some 400 Indians under his command, and sends to the Emperor in Manaus for an expert in balata [rubber].'

During the years in which Don Germano Garrido was consolidating his power, a new messiah arose on the Içana. This was Anizetto, whom Koch-Grünberg called 'a vagabond and hermaphrodite' of an unknown tribe and whom Koch-Grünberg's friend Otto Schmidt described as a small, ugly, middle-aged man. For some twenty-five years after 1875, Anizetto 'wandered about the Içana as a messiah and passed himself off as a second Jesus Christ. This started a great movement among the Indians who believed in him. He healed sicknesses by covering [patients] with leaves and anointing, and visited villages amid great ceremonies. He told his followers that they need no longer work in their plantations: everything would increase when he himself blessed their fields. People came from afar to consult him. They brought him everything they had, abandoned their work, and danced for days and nights on end in festival after festival.' The Baniwa successfully defeated the first punitive expedition sent from Manaus to catch Anizetto. But a second expedition took him, and he was forced to work in Manaus for a year, helping to build its cathedral. After this hard labour he was considered harmless and crazy and was released. Anizetto re-established himself on the Cubaté tributary of the Içana and regained considerable influence. His retreat, a village of six large but dishevelled huts, became a sanctuary for his devoted followers from the Baniwa and other peoples.

The Baniwa have always been a highly spiritual people. They believed that their creator Yaperikuli was 'the first Baniwa and the first human being', and it was easy for them to identify him with the Christian God, whom the missionaries called by the Tupi name Tupan. Anizetto and the other messiahs were tribal shamans who successfully blended Christian elements into their teaching. Recently a Baniwa shaman told Robin Wright that, during his training period, 'a shaman becomes like Christo: he makes the world, water, rocks, everything, like Yaperikuli made them. There are two rooms at the top of the cosmos, one next to the other and one is the shadow of the other. In one room is the shaman while Yaperikuli is in the next. Already the shaman becomes like Christ and wants to make and transform everything.'

In the late 1870s, another religious movement took shape on the Uaupés. This was led by an Arapaso shaman of the middle Uaupés who called himself Vicente Christo and claimed to speak to dead ancestors and to the Christian god Tupan, saying that he was God's representative and the father of the missionaries. Vicente Christo was a powerful personality who achieved a large following by charming Indians all along the river, and claimed that he could bring his disciples good health, protection, and relief from debt. He predicted that white traders and seringueiros would soon be evicted from the Uaupés and that exploitation would end. He also prophesied that missionaries would soon arrive and would help to protect the Indians.

This last prediction was fulfilled: in 1880 the Italian Friar Venâncio Zilochi from Piacenza started to revive the mission of Taraquá on the south bank of the middle Uaupés. But the missionary took a dim view of Vicente Christo. The young French explorer Henri Coudreau was there four years later, and he learned that 'at one moment, there was a proposal to arrest the prophet and send him for trial in Manaus. But for what crime? Some more practical regatão traders took Vicente Christo very affably with them, then put him in the stocks and had him locked up in the prison of Barcelos for some days. His prestige suffered as a result.'

By 1883 two other younger Capuchins reached the Uaupés: Friar Mathieu Canioni, the Corsican who had failed in his mission on the Purus; and Friar Giuseppe Coppi, who had just failed on the Madeira. These two eager Capuchins hurried up the river to persuade its Tukanoan tribes to assemble in villages and 'accept the laws of the missions. But they refused to submit and said that they wanted to retain their freedom. . . . We found [on the lower Uaupés] that none of them had much wish to unite in villages or to submit to a regular disciplined life.' It was only when they went far upriver on to the northern tributaries the Cudiari and Querari (now in Colombia) that they found more innocent Kobewa and Baniwa who willingly accepted their teaching. They planted crosses, baptised many children, and urged the tribes to build chapels. By the end of 1883 they claimed to have almost three thousand Indians in sixteen villages.

Friar Giuseppe Coppi was an energetic zealot. As he moved up the Rio Negro he had been shocked by its Baré Indians – 'drunken, lazy and immoral vagabonds. . . . Everywhere, religious indifference reigns to the highest degree.' But he blamed the oppressive traders and godless white men for this decadence. When he reached less contaminated Indians on the Uaupés, he was determined to do better. He rapidly developed his headquarters at the Tariana village Panoré. He soon had its sixty-three houses whitewashed and arranged along straight streets. He was enormously proud of a big new church that he had the Indians build, with three aisles, three altars, two pulpits and colonnades outside and within. Coudreau regarded Coppi as 'bizarre'. The missionary had filled his church and curacy with his own naive paintings, of such subjects as the Immaculate Conception, his native Siena, the Indians' Jurupari deity in hell, and the Crucifixion. He had built prisons for men and women and organised young Tariana into a police force wearing bonnets of his own design. One of his strange creations was a colonnaded cemetery – empty as yet – and a bridge whereby he passed from his fortified house into the tower of his church. Coppi had named the streets in Panoré village and numbered its huts.

Coudreau described Coppi as an 'active, inventive and authoritarian missionary'. When he replaced the ageing and gentler Friar Venâncio in August 1883, he had rapidly introduced forced-labour quotas instead of payment for work. He knew all about command and discipline, even though he spoke no word of lingua geral or any native language. The mission plantations flourished, and Coppi boasted that his Panoré was 'the largest and best ordered' of the Uaupés missions. He instituted a stern discipline, with morning and evening church assembly for the entire village and mass on Sundays. After breakfast, at dawn, the adults went to work and the children to school. The village was divided into quarters, each with a headman and assistants 'to maintain public and private order'. There was a curfew at night: after eight o'clock the Indians had to observe silence. This was to make it difficult for them 'to elude the vigilance of the missionary'.

Coppi disliked and despised the Tukano Indians. He wrote: 'I could confirm that, during the year in which I lived in their midst, they are very stubborn in their ideas, superstitious, diffident, hard to please, mendacious, loving idleness, given to immorality, vindictive, of short memory and unintelligent. They always agree and promise much, but do not keep their word. They are timid and docile, especially the Tariana, Baniwa and Kobewa.' He deplored their love of drink, particularly of the mildly fermented maize or palm-fruit beer called cachiri, and found them 'ferocious and terrible' when drunk.

This ignorant and insensitive reaction was in sharp contrast to that of other Europeans. We have seen how Alfred Russell Wallace was enchanted by the mysteries of Indian dances on the Uaupés. The Italian Count Ermanno Stradelli described the daily round of both sexes in an Indian village. This started at first daybreak, with everyone bathing in the river, making fires and food, the men going off to hunt and fish by the time the sun rose. Stradelli praised Indian generosity and lack of possessiveness about the land or its produce. He exposed the hypocrisy of the accepted view that Indians were lazy – for the Tukanoan tribes grew enough manioc to feed seringueiros throughout the region. 'It is those "idlers" who provide most of the manioc flour, often at ludicrous prices, for all the "energetic" inhabitants of the Rio Negro.' He admired the looks of these handsome tribes. After contact with whites, the men took to wearing trousers and shirts and the women skirts. Many Tukano contracted a skin blemish called purupuru that mottled their lovely coppery skins. This was probably a form of leishmaniasis transmitted by bugs living on forest mammals. Koch-Grünberg said that it began with white and black spots which gradually enlarged as the disease took its course. When he was with the Siusi of the upper Içana, a shaman and his wife 'were as black as Moors in many parts of their bodies and whiter than me in other places. The black patches feel hard and rough; the white are smooth and somewhat wrinkled and resemble burn marks.' 'The disfiguring skin disease purupuru, the native wildness of their facial features, and the European rags with which they drape themselves – all give a degenerate appearance to the otherwise well-proportioned bodies of these Indians.' Before being forced to wear clothing, the men of these Uaupés tribes wore only a bark or cloth support to their genitals.

Stradelli gave a delightful description of a typical Indian welcome to one of their great thatched houses. 'Immediately after your arrival you are offered the chief's hammock, which is next to the door. When you are seated, the men all file past one by one. They ask how you are, from whence you come, where you are going, and continue in this way with all your men. . . . Then it is the turn of the women. All the mothers of families come, each carrying a basket of manioc or tapioca cakes accompanied by the inevitable sauce of hot chili peppers, bia: they deposit it all on the ground in front of your hammock. They are followed by the youths and children, who come from the missions and ask for your blessing.' Once a visitor had eaten the cakes with their fiery sauce (which nearly ruined Stradelli's palate for good), he was accepted by the tribe. 'You are at home: you can come, go and do whatever you please and none will disturb you. But that freedom does not last long. Once the Indians' first feeling of respectful fear is gone, you become the victim of their curiosity. All of them want, like children, to see, know and touch everything. And the women and children, who were the most timid and reserved at the beginning, are the ones who do this most.'

The Capuchins soon clashed with regatão traders. During the

decades when missionaries were absent from the upper Rio Negro, these rascals had had a free hand among the Indians. Henri Coudreau described how traders would recruit Indians to gather rubber and forest produce, simply by giving presents to their chief. Each worker received a shirt, trousers and a Portuguese name, but no further payment for months of work. Some unscrupulous merchants would descend on a village, get its men blind drunk, and then force the women to sell their entire harvest of rubber in exchange for trinkets.

'The regatão generally seeks to exploit his men as much as he can, but they flee when the fancy takes them.' Recaptured fugitives were mercilessly beaten with spade irons up to a hundred times on their hands, or the soles of their feet – 'which prevents their running away but does not stop them paddling'. Traders had the run of Indian women by bribing the chiefs for their services. Tribal morality, which was normally strict, was undermined as a result. Coudreau said that 'more than one regatão goes up the rivers less for commercial profit than for the little pleasures of the voyage.' And when Coudreau reached a village with a military escort, half the population fled at the sight of the soldiers. 'All the women and young girls hid in the forest.'

At Taraquá, Coudreau was shocked by the sight of a drunken trader joining in a native cachiri beer party. 'The great chief of the tumult, president of the orgy, he sings idiotic songs and goes with feet and head bare, beside himself, drunk, accompanying the shouting band of his men, rascal caboclos from the lower Rio Negro who demand cachaça rum with great cries. He has already abused all the women in the place, and these now follow him, gambolling and stumbling, with their breasts exposed, dresses fallen and hair dishevelled like bacchantes.' To the fury of the local missionary, Friar Mathieu Canioni, this regatão charmed the Indians by playing tunes from *Lucia di Lammermoor* and other operas.

Far worse than the traders, in the eyes of the Capuchin friars, were the native shamans. Friars Giuseppe and Mathieu surprised some of these shamans or pagés in action at the village near the Arara rapids. The pagés were wearing ceremonial paint and headdresses, and were using their sacred objects of bone and stone, cigar smoke, a paxiuba palm flute and a maracá gourd rattle. They were singing a low and mournful incantation over a sick person. Giuseppe Coppi recalled: 'We stood watching the ceremony for about five minutes, but then we could not restrain ourselves at the sight of such deception. We interrupted; but they continued without paying any attention to us. We started to threaten them. The pagés ran off into the forest with their amuleto.'

Soon after this confrontation, the two zealous missionaries learned more about the religion of the people they were determined to convert. The Tariana, Tukano and Kobewa people had developed a ritual celebrated at dance festivals, with music from sacred flutes and appearances by figures wearing mask vestments. The Tariana themselves called these figures 'Kue'; but they became known to outsiders by the Tupi or lingua-geral word Jurupari. (This was a misnomer: Jurupari was a capricious wicked spirit feared among the coastal Tupi tribes of Brazil in the sixteenth century. The Jesuits adopted the term to mean the Devil in their teaching.) The 'Jurupari' worship of the Tukanoan tribes of the Uaupés revolved around a child ancestor who roamed the forests in the guise of a sloth or howler monkey. Both these furry mammals resemble human beings. Sloths are associated with the rainy season, for they appear most often during heavy rains. There was also some connection between sloths, howler monkeys and male puberty.

The Capuchin missionaries learned that Jurupari festivals were preceded by a three-day fast by the entire tribe. The ceremony itself lasted for three days. All the women and children were then banished to the forests for they must on no account see the sacred masks. Three shamans, wearing these masks, played paxiuba flutes to summon Jurupari. After an hour or two of music, Jurupari arrived, wearing a mask and carrying ornaments similar to those of the shamans. In the words of Friar Giuseppe Coppi, 'The Indians, particularly the older boys, describe it as having only three fingers on its hand [like a sloth] and with ape-like feet. When Jurupari enters the house all is silent. He goes around hitting one or another person with his baton. They present him with food and drink and he eats and drinks like the others. Finally, there is a signal for the festival to resume and he returns to the forest whence he came. After his departure the women return and all prepare the dance.'

The core of these rituals was the sacred mask worn by Jurupari and his shamans. The Uaupés tribes themselves called the mask 'izi', which is related to their word for howler monkey, or 'putsumaka' meaning 'sloth'; but, once again, it became known to outsiders by a lingua-geral word, 'macacaraua' meaning 'monkey hair'. Coudreau described it as 'a black sleeveless coat which descends to the waist. . . . It is provided with a head, shaped in a cone frustum, which acts as a mask with a hole for the mouth and two for the eyes. This mask is surmounted with a crown of feathers and has various ornaments.' An essential element in puberty initiation among these tribes is to shave the heads of girls at the time of their first menstruation. These izi masks were therefore made of a mixture of monkey fur and virgin's hair, skilfully and laboriously woven on to a base of tucum palm fibres. One of these magnificent and awe-inspiring holy masks is preserved in the Pigorini Museum in Rome.

The izi masks were strictly reserved for men. Coppi noted that 'when young men wish to see this object for the first time, they must fast for a month and be beaten until they bleed by the pagés. Women must not see it, on pain of death.' Any woman who deliberately or even accidentally saw the masks risked being poisoned by the shamans.

Friar Giuseppe obtained an izi mask from a renegade Tariana at Iauareté. He and Friar Mathieu then determined on a reckless attempt to smash local beliefs. They hoped that, by an act of criminal ethnocide, they might more quickly supplant Tukanoan religion with their own. The friar decided to use the mask 'to drive from the minds of those Indians the superstitions surrounding these objects'. On 21 October 1883, he assembled the Tariana children in the schoolroom of his mission of Panoré. At a signal, a youth entered wearing a sacred mask. 'The boys who recognised it started to clap their hands and shout "The izi! The izi!" The girls were surprised and tried to flee. On finding the exits locked, they tried to hide behind one another; but they nevertheless looked at the dreaded image. I began to reprove them for their superstition. Then, when those young people saw that the sight of Jurupari did not produce death as they had feared, they became bolder, had a good look at it and touched it.' The friar determined to compound his outrage. 'Encouraged by the success of my experiment, I planted a tall pole in the yard of my house on the following day. I mounted the mask on top of this and had it on view throughout the day. From time to time, I summoned one or other of the women to force them to look at the idol. But they, fearing the pagés and their husbands, fled and shut themselves in their huts. I then ordered them to emerge and obliged them to work in the plaza. But at the prayer hour, only fifty men presented themselves. They announced that the women had fled for fear of the izi.' The men tried to seize the mask, but the missionary locked it in his house.

On the following Sunday, Friar Mathieu Canioni had arrived from

Taraquá and the two missionaries determined on a more flagrant confrontation. The entire village was assembled in church for mass. After the service, Canioni left the pulpit and Coppi stationed himself near the door 'to maintain order. During the sermon, the Indians may have suspected what was going to happen and they grew agitated. This agitation spread from person to person and increased. Thus, when the mask was finally shown to them a veritable tumult erupted. Husbands surrounded the women, children wept in fright and clung to their mothers, and the pagés angrily threatened them with death and tried to drive the women from the church. They blew ritually to disperse the captive influence as they advanced towards me where I stood guarding the door. Others assaulted Friar Mathieu to wrest the image from him, but he courageously defended himself with the crucifix in his hands.'

The two missionaries ran to their house, where they had firearms. The shamans were outside, shouting, striking blows into the air and firing symbolic arrows towards their rivals. The missionaries decided that it was too dangerous to remain. They fled downriver next morning, and when they reached Taraquá they promised its chiefs and shamans that they would never again show Jurupari izi masks to women.

Rid of their missionaries, the shamans of Panoré purged the village by imposing a month's fast. They cleansed the place with ceremonial rituals. Some shamans felt that they should renounce the Jurupari cult and submit to the friars, but Coudreau said that this was countered by an aged shaman from Taraquá, who had a vision of Jurupari flying above the forest canopy during a rain storm. The vision, which was wearing an izi skin, said that he was a Jurupari who lived below in hell. He warned the old shaman that he risked joining him there. 'You will come there if you continue to behave badly towards the great Jurupari. Take care, or you will weep one day in the torments of my dwelling. . . . The mysteries are being profaned, the enemies of Jurupari triumph, you serve our enemies or are indifferent. The great and powerful Jurupari, the terrible Jurupari, is angry with you.'

The Capuchin missionaries tried in vain to re-establish their influence on the Uaupés. Henri Coudreau went back up the river with them in early 1884, protected by a strong military detachment. He recalled that Friar Mathieu 'amuses himself by carrying in his luggage a macacaraua [izi], the sacred emblem of Jurupari'. But it was the native religion that ultimately triumphed. Theodor Koch-Grünberg was on the Uaupés twenty years later and reported that all but three villages near the mouth of the river were deserted and overgrown with vegetation. The rash and foolish Capuchins had had to flee, 'and never again returned to the Uaupés. . . . Even Friar Venâncio, the quietest and most reasonable of the three, had to tear himself with heavy heart from his blooming creations. The converts scattered and returned to their former homes, which had not yet become strange to them. Since that time, no one has renewed the attempt, and the Indians of today have only a vague recollection of their pastors.'

Rio Branco–North Amazon

In the public pontificating about Indians and official despair about 'civilising' them, many saw missionaries as the only panacea; but the dearth of missionaries was dramatically illustrated in the 1846 report for the province of Pará – which then included the entire Brazilian Amazon. Only two missionaries were active in this immense area. One was Father Torquato Antonio de Souza, who controlled the former Jesuit missions near the mouth of the Xingu. Prince Adalbert of Prussia was most impressed by this young Brazilian priest when he visited the Xingu in 1842 with the young Count Bismarck. He found him enterprising and energetic. Father Torquato had worked among the Mundurukú and in 1840 was moved to the Juruna of the lower Xingu. 'His friendly and conciliating manner, together with the rich presents of earthenware vessels, glass beads, tools, etc., which he made to the Jurunas who occasionally visited Souza, soon attracted others of the tribe, and the Padre succeeded in gaining their confidence, and baptised a large number.' The missionary helped the Germans with their expedition up the Xingu; and they in turn delighted the Juruna by bathing naked – the Indians had never seen unclothed white men, least of all a Prussian prince and the future Iron Chancellor of Germany.

The other missionary in Amazonia in 1846 was more controversial. The Carmelite friar José dos Santos Inocentes was active near Fort São Joaquim on the upper Rio Branco in the far north of Brazil. He had united a mere thirty-three Wapixana, Makuxi and Sapará, who were engaged in growing manioc, corn and sugar and were said by the Provincial President to be well educated and acculturated. Friar José was a turbulent priest, despite the 'innocent saints' in his spiritual name. He had been sent up the Madeira to the isolated Fort

Principe da Beira as an army chaplain in 1832. A judge in Cuiabá was soon complaining that he had insulted Portuguese settlers by inventing a nickname for them. He was back in Pará during the troubled years before the Cabanagem revolt; and his extraordinary political manoeuvres resulted in his exile in 1839 to the Rio Branco mission.

After consolidating the few Indians living near Fort São Joaquim, Friar José moved up the Tacutu river and founded a mission called Pôrto Alegre on an island near the Rupununi river in British Guiana (now Guyana). He assembled a large number of Wapixana and Makuxi, but his village was dangerously close to that of the English Protestant missionary Thomas Youd. There were diplomatic protests between Great Britain and Brazil, as a result of which the mission was moved downstream closer to Fort São Joaquim. João Wilkens de Mattos said that Friar José dos Santos Inocentes zealously directed his mission 'to the great profit of humanity'.

One problem was that a large Makuxi village called Pirara lay on the portage between the Tacutu and Rupununi. It was thus on the seasonally flooded plain between the waters of the Rio Branco, which were clearly Brazilian, and the Essequibo which flowed north into British Guiana. It had been a principle of the eighteenth-century treaties of Madrid and San Ildefonso that the northern boundary of Brazil followed the watershed between the Amazon basin and rivers flowing into the Caribbean. It was therefore difficult to determine whether Pirara lay in territory belonging to Brazil or to British Guiana.

The Protestant missionary Youd had built himself a house at Pirara and started to convert its Indians. He withdrew, and the Brazilians occupied Pirara. In March 1840, Youd and José dos Santos Inocentes met at a rapid on the Rupununi. The rival missionaries were polite to one another; as Youd wrote in his journal: 'Thanks be to God that we were enabled to argue the several mission points at issue with great calmness; and the more so perhaps since we both well knew that these matters cannot be settled by us, but must be by the two Governments.' The Brazilians resolutely claimed the west bank of the upper Essequibo. The trouble worsened when a delegation of Indians from Pirara came to Youd soon after his meeting with the Brazilians. 'Several of the principal men of the different tribes of Indians came before me and stated in very strong language their entire disapprobation of my leaving them. . . . They declared they would never submit to Brazilian control, for they were English subjects and on English ground; that the Brazilians came with a lie in their mouth, saying the land was theirs. . . . "You must not go, the land is not theirs, they lie." ' A few days later, the Wapixana chief Ya-wa-imdapa came with a delegation including Tarumá and Carib-speaking Atorai. 'The Chief addressed me in equally strong language, but with tears in his eyes declaring that I should not leave them. . . . He says the Brazilians have already kidnapped one of his sisters, on which account he hates their very name, and dreads to think of being in any part of their territory.' Youd took the chiefs down to Demerara to make their case to the British governor. In the following year, 1841, the British sent a commissioner, William Crichton, to investigate. When he reached Pirara, he was welcomed by Friar José and Captain Leal of the Brazilian army. Many Indians came to the village to watch the negotiations: Crichton reported that 'the old people among them seemed much interested in what was going on from the very close attention they paid to everything which passed between the Padre and [me], especially during meals when greater facility was afforded them for observation.' The Brazilians agreed to withdraw from Pirara, but both sides felt that they could not reach a conclusion without a proper survey. This was performed in 1842 by the German-born explorer Robert Schomburgk, who had been sent by the Royal Geographical Society to investigate the remote parts of British Guiana.

After surveying the upper Tacutu and Maú (Ireng) headwaters of the Rio Branco, Schomburgk and his brother Richard went downstream to Fort São Joaquim itself, where they were very well received. Friar José joined the fort's commander in selling cattle, food and Indian headdresses and artefacts to the British visitors. As Richard Schomburgk commented: 'Could anyone blame the poor devils? Captain Antonio de Barros Leal had received no pay for four years, his garrison at the Fort for three years, and poor Father José nothing for ten years. What wonder then that they willingly seized the opportunity of emptying the full pockets of the enemy?'

A few months later, after the Schomburgks had failed to climb the mysterious table mountain Roraima, there was further friendly trading between Friar José and the British. Hearing that they were returning to the Caribbean coast, he asked them to bring him black cloth for his altar and glass shades for the lamps he kept burning in his two churches. 'After making this request, he brought out a large musical box which he assured us had hitherto given the only right tunes for the Mass, because without it his Indians could not now and nevermore bring out the responses.' The Schomburgks could do nothing to repair the worn springs and rollers of this box. 'He received this information almost with tears in his eyes and, if only to cheer him up again a little, my brother made him a present of a couple of bottles of wine which completely effected the purpose intended.'

Robert Schomburgk was back among the Wapixana of the Rupununi in 1843, and it is worth quoting his lyrical account of a visit to their village. On 6 May, he wrote 'Nothing could exceed the beauty of the morning. The sun rose partially covered by fleecy clouds, as if afraid to contend for the supremacy of the day against the dark hovering masses to the west; but when its rays fell upon the raindrops on the foliage, the scene was one of fairy land. The majestic Mora (*Mora excelsa*), refreshed by the late rains, was covered with a succession of leaves whose tints, varied with age, passed from yellow through red to dark green; while the splendid *Petrea* with racemes of bright blue flowers trailed from bush to tree, and with the orange-coloured *Combreta* gave variety to the surrounding scenery. We were now surrounded by mountains through which the river had forced its way.' An old chief greeted the travellers in tolerable Portuguese, and the young men and women of the tribe were brought up one by one to greet Schomburgk. He was impressed by the provisions of food and firewood in the village. The chief then took him to see his forest clearing. 'He showed me the pride of his heart, spots of cassava (*Janipha manihot*), some, as he said, six moons, others four moons in the ground. There were his yams, and there his tobacco plants and arborescent cottons of a size that would have astonished a planter from the south of the United States. . . . The old man could not sufficiently expatiate on the fertility of the soil around his village, in proof of which he pointed to the graceful curua-palm towering high above the adjacent forest trees.'

Schomburgk then turned south again and ascended the Essequibo to its source. Between June and August 1843, he boldly took his Makuxi guides across the watershed into unexplored country on the Brazilian side. He descended the Cafuini and returned up the Anamu, both headwaters of the Trombetas river. During this thrilling journey he made first contact with a number of tribes, all of which were courteous and hospitable to the strangers: Tarumá, and Carib-speaking Wai-Wai, Pianokotó and Tiriyó. He also saw the last remnant of the Aruak-speaking Mawakwa, whom his Makuxi called Maopityan or 'Frog people'. Schomburgk completed that expedition by recrossing the watershed and descending the Courantyne back into British Guiana.

The Pianokotó fled at the first sight of Schomburgk's party, fearing that he was coming to kill their men and steal their women. When, exhausted and hungry, the expedition finally made peaceful contact with a Pianokotó village, Schomburgk was impressed by their looks: 'I had seldom seen a finer set of men . . . some appeared to be 5 feet 8 inches in height; their limbs strong and muscular. That important piece of head-dress, the queue, was attended to with such neatness, that it would have done honour to a Parisian coiffeur of the old regime. . . . Neither male nor female were painted in lines, but their whole body, with the exception of the face, was covered with roucou [anatto] or red paint. The men wore a profusion of beads round their wrists and across their shoulders, and a band of cotton below the knee with a long tassel hanging from it. The ankles were tied with strips of palm-leaves, ornamented with red and black paint. Their waist was girded with a broad piece of bark, from which their waist-lap was suspended.' 'The greatest admiration is due to the waistlaps of the men, which are so firmly woven of indigenous cotton, that they would do honour to a European manufactory. They are the handi-work of the Pianokotó and Tiriyó dames. Their spindles, although simple, and the circular piece at the end, which sets it in motion, rather coarsely executed of bone, are nevertheless very neat and terminate in a piece of bone very neatly cut out, through which the thread is conducted.'

The missions near Fort São Joaquim did not flourish for long. Friar José dos Santos Inocentes ran his mission of Pôrto Alegre until 1846, when he was replaced by another Carmelite missionary, Antonio Filippe Pereira. 'From that year onward the Mission entered upon a new phase: the priest to whom it had been entrusted was not en-dowed with the vocation necessary for directing an establishment of that kind; he immediately displeased the Indians, who gradually withdrew themselves.' Having lost his parishioners, the missionary tried to restock Pôrto Alegre with uncontacted Yanomami Indians. President Francisco Coelho reported in 1849 that 'the missionary has recently made efforts to make the Indians who live in the forests of the upper Catrimani river descend and settle in the aldeia. . . . It is the missionary's intention to repopulate this place with those Indians.' Fortunately, he failed. The Yanomami survived intact, and are today the largest tribe of forest Indians in South America.

There was an attempt to revive the aldeia under a new priest in 1851, but 'little or no benefit accrued to the already decadent Mission from this appointment.' By 1852 the mission of the upper Rio Branco was almost devoid of Indians; they had left the dismal place to return to richer and freer hunting grounds. The government removed the missionary.

We have few records of what happened on that remote frontier. In 1857 Chief George Wishrop of the Atoraí in British Guiana made a formal complaint of Brazilian press-gangs seizing members of his tribe. 'Whenever these incursions are made by the Brazilians, the houses on the Rupununi are entered and the residents there treated most shamefully.' These atrocities were far too remote to be checked. The Governor of British Guiana admitted that 'these predatory incursions are at such a distance from our most advanced post as to entirely preclude even official cognizance of them, much more any attempt to check or punish them.' An English traveller called Dawson reached the Tacutu in 1858. He confirmed that 'the system of hunting the Indians for slaves is still continued by the Brazilians: each season, when the waters are high, numbers of the Wapixana are carried off. For the most part they are employed . . . constructing roads on the banks of the Rio Branco and other tributaries of the Amazon, where the rivers are impeded by rapids'. Such portages were built to help bring cattle from pastures of the upper Rio Branco down to Manaus. 'Some [Wapixana] who have escaped, give a sad account of their treatment. . . . There is now established in the neighbourhood of Fort St. Joaquim a religious house to which the young women are forcibly carried off.'

Some three hundred kilometres south of the peaceful Aruak-speaking Atoraí was a Carib tribe with a similar name but very different temperament: the Waimiri-Atroari. This warlike tribe has defended its forests north of Manaus with admirable tenacity, right up to the present day. In 1865 these tribes were victims of 'a blood bath and incredible cruelty' by an expedition under Manoel Pereira de Vasconcelos. Governors of Amazonas complained of attacks by the Waimiri-Atroari: on Tauapeçaçu on the lower Rio Negro not far from Manaus itself in 1863; on the town of Airão, somewhat farther up the Negro, in 1865; on their own river, the Jauaperi, in 1866; and on these same places and Pedreira in 1873. In that year the town of Moura was abandoned by its inhabitants and completely sacked by the Indians. Any canoes moving along the Negro were seized by the Waimiri-Atroari when they sallied forth from the Jauaperi river on their warlike campaigns. As so often elsewhere, the Waimiri-Atroari were reacting to aggression by 'civilisados'. The French traveller Marcel Monnier explained that they were provoked by traders who pretended to barter and then tried to seize Indians as forced labourers. Such traders entered Atroari territory under arms. 'They set fire to villages, led women and children off into captivity, and shot at the wretched men who tried to defend their huts against the invaders.

From that day onwards the war was ignited, and continued incessantly and implacably.' The Indians ambushed hunters and fishermen and shot them full of poisoned arrows, they attacked villages by
night, pillaged, burned and took prisoners.

The place most vulnerable to Waimiri-Atroari attack was a hamlet
called Pedreira, for it lay on the Negro immediately opposite the
mouth of the Jauaperi. The English engineers Charles Barrington
Brown and William Lidstone found a detachment of troops defending Pedreira when they visited it in 1874. They wrote that the tribe's
fierce independence had a long history. 'From the time that the Rio
Negro was first settled by the Portuguese to the present, these
Indians have refused to have any dealings whatever with them or
their descendants. Every expedition that has been made up their
river, for the purposes of trade or otherwise, has been immediately
attacked and driven back. It seems not at all unlikely that a slave-
hunting raid, perpetrated by the Portuguese many years ago upon
these tribes, has so embittered them, that, dreading another, they
are on the alert to attack anyone who comes into their territory.' An
Italian friar who tried to convert them in the 1850s had been killed.

The attack on Pedreira in January 1873 marked a new stage of
aggression by the Atroari, for it was a surprise attack apparently
motivated by greed for plunder. A large force of Indians launched
this night raid, during which they killed two women and a child.
'After taking every article of iron they could lay their hands on, such
as knives and axes, and playfully ringing the church bells, they
departed as suddenly as they came. Having been so successful in the
matter of loot they paid the village a second visit, during which they
removed the entire contents of a blacksmith's forge, brutally murdering the unfortunate owner and his boy. We paid a visit to the spot,
and saw how thoroughly they had devastated the interior of this
building, even extracting the nails and staples from the woodwork.'
The government's response was to send a launch up the Jauaperi,
armed with a pivot gun and soldiers ordered to shoot Indians at
sight. This punitive raid sailed up the Jauaperi for 150 kilometres to
its first rapids, but captured only an empty canoe whose paddlers
had escaped into the dense forests. The Atroari made further attacks
on Pedreira and nearby Moura. But in November 1873 the raiders
were pursued into the forest by Moura's garrison, trapped alongside
a lake and slaughtered. Only nightfall ended the massacre, and the
official report noted laconically that 'many were killed.' Twelve
canoes were captured. In renewed fighting the next day, the
Waimiri-Atroari defended themselves valiantly with bows and

arrows against guns. But the troops took cover behind tree trunks and gave no quarter. The Governor of Amazonas sent an armed flotilla under a Lieutenant Antonio de Oliveira Horta. 'He spent the entire year hunting Indians on the Jauaperi.' On 20 October 1874 his force killed more than two hundred Waimiri-Atroari, and on 21 November there was another massacre. More were killed next day, and on 23 November some troops returned to the site of the 'previous day's bloody drama. They found twenty-three wounded Indians there, all silent, hidden in the foliage of trees into which they had climbed. [The soldiers] took aim and fired. . . . All fell, with the exception of one who remained caught on a branch.' There were further killings of Indians in 1875 and in a battle on 20 December 1876.

Years of uneasy peace followed. The Waimiri-Atroari retreated up the Jauaperi river, pursued by occasional punitive expeditions. If they ventured down on to the Rio Negro, 'anyone who sees one kills him, which provokes the continuous war with these Indians. . . . Greeted with shots, they reply with arrows. But there is nothing barbarous about that: for these Indians' descents [on to the Negro] are not intended for robbery or assault, but rather to seek trade with the civilisados.'

The author of this conciliatory interpretation of Atroari behaviour was the remarkable Brazilian naturalist João Barbosa Rodrigues. A self-taught botanist, Barbosa Rodrigues became Brazil's leading expert on palms and orchids. He also developed a romantic admiration for Indians. Sent by the imperial government, he made a series of expeditions to Amazon tributaries in the 1870s. This was the heyday of physical anthropology, and Barbosa Rodrigues therefore carefully measured the limbs, skulls and heights of the many tribal Indians he met on his travels. He also made valuable studies of native folklore, dances, burials and artefacts. He gathered his collections of plants and ethnographic material into a museum and botanical garden in the booming rubber-trade metropolis of Manaus.

João Barbosa Rodrigues decided to try to do something about the Waimiri-Atroari, who killed two settlers at Moura in 1881 and were causing panic in the forests north of Manaus. He met a group of armed Indians on the Yatapu river near the Jauaperi and was sure that they were Waimiri. He won their friendship with cachaça rum and tools, and they promised to descend from their river and settle on the Negro, even though they told him that 'the whites are bad' on that river. Barbosa Rodrigues promised to return with more presents to complete this migration – which would, of course, have been fatal to the tribe. Luckily for the Waimiri, their would-be benefactor was frustrated. The President of Amazonas greeted his request for launches and presents for the Indians with incredulity. 'You are mad! Your temerity will be the end of you!' The steam launches requested by Barbosa Rodrigues were duly sent up the Jauaperi, 'but instead of fulfilling the promises made between me and the Indians, they took yet another proof of white treachery: a battalion of troops, cannon and machine guns.' This expedition returned and reported that it had killed no Indians. Barbosa Rodrigues was not so sure about this, for he obtained from the soldiers an Indian bow full of bullet holes at chest height. 'This made the tears run from my eyes. I saw how those who sought civilisation were greeted with fire and sword, and sacrificed.'

After this ugly failure, the provincial government allowed Barbosa Rodrigues to try gentler methods and he set out again in 1884. A naval launch was stationed at the mouth of the Jauaperi to prevent entry by adventurers who might wreck his attempted pacification, while Barbosa Rodrigues bravely paddled up the river in a canoe, with an armed escort, a captured Atroari boy interpreter, and plenty of presents. After a few days, he sighted Indians on the banks. 'His arrival was greeted by murderous cries. The Indians rushed down to the small beach where his boat had landed. Stone axes were brandished at the head of the audacious traveller. But he impassively presented his peace offerings to these furious men: brightly coloured cloth, knives and mirrors.' The attraction of trade goods and a conciliatory approach were immediately successful; the shouting abated and Barbosa Rodrigues was led to the Atroari huts as a friend. A few days later, peace was concluded. The Brazilian promised that the Indians would no longer be molested; they in turn promised to forget past injuries. As Barbosa Rodrigues was leaving, an old Indian took his hand and said: 'I am already old: I do not know whether I shall ever see you again, for I shall die. If I could, I would descend the river with you. But my children will go to you one day. You are a good white man. The Crichanas [Atroari-Waimiri] will not forget you.'

João Barbosa Rodrigues made an eloquent plea for a policy of leaving Indians isolated and unmolested. 'Inhumanity, persecution, gunfire, war and all the ravages of which the Indians are victims have caused them to be feared, intractable, vengeful and rancorous! An Indian's heart is a treasure. Leave it virgin, as untouched as the forests in which it is formed! Educate, but do not profane it. Do not take corruption, dishonour and slavery to the malocas! Respect Indians and you will be respected.' For a further few years, Barbosa

Rodrigues sought to carry out this policy of benign education of the newly pacified Waimiri-Atroari. He returned to the Jauaperi several times and was greatly helped in winning the tribe's confidence by his brave wife Constança. He initiated the tribe in the use of metal tools to make canoes and to farm, and he soon had the men making rectangular thatched houses instead of their superb conical communal huts. In return, he removed many tribal artefacts for his museum in Manaus.

Barbosa Rodrigues' initiative ended when he himself stopped visiting the Jauaperi. The settlers on the Negro continued to fear and hate the Indians. They told the passing French traveller Henri Coudreau in 1885 that 'the pacification by the botanist–apostle Barbosa Rodrigues has had curious results. The Waimiri now pillage batalhão river boats and isolated farms with impunity. The inhabitants of Moura and the lower Rio Negro are obliged to flee.' Trusting Barbosa Rodrigues' promises, eight canoe-loads of Waimiri went to fish peacefully on the Rio Negro. The young men of Moura treacherously attacked them and, as a result, Coudreau found that 'here they talk of nothing but the recent exploits of the terrible Waimiri – of the soldiers and settlers they have just massacred.'

By the start of the twentieth century, the Waimiri-Atroari were friendly towards visitors who approached them peacefully. An Austrian collector called Richard Payer visited the Waimiri in 1900 and again in 1902. Having traded a dog and other goods for their artefacts, he was surprised by how trustingly the women and children sheltered under the awning of his boat to escape a rainstorm. On his second visit, Payer suddenly came upon an uncontacted group of young Indians deep in the forest. 'They struck their chests with their hands and declared themselves as "Parime" or friends, and asked whether we were the same.' Peaceful contact and trading ensued, and Payer had the privilege of visiting the village of this tribe and watching its dances.

The atmosphere worsened again in 1905 as a result of 'a pointless slaughter by a punitive expedition from Manaus that was said to have cost the lives of two hundred Indians of both sexes and all ages'. Governor Constantino Nery of Amazonas sent a military expedition up the Jauaperi to punish the Waimiri for having evicted some seringueiros who invaded their territory and killed one of them. The punitive raid was led by militia Captain Julio Catingueira. 'He behaved like a criminal. He besieged some malocas and, since the Indians would not allow themselves to be arrested, set fire to them burning the people alive. He left the bodies of 283 Indians as fodder for vultures and wild animals, and took off as prisoners to Manaus eighteen men and one woman.' These wretches were kept in the barracks of the military police. Many citizens of Manaus recalled seeing them sadly wandering down to the river front to gaze at the forests on the far bank.

Theodor Koch-Grünberg said that the Waimiri came down to the mouth of the Jauaperi river during the rainy season to catch turtles, but withdrew far upriver during the dry months. The young men of Moura also went to catch turtles and would immediately shoot any Indian who showed himself. The German anthropologist was convinced that the tribe wanted peaceful contact. This friendly attitude was demonstrated in the welcome which the Waimiri-Atroari gave to two founders of the Indian Protection Service, Captain Alípio Bandeira and Colonel Bento Lemos, a few years later. But the tribe wisely resisted attempts to invade its territory. For a half century from the 1920s to the late 1970s, the Waimiri-Atroari killed all intruders. It maintained a heroic patriotic defence of its homeland, which had started three centuries earlier when the first whites penetrated this part of Brazil.

The Waimiri and Atroari tribes occupied the forests mid-way between Manaus and the fertile savannahs of the upper Rio Branco. Partly because of their presence, it was not until the late twentieth century that a road was finally cut through their forests to link Manaus and Boa Vista, the capital town of the territory of Rio Branco (now Roraima). Until recent times, communication with that northernmost part of Brazil was only along the Branco river, the broad artery of which was a reasonably convenient avenue – straight, deep, running north–south, and broken by only one set of difficult rapids.

The upper Rio Branco prospered and decayed in sympathy with the main Rio Negro, of which it is the largest tributary. It flourished in the late eighteenth century, when the Portuguese wanted to assert their occupation of this northern part of the Amazon basin. It was then that Fort São Joaquim was built to guard the junction of the Branco's main headwaters, the Tacutu and Uraricuera. Those distant rivers were explored and mapped by teams of boundary commissioners. The Indians who were briefly congregated in the lee of the fort soon vanished, wiped out by disease, forcibly moved to distant parts of Amazonia, or fled to the forests to escape forced labour. But the cattle that Manoel da Gama Lobo d'Almada introduced to the natural savannahs near Boa Vista ran wild and multiplied. The upper Rio Branco declined along with the rest of the

Amazon and Negro in the first half of the nineteenth century; its stagnation was revealed in the writings of the Schomburgk brothers in the 1840s. Colonial poverty was generally good for native tribes, for it meant less frontier pressure, even though the few colonists operating on the frontier were more lawless and uncontrolled by central government.

Two main tribal groups survived in this region: the Carib-speaking Makuxi and the Aruak-speaking Wapixana. Other Carib tribes – Paraviana, Paushiana, Taulipang and Sapará – had largely vanished, extinguished by the colonial onslaught. Both Makuxi and Wapixana, who disliked each other in the traditional enmity between Caribs and Aruaks, were on good terms with the white settlers because the two tribes were docile, offered no armed resistance and were prepared to work as paddlers or cowhands.

The Rio Branco was fortunate in possessing few *Hevea brasiliensis* trees, so it was never invaded by seringueiro rubber tappers. The Amazon rubber boom affected the Rio Branco only marginally. By the end of the nineteenth century, demand for meat in the booming city of Manaus caused a revival in cattle-ranching on the plains near Boa Vista. But cattle ranches were less damaging to Indians than other forms of frontier expansion: Indians found jobs as cowhands or boatmen on the meat barges, and they objected to such work less than to plantation labour.

In 1884 Henri Coudreau took passage in a boat manned by Makuxi and he wrote that it was difficult to imagine how empty the Rio Branco was at the time of his visit. In five hundred kilometres he saw only six malocas of Carib-speaking Paushiana – perhaps 250 Indians in the entire valley as far north as Boa Vista. That regional capital was a mere village.

The British geologist Charles Barrington Brown described the famous Fort São Joaquim in 1871: 'The fort, which is built of red sandstone on a low ridge, not much above the level of floods, has a large gateway in front, set back so as to be commanded from the battlements above. The walls are of considerable thickness, and the embrasures have been built in with masonry. There were five unmounted cannon lying about, one of which was of English manufacture. . . . The whole place was in a most untidy dilapidated condition, pigs, dogs, and fowls roaming about everywhere.' The Commandant, Captain Abreu, made a most generous gesture to Barrington Brown: he gave him a pint bottle of Allsopp's India pale ale – a treat that the Englishman had not tasted for 'five months and ten days'. Barrington Brown then had a gallop across the grassy plain south of the fort. He rode past 'large shallow ponds with rushes and lilies, tenanted by flocks of large white cranes and jabirus [storks], as tame as common geese to us on horseback. . . . The water which lies over this plain for a part of the year produces fine grass for the eighty or ninety head of cattle kept in the vicinity of the fort. Beyond the plain was ordinary elevated gravelly and sandy savanna, from the edge of which, looking across the marshy level, the old fort looked grim and lonely.' Coudreau said that the fort's five-man garrison spent most of their time on neighbouring ranches since the fort was flooded during the rains and uninhabitable from fire-ants during the hot months.

There was no priest in the entire Rio Branco valley. But there *was* plenty of cattle: twenty thousand head of cattle and four thousand horses on thirty-two public and private ranches.* Stradelli said that the government-owned fazenda of São Marcos occupied the entire peninsula between the Uraricuera and Tacutu rivers, stretching north for hundreds of kilometres to the unexplored Pacaraima hills. The fazenda of São José stretched from Fort São Joaquim eastwards towards the Rupununi and British Guiana. Between them, these two national ranches contained over five thousand cattle and seven hundred horses.

Count Stradelli noted that the government farms used only Carib Makuxi as cowhands. The most numerous of the tribes in contact with the whites, the Makuxi were regarded as good workers at jobs they found congenial, such as ranching or navigating river boats. The German traveller Grupe y Thode said that 'These are large heavy boats, which have great difficulty passing the rapids of the Rio Branco and then go on to Manaus in an even longer and harder journey.' Coudreau said that by 1885 forty cattle boats a year were descending to Manaus, each carrying between fifteen and thirty-five animals.

Robert Schomburgk described Makuxi as 'the most beautiful Indians of Guiana, possessing rich voices, fluent speech, cleanly habits, good morals and a love of order'. But the Italian Stradelli was more critical of Makuxi women, who were markedly smaller and more delicate than their men. 'They are rarely beautiful, although of their type a few could be described as not ugly. Their figures are slim and elegant as long as they are young.'

The Wapixana had once been more numerous than the Makuxi, but by the late nineteenth century they had been decimated. As Coudreau observed, 'It is curious to note that tribes who become acculturated fastest also disappear quickest. Such are the Wapixana, who became civilised faster than the Makuxi. Many of them speak Portuguese. The Makuxi are far more rebellious against civilised discipline. They are reluctant to teach their language to the whites. They are insolent and insubordinate. Conclusion: the Wapixana were the most important tribe of the Rio Branco a century ago but they now number scarcely a thousand. The Makuxi on the other hand are far more numerous today than a century ago. They form the most important tribe in the region: you can count three or four thousand of them.'

Both Wapixana and Makuxi were generous and hospitable to travellers. Charles Barrington Brown described how his party would approach a Wapixana village, with his Indians playing a tune on their bone flutes and shouting as they entered the village itself. 'They would then enter the principal house and sit down in a circle. The chief man of the place would rise from his hammock, walk up behind one and tap him on the shoulder, muttering a few words of salutation, which were responded to. He then passed on to the next, and solemnly went the round of the circle, holding a slight conversation with each, standing up behind the back of the man with whom he spoke.' This ritual was then repeated by other men of the host village.

'The Macusis [Makuxi] acted differently; they entered the houses noisily, giving three stamps on the ground, and uttering in a deep tone of voice the sounds "Too-too-too Hah-hah-hah". The people who greeted them did not touch them, but stood up in front and held short conversations . . . pouring forth a long and rapidly worded address. The Macusis addressed would keep up a constant fire of words such as "Enah! Enonombay! Oah!" etc., over and over again. These replies are equivalent to our "Yes; Yes, indeed; Yes, truly," etc.'

Barrington Brown recalled a typical evening in a Wapixana hut. 'The dim little fires beneath the Indians' hammocks gave just enough light to reveal the gloomy nature of the abode. The Indian men lay in their hammocks talking and smoking their bark cigarettes, while the women spun by hand or manufactured their bead dresses. An old woman sat over a fire near the hammock of my guide and in a dull, monotonous, whingy tone related a long story to him. As night comes on this whingy, complaining tone is always adopted in conversation by Indian women and children, and to a slight extent by the men, and is very curious. I got so tired of hearing the old woman's voice, that to try and break the spell I asked [my guide] what in the name of goodness was the old woman talking about. He replied that she was relating how, not long before our visit, the people of her village, including herself, made a pilgrimage to see the sorcerer of Wakopyong; that they were nearly starved to death owing to the great number of people there consuming all the food; and that after a lengthened stay they returned home to find their neglected fields contained but little cassava [manioc]; so that now they were on short commons until what they had planted had time to grow. . . . Many a night of this sort comes back to my memory as I pen these lines, and the recollection of them is on the whole, despite the cockroaches, not an unpleasant one.'

This same author wrote how enjoyable it was to travel with men of this tribe. 'The band of Wapixana Indians with me were very jolly fellows, full of fun and laughter, joking and chaffing each other incessantly.' As his party approached a village of Atoraí (Aruak-speakers like the Wapixana), they were met and led back to the aldeia by fifteen men headed by 'a drummer beating away at his instrument in a most lively manner. It turned out that they had a little drink on hand, and thus invited us to join in the festival. My men and Indians did join in, and drank as fast as the horrid decoction would be handed round. Weak as paiworie is in the amount of alcohol it contains, a bucketful or so will make a man drunk.' The Indians overcame this problem by drinking huge quantities and then vomiting it up so that their women could serve them more. 'Down it is gulped till a state of intoxication is reached. Hard old drinkers do not seem to feel sick during the operation, but laugh and seem to enjoy the fun of vomiting.'

In 1884 Henri Coudreau struck eastwards from Boa Vista towards the Guiana hills. For a thousand kilometres between the Rio Branco basin and the Atlantic Ocean, the geologically ancient Guiana shield remains one of the least explored and penetrated parts of South America. The low ranges of the Acaraí and Tumucumaque hills run from east to west. They form the watershed between rivers flowing north into the Guianas or south into the Amazon and they thus make a convenient northern boundary of Brazil, a natural geographical divide that is an international frontier according to the sensible principles laid down by the negotiators of the Treaty of Madrid in 1750.

The hills along the northern edge of Brazil are home to a series of Carib-speaking tribes, handsome, self-assured and generally hospitable people who have survived to modern times less shattered than native Indians in other parts of Brazil. These Caribs have geography to thank for their isolation and survival. The great southern-flowing rivers drop off the Guiana shield in rapids and waterfalls that form an effective barrier to movement upriver. Indians living below these falls were exterminated in particularly brutal wars and slave raids during the seventeenth century; but the settlers could not easily reach tribes living on the headwaters. The soils of this region were unsuitable for *Hevea brasiliensis* trees, so seringueiros had no incentive to penetrate beyond the lower rivers in search of rubber.

Few travellers or explorers reached Brazilian Guiana. Those who did brought back tales of great physical hardship but warm welcomes in Indian villages. Coudreau described the Carib-speaking Wai-Wai as 'a beautiful race, with noble traits, fine figures and majestic bearing. They belong to the aristocracy of the Guiana tribes. They are fairly tall and of a vigorous complexion, but despite this they are very gentle and fearful.' Coudreau reached Wai-Wai villages at the headwaters of the Mapuera branch of the Trombetas in 1884. He was in terrible condition after a tough journey scrambling over rocky hills and dense slippery jungle trails: exhausted, with severe eczema, swollen feet and a septic toe. When he reached one Wai-Wai village, Coudreau slept for thirty hours and a kind old chief said to him: 'You are not old, and yet your hair is white and your eyes are ill. Go home to your land. The paths of the savannah and forest are not good for white men.'

Thirty years later, William Farabee and his team from the University of Pennsylvania Museum reached a Wai-Wai village after a month's journey from Boa Vista. The whites and leaders of the visiting Indians were immediately given stools to sit on. 'All the men and boys of the village came and sat or stood near. There was no noise, confusion or excitement. Our visiting chief told the chief of the village all he knew about us, who we were, where we came from, where we were going and what our desires were. The chief asked him many questions, and when he was satisfied he went to the door of his house where all the women had gathered with his two wives and told them all that he had learned about us.' The women then brought four large bowls of fermented manioc drink and the chief held a bowl for each visitor in turn to drink. That evening the Wai-Wai performed a dance in the visitors' honour. Circles of men and girls danced forward and backward in opposite directions, to the music of a great trumpet, jaguar-bone flutes, rattles, rhythmic stamping and singing.

The Wai-Wai had fine ornaments of featherwork or bark, but nothing whatever of European origin. The men 'wear their hair like women, but rolled up in a white bark that presses the hair into a spiral, which makes this appendage look like a roll of tobacco'. Farabee admired 'one fine looking young fellow who was very proud of his physical appearance. Every morning after taking his bath, except when he was going to work or to hunt, he would oil and comb his beautiful long hair, twenty-eight inches in length, and slip on his well-decorated hair tube; then he would paint his face with a variety of designs. In the evening he would wash it all off and in the morning put on other designs, so changing his appearance that it was difficult to recognize him. He used more paint than all the others combined.'

Farabee's expedition made a long and gruelling expedition eastwards into the hills of Brazilian Guiana. It moved from the Wai-Wai to the related Parikotó on the upper Mapuera; thence on to the Pianokotó on the Anamu headwater of the Trombetas; and finally to their goal, the Tiriyó living in the Tumucumaque hills on the Brazilian–Surinam frontier and in low forest and open savannahs near the source of the Paru river.

All these tribes were Carib-speaking and with similar customs. Farabee and his men had the thrilling experience of being the first white men to see some of these peoples. On arrival at a village, they usually received the same elaborate and courteous greeting. Different tribes gave different reactions to the visitors' guns and matches, none of which they had ever seen. One chief asked Farabee to demonstrate his gun: he did not flinch at the noise of the shot, but was deeply impressed to see that it had pierced the wood of a soft tree. His men would not touch meat killed by shot, and feared that the whites were offering them poisoned food. Another group insisted on stripping Farabee and rubbing him from head to foot with cotton soaked in vegetable oil. He learned that this was a puberty custom intended to make boys grow strong – even though Farabee was over six feet tall and towered over his hosts.

At one Parikotó village the reception was hostile. As the expedition walked towards it from the surrounding forest, 'we found eight men lined up with their bows and arrows ready to shoot, and in front of them the chief with a large highly polished knife in his hand. It was a most formidable-looking array of men and arms. We had taken the precaution to leave behind in the canoes our guns and bows and arrows. The chief with his knife waved us aside to some logs, where we sat with our backs down the hill, facing the men. Everybody seemed wildly excited. The dogs were barking, the children crying and the women running about and talking fast and loud, but the men never said a word nor took their eyes from us nor put down their bows.' 'We endeavoured to reassure them by being as calm as possi-

ble with a forest of arrows pointing in our direction.' The expedition
trusted in the fact that it was unarmed, for 'an Indian, unlike some
civilized men, will not attack a defenseless man.' The Parikotó were
finally persuaded that the visitors meant no harm. They remained on
guard for two days, with armed men protecting their women; but
after that they entertained the Americans splendidly for two weeks.

When the expedition finally reached the Tiriyó, remotest of all the
Brazilian Guiana tribes, it received the customary welcome. First
came the speeches, with hosts and visitors facing one another. 'The
chief would talk for fifteen minutes without hesitation and then
suddenly stop for me to reply. Neither of us knew a word the other
said yet we understood each other perfectly.' Then came the food:
great cooking pots full of soup and boiled meat, which the guests ate
by soaking manioc bread or fished out with their fingers. Farabee
knew that his men must take the drink offered to them, even if they
disliked it. 'To make intoxicating drinks the girls chew cassava
[manioc] in order to mix the saliva with the drink and start fermenta-
tion. They scrape the tongue before beginning to chew and saturate
it with wild honey. The ones selected for this purpose are marked
with tattoo lines about the mouth. Fortunately the traveller learns to
like the drink before he sees it prepared. The taste acquired, it
doesn't matter, he must drink it.'

The Tiriyó staged entertainment of dances in which they imitated
episodes of daily life. 'Hunting scenes, jaguars chasing a herd of
peccaries, vultures eating dead animals, etc., all so well done that we
understood perfectly.' There were also fierce wrestling matches in
which rivals wielded strong whips. 'At a given signal they attacked
each other with their whips, making them crack like pistols about
their bare legs. When they could stand the punishment no longer
they dropped their whips and rushed at each other like mad.' Each
wrestler tried to lift his opponent until neither foot touched the
ground. Farabee recommended his readers to try this, as a challeng-
ing variation to traditional wrestling. But alongside such violent
sports, life in the Tiriyó village was calm and there was abundant
food. Although the Americans often took many people with them
from one village to the next, there was never any misconduct or
impropriety. 'There was no evidence of anger or resentment. We
never saw a child punished nor even one that needed it. The perfect
obedience of children is probably due to the custom of separation of
the sexes.'

Jules Crevaux, who approached these Carib tribes from French
Guiana to the east, watched an excruciatingly painful boys' initiation

ceremony among the Wayaná, who lived south-east of the Tiriyó on the upper Jari. The initiates danced all night in elaborate and beautiful costumes. Each candidate was then held by three men. 'One holds his legs, another his arms, and the third pulls his head brusquely backwards. The shaman then applies to his chest the stings of a hundred fire ants which are held in trellises by the middle of their bodies. These instruments of torture have bizarre shapes, representing quadrupeds or fantastic birds. A similar application is made on his forehead with wasps. The patient invariably falls into a coma and has to be carried to his hammock like a corpse. He is firmly bound to it with cords that hang down on each side, and a small fire is lit beneath him. The torment continues without interruption. The wretched victims are successively taken into a hut. Pain makes each of them writhe uncontrollably – their hammocks swing in all directions from the vibrations and make the hut itself shake until it seems about to collapse.'

This same explorer described his entry into a Wayaná village. He had to allay the suspicions of the chief, who was about to shoot him with an arrow when he landed from his canoe. As Crevaux approached the village, 'a band of dogs rushes at me: I have great difficulty confronting these ferocious animals. When I knock one out with my cane, another bites my calf. Elsewhere, two children see me and start crying in terrible fright. The smaller falls while running off, rolls on the ground and covers its eyes with its hands. Trumpeter birds, curassows and macaws all come to flutter about me. A small tame jaguar leaps onto my back with one bound and tears my bush jacket. [The chief] makes a gesture and all these animals retreat. Arriving at the large hut in the middle of the village, the chief's two wives bring me respectively a stool and an earthenware bowl containing the remains of lunch: a little boiled fish with plenty of chili pepper.' That night Crevaux watched a magnificent dance by a band of visiting Wayaná in full regalia. 'The men are covered in feathers, necklaces and belts of cotton or coati skin. Almost all have a form of peruque made of straps of black-painted bark. Some wear a form of cloak of floating strips hanging from their necks and falling to the ground.' The dancers had rows of rattling nuts on their legs to heighten the rhythm. They danced all night without interruption, apart from occasional drinks from gourds of cachiri beer.

In contrast to these scenes of tribes in their full glory, Olga Coudreau saw others on the verge of disintegration. (Olga was Henri Coudreau's widow; she continued exploring the northern tributaries of the Amazon after her husband's death from malaria in 1899.) She met a trembling old man on the Cuminá who told her he was the chief of the Pianokotó of the Paru and Imarara rivers. His small village was surrounded by a high earth rampart to protect it from attack by other tribes or by runaway black slaves. The old chief was generous in giving food to Madame Coudreau, but he admitted that he had traded away most of his dogs and hammocks to the Wayaná of the Jari, who in turn used them to obtain metal tools from blacks in Brazil or to the north in Dutch Surinam or French Guiana. Olga Coudreau was shocked by the dirt inside this old man's hut. 'Never in my life have I seen such an incalculable number of fleas as there were inside. It is difficult to imagine them. All types of those unpleasant insects had made a rendez-vous in this place – from the less irritating to the piercing jiggers of equatorial America. I could not see the earth beneath all these parasites, of a fine chestnut colour, who were awaiting the visit of my accommodating legs to make a comfortable meal. They installed themselves in my flesh and greedily bit and sucked my poor human blood. Despite the excellent bath I took when I left these Indians, I would have had difficulty ridding myself of their damned fleas without an energetic rub-down in eau de cologne.'

Below the protective barrier of waterfalls and raging rapids, these rivers were either 'dead', denuded of all inhabitants by slaving and disease, or the scene of fighting and the degradation of tribal Indians. Much of the trouble came from black slaves who had managed to escape from the tyranny of the slave plantations and had found sanctuary on the northern tributaries of the Amazon. Their numbers increased greatly during the Cabanagem revolt and its bloody repression during the 1830s. They formed themselves into black republics or mucambos, the greatest of which was Maravilha ('Marvel') on the Trombetas; but it was finally destroyed by the Guarda Nacional in 1855.

A report of 1862 said that there were no Indians whatever on the lower Trombetas, but a woodsman called Thomas d'Aquino had gone far upriver and made contact with a handsome, pale-skinned tribe – presumably the Pianokotó or Parikotó. Runaway slaves also reported that powerful tribes had evicted them from the upper river.

At times, mucambo blacks and Indians traded peacefully or intermarried. There is some black blood among surviving tribes of Brazilian Guiana, and Indian blood in blacks living on the northern rivers. But more often the two races clashed: there was bloody fighting when fugitive blacks were driven into Indian territory on the upper rivers.

The aged Pianokotó chief told Olga Coudreau that in about 1875 mucambo blacks had come up the Cuminá to his land on the Poanna (or Paru de Oeste), where they settled and made friends with his people. But then the blacks – escaped slaves themselves – tried to imitate their former white masters by enslaving Indians. One black made a large establishment and forcibly seized Indian women, whom he used as 'gentle slaves of a ferocious and blood-thirsty master. They obeyed under constant threat of whip lashes and when their work seemed inadequate the mucambeiro punished them with hideous barbarism.' Among the punishments he inflicted were beatings and forcing his victims to sleep out on cold nights in the stocks. The Indians rescued their women, only to have the black recapture them. The Pianokotó finally killed and decapitated their oppressor. Other blacks made friends with the Indians, giving them presents and pretending that they approved of the killing of the evil mucambeiro. They then invited the tribe to a large fishing party, luring men, women and children to a sandy island on the Poanna. They removed the Indians' canoes and opened fire on them with gunshot 'which decimated these defenceless wretches. They then ran up to finish off the wounded with their machetes, and the corpses were left as fodder for the vultures.' After this massacre, the blacks retreated down the Cuminá to avoid Indian vengeance. But they maintained their hostility. An old mucambo black called Lothário told Olga Coudreau in 1900: 'My white lady, you know perfectly well that Indians are not human beings.'

Blacks who fled to the upper rivers often carried alien diseases. When the French explorer Adam de Bauve approached the Tumucumaque hills in 1830 from the east (up the Oiapoque river which forms the modern boundary between Brazilian Amapá and French Guiana) he found many villages of Tupi-speaking Wayapí that had been abandoned because of disease. The village clearings were full of crops and fruit trees, but the people had fled. 'In many cases, I found platters and pots and heavy utensils which they had doubtless been unable to carry.' He finally reached a village of a hundred people, 'all looking ill – pale, sickly and weak. Most fled at our approach. There were many more women than men. . . . The chief confirmed what I had already noticed: that an epidemic had carried off the greater part of the people of the abandoned villages through which I had passed. He assured me that we would encounter the same isolation everywhere, for a great distance. Only apathy and despair had forced this group to remain at a place which they seemed to regard as destined soon to be their tomb.' The depopulation was worse when Jules Crevaux went up this Oiapoque river almost half a century later.

Crevaux recalled that the French engineer Bodin, who ascended the river in 1823, reckoned that he had seen five thousand people on it. When Crevaux went in 1877 to the source of the Oiapoque and across country to the Cuc headwater of the Brazilian Jari, he counted only two hundred Indians throughout his journey. 'If this decline continues, there will soon be no Wayapí left. Other tribes are on the verge of extinction. The Emerillons now number no more than fifty persons, and the Acoqua, whom Fathers Grillet and Béchamel visited [in 1674], have completely disappeared.' In the 1820s French missionaries calculated the population of Amapá (the land on the Atlantic coast north of the Amazon) at two hundred thousand; now in the 1870s Crevaux suspected that it contained no more than three thousand people.

Alien diseases penetrated far beyond the colonial frontier, carried inland to uncontacted tribes by other Indians. In 1837 that great explorer Robert Schomburgk had reached the source of the Essequibo. He left his canoes and had a 'three days' painful march' to the place where the river rose, 'a spot surrounded by high trees interwoven with lianes, so much so that we could not get sight of sun or stars. . . . We hoisted the British Ensign, which we secured firmly to one of the trees, there to remain till time destroys it, and drank Her Majesty's health in the unadulterated waters of the Essequibo, the only beverage within our reach.' But even here at the frontier between Brazil and British Guiana, disease had preceded the explorers. Schomburgk entered a village of Tarumá – a people who had fled to this remote refuge to escape the Portuguese of the lower Rio Negro. The village seemed deserted. But when Schomburgk looked inside a hut, 'what a shock I got on seeing some smallpox cases looking at me from out of just as many hammocks! One of these unfortunates who had got over the terrible disease, that had now spread so far inland, was already up and about once more. The scars that had been left gave the poor devil a still more revolting appearance, while the larger pits had taken on in general a dark black colour. . . . Smallpox is undoubtedly the most devastating and probably also the last scourge to seal the doomed extinction of the Guiana aborigines. Shocked and affected by the gruesome sight I hurried back to our camp.'

Explorers of these regions suffered appallingly from malaria. Adam de Bauve was so ill in one Wayapí village that the Indians were sure he was dying. They brought him chickens to eat, but would run off shouting if he tried to enter their huts. They were convinced – not without reason – that he was bringing contagion. Meanwhile his

42. *A canoe penetrating flooded forest.*

43. *Indians cut a passage for the explorer Henri Coudreau.*

44. *Fort São Gabriel guarded important rapids on the Rio Negro.*

45.   *A construction crew on the ill-fated Madeira–Mamoré railway.*

46.   *Railway engineers meeting Karipuna on the Madeira river in the 1870s.*

47. *Karl von den Steinen descending a rapid on the Xingu.*

48. *The professional Indian-hunter Martins with his victims, captive Xokleng women and children.*

49. *Indians of the Rio Negro during the rubber boom.*

50. *Modern Tukuna near Tabatinga on the Solimões, living in poverty.*

51. *Parintintin were formidable warriors.*

52. *The Makuxi village Pirara was disputed by missionaries from Brazil and British Guiana in the 1840s.*

53. *A Salesian missionary among Indians of the Uaupés river.*

54.   *A formal welcome in the village of Carib-speaking Wayaná.*

55.   *A Wayaná woman removing jiggers from Crevaux's foot.*

Above: Steinen's expedition camped among
ngu Indians, 1887.

Below: Steinen's expedition made the first
ntact with Kalapalo of the upper Xingu in 1884.

Right: Xingu Indians launching a bark
noe.

59. *The tense moment of Steinen's first contact with the Suyá on the Xingu, 1884.*

60. *Karl von den Steinen watching Bakairi flute players during his first exploration of the upper Xingu in 18*

friend Ferré was desperately ill in another village. 'Not knowing how to rid himself of [malaria], he arranged for cold water to be poured onto his head from a certain height. His fever was cut, but he continued for a long time to tremble so violently that he could not even lift a spoon to his mouth.' Crevaux also had bad attacks of malaria. He wrote: 'My allies the Indians abandon me precisely because I am feeble. . . . For ten days I have not been normal for an instant. In the mornings I am influenced by excitement that doubles my physical strength and my will; the rest of the time I tremble, suffer intense thirst, or sweat.' Henri Coudreau died of malarial fever on the Trombetas in 1899. His widow Olga and her men often suffered from the disease. Most of the rivers she surveyed – the Trombetas and its large tributaries Mapuera, Cachorro (or Kaxuru) and Cuminá, and the Curuá and Maicuru – were denuded of Indians. The few natives she met were often pitifully thin and yellow-skinned from malaria.

Imported diseases brought depopulation and destabilisation, which in turn provoked inter-tribal warfare. Farabee reported that the Chikena (Sikiana) of the upper Trombetas had been destroyed by Pianokotó because of disease. 'Their enemies had burned their village and killed all the people who were present at the time. A few had been away from home and as they returned they found the dead bodies of their friends and the burning village. They made their escape before being detected. The people of the village had been blamed for sending sickness to their neighbours. Men would live for ever but for diseases which are sent by enemies. This superstition is responsible for the deadly wars which have destroyed nearly all the people.'

Other Carib groups living farther down the Trombetas and on the Cachorro told the modern Brazilian anthropologist Protásio Frikel that their villages had become so decimated that they could no longer practise the cross-tribal marriages that prevented in-breeding. Tribes and villages merged as a result. The Kaxúyana told Frikel about the belligerent Kahyána: 'They were terrible, the horror of other tribes! They fought everyone and they also fought one another. It was not because of disease that they put an end to us. It was through fighting!'

Olga Coudreau deplored this internecine warfare. 'This lack of understanding or alliance between individuals or malocas, in their struggle for survival, will cause their disappearance, which is taking place at great speed. In a few generations, the Indians will be no more than a memory.' 'It is absurd to think that traders, administrators or colonists could transform these savages into civilised people.' 'For them the land is good, they are in a golden age, they have no worries, disappointments, desires or jealousies. When someone comes to violate the land of a tranquil maloca on the pretext of civilisation, it will be the end of the happiness they enjoy. We will teach them passions and grief that they do not now know. Why bring them tears?' 'These Indians have a right to exist and should not be condemned in advance, being forced to disappear or to live like seringueiros. They should be allowed to develop in harmonious heterogeneity, so that their native characteristics are not abolished.'

A few tribes of the Guianas have survived, protected by the difficulty of access to their remote villages. But the Makuxi, Wapixana and other Indians of Roraima were less fortunate. Theodor Koch-Grünberg revisited them years later and recorded in his diary: 'The Indians of Rio Branco are close to their end. Those who escaped influenza, which killed entire malocas, are now being liquidated for ever by balata-gatherers, gold prospectors or diamond seekers. The region around Roraima is thoroughly invaded by whites, blacks and detribalised mestizos from British Guiana, Brazil, Venezuela and God knows how many other countries. The few Indians who survive have been deprived of their rights and reduced to slavery. Their ingenuous happiness has gone, their solemn dances have ceased . . . the joyful playing of children on the sandy centre of the village by moonlight has ended. Happy are those who died in time.'

PART 4

1840–1910: Missionaries, Anthropologists and Indian Resistance

Botocudo

There had always been an isolated frontier not far north of the Brazilian capital Rio de Janeiro. This was among the Botocudo of the forested hills separating the Atlantic coast from the central Brazilian plateau. After Guido Marlière's humanitarian efforts in the 1820s, dealings with the Botocudo relapsed into ugly skirmishes between colonists and Indians.

A young Brazilian politician called Teófilo Ottoni vividly described the horrors of the years after Marlière's dismissal. In 1830 the Botocudo killed members of a settler family near Calhão. Neighbours of the dead formed a reprisal posse and obtained powder and shot from the provincial government. They enlisted Indian guides called Cro and Crahy and set off towards a Botocudo village called Capivara pretending to be a hunting party. They turned off by night and crept towards the sleeping village, where they carried out the customary murderous dawn attack. Ottoni explained that the first move of such raiders was to infiltrate the huts and try to seize bows and arrows piled near each family's fire. After disarming the besieged in this way, 'they proceed to the slaughter. They separate the kurucas [boy slaves] along with any pretty Indian girl, and these form the spoils. They descend without mercy on the others. The killers feel no more emotion than an executioner slipping a noose over the neck of the hanged. . . . [In the 1830 attack] the forces were hopelessly uneven. Resistance was impossible. The village became a slaughterhouse rather than a battlefield. The savages fired a few arrows in their despair but did not kill a single assailant.' Every small farmer had kurucas (a Gê word), for personal use or as items of trade. 'This cursed traffic in savages . . . was the cause of innumerable calamities. . . . Each cost a hundred milreis. In the market of the [coastal town of] São José appeared not only prisoners of war captured by the tribes who trafficked there, but also those tribes' own children who were snatched from them in a thousand ways.'

An official called Pedro Reinault was sent in 1836 to investigate the possibility of opening mines in forests between the upper Mucuri and Todos os Santos (All Saints) rivers. He reported that the territory was stubbornly held by the fierce Jiporok (or Gyporok) Botocudo. 'They made the utmost efforts to continue to roam independently over their immense possessions. Their presence and their atrocities terrified the few prospectors who sought to extract those riches.'

Reinault said that the great nation of Botocudo had reached the wooded hills between the sources of the Doce, São Mateus and Mucuri rivers only in about the 1780s. They had dislodged the original Indian inhabitants, all of whom had been forced to take sanctuary among the whites; the warlike Puri alone had resisted. But there were deep divisions within the Botocudo. The Naknyanuk, for instance, were just as terrified of the Jiporok as were the white settlers. When Reinault made his descent of the Mucuri, his first meeting was with over three hundred Naknyanuk at a river crossing. These had had contact with pioneer fazendeiros (whose cattle they tried to hunt) and were docile enough. Reinault's expedition distributed presents among them.

Reinault made a tough crossing to the Todos os Santos river and, exhausted and short of food, started down it in September 1836. This river ran into the Mucuri and, on the seventh day of the descent, the expedition met eighty savage Jiporok. There were twenty-five warriors among these and they started firing arrows. Reinault took his canoes out of range in the middle of the river and, by nightfall, had achieved a dialogue. He then distributed tools among the Jiporok. 'From what I could gather, these Indians had never had any knowledge of any civilised person. Nothing among their possessions revealed such knowledge. The most common and ordinary foods of the inhabitants of the province were unknown to them.' Reinault spent the night among these newly contacted Jiporok Botocudo, with his soldiers on guard and fearing an ambush; early next morning he escaped downriver. Farther downstream, the expedition was again attacked by Botocudo as it was passing a narrows. The canoes pulled to the far bank amid a hail of arrows. The leader had great difficulty restraining his men from shooting back; but he was convinced that any fighting would prevent colonisation of these rich lands. 'An interminable war would have begun, like that which still exists among the Botocudo of the Doce river, who almost always attack travellers even though they have been in contact with civilisation for so many years.' After a day of hostility, Reinault managed to convince the Jiporok that he had come to help them against another tribe; the shooting stopped at once, and he distributed presents, to the joy of the Indians. Reinault saw 'the large numbers of hostile Indians that infest the banks of the Mucuri as the only obstacle to opening river communications with the wretched district of Minas Novas'. This obstacle could easily be removed by a prudent man pacifying the tribe. 'Such a work of philanthropy and necessity would reopen the riches of [that river] to entrepreneurs.'

One acculturated Botocudo called José deserted from the Brazilian army and led a fierce group of Indians in the Chifre hills. The settlers enlisted another renegade Indian called Lidoro to woo this Chief José to a remote place and treacherously kill him. Then in 1838 Lidoro joined Crahy to guide a large force into the Serra do Chifre to destroy its village. 'Killing a village' was settler jargon for ambush massacres. Ottoni reported that ' "Villages were killed" on the Jequitinhonha, Mucuri and Doce in Minas Gerais and in Espírito Santo.'

During the 1830s and early 1840s the government reverted to a policy of armed opposition to the Botocudo. This was reasonably successful – from a purely military point of view. The main instrument of containment of the Botocudo was to arm and enlist their traditional enemies, the Maxakali. The military commander, Colonel Julião Fernandes Leão, gave the Maxakali a large reserve area on the Prates headwater of the Jequitinhonha. They were an industrious tribe and tried to become acculturated to European society. Maxakali pottery was used by colonists all along the Jequitinhonha; their canoes and paddles were in demand by local boatmen; and they themselves were excellent canoers, sought after to transport salt along the river. Ottoni reported in 1858 that 'the Maxakali became Christians, have a regular cemetery, and are trying to erect a church. . . . They live in regular tile-roofed houses. One of their chiefs, Captain Silva, is an intelligent man who can read and has already visited Rio de Janeiro.' By mid-century, the Maxakali had almost abandoned bows and arrows in favour of guns supplied them by Colonel Leão. This gave them an advantage over the fierce Botocudo, so that 'they have constantly helped the settlers in the repression of the Botocudo. . . . Guido [Marlière] was the father and friend of the Botocudo, but [Colonel] Julião is their conqueror and victor.'

Reading accounts of contact with the Botocudo during these years, there is a strong impression that the Indians wanted peace but were rightly apprehensive of European treachery. An official called Barbosa d'Almeida wrote an interesting account of a contact with an Indian group on the Mucuri in 1845. His expedition was moving along the river and heard Indian voices on the forested banks. A native interpreter was sent ashore to make contact and returned with three Indians. These were given presents of tools, food and fish, and other Indians emerged cautiously from the woods. 'They were delighted by the good treatment they received, and lost their deep apprehension. They covered us with embraces, clapped their hands and cried out "jacjemenu", a term that always serves to indicate peace and friendship.' The expedition's soldiers remained in the canoes on the far bank, and the Indians 'watched them with considerable fear, doubtless remembering the treachery of which they had been victims at the town of Prado and other places'. To calm them, the expedition leader ordered a soldier to play his violin, and the Indians danced happily to its music. Then occurred the magical moment when Indians sampled the cutting power of sharp metal. 'The axe was the tool that delighted them most. They seemed to know their use, for as soon as they received them they tested how well they cut on the trees. They disappeared at once, and then returned to seek new ones. They moved through the woods with the greatest speed and we saw them only when they were very close. They were all naked, the men robust and well built and of cheerful expression, with their ears pierced. The women were very thin and wore great wooden discs in their lower lips, which deformed them.' A priest who was with the expedition made a mission in a clearing on a lake called São Caetano. A carpenter made a great wooden cross, and seventy-five Indians assembled for a ceremony of foundation, with firing of shotguns and vivas to the Christian religion and the Emperor Dom Pedro. But this mission did not last for more than a few months.

There was more trouble in 1846. A frontier family called Viola had some Indian boy slaves or kurucas, including two sons of Chief Jiporok of the Botocudo who lived on the Urucu, the largest southern tributary of the Mucuri. A semi-civilised Indian 'interpreter' had gained an ascendancy over the Naknyanuk Botocudo, and he tried to force the Violas to pay him a levy for their kurucas or to hand back Jiporok's sons. The Violas refused. In 1846 the Naknyanuk managed, during a torrential rainstorm, to enter the Violas' house and steal their guns. They then surrounded the farm and killed eight members of the family. 'The attack against the Violas – although justified by the unlawful detention of Jiporok's sons – unleashed horrible reprisals. The Christians lured the savages into an ambush at a place called Mariano, two leagues above São José. They attacked them treacherously and made a heavy carnage. Sixteen Indian skulls were then sold to a Frenchman who said that he was acquiring them on behalf of the Museum of Paris.'

Teófilo Ottoni led his first expedition to the Mucuri in 1847, the year after this massacre. He returned captured Indian boys and a woman, as a peace offering to the Botocudo. This gesture, and lavish distributions of presents, enabled Ottoni to gain the friendship of Chief Jiporok. 'He was a brave and intelligent Indian – as much as Indians can be. I recommended to him that he should be tame and should not harm Christians. But he answered emphatically: "You yourselves keep tame! We are as placid as land turtles." And he was telling the truth. Jiporok and his tribe confidently followed my advice and started to present themselves to the Christians on the coast. They paid heavily for their faith in my words. Less than a year after our meeting and peace treaty, when they were at a place called Itaúnas near São Mateus, a so-called Christian called Salles treacherously murdered the good chief and fourteen of his tribe. He did this on a frivolous pretext, driven by hideous passion.' The remainder of Jiporok's people fled after this massacre, and it was not known in which forests they hid.

Ottoni had been a founder of the Brazilian Liberal Party, formed in 1840 to oppose the Conservative Regency that ruled Brazil during the minority of the future Emperor Dom Pedro II. Ottoni led a rebellion of Liberal deputies to protest against the Emperor's Conservative-inspired dissolution of the Chamber of Deputies in 1844. Although the revolt failed, its leaders were eventually granted amnesty. But Ottoni was losing his taste for politics. He decided instead to lead his expedition to the Mucuri river in the north-east of his native Minas Gerais.

Ottoni was deeply impressed by his first contact with Indians and realised that frontiersmen's reports of the ferocity of the Botocudo were grossly exaggerated. He wrote to the President of Minas Gerais: 'I am confident that the system of uninterrupted giving of presents will enable [us] to gain the goodwill and friendship of the savages. ... Treating savages with kindness is the infallible method of winning their friendship.' The Provincial President listened to this advice and ordered gentle methods in dealing with the Botocudo. But he stressed that the purpose was simply to pacify them in order to drive colonisation roads into their territory. And he nullified any good intentions by founding another military barracks at a place called Santa Cruz on the Preto headwater of the Mucuri. Various peaceful tribes, including the survivors of the Capivara dawn massacre, settled near the fort. Within two years the experiment failed. Far from being kind to the Indians, the soldiers remained totally idle and made the Botocudo do all forest clearing and farming labour. They also abused Indian women. In 1849 the Botocudo warned four soldiers with whom they had no quarrel to leave. They then killed the worst offenders, a Sergeant Coelho and three of his men. The vast region of the upper Mucuri was back in Botocudo control.

Teófilo Ottoni was re-elected as a representative of Minas Gerais in 1850. But his experience of Indians and exploration had made too deep an impression: he abandoned politics altogether and decided to devote his life to pacifying the Botocudo and colonising their lands with European settlers. Ottoni was back on the Mucuri in 1852. On 4 August his expedition made contact with the Naknyanuk Botocudo of Chief Poton, and Ottoni lavished presents on the tribe. The name Poton sounded like Ottoni, so the two leaders pretended to be related. Chief Poton 'accepted this relationship and told me to bring the rest of my relatives, for there was much land and it would suffice for all. I took him at his word. Two weeks later a great clearing was felled by the savage's people. This produced three magnificent fazendas, today [1858] being cultivated by over 150 slaves, and their owners live on excellent relations with [Poton's] people.'

Later in 1852, Teófilo Ottoni turned his political oratory on to Chiefs Timotheo and Ninkate. 'This latter chief had arrogantly declared that the Portuguese should content themselves with the lands that they had already taken! I comforted them and gave them presents. And that same evening they both asked me to clear a large plantation there.' Ottoni had studied the methods of William Penn in the United States and was struck by the fact that he had obtained land from an Indian tribe to found Philadelphia in the same way as Ottoni had duped the Naknyanuk. Ottoni therefore called his new settlement Philadelphia.

Chief Timotheo was taken to a frontier town and loaded with tools and presents. His tribe was settled on a stream near Philadelphia, on land 'registered' for it; but the remaining territory was all ceded to Ottoni's new Mucuri Company. A few years later, Ottoni wrote that 'Chief Timotheo and his tribe would now risk their lives to defend the lands they donated to the Company. I have done everything to ensure that they will never repent that donation. . . . These Naknyanuks are hard-working: they plant and reap and are a help rather than a burden to new settlers. They are constantly seen in the streets of Philadelphia selling poaia [ipecac or fever-root], sarsaparilla, skins of deer and other animals, sweet potatoes, cane and other produce. The Naknyanuks live in enviable harmony – the members of a tribe with one another, and tribes between themselves.' Ottoni was also impressed by the Indians' medical knowledge: they used genipap bark fluid to cure buboes and other roots to alleviate catarrhs and fevers.

Ottoni found that other chiefs of the Naknyanuk Botocudo were more wary of his plans to invade their territory. There was an attack on Ottoni's men in 1853 when they were cutting a trail near the headwaters of the Urucu river. There was a temporary peace, but the fighting resumed. A military post was established on the Urucu under a Lieutenant Mamoré, but it came under heavy Indian attack. Pojichá Botocudo killed an engineer called Robert Schlobach when he was working on a new road. Then there was a raid on the house of a Portuguese trader, thirty-three kilometres from Santa Clara. The trader's family was massacred and his store was looted. One daughter staggered for a few miles with her intestines exposed. 'Her horrible condition caused immense grief to all who saw her. She died hours later amid excruciating suffering.' There were frequent attacks on the farm of one Antonio Dias Araújo, and the road from Santa Clara became very dangerous.

The Botocudo developed a skilful method of ambush, with hides every ten paces along the forest paths. Three Indians would man the first hide. One fired through a hole in the foliage and the other two stood to fire over his shoulder. But if the victim escaped, the Indians signalled by bird calls and he was hit by the team in the next hide. The Botocudo fought with clubs and very powerful bows and arrows. The bows were almost the height of a man and made of very hard, heavy and strong airi-palm wood. The Canadian geologist Charles Hartt found that his strongest canoe-men could not begin to bend one of these mighty bows: 'no one but an Indian can use them.' War arrows were tipped with broad bamboo heads, hardened in the fire and razor sharp. 'It makes a terrible wound, and one particularly dangerous because of the concave shape of the arrow, which facilitates bleeding.' The Botocudo kept contact with one another in the forests using loudspeakers made from tail skins of giant armadillos.

Botocudo fighting skills could not match the settlers' guns. As Hartt commented: 'The injuries committed by the Botocudos on the whites are as nothing compared with the wrongs inflicted upon them by those who have dispossessed them of their home and have almost destroyed the race.' One otherwise respectable military commander told Ottoni how he had attacked a village in the classic manner. 'The results were what usually happens. So that there should be no doubt about his exploit, this Commander brought to São Mateus the repulsive booty of three hundred ears that he had ordered amputated from the murdered savages.' Hartt said that the once-numerous Botocudo at São Mateus had been killed off, hunted down like wild beasts by the settlers. One colonist told him that during his lifetime he had either personally or at his command caused 'the death by knife and gun and poison of over a thousand of these poor creatures!' As Ottoni confirmed, 'To the shame of civilisation, poison has been used against savages in the Mucuri region. One even hears horrible cases of entire tribes falling victim to measles, with which they were treacherously contaminated in order to exterminate them. They were given the clothing of people who were ill from the disease.'

There was often an uneasy symbiotic relationship between settlers and Indians. The natives wanted manufactured goods and food, and the colonists wanted labour. Tribal Indians would drift into fazendas which were being cleared at the edges of their forests. Those who were prepared to work for the colonists were fed from the farmer's stew pot. 'Others hunt, or eat leftovers from the workers' table. Such is the power of hunger and the terror that the memory of past slaughters holds over the savages, that these wretches allow themselves to be subjected to whipping, hand beating, and even to the stocks. Even today [in 1858] these are the civilising instruments used by Christian settlers. Not only do Indians submit to such punishments without resistance, they do not even flee from farms where they are given insufficient food.'

Charles Hartt gave a good description of Botocudo working on settlers' farms a decade later. 'The Indians have learned the use of rum and tobacco, of both of which they are very fond and which are rapidly working their ruin. . . . The Indians come into the settlements to beg, and they not unfrequently are employed to work on the fazendas, their service being voluntary. At São Mateus they are paid in victuals and rum; but on the Mucuri they have learned the use of money, which they call *pataca*. At São Mateus I saw both men and women at work with the negroes. They are not much to be depended upon, usually remaining but a few days on the fazenda, and then returning to their wild life in the forest. They are very lazy, and half a dozen are scarcely worth an able-bodied negro. They seemed very docile and good-natured; indeed, I was particularly struck with this last feature in their character. At their work they laughed and played jokes on one another, and in the house at their meals were quite as merry as the negroes. . . . They have no idea of *meum et tuum*, and they are particularly addicted to stealing bananas, corn, or anything else they happen to take a fancy to. They often come almost stark naked into Philadelphia and Urucu to beg.'

In 1857 Teófilo Ottoni had his men start to cut a road for 180 kilometres from the frontier town Santa Clara to his colony Philadelphia. A group of road workers suddenly found itself surrounded by a numerous tribe. 'The chief arrogantly declared to them that he wanted no road through his lands. He and his men then fired a great many arrows at them, from which three members of the expedition were seriously wounded.' Later that year, another group of Ottoni's men came across an Indian village. The inhabitants fled into the forest, but the Brazilian surveyor called out that he came from the very good captain who left presents hanging on cords in the forests. He had come only to ask permission to cut a road through the forest without taking any Indian lands. 'A voice answered: "If you are from that captain you do not need guns. Remove them." The party threw their weapons to the ground. A savage promptly emerged from behind a log, flung his bow in one direction and his arrows in another, and ran with open arms to embrace all the members of the party with the greatest effusiveness. He asked for their leader, and then declared that he was my friend and that he gave me permission to build a road, even if it were through the middle of his house. . . . This brave and generous chief was called Pojichá.'

The Indians were right to fear new roads, for these were certain to attract settlers. Various Botocudo tribes tried in 1854 to persuade Timotheo's Naknyanuks to kill Ottoni, his brother and other white leaders of the Philadelphia settlement in order to stop further invasion of Indian lands by the new road. But the Naknyanuks refused, and told Ottoni about the plan.

In 1857 a Swiss scientist and traveller, Baron von Tschudi, visited Philadelphia to see whether it would be suitable for Swiss immigrants. Tschudi and Ottoni made an expedition together and contacted the Jiporok Botocudo, survivors of the São Matheus massacre nine years earlier. The tribe had crossed a hundred kilometres of hostile Indian territory, to find sanctuary in the forested hills of the upper Mucuri. These Jiporok revealed that they had occasionally had Ottoni in an ambush but had spared him because he had been their friend in 1847. They also liked a local settler called Gama. 'They said that whenever Indians visited Gama's house his women all went to grind manioc to make flour to give them. Gama was very good. They had often seen him cutting trails in their woods, but had not spoken to him because they were on bad terms with the Portuguese.'

Senator Ottoni finally succeeded in building what Charles Hartt described as an excellent wagon road from Santa Clara to Philadelphia, with a mule path on to Minas Novas. Ottoni then set about attracting European colonists to his Mucuri Company. His agents vigorously sold plots of land to settlers from Germany (particularly Saxony), France and Switzerland.

Despite all the help from the Botocudo, Ottoni's colony did not flourish. Baron von Tschudi was unimpressed by the condition of the German settlers who had been lured there. Two years later there was a more damning report by the German medical doctor, Robert Avé-Lallement, who saw German and Alsatian colonists in lamentable condition at Ottoni's colony of Santa Clara. Many were ill and had no medical help. There were Dutch colonists at another settlement, the Colónia Militar do Mucuri, run by a Captain Barros. These wretched people had been particularly badly cheated and exploited. Avé-Lallement met Ottoni himself at Philadelphia and found him a friendly man. But Ottoni would not accept that anything was wrong in his colonies: he claimed that any criticism was lies by the settlers. Avé-Lallement did not agree. He wrote that Ottoni's agents had been selling under false pretences in Germany, offering tracts of rainforest and Botocudo lands as equivalent to good European farmland. He saw Ottoni himself as a crook, cheating the colonists and accepting money both from them and from government subsidies. Other contemporaries blamed the failure on lack of official support: Teófilo Ottoni was out of favour because of his liberal politics.[*]

Hartt gave a more balanced judgement of the Mucuri Company. 'The colonists appear to have been, to a very large extent, of very poor quality. Through the misrepresentation of the agents of the company in Europe, the colonists were led to expect to find themselves on their arrival in possession of a house and cultivated farm. It was a bitter disappointment to them to be sent into the virgin forest. Nevertheless, extensive clearings were made, and the villages of Urucu and Philadelphia were built.' Whatever the reason, Ottoni's Mucuri Company failed utterly and was liquidated with heavy debts in 1861. Hartt wrote that the land on the Mucuri was fertile and the idea of colonising it was sensible. 'It was owing to bad management on the part of the company, to the slanders of enemies, and to the bad character of a large part of the colonists themselves, that the enterprise has proved a failure.'

*

Avé-Lallement was a curious observer of Indians, an extreme racist convinced of the superiority of European civilisation. His attitudes echoed and exaggerated some of the writings of Spix and Martius forty years earlier. In February 1859 Avé-Lallement went inland from Philadelphia to meet the semi-acculturated Botocudo of Chief Poton. These Indians were very pale and seemed sickly and anaemic. Their bellies were swollen, perhaps from undernourishment. The German doctor saw the naked Indians as 'a repulsive anthill of viragoes and male equivalents: no woman a true woman and no man a perfect man in that horde!' He found their expressions indifferent and apathetic. Their dull eyes 'reflect nothing, absolutely nothing: they have the appearance of perfect idiocy.' They would not return the doctor's penetrating stares, and he took this to be from fear that the 'fixed look of a civilised man' would discover their defects and thus completely annihilate them. Farther inland, on the Ribeirão das Pedras, Avé-Lallement met a less contacted group of Botocudo at the farm of a settler called Gasinelli. These men seemed more muscular and had a better skin colour. 'The women, on the other hand, are horrible. With no feminine expressions in their faces, short and fat, they stationed themselves there with half-imbecile smiles and without the slightest sign of modesty or shyness. They presented to our gaze the entire fronts of their bodies, without thinking of the slightest covering or even bending their knees inwards. . . . Figures of women in . . . truly hideous shape!' The Botocudo men traded wild honey, ipecac fever-root and jaguar skins for manioc flour. The women, having nothing to trade, danced for the entertainment of the visitors. Avé-Lallement (who had earlier commented lasciviously on the superb naked bodies of black slave women) was appalled by the 'idiotic faces, lip discs in constant motion, bobbing breasts and complete nudity of the women (one of whom was in an advanced state of pregnancy and gave birth twelve hours after this dance), large scars on their shoulders from brutal treatment by their men, and their clumsy jumps – all this caused a truly horrible impression.'

Various travellers gave glimpses of Indians in this part of Brazil during the middle nineteenth century. Baron von Tschudi visited a fazenda opened by two mulatto brothers called Pego on the Suaçuí Grande headwater of the Doce. By treating the local Botocudo well, these brothers had won their friendship and respect – and had also enlisted them to help clear forest for the plantation. All this was ruined by a Capuchin missionary called Friar Bernardino, who reached the fazenda in 1848. Tschudi accused this friar of kidnapping two Indian girls, getting the Pego brothers arrested by spreading rumours that they were inciting their Indians to rebel, and then frightening off the Botocudo by his clumsy attempt to convert them. In the end Friar Bernardino seized the fazenda, sold its cattle, stole its contents, imported girls to form a nunnery where he lived 'a wild debauched life with them', and finally decamped to Bahia.

A German zoologist called Hermann Burmeister was with the Coroado and Puri in 1851. At the Aldeia da Pedra, on a bluff above the Paraíba do Sul, there were almost no Indians left in the main village. This was because the Franciscans who founded the mission in the early nineteenth century 'did not observe the Jesuits' sensible system of excluding all whites from Indian villages. They admitted Brazilians and Europeans equally. Thus, although there are a few Indians living nearby, the village is entirely inhabited by whites, blacks and mulattoes.' A Capuchin from Florence, Friar Florido de Castelo, prided himself on having baptised seven hundred Coroados, two hundred Puri and some Botocudo; but the Indians were indifferent to Christian religious ceremonial 'whose pomp and brilliance so attracts the blacks'.

Burmeister regarded the Coroados and Puri as civilised, but noted that their social position was inferior to that of the blacks. 'As with all Indians, they are interested only in their daily needs. They own nothing beyond what they carry with them. All their belongings fit into a kerchief, which they always carry, leaving their huts with bare walls.' They wore European clothes and hats, lived in thatched wood-and-mud houses scattered in the woods far from the roads, and hunted with guns rather than bows and arrows. Although they grew manioc, oranges and bananas, this was only to feed their families. 'Only a need for European clothes, which they now wear, forces them to work. They hire themselves out as day-labourers on nearby fazendas, to cut and transport wood. They carry logs to the river on a sort of train that belongs to the fazendeiro. Once in the water, the logs are bound together to form rafts. The Indians are excellent at this type of transport. They spend weeks on end living on the floating tree trunks. An entire family accompanies its head during this task.' They steered the log rafts skilfully along the river currents and through rapids. 'All these Indians are aquatic: they bathe daily, swim and dive with great skill, and are far cleaner and more hygienic than mulattoes or blacks. In this way they take the logs down the Pomba and Muriaé rivers to the Paraíba and thence to Campos and on to the sea. With the money they earn, they buy pieces of clothing, powder, shot and other utensils such as knives or scissors for daily use. That is all that a civilised Indian owns.'

To Burmeister, the young Coroados were 'distinguished by their serious and correct behaviour. They inspire confidence and are physically more agreeable than the blacks.' But when they grew older and became demoralised by frontier society, they were ruined by alcohol. The old men and women were 'arrogant, impertinent and bad-mannered . . . addicted to the vice of drink and thus repugnant and bestial. . . . Their drinking was communal. Each in turn brought a glass of cachaça and passed it from mouth to mouth until it was empty. Then it was another's turn! In a short time, men and women lay drunken and senseless on the ground. When fireworks exploded in a church festival, they uttered piercing cries in their drunken state and the spectators laughed as if at a funny spectacle. No one was upset by such scenes. The blacks particularly liked to incite the Coroados to drink more so that they could be entertained by scenes of animal brutishness. Such behaviour by the Indians gave great satisfaction to the blacks, for it made them consider themselves far superior.'

Burmeister noted that Indian men and black women despised one another. But 'a sensual Indian woman prefers a black, and he prefers her. This is easily explained for physical reasons. . . . It is well known that the erection of a certain organ is very large among blacks whereas Indians are of delicate build and are weaker than Europeans in this particular.'

With the collapse of Teófilo Ottoni's Mucuri Company, the government turned to missionaries for help with the Botocudo. These fiercely independent Indians had resisted 250 years of attack by colonists trying to push inland from the Atlantic seaboard: the savage decree of 1808 which declared open war on all Botocudo; the conciliatory approach of Guido Marlière; containment by frontier forts; and an assault on their lands by European settlers of the Mucuri Company. They now had to endure Italian Capuchin missionaries.

The first two missionaries, Friar Serafim de Gorizia, aged forty-three, and the twenty-seven-year-old Friar Angelo de Sassoferato, reached Philadelphia in 1873. Since the failure of Ottoni's colonisation company in 1861 the region had been in anarchy. The provincial director of Indians reported that in three years between 1869 and 1872 over eight hundred Indians had been killed, either by whites or in inter-tribal fighting. Families of pioneers who penetrated Indian lands to open new farms had disappeared without trace. Some groups of Botocudo were well led, often by semi-acculturated

Indians who deserted from the Brazilian army. Other groups were deceived by the settlers and treacherously slaughtered, as had happened at São Miguel on the Jequitinhonha and at the Ribeirão das Lages, where not even suckling infants were spared. 'In one place they were exterminated, in another they were reduced to virtual slavery and were then considered "tamed".'

Chief Poton of the Naknyanuk Botocudo advised the newly arrived Friars Serafim and Angelo where to build their mission aldeia. He chose a site in hills above the Itambacuri river, thirty-six kilometres south of Philadelphia. It was a beautiful place, with sweeping views over the river, and it proved excellent for growing rice, sugar, corn and black beans. Settlers and Indians worked together to fell a great clearing from virgin forest. There was much suffering and hunger building a cattle trail from Philadelphia to the new mission. Friar Serafim recalled that 'the mosquitoes were insufferable. They were a martyrdom for us, buzzing even in the smoke of our fires and causing us such fatigue that within a few hours they would leave us nervous and exhausted.'

The Itambacuri mission was initially stocked by Botocudo of Chief Pahóc, a powerful leader with eight hundred warriors in his immediate control and a further hundred in outlying villages. These were from the Krikatí, Mucuri and Nhanhan sub-tribes. Chief Pahóc had been in contact with whites for many years. His daughter Umbelina had married a Brazilian called Félix Ramos da Cruz, who acted as interpreter. In 1870 Pahóc took a hundred of his Indians to visit the civil director of Indians of Minas Gerais at Ouro Prêto, and the following year he called on the directors of Indians at Philadelphia. In the years after forming the mission, the Italian friars enlisted settlers (who badly wanted the Indians pacified) to help assemble Indians there. 'We worked ceaselessly to call and attract various tribes that were scattered in the forests and lead them to the central aldeia. Some were very numerous, but others already badly diminished.'

Freshly arrived from Italy, the two Capuchins underestimated the seriousness of cultural shock among Indians driven too quickly into acculturation. They determined on a disastrous policy of miscegenation. The younger friar wrote that 'Friar Serafim immediately became convinced that the Indians should not be treated as an isolated people, separated from the civilised [Brazilian] nationals. This would have prejudiced the objective that we and the government had in mind. He therefore immediately opened schools for both peoples, mixing them up as if they were a single race. He also promoted marriages between them, for he considered this to be the only sure means of assimilating the pure Indian race. The government also acknowledged this. Teaching in our schools always consisted of primary instruction, catechism, and manual or agricultural work. Three or four years after their foundation, our schools were already regurgitating boys and girls of both races.'

Within two years, the Itambacuri mission had three hundred warriors and their families. In 1875 Chief Pahóc's son-in-law Félix Ramos helped attract five hundred men, women and children of the Ponchão sub-tribe. They migrated to Itambacuri after a long journey; some remained in the mission and others settled in forests near the town of São Mateus. By 1877 there were 570 Indians in the aldeia and a further three thousand in intermittent contact in the surrounding forests. The two missionaries had a staff of twenty-two helpers and labourers, but they themselves energetically wielded axes and hoes. Visitors were impressed that in four years they had created a village of twenty tiled houses and over a hundred thatched huts, neatly arranged along streets lined with coconut palms, and surrounded by thriving plantations. The friars were tireless in teaching the children and hearing confessions, and at a special mass they congregated two thousand Indians and whites. By 1884 the missionaries themselves boasted that they had 890 Indians settled in various aldeias, alongside nine hundred poor Brazilian labourers. They had instigated 106 marriages between Indians and Brazilians. There were also 520 unsettled Indians in the Itambacuri region. A group of colonists even wrote to the Emperor praising the work of the Capuchins. They said that four groups of Indians settled at Itambacuri were 'generally civilised. The Indian children are taught their first letters and the arts of carpenters, blacksmiths and joiners; the older ones are established farming their own lands. A great number of national colonists is established in the territory of that aldeia. Over a hundred marriages have taken place between Indian women and national men: these are the most effective guarantee of the progress of that settlement.'

There were, however, serious problems. There was danger from hostile tribes and even from Araná Indians of a rival mission on the Doce river. Friar Serafim was so alarmed by these Araná, who were armed with guns, that he obtained a military contingent of twenty soldiers to guard his mission. The troops helped build its houses. He later incorporated some Araná into his aldeia when their missionary died in 1875. Support from the provincial government was patchy. Much financial help had been promised at the outset, but by 1874 the authorities were already saying that no more money was available 'because of the unsatisfactory state of the provincial coffers'. The missionaries vigorously demanded money for tools, seeds, cloth with which to dress naked Indians, and materials to build a large church.

A more serious problem came from the colonists. These were desperate for Indian labour on their farms and resented the way the Italian missionaries used Indians to tend their mission's plantations but denied these workers to the surrounding fazendeiros. They wanted the Indians to remain in the forests 'from which they could summon them at any time to work on their clearings, in exchange for illusory trinkets and copious cachaça'. Friar Serafim complained that settlers tried to lure Indian children into their households 'in order to employ them one day as slaves'. An official report of 1879 admitted that when slavery of blacks was abolished, local farmers 'thought that they could easily resolve the problem by substituting Indians for slaves. For they considered Indians as "bad beasts", whom they must either subjugate and use for labour, or eliminate.' Some settlers organised a campaign of vilification against the missionaries. They enlisted the brothers of Teófilo Ottoni (who had died in 1869, broken in health and financially by his Mucuri experiment). In 1882 Counsellor Cristiano Ottoni attacked the missionaries in a speech in the provincial Assembly. He accused them of squandering money to entertain the local bishop and of failing to pursue his late brother's policy of attracting and pacifying Indians.

The Capuchin missionaries had an ambition: to attract and convert the fierce Botocudo of Chief Pojichá, the brave chief whose men had harassed the building of the road to Philadelphia but who had made temporary peace with Teófilo Ottoni in 1857. Since then, Chief Pojichá had died and his warriors remained independent and invincible. Brilliant archers who used long bows, these Botocudo moved swiftly through the forests, sleeping on the ground and eating game raw, and were masters of camouflage and ambush. Their communal malocas were well hidden in the darkest depths of the forest, far from rapids so that they could hear any noise. They controlled the forests between the headwaters of the São Mateus and Itambacuri rivers. There were thought to be six groups of these Pojichá Botocudo, who called themselves Krekmun and Kreché, including some two hundred naked and hostile hunter–gatherers near the São Mateus and about eighty more acculturated Urucu on the Todos os Santos river.

As early as 1875, Friar Serafim obtained from the provincial authorities a pardon for the Pojichá for any 'crimes' committed in defence of their territory. But it was not until 1884 that this fifty-five-

year-old missionary finally made contact with the tribe. Friendly
Indians guided him for forty kilometres into the forest. The younger
Friar Angelo described the exciting and potentially dangerous moment of contact: 'It is impossible to describe the wonder and admiration with which Friar Serafim's presence filled the Indians. He was a
tall, robust man, ruddy, bearded, dressed in the Franciscan habit,
unarmed, wearing a crucifix on his chest, full of majesty but utterly
captivating. It was not difficult for the chief to be convinced that this
strange figure in front of him was a friend. He gave a strong and
protracted whistling call – the conventional signal, that echoed for a
long time in the depths of the forest – which summoned the tribe
with surprising speed. Indians suddenly emerged from all sides. The
missionary, smiling and without losing his habitual calm and serenity, found himself as if by magic a prisoner in their midst. He then
offered them presents and everything he had brought to eat, and
received in return half-roasted monkey.'

The friars led this group of Pojichá back towards their mission.
The journey involved spending a night in the town of Philadelphia,
whose population rushed to see the unexpected sight of the Indians
whom they had feared for so long. They professed to be full of
admiration at the courage of the missionaries who had achieved this
pacification. But it was equally clear that many wished to settle
vendettas and remove future danger by lynching the Pojichá. Philadelphia's police chief lodged the tribe in a walled enclosure, theoretically to protect them but in fact to trap and slaughter them and
discredit the missionaries. Friar Serafim had a long meeting with the
police chief to persuade him to desist. There was heavy rain during
the night, but the Pojichá noticed the suspicious movement of armed
soldiers outside their compound. When they saw the gate to the
compound being shut they became convinced of treachery and prudently climbed the wall to escape into the forests. They left behind
one sleeping boy, and the friar got this young Indian to lead him to
the tribe in the woods. The Botocudo were now sure that Friar
Serafim was an accomplice of the soldiers, determined to lure them
into a treacherous ambush. They greeted him with a volley of arrows,
which he braved and tried to convince them that he, at least, was a
friend.

Later in 1884, some chiefs of the nomadic Pojichá visited Itambacuri aldeia and decided to bring their people to live alongside it. The
mission had an obvious appeal, with its plantations of food and its
apparently abundant supply of metal tools. So in 1885, the missionaries made a fresh attempt to seduce the main group of Pojichá

to move to Itambacuri. This time they sent trusted Indian interpreters. The tribe clearly wanted peace, and accepted the invitation. It chose a trail via the São Mateus river to avoid Philadelphia, and set out along this in torrential rain. The trail passed by the farm of one José Teodoro Dias. This settler hid his armed sons near his banana grove and, when two Indians asked for bananas, they were lured into the grove and shot. There was a fierce fight with the rest of the tribe. As the Pojichá ran off through the forest, they came across a party of eight mission Indian interpreters, assumed that these were part of the treacherous plot, and killed and mutilated them. A police enquiry at Philadelphia accused the missionaries of responsibility for the battle. The chief of police was part of a group of frontiersmen who wanted to demolish the mission and acquire its Indian labour. Another anti-missionary settler was Leonardo Ottoni, one of Teófilo's brothers. On 3 October 1885 this Leonardo invited thirty-eight leading Pojichá to his Fazenda da Liberdade. Generous quantities of cachaça helped Ottoni allay the Indians' suspicions, and all thirty-eight Pojichá braves, including two chiefs, were massacred. Cruelly decimated, the shattered remnant of the tribe fled into the forests of the Aimoré hills. As Friar Serafim wrote: 'The Indians cannot be blamed for wandering through the forest like wild animals . . . after having been provoked, persecuted, condemned to public scorn and hunted down like dangerous beasts.'

Three years later, Friar Serafim made yet another attempt. He took Indian interpreters and boldly followed the trails to the São Mateus river. Incredibly, given the wretched history of white treachery, he succeeded. The Pojichá were united and the missionary triumphantly led back an army of two hundred warriors, painted with red urucum dye and armed with bows and arrows. He settled these new arrivals in an aldeia some distance from his main mission. The Capuchins boasted that they had now finally freed the vast region of the upper Mucuri from Indian incursions: settlers could farm their usurped land without fear. The Pojichá men were given tools and taught how to farm. Their children were removed for instruction in the main mission school and by June 1888 Friar Serafim proudly reported that 'the young in particular have lost their bad habits. They apply themselves patiently to agricultural labour and to light industry in cotton spinning.'

In 1890 there was yet another terrible drought in the north-east of Brazil. Refugees fled from Ceará and drought-stricken parts of Bahia. Some men went to work as rubber tappers in Amazonia, but many families migrated south. They heard of the good work of the

Italian missionaries and many headed for Itambacuri. The mission's original population was swamped by new arrivals and rapidly trip-led. The missionaries made great sacrifices to house and feed the refugees, but their work was made more difficult by the southward spread of the drought into Minas Gerais. Despite this, by 1893 Friar Angelo was able to boast that their Indians had increased to 2500, many of whom were intermarried with neo-Brazilians. The mission had helped to expand the Brazilian frontier and had brought credit to the Franciscan order. 'We felt satisfied and jubilant, for our sacrifices redounded in an achievement pleasing to God and useful to Brazil. Subventions paid to us by the government, and the school grant which had multiplied with the development of the settlements, were all employed in successful Indian conversion, in building useful works and improving the colony. Our work, with divine blessing, yielded marvellous results. Itambacuri grew and prospered to such a degree that it caused admiration and wonder among all who visited it.'

No sooner had this self-congratulation been written than the mission of Itambacuri was struck by disaster. In mid-1893 there was an epidemic of measles and fevers. As always, tough Indians had no inherited immunity against such imported diseases, and men, women and children succumbed. On one day alone, eighteen died. The missionaries were powerless to help and merely blamed their Indians for jumping into the river to cool their fever. The Indians were already demoralised and discontented because they were denied the solace of alcohol. The tragic epidemic brought this discontent to a head: there was a plot to kill the missionaries, drive out the settlers, and for the Indians themselves to take control of Itambacuri.

One morning, Friar Serafim issued a large quantity of cloth to the Indians. Friar Angelo told one of the chiefs to go and work, saying that it would be a consolation for the chief to leave something for his children when he died, for we must all die. The chief answered harshly: 'Yes, we must all die. But you will die first and I will die later.' That evening, 24 May 1893, Indians painted with urucum crept through the cemetery towards the missionaries' garden. When the friars strolled in the garden after mass, both were wounded by arrows. Friar Angelo grabbed a gun and fired towards the attackers, but was greeted by a shower of arrows. Indian boys interned in the missionaries' house ran to join their people. Hearing the shot, settlers ran out and mounted a defence of the mission buildings while others rode to Philadelphia for help. The Botocudo had assembled seven hundred men, but these were driven off by an armed posse and twenty well-armed soldiers from the town. The Botocudo destroyed and burned as much as they could before retreating, but they were overtaken by a punitive expedition. In the ensuing battle some Indians were killed, sixteen were captured and the remainder escaped. The sixteen captives were all condemned as ringleaders of the plot, and imprisoned.

There was an hysterical press reaction, with exaggerated stories of white deaths and indignant editorials about barbaric ingratitude by the savages. The head of the Capuchin Order sent congratulations from Rome and special privileges for the two missionaries. And a contemporary anthropologist, Alexandre de Mello Moraes, wrote that 'from a moral and intellectual point of view, the Botocudo are an expression of the human race at its most inferior. . . . They have great difficulty in adapting themselves to a civilised environment. They are also about to be extinguished as a race: it is probable that within half a century it will be impossible to find a pure specimen.' By retreating to their forests, the remnant of the once-powerful Botocudo tried to prevent this extinction.

Mello Moraes imagined that he understood the effects of cultural shock. 'The nostalgia of savages brusquely removed from the vastness of the forests and from their villages is accompanied by . . . serious physical symptoms. [They suffer] loss of appetite, disturbances of secretions, visceral disorders, hallucinations, hepatitis, sadness mixed with sombre melancholy, oedemas, and calm that becomes taciturn. They refuse what is offered to them, become upset without cause, and are obstinately silent. But if someone talks to them in the language of their forests, they breathe deeply and feel happy.' Mello Moraes saw this desolation in a romantic light: 'At night, when the stars twinkle and the moon sheds its pious radiance on sleeping nature, savages can be seen here and there leaning over the rivers, dipping their memby-reed flutes into the waters to make them more plangent. They lament in those dolorous sounds all the woes they find on earth. They play on and on forever, until they are exhausted or dawn breaks!'

Missionary Zeal,
the Tocantins–Araguaia Frontier

In 1846, newly imported Italian missionaries sought to establish themselves on the Tocantins frontier of central Brazil, just as they were trying in other parts of the country. Their arrival was welcomed by President Ignácio Ramalho of Goiás, who hoped that missionaries would bring new impetus to Indian pacification. He wanted to stop the sterile policy of sending punitive raids against the tribes of the Tocantins and Araguaia. Many frontier towns had been destroyed or abandoned because of Indian attack. But Ramalho blamed 'not only the ferocity of those wretches, but also the futile methods with which we tried to tame them. Far from achieving their intended purpose, these [punitive expeditions] turned them into irreconcilable enemies of the civilised classes.' This perceptive President also realised that it was folly to move Indians from their homelands into remote aldeias near colonial towns. Such aldeias are 'very expensive and cannot prosper. One cannot successfully dislocate a horde of savages from the place where they are established. Nor can one achieve a rapid change in their customs or subject them to regular work, when their habits are different. I therefore consider that the best system to adopt . . . is to found aldeias in places with which they are familiar. They can then acquire social needs, gradually and imperceptibly.' The President hoped – perhaps ingenuously – that aldeias located in the tribes' own territory, coupled with peaceful methods of attraction, 'would gradually convince them that the civilised race does not want their destruction, but rather their well-being. . . . This method is preferable to the usual one of attempting to subject them by force to a state of sociability. I do not attribute the ferocity of the Indians to their nature or to the barbaric customs observed among them. It is due to the bandeira raids and other acts of violence that have been employed to bring them to our society by terror.'

President Ramalho's new plan resulted in the foundation of three aldeias on the Araguaia river. There was Jamimbu, created for nomadic riverine Karajá on the upper Araguaia. To the surprise of the provincial government, this led to a peaceful approach at the end of 1846 by a group of the dreaded Chavante. 'They appeared at a place called Salinas [on the upper Araguaia] requesting peace and the protection of the government. This was certainly because they had seen the Karajá being protected and given presents.' An Italian Capuchin, Friar Sigismundo de Taggia, was sent to try to convert these Chavante. He took a group of them on an embassy to the provincial capital Goiás, where their chief was given a Brazilian uniform, a knife, cloth, other clothing and 'a second-hand cocked hat, bought for two milreis'.

Friar Rafael de Taggia was another Capuchin from the same north Italian town. He was installed among the Krahó near Carolina on the Tocantins in 1846. We saw how the Krahó helped the cattlemen of Carolina defeat other tribes at the beginning of the nineteenth century. Since then, Carolina had expanded but the Krahó had declined disastrously from disease and alcohol. By the 1840s they were considered an impediment. They were occupying good potential cattle land upriver from Carolina. Friar Rafael was therefore enlisted to remove the troublesome Krahó, and the settlers of Carolina even subscribed 424 milreis to help the missionary in this nefarious work. In 1849 he succeeded in persuading eight hundred Krahó to move two hundred kilometres up the Tocantins to a new location at the mouth of the Sono (Sleep) river. This new site was named Pedro Afonso after the Emperor of Brazil. Friar Rafael himself explained that 'they lived peacefully on their lands [near Carolina]. But having given cause for complaint to the fazendeiros they were removed and now compose the aldeia of Pedro Afonso.'

In this new area the Krahó formed a buffer to protect Carolina from Chavante or Cherente attack from the south. Padua Fleury, who was President of Goiás in 1848 and 1849, hoped to build a road down the east bank of the Tocantins to Pedro Afonso. He described the Krahós' new territory as containing 'many good pastures for raising cattle and horses and forests suitable for agriculture, and it is healthy.' But in reality the Krahó were exiled for expediency, for the sole benefit of the colonists of Carolina.

Friar Rafael wrote about his work with the Krahó, and revealed the same frustrations and incomprehension of Indian society that had emerged so strongly from Jesuit reports in earlier centuries. Dismissing the tribe's spiritual beliefs, he wrote that 'they live without religion' but have only superstition. 'Since religion is the fundamental basis of political and moral education, it is evident that these Indians are a brute people devoid of education. . . . They train their children only in skills useful to them: to be good runners, good archers and good hunters.'

The missionary's greatest problem was disease. Indian shamans are judged largely by their ability to heal and to predict the future. Christian missionaries have always been assessed by their native congregations for these same powers. Modern missionaries rely on sophisticated medicines and manufactured tools to buttress their religious teaching. The tragedy for the Krahó was that they were decimated by epidemics in 1849 and 1850, soon after moving to Pedro Afonso. With his limited medical knowledge, the Italian missionary was powerless to save them and the tribe lost a fifth of its population. Catholic missionaries always attach great importance to administering the last rites to dying parishioners, but the ritual was misconstrued by the stricken Krahó. 'They say that being baptised is tantamount to shortening their lives, and that baptism kills them. We missionaries have to administer this necessary sacrament to dying children by force. The chiefs have issued orders in the village, forbidding anyone to tell the missionary about sick people. They consider our medicaments to be sorcery. People thus die without treatment.'

Despite this terrible disaster, Friar Rafael gained the affection of the Krahó. He described them as 'very faithful and fond of the missionary who is entrusted with their government. They are always ready to lose their lives for love of him.' James Wells, who travelled on the Tocantins shortly after the friar's death in 1875, heard only good about him. After moving in with the Krahó, Friar Rafael 'met with a rough reception at first and was for a long time in daily danger of losing his life, but his tact, patience, and kind and gentle nature gradually so gained the obedience and good-will of these wild sons of the forest, that he was enabled to baptize them in the Roman Catholic faith, and teach them a few habits of industry, agriculture, and to provide for the coming morrow, yet still they wear only their natural garments, i.e. their skin and a few feathers stuck in their hair for state occasions; possibly the poor friar has nothing to dress them with, and wisely sees no shame where none exists.'

The mission of Pedro Afonso proved too fertile. Settlers soon poured into this part of the Tocantins valley. Friar Rafael once again performed the dubious task of moving his Krahó away from a rich colonial frontier. 'In 1850 the first Brazilian settlers appeared amongst the Indians [at Pedro Afonso], who two years afterwards, accompanied by their beloved pastor, sought a more congenial existence in the wilderness on the borders of the Rio do Manoel Alves Pequeno.' Friar Rafael did not press the conversion of the Krahó too violently. He explained to the Provincial President in 1859 that he had 'few hopes for his efforts towards the religious and civil education of his catechumens. . . . He was attempting only to keep the natives in a state of peace, and to serve as parish priest for the new settlers' who were flooding into Pedro Afonso. He hinted that he preferred to be vicar of the frontier settlement to trying to convert reluctant Indians. President F. J. da Gama Cerqueira commented angrily that 'he is forgetting what concerns catechism – for *making the Indians Christian seems to him a task beyond his capacity.*'

The Krahó themselves recall the main legacy of twenty-seven years of missionary activity as intermarriage with black neo-Brazilians. Chief Major Tito, who became famous for his wealth and was finally murdered by colonists, had African blood, as have most Krahó chiefs to the present day. The Krahó are still in their new location, reasonably intact and with many of their tribal customs still functioning. Their survival is due to their own resilience, the barrenness of the sandy campo to which they were exiled, and the collapse of the mission after Friar Rafael's death in 1875. By the late nineteenth century this tribe was pagan again.

The settlers who drove the Krahó from Pedro Afonso were an unattractive lot. James Wells described them as extremely indolent and their homes as decrepit and dirty. The huts of the town were scattered over a large area, surrounding 'a little church of whitewashed adobe walls and tiled roof, extremely plain and as unpretentious as a white box'. The English traveller met a local potentate: 'His eyes gleamed in their cavernous sockets at my questions, and he replied with a chuckle that, after all, he was credited with twenty-two deaths. . . . "And the rest? and the rest?", he said, bending forward his head with a jerk, and peering into my face, at the same time giving me a dig in my side with his claw-like fingers. . . . He wants to be affable and hospitable, but it is impossible to resist a feeling of loathing at the repulsive figure and murderous rascal. . . . I believe he is a madman.' This capitão's farm had a few naked Indians. Wells was told that the boss was in the habit of raiding nomadic tribes between the Tocantins and Araguaia, where 'he and a few congenial natures slaughter them like beasts of prey, and bring away the children as captives.' As we have seen, although Brazilian laws were fairly just on paper, they were unenforceable on such remote frontiers. 'In practice . . . in the far interior of Brazil, any local magnate can commit with impunity the grossest crime, provided he has influence and can afford to pay.'

In 1851 Friar Rafael sought to extend his mission to the Cherente tribe living south of the Krahó. In the previous year a large group of Cherente had moved down to settle near the mouth of the Piabanhas (Areias) river, 140 kilometres up the Tocantins from Pedro Afonso. They were led by a chief called Cassiano, a white man who had been captured as a boy and raised in the tribe. Their move was inspired by friendly contact with one Colonel Vicente Ayres da Silva, who had visited their villages during a prospecting expedition up the Sono river: the Cherente were tired of hostilities with the settlers and followed this first white man who had shown them goodwill. When Friar Rafael visited the Cherente, there were over two thousand of them at a place called Teresa Cristina. They had been badly decimated by frequent epidemics and by bandeira raids on their villages. Friar Rafael commented that 'They are, however, very prolific and now that they continue to live in peace they have clearly multiplied – to such an extent that the government will have to make provision for their support.' James Wells said that in 1870 a Cherente chief baptised as Gabriel made the long journey to Rio de Janeiro to visit the Emperor Dom Pedro II, who had a romantic affection for Indians. 'They returned pleased with their visit and loaded with presents.' When Friar Rafael was paralysed by a stroke in 1875, his fellow missionary Friar Antonio de Ganges took him upriver to Teresa Cristina to die among the affable Cherente.

Wells wrote of the missionaries that 'every-one spoke of these self-sacrificing men in terms of affection and respect.' But the new Italian Capuchins were not all successful. In 1851 the President of Goiás complained that Friar Rafael was the only one of four Italian missionaries in his province who had bothered to reside among the Indians. The others 'remain stationary in the places where they establish their domicile'. A few years later, another Provincial President complained about the laziness of the Italian Capuchins. President Gama Cerqueira said that Friar Antonio de Molineto was spending many months each year in the city of Goiás rather than among his congregation of Cherente. In 1862, President José Pereira de Alencastre said how disappointed he was in the performance of the Capuchins. He wanted to remove all managerial and financial functions from them. This particular President felt that missionaries harmed Indians by making them change their customs. But his proposed solution to the Indian 'problem' was ruinously impractical: he wanted more colonisation in Indian territories. Settlers would inspire the natives through 'friendly commercial dealings. . . . Such nuclei of colonisation would cause commerce, agriculture and industry to appear. They would regenerate the aboriginal race which is so profoundly corrupt and, devoid of ambition or wants, lives abandoned to purely animal instincts.'

An example of the missionaries' incapacity involved contacts with hostile Chavante beyond the Araguaia frontier. President Gama Cerqueira wanted Friar Antonio de Molineto to try to found a mission among the Chavante of the Tesouras (Scissors) river. But the missionary 'refused absolutely: for he said that he was well aware of the wicked nature of those savages'.

In 1856, Friar Sigismundo de Taggia, the missionary in charge of Jamimbu aldeia on the upper Araguaia, made a fresh attempt up the Rio das Mortes (River of the Dead). He took his resident Chavante chief Felipe, some tame Indians, soldiers and settlers for three hundred kilometres up the Mortes. Friar Sigismundo then sent his tame Chavante to scout ahead towards the uncontacted Chavante. The mission Indians found a village after two days' march. Its young men were off hunting peccary, but there were some women and elders. 'When they reached the village an old man wanted to shoot arrows rather than talk to them. Despite this, they succeeded in surrounding and conversing with him, and Chief Felipe made him see that he was his relative, that he had come with the missionary to bring gifts and not to fight, and that they wanted peace. The old man replied that Christians were very bad: when the Chavante had been at Carretão aldeia they suffered [many punishments and tortures].' The expedition decided to retreat rather than await the return of the tribe's warriors. Before leaving, it stole some mats, arrows and other artefacts.

On its return towards Friar Sigismundo's canoes, the party stopped for the night and was ambushed by Chavante. A corporal and soldier were clubbed to death while asleep. A skirmish ensued in the dark. The wild Chavante were driven off by gunfire and some were killed, but one warrior successfully fired back with a gun taken from the dead corporal. Back at Jamimbu, Friar Sigismundo asked the authorities for weapons for another attempt. President Cunha sent twelve guns, six hundred cartridges and fifty flint-locks. But he advised the timid missionary to go in himself next time, and not leave the contact to imprudent men who stole Indian possessions.

Missionaries were doing no better downstream on the Tocantins Araguaia. The aldeia of Boa Vista, on the left bank of the Tocantins some 360 kilometres downriver from Carolina, had a chequered history. It started in 1841 with only eleven people, but by 1848 had received an influx of two thousand naked Apinagé. It became a fine source of labourers and beautiful women for the growing nearby settlement of Boa Vista. In 1850 a President of Goiás called this Indian village 'the cellar where the civilised inhabitants of the Camp of Boa Vista go to replenish themselves'. By the following year, Boa Vista had almost three thousand Apinagé; but its Italian missionary, Friar Francisco do Monte San Vito, lived far from the Indians, preoccupied with founding a rich church in the colonial settlement. By 1857 its population was down to six hundred. At the end of that year, Boa Vista's warriors took the guns they had traded with the settlers and crossed the Tocantins to settle old scores with the Gaviões (Hawks) Timbira of the east bank. They made a 'horrible slaughter' of the Gaviões and brought back almost a hundred children as captives. Friar Francisco told the Provincial President that he had 'distributed these among the inhabitants of the town of Boa Vista, for them to be baptised'. This was, of course, a euphemism for slavery as household servants. President Gama Cerqueira commented: 'This simple fact is sufficient to give a rough idea of the state of those missions and the degree of interest that their missionary–director takes in them.'

Farther down the Tocantins, where the river turns west toward its junction with the mighty Araguaia, a military presídio called Santa Thereza (later renamed Imperatriz) was founded in 1848. The Carmelite brother Manoel Procopio took over missionary work among the neighbouring Krenyé Timbira – another Gê-speaking tribe closely resembling the Apinagé, Krahó and Canela – and ran the mission for a number of years without great success. By 1859 the Krenyé there were reduced to fifty or sixty poor and undernourished Indians; and in the 1860s they fled north-eastwards to settle on the upper Gurupi river. They told the contemporary traveller Gustav Luiz Dodt why they had emigrated: some settlers attacked their village while its men were absent, abducting a number of children; in revenge, the Krenyé attacked a neighbouring fazenda and killed seven people. They themselves fled to escape reprisals.*

The provincial authorities, keen to push the frontier westwards from the Tocantins to the Araguaia, sought to enlist missionaries for this expansion. Brother Manoel Procopio had fleeting contact with the fierce Krikatí or Gaviões tribe of Timbira. For a few years between 1848 and 1854 the Gaviões used to visit Santa Thereza, and three hundred of them even settled briefly to the north of this mission.* By 1855 they were gone. That year's presidential report for Pará described the mission as being in a state of complete decadence. A report of 1865 said that the local Indian director was determined to try to pacify the Gaviões Krikatí who 'raided and sacked cattle and farming ranches' all the way from Leopoldina to the Chapada (Plateau). At least six large villages of Gaviões were known: that of Chief Governador had a thousand inhabitants and that of Chief Belisário six hundred. By contrast, when the director of Indians visited a village of two hundred Pukobye and Krikatí 'who seemed to have been pacified for a long time . . . they were already in extreme misery.' As always, tribes flourished in the forests but were morally and physically destroyed by acculturation. The Gaviões, like the Chavante far to the south, decided to resist white colonisation. Their warriors defended their forests on both banks of the lower Tocantins until the second half of the twentieth century. This wise decision ensured their survival as a reasonably vigorous tribe until recent times.

Dr Rufino Theotino Segurado sailed down the Araguaia in 1846 and had very friendly contact with the Karajá. One chief climbed on to Segurado's boat 'unarmed and with a confidence I found admirable. . . . In all their actions they showed a limitless confidence in us.' There was an exchange of the white men's tools, beads and tobacco for Indian fish, gourds, bananas and pineapples. The Indians voluntarily helped Segurado's expedition, pulling its boats and carrying loads.

Downriver, Segurado met Chief Carô of the Xambioá (pronounced Shambioá) Karajá. The old man was distinguished from the rest of his men only by an old straw hat, a gun, and a pair of trousers which he wore as a cape on his shoulders. Segurado asked Chief Carô if he wanted the whites to settle on the Araguaia with their oxen and horses; and the chief said that he would welcome this. He then paused, thought for a moment and 'suddenly raised his head and said: "Presídio, no." ' Segurado explained that any settlement must include a stockade and garrison. 'He then said to me heatedly, in a loud voice: "Presídio, no, not want. . . . Padre, no; turi (Christian), no; ox, no; horse, no." It is easy to see from this sudden change in the Indian's thinking that he had not forgotten the cruelties against [the Karajá] by a rash commander of the extinct garrison of Santa Maria.

It would not be easy to establish a presídio near these villages.'

Santa Maria was the fort guarding the main rapids on the Araguaia that the Karajá and Chavante had destroyed in 1813. It was revived in 1852 but almost immediately burned by Indians. In 1858 it was rebuilt for the third time. When the Indians again burned it in 1861, an aggressive President of Goiás determined to take stern measures. President Aragão e Mello said: 'I resolved to raise to forty the number of troops in the garrison and to add to them some condemned convicts from the prison of Goiás. These will go there to serve their sentence . . . and will also help defend the presídio.'

The missionary Friar Francisco do Monte San Vito was also sent to this frontier. Although earlier presidents had condemned his laziness among the Apinagé of Boa Vista, Friar Francisco was now in favour. He went to Santa Maria in 1859 and spent the following year preparing a punitive expedition with a Guarda Nacional captain against Indians near the fort. But it was the Indians who struck first with a pre-emptive attack. 'They burned what he had built, killed two people, and put the missionary himself and the rest of his men to flight.' Friar Francisco did not wait to bury the dead. He fled back east to Boa Vista on the Tocantins and wrote from there accusing the Karajá of the attack. The Provincial President agreed. 'These Indians appear tame. . . . However, they are profoundly deceitful. They lose no opportunity to destroy any establishments founded in the territory they inhabit.' Friar Francisco do Monte San Vito returned to Santa Maria and developed the settlement with some forty houses of colonists and a fortress-like church. He died in 1873 and was not replaced; the military garrison was withdrawn from Santa Maria.*

In 1863 João Couto de Magalhães, then a young lawyer, descended the Araguaia and fell in love with this mighty river. During the rainy months, from October to May, the Araguaia fills and is as broad as a gently flowing, tawny-brown lake. There is a thin fringe of forest along the banks but open campo or cerrado scrublands on the plains beyond. In the dry season the river changes character. Its waters fall to reveal immense sandbanks, often stretching for hundreds of metres to the river's distant channel. On this hard ribbed sand, the riverine Karajá build small barrel-vaulted thatch shelters.

During his first expedition to the Araguaia, Couto de Magalhães saw the decaying village of Estiva, six kilometres north of the abandoned mission of Salinas. Friar Sigismundo de Taggia had been in charge of Estiva and Salinas for sixteen years, but by 1862 he had only two hundred Indians, mostly Chavante with some Karajá and two Canoeiro. He was a benign missionary who allowed his Karajá to

wear no clothes. Couto de Magalhães reckoned that there were seven
or eight thousand Karajá and related Xambioá, Karajaí and Javaé in
seventy villages along a thousand kilometres of river. Apart from the
handful at Estiva, none was in contact with missionaries.

When Couto de Magalhães later tried to fulfil his vision of developing the Araguaia, he created the town of Leopoldina (now
Aruanã) where the road from Goiás to Cuiabá crossed the river – his
hope being that Leopoldina would become the provincial capital. He
introduced paddle steamers and created an imposing steam navigation company of the Araguaia in 1871. Old Friar Sigismundo, exhausted from his years of missionary work, was sent downriver to
found a mission at São José do Araguaia (former Jamimbu). He was
told to organise the vigorous Karajá, who would supply food for the
steamships and help guide boats through the rapids. For a time São
José was 'a centre of evangelisation', with bands of Karajá camped
on the wide beaches nearby. Steamers plied the empty Araguaia.
They sailed north from Leopoldina down the river to a line of tiny
presídios: São José, Santa Isabel do Morro (mid-way down Bananal
island near the mouth of the Rio das Mortes), Santa Maria, Sham-
bioás and São José dos Martírios. All along the Araguaia, the Karajá
were encouraged to bring logs for the steamers' boilers and were to
be paid in tools, tobacco, clothing and salt.

Couto de Magalhães even founded a school for Indian children
called Colegio Isabel, a few miles downriver from Leopoldina. This
school was supposed to educate a contingent of Indian children
who would promote the colonisation of the Araguaia. Couto de
Magalhães hoped that the day would come when travellers would
find in any Indian village 'ten or a dozen people who speak both our
language and the native one, who can read and write, who are
Indians by language and blood but are Brazilians and Christians in
ideas, sentiment and education'. Of course, the intention went far
beyond helping travellers. The school's founder assumed that a tribe
whose children had been educated in this way 'would, following the
laws of human perfectibility, transform itself . . . sufficiently to begin
to be useful'. When the school was founded in 1871 it had twenty-one
Indian children of both sexes, from the Karajá, Kayapó and Gorotire
tribes. The number of children grew steadily until by 1879 there were
fifty-two pupils, who now included Chavante, Tapirapé and Guajajara. Visitors reported that the children were good at reading and
writing Portuguese but bad at mechanical skills. Some tried to run
away. By the late 1880s Couto de Magalhães was gone from Goiás,
and Isabel school collapsed. A French missionary wrote that 'it did

not produce the hoped-for results. Many children who boarded there died. For this or some other reason, parents refused to send more children there. Almost all who survived hurried back to their forests as soon as they left the Colegio, to resume a savage life.'

Couto de Magalhães' dream was an illusion. Although the Araguaia river teems with fish, its banks are often too arid to support settlement, and its waters rise and fall too dramatically to sustain river traffic. When Couto de Magalhães left Goiás his colonial empire quickly vanished. Leopoldina was racked by malaria and by 1890 was in decay, Isabel school was gone, and the presídios were abandoned. The steamship line was operated by different concessionaires, one of whom was an American; but in 1900 its three steamers were sold by public auction.

Much of the failure of the Araguaia frontier lay in the mismanagement of the presídios. Couto de Magalhães wanted desperately to win over the river's tribes – he even founded his own Catechism Service to try to convert them to Christianity. But his efforts were totally nullified by the brutal behaviour of the presídio garrisons. These isolated stockades were manned by soldiers whose tour of duty there was a punishment and by convicts from the frontier jails. By 1880 the garrison of Leopoldina had been withdrawn. The small village of São José do Araguaia (former São Joaquim do Jamimbu) still had a few docile Chavante and Karajá, living together in one large hut. But the main centre for Indian activity was Santa Maria do Araguaia, 160 kilometres downriver or north of the northern tip of Bananal island. It lay in an area relatively full of Indians (Karajá and northern Kayapó) and was also strategically located for river commerce. President Souza Spinola described Santa Maria in 1880 as 'an essential base for colonising efforts'. But he lamented the fact that this presídio 'has been the theatre of the most bloody fighting against Indians. Santa Maria do Araguaia has a long history of disasters and deceptions. Founded three times and dissolved as often: once by government decision; once for lack of resources; and finally attacked by the savages who inhabit both banks of the river.'

We have seen how condemned men from the prisons of Goiás were sent to Santa Maria in 1861 after the Indians had again burned it and how Friar Francisco do Monte San Vito fled from an encounter with the Karajá there. Five years later, another President wrote to the fort's commander urging him: 'Seek to prevent the [Indians] having much contact with your soldiers or ill-educated people, so that they have no reason to complain about us but will instead become convinced that we esteem them.' This President also sought to stop a nasty traffic in Indian children: local settlers were trading tools and tobacco for Kayapó children. President Gomes Siqueira ordered that anyone who obtained children in this way should be sent to Goiás for trial, for 'this traffic constitutes the crime of reducing free persons to slavery'.

There was a steady turnover in presídio commanders, and their garrisons continued to consist of the toughest and most disreputable soldiers. Finally, in 1881, President Leite de Morais decided to remove these costly and useless forts. 'The soldiers treat the Indians like beasts. A short while ago I received news that the commander of one presídio had, for no reason whatever and without any aggression or provocation, crossed to the left bank of the Araguaia and destroyed the little huts of some savages. . . . Uniforms and swords should be withdrawn from the banks of the Araguaia and Tocantins and replaced by axes and knives. Soldiers never were and never will be catechisers. Until we introduce these reforms, it is a thousand times better to leave the savages alone in their forests and rivers.' This Provincial President hoped that the Indians could be won over by trade. He opposed giving presents, which 'do not civilise, but corrupt', but he admired the way the Karajá greeted steamers with logs they had cut in return for axes, scythes and knives. 'They do not flee when the steamer approaches. The smoke does not terrify them: it is the symbol of peace.'

The Italian Capuchins did little to help. Most of these missionaries reached Brazil totally unprepared for rough life on the frontier. They disliked living in the wilds and were too rigid and arrogant towards the tribes they wished to convert. In 1872 Couto de Magalhães sent Friar Savino of Rimini to run a new aldeia among the Xambioá Karajá. After a while, someone stole a hundred sacks of salt belonging to the steamship company. 'The missionary imprudently gathered some of his men and took them to obtain satisfaction from Chief Deorodós for the missing salt. Deorodós became irritated by the insult that the friar did by calling him and all his tribe "thief". The chief brusquely answered: "We have nothing to do with your salt!" and threw himself at Friar Savino. He, in a rapid movement, grabbed his arms and started a corporal fight. At that moment one of Friar Savino's men struck a deep machete blow at the Indian's spine. He was prostrated, never to rise again. Deorodós, chief of the tribe, was dead. The furious Indians swore to avenge the death of their chief.' The Italian friar was sent to Goiás for trial, but was acquitted by a jury. He returned to the Xambioá and told their new chief that he would be their friend if they behaved. 'But if you attempt to offend me, remember that I will exterminate you from the face of the earth, and will thus remove the greatest obstacle to commerce and civilisation that exists on the Araguaia!' Official reprisals by the local garrison, acting on orders from the missionary, resulted in the deaths of thirty Indians and the wounding of as many more.

During these years, the southern Kayapó were provoked into action against settlers invading their lands. These were the descendants of the once-fierce Kayapó who had agreed to settle in aldeias near Goiás in the 1780s. They had then been the pride of the colonial authorities. No expense had been spared to create model villages for these Indians, to prove that royal officials could pacify and convert Indians as successfully as the disgraced Jesuits. We have seen how the model villages had declined by the early nineteenth century. In 1862 the President of Goiás reported that southern Kayapó were attacking settlers' farms on various rivers in the south of the province. 'It is thought, with reason, that these Indians belong to the extinct aldeias of Santa Maria [Maria I] and São José de Mossâmedes. They were expelled from there a few years ago without any plausible motive.'

Eighteen years later, the authorities were still worried by Kayapó attacks on ranches near the Verde and Bonito rivers. President Souza Spinola praised these Indians and defended them in his report of 1880. He admitted that their territory was 'one of the most suitable areas in the province for raising cattle. Because of this it has been progressively settled . . . and it is regrettable that the settlers should be exposed to attacks by the Kayapó savages. Ever since colonial times these natives have been attacking the Christian population – and vice versa.' Indians had recently killed a frontier family and the colonists organised a reprisal raid before the President could stop them. 'It is cruel to wish to exterminate these Indians, who belong to a large and strong nation and who work very hard. They are the best rowers on the Araguaia, robust and audacious workers. If they have attacked us, they have also been treated mercilessly by the Christians. Your Excellency cannot imagine how many atrocities our people have committed against the Indians, even recently. Such atrocities receive no publicity and it is difficult for my presidency to learn about them. The biggest obstacle to catechism is not the Indians' hatred of the Christians, but the latter's hatred of them.' The situation deteriorated. Conflict between settlers and Kayapó was most acute in the rich valley of the Bonito river, which a contemporary described as 'effectively the heart of Caiaponia, a region that has since time immemorial been considered as the cradle of the

Kayapó Indian nation'. The French missionary Étienne-Marie Gallais said that the settlers' invariable attitude to Indians was 'The Indian is a bad beast' and it was an act of charity to clear the land of them just as it was a service to humanity to destroy snakes or jaguars.

The authorities established a small fort called Macedina guarding the passage across the Araguaia of the Goiás–Cuiabá road (near modern Barra do Garças). The Kayapó once tried to attack the fifteen men of this outpost, but although hundreds of Indian warriors made a brave assault, they were driven off by gunfire. By 1886 the colonists of Rio Claro, a tributary of the Araguaia between Barra do Garças and modern Brasília, became exasperated by Indian attempts to defend their homeland. 'One day the able-bodied men armed themselves and organised an immense raid.' They ascended the Araguaia and Caiapó rivers in a flotilla of light boats full of ammunition and food. The raiders split, with one group moving along either bank and the flotilla liaising between them. The Indians fled, abandoning three villages. 'They left in them only some old women, children and sick people incapable of flight. These were all pitilessly massacred.' The Kayapó in revenge harassed the expedition as it retreated. During the ensuing years they attacked settlers' farms with increased fury.

By the end of the Brazilian Empire (the Emperor Pedro II abdicated in 1889), the Kayapó were threatening the city of Goiás itself. 'The authorities were alarmed by this and wondered whether they might use missionaries to calm the turbulence of these dangerous savages.'

The Bishop of Goiás turned to a French missionary, Friar Gil Vilanova, a thirty-seven-year-old Dominican from Marseilles who had just reached this part of Brazil. Vilanova spent some months in 1888 trying unsuccessfully to contact the southern Kayapó of the Rio Bonito; but he later made his name as the 'Apostle of the Araguaia' for his work among the northern Kayapó nine hundred kilometres to the north.

During these decades, the Brazilian frontier had started to clash with the northern Kayapó. The northern branch of the Kayapó nation still survives in the densely forested hills west of the Araguaia. A series of tribes lives between the middle Araguaia, Xingu, Iriri and Tapajós rivers. Tough Gê-speaking warriors, these northern Kayapó finally ceased fighting the neo-Brazilians only during the decades after the 1950s. Their main protection has been the heavy forest cover of their territories: for, unlike the southern Kayapó and other Gê-speaking tribes of the central Brazilian plateau, many of the northern Kayapó live in high hyleian rainforest. Their lands are less coveted by cattle ranchers than the more open campo and cerrado plains to the south-east.

The first references to the northern Kayapó seem to have been to a group called Nhyrkwaje, which lived between the lower Tocantins and Araguaia. This tribe suffered from the settlers of Carolina as early as 1810, and apparently migrated westwards to escape the whites. By mid-nineteenth century, travellers were talking of the Kayapó as living west of the Araguaia, a few days' march from the presídio of Santa Maria. The Kayapó were regarded as enemies of the Karajá who dominated the river itself. By 1867 the commander of the stockade of Santa Maria reported sporadic contacts with the Gradaú group of Kayapó. The Indians were trading peccaries and children with the settlers in exchange for metal tools and glass beads. The Provincial President ordered that the traffic in children must stop. He told his local commander to do everything possible to achieve 'peace and good harmony with those Indians'.

There was occasional conflict. A Kayapó chief known as Pedro held some Christian captives. The Provincial President authorised his military commander to take an armed escort to ransom these, but to try to avoid any conflict or reprisals. During the 1870s Kayapó children were taken to Couto de Magalhães' college on the upper Araguaia. But when some children died of malaria and others tried to escape back to their villages, their tribes refused to send more. In 1876 an internecine feud decimated the Kayapó living opposite the presídio. Chief Wanaô of the Gradaú had a quarrel with the Gorotire Kayapó who lived to the west. The Gorotire stole some of his pigs, and the chief led a hundred of his men and thirty women on a reprisal raid. Twenty days later, Chief Wanaô limped back with only eight followers. 'He said that they had been defeated by the Gorotire and the rest had stayed there, either dead or prisoners.'

In 1879 President Souza Spinola of Goiás travelled down the Araguaia river in one of the new steamships. The commander of Santa Maria had given presents to the Kayapó and arranged for chiefs from five of their tribes to meet the President. Souza Spinola recalled that 'they asked for peace and friendship, and wanted to settle close to us. They are, however, afraid of the Christians who are always persecuting them with raids, killing their wives and children. One showed me his foot and I saw a deep scar.' The Indians told about a battle against a mass of settlers armed with rifles. The Kayapó men managed to escape with some wounded, but the Christians killed ten women and two children. These Kayapó promised to settle a few miles west of the Araguaia beaches, in a fertile region of savannah and forests. They asked for agricultural tools, cattle, pigs and breeding mares. As so often, the main obstacle to peaceful relations with Indians lay with the settlers. The commander of Santa Maria called for immediate reinforcements, 'not because of the numerous tribe of savages, from whom he fears nothing, but because of national colonists'. A group of Kayapó were duly settled across the river from the presídio, but the experiment was short-lived. In 1881 the Kayapó could not resist making a surprise attack on their traditional enemies the Karajá. The commander of Santa Maria fort went to reprimand them, but the Indians escaped to the west. When the great German ethnologist Paul Ehrenreich sailed down the Araguaia in 1888 there was no contact with these Indians. They were 'powerful, warlike tribes who continue to be completely undisturbed by European influence and are not about to be rapidly drawn into the bosom of civilisation'.

Friar Gil Vilanova made a fruitless attempt to contact the northern Kayapó in 1891; but he returned in 1896 and was more successful. At the Barreiras rapids thirty kilometres upriver from Santa Maria, he managed to contact some Kayapó of Chief Paracantí. He organised a great banquet. These Indians had never seen cows or tasted their meat. A settler later recalled how Friar Gil had killed 'all the cattle needed to satisfy the appetites of all the stomachs of the Indians whose confidence he wished to win'. Having fed the tribe, Friar Gil seduced it with lavish promises. He explained that he planned 'to build a great house, a quicré such as they had never seen, within which he would reunite all the children of the tribe and would teach them to live well'. Chiefs Paracantí and Beca accepted, and immediately wanted to hand over their children for this fabulous education.

Gil Vilanova founded his mission for the Kayapó in May 1897 at a place he named Conceição (Conception) do Araguaia, on the west bank ninety kilometres downstream of the frontier town of Santa Maria and opposite the presídio of the same name that was destroyed in 1813. Five hundred Kayapó settled in a village a kilometre from the mission. Unfortunately for the Indians, the settlers also liked the new foundation, which was on a high bluff overlooking the river. By 1898 there were a thousand civilisados at Conceição, many of them refugees from civil wars in Maranhão following the proclamation of the republic. Friar Guillaume Vigneau arrived in that year and helped Vilanova build two vast thatched sheds: one in which to house fifty Indian children, the other in which to feed them. Each boy had a hammock, blanket and clothing; food was provided for the boys and for a procession of adult Indians who came daily to visit them. 'The system adopted in the work of catechism consisted of paying most attention to the children, taking them at the most tender age before they had contracted the habits of a savage life, and then giving them a Christian education.'

Vilanova himself described the strict regime he imposed on his school. 'At six, rise, prayer, coffee; classes from seven to 10.30; at eleven, lunch, recreation, and a walk through the aldeia under the direction of a dedicated employee; at 4.30, dinner. They go to bed at eight in the evening, and before that the children remain in the company of a missionary. That is the moment to talk to them about God and prepare their souls for the grace of baptism.' It was a deliberate return to the cradle-to-grave discipline of the Jesuits expelled 140 years previously. It was also a precursor of the great seminary-like missions established by Dominicans and Italian Salesians elsewhere in twentieth-century Brazil.

The French missionary was determined to break Kayapó tribal culture as quickly as possible. He boasted after a few years that his young pupils 'are now more disciplined: they attend school regularly and have all learned to speak Portuguese, as well as the first prayers and some responses to the catechism. Some are starting to read and write.' He regarded this as a 'great advance' on their previous way of life. They had lived in 'absolute isolation in the depths of the forests, where they lived naked, without shelter, at the mercy of their hunting; their antipathy to civilised man had reached hatred; their absolute ignorance of the Portuguese language; the war they declared against any who sought to set foot in their territory.' The ignorance, of course, was in the mind of the missionary. Far from being without shelter or short of food in their homelands, the Kayapó were excellently nourished and with a culture whose artistic and intellectual achievements far excelled the ignorant and often brutal alternative offered to them on the margin of frontier society.

Friar Gil said nothing about freedom. He appeared to be unaware that his determination to supplant tribal beliefs with those of his own religion and the attempt to settle a semi-nomadic people alongside frontiersmen were a denial of that people's liberty. He and his fellow missionaries did, however, sense that something was wrong. Friar Étienne-Marie Gallais wrote that 'from time to time, even after we thought that Indians had been conquered for civilisation, they are consumed with nostalgia for the savage life. A curious need for absolute freedom impels them towards the forest, and they will sacrifice any material advantages to satisfy that need. One of our greatest problems . . . was to combat this instinct and to hold them in Conceição.' It was difficult to discipline the young Indians. 'At the slightest dispute, they threw their clothes at [Vilanova's] head and returned to their aldeia.' Angry and frustrated missionaries condemned the Kayapó as 'inconstant and undisciplined, gluttonous and thieving, fickle and vengeful', but Friar Gil was portrayed as a paternalistic and generous figure, 'overindulgent towards his pupils, unable to refuse them anything, treating them rather like animated children'. Such kindness gained Vilanova the love of his Indians, and they accepted whatever he told them about Christian teaching. He had the sense to teach that heaven was a place full of knives, machetes, turtles, bananas and water-melons. He also allowed tribal life to continue unmolested in the main aldeia. When the German anthropologist Fritz Krause visited Conceição in 1908 he found, for instance, that only a few mission-trained young Indians wore clothes, and then only when a stranger was visiting.

The early years of Conceição de Araguaia were hard, until Friar Gil had the good idea to look northwards to the provincial government of Pará for funding. Pará was rich from rubber profits, and its government was delighted to learn that missionaries were subduing a potentially dangerous tribe on its southern frontier. The French missionary made an annual journey downriver – braving the rapids and malaria of the lower Tocantins – to seek official subsidies and private charity from Belém. In 1902 he took a boatload of Indian artefacts to sell in the city. He also tried to make his congregation develop plantations of the low-grade maniçoba rubber trees near the mission. After so many decades of failure by missionaries the experiment at Conceição rapidly gained fame in Brazil. In late 1902, Friar Gil Vilanova returned to France to lecture about his success and to raise funds. But the two founders of Conceição soon succumbed to malaria, which raged among the rubber seringueiros on the lower Tocantins. Guillaume Vigneau died in 1903 and Gil Vilanova in 1905 on his way back from Belém in one of the mission boats. The mission continued, under fresh French Dominicans. Conceição do Araguaia also survived as a colonial town and is now a fast-growing city.

The mission on the banks of the Araguaia affected only the Irã-Amranire (then known as Gradaú) tribe of Kayapó, a people who had migrated westwards from the right bank of the Araguaia. Their partial conversion had relatively little effect on other northern Kayapó tribes. Gil Vilanova told the French explorer Henri Coudreau that the wild Xikrin Kayapó lived north-west of Conceição on the Caeté headwater of the Itacaiuna river; Coudreau confirmed that there had been several contacts with members of this tribe on the lower Itacaiuna during the 1890s. The Xikrin have survived relatively unmolested: they still occupy their original habitat; their main contact with the rest of Brazil was through French Dominicans and is now with the Indian Foundation; but they are under serious threat from the gigantic iron-ore deposits discovered in the 1970s in the nearby Serra dos Carajás.

The northern Kayapó heartland lay between the Fresco and Riosinho tributaries of the Xingu, 250 kilometres west of Conceição. Although the missionaries of Conceição knew that the Gorotire Kayapó lived in those forests and savannahs, it was several decades before any lasting contact was made with that tribe. The Kayapó were, however, fragmenting because of internal conflicts. At about the time of Vilanova's death, there was a bitter quarrel between two chiefs of the large Gorotire tribe. The quarrel was resolved in a duel fought with murderously heavy war clubs. The defeated chief Motere survived and led his people westwards across the Xingu, forming a splinter group that called itself Mekragnoti or 'People who paint their upper faces with red urucum'. After 1910 fighting continued between these Mekragnoti and the Gorotire. In about 1918 the Mekragnoti migrated farther west, to settle on the upper Iriri and Curuá: a move that brought them into conflict with other Gê-speaking tribes (such as the Kruatire (Suyá) and Kreen-Akrore or 'Shaven-heads'), with non-Gê tribes of the Xingu, and with some rubber gatherers who were penetrating the lower Curuá.

The Belgian anthropologist Gustaaf Verswijver has gathered tribal legends from the Mekragnoti about those years of migration. These tribal histories tell of peaceful trading contacts between the Gorotire and the Tupi-speaking Juruna of the Xingu. The Juruna had been in contact with white colonists for centuries – they were one of the first tribes to be contacted by the Dutch and English near the mouth of the Xingu in the seventeenth century and were later subjected to Jesuit mission rule. During the nineteenth century, the Juruna gradually migrated up the Xingu towards their present location within the Xingu Indian Park near the upper river. They co-operated with rubber gatherers and this gave them access to European trade goods. The Kayapó had developed a passion for glass beads – which they still adore, particularly to bedeck their women and children. A trade developed between the powerful Gorotire Kayapó and the Juruna, and Kayapó legends tell of successful acquisition of 'little white, yellow, green and pale blue beads . . . and many dark blue and big white beads'. The legends also describe warfare, treachery and massacres, interspersed with periods of friendly trading between the Juruna and Kayapó. Another modern friend of the Gorotire Kayapó, a former Indian Protection Service official called Cícero Cavalcanti, was told about conflicts between the Indians and rubber gatherers on the Araguaia at the start of this century. The rubber men marched inland from the river with mules to carry their supplies, and the Gorotire could not resist killing some of these unknown and tempting animals which also damaged the tribe's corn crop. In revenge, rubber men shot at the Gorotire with their Winchester rifles. Although they were tough and brave warriors, the Kayapó realised that their bows and arrows and clubs were no match for carbines. 'They therefore began to carry off rifles whenever they could, and were learning to use them.'

The unequal fighting caused the tribe to withdraw from the Araguaia plain westwards to a rich plateau which Kayapó had been occupying since the mid-nineteenth century. This area, of the Fresco, Vermelho and Riosinho tributaries of the Xingu, has remained the heartland of the northern Kayapó. It is a region of forest and savannah, with beautiful hills and waterfalls to the south. There is now a continuous Kayapó reserve territory stretching from the Kokraimoro at the Serra Encontrada to the Kuben Kran Kegn and Gorotire and the recently separated villages of Kikretum and A'ukre all on the mid-Fresco river.

Bororo Surrender

Other Italian missionaries tried to convert the Bororo of Mato Grosso, sixteen hundred kilometres to the west of the Botocudo. By the late nineteenth century, the western Bororo (the Cabaçal west of Cuiabá and the Plains Bororo to their south) had long since seen their plains occupied by vast cattle ranches. These Bororo had become fine cowhands. They rode horses and mules excellently and were skilled at lassoing – they would ride close to wild cattle they wished to catch and were often gored. Decades of proximity to civilisation had brought these western Bororo only rum and moral collapse. Bororo men treat their women badly, and it was customary for men to offer women to anyone from whom they wanted a favour. Júlio Koslowski, who visited them in 1894, said that when a friend of his spent a night in one of these villages 'he was offered so many women by their husbands who wanted rum' that he had to seek protection in an old man's hut. The big ranches were full of Paraguayan and Brazilian cowboys, who did nothing to improve the Indians' morals. The great German anthropologist Karl von den Steinen described these people in 1887 as 'a decadent and wretched community: it could not survive civilisation, its syphilis and cachaça.'

Just beyond the western Bororo were the Paresi and Kabixi (pronounced Kabishi), once-docile Aruak-speaking Indians who had been taken off in droves for slavery during the eighteenth century. These now found that the old gold-mining communities of Vila Bela (Mato Grosso city) were exhausted and almost depopulated. Severino da Fonseca said that, during the 1870s, these Indians 'realised that the time had come for their revenge. They began their depredations and assaults. Isolated farms and their peaceful inhabitants were the first to be attacked. The Kabixi have gradually destroyed all the mining camps and most of the places that formed the district of the old city of Mato Grosso. . . . The last of these, São Vicente Ferrer, was destroyed by them in 1877. A few years ago they burned the Guaporé bridge and slaughtered the guard of the Jauru registro. They have also attacked Casalvasco more than once, and have robbed and burned houses in the city of Mato Grosso itself.'

A far more stubborn and effective resistance was made by the eastern Bororo, known to themselves – as we saw – as Orarimugu but to Brazilians as Coroado. These tall, powerful and handsome warriors defended forested lands between the São Lourenço headwater of the Paraguay and the upper Araguaia rivers. They thus cut the direct road link between Goiás and Cuiabá. We have seen how they were victims of countless raids and campaigns. 'Their atrocities, robberies and burning, and killing and capture of settlers' were said to occur almost every year during the 1870s and 1880s.

One President of Mato Grosso tried a desperate experiment in 1873. He enlisted the docile Terena of southern Mato Grosso to pacify the fierce Orarimugu Bororo. Chief Alexandre Bueno marched north with seventy warriors. His peaceful overtures failed, and his men then went on the warpath. They brought back a sackful of ears and two Bororo women and two children whom they had captured on a forest trail. A later President roundly condemned this policy of aggression. He handed the captives over to the Orphans Judge in Cuiabá. 'The Terena chief's expedition has, far from curbing the devastations of the [Coroado Bororo], on the contrary contributed to their resurgence. It exasperated them so greatly that they have returned to their raids up to the environs of this capital [Cuiabá].' This President regretted the money wasted on the Terena adventure. He sent the Terena chief back to his territory and 'relieved him of the commission which he himself had called "Expeller of Indians" '.

Steinen wrote that 'during the years 1875 to 1880 the Bororo were said to have burned 43 houses, killed 204 people (134 men, 46 women, 17 children and 7 slaves) and wounded twenty-seven people. . . . There is no record of how many Bororo were killed, but there is no doubt that reciprocal vengeance played a large role.'

Another solution was attempted in 1879. Military detachments were posted close to Bororo territory. Their commanders were ordered 'to repel the incursions of the Indians and to organise flying patrols in co-operation with the farmers themselves. In this way, by employing the greatest vigilance throughout the threatened area, the assaults of those treacherous enemies could be avoided. For they attack only by surprise and flee as soon as any serious resistance is offered.' This bold plan did not work. The Provincial President admitted that the flying patrols did not live up to his hopes. He was soon asking the imperial government for funds to hire 'suitable men, woodsmen who are accustomed to life in the forest and do not fear Indian ambushes . . . a rural guard, permanently maintained and well paid'.

Despite this search for fearless woodsmen, it was the Bororo who were in the ascendant. In 1878 alone they killed five people near the São Lourenço, left nine dead and six wounded in Brotas, three dead in Guia, one wounded at Vila Mendes near Cuiabá, and two dead and two wounded at Chapada. Sheriffs in the frontier villages were busily arming settlers and organising reprisals. The Bororo easily repelled such expeditions, often ambushing troops sent against them. 'One white man who had cruelly killed two Bororo children was systematically tracked for four years until the Indians succeeded in surprising him without military protection and seizing him. Not content with killing him, they tortured him and crushed his body.'

Pacification of the eastern Bororo seemed impossible until in 1885 Dr Joaquim Galdino Pimentel was appointed President of Mato Grosso. Pimentel was interested in Indian affairs and was convinced that even the most indomitable tribe would respond to kind treatment. A number of captured Bororo women were held in Cuiabá, and he sent these with a military expedition led by Ensign Antonio José Duarte. 'These seven Indian women were now civilised. They left their children among us and accompanied the force as missionaries of peace. They were to convince the Indians of that region of the utility and advantages that civilised life had to offer them.' Once in the forests, the women went ahead. They removed their clothes and painted themselves with red urucum. Their tribe was overjoyed to see them, and they were welcomed with three days of feasting. The women succeeded only too well in their mission. The entire tribe of four hundred decided to accompany them; but in the event there was room in the expedition's launch for only twenty-eight.

Ensign Duarte recalled that he did not have enough clothing to dress all these Indians, so he borrowed items from his troops. 'Their entry into the camp took place at seven in the evening – an unsuitable hour to receive a barbaric and armed group, but what else could I do? . . . I arranged my force in the best order, taking up appropriate positions. They all entered my camp armed, with the civilised Indian women coming in front. Each man came up to me and surrendered his weapons, extending both hands and grasping mine with considerable strength.' Everyone in Cuiabá was surprised and delighted by this success. A local magazine wrote: 'Undeniable proof of this sentiment is the majestic escort of ladies and gentlemen of both political parties, including the Provincial President and many authorities and functionaries, which greeted the expedition when it entered this city, from the bridge over the Coxipó river, where they were awaited, to the building called Couto de Magalhães camp on the bank of the Cuiabá river, where all the Indians are conveniently lodged.' The city council praised President Pimentel, and an effusive letter of congratulation came from the Corumbá Immigration Company, which was trying to attract European colonists to the region. The Bororo stayed in Cuiabá for forty-four days. 'Throughout the time of their stay among us, the Indians were given presents and welcomed by the populace. They walked through the streets of the city, entered houses, and returned contented to their camp on the banks of the Cuiabá river, where they spent a happy time. His Excellency [the President] visited them almost daily, gave them many gifts, offered them meals in his palace, and was their godfather on the occasion of their baptism, a ceremony that took place in the Church of the Rosary on 29 June 1886.' The Bororos' young chief Moguyokuri was described as 'a practical Indian, 1.9 metres tall and, despite some inherent brutality, a naturally genial gentleman.' But Steinen dismissed as rubbish local press reports that this chief used to give the President gifts, smiling with pleasure as he did so. When the Bororo left Cuiabá, they were seen off at the river bank by the President, the police chief, the military commandant and other dignitaries. The local press reported that 'a musical band played beautiful marches, appropriate to the parade.'

Back on the São Lourenço river, more Bororo filed out of the forests and were clothed by Ensign Duarte. As he saw it, they had 'resigned the savage life to embrace that of civilisation'. They celebrated the change with a night-long dance, to the music of horns and punctuated by 'frightening grunts'. The Bororo were then assembled in a 'Military Colony' called Tereza Cristina on the banks of the São Lourenço. Ensign Duarte was in command, and he instituted an extraordinary system of acculturation: officers, soldiers and Indians lived together in a wild round of dances, drink and promiscuity. Karl von den Steinen visited Tereza Cristina two years after its foundation. He watched a moonlit dance between the soldiers and mulatto and Indian women. 'They were making music with accordions, plates and forks – expansive merriment everywhere!' When a cow was slaughtered, its meat and bones were heaped on its skin. The

Indian men, women and children waited alongside carrying baskets. An officer gave a signal, and the mob of Indians rushed at the meat like a pack of wolves. The tribe became hopelessly addicted to cachaça rum. Von den Steinen was amazed to see Chief Moguyokuri come to the junior officers dressed in a red woman's blouse and a white linen jacket, demanding cachaça. He finally got his bottle of rum, and was equally successful whenever he woke up the officers late into the night. Cachaça was, of course, also the currency for the seduction and prostitution of Bororo women.

Steinen said that Duarte was truly ' "the god of the Coroados". He gave them everything they wanted and kept them quiet by this simple method, which did not cost him much.' The provincial government provided funds, and Lieutenant Duarte profited by selling supplies to his men at inflated prices. The German anthropologist was shocked to find no teaching of Bororo children, no training in agriculture or religious instruction. The Bororo lived in small rectangular huts arranged in rows around a central plaza. At the time of Steinen's visit there were two hundred Indian warriors with their wives and children, and fifty Brazilians with their women. The Bororo were very casual about the shoddy clothes, blankets and tablecloths they had been given in Cuiabá. They discarded most items of clothing or used them to carry fish or meat. 'They never dreamed of washing their linen: their shirts looked as mud-coloured as their bodies or as the earth or the huts.' Spoiled and demoralised by the new regime, the Indians refused to farm. They ate the soldiers' crops as fast as they grew, cutting and sucking ripening sugar cane, digging up growing manioc, or cutting down piquiri trees to get at their fruit.

One of the Bororo women who had shed her clothes and persuaded her tribe to surrender to Ensign Duarte was called Rosa Bororo. This formidable woman lived on until 1913 in a village of the Bakairi, of which her son had become chief. But she came to regret her mediation in 1885. Before dying she advised her son: 'Do not trust the whites. They are men who control the lightning, who live without a homeland, who wander to satisfy their thirst for gold. They are kind to us when they need us, for the land that they tread and the plains and rivers they assault are ours. Once they have achieved their goals they are false and treacherous.'

Frontier fighting against the eastern Bororo was not finished. In 1890 a settler from Goiás attracted two hundred Indians and led them to a well which he had poisoned. The Indians drank deeply from the apparently clear water and all died. The Brazilian press roundly condemned this atrocity – but Czech and French anthropologists noted that 'as usual, this act was not punished by the representatives of civilisation, the Bororos not being Christian.' The Bororo naturally retaliated. 'To avenge this horrible and inhuman crime . . . the Indians in turn slaughtered all civilisados who could not resist their attacks. In these surprise attacks, whole families perished and large numbers of cattle suffered hunger.' The entire family of one white-bearded settler, Emanuel Ignacio, was surprised in his farm near the Araguaia. The patriarch was clubbed to death in his hammock and his sons, daughters and grandchildren were transfixed by long spears. A black servant woman returned from fetching water and found the gruesome scene. She crept into the house and found Ignacio's gun, which she fired at the Indians who were ransacking the place.

It was on this turbulent frontier that Cândido Mariano da Silva Rondon – a man destined to become the greatest champion of native rights – had his first experience of Indians. The Brazilian government was determined to link Cuiabá to the east coast by a strategic telegraph line. This had been completed as far west as the Araguaia river and it now had to cross the dangerous territory of the eastern Bororo. An enlightened army engineer, Major Ernesto Gomes Carneiro, was put in charge. He chose as his adjutant the twenty-five-year-old Lieutenant Cândido Rondon, a young officer who had graduated top of his class at the Escola Militar in Rio de Janeiro and had just obtained a degree in mathematics and natural sciences at the senior war college. He had also played a role in the bloodless revolution of 1889 which ended the Brazilian Empire and introduced the republic. Yet he was from Mato Grosso, born in a humble village near Cuiabá; and his great-grandmother was a Plains Bororo.

Rondon reached Cuiabá in April 1890 and by July the line of new telegraph poles had advanced 130 kilometres to the east. The route was now entering the lands of the hostile Bororo. Major Gomes Carneiro chose Rondon to push forward on a reconnaissance with him. At times they were reopening an old trail abandoned because of Indian attack. At other times they were exploring, cutting into virgin forest and savannah. They pressed forward, riding their mules from daybreak to late afternoon, and camping with the mules still wearing halters and with sentries and guard dogs posted. During this expedition, Rondon came to worship his superior officer. Gomes Carneiro was a brilliant leader and an ardent naturalist who taught Rondon the names of plants and animals. Above all, he was humane, with a

new conciliatory approach to Indians. He fixed notices to his telegraph poles forbidding anyone to try to kill the Bororo or expel them
from their land. He even declared that 'no one should ever shoot at
Indians even to frighten them.'

As the expedition advanced, there were increasing signs of Indians: hunting shelters, broken twigs, remains of recent fires. Near the
headwaters of the Barreiro, a tributary of the Garças ('Herons') and
Araguaia, the two officers became convinced of the presence of
Bororo and carefully corralled their mules. Rondon later recalled
Major Gomes Carneiro waking him in the middle of the night and
calling softly to him: ' "Cândido, are you listening?" The forest was
becoming animated. At some distance around our campsite apes
yelled and howler-monkeys roared, prego macaques were whistling,
jaós [large game birds] and partridges were chirping . . . it was as if
all the wildlife around us was conversing. "I can hear the chirps of
partridges – but they do not chirp at night like jaós. Apart from that,
it is not natural for all the animal life to decide to converse at this
hour of the night." "What do you think, then?" "That these are
Indians communicating to one another at a distance." Gomes Carneiro got up. "I am determined never to fight Indians. Besides being
unjust, it would prejudice the results of our expedition. We have
only one recourse: to strike camp and leave. We can thus give the
Bororo a victory, for they are planning to avenge on us the armed
attacks of which they have been victims." ' So the expedition extinguished its fires, gathered the animals from their corral, and moved off
in darkness before the Bororo could launch their dawn attack. The
reconnaissance successfully reached the Araguaia, and during the
following year Rondon and his men erected the telegraph line, often
working in appalling conditions, without food, drenched in tropical
rains and buffeted by lightning storms. Rondon paid tribute to
Gomes Carneiro almost seventy years later. He called him 'my
beloved master of the sertão. There you taught me to be a soldier. . . .
It was with you that I learned to love Indians, partly by pondering the
orders you enforced to defend and protect them, along the telegraph
line through Bororo country, but also by your thrilling example of
yielding in the face of the warnings that Indians nobly give to invaders of their lands before making them know violently that their
presence is disagreeable.'

A new Italian missionary order now appeared in Mato Grosso: the
Salesians, founded in 1859 by the Italian San Giovanni Bosco in
honour of the Swiss saint François de Sâles, Bishop of Geneva in the
late sixteenth century. In 1895, when it had become obvious that

military rule of Bororo villages was a disaster, the provincial government invited Salesian missionaries to take charge of Tereza Cristina. They found its Indians addicted to a daily ration of cachaça, which the soldiers paid them for their labour. The missionary, Father Giovanni Balzola, was determined to stamp out alcohol, even though the Bororo depended on it for spiritual inspiration and social release. One Salesian wrote: 'The soldiers were gradually reduced in numbers. The first concern of Dom Balzola and the other missionaries was to teach work by example. They themselves worked in the fields from morning to evening. They were thus able to reduce and gradually suppress the use of pinga [rum].'

But the attempt was too violent, and the missionaries proved unable to extirpate drinking and dancing, which the Indians so greatly enjoyed. Balzola himself claimed that he proceeded gradually: 'We were accustoming them to work, but at that time we avoided anything difficult. We ourselves had to spend the day working with them, to encourage and teach them how to use farm tools and methods. Even when I was absent for a while on pious observance, I would have to interrupt perhaps to put a handle on a hoe or to adjust an axe or other tool, which they continually broke by their rough way of using them.' All this was too disagreeable for the Indians. Thus, although Father Balzola was quite well liked, his prohibition of alcohol and insistence on work produced an uprising that threatened his life. By 1898, the provincial authorities decided that the Bororo had been progressing better under lay rule. They asked the Salesians to withdraw. A lay director, Manoel Canavarões, was installed at Tereza Cristina, only to make the rather surprising claim that he could do nothing with the Indians because they had become too idle under missionary rule.

An American called Cook was able to visit eight villages of unacculturated Bororo in 1900. He reached the Ponte de Pedra (Stone Bridge) tributary of the São Lourenço after a gruelling eight-hundred-kilometre ride from Goiás. 'The last sixty or seventy miles was through an exceedingly wild and almost unknown region of forest and dense bush that made travelling almost like pushing through a network of barbed-wire sieves, where we were constantly raked and torn, and were drenched by the daily thunderstorms.' Other parts of Bororo territory are far more beautiful. Their plateau is part of the geologically ancient central Brazilian shield. Its weathered sandstones are cut into dramatic table mountains, with cliffs visible for miles across the low forests. From the tops of these flat mountains there are sudden, unexpected and sweeping views into hidden valleys or across immense plains.

Cook made his journey with a Brazilian explorer called Antonio Cândido de Carvalho, who was well known to the Bororo. The Indians soon appeared in large numbers at the explorers' camp, hoping for presents. 'They pour in upon us regularly at the break of day and stay faithfully till the shadows of night begin to deepen. . . . They recline on our boxes, sprawl on our tables . . . squat on the ground, and hunch down around our pot as it boils, always leaving a patch of [red] paint wherever they sit or lean. Some smoke, others lazily pick and eat the kernels from a roasted ear of corn, others nibble the white cheese-like heart of a diminutive palm. . . . The boys devour bits of fish roasted black, or shoot at a stick or a stump with their crude bows and arrows.'

Many things about the Bororo impressed Cook. He admired their brilliance as swimmers and fishermen. They fished very successfully with nets and harpoons. 'A Bororo will remain in the water an hour or two continuously, and return ashore with six or eight large fish. They have learned to turn their bodily strength to the greatest account while in the water.' Bororo women were particularly hard-working, and the men knew all the plants and creatures of the forest. 'They are communistic, and therefore little inclined to attempt any-thing extensive in the way of agriculture or to provide a stock of food. For if one family should do this, it would only be to divide the harvest with the rest of the community and leave themselves with nothing for the morrow. There is thus no incentive for labor, except when hunger drives them in search of food.'

Cook described the very elaborate Bororo funeral ceremonies, and the tribe's many songs and dances. He could not understand the faith-healing role of the shamans, whom he dismissed as opportunis-tic charlatans. After one song, he watched fascinated as the singers moulded a mixture of black earth and ash 'and made animals in relief on the ground, especially the tapir which they were to hunt next day. This is also a tribute of honor to the animals. . . . As they had seen men hunting on horses and admired this method, they formed a horse in relief with a man mounted on it.'

As a visiting male, Cook was allowed into the great central hut, which he described as the 'bachelors' hall/workshop for making arrows'. 'It is entered through an opening at each end, like a hole in a haystack, and within is always damp, gloomy, and foul smelling.' Family huts were no better. 'Deep gloom reigns within these huts. They are made dark that they may be free from flies, and are dens of rubbish and filth. Stuck into the roof are bows and bundles of arrows, war clubs, fishing gear, and instruments and ornaments not in use. The occupants of this human lair are sprawled on a palm-leaf rug, with a log of wood . . . for a pillow, and sleeping or gnawing an ear of corn, a bit of fish or vegetable, or sitting tailor fashion making beads, arrows or other objects, or kneeling by the little fire preparing food.'

There was continued fighting with the uncontacted Bororo. A fazendeiro called Clarismondo used to have good relations with part of the tribe, who would occasionally visit his farm and be given food. On one visit things went wrong. The Indians asked for more rapadura – hard brown sugar – but were refused. A fight ensued, during which Clarismondo was wounded but fought back, his younger brother was killed, and his mother and other relatives wounded by Indian clubs. The Bororo were driven off with several dead. Not content with this, Clarismondo determined on vengeance. The government refused to help him, but in 1902 he assembled sixteen friends, heavily armed, and they tracked the Indians along the Barreiro. They saw two Indians fishing and silently followed them to their village. The usual dawn attack followed, with Indians shot down as they ran from their huts. A Salesian missionary wrote that 'the civilisados, drunk with blood and vengeance, spared no one. Those who managed to hide in the tall trees were discovered and became living targets: when their bodies fell heavily to the ground they were reduced to shapeless masses.' The ground was covered in dead bodies. In this and another similar attack, Clarismondo's gang massacred over a hundred Bororo of all ages and both sexes.

The Salesians now returned, though they were not yet allowed to resume their administration of Tereza Cristina. Those who visited this colónia in 1905 found it a sombre place, with a cemented house for the director, a telegraph station, and a row of five small clay-and-thatch huts occupied by mestizos and a Guató Indian family. Nearby was a round 'catechism hut', and the Bororo of Chief Dotte lived in six other huts. Most of the Indians lived farther up the river, and they were developing good plantations of maize, manioc, sugar cane and rice.

The Salesians moved on to the Barreiro river and managed, despite Clarismondo's massacres there, to attract some Indians. Father Balzola overcame the suspicious hostility of these Bororo and created a mission called Santo Cuore. In 1908 other Bororo were raiding new farms on the Vermelho. The Provincial President wrote to ask the Salesians to help, and Father Balzola managed to persuade the Indians to stop their vendetta against the whites. He boasted that 'a good many even entered the service of the fazendeiros. The men tended their cattle and the women did domestic work.'

From then on, the Italian missionaries rapidly expanded their domain. By 1911 all former territories of the Bororo belonged to the Salesians. Children were isolated from their parents to receive special intensive religious training. The Indians lived in wattle-and-daub houses which were manifestly inferior to their traditional huts. Most seriously, the rectangular layout of the missions undermined Bororo social custom, which depended on a circular plan with divisions into clans and moieties (each moiety occupying a side of the circle of huts) and a central men's hut. The Bororo were thoroughly detribalised. In return, they gained food from the mission's extensive plantations – which they of course worked. Henry Savage-Landor, a boastful English explorer, visited one Salesian mission in 1911 and was impressed by its neat buildings and surrounding farmlands. 'I inspected the buildings where useful trades were taught to the Indians of both sexes. Weaving-looms and spinning-wheels had been imported at great expense and endless trouble, as well as blacksmiths' and carpenters' tools of all kinds. . . . What pleased me most of all was to notice how devoted to the Salesians the Indians were, and how happy and well cared for they seemed to be. They had the most humble reverence for the Fathers.' Savage-Landor was pleased by the sight of a tidy European garden and the incongruous sound of Bororo children playing Verdi songs on brass and stringed instruments.

After some years of such activity, the Salesians were able to claim that they had opened the vast region inhabited by the eastern Bororo to white colonisation. When they arrived there, 'it could not be securely inhabited by whites nor even safely crossed by them without a strong military escort. Now, by contrast, the plateau of Mato Grosso east of Cuiabá is rapidly being settled by fazendeiros, and numerous diamond prospectors visit diamond-bearing deposits of the Garças basin with impunity.'

Xingu

On 11 August 1884 there was a thrilling contact with unknown Indians in the heart of Brazil. For once, this discovery was made not by adventurers, rubber tappers or surveyors, but by anthropologists in sympathy with the people they were meeting. The leader of the expedition which made this momentous contact was Karl von den Steinen, a twenty-nine-year-old German who had gained anthropological experience on the Marquesas Islands in the South Pacific and was returning to Europe from a German expedition to the remote Antarctic island of South Georgia. Steinen persuaded the authorities in Cuiabá to allow him to march his team north-eastwards to the headwaters of the mighty Xingu river. His expedition was given an escort of twenty-nine soldiers as protection in a totally unknown region.

It was extraordinary that the Xingu was still unexplored in the late nineteenth century. All the other major southern tributaries of the Amazon had long since been mapped, travelled and even settled. The lower Xingu had had a Dutch fort in the early seventeenth century and Jesuit missions during the following 150 years. It had been sporadically settled; explored in 1843 by Prince Adalbert of Prussia and the young Count Otto von Bismarck; and exploited by rubber tappers. But all the upper Xingu was still terra incognita. Steinen himself exclaimed: 'One often wonders how it is possible for a river that emerges so close to [Belém do] Pará, a mile wide, completely free of any island, a grandiose mass of crystalline water full of fishes, whose banks are without doubt among the most fertile in Pará . . . can be known for only a small part of its course.'

Steinen's expedition consisted of three Germans and six Brazilians, in addition to the military escort, which departed after the headwaters of the Xingu had been reached. It was carried across the scrubby plains of northern Mato Grosso by nine mules, twenty-five oxen and six dogs. The team went first to a village of christianised Carib-speaking Bakairi who lived on a source of the Paranatinga (Teles Pires): fifty-five people in ragged shirts, trousers and dresses who had been in contact with the Brazilians of Cuiabá since 1820. The German anthropologists got on well with the Bakairi chief Captain Reginaldo, who wore the Brazilian army uniform that was the badge of office of chiefs of acculturated tribes. It was known that there was a group of uncontacted Bakairi on the Xingu, so Steinen persuaded Chief Reginaldo and some of his men to accompany the expedition. They marched eastwards and, after two weeks, reached the Batovi (Tamitatoaia) headwater of the Xingu, built eight jatobá-bark canoes, and set off down the unknown river.

The expedition sailed for seventeen days down the beautiful empty Batovi, camping on islands or sandbanks or in the screen of trees that hides its banks from the more open campo undergrowth beyond. On 11 August, just as they prepared to tackle another set of rapids, they were surprised to see an Indian canoe tied to the bank. They were about to experience the excitement, and danger, of contact with an unknown tribe. 'Where are the Indians? We all assemble and, leaving three men to guard the canoes, advance with weapons in our hands. The ground is strewn with jatobá fruit, but a well-defined path leads inland. We pass a tree on whose bark are crudely carved figures of a man above and a woman below, half life size. Our column marches silently through the forest. The narrow path is interrupted; there is a clearing.' This proved to be a half-cleared roça, with tangled felled trees and branches being burned ready for planting, which explained a column of smoke that the expedition had seen for the past few days. 'We clamber cautiously over this clearing and march again along the forest trail. "Beiju", one man whispers and triumphantly points to some crumbs which give us a vision of new food supplies. "They have beijus [manioc bread]", each man whispers to the one behind him.' There is an arrow leaning against a tree. 'We become more serious and even the blacks, who had tried to pluck up courage through conversation, now march forward without saying a word. From time to time there are small fires, either alight or extinguished. We have already been going for three-quarters of an hour. But look: another clearing! A lovely cluster of bocaiuva palms loaded with fruit; grains of corn on the ground; another small patch of forest, and "Houses" calls the front man. Three beehive-shaped huts are visible and the one in front, at the end of our path, has its low door open. We can make out some heads in the darkness. An entirely naked Indian emerges, young and well built, shuts the door and comes towards us, holding horizontally a long arrow shaft without its point. I tell Antonio to greet him in Bakairi. Antonio, hardly able to breathe, calls out "Kxulino!" and, thank heavens, the Indian answers in Bakairi. He advances anxiously to Antonio, leans against him, and the two walk onward embracing one another, both talking at once, and both trembling all over their bodies from a mixture of fear and excitement. We are all overcome with a happy feeling of relief.'

During the following days the expedition had the magical experience of first contact with a hitherto-unknown people. The Germans were impressed by the quality and artistry of Bakairi handicrafts – intricate baskets, wooden stools carved in animal shapes; combs of creeper spines bound together with consummate skill, shell necklaces and superb feather ornaments of brilliant blues and reds from macaws, white from egrets, black from wild turkeys, and green, yellow and scarlet from parrots. They were entertained by the booming of sacred flutes, and participated in moonlit dances to a hypnotic rhythmic stamping and drumming. They admired the handsome Bakairi: the men totally naked, their athletic bodies muscular from constant wrestling, hunting, fishing and forest clearing; the women with long, shining black hair and equally naked apart from uluris, tiny triangular coverings so small that they fitted within the lips of their hairless genitals. Karl von den Steinen wrote an admirable description of these anthropological marvels in his classic *Durch Central-Brasilien* (*Through Central Brazil*).

Almost more important than Steinen's details of Xingu Indians' customs and possessions was his attitude to the Indians themselves. Although he appreciated their edenic simplicity and the beauty of their country, he was no romantic of the 'noble savage' school. He portrayed Indians as real people, intelligent and resourceful but with the usual virtues and defects. Individual Indians emerge from his narrative as distinct personalities. They were shown to have a good sense of humour, capable of being callous or timorous, and were quick-witted. Such treatment was a refreshing contrast to the abstract pontificating about the native problem by so many theorists who had no intimate contact with tribal society.

Steinen noticed how the Bàkairi reacted to their first sight of white men. 'One cannot say that the barbarians expressed great amazement about us. They generally paid no attention to the colour of our skins or to our beards. They freely admired the clothes, machetes and binoculars – but like children who take Christmas presents as though they had experienced it all before. A demonstration of shooting provoked great fright among them. the women ran off and the men crowded together and laughed embarrassedly when they saw our merriment. But to prevent a repetition, they insistently begged us: "Ala, ala – enough." Our dogs, which were strange to them, so appalled [one Indian] that he showed a determination to shoot them dead.' Steinen concluded that 'these Bakairi "savages" are skilful, lively and certainly very agreeable. They do not steal, even though we had brought veritable treasures. They use no strong drink and refuse tobacco.'

The upper Xingu is unique among surviving Indian regions of Brazil in having a cluster of tribes of different languages which live together in relative harmony. These tribes trade with one another, occasionally intermarry, fight only rarely, and regularly compete in intertribal games – contests of wrestling and archery. Through centuries of contact, they have come to resemble one another closely in ornaments, haircuts, houses, artefacts and customs. There are tribes speaking the main languages of native Brazilians: Tupi-speaking Kamayurá and Aweti; Carib-speaking Bakairi, Nahukuá, Kalapalo and Kuikuro; Aruak-speaking Mehinaku, Yawalapití and Waurá; and Trumai and Txikão, whose languages are 'isolated' or different from the main linguistic trunks. These tribes all live on the fan of small rivers that form the headwaters of the Xingu. A few days' canoe journey down the broad main river live the Gê-speaking Suyá; and soon after Steinen's visit, the Gê-speaking Txukarramãe Kayapó migrated upriver into this area.

The 1884 expedition had the privilege of contacting a number of these tribes. After a few days with the Bakairi, it visited the now-extinct Aruak-speaking Kustenaú. Steinen noted that this group used hammocks of buriti-palm fibre, superior to the cotton hammocks of the Bakairi and a sign that this Aruak tribe had migrated up the Xingu from the Guianas and Caribbean far to the north. The German anthropologist traded a hammock for a couple of kitchen knives, after strenuous haggling. 'The women here take part in the conversation. They participate in the bargaining without being asked, and are always sure not to give anything away. I bear no grudge against the owner of the hammock, a young lad whose crafty and impudent expression reminded me of the shoplifters in Berlin police files. He was newly married. His wife was about twenty-five, with large shining eyes: sitting there in her youthful happiness, she swung in her hammock and talked to me with animation.'

This was an expedition of pure exploration. Its members were not sure whether they were on the waters of the Xingu or Tapajós until they encountered large tributary rivers entering from the west. On 30 August they emerged from the headwaters on to the wide waters of the great Xingu river. 'We had for a long time been wandering as if in an enchanted garden: we could not escape from the dense vegetation and narrow devouring pathways. We had suddenly reached a broad, straight avenue.' They were delighted to be briefly freed from 'these men who think only of the present, this inexhaustible foliage, the swarms of insects, all the endless exuberant world of the tropics.'

They had further exciting encounters with new tribes. One morning the Trumai suddenly appeared. A long line of canoes emerged slowly and silently on to a curve of river in front of the expedition's camp. 'Two Indians stood motionless in each canoe, with their bows ready, while a third sat in the middle and scarcely seemed to move his paddle. We counted fourteen canoes and forty-three people. In perfect order, as if performing a carefully rehearsed theatrical production, the long narrow vessels glided noiselessly towards the forested far bank, well away from our beach.' The Trumai warriors were naked, painted in black and red dyes, and wearing white feather headdresses. They did not speak or give any commands. Then they suddenly broke the silence with a show of aggression, beating their chests, shouting fanatically and swaying their bodies and legs. Steinen commented: 'Had any of us been even half so excited, while standing in a canoe, we would immediately have fallen helplessly into the water as soon as we tried to copy them! But we were on solid ground and the example was infectious. So we also howled and roared and beat our chests.' When the German party shouted in Bakairi there was no response; but when Steinen recalled two words of Trumai that he had been taught, the Indians became friendly. After a debate, they paddled over to the beach and landed. 'Each of us grabbed one of them by the arm, whereupon another of them quickly attached himself to our other arm; and in this way we walked fraternally up to our camp.'

All seemed to be going well. Then one of the German guns was accidentally fired. 'What panic! Did they fear that the earth would open and swallow them up? That was elementary terror: there was no question that we controlled the thunder and lightning. With a few bounds they were all back in their canoes, pushed off, paddled with all their might, shouting, and only calmed down when they were back in the middle of the river.' No friendly gesture could lure the Trumai back. It was then discovered that they had run off with

'Manuel's pistol, Castro's, Wilhelm's and Antonio's hats, Quintiliano's shotgun, the soldering iron and I don't know what else! It seemed incredible that they could have grabbed so many things in such a short space of time.' The Indians had either thought that they were trading their manioc bread for these objects, or they might simply have been examining them. The expedition's military escort pursued the retreating Trumai, fired a volley, and recovered the missing items when the Indians landed and abandoned their canoes.

The delicate and dangerous business of contacting this tribe had miscarried. Steinen was naturally sad at the failure. But he was also relieved, for the Bakairi had warned that the Trumai were known to receive strangers well, surreptitiously take their weapons, and then suddenly attack them. 'The narrators also added that these Indians used to pull their enemies' arms out of their sockets – "poc, poc, poc" – tie their hands and throw their helpless bodies into the river. Thank heavens we escaped a similar fate.'

Three days later, on 3 September 1884, the expedition contacted yet another unknown tribe. They had sailed on down the broad Xingu. At that time of year – the end of the dry season – there would have been wide sandbanks exposed below the towering vegetation on either bank. They started to see huts and people on the shore. Suddenly five long canoes appeared from a side stream, full of women and children returning from a plantation with greenery, manioc and fruit. The women were appalled by the sight of men from an alien world. 'They propelled their canoes hastily to the bank, snatched up their children and, with the smallest infants on their left hips, ran shrieking into the forest to reach their huts overland.' One canoe containing three men and one fat old woman allowed the strangers' canoes to approach it. The expedition then paddled straight towards the tribe's village. This was another moment of first contact, thrilling and dangerous for the Europeans but a terrible shock for the native tribe. Steinen was pleased to see that the men of this tribe wore lip discs: a sure sign that they were the much-feared Kayapó tribe called Suyá.

'What confusion among these primitive people! Some forty men had assembled there, all naked, their bodies streaked unartistically with black and red dyes, some with white or orange feather head-dresses, some with loose, tangled hair hanging down to their shoulders. All were armed with bows and arrows and also clubs. All had their lower lips monstrously deformed by discs, painted red on top, that projected horizontally in front of their teeth like small salvers. None kept his mouth still for an instant. . . . "Suyá. Suyá.

Tahahá Suyá. Tahahá Suyá." The roaring of the frenzied pack always finished with these words repeated in every key. They brandished their weapons and leaped about with their eyes fixed on us.'

Steinen went at the front of the lead canoe with Dr Clauss, bravely prepared to land and trying to demonstrate their good intentions through sign language. The Suyá's outrage increased. They were in disaccord. 'Two were so agitated that they had a fight and then jumped on to two boulders that lay in the water and gesticulated violently. Every movement was accompanied by their "Tahahá! Tahahá!" They pointed out their bows, and pressed their left hands in quick succession down their chests, arms and legs, as if they wanted to make it clear to us that our weapons and clothing seemed suspicious to them. I laid down my gun and my intelligent Suyá [interpreter] immediately followed my example, placing his bow and arrows on the ground, clapped his hands and shouted "Tahahá! Tahahá!" But they would not let us land. At our slightest movement to do so, their agitation grew to a crescendo. In an unequivocal manner, all their arms pointed downriver as if to say: "That way: your route is that way." Meanwhile Castro and the others approached. The Indians' most suspicious looks were aimed at our dogs, for it would have been entirely contrary to dogs' general nature to remain as quiet observers in the midst of all that din: they were barking with all their might and in their exasperation we could scarcely prevent them from jumping ashore to create unholy problems with these redskins.'

Steinen's expedition had to withdraw to the far bank of the Xingu. A Suyá canoe then followed them and the tribe's suspicions were allayed in the usual way: by the attractions of barter. Steinen himself waded out into the water to proffer a flannel shirt, and when this was finally exchanged for some sweet potatoes the spell was broken. 'Soon other Indians approached; there was much shouting to the far bank, and all went well. They landed; in no time a lively trade was in progress.' Feather headdresses were bartered for trade goods, including fish-hooks, which were new to the Suyá but which they pretended to understand. The fraternisation between the two alien races continued far into the night on that sandbank. Steinen imagined how this amazing encounter would enter Suyá legends: tribal bards would tell of the brief visit by strange people, but they could show knives, mirrors, fish-hooks and axes as tangible proof of their reality.

The anthropologists later visited the Suyá village, a place of some 150 people living in nine straw huts. The Germans introduced the

concept of drawing on paper to the Suyá, and the Indians made
fluent, geometric designs of familiar objects. One man also drew an
excellent map of the upper Xingu in the sand, with rapids, waterfalls
and the villages of every tribe neatly marked along the winding
course of the river. The Suyá were also invited to draw the German
expedition and did so in a novel way. We have pictures of Steinen's
team, standing in a group photo looking remarkably modern, with
full beards, broad-brimmed floppy straw hats, open-necked long-
sleeved checked shirts, tough baggy trousers, and boots or sandals.
The Suyá drawing of this group showed the men's unkempt hair and
bushy beards. But their matchstick bodies wore no clothing whatever: instead of clothing, the native artist carefully drew a fine set
of genitals on each European!

Suyá women also surprised the Germans by their candour. Three
women once visited the camp in a canoe, with two of their men.
'The women came in the simplicity of paradise, and no less innocence. They wanted to have intimate relations with us – something
that did not conform to our rigorous discipline! Their male companions demonstrated this desire by sign language that could easily be
understood by all peoples at all times. . . . The women were completely naked and were neither young nor beautiful, but they were in no
way promiscuous or embarrassing. Their naturalness was truly asto-
nishing. They landed from the canoes and washed themselves in the
most open manner, thus demonstrating that they still had a naive
innocence that critics deny to the Medici Venus.'

Steinen was intrigued by Indian nakedness and by his reactions to
it. He sought to convey to his nineteenth-century readers how natural and unshocking it seemed. 'After a quarter of an hour a visitor is
no longer aware of this wicked nakedness. But if you do deliberately
remember it and ask yourself whether the naked people – fathers,
mothers and children who stand around or walk about so innocently
– should be condemned or pitied for their nakedness, you must
either laugh at your question as something utterly absurd or protest
against it as unworthy. From an aesthetic point of view lack of
covering, like truth itself, has its pros and cons: young healthy
people may look enchanting in their unconstrained movements, but
the old and sick are often dreadful in their decay.'

On a later return to the Xingu, he was struck by the beauty of a
young Bakairi mother. She had 'a finely cut European face with full
lips, lightly reddened cheeks framed by thick waving hair, and the
most beautiful eyes I had seen in all Brazil – which is saying a great
deal. They were large eyes whose lovely look contained no coquetry,

but whose piercing fire blazed with a full, naively tender impact –
and a spark of innocent lasciviousness. . . . With a body that had
never been laced up or mishandled, she really looked like a young
mother Eve. Sadly, she scratched her head too often. This may
sometimes have been done from embarrassment, but lice also contributed to cause it.'

Along with nudity went a candour about sex that was a revelation
to Steinen's puritanical and often hypocritical contemporaries. 'Our
natives have no secret parts of their bodies. They joke about them in
words and pictures with complete frankness that it would be idiotic
to regard as indecent. . . . Some of them celebrate puberty for both
sexes with noisy festivities during which they actively demonstrate
interest and exuberance about their "private parts". If a man wants
to tell a stranger that he is another's father or a woman to demonstrate that she is a child's mother . . . they touch the organs from
which life springs, with instinctive and natural openness.'

The corollary to Indians' nakedness was their attitude to European dress. Steinen described a Bakairi warrior's embarrassment
when he needed help trying on some trousers – he tried to put them
on backwards and over his head. Another Bakairi had difficulty
taking off a jacket. 'Our clothing was just as remarkable to these
good people as their nakedness was to us. When I went to bathe I was
accompanied by men and women and had to permit all my layers of
clothing to be minutely examined. They had no idea that their
curiosity might upset me.' The Indians admired a tattooed kiwi that
Steinen had acquired in the Pacific, 'but to my satisfaction, they were
visibly disappointed that there were no greater marvels under my
careful and curious wrappings.'

Karl von den Steinen wrote superb ethnographical accounts of all
aspects of Indian life. He particularly appreciated the glories of
Indian culture. He was interested in the origins of their decorations,
the skill and artistry of their manufactures, their invention of ceramics and of the twirling stick for making fire, the reasons for their
body painting and plastic representations, their magic, and their
masks and dances. He told Bakairi myths and legends with great
sympathy and understanding: he penetrated the primitive imagination far more effectively than any previous investigator.

Steinen wrote classic books about his two journeys to the Xingu:
Durch Central-Brasilien described the first expedition of 1884–5 and
Unter den Naturvölkern Zentral-Brasiliens (*Among the Natural Peoples of
Central Brazil*) about his return in 1887–8. His revelations had greater
impact because he wrote in such a lively style, often humorous,

unpompous, direct, and remarkably free of abstract theories for a German academic of his age. His love of Indians pervaded his narrative and treatment of scientific questions, but he was no romantic. Steinen's Indians gained credibility because he criticised their many failings.

Since they have no writing, Brazilian Indians are accomplished orators and storytellers in the tradition of Homeric bards. Tribal elders smoke on the village plaza every night, men gossip in men's huts, and families chat while they rest in their hammocks. Some of the first visitors to Brazil in the sixteenth century managed to record vivid Indian speech. But since that time any wonder or admiration about Indians had long since disappeared. Other nineteenth-century travellers pontificated about the Indian problem or described the curiosities of tribal life, but Karl von den Steinen was the first to allow the Indians themselves to speak. He tried to recapture their repetitive talk and graphic gestures. His account of a geography lesson from the Bakairi is a good example:

'That most important concern of mine, the geography of the Culiseu river, was thoroughly dealt with. The river was drawn in the sand and the tribes were named and indicated by grains of corn. . . . But what a difference between a printed Baedeker and this gesticulation, this spoken picture, this enumeration of day's journeys that creep relentlessly farther stage by stage! The second Bakairi village is some days' journey from where we were. . . . You don't rest much in the good old days that I was experiencing here. First you get into your canoe, *pepi*, and paddle, *pepi, pepi, pepi*. You row with paddles, left, right, changing sides. You reach a rapids, *bububu*. . . . How high it falls: his hand goes down the steps with each *bu*, and the women are fearful and cry "pekoto, ah, ah, ah. . . !" There the *pepi* must plunge between the rocks – a hard stamp on the ground with his foot. With what groans it is pushed through, and the *mayaku*, the baskets of baggage, are wearily carried overland – once, twice, three times, on the left shoulder. But you climb aboard again and paddle, *pepi, pepi, pepi*. Far, far – his voice lingers *ih*. . . , so far *ih*. . . , and he pushes his mouth out into a snout and pulls his head down hard into his neck. He demonstrates how the sun sinks in the heavens, *ih*. . . . The sun sinks over there, until – he holds his hand out as far as possible and draws an arc towards the west, ending at the point in the sky where the sun stands when – *lah*. . . *a* – you reach the landing place. Here we are with the "Bakairi, Bakairi, Bakairi!" "*Kura, kura!*" Here we will be well received.'

The 1884 expedition visited a number of Suyá villages. At one of these they committed the solecism of entering the elders' council hut uninvited and thus competing with the shaman. The Indians politely but firmly indicated that the Germans should leave. So they set off down the Xingu on 6 September, only one month after first entering the enchanted lost world of the upper Xingu. They found that the Suyá had stolen their belongings on a massive scale – Indians are generous with their possessions, sharing what they have in their communistic society, so that they resented strangers visiting their villages with many objects that they were unwilling to leave behind or barter. The Germans dug up some of their belongings that the Suyá had surreptitiously buried in the sand; but as they left, they saw the Indians dig up many more. A Suyá chief guided the expedition for the first few days. He wanted Steinen's men to join his warriors in a combined attack on the Trumai. He proposed that they hide in the forest and launch a surprise attack on the Trumai village, using the Europeans' guns. 'All the [Trumai] men would be killed, but the women . . . would be distributed, half among us and half among the Suyá – each of us would get more than one woman!'

The Suyá had warned the Germans that nine days' journey downstream from their territory the Xingu river cascaded over a great waterfall. A Suyá had shown the river falling vertically from the sky, had laughed disagreeably, shaken the prow of their canoe, and seemed to say: 'Ha! There you people are going to plunge to your deaths! Good luck to you!' Tens of thousands of biting blackfly, pium (simuliidae), breed in these rapids. I myself recall dense clouds of these infuriating insects attacking us when I once visited these rapids with the great explorer and Indianist Cláudio Villas Boas: the bare back of the man in front of me in the canoe was covered in pium and speckled with hundreds of red spots from their itchy bites. Steinen suffered from the same irritant, as his expedition unloaded its canoes and plunged through the turbulent waters. He decided that these rapids were geographically so characteristic and ethnographically so important 'that we could only give them the name Von Martius Rapids, in honour of our compatriot who was at the forefront of all Brazilian research and exploration.'

The Von Martius Rapids formed an effective barrier to the spread of civilisation up the Xingu. Thanks to them, the tribes of the upper Xingu had been uncontacted before 1884, and these rapids have helped to protect the cultures of the Xinguano peoples to the present day. When Steinen's expedition passed the rapids, it found the Juruna of the lower river depopulated, demoralised and impoverished from their contacts with the rubber boom. The Juruna welcomed the German explorers amiably enough, but the tribe was becoming addicted to alcohol. It was gradually migrating up the river to escape from the advancing frontier. Twelve years after Steinen's visit, a pathetic Juruna chief told a French traveller that his people were poor and frightened. 'It is our destiny to be always in flight. In the past we fled from wild Indians, and now from our "dear protectors" the civilisados. Soon those gentlemen will have none of us left to protect. The last Juruna will soon carry off forever the soul of our race.'

The Juruna represented a classic example of a tribe fleeing before a threatening frontier. In the seventeenth and eighteenth centuries this populous tribe lived near the mouth of the Xingu and came under Jesuit missionary control. When Prince Adalbert of Prussia visited them in 1843 they had migrated upriver beyond the great bend in the lower Xingu. There were reckoned to be two thousand Juruna in nine villages near the modern town of Altamira. At that time, part of the tribe was tended by the energetic missionary Father Torquato. The provincial government of Pará revived this mission in 1859 and it lasted until 1880, though it was not a great success, with no more than 250 Indians. By the time of Steinen's descent in 1884 he saw 205 Juruna in five villages. These people were demoralised but still kept much of their independent culture. The worst decline came with the impact of rubber gathering during the next decade. By 1896 there were a mere 150 Juruna, emaciated, dressed in ragged clothes, and in bondage to the rubber barons Raymundo Marques and the Gomes brothers. In 1910 part of the tribe tried to flee up the Xingu to escape another rubber boss, but were pursued by armed gunmen. The Juruna also came under pressure from the warlike Kayapó who, as we have seen, had migrated westwards from the Araguaia. In 1916 the sad remnant of the Juruna made the wise decision to migrate up the Xingu to settle above the great barrier of the Von Martius Rapids. This saved them. The surviving Juruna now live at Diauarum in the sanctuary of the Xingu Indian reserve.

The nearby Tacunyapé suffered a worse fate than the Juruna. In the seventeenth century, this affable and docile tribe occupied the forests east of the lower Xingu, opposite the Juruna on the river's left bank. The Tacunyapé lost men in battles against the Juruna and Kayapó. But their worst devastation came from malarial fevers. Five hundred of them were settled in a mission in 1859, but by 1863 deaths from disease had reduced them to 150. Steinen saw only seventy in 1884 and Coudreau met forty a decade later. In that year, 1894, they were struck by smallpox or measles, and by the end of the century this once-industrious and artistic tribe was extinct.

Karl von den Steinen returned to the upper Xingu in 1887 and made first contacts with more of its tribes. His thrilling discoveries had a great impact. His sympathetic attitude to the Indians helped introduce a new and kinder approach, foreshadowing the conciliatory and protective methods attempted by the Brazilian army officers Gomes Carneiro and Cândido Rondon among the Bororo a few years later. Steinen's writings also opened a new era in Brazilian anthropology. From his day onwards, specialists started to study specific problems or individual tribes. He also inspired a generation of brilliant German anthropologists, some of whom accompanied his expeditions: Paul Ehrenreich, Hermann Meyer, Max Schmidt, Fritz Krause, Theodor Koch-Grünberg (among the tribes of the upper Rio Negro) and the great Curt Unkel.

A series of expeditions tried to follow Steinen into the magical world of the upper Xingu. The western, acculturated Bakairi suffered from these attempts. In 1889 a Captain Telles Pires took many Bakairi men as paddlers on an expedition down the Paranatinga, but the entire expedition died – including the Bakairi chief and his son. The river was renamed Teles Pires in honour of the luckless leader. In 1897 a Colonel Paula Castro took an expedition to the Culiseu headwater of the Xingu, searching for a legendary gold-mine called Los Martirios. This same Castro returned in 1899–1900 with a large government-financed expedition, ostensibly to cut a trail along the watershed between the Xingu and Araguaia but in reality to search for the mythical mines. It was a similar lost city of crystal that lured Colonel Percy Fawcett to his death among the tribes of the upper Xingu in 1925. Many more Bakairi died on Castro's sorry enterprise, and its leader went mad.

In about 1898 five Americans penetrated as far as the Suyá, who appeared to welcome them, but when the visitors were seated in a hut the Indians struck each man from behind with a club and killed them all. This tragedy was witnessed by a Mehinaku boy: the Suyá themselves remained hostile to all strangers until the mid-1960s.

The shattering of the Xingu's isolation also damaged the uncontacted half of the Bakairi tribe, which was living on the Culiseu. When Steinen first saw them in 1884 they welcomed him as a splendid tribe, proud and happy, with its society functioning perfectly. By 1899 another German anthropologist, Hermann Meyer, reported that these eastern Bakairi had almost disappeared. The corrosive influence of the western Bakairis' 'civilisation' had been too strong. 'This tribe is fallen into extreme decay. Its third village has disappeared completely. The inhabitants of the first and second have exchanged their beautiful houses for miserable huts, and for their subsistence have abandoned themselves almost entirely to reliance on deliveries from the [western] Bakairi of the Paranatinga – so that it was absolutely impossible for us to obtain food there. Through trade with the tame relatives of their tribe, they have obtained a knowledge of easily cultivated crops, but they are too idle to farm them. A large part of them has already moved to settle near the Paranatinga village. It will not be long before the last Bakairi has disappeared from the Culiseu.'

This Hermann Meyer led two expeditions to the upper Xingu, in 1895 and 1899. He chose to explore two headwaters of the river that, sadly for him, contained many tough rapids and malaria, but no Indians. His expeditions thus revisited only the same tribes first contacted by Steinen and added nothing to ethnographic under-standing of them. But his team did have magical moments among the Xingu Indians. After a gruelling descent of the Ronuro, they finally made contact with a tribe. 'A slim, pale-blue column of smoke climbed quietly out of the forest into the sky about three kilometres from us. It was a truly thrilling moment. Our canoes glided noise-lessly, in good order, from the shelter of an island into the mirrorlike open water. To the right appeared the mouth of the Batovi [Tamita-toaia] river, and immediately afterwards a view of the main Xingu opened up. . . . No one had yet noticed us. Happy laughter and chatter sounded towards us, breaking the solemn stillness of the evening in that magnificent scenery. We could clearly see a naked young man innocently occupied with a canoe. Then he looked up, started in amazement, and in that idyll a bomb could not have been more dramatic than his shout to warn his people of the approach of so many canoes.' Peaceful contact was soon established, and Meyer discovered that he was among the Kamayurá.

A few days later, Meyer's expedition visited the Trumai. This people were more nomadic and culturally less advanced than the majority of Xingu tribes. It was also suffering from attack by the belligerent Suyá – the warriors who had proposed to Steinen that he join them in destroying the Trumai. But Meyer's men enjoyed their stay with the peaceful Trumai. After a day of ethnographic study, 'towards evening it is most agreeable to bathe in the nearby river or lake. Half the young men and boys accompany us. There is a lively splashing, diving, spraying and swimming, watched in innocent delight by the village beauties who have come down to fetch water in huge gourd pitchers. We then sit for another hour or so among the groups who chat unconcernedly in front of their huts. We readily let the young people question us about all manner of things. But they do not allow this to disturb their work. Young women turn their spindles, brothers and sisters eagerly search in one another's thick hair, the head of the household smokes a cigar, children thread bead necklaces, and a young lad plays a pan pipe. Dogs and tame parrots sit peacefully near one another. The day ends either with a dance in our honour in which even the women participate, or an endless flute concert.'

The authorities in Cuiabá tried to dissuade a young German called Max Schmidt who wanted to visit the Xingu alone in 1901. But Schmidt persisted and eventually made the overland journey to the Xingu with only five Bakairi Indians, horses and oxen. He commented on the frustration of leading a group of Indians: 'If there is a difficult river crossing or some task to be accomplished in which each man can show his strength and skill, they are excellent and even amazing. But for routine daily work! One wants to fish, another to hunt, and all of it naturally at precisely the wrong time.' The trek across the campo savannah, building of bark canoes and short river journey to the first Bakairi village on the Culiseu took almost two months.

Schmidt approached the Bakairi village with his acculturated Bakairi making welcoming calls and he himself playing the German tune 'Margareta, Mädchen ohne gleichen' on his violin. He was well received in this and another Bakairi village, because he handed out presents of beads and showed the Indians their pictures in a copy of Steinen's book. Things went wrong when Schmidt visited other tribes. He tried to barter for headdresses and artefacts at the river port of the Nahukuá, but many of his trade goods were stolen. Indian women even stole back objects they had bartered with Schmidt in order to trade them a second time. 'The contact with the Nahukuá in their own port produced the effect of an assault rather than a visit.' Some Nahukuá borrowed his canoe to go fishing, but on their return he found that they had forced the lock on a chest and taken its contents of beads, fish-hooks (which they were just learning to use) and other tools.

Things grew worse when Schmidt paddled on to the village of the Aweti. As he walked inland to their village, Aweti porters simply vanished into the woods with his loads. Schmidt and his tame Bakairi were stripped of many belongings during the night. When he went to bathe, he returned to find the Aweti chief handing out all their remaining clothing to his men. The Indians could not understand Schmidt's possessiveness and continually tried to grab his machete. He eventually decamped to his canoes, erected an oxhide shelter and 'laid out every firearm that we possessed, ready for defence behind the shelter and near our open cartridge box. Counting my revolver and [the Bakairi] André's pistol, we each had eleven shots ready to fire.'

The Aweti eventually arrived with some loads of food, but without Schmidt's other belongings. Schmidt decided to flee, paddling furiously down a labyrinth of small channels towards the larger river. 'Oh, exhausting fight for life! We paddled with all our strength for two days' to reach the Culiseu. The Aweti then surprised Schmidt by appearing in their canoes with many of his loads and his ethnographic collection. They even helped to paddle him upriver. There was more trading with the Mehinaku, but Schmidt had little left to barter. He disposed of his last buttons, the glass plates from his camera, and his beloved violin – now useless because in a moment of confusion he had sat on it in a hammock.

Salvation came at the Bakairi village. Schmidt was starving, his feet ulcerated, his clothes in ribbons and he himself stricken with malaria. He had a fevered week, awoken from his delirium by Indians dancing, stamping their feet and singing near his hammock. The women pestered him for presents although he was too weak to respond. But he was pleased to awake from one fever to see 'the beautiful Tuirki, a slender young girl with a figure still in its first bloom, who was well aware of her charms. She smilingly handed me some of those tiny uluris of bark fibre which constitute the only item of female clothing and are no bigger than a vine leaf. The giver herself was also equipped only with one of these.' Max Schmidt eventually left the Xingu after a disastrous six weeks among its Indians. He had learned that these tough tribes should not be underestimated. When the Mehinaku demonstrated how the Suyá had clubbed the five Americans in 1898, they indicated that Schmidt was lucky not to have suffered the same fate. It was a lesson that Colonel Fawcett failed to heed when he blundered on to these rivers in 1925.

The Paraguay River

South of Cuiabá and the homelands of the Bororo, the Paraguay river formed a frontier between Portuguese Brazil and the empty vastness of the Chaco in what are now Bolivia and Paraguay. A fan of headwaters form the great river – the Cabaçal, Jauru, Cuiabá and São Lourenço, all inhabited by Bororo. South of these, the middle Paraguay is broken by a labyrinth of lakes. During the rainy season it overflows into the world's largest swamp, the Pantanal, which floods twenty thousand square kilometres of land along six hundred kilometres of the river's course.

The lakes, channels and spongy islands to the north of the Pantanal are home of a strange and highly aquatic tribe called Guató. Shy and solitary, they had been in intermittent contact with Spaniards and Portuguese since the sixteenth century. By the time of the Imperial Russian expedition of Baron Langsdorff in 1826, the Guató were outwardly fairly acculturated. The men wore cotton trousers and the women cotton skirts. These clothes were obtained by trade with Brazilians but, as the Indians had no soap, they soon degenerated into filthy rags. Although few in number, the Guató were handsome and warlike. Langsdorff noted in his diary that 'Both Guató men and women have pleasant features: their skin is dark brown, tanned by the constant action of sun and wind.' Hércules Florence, one of Langsdorff's artists, reckoned that there were only three hundred Guató, unless there was another large village hidden deep in the swamps.

The Guató economy depended on hunting. Moving swiftly in canoes loaded to the brim, the Guató were deadly shots with their bows and arrows. Their main food was alligators and fish; but they traded jaguars, monkeys and otters that they hunted successfully on their islands. 'They have absolutely no sense of religion. . . . The Guató still live in a state close to savagery. When hunting and fishing, they are the best shots of all Indian tribes. They are dirty and unscrupulous, and continually roam from place to place with several settlements near the river.' But to the artist Florence, the tall, attractive and taciturn Guató were 'the most admirable of all tribes'.

Twenty years later, the Count of Castelnau was equally impressed by the tribe. He also found the men very handsome, with their aquiline noses, long flowing black hair, occasional moustaches and beards, and large Caucasian eyes. He persuaded the Guató to guide him into their maze of lakes and channels. When far from colonists, the tribe went naked apart from small cloths over their genitals. Tall and muscular, they were very strong. Constant paddling gave them magnificent physiques. Guató women were equally attractive but seemed to Castelnau to be melancholy, with the sad expressions of slaves. Guató men were polygamous with up to a dozen wives, and fiercely jealous. Gentle in speech and manners, they preferred a solitary life, with each family group isolated amid their vast expanse of marsh and floodlands. During the flood season they lived for weeks on end in their canoes; and when the Pantanal was drier they contented themselves with simple shelters.

Castelnau tested the Guató's legendary skill as archers, and was duly amazed by their ability to hit birds flying far overhead, or fish and alligators moving through the swamps. They attacked jaguars by hand, hitting them with arrows fired from huge 2.5-metre bows and then closing in with four-metre-long bone-tipped lances.

The French traveller was also impressed by Guató intelligence. Contrary to Langsdorff's impression, he found that they did believe in God and an afterlife. They also counted to infinity, unlike most Indians, whose arithmetic stopped at five or six. Henrique de Baurepaire Rohan, who sailed down the Paraguay in 1846, found the Guató to be tough but honest traders. One Indian kept asking to be given some of Rohan's belongings but was refused. 'He doubtless attributed this to stinginess on my part and made this mortifying comment: "I am asking because I am poor. But I see that you are even poorer than I." ' By mid-nineteenth century the Guató were well regarded by Brazilians as a docile and friendly tribe. Rohan understood why they chose to be so isolated. 'Love of independence keeps them in these solitudes where none disturbs them. In this sense they are happier than some sedentary tribes, to whom civilisation has revealed only its side that is least agreeable to simple men.'

By the 1860s, Augusto Leverger (a President of Mato Grosso with a keen understanding of its Indians) described the Guató as 'loyal and inoffensive. . . . Almost all their adults speak Portuguese more or less fluently. As soon as they sight some vessel they immediately approach and accompany it, sometimes until nightfall. They hope to be given goods: salt, tobacco, the remains of a meal, or above all cachaça. They also trade with our people, exchanging the produce of their hunting – such as skins of jaguar, howler monkeys or otters, wax, wild honey, etc. – for the above articles or for axes, spears, knives, fish-hooks or cotton cloth. They sometimes enlist for work in canoes and are very useful for hunting, fishing or navigation over flooded land.' But, despite their fluency in Portuguese and their being on 'more or less intimate terms with us, they show little inclination to renounce their way of life.' Leverger doubted whether the Guató would ever become assimilated into Brazilian society.

The isolated tranquillity of the Guató was shattered by two disasters. One was a war against the eastern Bororo, who lived upriver of them on the São Lourenço. An old chief called Fernando told Júlio Koslowski about this tragic feud. He blamed the Bororo for starting it, with attacks (sometimes in large numbers) on Guató families in which men were killed and women abducted. When the Guató became aware of this invasion, they united and drove the Bororo off in bloody skirmishes. The Guató sought vengeance by penetrating Bororo territory where they caught many prisoners in raids and ambushes. The captives were ceremonially executed, one at each place where a Guató had been killed, 'thus procuring the peace of the soul of the dead man'. But the small Guató tribe was diminished by this protracted vendetta against its larger neighbour.

Then came a more serious disaster. In 1864, when the Paraguayan dictator Marshal-President Francisco Solano López went to war against Brazil, Paraguayan troops invaded Mato Grosso and swept up the Paraguay river. A Paraguayan warship anchored near the Guató homeland of Lake Gaíba. The invaders tried to persuade the tribe to move to an attractive country of fine rivers within Paraguay itself. The Guató suspected that this was a trick. Their envoy went daily to the warship but he procrastinated in the negotiations. Finally the Paraguayans, angry and frustrated by the delays, bayoneted the envoy and threw his body into the river. A hidden Guató saw what happened, and the tribe assembled in a vain hope of luring their enemies into the narrows of their swamps. The Paraguayans avoided the ambush and withdrew. But they left a deadly legacy. 'The unfortunate Indians fell into the claws of a more terrible adversary: smallpox. Almost all the tribe succumbed, victims of this disease.' Only a few isolated Guató survived. Júlio Koslowski met these in 1894 and was told by an old lady, in a sad and emotional voice: ' "The pox finished everything, everything." Her eyes filled with tears as she recalled the tragedy, for she had watched almost all her people disappear in a short time.' Later that night, the aged Guató men and women drank quantities of cachaça and 'became happy and sentimental. A circle of men and women sat around my hammock, weeping and lamenting the ruin of their tribe and their personal misfortune. . . . The old man told me that they needed strong drink from time to time, to expand their spirits from the oppression and woes they felt.'

Farther south along the Paraguay river, the Brazilians had defended this western frontier with forts – Corumbá, Albuquerque and Coimbra, all of which were on the western or right bank of the river, facing the vast expanses of the Bolivian Chaco. This part of the Pantanal was the home of the magnificent horsemen the Guaikurú or Cavalleiros, whose murderous charges had once been the terror of Spaniards and Portuguese alike. Alongside them lived their surrogates, the docile Guaná, a prolific people who acted as almost voluntary slaves to the aristocratic and warlike Guaikurú. We have seen how, after fighting successfully throughout the eighteenth century, the Guaikurú came to terms with the Portuguese. A formal peace treaty was signed in 1791. By the nineteenth century the Guaikurú were reduced both in numbers and in military strength. Of their various divisions, the one about which we hear most is the Kadiwéu (a Tupi word for a group formerly called Mbayá). Their associates, the symbiotic Guaná, are now reduced to the Terena and Kinikinao sub-tribes.

In the early decades of the century, the Kadiwéu lived in the plains of southern Mato Grosso between the Bodoquena hills and the Apa river, which was and still is the frontier between Portuguese and Spanish dominions. They successfully exploited the rivalries between Brazil and Paraguay. At one time they forced the Paraguayans to evacuate Fort Olimpio (former Fort Borbón), their main northern stronghold in the Chaco. There was a peace; but in 1818 the Kadiwéu again went on the offensive, driving the Paraguayans out of all lands almost as far south as Concepción. But the Indians' fighting tactics were inflexible and they suffered from lack of military command or strategy. The Paraguayans learned to deal with their attacks, garrisoned their frontier forts, and drove the Kadiwéu north into Brazil.

When Langsdorff's expedition reached the Paraguay river in late 1826, it found the Guaikurú involved in what proved to be their last hostilities against the Brazilians. An isolated farmer and some Portuguese soldiers had been killed. The Kadiwéu abandoned aldeias near Miranda and Coimbra and were said to have four thousand men under arms. They had stolen five hundred horses from the old portage at Camapuã and were raiding Guarani-speaking Kaiwá and Gê-speaking Kayapó for children and slaves. The Russian expedition encountered fourteen large canoes taking three hundred soldiers and militiamen downriver from Cuiabá to subdue this tribe. But Hércules Florence reported that the Emperor had given express orders that the Guaikurú were to be treated leniently.*

When Albuquerque became a parish in 1833, it had a garrison of forty soldiers, twenty-six other Brazilians, and over two thousand Indians living nearby. There was one aldeia of Guaikurú, one of Guaná and one of Kinikinao – the latter two groups being related to the Terena whose aldeia was not far to the east up the Miranda river. The French expedition of Count Castelnau visited Albuquerque in 1845 and found its Indians peacefully assimilated. The Guaikurú were mostly converted to Christianity, but were almost naked and lived in open-ended thatch hangars – which is the preferred housing of the surviving Kadiwéu to this day. Their main industry was the sale of hammocks woven by the women.

While Castelnau was with them, a group of wilder Kadiwéu rode in from battles against other tribes of the Chaco. These were tattooed with traditional geometric designs, and the women's breasts and horses' flanks also had tattoo marks of their clan chiefs. All wore silver necklaces obtained from plunder. They were nomads, constantly on the move, with families, tents, possessions and even dogs mounted on their horses. 'They live only from disorder and pillage and often commit appalling massacres. At times they are in the lap of abundance and squander in a few days what could have lasted for entire months. At other times they live only off reptiles and insects.'

The Guaikurú living near Fort Coimbra demonstrated a mock attack for the horrified French visitors. The warriors were 'almost naked, painted in black and white, armed with long lances with pointed iron heads and some with guns. They leaped on to horses almost as savage as themselves, which they steer only with a rope around the lower lip, and set off at a gallop. . . . They wheeled and executed a charge, firing their guns and arrows. Then, reaching the village square, they dismounted with great agility and jumped on to the men there. After flattening them they pretended to cut off their heads. This scene was accompanied by dreadful howling and had a savage appearance that froze one with horror!'

At another place, Castelnau watched a more dignified Guaikurú festival. There were wrestling and boxing matches between both men and women. The boxers spilled much blood, but did little harm to one another. A large quantity of cachaça was consumed. There was then a more elegant tournament by plumed, naked men on galloping horses trying to pierce a ring with their sabres. The French admired the dignity of the principal chief of the Guaikurú, despite his somewhat comical dress: a three-cornered hat worn over his long flowing hair, a black habit inherited from his grandfather, no shoes, and white breeches worn back-to-front.

These proud displays were a sham. The haughty Kadiwéu and other Guaikurú were becoming an anachronism. Their former slaves, the Aruak-speaking Guaná (Kinikinao and Terena), were on the other hand multiplying and flourishing. An industrious agricultural people, these established good relations with frontier settlers. They had fine plantations of corn, celery, manioc, sugar cane, cotton and tobacco. Their women made splendid cotton blankets and hammocks, which were sold as far afield as Cuiabá, along with Terena belts, braces, saddles and fish. Many men worked as paid labourers in settlers' plantations.

With their pale skins and lack of tattoos or body paint, the Guaná Terena appealed to Europeans. Hércules Florence admired the women's good figures and fine teeth. But he regarded this hardworking tribe as cowardly and thieving, and he was appalled by the way its men prostituted their women out of sordid self-interest. Guaná women 'are totally unbridled, the more so because their own husbands are devoid of any jealousy: they offer them to strangers with the greatest facility, in return for some money or pieces of cloth.'

By the 1840s the villages near Albuquerque were very detribalised. The Guaná aldeia consisted of sixty-five huts in rows around a square. A cross stood in the middle of the plaza, and the houses were of wattle-and-daub with thatch roofs in the Brazilian manner. There was even furniture inside, with beds of leather slung on wooden frames. All the Indians spoke Portuguese and professed Christianity. Around the village were their plantations and herds of horses and sheep. The nearby village of some eight hundred Kinikinao was equally impressive, although its Indians were slightly less acculturated than the Guaná. The French also visited the vast village of the Terena, on a lake beyond the wide plain of the Miranda valley. One village had 110 huts in long rows, with a population approaching two thousand, and there were a further thousand Terena in villages nearby. These Indians were more warlike, naked and with fine body painting similar to that of the Guaikurú; but they were as industrious and prolific as the other Aruak tribes of the Paraguay.

The Terena had been a warrior tribe, despite their subservient alliance with the Guaikurú. When Castelnau saw them in 1845, they had just arrived at Miranda from the plains of the Chaco. He described them as 'a nation of warriors who have preserved all the customs of their fathers. . . . Among their possessions there are still objects which they took from Spaniards whom they massacred.' Even after their settlement at Miranda, we hear of Terena slave raids to capture women and children from the peaceful Guarani-speaking Kaiwá (Caiuá) to the south.

Italian Capuchins tried to establish themselves among the Kinikinao at Albuquerque, among the Terena at Miranda and even among the proud Kadiwéu. The missionaries were active by 1850; but a revolt by the garrison of Coimbra in 1851 forced them to abandon their attempt. By 1856, the remaining mission among the Kinikinao 'was not prospering. A deplorable fatality has meant that for the past three years the plantations have failed. The resulting hunger has forced the adult Indians to scatter, and the children rarely attend school since they also have to provide for their subsistence.' But this tribe did not revert to its former state: its members sought work on ranches or as river canoe crews. So by 1862 the Kinikinao mission had recovered. A president of Mato Grosso reported that these were 'Indians of excellent disposition, who are now providing various services for society. They work as labourers on farms or cattle ranches, and rowing canoes which navigate between ports of the lower Paraguay and this capital city [Cuiabá].'

These Aruak-speaking peoples were regarded by the authorities as the only model Indians. Augusto Leverger, who was also an experienced Indianist and historian of Mato Grosso, reckoned that in 1863 there were twenty-four thousand assimilated Indians in the province out of a total population of sixty-five thousand. He felt that there was little to be gained from most of them. The exceptions were the Guaná, Kinikinao and Terena. These 'already provide valuable service for us. Living among us as they do, one may presume that future generations will be even more useful; and it will not be long before they melt into the mass of our population.'

By mid-nineteenth century, the largest remaining group of Guaikurú was the Kadiwéu. There were thought to be eight hundred of them, roaming in bands on both banks of the Paraguay river below Coimbra. They were still nomadic, moving camps swiftly and frequently. They hunted, fished and raised their beloved horses, but they still refused to work at demeaning agriculture. They occasionally attacked neighbouring tribes, but had stopped fighting whites because of their superior firearms. A report on the Indians of Mato Grosso said that the Kadiwéu tribe 'preserves traces of the proud and bellicose spirit of its ancestors. . . . The most characteristic traits of the Kadiwéu are presumption and haughtiness. They occasionally appear in various towns to trade their horses and rope for alcohol, hatchets, knives, cotton cloth, calico, baize, and silver for the bangles with which they decorate themselves.'

The American soldier of fortune John Henry Elliott made a painting of a group of Kadiwéu in 1847. They were mounted on superb horses and had many more loose horses in their convoy. Their long hair was tied at the back, their faces painted in black and red, and they wore only sarong-like skirts fastened at the waist by lasso cords. Their weapons were long lances and swords held in shoulder scabbards. 'Most of the men were tall and thin with an arrogant and disdainful look, affecting a certain air of superiority.'

The isolation and relative tranquillity of the Paraguay river frontier was shattered in 1864, when war broke out between the Republic of Paraguay and Brazil, which in 1865 became a war between Paraguay and a Triple Alliance of Brazil, Argentina and Uruguay. That war was caused by the pretensions of Paraguay's dictator López, whose Napoleonic ambitions far outstripped the resources of his tiny landlocked country. The war raged for six years with savage ferocity. The Guarani Indians of Paraguay – descendants of the Jesuits' converts – bore the brunt of the fighting and their courage and stamina were amazing. By 1870 Paraguay had lost more than half its population and only twenty-eight thousand men remained alive. Because the War of the Triple Alliance coincided with the American Civil War, it has been eclipsed; but it contained the first use of many ingredients of modern war – torpedoes, trenches, barbed wire and aerial observation by balloon. As with the American war, it started with successes for the underdog; but the gallant smaller side was the eventual loser. Most of the fighting was on Paraguay's southern and eastern frontiers. The weight of the Brazilian and Argentine armies and navies drove López' brave Guarani soldiers inexorably back until their country was overrun.

In December 1864 the Paraguayans sent a large force of cavalry and an infantry battalion across the Apa river into southern Mato Grosso, and three thousand men in a flotilla of ships up the Paraguay river. The fort of Coimbra made a brief resistance, but on 28 December its four hundred men slipped away under cover of darkness. The other forts were easily captured by the Paraguayans, whose ships sailed far north. One Brazilian warship was captured in the São Lourenço river, and Cuiabá itself was spared only because its river was too shallow for the Paraguayan steamers.

The various Indian tribes reacted differently to this war between the colonial powers. The shy and solitary Guató did nothing to help the fleeing garrison of Coimbra. But as we have seen they resisted Paraguayan blandishments to move to the Paraguayan heartland – and fell victims to the terrible epidemic of smallpox introduced unwittingly by the invaders. The Guaná and Kinikinao near Albuquerque were less astute: many of them did migrate close to Asunción where they dwindled from disease and failed to return. These tribes were badly affected by the war. Those who did not move southwards dispersed and only a few survived to take refuge among their kindred Terena. Their missionary, Friar Angelo de Caramonico, was imprisoned and killed by the Paraguayans.

The Paraguayan invasion of Mato Grosso was violent and bloody. There are terrible accounts of massacres, rapes and pillaging by the invading forces. In this fighting, both Indians and whites suffered, and were forced into common cause. Many were driven to seek sanctuary in the Serra do Maracaju, the line of hills between modern Aquidauana and Campo Grande. Those Kinikinao who had not gone to Asunción co-operated most closely with the Brazilians. The related Terena at first remained isolated and uncommitted; but later they too had to flee and join guerrilla groups operating in the hills.

The proud and warlike Guaikurú Kadiwéu were ambivalent. At the outset of the war, the Paraguayans overran a tiny Brazilian garrison at Pão de Açucar (Sugar Loaf) Fort on the Apa river. The first instinct of the Kadiwéu was to kill the fugitive Brazilians; but they decided instead to protect them. The warrior horsemen thus escorted twenty-five Brazilian soldiers through the forests and swamps north to Cuiabá. 'After the most painful hardships and when they were already thought to be dead, the mourned victims appeared [at Cuiabá] surrounded by Indians. This unusual escort had mitigated the suffering of those unfortunates by many acts of kindness. The Brazilian government, always ready to reward generous actions, lavished presents on the Indians. The initiator of that praiseworthy action [Chief Lapagate] was awarded the honorary rank of Captain. . . .' Years later the old Emperor Dom Pedro II asked General Francisco de Mello Rego: 'How are my friends the Guaikurús? What news of them?' Mello Rego, who was President of

Mato Grosso, answered: ' "Few remain and they live dispersed. They are suffering the same fate as the other Indians of Mato Grosso." "Well, they deserve much from us and, out of gratitude alone, we should not let them reach this state," said the Monarch. . . . He was perhaps the only Brazilian who showed that he appreciated the full worth of the services they gave us.' It was thanks to an imperial donation that the Kadiwéu received title to the rich pasture of Nalique in the Bodoquena hills, which they still possess. The Terena also felt that their tribe's defence of its lands near Miranda reinforced their right to that territory.

The Brazilians were humiliated by the loss of southern Mato Grosso – even though all the important fighting of the war took place far to the south, on the lower Paraguay and Paraná rivers. An expedition was mounted in São Paulo early in 1865. It marched very slowly westwards, across the barren forests of Mato Grosso. It reached Miranda only towards the end of 1866, and then marched south against Paraguay the following year. Five thousand men were in this column and, according to the engineer Colonel George Thompson who was fighting on the Paraguayan side, 'the Indians of the province were also armed with rifles, but, instead of fighting with them, used them to shoot their game.' The expedition crossed the Apa and entered northern Paraguay, but it was a disaster. A Paraguayan force caught it at a ranch called La Laguna, and the Brazilians suffered a long and devastating retreat. In the end, only seven hundred emaciated survivors staggered back to Brazil. One of these was Alfredo d'Escragnolle Taunay, nephew of the artist who drowned on Langsdorff's Russian expedition and later to become one of Brazil's most famous historians. Taunay described the harrowing retreat in a magnificent book. He was not flattering about the Kadiwéu, who used the war to revert briefly to their former belligerence towards all colonists, assuming 'an attitude hostile to any white man, now attacking the Paraguayans on the line of the Apa, now assassinating whole families [of Brazilians] on the Bonito.'

The Paraguayan War caused damage to the Indians of southern Mato Grosso beyond the immediate devastation of the invasion. The Guaná and Kinikinao had suffered from their exodus and the Guató from smallpox. But the tribes who remained – notably the Terena and Kadiwéu – were victims of a wave of colonial settlement in the aftermath of the fighting. After the defeat of Paraguay in 1870 the Brazilian government was eager to populate its western frontier. Before the war, the first cattle ranches had spread westwards from São Paulo and the cattle 'triangle' in Minas Gerais, across the endless forests of southern Mato Grosso: any cattle on the Paraguayan frontier had come from the plains of the Chaco or the savannahs of Paraguay. This invasion accelerated when Brazilian soldiers saw the fertile Miranda and Aquidauana valleys for the first time. Many troops were demobilised in the region and decided to remain there. The result for the Indians was a half century of invasion and oppression which they still refer to as 'the time of captivity'.

The Terena were particularly vulnerable. Not only did they occupy fertile and accessible land which they had successfully cultivated but they themselves were also sought after, for Terena men were excellent cattle hands, and their women were attractive and considered promiscuous. They were victims of fake debt bondage. One fazendeiro used to assemble his Terena cowboys every year and read out each man's debts. He then performed an extraordinary act of spurious generosity, lowering each Indian's debt. 'In fact', an official report noted, 'the wretched cowhands owed nothing to the usurer.' The Indians, like their compatriots in Amazonian rubber seringals, could not change employment unless a new master paid off their debts. The same report commented: 'There thus arose a new form of slavery, maintained and enforced by the state police. . . . It is curious that in towns and settlements the police are always in the hands of the fazendeiros themselves, who are the authorities, justices of the peace, sheriffs and deputy sheriffs. Soldiers are recruited by them and thereafter are considered as their personal retainers. The fazendeiros supply their food and receive their pay and rations. The soldiers serve them as cowhands and labourers, performing all the work that the fazendeiro, as police chief, orders.'

The Kadiwéu also suffered during the late nineteenth century. In 1904 an old shaman described the thirty years of decline in a moving account to a visiting anthropologist, the Italian Guido Boggiani who lived with the Kadiwéu in 1892 and found them financially and socially impoverished. They were split by internal feuds and their numbers were drastically reduced. Paradoxically, this sad period witnessed an artistic flowering among these Indians. It was at this time that they started to make pottery of remarkable plasticity, in fine shapes with startling geometric incisions and colouring. They are now recognised as some of the most skilled potters of South America. They also started making combs and other objects. Their most vivid artistic expression had always been in body tattooing and painting. Castelnau in 1845 had first noticed a tendency to asymmetry in Kadiwéu body painting – men and women quartered their bodies in different coloured squares, and their elaborate tattoos differed on either side of their limbs and bodies. When a Brazilian warship first sailed up the Paraguay river in 1857, the Kadiwéu immediately imitated the uniforms, braid and anchors of its officers in their decoration. Such imagination and innovation flowered by the 1890s. Boggiani sketched men and women embellished with baroque volutes, fine geometric maze designs, diagonal step motives and concentric circles. Forty years later, the great French anthropologist Claude Lévi-Strauss got Kadiwéu women to draw their own body designs. He reported that 'the face, after being halved, quartered – or sometimes perhaps divided obliquely – is lavishly decorated with arabesques which are drawn as if on an even surface, no attention being paid to the eyes, nose, cheeks, forehead or chin. These skilful compositions, which are asymmetrical yet balanced, are begun at any one corner and completed without hesitation or correction. . . . Among the four hundred designs I collected, I did not notice two alike.'

The period of oppression was somewhat mitigated in 1903, with the arrival in Terena territory of the remarkable young army engineer Lieutenant Cândido Mariano da Silva Rondon, who, with his team of engineers, had completed his harrowing three-year expedition pushing the telegraph line from Cuiabá south to Corumbá, driving wires and poles through the dense forests and swamps of some of Brazil's most forbidding terrain. When he reached Miranda, Aquidauana and Ipegue, Rondon was appalled by the condition of the Terena. He found the ancient Kinikinao aldeia abandoned and invaded by settlers, and sought to restore it. He also organised the demarcation of various Terena aldeias that were being engulfed by encroaching cattle ranches. Chiefs such as Manoel Pedro and Macolino Wollily were appointed for the Terena of Bananal (east of Miranda), and they organised the demarcation of this village, which is still the heartland of the Terena. At nearby Ipegue Rondon assembled some Terena. He recalled: 'I spoke to them about the desirability of moving to join their chief and resuming their ancient way of life. They were satisfied with the guarantees I gave them and promised to return to their village.' It was something unheard of, a radical new approach, for a Brazilian army officer to encourage Indians to resume their ancient way of life. Without their land, the Terena could never rescue their tribal society. It was thus the protection given by Rondon's telegraph commission that has helped the Terena survive to the present day as a cohesive – and politically active – tribe.

23

Kaingáng Defiance

In the far south of Mato Grosso lived a group of Guarani-speaking Indians, survivors of the Guarani who had been converted by Spanish Jesuits from Paraguay in the seventeenth century. As with other Guarani, these Kaiwá were industrious and gentle people. They suffered as a result, falling victim to raids by the warlike Guaikurú and even by the Terena who wanted Kaiwá women and children.

In 1830 one group of Kaiwá made a long migration eastwards, across the mighty Paraná river and over the fertile plains around Curitiba. They then retreated into the forests on the south bank of the Paranapanema. In 1844 some of these Kaiwá appeared on a fazenda belonging to a remarkably humanitarian landowner, Silva Machado, Baron of Antonina. He received the Indians with presents instead of the usual gunfire, had an eighty-kilometre path cut to reach the rest of the tribe, and then organised a mission called São João Baptista for them under the care of a Capuchin friar. Baron Antonina saw it as his philanthropic duty to convert and civilise these Indians, and the Kaiwá responded enthusiastically. When the baron himself visited their mission village, they prepared a house decorated with branches and flowers and adorned themselves in their finest feather headdresses. 'They appear to love him to an extreme, for they appreciate how much this great patriot and useful citizen has done for their benefit. As part of his outstanding philanthropy he banished their hunger at his own expense and preserved them from the rigours of nudity. The noble baron greeted them with affection and distributed rum, tobacco, brown sugar, salt, clothing, beads, etc. among them.'

The baron himself led an expedition in 1845 which descended the Verde and Paranapanema rivers (between the modern states of São Paulo and Paraná). It saw smoke on the Tibagi tributary of the

Paranapanema. Some members of the expedition jumped ashore and followed Indian trails until they sighted a group of Kaiwá, mostly women and children. These were 'in a clearing, surrounding a fire, with an enormous basket of palm hearts, many jacu [game birds] and peccaries dead beside it.' The explorers decided to take the Indians by surprise. 'Mr Lopes and Mr Vergueiro jumped unexpectedly into the midst of this gathering, like beings risen from the earth. [The Indians] were stupefied. The invaders used that instant to give coloured and golden beads to some and throw beads to the rest. At the same time, the remainder of our men appeared simultaneously on all sides of the clearing: they had run up with the speed of lightning, well armed and supposing that the first men were in grave danger. The bugres succumbed at this simultaneous apparition, at the sight of the weapons, and at their ignorance of our small number. They fell to their knees, raised their hands to heaven and demonstrated their terror. But we greeted them with embraces and removed our firearms for which they seemed to have an exaggerated knowledge. We gave them many axes, sickles, knives, fish-hooks, beads, mirrors and other trinkets.' The tribe had fourteen huts and about seventy people. 'All the men were tall and well built, and the women pretty rather than ugly, with one of great beauty.'

Baron Antonina organised another expedition in 1847 to try to contact remoter groups of Kaiwá: he wanted to persuade them of the 'benefits' of abandoning their migratory life and settling in an aldeia. This expedition included the young American sailor John Henry Elliott, who had settled in southern Brazil after adventures in the American and Brazilian navies. Baron Antonina also hired a Paraguayan Guarani guide called Joaquim Lopes to speak to the tribe and load it with presents. Chief Iguajurú of the Kaiwá, who had four thousand Indian followers, was impressed. He himself accepted baptism with the name Chief Libanio and his people imitated the Kaiwá of São João Baptista in calling Antonina 'Pagé Guaçu' or Great Shaman. Chief Iguajurú decided to accept an invitation to settle his people, close to a military outpost that was being built at Jataí on the Tibagi river to protect this crossing between Brazil and Paraguay. Soon seven chiefs and five hundred Kaiwá assembled in their forests and were ready to embark on canoes organised by the Paraguayan Guarani interpreter. But the plan failed. The Kaiwá had arrived without food, and an expedition sent from Curitiba with supplies for the newly arrived Indians took over two months on the difficult journey in heavy rains. Some Kaiwá converts on the relief expedition 'fled because of ill-treatment they were given on it. They went as fugitives to their own people and told them of the sufferings they had endured and the bad treatment given them – which was very different from what they had been promised before their departure.' Not surprisingly, the Kaiwá who were assembling and ready for pacification took fright at this and dispersed back into their forests.

Next year, 1848, the guide Joaquim Lopes again made contact with Chief Libanio's Kaiwá. Lopes was impressed by the tall, athletic chief, with his frank, magnanimous expression and intelligent conversation. He found the Kaiwá to be delightful people, good-looking, generous and very friendly. The men wore small plugs of amber-coloured stone in their lower lips, but the women dressed in cotton shifts not unlike those of mission Indians – doubtless a legacy from the distant past when they had been under Jesuit rule. They also adorned themselves with beads, molluscs and bone ornaments. But they lived in fear of both whites and other Indian tribes, not even daring to keep dogs or chickens lest they might make a noise that would betray the tribe's location. The Kaiwá lined up to receive Lopes and he gave them presents. 'I placed a red cap on the head of the chief and girded his shoulders with a bandolier that [Baron Antonina] had worn when commander-in-chief of the National Guard. He appeared well pleased with these presents, to the extent of marching a few paces from side to side with his body leaning backwards.' But, despite all the presents and blandishments, he did not move his people to live near the colonial frontier.

Most Kaiwá fled whenever they saw whites. On one occasion, however, Joaquim Lopes surprised a canoe of Kaiwá who were fishing. One garrulous woman 'never stopped talking to my interpreter to persuade me of her happiness at meeting white men who did not harm them but who treated them very well'.

Baron Antonina did not give up easily. He sent John Elliott off again in 1852, and the American wrote that the disastrous attempt of 1847 had not discouraged the baron from 'his laudable attempt to annexe a village of Indians to the military outpost of Jataí, whose establishment was entrusted to him.' So Elliott sailed down the Paranapanema, equipping himself at Jataí fort with sixteen armed men, plenty of presents and four canoes. He found various groups of Kaiwá wandering disconsolately in forests near the Pirapó to the south of the Paranapanema, and, using Guarani interpreters, managed to assemble some two hundred of them. He made a rousing speech. 'I told them that in their former homeland they lived in continuous misery, having suffered a shortage of food for a long time, besides being always assailed by fear of the enemies who surrounded them – Paraguayans to the south, ferocious Guaikurú and treacherous Terena to the west, barbarous Coroados [Kaingáng] to the east – all of whom waged war on them, killing their men and carrying off women and children to captivity. After that I described to them in detail the abundance they would find on the banks and forests of the Tibagi, full of palm hearts, rich in fruit, game and honey, with the river abounding in fish, and finally that there they would encounter the generous and protective hand of the Pagé Guaçu [Baron Antonina] who would defend them from their enemies and succour them in their necessities.'

Such a speech could hardly fail. The Kaiwá set off with Elliott, the men on land and their women in canoes with the white men. It rained incessantly and hunting was difficult. The tribe moved slowly, with nightly singing and dancing. The Indians were suspicious, often threatening to run off and exhausting Elliott's supply of presents and patience. He was afraid of an attack by 'over a hundred savage sagitarians, ready to shoot their arrows at the first signal from their chiefs'.

The expedition finally reached Fort Jataí after a gruelling forty-one-day ascent. It was given a tumultuous welcome, with a continuous fusillade of guns to applaud the new arrivals. 'This lively reception was answered by the blowing of cornets, bugles and flutes that I had with me and with other Indian instruments. They produced a thunderous fanfare that greatly delighted the Indians.' Some cattle and oxen appeared. 'Since the Indians had never seen these animals their fear and admiration was tremendous when they caught sight of them. They ran off terrified and climbed into the trees.' The six hundred Kaiwá brought by Lopes and Elliott were settled in an aldeia called São Pedro de Alcantara.

In 1866 the Paraguayan War inspired renewed efforts to drive a road or river route down the Ivaí from Paraná westwards to Mato Grosso. The Brazilian government employed the German engineer Joseph Keller and his son Franz to explore this region and report on its tribes. They reported that the extensive lands between the eastern tributaries of the Paraná – the Paranapanema, Ivaí and Iguaçu rivers – were full of fish and game and thus sheltered numerous bands of Indians. Few of these were Kaiwá, the majority of whom were far from the colonial frontier to the west of the Paraná. The few wild Kaiwá still living to the east of that great river were under a chief called Cuyabá. They sometimes visited an aldeia called Parana-panema to trade their delicious honeycombs, tanga skirts and hammocks for knives.

Franz Keller painted the Kaiwá chief Pahy wearing 'a headdress of yellow feathers of the most elegant and picturesque shape, in which he appears on formal occasions. These Indians' character is an interesting mixture of affable and suspicious qualities. Thus, more may be achieved with them through gentleness and peaceful words than through arrogance and force.' Keller praised the brilliance of the Kaiwá in navigating their canoes through turbulent rapids. The old Chief Libanio was still alive in 1866 at the aldeia of São Pedro de Alcantara. But he had been eclipsed by the director of Indians and 'excessive use of alcoholic drinks has stripped him of his remaining influence over the people in the aldeia.' The settlement was still functioning in 1881, when Colonel Francisco Quadros described its 'domesticated' Kaiwá as useful citizens. He praised 'the service they give to people navigating the Paranapanema'.

The main Kaiwá tribe, living far to the west between the Paraná and Paraguay rivers, was equally docile and acceptable to the colonists. In 1864, at the start of the Paraguayan War, the Capuchin missionary Friar Angelo de Caramonico was removed from running the Kinikinao mission on the Paraguay river because of serious allegations against him. He sought to justify and redeem himself by contacting the Kaiwá near Dourados in southern Mato Grosso. After a long expedition, Friar Angelo returned to Cuiabá with Kaiwá and Guarani chiefs. The Provincial President was impressed. He noted that the friar had done this 'partly to prove what efforts he had made to fulfil his mission, and also so that I should hear from the chiefs themselves that they and all their subjects definitely wished to settle in regular aldeias at the government's discretion'. By 1872, a report on the Indians of Mato Grosso described the Kaiwá as numerous, peaceful and sedentary, although little known. It even said that some people claimed that the Kaiwá were 'consistent in whatever they undertake – an extremely rare quality among savages'. This quiet tribe survives to this day, on a 3600-hectare reserve near the town of Dourados.

When the Kaiwá crossed the Paraná in their migration towards the Atlantic Ocean, they entered the territories of two formidable tribes: the Kaingáng in what are now the states of São Paulo and Paraná, and the related Xokleng to the south in Santa Catarina. Franz Keller noted the contrast in character between the two native races. 'The Kaingáng are just as frank and bold as the Guarani and Kaiwá are timid and reserved. They are an eminently warlike people. If they have no one to fight, they use hunting as an outlet to demonstrate their strength and cunning. It must be acknowledged that in hunting tapirs and peccaries they achieve rare perfection. The weapons they use in these pursuits are finished with extraordinary skill. Their long bows are all veneered with bark from imbé lianas and their arrows are made of a wood of great elasticity and worked so well that they look machine-made.' Their games were equally violent. Keller watched Kaingáng from two aldeias in north-western Paraná compete against one another. They met on sandy ground and each side had a pile of short cudgels made of hard, heavy wood and sharpened at both ends. The two teams hurled these clubs at one another with such force that they often caused serious wounds.

The missionary efforts of Francisco das Chagas Lima, who worked among one group of Kaingáng between 1810 and 1828, achieved little, frustrated by lethal epidemics, by the tenacity with which the Kaingáng clung to their tribal customs, and by the aggressions of colonists encouraged by the royal edict of 1808 which declared open war on the Kaingáng. At that time, settlers pushing west from Curitiba had penetrated the rich plains of Guarapuava.

Soon after the abdication of the first Emperor of Brazil, Pedro I, a law of 27 October 1831 revoked the anti-Kaingáng decree of 1808. Indians who had been enslaved under that law were to be freed – but instead of a return to their tribal societies, they were placed under the protection of justices of the peace and were considered as legal orphans. This was a disguised form of slavery. Documents survive about the fate of a group of Kaingáng who lived on the Itapetininga plain and the Juquiá river, mid-way between the towns of São Paulo and Curitiba. In 1835 seven families of these Indians were delivered to the Orphans Judge of the coastal town of Iguape. He promptly distributed the Indians among townspeople, who were to 'clothe and support them and at the same time try to employ them in useful pursuits. The citizens would be reimbursed for any expenses they might incur over them. This would serve to accustom [the Indians] to work. . . .' Most of this group of Kaingáng died in a measles epidemic in 1842; others fled back to their forests.

An influential champion of Indians now appeared in São Paulo. José Joaquim Machado de Oliveira had briefly been President of Pará in 1831–2, at a time when the Amazon was about to plunge into the Cabanagem rebellion. His attempts to deal sympathetically with the social injustices of Pará led to his removal: Portuguese landowners, merchants and local politicians had combined against him.

In 1846 this remarkable politician and historian was named as director-general of the Indians of São Paulo, a new position created by the imperial Indian law of 1845.

Machado de Oliveira realised that radical reforms were needed before the Indians could ever be successfully incorporated as useful citizens of Brazil. Protection of Indians must begin with their land. Without land, any tribe was vulnerable to abuse and unable to feed itself. When the Emperor Pedro II visited São Paulo, Indians from several villages sent him 'complaints about unjust seizure of lands they considered their rightful property'. Machado de Oliveira demanded that the Provincial President appoint a lawyer to help the Indians recover their land. But the man who was appointed, J. A. Pinto Junior, was a provincial deputy whose sympathies were with the landowners and settlers.

In 1848 Machado de Oliveira made a powerful appeal to the provincial legislature. He lamented that the history of Indian aldeias was everywhere the same. A settlement was made for the Indians, with land and false promises. 'But shortly afterwards these poor savages, without guidance or protection, enclosed, mistreated and despoiled of their property, either vegetate in poverty or run away to the forests. They take with them, from their contact with civilisation, nothing more than a few vices that they had not known before. . . . I have seen places where hundreds of native families were farming a few years ago and where hardly more than one or two individuals are now to be seen, and these so degraded that it induces a feeling of disgust. I do not know what fatality dooms this unfortunate race to disappear completely from the face of the earth.' An attempt was made to revive four Indian reserves near São Paulo, but when the tribal families were reunited it was found that the land that belonged to them was hopelessly invaded by squatters and intruders. The lawyer did nothing and was given no funds for a legal defence. As the Provincial President commented, 'anyone familiar with the chicanery of our courts and the delays and innumerable postponements involved in this kind of legal action . . . has no reason to expect much when the parties are a few poor Indians.'

It was still the dream of Brazilian governments to fill their vast country with European immigrants. There was an idea that the hardy peasants of central Europe would provide the tough, hardworking labourers needed to transform Brazil into an agricultural paradise as flourishing as the United States in North America. We have seen how Teófilo Ottoni wasted his career and fortune on colonisation schemes in Minas Gerais. Other groups of Europeans were being attracted to Pará on the Amazon and to the province of São Paulo. But the most promising lands were in the far south – in Paraná (a province separated from São Paulo in 1853), Santa Catarina and Rio Grande do Sul – where, being farther from the Equator, the climate was more temperate, similar to conditions in Europe. Southern Brazil was relatively empty, and it was also a region that the Emperor wanted to populate as a buffer against the Spanish-speaking republics to the south.

In the Itajaí valley of Santa Catarina, for instance, the coastal town of Itajaí was founded in 1820; in 1829 a colony called São Pedro de Alcantara was created with 154 families of Germans from Bremen; in 1836 Colónia Itajaí was founded, with a detachment of footsoldiers to protect it from the Xokleng (by 1854 this colony had fifteen sugar mills and twenty manioc farms); in 1845 there was a short-lived Belgian colonisation scheme; and in 1850 Dr Hermann Blumenau started the Colónia of São Paulo de Blumenau, helped by a recruiting agent whom the Brazilian government had sent to Prussia. Blumenau originally planned a large settlement, but when he sailed in 1850 he took only sixteen pioneers. More arrived in 1852 and, after many initial struggles, there were a thousand people in his settlements by 1860. A military colony called Santa Teresa (now Catuira) was founded on the Itajaí do Sul river to protect Blumenau from Xokleng: in 1854 this fort had forty-three soldiers, fifteen women and five children. Trails were cut to link Blumenau to Dona Francisca (now Joinville). The Paraguayan War of 1864–70 and the Franco–Prussian War of 1870–1 slowed the development of these German colonies, but they prospered thereafter and Blumenau became a município in 1880. Other colonies were founded in southern Brazil by Americans and English, Germans and Italians, and Swiss.

All this frontier activity threatened the Kaingáng and Xokleng. In 1852 the President of São Paulo summed up the hardships of Indians in western Paraná and Santa Catarina as 'the ill-starred history of the settlements of Palmas and Guarapuava, which were successively broken up and abolished after the Indians belonging to them had been murdered and robbed of the land which had been granted to them.' This President wanted to recreate Indian settlements along the Iguaçu river – a strategic route for a new road from Paraná to the mission provinces of Argentina and Paraguay – but he could see no hope of financing the many legal actions needed to reclaim the land, or of persuading the Kaingáng 'to overcome the distrust felt as a result of what has happened there'.

In the 1830s frontier settlement was spreading westwards from

Guarapuava. The colonists here had established good relations with the Kaingáng of Chief Viry. Thus, when in 1838 they pushed south across the Iguaçu river and discovered the rich plains of Palmas, they used Viry's Kaingáng to help attract the Kaingáng of this part of Santa Catarina.

One tactic adopted by the colonists was to enlist Kaingáng chiefs to fight their compatriots. In 1843 the Kaingáng Chief Victorino Condá of Guarapuava was encouraged to attack the Kaingáng who were massing near Palmas to the south. A group of Palmas Indians tried to escape to the sanctuary of the Guarapuava aldeia, but Condá and the local military force pursued and 'twenty or more unarmed Indians of both sexes were murdered without offering any active resistance.' Chief Victorino Condá was rewarded with 220 milreis, put in command of the Kaingáng he had defeated, and recognised officially as a bugreiro or Indian-hunter. Chief Viry of Guarapuava succeeded in this nefarious role. Although the settlers forced him to leave Guarapuava, he took his people south to Palmas and by 1856 was demanding uniforms, pay and recognition as a bugreiro.

In 1845 a group of settlers from Paraná under one Rocha cut southwards across the upper Uruguay river to the valley of Nonoái in northern Rio Grande do Sul. Other colonists soon followed. At this same time Baron Antonina, protector of the Kaiwá, was driving a road westwards from the Jacuí river into the uplands of Rio Grande do Sul. Ever since the expulsion of the Jesuits, the western part of this province had been in ruins: its rich pine forests and savannahs were ripe for colonisation in the mid-nineteenth century. Chief Victorino Condá, meanwhile, had moved even farther south to Nonoái, where he continued to fight for the colonists.

While chiefs such as Viry and Victorino Condá sided with the settlers, others continued to fight fiercely. The Kaingáng of Santa Catarina recalled those early clashes in their oral traditions: 'In those days our people had no metal tools. Chief Combró knew that the white men had axes and knives . . . and, wishing to acquire them, he killed the occupants of the first house he encountered. When the whites discovered this . . . they attacked his shelter.' Chief Combró retaliated by pursuing his white enemies and, after his death, his sons Tandó and Cohí continued the warfare. They were particularly angry with the 'tame' Kaingáng who were fighting for the colonists. Those mercenaries eventually killed Tandó, and the unacculturated Kaingáng 'suffered great reverses and reprisals by the settlers aided by chiefs Condá and Viry'. Another 'tame' Kaingáng leader was Chief Doble. He went to the provincial capital with part of his tribe and an escort of thirty 'savage' Kaingáng, in order to receive the rank of brigadier and other rewards from the President. But one of the German colonists, Reinhold Hensel, said that 'during their stay at Pôrto Alegre they were infected by smallpox poison. The disease manifested itself only after they returned to their settlement, and it thus caused great devastation among them.'

By 1857 the Vice-President of Paraná reported that the Kaingáng of Palmas were tame, completely idle and always ready to take up arms against their fellow Indians. A decade later, another President was still hoping to conquer, give religious instruction and ultimately 'civilise' all the Kaingáng; he wanted Indians to acknowledge the superiority of civilised men.

Brazil's southernmost province, Rio Grande do Sul, had always been a battleground between the Portuguese and Spanish empires. We have seen how the region of the former Jesuit missions in the west of Rio Grande do Sul lapsed into anarchy with the depredations of successive armies and warlords. There was thus a military flavour about this province and frontier area. There had also been a long and bitter popular rebellion of the 'Republic of Piratini' between 1835 and 1845.

The southernmost Kaingáng aldeia of Nonoái was created soon after the imperial victory over these rebels, and a company of foot-soldiers was therefore garrisoned near the Indian village. Chief Victorino Condá was awarded the rank of captain and encouraged to keep his men under arms. In 1848 there were 144 Indians settled at Nonoái; but in the following year another group of six hundred Kaingáng were being forcibly moved there by the soldiers. It became official policy to make Nonoái a collection centre for all natives of the region. Guarani were mixed with their former enemies the Kaingáng in this aldeia, and in 1854 all Chief Doble's surviving Kaingáng from Guarita were being forced or persuaded to transfer to Nonoái. Not surprisingly, there were serious tensions. Doble's Kaingáng were attacked by their uncontacted compatriots from the forests beyond the Uruguay. In 1854 the President of Rio Grande do Sul said that Nonoái was threatened by 'an invasion by intruders hostile to its director and who try to divide its Indians with their intrigues'.

By the following year, Doble's people and those who had been moved to Nonoái in 1849 were resisting their internment in this camp. They were being forced to work on a new road being cut from Cruz Alta across western Santa Catarina to Palmas in Paraná. Such roads were and are still the most potent means of penetrating virgin country. A later President of Santa Catarina argued that 'the best way to drive away Indians would be to open up and populate roads, and assign forces to defend the more accessible places.' The pacified Indians of Rio Grande do Sul were thus helping to subdue the remaining hostile tribes by building roads, just as they did by fighting for the colonists. As Carlos de Araújo Moreira Neto, the leading historian of nineteenth-century Brazilian Indians, pointed out: 'this means that the Indians of Nonoái were working for their own inevitable domination and eventual extermination.'

The attempts to transfer and assemble disparate groups of Kaingáng into one settlement incapable of providing them all with the necessary hunting grounds, and the conflicts between tame and hostile tribes, led to serious inter-tribal fighting and disruption during the late 1850s. In 1855 Nonoái's population had been swollen to almost a thousand, with as many as six groups led by their respective chiefs. At the end of that year there was a raid on a colonist's farm, apparently carried out by the Indians of two of these chiefs. They were pursued by the militia, aided by the Kaingáng of two 'loyal' chiefs; the two hostile chiefs Nicofe and Manoel Grande were respectively killed and captured; and their relative Victorino Condá left Nonoái to return to Palmas, whence he launched attacks on his former fellow tribesmen at Nonoái. Chief Viry, who was still at Palmas, helped Condá in these skirmishes, while Chief Doble kept his people apart in Vacaria. In 1859 the peoples of Chiefs Doble and Chico were relocated in a new settlement called Santa Isabel near Cazeros military colony. These Kaingáng were in wretched condition, short of water and settled on poor land, and they petitioned to be returned to Nonoái.

By the 1860s Nonoái's population was much reduced by these migrations. President Fernandes Leão made 'gloomy forecasts about the future of the province's settlements' and admitted – contrary to official policies of the day – that rapid and compulsory acculturation of Indians into 'the customs and occupations of our society will mean their death'. By the end of that decade, Reinhold Hensel wrote that the Kaingáng no longer inhabited the extensive forests of the plateau and low hills bordering the Uruguay river that separates Rio Grande do Sul from Santa Catarina. Although they had once been greatly feared by the German colonists, 'today they seem to be entirely repulsed and are limited to the provinces of Paraná and Santa Catarina where the colony of Brusque is particularly exposed to their ravages.'

When the German traveller Max Beschoren visited Nonoái five

years later, he found a thriving colonial parish with the Kaingáng
aldeia some distance from the town. There were now three hundred
Indians at Nonoái, with only fifty warriors among them. They lived
in a cluster of simple thatched huts built of a variety of materials and
with almost no furniture. They seemed contented enough, with
plenty of game to hunt, living surrounded by dogs, pigs, hens and
parrots. In winter almost all the men went off to the woods to gather
herva maté for the aromatic tea so beloved of Argentinian gauchos:
this earned them enough to live on and buy cachaça.

To the west of Nonoái, Beschoren visited Campo Novo, a rich
plain on the Turvo tributary of the Uruguay. This valley had been
discovered by colonists in 1834, but their attempts to settle it were
stoutly resisted by the resident Kaingáng of Chief Fongui. He killed
many settlers in frontier warfare, but then had a change of heart and
decided to come to terms with the invaders. 'The settlers at once
forgot their old hostility and gave their former enemy food, clothing,
etc. and thus became friends.' Fongui and his people were moved to
Nonoái in the late 1840s and helped government forces pursue their
'rebellious' compatriots. But Fongui came to dislike Nonoái and led
his tribe back to their former homes on the Turvo. His village
consisted in 1875 of two rows of well-built wood and tile houses.
Beschoren made friends with this very old gentleman, who although
he was well into his eighties could still walk long distances with ease
and kept three wives and many children. His people were well
clothed and housed. They prospered from gathering herva maté but
were badly addicted to cachaça. Old Chief Fongui dealt severely
with drunks, tying their hands between their knees and dumping
them in the bushes to sober up.

Fongui's acculturated Kaingáng often traded with their uncontacted compatriots who lived in the pine forests on the right bank of
the Uruguay in Brazilian Paraná and Argentine Missiones. But the
isolation of these people was broken in the following decade. The
Brazilians wanted to push a road into the far west of Santa Catarina.
They founded military colonies to protect this strategic route: at
Chopim (now Xanxerê) and at Chapecó opposite Nonoái on the
north of the Uruguay in 1881, and at Iguaçu near the mighty waterfalls in 1888.

The Kaingáng who fought for the settlers were remarkably effective.
In 1856 Chief Viry's forces attacked uncontacted Kaingáng in the
Piquiri valley in western Paraná. Viry's men 'killed many of their
warriors, captured some others and burned their huts. Disheartened

by this and other reverses, a large number of them came to seek our friendship. They presented themselves in 1858 at the military colony of Jataí. . . . The government sought to settle them in the aldeias of São Jerónimo and later also in São Pedro de Alcantara. A large number of them still lives quietly and industriously in São Jerónimo. But those of São Pedro de Alcantara, however, were disgusted by the behaviour and speculations with them of Friar Timotheo de Castelnuovo. They therefore withdrew and now [in the mid-1860s] live peacefully in the forests of the Tibagi and Ivaí valleys.' Franz Keller was also convinced that the Kaingáng of chiefs Manoel, Gregório and others had decided to cease fighting and enter the aldeias of western Paraná because of defeats by the Kaingáng mercenaries fighting for the whites. 'Assaults on the road south [from the Ivaí] also ceased completely . . . from fear inspired by the chiefs or famous captains Viri and Victorino Condá. . . . [Their tribe] was armed with guns and waged cruel but effective war on its brothers in the wilds near the Palmas plains.' Keller recalled that there had been bloody fighting between colonists and settlers in western Paraná. During the years when the Kaingáng were proscribed by law, killing an Indian was considered no different to hunting a jaguar.

In the 1860s official attitudes changed and there was fresh effort to turn these Indians into wage-earning labourers. Aldeias were established: at São Pedro de Alcantara and São Jerónimo on the Tibagi, and at Paranapanema on the site of the long-abandoned Jesuit mission of Santo Ignacio where the Tibagi flows into the Paranapanema. The government devoted funds to buy trade goods and tools for the Kaiwá and Kaingáng in these villages. Keller praised the Italian Capuchin missionary for the initial success of São Pedro de Alcantara. 'At the outset, fighting seemed imminent at times. But thanks to the tact of the worthy Director, Friar Timotheo de Castelnuovo, the critical period passed. The Kaingáng – two hundred of whom had on different occasions approached intending to launch an attack – finally decided to build a hut near the centre of the aldeia. Today, although still far from civilised, they have at least entirely abandoned their old ideas of robbery and killing. They live peacefully in the same aldeia alongside the Kaiwá – although one cannot say that there is genuine friendship between the former enemies.'

In the early 1860s, São Pedro de Alcantara had a population of five hundred Kaingáng and four hundred Kaiwá and Guarani. But the village was close to the military colony of Jataí and therefore attracted settlers. Friar Timotheo, who encouraged such colonisation, wrote a curious letter to the Provincial President in 1871 in which he happily recalled the days when he had been confronting hostile Indians and had therefore enjoyed government support. 'Times have changed: the Indians have ceased to be savage, they have fraternised with us, have been learning our trades and adopting our customs.' Friar Timotheo complained that Indians outnumbered settlers and missionaries by five to one at São Pedro. They were therefore exhausting his slender resources, and were too numerous for him to convert. Ten years later, however, there were more settlers and fewer Indians at this mission. A report of 1881 said that it contained 210 Kaingáng and 378 Kaiwá Guarani, but also 43 blacks, 134 mixed-blood colonists, and 3 missionaries 'of pure European blood'. The aldeia of Paranapanema was extinguished in 1878 and the other Indian villages of western Paraná were eventually swallowed in the same way by the advancing frontier.

To the south, in Santa Catarina, the Kaingáng initially welcomed Capuchin missionaries who arrived in their midst in the late 1840s. The Italian friars came with plenty of clothing, seeds and agricultural implements. The Kaingáng in turn seemed delighted by the trappings of Christianity. They enjoyed singing in the church choir, and natives participated in the mass as sacristan and other officers. But when frontier relations deteriorated into fighting, the missionaries were less successful. Two Italian Capuchins tried to convert the Xokleng of the interior of Santa Catarina in 1868, but their missions at Lages and Itajaí achieved few converts.

In 1885 there was another failure, by the Capuchin Friar Luiz de Cemetille. The trouble was that the missionaries refused to plunge into the forests. They preferred the comforts of Penápolis, where they had been given a large convent estate. 'The friars kept the convent and lands, which they later divided into lots for sale; but they never approached the forests of the Indians and took no step to call these to peace.' Friar Luiz de Cemetille excused his failure to convert the Kaingáng by claiming that nature had been too liberal to them. When Friar Luiz tried to make the old chief Aropquimbe give up his four wives, the chief refused because the wives were a symbol of his valour as a warrior. He explained that he did not live among the whites 'to find happiness, for he was happier in the virgin forests where the game, fish and fruit were more abundant, and there never failed to be enough food to support him and his numerous family. The true reason for his staying among us was because he could no longer do without our tools. It was now too late for him to accept a new religion, for he was an old man – so old that he could not learn to make the sign of the cross. In the end he left with a guffaw of laughter, slapped me on the back, and said a sarcastic farewell.' This Capuchin missionary felt that the Kaingáng could be persuaded of the virtue of work only by ambition to acquire objects. Conversion of such Indians would be very slow: it was probably impossible among adults, but might succeed if missionary efforts were concentrated on children.

In the 1880s there was a further drive westwards by the frontiersmen of Paraná. The Camé Kaingáng of the Piquiri river sought help from the colonists of Guarapuava against hostile Indians to the south of them near the mouth of the Iguaçu – the region near the magnificent Iguaçu waterfalls. The authorities naturally welcomed this alliance. The Indians of the Piquiri would become 'vigilant guards' to protect Guarapuava; and they could help in the exploration of the unknown lands between the lower Piquiri and Iguaçu rivers. The Camé Kaingáng were marvellously co-operative. By 1883 they had won over 'other remote hordes, from the plain of Moirão to the heights of Sete Quedas. This conquest proceeded so rapidly that when citizen Norberto Mendes Cordeiro and other explorers went from that plain and on to the Sete Quedas, he found loyal [Indian] friends and auxiliaries, who vied with one another to be the first to offer hospitality to the daring frontiersman and his intrepid companions.'

Another explorer, José do Nascimento, penetrated the plains of Jusquiá west of Guarapuava in 1886 and parleyed with six Kaingáng chiefs from the Piquiri. Nascimento tried to persuade these Indians to move to the Ivaí river near the colonial settlement of Teresinha. But the Kaingáng quickly refused: they did not want to leave their homelands, where their ancestors were buried and which they regarded as richer in game than the Ivaí. They did, however, want to be able to make their own cachaça rum. 'They ask to be given a sugar mill and other equipment necessary for treating cane, tools, and some Portuguese . . . among whom should come smiths, carpenters and other artisans who would teach them to work and farm – for which they show much inclination and energy: for there is no laziness among these people, as many claim.' This same Nascimento also visited more acculturated Kaingáng near Tibagi. He found them deeply worried that their lands were threatened by encroaching settlers. They clapped with delight when he reassured them that they would be protected. He also noted that they greatly loved the blacksmith of Tibagi, Carlos Schneider, who made no charge for repairing their tools.

The colonists of Santa Catarina formed an infantry militia in 1836 and this continued until its disbandment in 1879. Its role was to protect frontier settlements and launch official raids into Indian territory. But the militia was poorly armed and ineffective. The job of exterminating Indians was soon taken up by the professional hunters known as bugreiros. Such paid killers tried to surprise Indian villages when the men could be killed in their sleep. They brought back only the women and children. Captive women were exposed to public curiosity as they were brought back in carts and, according to a citizen of Blumenau, Dr Hugo Gensch, the bugreiros even 'charged money to show the women's sexual organs'. Notorious bugreiros included João Bento, Martins, Veríssimo, Maneco Angelo and Natal Coral; but the most famous was Martinho Marcelino, who was paid by the provincial government of Santa Catarina to decimate Xokleng and who killed more Indians than all the others put together, often slaughtering hundreds in a single raid. Eduardo Hoerhan described a typical attack: 'They took infinite precautions, for it was essential to surprise the Indians in their huts when they were fast asleep. They took no dogs. They followed Indian trails, discovered the huts, and without talking or smoking awaited the propitious moment. They launched their attack as day was about to break. Their first concern was to cut the bowstrings. They then made their slaughter. You must appreciate that the Indians were awoken by shooting and machete attacks and had no chance to defend themselves. The assailants' entire heroism consisted of cutting inert flesh of people terrified by surprise.'

Official attitudes to the Kaingáng and Xokleng became increasingly hostile and strident. In 1858 the Marquis of Olinda, who was Interior Minister, admitted that most Indians in Brazil 'are marching towards rapid annihilation. In general, lands belonging to Indians have been invaded by powerful neighbours, taken by town councils, and even sequestered by municipal judges. . . . The wretched Indians find themselves persecuted and oppressed almost everywhere. What I have demonstrated is nothing less than the martyrdom of the primitive inhabitants of Brazil.' The next minister took a very different view of land rights. He declared, 'The wandering Indians of these regions are constantly threatening the property rights and even the lives of the civilised inhabitants.' In the following year, the imperial minister responsible for Indian affairs described the Xokleng as 'so ferocious, indomitable and blood-thirsty that they dispel any hopes of converting them to the customs of our society. . . . It is felt that only armed force can dominate them. This will mean that they are obliged to live in subjection (that is, in a servile state) and their children will be raised in different habits to their parents' barbarity.'

It was feared that Indians who defended their lands would discourage European immigrants. 'Indians who disturb the colonists in their agricultural labours are aggravating unfounded or true accusations against emigration to Brazil.' The President of Santa Catarina was even more outspoken. He declared that 'these barbarians who spare neither women nor children, who think only of robbing us or attacking us in ambushes, can never be treated with kindness and consideration. . . . I am increasingly convinced that it is practical, even necessary, to snatch the savages by force from the forests and place them somewhere whence they cannot escape. In this way we could protect the farmers from these murderers. We might even make useful citizens of these barbarians' children.' So when the German consul in Santa Catarina proposed that persons be hired to 'put the assailants to flight', his idea was accepted: one Manoel Alves da Rocha was hired as a bugreiro at a salary of 300 milreis a month, to be provided partly by the settlers and partly by the government.

Despite all the outcry among the colonists, the balance of terror was heavily in their favour. The settlers of Guarapuava and Palmas assembled against the Kaingáng in 1859 and made a great slaughter among them: the defeated survivors took refuge alongside the Kaiwá at Jataí. But Colonel Francisco Quadros felt that 'the savage cruelty of the explorers of the forests and wildernesses of São Paulo was the sole reason why these poor people have not yet thrown themselves into the arms of our civilisation.' José Deeke combed through the reports and newspapers of the German colonists of Santa Catarina and found that in the sixty-two years from 1852 to 1914 the Xokleng had made only sixty-one attacks, in which they killed forty-one whites and wounded twenty-two. He argued that the Xokleng often came in search of food or metal for their arrow-heads. Others approached the whites out of mere curiosity. 'The natives did not come with the direct intention of killing. Hatred for the whites and blood-thirsty vengeance, of which they are accused, are mere fiction. The natives want only to obtain the articles they need, such as metal tools or cloth. Without doubt, however, they feel no inhibition if it is necessary to despatch a white to the other world; but that was not the purpose of their assaults.'

By the end of the Brazilian Empire in 1889, the Kaingáng and Xokleng of southern Brazil were in a miserable condition. Nonoái in Rio Grande do Sul was much reduced, partly because it had ceased to be an assembly point – various sub-tribes of Kaingáng were dispersed to other aldeias, which was probably to their benefit. But such smaller aldeias were extinguished when they clashed with the demands of colonial landowners. The last presidential report, of 1889, revealed that the Indians were working on road gangs to open the interior of the province to settlement. Their supervisors were salaried, but the Indians themselves were forced to work only 'in exchange for their daily food'.

In Santa Catarina, many Xokleng were still resisting German colonists' expansion inland. There was official support for the policy of hiring bugreiros to hunt down and exterminate hostile Indians. A. F. de Souza Pitanga, a magistrate in the interior of the province at that time, was disgusted by the settlers' loathing of wild Indians. 'The common people call them by the significant name "vermin". During my tenure of the judicial district of Coritibanas in Santa Catarina, I had to declare publicly by legal decision that anyone who attempted an attack which they ingenuously call "beating up bugres" would be punished under the penal code, in order to stop such attacks.'

The Provincial President Francisco da Rocha tried to analyse the Indian problem in his report for 1887. His conclusions were profoundly pessimistic, but accurate for some tribes. He was not impressed by religious conversion: there were far too few missionaries for it to be effective, and he considered tribes like the Xokleng too wild to be capable of instruction. They were too nomadic to be pinned down in one settlement, and their existence as hunter–gatherers made them too 'primitive' for Christianity. The Xokleng were formidable fighters, 'who steal up like deer or snakes' and attack from ambush 'with infernal yells and blood-curdling laughter' if they felt strong enough to win; otherwise they fled silently through the trees. But armed force was not the answer. If subdued by military conquest, such Indians would become desperate, would flee and exact 'barbarous revenge'. President Rocha blamed Brazilian society for its intolerance to Indians, and acknowledged that tribes who were forced to coexist 'are overcome by a profound melancholy which destroys and kills them'. His proposed solution was illogical and unjust. He wanted to drive Indians farther from the frontier by opening roads into their territory, sending in colonists and establishing military outposts. The Indians would withdraw before the advancing frontier until their last refuges were occupied, at which time they would be forced into a final confrontation with Brazilian society. This is precisely what is happening today to the last tribes being contacted in the innermost depths of Amazonia.

Early in the twentieth century, Dr Hugo Gensch of Blumenau was a respected member of the German settler community who deplored and opposed the atrocities of the bugreiros. Gensch shocked an anthropological congress in Vienna with his reports of murders, rapes and enslavement of Kaingáng and Xokleng. He even published photographs of bugreiros with their frightened and pathetic women and children captives. Gensch was vilified as an Indian-lover by the other colonists. In order to prove the innate intelligence of Indians, Gensch acquired a ten-year-old Xokleng girl called Korikrã. He adopted her as his daughter and decided to give her a European education. She was christened Maria and Gensch taught her French and German, took her to Paris and Buenos Aires, and was inordinately proud of his experiment with her.

Years later, an Indian service official called Eduardo Hoerhan brought a hundred newly pacified Xokleng to Blumenau. Maria Korikrã's father and relatives went to see her. There was an embarrassing scene when the forest Indians removed her blouse to find an old scar, sought a tribal mark on her foot, and undid her hair to make her more recognisable. She refused to acknowledge them. Her angry father said: 'I see that you are ashamed of me, ashamed of all your people.' He showed his large hands and said: 'These hands carried you many times. These hands lifted your body up into the pine trees to pick the seeds you ate. These hands of mine raised me up into many trees to gather the honey you ate. Honey, you understand, honey! honey! which went down your throat – here' and he ran his hand violently down Maria's neck, to her disgust. 'The old man took Maria's aunt and held one of her breasts in his hand and said: "Look, these breasts fed you, these arms cradled you." The old man became filled with hatred and disgust. He went up to his daughter and pushed her away violently. Turning to Eduardo Hoerhan he said: "She is of no further use to us. But she could still serve you. Take her and bring her to your white house [in our village] and impregnate her many times. She can no longer perform for us, but she still could for you." ' Hoerhan did not follow this advice and no colonists were prepared to marry an Indian woman. Maria Gensch died unmarried, aged forty-two.

The northernmost limit of Kaingáng territory lay in the interior of the modern state of São Paulo, between the Paranapanema and Tietê rivers. Unfortunately for these Indians, the second half of the nineteenth century saw a coffee-growing frontier push inexorably into their homelands. Coffee had originally been grown in Amazonia, but it was found to flourish better in the cooler latitudes of São Paulo. At first coffee fazendas developed along the upper Paraíba, from the city of São Paulo towards Taubaté. This was the territory of the Puri, who had long since been pacified and destroyed. But after 1850 settlers clashed with Kaingáng Indians in the Avanhandava savannahs. Other colonists migrated south from Minas Gerais into the fertile Campos Novos (New Plains) west of Botucatu and into the region between the upper Peixe (Fish) and Paranapanema rivers.

In 1867 an English company built a railway from the port of Santos up the steep escarpment on to the plateau at Jundiaí. By 1872 this line was extended westwards to Campinas and then beyond towards Kaingáng territory. It was found that the interior of São Paulo had patches of violet-coloured terra roxa soil formed by decomposing basalt. This soil, together with the altitude of five hundred to nine hundred metres, proved perfect for growing coffee, demand for which was increasing hugely in Europe and North America. Technical improvements in coffee production enabled planters to manage without slaves, and the new railway allowed them to carry the beans to market without long mule trains. All this meant that there was a rush of colonists, which reached a crescendo between 1880 and 1910. The coffee frontier was highly damaging to Indians, for coffee plantations demanded all the available land, without providing a role for Indian labour.

The Kaingáng of São Paulo tried desperately to resist this invasion. They were reasonably successful near Campos Novos, around the headwaters of the Peixe and Feio rivers, and west of Bauru. The first coffee planter at the Ribeirão de São Matheus was killed in 1872, and for a time the area was abandoned by settlers. Gustav von Koenigswald wrote that 'the whites greatly fear the Coroados [Kaingáng] and people on the Indian frontier are never safe from their attack. . . . They strike sporadically, plundering and killing on isolated farmsteads before disappearing back into the forests.' Inevitably, the settlers responded by batidas, murderous raids into Indian territory. They also hired professional killers. 'In 1888 the bugreiro Joaquim Bueno poisoned with strychnine the pools of drinking water of a Kaingáng village in the sertão of the Paranapanema, causing the deaths of some two thousand Indians of all ages. This fact was narrated by Bueno himself, who remained unpunished.' The government also maintained military outposts near Kaingáng territory, notably Avanhandava and Itapura to protect portages around the rapids of those names on the lower Tietê.

The fighting intensified when the government sought to push the railway westwards towards the Paraná and Mato Grosso at the beginning of the twentieth century. Rail gangs clashed with Kaingáng Indians, and no quarter was given by either side. In one incident in 1907 a train came along the new line 'carrying the bodies of five men whose heads had been decapitated by the Indians. Needless to say, all the workers disbanded. On another occasion two groups of sleeping men were massacred.' Retribution was swift. On 16 October 1908 the *Correio da Manhã* newspaper in Rio de Janeiro reported: 'It is horrible what the workers of the Estrado de Ferro Noroeste [North-west Railway] are doing to the unfortunate [Kaingáng] Indians of the region between Bauru and Avanhandava. Their massacre is a kind of sport – a highly entertaining form of game hunting. Several days ago, according to witnesses, a group of these Indians was celebrating in their own manner the rites of a wedding ceremony, when suddenly they were attacked by railroad workers who slaughtered men, women, old people and children. They spared only one young girl whom they abused in a most barbarous fashion before proceeding to ransack the encampment.'

This particular massacre was fully reported by one of its members, João Pedro. The raiding party consisted of thirty-one men, heavily armed with Winchester 44-calibre carbines and shotguns. They advanced for four days before silently approaching a Kaingáng village as night was falling. The Indians were holding a festival around a fire in the middle of their village, which the attackers deduced was a marriage ceremony 'because one girl appeared to be the centre of attention and was more adorned than the others. The Indians danced and sang happily, entirely unaware of the horrible catastrophe that awaited them.' The watching attackers were impressed by the cleanliness and efficiency of the Kaingáng village, with its well-swept open ground, tidy huts and skilful thatch architecture. 'They were particularly surprised by the constant friendliness maintained throughout the festival, with open laughter and playfulness between the Indians. They could even notice from their hiding places the variety of characters, some gayer and others more withdrawn. The former often teased the latter, and they noticed some of the elders among the extroverts, but no discord arose from this.' The black bugreiro João Pedro told Lieutenant Pedro Dantas of the Commission of Enquiry: 'They almost seemed like real people, Lieutenant.'

The Kaingáng festival continued all night. Just before dawn, the bugreiros decided to launch their attack, fearing that they would be discovered in daylight. As Lieutenant Dantas reported: 'The first general volley was fired. One may appreciate its murderous effect if you know what good marksmen these people are, and consider how long they had to prepare their aim at leisure, each selecting one person so that the killing would not strike only random targets. Various other volleys were fired in addition to that one. The poor Indians did not have a chance. They awoke under attack and were completely disorganised by that cowardly and unprovoked aggression. Some affirm that over a hundred lives were sacrificed there: for the first volleys were followed by a machete attack that spared nobody.' When the raiding party returned, its leaders kept quiet but the lesser members could not resist boasting. 'They claimed to have made a clean sweep, and even proved their achievement by exhibiting ears cut from their victims!'

A Czech anthropologist, Vojtěch Frič, was in Paraná in 1906 and roundly condemned the German colonists for its frontier conflicts. Such colonists had bought Indian land for ludicrously low prices, and they were the first to complain vociferously of threats of Indian attack. 'It is enough for an Indian to approach a fazenda and call out loudly – no one understands what he is saying – for a soldier to be sent against him. Not only that, private individuals led by an Italian also undertake to punish the "evil, dangerous savages", just to have the pleasure of killing people. This sort of thing happens every day throughout [Kaingáng] territory. Every Indian who is found is shot. Entire expeditions have been organised to kill savages and steal small children who are then sold for 100 milreis apiece. This is happening in this century in the civilised states of Brazil!' One bugreiro called Antonio Adão was carrying a five-year-old boy back from an ambush, intending to keep him as a slave. The boy kept clawing at his captor's back. Adão finally lost patience, swung the boy into the air by a leg and let him fall on to his dagger. The Indian child was left there, impaled, to be eaten by vultures or forest animals. Alípio Bandeira, an early official of the Indian Protection Service of 1910, said that many Indian women were raped before being killed or burned in such raids.

Frič met bugreiros in the interior of São Paulo who decorated their Winchester carbines with Indian teeth. 'They earn up to 130 marks for every pair of human ears, and make a living exclusively from hunting "bugres". It is painful to hear such bestial men describe their forest expeditions: "It is beautiful to watch how an Indian who has been picked off in a high tree falls down from branch to branch and then lies dead on the ground." ' When such bugreiros were asked whether Indians could speak, they would answer: 'Yes, sir, they talk and look like people; but they are beasts of the forest.'

Extermination or Protection?

Throughout the second half of the nineteenth century, Brazilian Indians were declining in numbers and being forced to retreat to the innermost recesses of that vast country. Although some powerful tribes – Bororo, Kaingáng, Waimiri-Atroari, Chavante, Kayapó – fought stubbornly, others succumbed. Indians were becoming curiosities rather than a serious threat. With this decline in their political importance came a change in attitudes. Now that there was nothing to fear from Indians, urban intellectuals could afford to romanticise about them.

At one literary extreme, there were still writers who regarded Indians as an inferior race, an anachronistic impediment to the progress of modern Brazil. Francisco Adolpho de Varnhagen was the Macaulay of his age, author of a monumental general history of Brazil; but his views on Indians were tough and uncompromising. He himself had once been frightened by the threat of Kaingáng attack when travelling in Paraná. In a pamphlet published in 1850, Varnhagen poured out his 'indignation against the damned hypocrisy of pseudo-philanthropy. Is it true philanthropy for us to consent that the sons of the blessed territory of Brazil should be devouring one another in the forests and whenever possible attacking the civilised citizens of the Empire?' His 'prompt and sure' solution was to 'educate' Indians by force. 'Because of their moral incapacity, wild Indians should be declared pupils of the nation.' Captured Indians should be put to work on public labour projects or distributed among settlers' families as domestic servants.

Varnhagen equated tribes who fought to defend their lands with civil rebels. 'Wild Indians, those who with no present provocation keep the provinces in which they live in a permanent state of civil war, invade our fields, murder their owners or settlers or slaves, prey on their cattle, impede the opening of roads and freedom of communications' should be crushed as rebels. 'These and all other barbarians . . . prove docile and obedient only when defeated; just as they grow bold and threaten us when treated kindly.' 'If we consider Indians outside the social contract, if we judge them to be a foreign nation that threatens and molests us, we have every right to conquer them. There is no right of conquest more just than that of civilisation over barbarism. . . . Let us subject our savages, let us educate them forcibly, and fifteen or twenty years hence when they need no more tutelage let us make useful citizens and good Christians of them.' 'But you may say that the Indians are outside the Constitution "because of their moral incapacity". I would reply that the same applies to madmen. And yet you *lock them up* in an asylum.'

This historian fully approved of European conquest of the Americas. 'Our people learned by experience . . . that the right way to treat barbarians was to use force to impose the necessary tutelage that would make them accept Christianity and adopt the habits of civilised life. They either had to conform to this system or leave the land. Such are our convictions.' He quoted with approval the view of a Brazilian bishop that 'slavery and subordination are the first steps in the civilisation of nations.' 'Far from condemning the use of force to civilise Indians . . . we must resort to it today . . . for the benefit of these unfortunates. Even when reduced to the condition of African slaves in our society, they enjoy more tranquil and secure lives than that afforded by the fearful and dangerous liberty of their forests.'

Varnhagen's belligerence echoed that of some provincial presidents and most frontier colonists. But the reactionary historian was immediately opposed by other liberal intellectuals. João Francisco Lisboa published a review called *Jornal de Timon* in the northern province of Maranhão from 1852 to 1855. This rebutted all Varnhagen's polemics. Lisboa wrote in defence of Indian freedom. He argued that Indians were the original and rightful lords of Brazil and condemned their subjection and enslavement. Another champion of the Indians, D. J. G. de Magalhães, said that Varnhagen was wrong to depict Indians as savages intent on vengeance on neighbouring tribes. Magalhães quoted early accounts of Brazilian Indians to show that they had a fine sense of law and social order and that tribes were governed democratically by their councils of elders. Anyone with experience of Indians knew that Varnhagen was writing rubbish.

The angry debate between Varnhagen and Lisboa coincided with a new literary movement in Brazil: indianism. The glorification of Brazilian Indians burst with the force of a new revelation in the poems of Antonio Gonçalves Dias. It was no accident that this great poet was also from the northern province of Maranhão, where Indian blood and culture were engrained in the population and its way of life, and uncontacted tribes lived in forests not far to the west. Gonçalves Dias published his first book of poems, *Primeiros cantos*, in 1847 and his third, *Últimos cantos*, in 1851, all while still in his twenties. He had already taught himself the Tupi language and he filled his poetry with its melodious words. Far from resenting his Indian past, Gonçalves Dias gloried in the cultural heritage and courage of Maranhão's native ancestors.

The indianist movement gained immediate acceptance. It appealed to nineteenth-century romanticism. It also assuaged feelings of frustration or humiliation among Brazilians recently emerged from colonial rule to independence. On the one hand, Brazilian politicians and businessmen wore starched collars and frock coats in the tropical heat, and their Emperor behaved with British dignity. But many secretly suffered from having mixed blood, and they resented the way in which Europeans – whom they admired and imitated – despised the tropics, the 'colonies' and the New World of the Americas. Now the indianist writers glorified and ennobled tropical nature and its primitive inhabitants. Brazil was portrayed as a virgin country full of youth and vigour. At the same time, the indianist myth reinforced the European sophistication of educated Brazilians: it was a romantic movement of obvious European origin. It regarded Indians as heroic victims of oppression, but it also viewed them as alien curiosities, members of 'the American people, now extinct'.

Indianist literature may now be criticised for being too artificial and repetitive, too steeped in romantic notions of the noble savage or edenic nature. But in its day it had a revolutionary effect. Gonçalves Dias and his contemporaries Gonçalves de Magalhães and the novelist José de Alencar all tackled the new idea of conflict of races. Writing about the valiant Guaikurú in 1882, Claudio Soido quoted Gonçalves Dias' poem 'Canção do Tamoio' ('Song of the Tamoio', about the tribe which resisted Portuguese colonisation of Rio de Janeiro in the 1560s) because it praised the bravery of a captured Tamoio facing execution. The greatest champion of the Indians, Cândido Rondon, loved to quote the same poem about the threat posed by European invasion: 'Don't you understand what the monster is seeking? Don't you understand why he has come, what he wants? He has come to kill your brave warriors, to seize your daughter and wife! He has come bringing heavy shackles from which the Tupi tribe will groan. The elders are going to have to serve as slaves – even the shaman will eventually have to be a slave! You will flee, seeking refuge: a sad refuge in the dense wilderness. . . . Oh shame! oh ruin!'

Indianist authors tended to look to the romantic past rather than at the ugly reality of the contemporary Brazilian frontier. Gonçalves de Magalhães wrote a magnificent epic poem, 'A confederação dos Tamoios' ('The Tamoio Confederation', 1856) about the attempt by tribes near Rio de Janeiro to expel the Portuguese colonists in the sixteenth century. In this poem the Indian leader Ambiré and his wife Iguaçu both sacrifice their lives in the struggle for freedom. Gonçalves Dias described that same resistance in his 'Canção do Tamoio'. His interest in native Indians as men of nature and his own nostalgia for his beloved Brazil emerge in his 'Timbiras' (about the tribes of western Maranhão) and 'I-Iuca-Pirama'. In 'O canto do índio' ('Song of the Indian') Dias examined the inner conflicts that rend tribal societies. He understood Indian protest against the invasion of their land and the trauma of cultural shock. In his poem 'Marabá' he expressed the anguish of a half-caste woman repudiated by her own people.

The third great Indianist writer, José de Alencar, was another northerner, from the province of Ceará. Alencar was a novelist, essayist and politician with a wide audience. He sought to write *Brazilian* prose, introducing colloquial idiom and many words of Tupi origin into his vocabulary. His novel *O Guarani* (1857) was also about vanished coastal tribes, but in it he created a magnificent fresco of Indian life. His short stories *Iracema* (an anagram of America, about an innocent Indian girl, written in 1865 and translated into English as *Iracema, the Honey-Lips* in 1886) and *Ubirijara* were other masterpieces of romantic Indianist literature, highly sympathetic to native tribal society. Alencar had previously attacked Magalhães' poem on the Tamoios, in an essay published under a pseudonym. This stirred up a famous literary debate among intellectuals, joined by the Emperor Dom Pedro II himself. From it emerged Alencar's vivid, musical style and his rich use of Brazilian language.

Literary awareness of Indian qualities was reflected in a more sympathetic official attitude. As the nineteenth century drew to a close, provincial presidents wrote more kindly about the Indians in their regions. They condemned those who oppressed Indians and longed to find solutions to the 'Indian problem'. But this shift to a more liberal approach was not translated into legislation. There were no important laws about Indians after the basic Indian legislation of 1845 and the Law of Lands of 1850. For forty years, almost the only edicts that involved Indians were decrees abolishing old and defunct missions and selling off their lands.

There was no improvement when Brazil became a republic in 1889. The Positivist Church – a sect based on the teachings of Auguste Comte which preached a system embracing all aspects of an individual's private and public life – was very influential in Brazil at this time. The Positivists proposed that parts of the country should be designated as 'American states of Brazil . . . composed of fetishist hordes scattered about the Republic'. Such states would be protected against any abuse of their lands or native peoples. The Republic of Brazil would 'maintain amicable relations with them, which is nowadays recognised as a duty between enlightened and sympathetic nations'. But this radical idea did not appear in the Republican Constitution of 1891. This legislation in fact made no mention of Indians, as we have seen. It dealt them a lethal blow by removing their legal right to tribal lands: for without land no tribe could support itself or survive intact. The Republican Constitution transferred ownership and political control of 'unoccupied land' (terras devolutas) from central government to the states. It abolished any special protection of Indians and handed them over to the state governments, which were composed of their traditional enemies the frontier settlers and landowners. Humberto de Oliveira commented that Indians were thus 'cruelly tricked out of the ownership of their lands'.

Article 6 of the new Civil Code equated Indians with young males aged between sixteen and twenty or with married women. It declared that they were 'incapable' with regard to certain acts – customs which might be acceptable to tribal society but were contrary to ordinary Brazilian law. The new Republican Constitution separated church and state. This meant that the church no longer enjoyed official status and missionary activity ceased to be a government service. The way was opened for Protestant missionaries to start operating among Brazilian Indians.

The devolution of power from central government to the states helped to spur a new westward push of the frontier. During the first two decades of the Republic, migration into central Brazil intensified after years of stagnation. In Amazonia the rubber boom was reaching its climax. Seringueiros poured into Acre and the uppermost headwaters of the Amazon rivers in search of hevea trees. The fast-growing city of Manaus inspired renewed cattle ranching on the Rio Branco and agricultural plantations on the upper Rio Negro. The abolition of black slavery in 1888 caused a labour shortage on sugar and coffee estates, so that Brazil actively encouraged European immigration. World demand for coffee pushed the frontier westwards in the states of São Paulo and Paraná. Many of the new European colonists carved farms out of former Indian forests in the southern states of Santa Catarina and Rio Grande do Sul and in Botocudo territory on the central coast. Huge plantations of the aromatic tea herva maté were created in southern Mato Grosso. With the introduction of refrigerated meat, cattle ranching in southern Brazil became big business. Many smaller farmers were driven out and sought new land on the western frontiers. All this activity was highly damaging to the Indians.

The government helped the new inward expansion by promoting railway construction. The most famous railway projects were the North-west Railway into the interior of São Paulo and the notorious Madeira–Mamoré Railway deep in Amazonia; both of these clashed with Indians whose lands they were invading. It was also felt necessary to unite the immense territory of Brazil with a network of strategic telegraph lines. We have seen how Cândido Rondon had his first contacts with the Bororo during the laying of the telegraph line from Goiás to Cuiabá in the 1890s. He went on to lead the team laying the line from Cuiabá south to Corumbá through the swamps of the upper Paraguay in 1900–4. In 1906 Rondon was ordered to push another telegraph line north-westwards from Cuiabá across unexplored country to the Madeira river. This fantastic assignment brought him into contact with unknown groups of Nambikwara and Tupi-Kawahib Indians. It also involved surveys of thousands of kilometres of newly discovered rivers and was to make Rondon one of the greatest explorers of the twentieth century. Official geographical explorations were active in other parts of Brazil and their scientists and surveyors sometimes clashed with Indians.

In contrast to these government activities, lawlessness continued in remote parts of the Brazilian interior. There was fighting for land when huge, ill-defined estates were invaded by squatters or broken up into smaller plots or agricultural colonies. Grileiros were land speculators who dealt in bogus land titles or resorted to force to evict settlers or Indians. Cangaceiros were marauding gangs of bandits who roamed the dusty sertão, the backlands of north-east Brazil. They terrorised isolated farmsteads, extorted ransoms and sometimes posed as champions of the poor against the powerful. Bugreiros were professional killers hired to exterminate Indians who resisted frontier expansion. Thousands of Syrian traders known as mascates peddled and bartered in the villages of the interior. Immoral and exploitive men, these were the equivalent of the regatão traders and aviador rubber dealers of Amazonia.

It was during these eventful years that a handful of Brazilian liberals evolved a radical new approach to the treatment of Indians. There had been excitement about discoveries of new tribes during the final decades of the nineteenth century. The Xingu Indians contacted by Steinen, Ehrenreich, Meyer and Schmidt, the tribes of the upper Rio Negro seen by Koch-Grünberg, and those of Brazilian Guiana visited by Barbosa Rodrigues, Coudreau and others, were all shown to be good people, hospitable, generally peaceful, and with ordinary human emotions which contrasted with the romantic fantasies of the indianist writers. Unfortunately, most of these discoveries were made by foreigners and the brilliant books of Steinen and Koch-Grünberg were published in German.

Rondon's explorations were different. He was a true Brazilian, an army officer, a Positivist, and a patriot who had played a role in the formation of the Republic. Rondon was a man of action, a heroic explorer. His adventures were fully reported in the Brazilian press, and whenever he emerged from the jungles and lectured in Rio de Janeiro, the city's largest concert hall was packed with everyone from the President down. Everything that Rondon said and wrote was steeped in his affection for Indians and his conviction that conciliation and kindness were essential in pacifying and contacting new tribes. As a Positivist who appreciated the merits of Indian culture, Rondon opposed missionaries. His humanitarian views came from a dynamic officer of admirable character, and not from an academic anthropologist.

Rondon started driving the telegraph line north-westwards from Cuiabá in 1907. He was penetrating the watershed between the Amazon and Paraguay river basins, a country of dense forests near the rivers and more open campo and cerrado on the plateau. This vast region is now named Rondônia in his honour. He established good relations with the Paresi and Cabixi tribes but had thrilling adventures with the uncontacted Nambikwara. When scouting ahead with three companions, Rondon was shot at by Nambikwara. His saddle and carbine, transfixed by Indian arrows, are still preserved in Brazilian museums. Rondon was a tough officer and a stern disciplinarian. He ordered his men, when attacked by Indians: 'Die if you must, but never kill!' Rondon's soldiers might fire into the air but must never shoot back at Indians. This policy, together with the usual presents, won over the Nambikwara during the ensuing years of exploration. In an article in one of Brazil's leading newspapers, Rondon wrote: 'From the depths of this endless forest . . . I assure you that the Indians, no matter what their tribe, are as susceptible as the most civilised westerner to love and goodness – not to mention their intelligence, so commonly recognised since colonial times.'

Back in the coastal cities, a few well-wishers were starting to create a pro-Indian movement. A remarkable woman called Leolinda de Figueiredo Daltro had in 1903 formed the Association for the Protection and Assistance of the Natives of Brazil, in conjunction with Sérgio de Carvalho of the National Museum and Henri Raffard of the distinguished Brazilian Historical and Geographical Institute. Leolinda Daltro had given up a teaching career and spent five years from 1896 to 1901 among the tribes of the Tocantins and Araguaia rivers. A firm believer in lay contact with Indians, Daltro clashed with the missionaries and was evicted from Goiás. She brought five Indians back with her – representing the Guarani, Guajajara, Cherente and Krahó tribes – and gave these a full education. Her Association did not prosper, but her adventures among the Indians gave her a certain fame.

The pro-Indian campaign was pursued in the learned societies. In 1908 there was an international congress of Americanists (academics studying Latin America) in Vienna. The young Czech anthropologist Vojtěch Frič stunned this assembly with his first-hand revelations of atrocities against the Kaingáng and Xokleng in Santa Catarina and Paraná. He described murders and rapes by professional bugreiros, slave hunts, contamination of tribes by clothing impregnated with smallpox, and enslavement of Indian children in settlers' households. These horrors were being perpetrated in a part of Brazil heavily colonised by Germans. Frič asked the Congress to vote that Indians were human beings and that warfare against them was unworthy of civilised twentieth-century man. His revelations were dismissed as exaggerations by Brazilian diplomats and German newspapers. It was implied that, as a Czech, Frič was hostile to German colonisation. Some German delegates to the Congress challenged Frič's scientific standing on points of detail about tribal linguistics. After an acrimonious debate, the Congress merely sent a petition to the Brazilian government requesting the abolition of Indian slavery in Santa Catarina.

Later in 1908, the *Revista* of the São Paulo Museum published a translation of a study of the Indians of that state by the museum's director Hermann von Ihering. This paper, originally written in English for the St Louis Exposition of 1904, contained a terrible passage about the fate of the Indians. In the original article, Ihering had predicted that the only possible end for the Indians was extermination. This was slightly mistranslated in the Brazilian version. It read: 'The present-day Indians of the state of São Paulo do not represent an element [that contributes either] to labour or progress. Because no serious or sustained labour can be expected from the Indians of this or any other state of Brazil, and because savage Kaingáng are an impediment to the colonisation of the backwoods regions they inhabit, it seems that we have no alternative but to exterminate them.'

Ihering's paper was immediately attacked by Sílvio de Almeida in an article on the front page of São Paulo's leading newspaper. Almeida assumed that Ihering had recommended rather than predicted Indian extermination. He condemned the German scientist as cold and inhuman. He contrasted German efficiency with the warmth and generosity of Brazilians. A month later another Positivist writer, Luis Horta Barbosa, continued the campaign in another leading newspaper. He urged patriotic Brazilians to condemn 'this ruthless and barbaric theory of a scientist alien to our sentiments and to our best instincts'. Horta Barbosa pointed out that Indians *did* work, in the collection of food for themselves and on some tasks for the government. He argued forcibly that Brazilians had a moral duty to help Indians, who were the original inhabitants of the country and who had been victims of centuries of terrible oppression.

In a brilliant thesis, the American historian David Stauffer has shown how skilfully the Indian sympathisers exploited anti-German feeling among Brazilians. Ihering tried to defend himself in a newspaper article. He explained that he admired Indian culture and respected the efforts of Jesuits and others who had tried to help them in the past. Ihering thought that, given a choice, most Brazilians would support their own compatriots against the outlandish and alien Indians. 'As a citizen, I cannot stand by and watch the march of our entire culture halted by Indian arrows. The life of a woodsman and colonist is certainly worth more to us than the life of a savage. The fate of the Indians is certain. Many of them will accept our culture; the remainder will continue to be our enemies and as such will gradually disappear.' Ihering repeated this message in a lecture to a learned society in São Paulo. He challenged Frič's revelations about bugreiro atrocities. He argued that colonists had every right to employ skilled woodsmen. 'Threatened and assaulted, the colonists have taken vengeance through organised expeditions against the Indians. Doubtless in the course of these attacks and reprisal expeditions the whites have also committed atrocities, but this occurs in other wars and revolts [elsewhere in the world]. It is absurd to expect things to be different in Brazil. It is our duty to protect and educate Indians who submit to our civilisation. But those who oppose our culture do not deserve the same consideration.'

Ihering stubbornly refused to correct the impression that he was advocating the extermination of Indians. He badly misjudged the mood of urban opinion in Brazil when he championed colonists against native Indians. The debate gathered momentum. The learned society of the town of Campinas in rural São Paulo led the way with impassioned speeches about the need for charity to Indians. The romantic idea of the noble savage was revived, and past wrongs against Indians were remembered. The pro-Indian recommendations of the patriarch of Brazilian independence, José Bonifácio, were reiterated. In another article, Sílvio de Almeida wrote: 'I believe that there will never be justification for usurping the much reduced territory that still remains to the rightful owners of all this vast and ancient land of Brazil.' The head of the Positivist Church wrote to the President of Brazil warning him that Ihering had preached 'the extermination of Brazil's natives. This means that he dares to recommend the murder of thousands of innocent persons.'

In December 1908 the staff of the National Museum in Rio de Janeiro – academic rivals of Ihering's Museum in São Paulo – were inspired by their director Professor Domingos de Carvalho to publish a statement deploring Ihering's views and defending the rights of Indians. They declared: 'Now that the director of a national scientific institution . . . is trying to encourage violence in the interests of colonial expansion, the staff of the Museu Nacional feels obliged to protest – certain, however, that the public will not permit the victory of this criminal idea.' The head of the Positivist Church wrote an article in support of this protest. Leolinda Daltro had her five acculturated Indians sign a statement assuring Ihering that tribes fought only in defence of their homelands. Daltro herself argued in a lecture that Indians were 'intelligent, kind, grateful, obedient and thirsty for instruction. They respect justice and derive pleasure from their manual labour.'

Hermann von Ihering wrote a final violent newspaper article before withdrawing from the debate. He still sought to present the problem as a choice between the lives of settlers or of savage tribesmen. 'Since ruthless warfare is being waged between these Indians and the pioneers of Brazil's modern culture, one may either . . . side with the natives and sacrifice the woodsmen and colonists, or join us in requesting protection for these frontiersmen, thereby approving the extermination of uncivilised forest Indians.' Ihering also condemned acculturated Indians as lazy and useless. 'It will not make the slightest difference to culture and progress . . . if such natives continue to exist or not.' He called Indians depraved and even quoted General Custer's notorious remark that the only good Indian was a dead one.

After this outburst, Hermann von Ihering remained silent. He was a meticulous scientist, specialising in molluscs, and a diligent museum curator who liked to acquire collections of Indian artefacts. But his views did not prove palatable to educated Brazilians. This was a time of aggressive, jingoistic German imperial expansion. A German foreign minister had outraged Brazilians by including the German settlers of south Brazil in a list of his country's colonial achievements. Thus, as a German, Ihering was a perfect scapegoat for Brazilians' feelings of guilt about the treatment of Indians. The pro-Indian lobby made brilliant use of this convenient foreign villain in mobilising public opinion to their cause.

Having won the moral debate, the Indianists turned to the more practical question of what should be done. Throughout 1909 proposals for new Indian legislation were drafted. In March, the learned society of Campinas created a Commission to Promote the Defence of the Indians. This new commission issued a pamphlet aimed at Brazilian public opinion. After cataloguing the centuries of abuse of Indians, the pamphlet demanded that native lands (which were still officially deemed to be 'unoccupied') must be protected. Only after their lands were secure could Indians be incorporated into Brazilian society. This was absolutely correct: to this day, land remains the crucial factor in Indian survival. No tribe can keep its cohesion and cultural identity without its lands for hunting, fishing, gathering and farming.

There were increasing calls for central government action. There should be a federal service responsible for Indians throughout Brazil. This point was made strongly at the First Brazilian Geographical Congress, held in Rio de Janeiro in September 1909. The new young President of Brazil, Nilo Peçanha, attended the opening of this congress, and a journalist from Minas Gerais called Nelson de Senna tried to awaken his enthusiasm by delivering an eloquent paper about the Indian problem. Senna described atrocities against Indians in graphic detail. He called for protection of Indian lands; he also exposed Brazil's lack of any coherent Indian policy and urged federal government action to win Indians' trust by patience and kindness. This was the same message that Colonel Cândido Rondon was propagating during 1909 in newspaper articles about his thrilling explorations.

Another fundamental issue remained to be tackled: whether contacts with Indians should be carried out by missionaries or by laymen. It was the same problem that Pombal addressed in 1757 when he transferred Indian affairs from Jesuit missionaries to lay directors. The influential Positivist Church and the Freemasons argued for non-religious protection of Indians. Ardent Positivists such as Cândido Rondon, Tito de Lemos and Luis Horta Barbosa wanted to remove both Catholic and Protestant missionaries from Indian tribes. They were joined by Leolinda Daltro (who had seen the damage done by missionaries on the Araguaia) and her anti-clerical friends. One of these, Antonio Simoens da Silva, addressed the Geographical Congress and described foreign missionaries as 'groups of veritable exploiters of ignorance and poverty.'

The missionaries also had powerful supporters. The Campinas Commission to Promote the Defence of Indians was unable to confront the problem of missionaries versus laymen because it contained leading Catholics, Protestants and Positivists. Squabbles between the two factions even brought about the collapse of Leolinda Daltro's Association for the Protection and Assistance of the Natives of Brazil. Norberto Jorge read a paper to the Geographical Congress in which he condemned Ihering but praised the missionary orders. He said that excellent work was being done by the Salesians among the Bororo of Mato Grosso, by Gil Vilanova's Dominicans on the Araguaia, and by Benedictines among the Makuxi and Wapixana of the upper Rio Branco. He looked back to the achievements of the Jesuits and deplored their expulsion by Pombal. He urged the government to increase its financial support of missionaries.

At its final session on 15 September 1909, the Geographical Congress recommended official protection of Indians throughout Brazil. It insisted that the authorities at all levels must uphold Indian rights, stop abuse of Indians, and try to prepare them for a place in Brazilian society. Leolinda Daltro then rose to propose that the Congress 'request the civil authorities to establish a programme of secular education of Indians, with the help of the Republican government since such instruction was the only one compatible with the statutes of its constitution'. After heated discussion, Daltro's motion was approved by a small majority.

By the end of 1909 the government started to respond to this well-orchestrated campaign. President Nilo Peçanha was an energetic lawyer still in his forties. He enjoyed the support of the big land-owners and these began to listen to the arguments that mestizos and Indians might be trained to fulfil their labour needs – which had been acute since the abolition of slavery. In 1909 President Peçanha created a new Ministry of Agriculture, Industry and Commerce, and appointed as minister one of the richest and most dynamic young politicians in Brazil. Rodolfo Nogueira da Rocha Miranda personal-ly managed vast estates which he had inherited in the interior of São Paulo, and turned them into the finest coffee plantations in the country. He was genuinely concerned about the welfare of rural workers and former slaves. Powerful and popular within the Repub-lican Party, Rocha Miranda determined to use his influence to push through Indian reforms without too much debate within or outside the government.

On 24 January 1910 Rocha Miranda paid an official visit to the National Museum in Rio de Janeiro and took special interest in its exhibits of Indian artefacts. He made an important announcement: he wanted to mobilise the skills and energies of the Indians. He would protect their ownership of their lands and would grant them the same privileges as were enjoyed by immigrant colonists. Also, he would make no attempt to supplant native religion or culture with any other. Rocha Miranda then sent his friend Clodoaldo de Freitas to Maranhão in order to suggest methods of protecting Indians and to assess the amount of land required in their reservations.

On 6 February 1910, two weeks after Rocha Miranda's declara-tion, Cândido Rondon sailed into Rio de Janeiro from the Amazon. He was given a tremendous reception. Four launches filled with generals, cabinet ministers, senators, congressmen and academics went out to greet his ship. As Rondon landed he was welcomed by military bands, by schoolgirls in national colours throwing petals, and by an eloquent speech from Leolinda Daltro. The newspapers were full of articles about the exploits of Rondon and his telegraph commission. After recovering from a bout of malaria, Rondon visited President Peçanha and took with him Libonio, son of a Paresi chief, whom Rondon had made a major in the Brazilian army because of his help to the telegraph commission.

Meanwhile the Minister of Agriculture, Rocha Miranda, was also receiving a favourable press. There was some opposition to the idea of civilising Indians; but almost all comment was in their favour. Rondon's sympathy to native cultures and the success of his gentle methods were stressed repeatedly in articles about the great explorer. There was no strong protest from either the missionaries or the anti-Indian lobby.

On 25 February Rondon visited Rocha Miranda at his ministry and the minister asked him to organise the government's new Indian Service. Rocha Miranda needed Rondon's prestige to make the Service succeed. He repeated his request in a letter to Rondon on 2 March, in which he stressed that the new Service would be specialised and professional, based on republican principles, and free from racial prejudice or religious proselytising. Rondon wrote a letter of acceptance a week later. He welcomed Rocha Miranda's initiative and agreed to lead the new Indian Protection Service on six conditions:

1 Indians would not be forced into rapid acceptance of full Christian doctrine or white civilisation.
2 No religious indoctrination or other metaphysical or scientific system should be used in trying to incorporate Indians into the national society.
3 The new service would be a form of inspectorate to supervise private or public initiatives.
4 The main responsibility of the new service would be the protection of Indian land. Territory stolen from tribes should either be returned to them or they should be compensated by equivalent land nearby.
5 Cattle and farm implements should be introduced to tribes, in order to inspire them to change to a more settled way of life. But whites should be sparing about giving advice to Indians and should ensure that their advice was wanted and did not conflict with Indian custom. Indians did not appreciate abstract advice of no obvious benefit to them.
6 The officers of the new service should make contact with nomadic tribes, seeking to ease or prevent inter-tribal or frontier warfare. These officers must be selfless and devoted to the interests of the Indians. Such a spirit was essential – more important even than the methods they used.

Rocha Miranda telegraphed acceptance of Rondon's conditions on 15 March. The minister also tried to enlist the approval of state governors. He wrote to them arguing that support for his new Service appeared to be 'so universal and unequivocal that I am convinced that . . . it represents a lofty national aspiration'. He praised the Indians for their refusal to bow down under barbarous captivity, and he asked the state governments to give the Indians 'the protection they deserve as human beings and the benevolent assistance they merit as helpless rustics'. All the governors accepted Rocha Miranda's proposal, and most wrote with enthusiasm, promising land and education to their Indians. Messages of support were also received from republican organisations, masonic lodges and academics – all wanting a secular service.

It was only now that the missionary forces mounted a rearguard action. In a series of newspaper articles, they dismissed Rocha Miranda's plan as impractical. They argued that although Rondon himself was of irreproachable character and dedication, he could never find other equally disinterested laymen. Only missionaries inspired by Christian faith would devote their lives to the Indian cause. Other articles deplored the attempt to replace established Christian beliefs with the new Positivism. The debate also raged in the learned societies. As a result of these pressures, the regulations of the Indian Service made no mention of faith or philosophy and did not criticise missionaries.

The regulations were drafted during May and a Statement of Intent was submitted to the President in June. It reiterated the dismal history of mistreatment of Brazilian Indians, contrasting Brazil's neglect of its Indians with the greater efforts of the United States, Chile and Argentina. The draft was approved by President Nilo Peçanha as Decree no. 8072 on 20 June 1910. The new Indian Protection Service was formally inaugurated on 7 September, Brazil's Independence Day, amid optimistic speeches by the Service's author, Rocha Miranda, and its first head, Cândido Rondon. It was the start of a new era for the Brazilian Indians, a century and a half after Pombal's Law of Liberty. And although the Indian Protection Service was to have a chequered career and to end in disgrace, it undoubtedly saved the people, culture and land of many tribes.

By 1910 there were certainly less than a million tribal Indians in Brazil. In 1760, at the time of the expulsion of the Jesuits and the start of the Directorate, there were probably twice that number. There had already been a tragic decline from the 3.5 or more million inhabitants of Brazil at the time of the first European colonisation in the sixteenth century. We know the reasons for that tragedy: deaths from imported diseases; deaths in battle or from overwork and oppression; collapse of the birthrate from the traumas of cultural shock, of dislocation or of invasion of tribal lands. By 1910 the demographic catastrophe of the native Brazilians was irreversible: Brazil, along with the rest of the Americas, would never be decolonised. At a time of explosive growth in the world's population, pure Indians in Brazil had actually declined to a point of numerical insignificance.

Vanished tribes had once covered the immense territory of Brazil in a kaleidoscope of nation-states, differing from one another only in language and details of social custom. The lost tribes left a legacy of attitudes, foods and artefacts, behaviour, words and place-names that help give modern Brazil its peculiarly attractive national character. Their blood mixed with that of immigrant blacks and whites to create the unique genetic blend of many present-day Brazilians. But individual Indians and entire tribes stubbornly refused to adapt to the invading civilisation. They wanted no part of the aggressive, materialistic, competitive, sophisticated and utterly alien society that was occupying their continent. Some tribes fought heroically to defend their lands, their freedom and their way of life. Others tried to accommodate to the new values, but failed. They eventually offered passive resistance, clinging to vestiges of their tribal systems. This condemned many to poverty at the base of frontier society. Their intransigence caused despair among well-wishers convinced of the inevitability of progress towards European–Christian civilisation. There was something admirable in the independent but identical reaction of so many different tribes: rejection of the new values being offered or imposed upon them, because of conviction that their ancient and proven ways were better for them and more appropriate to the land in which they lived.

APPENDIX ONE

Travellers and Explorers
Who Had Contact with Indians

Travellers, scientists and artists who visited Brazilian Indians, presented in chronological order. For their publications, see Bibliography. Before each entry are the dates of the period during which the subject was most involved with Indians.

1761–3

João de São José Queiroz. A Benedictine friar, he became Bishop of Pará immediately after the expulsion of the Jesuits, to whom he was violently opposed. Bishop São José Queiroz made pastoral visits to his diocese in 1761 and 1762–3. He sailed up the lower Amazon, seeing Mawé and other acculturated tribes in its villages. On the lower Xingu he visited former Jesuit missions now called Souzel, Pombal and Melgaço, where he saw Juruna, and Arequena, Manau and other Indians resettled after expulsion from their homelands.

1774–5

Francisco Xavier Ribeiro de Sampaio. As Ouvidor (Magistrate) and Intendente Geral of Rio Negro, he travelled up the Amazon, Solimões and Negro in 1774–5. He visited Pasé, Jurí, Miranya and Tukano on the Solimões and its tributaries, Mawé on the Amazon, and Manau, Baré and other tribes on the Negro. He urged directors of Indian villages to 'descend' more uncontacted tribes to restock their diminished aldeias.

1784–92

Alexandre RODRIGUES FERREIRA (1756–1815). Born in Salvador da Bahia, but studied natural history in Coimbra in Portugal. Sent as a naturalist on the Portuguese boundary commission to the Amazon in 1783, aged twenty-seven. Late 1784–5, he went up the Negro to Marabitanas; 1785–6 visited the Içana and Uaupés rivers; then in 1786 up the Branco to its sources, the Tacutu and Uraricoera. In March 1787 he was on the Aracá river, then up the Solimões. Ferreira wrote ethnographic studies of the Cambeba (Omagua), Katawishí and Mura of the Solimões, Miranya (Bora) and Jurí of the Içá–Japurá, Mawé and Karipuna of the Madeira and Warekena of the upper Negro, as well as essays on native pottery, pipes, masks and huts, and his famous *Diary of a Philosophical Journey through the Captaincy of Rio Negro*. In 1788–90 he travelled from Barcelos on the Negro, up the Madeira and Guaporé rivers to Cuiabá in Mato Grosso. In 1790–1 he visited the Paraguay and Jauru rivers and described the Guaná (Terena) and Guaikurú. He returned to Belém in Pará and thence to Portugal in 1792. Ferreira then held various posts in the Royal Botanic Gardens and as administrator of the royal estates near Lisbon, and later in the Customs. His reputation suffered because his writings and collections were dispersed and published only patchily after his death in Lisbon aged fifty-nine.

1781–1809

Ricardo Franco de Almeida SERRA (1750–1809). A Portuguese infantry officer, Captain Almeida Serra was sent to the Amazon in 1780 as part of the boundary demarcation team led by João Pereira Caldas. Early in 1781 he was sent to map the sources of the Rio Branco, during which he worked with Makuxi and Wapixana. In 1781–2 he made a tough journey up the Madeira–Guaporé route to Vila Bela in Mato Grosso. He was then sent on various exploratory expeditions: to the Barbados valley in 1783; Grão Pará hills and Jauru valley; mapping the Guaporé and its Galera and Sararé tributaries, and the Juruena. In 1786 Serra explored various Paraguay tributaries. In 1790 he was on the Parecis hills. During these explorations he was in the territories of Bororo, Paresis, Guató and perhaps Nambikwara. In 1797 he defended the Miranda valley against Spanish attack, and he commanded Fort Coimbra until his death from malaria at Vila Bela in 1809, aged fifty-nine. Serra wrote important studies of the Guaikurú, Kadiwéu and Guaná (Terena). Although a bachelor, he had two children by his companion, a Terena woman baptised Maria.

1809–10

John MAWE (1764–1829). Born in Derbyshire. A mineralogist, he sailed to Cadiz and Montevideo in 1804–6 but was captured because of Napoleon's invasion of Spain. In 1807 Mawe sailed from Montevideo to Santa Catarina and Rio de Janeiro, aged forty-two. In 1809 he visited the Canta Gallo gold washings near the Paraíba and saw some Coroado and Puri. In 1809–10 he was one of the first foreigners allowed to penetrate Minas Gerais and the diamond district on the upper Jequitinhonha, seeing some Botocudo. He returned to London in 1810 and ran a mineral shop there until his death aged sixty-five.

1809–21

Wilhelm Ludwig, Baron ESCHWEGE (1777–1855). Born near Hesse. After some years in Portugal as head of mines, Eschwege went to Brazil in 1809 aged thirty-two, as director of the royal mining companies. He became an authority on Brazilian geography and natural resources. He knew the Bororo in aldeias on the Aragauri (Velhas) and other Indians of Minas Gerais. Eschwege visited Puri-speaking Coroado of Xapotó near the Southern Paraíba river and Botocudo in northern Minas Gerais. He returned to Germany in 1821 and wrote many books on geology and mineralogy as well as an account of his travels.

1811

Henry KOSTER. Born in Portugal, but the son of a Liverpool trader whose business he continued. A sugar dealer, Koster went to Recife in 1809. In 1811 he visited some Gê-speaking Cariri in the villages of Aronxes and Masangana in Ceará and saw some acculturated Indians in São Luis do Maranhão, before returning to England later that year.

1812

Charles WATERTON (1782–1865). Born at Walton Hall near Leeds in Yorkshire. From 1805 to 1813 he was in British Guiana, managing some family estates in Demerara. In 1812, aged thirty, Waterton went inland to collect plants used in curare poison. During this journey he penetrated the northern tip of Brazil and visited Fort São Joaquim on the upper Rio Branco. He travelled with Aruak and Makuxi Indians. Waterton returned to England in 1813. In 1816 he sailed to Pernambuco and Cayenne. He revisited the interior of British Guiana in 1820 and again in 1824, collecting and observing forest wildlife. He returned to England to run his estate at Walton Hall, observe his American animals, and write about natural history.

1813–29

Guy (Guido) MARLIÈRE (*c.*1769–1836). A French officer, Marlière joined the Portuguese army during the Napoleonic War in 1802. He accompanied the Prince Regent's court to Brazil in 1808. He was sent inland to northern Minas Gerais in 1813 to investigate relations between Coroado, Coropó and Puri Indians and missionaries at São João Baptista do Presídio. He showed an affinity with Indians and later that year was appointed captain-general of the Indians of that parish. Promoted steadily, by 1823 Marlière became a lieutenant-colonel and director-general of all Indians in Minas Gerais. He controlled some 4300 acculturated Indians in seven villages. Marlière was famous for his pacification of the hostile Botocudo of the Rio Doce between 1819 and 1829. He reversed the policy of military expeditions to subdue the Botocudo, but won the tribe's friendship by gentle methods of attraction. Much praised by foreign visitors and many royal officials, but his championing of the Indians also won him enemies. Marlière was dismissed in 1829, but lived on his fazenda Guidovale until his death aged about sixty-seven in 1836. He wrote no book, but many reports and letters.

1814–23

Francisco de Paula RIBEIRO (1780?–1823). A Portuguese army officer, Ribeiro was sent in 1814–17 to command a small fort called Principe Regente at the confluence of the Alpercatas and Itapicuru rivers in southern Maranhão, on a new trail between Maranhão and Pastos Bons near the northern tip of Goiás. In 1815 he made a famous expedition to demarcate this frontier region. He was in contact with many tribes with whom he was invariably sympathetic, and he was an excellent ethnographic reporter. Ribeiro saw Krahó,

Akwê-Chavante and Apinagé on the Tocantins as well as many little-known tribes of western Maranhão: Canela and many different groups of eastern Timbira (Porokamekra, Kilkatí, Pukobye, Krenyé, etc.) and Tupi-speaking Guajajara. Four years later he wrote an account of the Pastos Bons region. He left vivid accounts of raids and epidemics that destroyed Indians. When Brazilian independence from Portugal was declared in 1822, Major Ribeiro was sent by the Portuguese government to stop rebels from Goiás reaching Pará. He held out for some months but was surrounded by a force of frontiersmen and Krahó and Apinagé, captured and taken to Carolina for execution by these rebels in 1823.

1815–17

Georg Wilhelm FREYREISS (1789–1825). Born in Frankfurt-am-Main, but he became interested in natural history in Sweden. He reached Brazil in 1814, aged twenty-five, and travelled to Minas Gerais with the geologist Baron Eschwege (q.v.). Early in 1815 Freyreiss went from Mariana to see Puri near Santa Anna and Coroado and Coropó near the presídio of São João Baptista. From late 1815 to 1817 he travelled up the coast from Rio de Janeiro to Bahia with Prince Maximilian zu Wied-Neuwied (q.v.) and Friedrich Sellow, collecting mammal and insect specimens and visiting some acculturated Botocudo and Camacan. Freyreiss then helped to found a German colony called Leopoldina in southern Bahia and died there in 1825, aged thirty-six.

1815–17

Maximilian Alexander Philipp, Prinz zu WIED-NEUWIED (1782–1867). Born at his family's estate at Wied near Bonn, he studied natural history at Göttingen and went to Brazil in 1815, aged thirty-three. Wied-Neuwied visited Coroado and Coropó at the mission of São Fidelis and newly contacted Puri nearby on the Paraíba do Sul in 1815. From late 1815 to 1817 he travelled up the coast from Rio de Janeiro to Salvador da Bahia, partly with Freyreiss and Sellow, visiting Botocudo and Camacan on the Belmonte (Jequitinhonha) river, Camacan near the Pardo, Pataxó and Cariri on the Paraguaçu river. Wied-Neuwied wrote one of the best accounts of the natural history and natives of Brazil. His chapter on the Botocudo is credited as the first serious anthropological monograph on any Brazilian tribe. He also made tribal vocabularies and studied physical anthropology. In 1832–4 he travelled on the Mississippi and Missouri rivers.

1816–31

Jean-Baptiste DEBRET (1768–1848). Born in Paris. Studied painting under his famous relative Louis David and exhibited paintings during the Napoleonic era. Debret accepted an invitation from King João VI to join a group of French savants who reached Brazil in 1816, when Debret was forty-eight. As an elderly court artist, he saw groups of Botocudo, Puri and Pataxó who were brought to Rio de Janeiro. But it is doubtful whether he ever travelled at all, apart from a possible visit to the Puri at Canta Gallo on the Paraíba do Sul and a journey in south Brazil in 1827. Debret returned to France in 1831 and produced three famous volumes of vivid pictures of the Brazilian court and daily life. In both his pictures and writings about Indians, Debret plagiarised blatantly from Wied-Neuwied, Spix and Martius and others, and he copied ethnographic objects in the Imperial Museum in Rio de Janeiro.

1817–22

Augustin (Auguste) François César, provençal de SAINT-HILAIRE (1779–1853). Born and died in Orléans. Saint-Hilaire started as a businessman but changed to botany. He reached Brazil in 1816, aged thirty-seven, in the entourage of the French ambassador, the duc de Luxembourg. In late 1817 he saw some Coroado near the Paraíba. Also in 1817 he went to Minas Gerais with Baron von Langsdorff (q.v.), then north to Diamantino on the upper Jequitinhonha where he visited Botocudo. In 1818 he travelled up the coast to Espírito Santo, visiting Waitaká at São Pedro dos Indios, Tupinikin at Benevento and Vila Nova (Almeida), and the Botocudo being attracted by Guido Marlière (q.v.) on the Rio Doce. In 1819, Saint-Hilaire travelled across southern Minas Gerais to Goiás, visiting Kayapó at São José de Mossâmedes and on his return towards São Paulo aldeias on the Araguari (Velhas) river which had been stocked in turn with Bororo, Karajá, Tapirapé and Chikriabá. 1820–1: south to Paraná, Santa Catarina, Rio Grande do Sul and Brazilian Cisplatina (Uruguay) to see Guarani of former Jesuit missions in western Rio Grande do Sul. Saint-Hilaire returned to France in 1822, to become professor of botany in Paris and a member of the prestigious

Académie des Sciences. He wrote extensive and delightful accounts of his six years' travels in Brazil.

1818–19

Johann Emanuel POHL (1782–1835). Born in Kanitz in Bohemia and studied medicine and botany, which he taught in the University of Prague. Pohl reached Brazil in 1817, aged thirty-five, in the entourage of the Habsburg Archduchess Leopoldina. In 1818 he travelled across southern Minas Gerais to Goiás where he visited Kayapó in the aldeia São José de Mossâmedes and Chavante in Pedro III (Carretão). He was then one of the first foreigners to descend the Tocantins and see Krahó and Apinagé beside Cocal Grande near Carolina. He returned to Goiás, thence to Minas Gerais, visiting Minas Novas on the upper Jequitinhonha where he saw Maxakali and Botocudo. Pohl returned to Austria in 1821. He died in 1835, aged fifty-three, after the publication of only the first volume of his travels.

1818–34

Johann NATTERER (1787–1843). Born in Vienna, he learned taxidermy and zoology from his father, who was the court falconer. Natterer also became a fine artist, and worked in the imperial natural history collection. He accompanied Archduchess Leopoldina to Brazil in 1817 as a zoologist, aged thirty. After a journey near Rio de Janeiro with Pohl, he travelled by the river route towards the Paraná and Paraguay in 1818–19. In 1820 and 1821 he collected in Paraná and near Rio de Janeiro. In 1822–3 he went across-country from São Paulo to Goiás and Cuiabá, seeing Bororo. After a year in Cuiabá, Natterer spent 1826–8 travelling on the Paraguay and Guaporé rivers and recovering from a severe attack of malaria. In 1829 he went from Cuiabá, down the Guaporé and Madeira rivers, in 1830–2 up the Rio Negro to the Uaupés, Içana, Casiquiare Canal and other tributaries of the upper Negro, living with Baniwa, Tukano, Tariana and other tribes. In 1831–2 he was on the Branco and Mucajaí, and in 1832–4 at Manaus and on the Solimões. In 1834, Natterer descended the Amazon to Belém and thence in 1835 back to Vienna, taking a gigantic collection of natural history specimens including some 1900 native artefacts from seventy-two tribes. He compiled sixty glossaries of tribal languages but sadly wrote no ethnographic reports or popular account of his remarkable travels. He probably saw more tribes than any other visitor to Brazil. Natterer married a Brazilian girl at Barcelos on the Negro and had a daughter by her; but Wallace (q.v.) claimed years later that he met an illegitimate daughter of Natterer and an Indian woman at Guia on the Içana. Back in Vienna, Natterer worked in the Imperial Museum of Natural History but he died of a lung complaint in 1843, aged fifty-five. His magnificent ethnographic collections are in the Museum für Völkerkunde in Vienna, but most of his papers and diary were lost in a fire during the revolution of 1848, five years after his death. Koch-Grünberg (q.v.) saw some of Natterer's notebooks in a private collection in Vienna.

1818–20

Carl Friedrich Philip von Martius (1794–1868). Born in Erlangen in Bavaria. A botanist, he became a fellow of the Bavarian Academy of Sciences. King Maximillian Joseph of Bavaria sent him with Spix (q.v.) to Brazil in 1818 in the suite of Archduchess Leopoldina, with instructions to investigate tribal Indians as well as natural history. In 1818 they went from São Paulo to see Wayaná at Aldeia da Escada near Jacaré. Thence to Minas Gerais, visiting Botocudo at the presídio of São João Baptista on the Xipotó river and wilder members of the same tribe near Minas Novas on the Aracuaí (Jequitinhonha). They went inland to Montes Claros and the upper São Francisco, and then across south-western Bahia to descend the Paraguaçu to Salvador da Bahia. They visited São Pedro de Alcântara in Ilhéus to see acculturated Tupinikin, Guerens and Camacan. In 1819 Spix and Martius left Salvador north-westwards to Juazeiro on the São Francisco, seeing a remnant of Timbira at an aldeia near Oeiras in Piauí and wilder Timbira from the upper Mearim at Caxias. They descended the Itapicuru river to São Luis do Maranhão. The two Bavarian scientists were the first non-Portuguese Europeans to obtain permission to visit the Brazilian Amazon. They started upstream in August 1819 and saw Mundurukú, Mawé (and Parauiana relocated from the upper Rio Branco) at Vila Nova da Rainha (Parintins), on Tupinambaranas island and at Canomã and Maués aldeias. They saw nomadic Mura nearby on a sandbank and also near Manaus. They travelled up the Solimões, seeing various acculturated tribes, especially at Ega (Tefé). The travellers divided in December 1819: Martius went up the Japurá for two months, seeing Aruak-speaking Pasé, Yumana and Kayuishana, Koeruna, and Tukana-speaking Kueretú near the frontier with modern Colombia. Martius was impressed by the unacculturated Yurí and Miranya he saw on this excursion. Reunited at Barra (Manaus) in March 1820, the two Germans rapidly descended the Amazon, revisiting some Indian villages, and left Belém for Europe in June with a vast collection of natural history specimens and Indian artefacts. Martius' subsequent writings and lectures formed the basis of modern Brazilian ethnography and tribal linguistics – even though some of his theories about Indian origins and decadence are now discredited. By comparing tribal vocabularies, Spix and Martius first classified Brazilian Indians into linguistic trunks. They also studied Indians' physical constitutions, illnesses and treatment, and social organisation. Although they spent under three years in Brazil, Spix and Martius had a profound influence on Brazilian studies. Martius collected 6500 species of plants, which formed the basis of the gigantic *Flora Brasiliensis* on which almost every botanist worked throughout the nineteenth century.

1818–20

Johann Baptist von Spix (1781–1826). Born in Hochstadt in Bavaria. A zoologist, Spix was the older and senior naturalist on the Bavarian mission of 1818–20, but died soon after returning to Germany. Spix made the same journey as Martius (q.v.) and they wrote jointly about their travels. They separated between December 1819 and March 1820: Spix went up the Solimões to Tabatinga where he saw Tukano, thence downriver to Manaus and up the Rio Negro to see some remnants of Baré and Manau in former mission villages.

1824–9

Georg Heinrich, Freiherr von Langsdorff (1774–1861). Born in Rhein-Hessen and studied medicine and surgery at Göttingen. A keen naturalist, Langsdorff obtained a place on the Russian circumnavigation led by Admiral Adam von Kruzenstern, 1803–6. During this he visited Brazil briefly in 1803–4. He joined the St Petersburg Academy of Sciences in 1808 as a zoologist and botanist. Langsdorff was appointed the first Russian consul-general to Brazil 1813–20. During these seven years he was host in Rio de Janeiro to almost all visiting scientists. Langsdorff then returned to Russia and persuaded Tsar Alexander I to back a scientific expedition to Brazil, with himself as leader. He returned to Brazil in 1822, aged forty-eight, and recruited a strong team of scientists and artists. (The artists included Moritz Rugendas and later Adrien Taunay and

Hércules Florence (qq.v.).) Excursions were made from Rio de Janeiro, notably to Minas Gerais in 1824. The main expedition went inland only in 1825: from São Paulo down the difficult Tietê river, seeing some southern Kayapó on the Paraná; thence across to the Paraguay, visiting Guaná (Terena) and riverine Guató. In 1827–8 the expedition spent many months in Cuiabá, visiting Bororo groups nearby. It then embarked on the difficult descent of the Arinos–Tapajós, visiting little-known Apiaká and Mundurukú groups. Langsdorff suffered severe malaria and was accused by some of his young companions of going mad. He was taken back to Germany in 1830 and lived for a further twenty years. It is not known whether he regained his sanity, but he never published the results or wrote an account of his important expedition.

1824–5

Johann Moritz RUGENDAS (1802–58). Born in Augsburg to a family of artists and engravers, he studied art in Munich under Lorenzo Quaglio. Rugendas went to Brazil aged nineteen in 1821 as an artist on the Langsdorff (q.v.) expedition. He went to Minas Gerais in 1824 with Langsdorff, where he saw Puri, Camacan and Botocudo. He disagreed with the erratic Langsdorff and refused to accompany his main expedition. After a few months in Rio de Janeiro, Rugendas was summoned home in 1825 by King Maximilian Joseph of Bavaria to illustrate the travels of Spix and Martius. He took 500 drawings, some of which were later published as engravings in Paris in his famous *Voyage pittoresque*. The engravings were beautiful, but the picture of Indian life was somewhat romanticised. Rugendas later travelled and painted in Mexico, 1831–4, and in Chile, Peru, Bolivia and Brazil, 1834–47. He was one of the finest artists ever to work in South America.

1825–9

Hércules FLORENCE (1804–79). Although born in Nice to an artistic family, Florence taught himself painting. Orphaned young, he went on his travels. This took him to Rio de Janeiro where he was working in a bookshop when he answered Langsdorff's (q.v.) advertisement for an artist for his scientific expedition of 1825–9. He joined aged twenty-one as baggage master and auxiliary artist. Florence made beautiful and highly accurate drawings and paintings of Terena, Guató, Bororo, Apiaká and Mundurukú, most of which are now in

Leningrad. His diary of the expedition was published in 1875 shortly before his death. After the expedition Florence married a Brazilian girl and lived in Rio de Janeiro.

1825–8

Aimé Adrien TAUNAY (1803–28). The son of the distinguished French artist Nicolas Antoine Taunay, Adrien accompanied his father on the scientific voyage of the frigate *Uranie*, sent by the French government on a voyage of circumnavigation. Shipwrecked in the Falkland Islands, the Taunays settled in Rio de Janeiro in 1820. Langsdorff (q.v.) recruited the younger Taunay, aged twenty-two, as official artist of his expedition after Rugendas (q.v.) refused to go. Taunay made some fine paintings of Kayapó, Guató and Bororo Indians, but drowned trying to swim the Guaporé river in 1828.

1825–57

João Henrique de Wilkens de MATTOS (1784–1857). Born in Barcelos, Rio Negro, the son of a surveyor on the boundary commission, Sergeant-Major Severino Eusebio de Mattos. He was an infantry officer in Pará and Amazonas, and a notable artist. He performed many difficult missions in remote parts of Amapá, French Guiana, Brazilian Guiana and Rio Negro. In 1825, he reported on the frontier forts of Tabatinga on the Solimões, where he saw Tukano, and São Joaquim on the Rio Branco, among Wapixana and Makuxi. Mattos fought in the Cabanagem rebellion, 1835–9. In 1845 he wrote a detailed report on the decadence of Rio Negro and its Baré and other Indians. He died of malaria at Cucuí on the upper Rio Negro, aged seventy-three, when reporting on messianic disturbances among the tribes of the Uaupés and Içana.

1827–8

William John BURCHELL (1781–1863). Born in London and learned botany from his father, who owned the Fulham Nursery Gardens. On Saint Helena island from 1805–10 as a merchant, and founded its botanical gardens. Then from 1811–15 made an extensive expedition from South Africa into unexplored territory. Burchell went to Brazil in 1825, aged forty-four, as a botanist attached to the British envoy Sir Charles Stuart. After travels near Rio de Janeiro and in Minas Gerais and São Paulo, he went overland to Goiás in 1827. He descended the Tocantins to Pará in 1828, visiting and drawing Krahó and Cherente and making magnificent botanical collections.

1828

Dr Robert WALSH (1772–1852). Born in Waterford, Ireland. Walsh was ordained as an Anglican curate and qualified as a medical doctor. He travelled in Turkey and Russia before visiting Brazil in 1828, aged fifty-five. He went to investigate the horrors of the slave trade, being an ardent abolitionist. He saw some Puri at Valença and Aldeia da Pedra on the Paraíba, and went on to Ouro Prêto in Minas Gerais. He returned to Ireland as a country curate.

1828

Henry LISTER MAW (b.1804). A British naval lieutenant in HMS *Menai*, Lister Maw descended the Amazon from Peru in 1828. He entered Brazil at Tabatinga and left from Belém do Pará. He saw acculturated Indians along the banks of the Amazon and was shocked by their condition. Maw retired from the navy in 1834.

1835

Lieutenant William SMYTH (b.1800) and Lieutenant Frederick LOWE (b.1811), British naval officers on HMS *Samarang*. Smyth and Lowe organised an expedition from Lima to the Peruvian Amazon rivers in 1834. They entered Brazil at Tabatinga in 1835 and descended the Solimões, visiting acculturated Jurí at Santo Antonio near the mouth of the Içá, Kayuishana at Tunantins, and Katawishí at Coari near Ega (Tefé). They also witnessed the Cabanagem revolt in Pará. Smyth went on to serve under George Back in arctic exploration in HMS *Terror* and retired as captain in 1843. Lowe retired as commander in 1845.

1838–9

Daniel Parish KIDDER (1815–91). Born in Darien, New York, Kidder became a Methodist minister and was sent to Brazil as a missionary in 1837 when he was twenty-two. He travelled inland from Rio de Janeiro and then to Belém do Pará for three years, trying to make Protestant converts. He was shocked by the treatment of caboclo Indians; but he also deplored the Cabanagem revolt. He returned to the United States in 1840 and served as a clergyman and theology teacher in New Jersey and Illinois.

1839

George GARDNER (1812–49). Born in Glasgow, Gardner qualified as a medical doctor but became a botanist, studying under Sir William Hooker. He sailed to Brazil on a plant-collecting expedition in 1836, aged twenty-four. After collecting near Rio de Janeiro, he sailed north to the São Francisco river and went inland from Pernambuco to Piauí and northern Goiás. In 1839 he saw the decaying mission of Duro on the Manoel Alves tributary of the Tocantins, where Akroá and Krahó lived in fear of attack by Cherente. He returned to England in 1841, then went to India and Ceylon (Sri Lanka) where he founded a botanical garden but died aged thirty-seven.

1838–42

Sir Robert Hermann SCHOMBURGK (1804–65). Born in Freiburg-an-der-Unstrut, Prussia, the son of a Protestant minister. He started a business career in Naumburg, and then went to New York and Virginia trading in tobacco. In 1830 Schomburgk moved to the West Indies and made a marine survey of Anegada in the Virgin Islands. The Royal Geographical Society was impressed by this map, and employed him to explore British Guiana (Guyana), which he did from 1834 to 1839. On his third expedition he entered Brazil by the Tacutu river in 1838, guided by Makuxi. From Fort São Joaquim on the Rio Branco, Schomburgk explored up the Surumu to Mount Roraima, meeting Wapixana, Arekuna, Purukotó and other tribes. He then went up the Uraricoera and Parima rivers to the upper Orinoco; thence through the Casiquiare Canal to the upper Negro. In 1839 he descended the Negro and ascended the Branco, to return to Fort São Joaquim and to Guiana down the Essequibo, seeing only acculturated Indians. In 1841 he returned to demarcate the western boundary of British Guiana. In 1842 he explored to the source of the Tacutu, among Wapixana and Atoraí, and other southern boundaries of British Guiana. Then up the Cotinga to Mount Roraima again, returning via the Pirara and Essequibo. Schomburgk became a British subject, was knighted in 1844, worked for the Colonial Office, and was then consul in the Dominican Republic (1848–57) and Thailand (1857–64). He retired in 1864 and returned to Germany, where he died in Berlin aged sixty-one.

1842

Moritz Richard SCHOMBURGK (1811–90). The younger brother of Robert Hermann, whom he accompanied on the expedition of 1841–2. A notable botanist, Richard also wrote a journal of this expedition. Both he and his brother were shocked by abuse of Indians by the Brazilians. After the attempt on Mount Roraima, Richard visited Fort São Joaquim in December 1842, returning to Guiana via the Tacutú–Essequibo route. He returned to Germany; fled for political reasons in 1848, to South Australia; started cultivating vines for wine-making; and became director of the botanical gardens of Adelaide, where he died aged seventy-nine.

1842

Prinz ADALBERT von Preussen (1811–73). Born in Berlin, a nephew of King Friedrich Wilhelm III of Prussia. After travels in various Mediterranean countries, Adalbert sailed to Brazil in 1842, aged thirty-one. Having visited Puri on the Paraíba inland from Rio de Janeiro, he sailed to Belém and took a small boat up the Amazon and Xingu rivers. His companions or aides-de-camp included Second Lieutenant Count Otto von Bismarck (1815–98), the future Chancellor of Germany, who was then aged twenty-seven. After visiting the mission of Souzel on the lower Xingu, the Germans went upstream to see various groups of Tupi-speaking Juruna and Tacunyapé. At the farthest south on their brief expedition they entered unexplored country. They returned to Germany early in 1843. Prince Adalbert became an admiral, and died in Karlsbad aged sixty-two.

1843–7

Francis Louis Nompar de Caumont de Laporte, comte de CASTELNAU (1810–80). A founder of the French Entomological Society, Castelnau travelled in the United States, Texas and Canada, 1837–41. He was then sent by King Louis-Philippe to lead a French scientific expedition to South America. The expedition reached Rio de Janeiro in 1843, when Castelnau was thirty-three. Later that year, it travelled across Minas Gerais to Goiás. Castelnau saw a few Chavante and Cherente at Carretão and Salinas aldeias. In 1844 he descended the Araguaia river, seeing many Karajá, Javaé and Xambioá. He visited Apinagé at Boa Vista mission near Carolina, and ascended the Tocantins to return to Goiás. Then west to Cuiabá, seeing some Bakairi at Diamantino on the upper Arinos. Early in

1845, the expedition went down the Cuiabá and Paraguay rivers to the border with Paraguay, seeing Guató, Kadiwéu (Guaikurú), Terena and Guaraní-speaking Kaiwá. They returned upriver and crossed to Vila Bela (Mato Grosso City) on the Guaporé, seeing some Cabaçal Bororo on the Jauru. Castelnau wrote good linguistic and ethnographic studies of the Bororo and Guató. The expedition crossed into Bolivia in mid-1845 and thence to Peru. It re-entered Brazil at Tabatinga on the Solimões in January 1847. Castelnau rapidly descended the Amazon, seeing only some acculturated Pasé, Kayuishana, Juri and other tribes. From Pará they went to French, Dutch and British Guiana and various Caribbean islands before returning to France. Castelnau became a diplomat, serving as French consul in Salvador da Bahia, where he wrote a monumental fifteen-volume report on his expedition, then in Cape Town and Bangkok, returning to France in 1862. He was sent to Australia as consul, and died in Melbourne aged seventy.

1845–50

John Henry ELLIOTT (1809–*c.*1870). Born in the United States, to an American father and English mother. Elliott served in the United States and then the Brazilian navies. Captured in the Cisplatine campaign of 1827, he escaped after two years and settled in Curitiba, Paraná. He accompanied the President of Paraná, Barão de Antonina, inland in 1845 to explore the Ivaí, Paranapanema and Paraná rivers. They visited both pacified and uncontacted Xokleng and Kaingáng. He went on another expedition with Antonina to the Ivaí and Tibagi rivers in 1847, on which they contacted some Kaiwá (Caiuá). Elliott was sent back in 1852 to attract this group. He found them on the Paranapanema and brought them back to settle on the Jataí. He wrote descriptions of these expeditions and drew pictures of the tribes, as well as of the Guató and Guaikurú he saw on the upper Paraguay in 1847 and 1850. He lived in Curitiba until at least the late 1860s.

1846

William EDWARDS (1822–1909). Born in Hunter, New York, and acquired a love of nature in the Catskill Mountains. He studied law. In 1846, aged twenty-four, Edwards travelled up the Amazon from Belém to Barra (Manaus). His enthusiastic description of Amazonian flora and fauna inspired Wallace and Bates (qq.v.). He employed Mura paddlers and observed acculturated Indians along the banks of the Amazon, but his attitude to them was unsympathetic. Back in the United States, Edwards was active in the law, in opening coal mines and building railways. He wrote a monumental work on butterflies of North America.

1847–61

Teófilo Benedito Otoni (1807–69). A Brazilian deputy, he was a founder of the Liberal Party in 1840, formed in opposition to the Regency that preceded the reign of Emperor Dom Pedro II. He supported a Liberal revolt against the dissolution of the Chamber of Deputies in 1842. The revolt failed, but Otoni and others were granted amnesty in 1844. In 1847 he led an expedition to the Mucuri river in north-east Minas Gerais and pacified some Botocudo with presents and kindness. He was re-elected in 1850 as a representative of Minas Gerais, but he withdrew from politics to devote himself to founding a colony on the Mucuri. In 1852 Otoni made a first contact with the Naknyanuk group of Botocudo, and in 1856 they helped him clear forest and build a road to his settlement, which he called Philadelphia (now Teófilo Otoni). He also had contact with long-settled Maxakali. His Mucuri River Company attempted large-scale colonisation, attracting immigrants from Saxony in Germany; but it suffered many disasters despite Indian help. The company was liquidated in 1861 after utter failure and political opposition, and this ruined Otoni's own fortunes and health.

1849–52

Alfred Russell Wallace (1823–1913). Born in Usk, Monmouthshire, Wallace became interested in botany and, while teaching in a school in Leicester, met Henry Bates (q.v.), who introduced him to entomology. The two young naturalists decided to sail to the Amazon, reaching Pará in 1848 when Wallace was twenty-five. In 1848–9 they collected near Belém, on the lower Tocantins, and near the mouth of the Amazon. In late 1849 Wallace and Bates went up the Amazon to Manaus, visiting the former missions of Vila Nova (Parintins) and Serpa. After many months in and near Manaus, Wallace went up the Rio Negro in August 1850. He ascended to near the headwaters of the Negro, among the Baniwa in Venezuela. On his return in June–July 1851 he explored far up the Uaupés into Colombia, seeing various Tukana-speaking tribes such as Kobewa, Tariana and Wana-

ná. Returning downriver to Manaus in September, he went back up
the Negro and Uaupés, again going far upstream beyond Iauareté in
early 1852. Wallace suffered severe malaria and dysentery on this
journey, but recuperated in a village of 'absolutely uncontacted
savages'. He descended the Uaupés, Negro and Amazon and sailed
from Pará in July 1852. The ship carrying him to England burned at
sea: Wallace was eventually rescued but all his collections of specimens, drawings and notes were lost. Wallace then went to south-east
Asia, collecting and writing in the islands of the Malay Archipelago
(Sarawak and Indonesia). He is famous for the Wallace Line dividing
fauna in this archipelago, and is recognised as co-discoverer with
Charles Darwin of the principle of evolution by natural selection. He
died in Dorset aged ninety.

1849–59

Henry Walter BATES (1825–92). Born in Leicester. While working in
a drapery business, Bates taught himself entomology. He made
friends with Alfred Wallace and they decided to collect on the
Amazon together. They reached Belém do Pará in 1848 when Bates
was twenty-three. They remained collecting near Belém and on the
lower Tocantins and Amazon until late 1849, when they started up
the Amazon. In January 1850, Bates visited a settlement of Mura
near the mouth of the Madeira. When Wallace went up the Negro in
March 1850, Bates went up the Solimões, visiting some Pasé near
Ega (Tefé) and making excursions nearby. In March 1851 he descended the Amazon to Belém and then went in November to settle
for over three years at Santarém. Bates often collected on the lower
Tapajós and saw Mundurukú there. In May 1855, Bates went up the
Amazon again and settled for four and a half years at Ega. He made
several excursions, notably in late 1856 when he went upstream to
Tabatinga where he witnessed a Tukano initiation ceremony. He
finally sailed back to England in 1859 after eleven years on the
Amazon, with huge collections that included over three thousand
new species of insect. He wrote his famous book of travels and many
papers on entomology. Bates married, and in 1864 became the first
paid Secretary of the Royal Geographical Society, a post he held with
distinction for twenty-eight years until his death aged sixty-seven.

1849–55

Richard SPRUCE (1817–93). Born in Ganthorpe near York and became a mathematics teacher at a school in York. A self-taught botanist, Spruce collected plants in the Pyrenees. Hearing of the success of Wallace and Bates (qq.v.), he followed them to the Amazon, arriving a year after them in 1849, aged thirty-one. In October he took a steamer to join them at Santarém, where he spent a year collecting plants and learning Portuguese and Tupi-Guarani. In October 1850, Spruce went up the Amazon to Manaus, seeing Munduruků and Mawé at Luzéa (beside Maués) and various acculturated Indians in riverside settlements. In November 1851 he went up the Negro employing only pure Baré, Tariana and Manau as his paddlers. From August 1852 to March 1853, he explored the Uaupés and saw many Tukano groups. He used Tariana as his plant collectors. Spruce went on up the Negro and through the Casiquiare Canal to explore many tributaries of it and of the upper Orinoco and Negro inside Venezuela. After remarkable adventures and achievements, Spruce re-entered Brazil at the end of 1854. Descending the Negro to Manaus, he then sailed up the Solimões in March 1855, to Iquitos in Peru. He spent many months collecting plants in the Peruvian montaña and Amazonia. He was then in the Ecuadorean Andes from 1857 to 1860 and on the coast and mountains of Peru from 1861 to 1864. Returning to England, Spruce wrote notable papers on botany. Although he published no account of his travels, his friend Wallace published a narrative based on Spruce's letters and journals, after Spruce's death aged seventy-six in 1893.

1851

Hermann BURMEISTER (1807–92). Born in Stralsund in Prussia, he became professor of zoology at the University of Halle. Burmeister came to Brazil in 1850, aged forty-three, in order to visit the famous Danish palaeontologist Peter Wilhelm Lund. In April 1851 he went inland to the southern Paraíba and saw some acculturated Coroado and Puri at the Aldeia da Pedra. Burmeister went on to spend some weeks with Lund at the caves of Lagoa Santa, and five months at Congonhas recovering from a fall. He later travelled in Argentina, wrote about Argentine fossils, and became director of the Museo de Buenos Aires, in which city he died aged eighty-five.

1851

William Lewis HERNDON (1813–57). Born in Fredericksburg, Virginia. A United States naval officer, Herndon commanded a steamer in the Mexican War of 1847–8. In 1851 he and Lieutenant Lardner Gibbon were sent by the American government to investigate the commercial potential of the Amazon. Herndon descended the main river from Peru, while Gibbon entered Brazil down the Madeira from Bolivia. Herndon was unimpressed by the Tukano he saw near Tabatinga, Jurí near São Paulo de Olivença, and Mura near the mouth of the Negro. (Their joint report to Congress also quoted from an account of the Mundurukú and Mawé on the Tapajós by the French traveller Alphonse Maugin de Lincourt.) The two naval lieutenants praised the commercial potential of the Amazon and encouraged its colonisation by non-Indians. Herndon was promoted to commodore and captained steamers in the Caribbean. He was drowned aged forty-four, going down when his ship was wrecked in a storm off Cape Hatteras, after Herndon had saved most of his passengers.

1857

Johann Jakob, Baron von Tschudi (1818–87). Born in Glaris to a distinguished Swiss family, he studied natural sciences at Neuchâtel and medicine at the Sorbonne in Paris. He spent five years in Peru, studying Inca antiquities and Quechua Indians.In 1857–9, Tschudi returned to South America, to travel in Brazil, Argentina, Chile and Peru. He was in Brazil in 1857, where he saw some miserable Coroado and Coropó near São Fidelis on the Paraíba and bands of Botocudo on the upper Mucuri in Minas Gerais. He visited the colony of Teófilo Otoni (q.v.). In 1860 he was appointed Swiss minister in Brazil and travelled throughout southern Brazil seeing Swiss immigrants. He later became Swiss ambassador in Vienna, and was famous as a zoologist.

1858–9

Dr Robert Christian Berthold Avé-Lallement (1812–84). Born in Lübeck. A medical doctor, he went to Rio de Janeiro in 1837. He travelled inland through much of Brazil in 1858–9, ascending the Jequitinhonha and seeing Botocudo at Teófilo Otoni's colony Philadelphia on the Mucuri. Avé-Lallement was violently critical and uncomprehending of Indians. Moving on to the Amazon, he saw some acculturated Tapuio along the main river, as well as a group of Mura near Serpa on the Madeira and some Tukano at Tabatinga on the Solimões. He wrote a book on tropical plants as well as an account of his travels.

1858–60

Antonio GONÇALVES DIAS (1823–64). Born in Caxias, Maranhão. After studying law at Coimbra in Portugal, Dias entered government service in Brazil. He was sent to study education systems in Europe, 1854–8. On his return, he joined the Imperial Scientific Commission to Ceará (known to its critics as the Comissão das Borboletas, 'Butterfly Commission') as head of the ethnographic section, 1858–9. They saw Tupi-speaking Potiguar and Dias wrote a Tupi diction- ary. He went on to spend six months on the Amazon in 1860, seeing Mawé, Mundurukú and Mura. He was famous as a poet and play- wright, and had a romantic vision of Brazilian Indians. His poems *Primeiros cantos* and *Os Timbiras* helped to launch the indianist literary movement. Gonçalves Dias returned to Rio de Janeiro in 1861, ill from his Amazon expedition. In 1862–4 he travelled in Europe, but was drowned in a shipwreck on his return, off the coast of his native Brazil, aged forty-one.

1861–9

William CHANDLESS (1829–96). Born in London, Chandless read classics at Cambridge, then studied law. In 1854 he travelled across the Rocky Mountains in a waggon train to California. In 1858–61 he travelled in Argentina, Chile, Colombia and other Andean coun- tries. He then resided at Manaus for many years while exploring southern tributaries of the Amazon. In 1861 Chandless ascended the Tapajós, Arinos and Juruena rivers, visiting Mawé, Mundurukú and Apiaká villages along their banks. From June 1864 to February 1865 he explored the Purus river, going farther upriver than previous Brazilian explorers. On the lower Purus he met some Mura and Paumarí; farther upstream, he contacted Ipurinã, Maniteneri and Kanamarí. One headwater of the Purus is now named after Chand- less. In 1865 he explored the longest tributary of the upper Purus, the Acre river, seeing two small tribes that may have been Takana- speaking Kapechene and Araona. In late 1867 he sailed up the Juruá, visiting a Katawishí village on the lower river and then seeing no Indians until some Araua, Canibo (Kuniba) and Kanamarí on the upper river. He had a near-battle with Nauá, not far from the Javari and the Peruvian border. In 1869 Chandless accompanied a Brazilian expedition to map the lower Maués-Açu, Abacaxis and Canumã rivers, seeing only acculturated Mundurukú on them. Chandless published reports of his expeditions and ethnographic observations only in the *Journal* of the Royal Geographical Society.

1862–76

Dr José Vieira COUTO DE MAGALHÃES (1837–98). Born in Diamantina, Minas Gerais. He obtained a doctorate in law and became president successively of the provinces of Goiás, Pará and Mato Grosso, 1862–8. In 1862, aged twenty-four, he went down the Araguaia in a small boat, visiting Chavante in Estiva aldeia and Karajá and Tupi-speaking Anambé of the lower Tocantins, from whom he learned Tupi legends. He persuaded Kayapó tribes to settle near the main Araguaia, by good treatment of them and their children. He founded Isabel College, on the upper Araguaia, for selected Indian children, hoping to use educated boys to convert their tribes. Couto de Magalhães also established fortified presídios and steamship navigation on the Araguaia and Tocantins. He wrote an account of his many expeditions, a book of anthropological theory in 1874, and his famous *O selvagem* about methods of acculturating Indians and about their legends. He was particularly impressed by the Mundurukú and Mawé of the Tapajós, Apiaká of the Arinos, and Guató and Guaikurú of the Paraguay. He fought as a general in the Paraguay War, and was president of São Paulo state after the republican revolution of 1889.

1863–7

Franz KELLER (1835–90). Born in Mannheim, he graduated as an engineer and also studied painting. He went to Brazil in 1856 when he was twenty-one, to accompany his father who was building a railway in Minas Gerais. He worked with his father on the railway and river surveys. They explored the Paraíba in 1862; the Paranapanema, Ivaí and Tibagi in 1863; and, during the Paraguay War, the Iguaçu in 1866. During these expeditions they studied and painted Kaingáng and Kaiwá (Caiuá). In 1867 they were sent to survey the rapids on the Madeira and saw some of its Karipuna. Franz Keller married and added his wife's surname, Leuzinger, to his own. He returned to Germany in 1873.

1865–6

Jean Louis Rodolphe AGASSIZ (1807–73). Born in the Canton of
Fribourg, Switzerland. Qualified as a medical doctor, but became a
keen naturalist. After the death of Spix in 1826, Martius gave his
great collection of Amazon fishes to Agassiz to study and classify.
Agassiz went to Paris in 1830, working under Cuvier on comparative
anatomy: he published a monograph on fossil fish. From 1832 to
1845 he was professor of natural history at Neuchâtel, and his work
included a trip to study glaciers in Britain in 1840. In 1845 Agassiz
moved to the United States and became professor of natural history
at Harvard University, where his lectures on glaciation and natural
history were very popular. He believed in the immutability of species
and opposed Darwin's theory of evolution. In 1865 the financier
Nathaniel Thayer sponsored an expedition to Brazil led by Agassiz
to support his theory. The expedition reached Rio de Janeiro in April
and the main party went up the Amazon from August 1865 to
February 1866. Agassiz and his wife Elizabeth saw some acculturated Mawé, a school for Indian children in Manaus, Mundurukú on
the Maués river, Tukano near Tabatinga on the Solimões, and numerous groups of tapuia. They measured Indian physiques in villages
along the main Amazon. Part of the expedition collected on the
Tapajós, others on the Içá and Jataí, others on the Rio Branco, and a
team of geologists worked in Minas Gerais. Agassiz returned to the
United States in 1866 with a good impression of Indian character
and problems, but confused notions of racial mixing.

1865–78

Charles Frederick HARTT (1840–78). Born in Canada and trained as
a geologist. He joined the Thayer–Agassiz expedition of 1865–6 and
investigated the geology of Minas Gerais and southern Bahia. He
saw many Botocudo, Camacan and Tupinikin and wrote a study of
Botocudo history and ethnology. He returned to Brazil in 1867 to
visit the coast between Pernambuco and Rio de Janeiro, and wrote
about Brazil's geology and physical geography. In 1870 he persuaded the financier Junius S.Morgan to back the Morgan Expedition, which worked in Brazil for a decade, seeking to prove that the
Amazon basin was not of glacial origin. Hartt then led the Imperial
Geological Commission. He wrote a summary of the ethnography of
the Amazon valley, made a fine compilation of Mundurukú legends
and was the first to appreciate the importance of Indian mythology.

He wrote about Indian art and rock engravings. Hartt also worked on excavation of ancient sambaqui mounds (shell middens) on Marajó island in the mouth of the Amazon. He died of yellow fever, aged thirty-eight, after notable work on Amazon geology.

1867

Sir Richard Francis Burton (1821–90). After his famous Middle Eastern and Indian travels, his visit to Mecca, his expedition across Somalia, and to seek the source of the Nile with Speke, Burton was sent as consul to Santos, in 1864, when he was forty-three. In 1867 he travelled inland to northern Minas Gerais and then descended the São Francisco river. His only contact with Indians was at São João dos Indios, near the confluence of the Verde and São Francisco, where there were remnants of Chavante, Xikriabá and Kariri. Burton was later consul in Damascus, and died in Trieste.

1870–7

George Earl Church (1835–1910). Born in New Bedford, Massachusetts, Church became an engineer. After building railways in Argentina in 1857–60, fighting with distinction in the American Civil War and covering Juárez' war against Maximilian in Mexico in 1866–7, Colonel Church was engaged by the Bolivian government to try to build a railway bypassing the rapids on the Madeira river, in order to gain an outlet for Bolivia's rubber. He obtained a concession from Brazil and floated the Madeira and Mamoré Railway Company; in 1871 he started work in the territory of the Tupi-Kawahib (Parintintin) and Karipuna. Despite all Church's efforts throughout the 1870s, the railway project failed. He was later active in Ecuador, Venezuela and Costa Rica and wrote a survey of the native tribes of South America which was published in 1912 after his death.

1870–85

Herbert Huntington Smith (1851–1915). A geologist, born in the United States, Herbert Smith was Charles Hartt's (q.v.) assistant on the Morgan Expedition of 1870. He visited Mundurukú and other tribes of the lower Amazon. On his second visit to Brazil in 1873–7, Smith studied fauna near Santarém and then succeeded Hartt as head of the Imperial Geological Commission. In 1877 *Scribner's Magazine* sent him to report on Pará and Rio de Janeiro. He returned to

Brazil in 1881 and spent four years in the interior of Rio Grande do Sul and then on the upper Paraguay. He made vast collections of insects and birds. He lived for four months among the Kadiwéu of Southern Mato Grosso, and studied their ceramics.

1874–84

João BARBOSA RODRIGUES (1842–1894?). Born in Rio de Janeiro. He dedicated himself to botany and ethnography, both of which he had taught himself. He was sent by the imperial government in 1871 to do scientific studies in Pará and Amazonas. In 1875 he published a series of reports on his explorations of the rivers Capim, Tapajós and northern tributaries of the Amazon: Trombetas, Urubu, Jatapú and Nhamundá. He wrote books on palms and orchids and identified many new species of both. Barbosa Rodrigues also studied Indian dances, folklore, burials, weapons and artefacts. He published monographs on the Tembé of the Capim in Pará, Mundurukú and Mawé of the Tapajós, and Tukano of the Solimões, all in 1882 as part of Ladislau Neto's notable Anthropological Exhibition in Rio de Janeiro. He also made physical anthropological measurements of the Miranya of the Japurá, Kayuishana of the Solimões, Arara of the Madeira, Pariki of the Jatapú, Arauakí of the Uatumã, and Puri of the Mucuri in Minas Gerais. In 1884 Barbosa Rodrigues founded the botanical gardens of Amazonas in Manaus, and he included important ethnographic collections in his museum. In 1884 and on two later journeys, he made peaceful contact with hostile Waimiri (then called Crishana or Yauaperi) of the Jauaperi tributary of the lower Negro. His heroic wife Constança helped him in this dangerous pacification. Barbosa Rodrigues also wrote romantic poetry about Indians.

1877–9

Jules CREVAUX (1847–82). Born in Lorquin, Meurthe, in France, Crevaux became a doctor in the French navy, and was wounded in the Franco-Prussian War in 1871. He worked in French Guyane (Cayenne) treating yellow-fever victims and determined to be the first explorer to reach the Tumucumaque hills on the Cayenne–Surinam–Brazilian border. In 1877 he crossed from the Maroni on to the upper Jari, among Wayaná, and was the first European to descend the Jari. After a brief return to France, Crevaux went up the Oiapoque in 1878 among the Tupi-speaking Wayapí then across to the Jari headwaters among the Carib Wayaná and approached territory of the Tiriyó. He moved on to the upper Paru and made a first descent of it, seeing many Wayaná and Ataraí villages. In 1079 Crevaux took a steamer up the Amazon and up the Içá–Putumayo, seeing some Tukano, and Witoto in Colombia. He crossed to the Caquetá and descended it to the Japurá, visiting Carijona (Karihona). In 1880–1 he was on the Magdalena and Guayabero rivers in Colombia and the Orinoco in Venezuela. In 1882 he intended to explore the Xingu, but was killed by Toba in the Bolivian Chaco before reaching it.

1881–6

Ermanno STRADELLI. Born in Italy. He visited the Uaupés and Tiquié rivers of the upper Negro in 1881 and again in 1882, seeing Desana, Tariana and other Tukana-speaking tribes, as well as nomadic Maku. Stradelli was sympathetic to Indian culture and religion, and very critical of the behaviour of Italian missionaries. In 1886 he revisited the upper Negro, seeing Baniwa on the lower Içana and the decline of settlements along the main Negro. He then joined a Brazilian military inspection of the Rio Branco, seeing Wapixana and Makuxi settlements near Fort São Joaquim.

1883–99

Henri-Anatole COUDREAU (1859–99). Born in Sonnac, Charente-Maritime, France. He taught geography in Reims and then entered the colonial service and was sent to Cayenne, French Guiana, in 1881 when he was twenty-two. In 1883 he crossed from the Oiapoque and entered Amapá down the Araguari, seeing Carib-speaking Galibí and Tupi-speaking Emerillons (Wayapí). In 1884 he went from Manaus up to the Uaupés seeing Tariana, Tukano and Maku. Thence in 1885 to the Rio Branco and then north-eastwards to the unexplored sources of the Urubu and Trombetas. During this journey he made contact with Wapixana, Makuxi, Atoraí, Wai-Wai and Tarumá. Returning to France, he held a chair of geography at the Sorbonne, 1887–8. In 1888 he explored the Tumucumaque hills on the Brazilian–Guiana frontier, going up the Maroni river among Wayaná and Tiriyó. In 1890 Coudreau explored all the tributaries of the Oiapoque river, which separates Brazil from French Guiana, seeing various Wayapí tribes, and briefly entering the upper Jari among the Wayaná. In 1895 the government of Pará, at the instigation of José Verissimo, hired Coudreau to explore and map its rivers. From July 1895 to January 1896, he was on the Tapajós, seeing acculturated Mundurukú, Mawé and Apiaká. In 1896 he was on the lower Xingu and saw some Juruna. In 1897 Coudreau was on the Araguaia, visiting some Karajá, and then went up the Itacaiunas tributary of the lower Tocantins, close to the Xikrin Kayapó. In 1898 he was on the Anapu, west of Belém near the mouth of the Xingu; but saw no Indians. In 1899 he explored the Nhamundá and Trombetas rivers north of the Amazon, the latter as far as the mouths of the Cafuini and Anamu. He saw no Indians on this trip, but died of malaria during the descent, aged forty. Although Coudreau boasted of having seen twenty-two tribes and published vocabularies of the Wayaná, Aparaí and Wayapí, he came to despise Indians. He regarded them as an inferior race doomed to disappear before the 'progress' of European colonisation. He was accompanied on many of his expeditions by his wife Olga (q.v.), who continued his explorations after his death.

Olga COUDREAU, wife of Henri Coudreau (q.v.), accompanied her husband during his later expeditions and was with him when he died of malaria on the Trombetas in 1899. Madame Coudreau then continued the explorations on behalf of the government of Pará, always on northern tributaries of the Amazon. In April–September 1900 she travelled up the Cuminapanema, visiting Pianokotó near its headwaters. In 1900–1 she was on the Curuá, another river between the Trombetas and Paru. She explored the Mapuera tributary of the Trombetas in April–December 1901 and had friendly contact with Indians, probably Wai-Wai; on the Maicuru in 1902–3; and Canumã in 1905–6.

1884, 1887–8

Karl VON DEN STEINEN (1855–1929). Born in Mülheim in the Ruhr, he studied medicine and psychiatry in Berlin and Vienna. 1879–81: on a world circumnavigation, during which he was taught by the ethnographer Adolf Bastian and studied Marquesas islanders in the Pacific. 1882–3: on German expedition to South Georgia in Antarctica. On the return from this, in 1884 when he was twenty-nine, Steinen went up the Paraguay river to Mato Grosso. He left Cuiabá in May with a military escort and other scientists, including his cousin Wilhelm von den Steinen. They visited acculturated Bakairi on the Paranatinga and then crossed the campo to the Batovi headwater of the

Xingu. Here they were the first to contact other Bakairi, Waurá, Trumäi, Kustenáu and, further down the Xingu, Suyá and then already-contacted Juruna and Takunyape, before reaching Bolóm in October after the first full descent of the Xingu. Steinen's observations refuted earlier notions that Indians were stupid, humourless or in any sense abnormal. He returned in 1887, leaving Cuiabá in July and penetrating to the Batovi and thence to the Culiseu, revisiting the tribes seen three years earlier, as well as Kalapalo, Mehinaku, Auetí, Kamayura and Yawalapiti. After considerable ethnographic observations, his team was forced by illness and lack of food to return to Cuiabá at the end of 1887. He then visited some Bororo in 1888. Steinen returned to Germany and became professor of anthropology at Marburg and later Berlin, where he organised the South American section of the ethnological museum. He died in Cronberg in the Taunus, aged seventy-four.

1887–8

Paul EHRENREICH (1855–1914). Born in Berlin, and studied anthropology. When he was thirty-two, Ehrenreich accompanied Karl and Wilhelm von den Steinen (q.v.) on their second expedition to the headwaters of the Xingu, July–December 1887, during which they contacted many new tribes. When Steinen returned to Germany in mid-1888, Ehrenreich went overland to the upper Araguaia, where he saw some tame Kaiapó. He descended the Araguaia, spending a week with the Karajá and visiting newly contacted Kaiapó; then from Belém up the Amazon and Purus, on which river he saw some Paumari, Yamamadi and Ipurinã. Back in Germany, Ehrenreich published two papers in 1891 that brilliantly summarised the spread and linguistic divisions of Brazilian Indians. He became Professor of Ethnology at Berlin University in 1911.

1895–9

Hermann MEYER (1871–1932). Born in Hildburghausen in Germany. Inspired to study anthropology by Steinen (q.v.), he led a seven-month expedition to the upper Xingu in 1895 when he was twenty-four. After visiting the western Bakairi, the expedition explored the Ronuro headwater of the Xingu and returned up the Culuene, visiting Kamayurá, Trumai, Aweti and Nahukuá. Meyer returned in 1899 and tried to explore the Formoso, the Xingu's westernmost headwater, but after much hardship revisited the Culiseu and Culuene

tribes, including Mehinaku and Yawalipití. Meyer studied comparative Indian bows. He worked in the Bibliographical Institute in
Germany and died in Leipzig aged sixty-one.

1901–27

Max SCHMIDT (1874–1950). Born in Altona, Hamburg. Read law, but
was inspired by Steinen (q.v.) to study anthropology. In 1901
Schmidt, aged twenty-six, went with a few Bakairi alone to the upper
Xingu. He visited the Bakairi, Aweti, Nahukuá, Mehinaku and Trumai but the tribes stole his trade goods and he had to retreat, sick
and hungry. He saw some Guató on the Paraguay on his return
journey. In 1910 he was back in Brazil and followed Rondon's telegraph line to study the Paresi-Kabishi, then descended the Jauru and
revisited the Guató. In 1914, Schmidt was in Mato Grosso and
Paraguay studying Aruak tribes, and in 1918 he became professor of
ethnology in the University of Berlin. He returned to Brazil in 1926
and went from Cuiabá to the Paranatinga and Vermelho rivers to
study the Kayabí; then with SPI (Indian Protection Service) officials
to Humaitá to see the newly contacted Umutina; and revisited the
Bakairi and Guató on his return down the Paraguay, collecting
artefacts for the Berlin Museum. After 1929 he settled in South
America, first in Cuiabá and then in Asunción, Paraguay, where he
died aged seventy-six.

1899–1924

Theodor KOCH–GRÜNBERG (1872–1924). Born in Grünberg near
Giessen in Hesse. Inspired by Steinen (q.v.), he joined Meyer's (q.v.)
second expedition of 1899 to the tribes of the upper Xingu. He
studied the language of the Kadiwéu Guaikurú on the Paraguay and
wrote his doctoral thesis about it. In 1903 he was sent by the Berlin
ethnological museum to collect on the upper Rio Negro. He went up
the Içana, seeing Baniwa, Baré, Warekena and Siusi and Kuati far
upstream. He crossed to the Caiari–Uaupés and lived with the
Wananá and other Tukana-speaking tribes. He also observed some
nomadic Maku. After descending the Uaupés, Koch-Grünberg then
went up the Tiquié among its Desana, Tukano and Tuyuka, and
contacted some Bara far upriver. He often used Tariana paddlers on
these two years of expeditions. He returned to the far north of Brazil
in 1911–13. He went towards Roraima among Makuxi and Taulipang, then in 1911–12 up the Uraricoera among the Purukotó,

through Yanomami territory, where he saw some Maku, and over the watershed on to the Mereuari headwater of the Orinoco. He explored the Ventuari among Yekuaná, then passed through the Casiquiare Canal and descended the Negro in 1913. He published an important six-volume study of the life and mythology of these and the Makuxi and Wapixana, and of his explorations in northern Brazil, Venezuela and British Guiana. Back in Germany, Koch-Grünberg became professor of ethnology at Freiburg and then director of the Linden Museum in Stuttgart. In 1924 he returned to join Hamilton Rice's expedition to the source of the Orinoco, but died of malaria on the Rio Branco, aged fifty-two. Koch-Grünberg was a brilliant observer and anthropologist and a sympathetic friend of the Indians.

1904–5

Euclides da CUNHA (1866–1909). Born in the province of Rio de Janeiro. After an early career of journalism and in the army, he took part in the suppression of the Canudos revolt in the interior of Bahia in 1897 and wrote his famous *Os sertões* about the campaign. Chief of the Brazilian–Peruvian boundary commission of 1904–5, Cunha explored the upper Purus and wrote a report about it and its tribes. After touring Amazonia for the government, he returned to academic and literary posts, but was shot by an assassin when aged forty-three.

1890–1950

Cândido Mariano da Silva RONDON (1865–1958). Born in Mimoso south of Cuiabá, Mato Grosso. His great-grandmother was a Campanha Bororo. Both Rondon's parents died before he was three and he was brought up by an uncle in Cuiabá. Success at school won him a place in the Escola Militar in Rio de Janeiro and then in the Escola Superior de Guerra where he graduated as an engineer officer. Played a minor role in the creation of the republic in 1888. In 1890–1 he was building a strategic telegraph line east from Cuiabá towards Goiás through territory of hostile western or Coroado Bororo with his mentor Major Gomes Carneiro. After some teaching in the military academy and work on road-building and telegraph lines (1893–8), he returned to build a telegraph line south from Cuiabá through the Pantanal to Miranda and Aquidauana, 1900–5. He worked with Bororo helpers, contacted Uachiri (Guachí) and rescued Terena dispossessed of their lands. In 1906–10 Rondon led the heroic drive of the telegraph line north-west from Cuiabá towards the Madeira river, helped by Paresi and with dangerous encounters and eventual contact with Nambikwara. In 1910, back in Rio de Janeiro, Rondon accepted Minister Rocha Miranda's request to run the new Indian Protection Service. In 1911–13 he continued telegraph construction and vast explorations of rivers by his Commission in what is now Rondônia. He led an expedition in 1913–14 to take ex-President Theodore Roosevelt down the Dúvida (now Roosevelt) river. He completed the telegraph link to the Ji–Paraná and Jamari valleys in 1914–15. From 1915 to 1919 he carried out further surveys and exploration in Mato Grosso. In 1927–30, Rondon was charged with surveys of all Brazilian frontiers, which brought him into contact with many tribes, including Wapixana, Yanomami, Maku, Mayongong (Iekuana), Pianokotó, Tiriyó and Wayaná. He led a mixed boundary commission in 1934–8 on the Brazilian–Colombian frontier, which involved contacts with Uaupés tribes such as Tariana, Kobewa, Baré, Wananá and Hohodene. As director of the Indian Protection Service, he visited the tribes of the Xingu and most other parts of Brazil. Rondon was one of the greatest explorers of the twentieth century and an outstanding champion of Brazilian Indians. He died in Rio de Janeiro aged ninety-three, a marshal of Brazil, recipient of many geographical and humanitarian medals, and honoured with a special funeral ceremony by the Bororo.

APPENDIX TWO

Chronology

1750	Treaty of Madrid fixes boundaries between Portuguese and Spanish empires in South America
1754–7	Governor Francisco Xavier de Mendonça Furtado's first journey up the Amazon
6 June 1755	Pombal's Law of Liberty for Indians
7 June 1755	Law removing missionaries from temporal control of Indians
1755	Karajá slaughtered on Bananal island in the Araguaia by Pinto da Silveira
1756	Spanish–Portuguese army destroys Guarani of Sete Povos missions at Caibaté in Rio Grande do Sul
1756–63	Seven Years' War: Portugal at war with Spain after 1760
1757	Mendonça Furtado's Directorate legislation for Amazon Indians
1757–9	Akroá of northern Goiás defeated and settled in Duro and Formiga aldeias
1757	Native rebellion at Lamalonga on middle Rio Negro
1758	Mendonça Furtado's second journey up Negro, meets Spanish boundary commissioner
3 Sept.1759	Jesuits expelled from Portuguese empire
1762	Forts started at São Gabriel (Uaupés) and Marabitanas on Negro
1763	Capital of Brazil moved from Salvador (Bahia) to Rio de Janeiro

1764–5	Defeat of Guenguen and Akroá in Piauí
1767	Jesuits expelled from Spanish empire
1767–70	Explorations of Guarapuava plains in Paraná
1768	José Monteiro de Noronha on Rio Negro
1774	Portuguese capture Spanish troops on upper Rio Branco
1774–5	Francisco Xavier Ribeiro de Sampaio journeys on Negro, Solimões
1775	Start of forts São Joaquim on Branco and Coimbra on Paraguay
1775	Pinto da Fonseca expedition makes peace with Karajá on Araguaia
1777	Marquis of Pombal dies. Queen Maria I succeeds King José I
1777	Treaty of San Ildefonso redefines boundaries of Brazil: Sete Povos missions returned to Spain
1778	Guaikurú attack Fort Coimbra. Start of Fort Albuquerque on Paraguay
1781	Guaikurú make peace treaty with Portuguese
1781	Southern Kayapó settle in aldeias near Goiás
1781–7	Boundary commissioners explore upper Negro, Branco, Uaupés, etc.: Requena and Chermont on Japurá, 1782; Alexandre Rodrigues Ferreira's naturalists' expedition, 1784; explorations by Almeida Serra, Silva Pontes, Gama Lobo d'Almada, Lacerda e Almeida
1783–90	Ricardo Franco de Almeida Serra explores upper Guaporé, Paraguay rivers
1784 and 1787–8	Bishop Caetano Brandão journeys on Amazon
1785	Mura surrender on the Solimões, Madeira and Negro
1787–8	Chavante settle at Carretão (Pedro III) aldeia north of Goiás
1788	Report by Judge Pestana da Silva condemns Directorate system
1790	Makuxi of upper Rio Branco 'rebel' and are exiled
1792–3 and 1797	Thomas de Souza Villa Real journeys on Araguaia and Tocantins
1795	Mundurukú of Tapajós surrender, settled on lower Tapajós and Amazon
1797	Fort of São João das Duas Barras at junction of

	Araguaia–Tocantins
12 May 1798	Abolition of the Directorate
1798	Punitive raid slaughters Wapixana and Paraviana, upper Branco
1799–1800	Puri of Paraíba settled in Queluz mission
1800	Alexander von Humboldt refused permission to enter upper Negro
1801	Portuguese recapture Sete Povos missions, in 'War of Oranges'
1806	Peace with Camacan Botocudo in Ilhéus (southern Bahia)
1808	Portuguese royal family sails to Brazil
13 May 1808	War against Botocudo; 5 Nov. War against Kaingáng
1809	Pinto de Magalhães wins over Krahó, founds Carolina on Tocantins
1809–12	Expeditions into Guarapuava in Paraná, some Kaingáng surrender
1810–28	Fr Chagas Lima's mission among Kaingáng in Paraná
1813	Karajá, Chavante and Apinagé destroy Santa Maria on Araguaia
1813–18	Guido Marlière among Coroado, Coropó and Puri in Minas Gerais
1815	Treacherous slaughter of Timbira near Carolina on Tocantins
1815–16	Prince Maximilian of Wied-Neuwied travels in Brazil
1816	French Ambassador brings Saint-Hilaire, Debret and others to Brazil
1816–19	Fighting between Brazilians and Paraguayans devastates Guarani
1816–22	Fighting against western Bororo near Cuiabá
1817	Future Empress Leopoldina reaches Brazil, bringing Spix, Martius, Natterer, Pohl, etc., in her entourage
1817–20	Travels by J. B. von Spix and C. P. F. von Martius from São Paulo to upper Amazon and Negro
1819–29	Marlière's pacifications of Botocudo on upper Doce
1821	José Bonifácio d'Andrada e Silva's essay on

	civilisation of Indians
1822	Dom Pedro I declares Independence of Brazil
1823	Charles Macintosh invents waterproof rubber material
1826	Brazilian officials report to Emperor about Indians
1826–8	Baron Georg von Langsdorff's Imperial Russian expedition to Cuiabá and down Arinos–Tapajós
1831	Abdication of Emperor Pedro I, Regency for boy Emperor Pedro II
1831	Repeal of edicts of 1808 against Botocudo and Kaingáng
1835–6	Cabanagem rebellion: Cabanos occupy Belém do Pará
1836	Cabanos capture Manaus and hold it for some months
1838	Mura kill Bararoá and government forces
1839	Amnesty ends Cabanagem rebellion
1839–42	Expeditions by Robert and Richard Schomburgk in north Brazil
1840	Accession of Emperor Pedro II
1840	First Italian Capuchin missionaries reach Brazil
1842	Priest Silva Fraga converts some Cabaçal Bororo
1842	Prince Adalbert of Prussia and Count von Bismarck on Xingu
1843–56	Kaingáng chiefs Condá and Viry help colonists fight other Kaingáng in Palmas and Nonoái (Santa Catarina and Rio Grande do Sul)
1844–52	Attempts by Baron Antonina to settle Kaiwá in Paraná
24 July 1845	Imperial law on Indians
1846	Italian Capuchin missionaries reach Tocantins
1846	Count de Castelnau on Araguaia and Tocantins
1846–65	Indianist literary movement flourishes with Gonçalves Dias, Gonçalves de Magalhães and José de Alencar
1848	Henry Bates and Alfred Wallace reach Amazon; Richard Spruce arrives in 1849. Wallace leaves 1852, Bates 1859, Spruce 1864
1849, 1852	Friar Rafael de Taggia twice moves Krahó on Tocantins

1850	Blumenau German colony founded in Santa Catarina
1850s	Coffee frontier spreads westwards in São Paulo province
1851–2	US naval lieutenants Lewis Herndon and Lardner Gibbon on Amazon
1852–3, 1858–9	Santa Maria presídio on Araguaia twice built and destroyed by Karajá or Kayapó
1852–61	Teófilo Otoni's colony Philadelphia among Botocudo of Mucuri
1852–4	Carmelite Fr Bene active among Indians of Uaupés and Içana
1852–5	Colonias of Leopoldina, Januária, Capivari in Maranhão interior
1857–9	Messiah Venâncio Christo active on Içana and Uaupés
1857	Brazilian scientific/ethnographic expedition, Piauí and Amazon
1859	Slaughter of Kaingáng by settlers from Guarapuava
1860, 1867	Rebellions by Guajajara (Tenetehara) in Maranhão
1861	Failure of Otoni's Mucuri colony among Botocudo
1863–75	Fighting against Waimiri-Atroari of Jauaperi, lower Rio Negro
1864–70	Paraguay War: Paraguayans invade Mato Grosso, infect Guató with smallpox, damage Guaikurú, Terena
1864–5	William Chandless explores Purus, Acre; 1866 explores Juruá
1865–6	Louis Agassiz and Charles Hartt on Thayer Expedition
1866, 1868	Brazilian–Peruvian boundary commissions on Javari
7 Dec.1866	Imperial decree opens Amazon to foreign shipping
1870–3, 1879–81	Unsuccessful attempts by Col. George Church to build Madeira–Mamoré railway
1871	Couto de Magalhães founds Leopoldina, Colégio Isabel and steamship line on Araguaia
1871–4	João Barbosa Rodrigues explores Trombetas

	and other rivers
1872	Railways started westwards from Campinas into Kaingáng territory of São Paulo province
1873–85	Fighting against Eastern Coroado Bororo
1873–93	Capuchin missionaries found Itambacuri mission among Botocudo
1875	Henry Wickham steals rubber seeds from Amazonia
1875–8	João Severiano da Fonseca's journey around Brazil
1877	Severe drought in Ceará increases seringueiro migration
1877–8	Jules Crevaux explores Jari and Paru rivers
1879–84	Col. F. X. Lopes de Araújo explores Brazilian–Venezuelan frontier
1880–3	Italian Capuchins' failed missions on Uaupés
1881	Closure of presídios on Araguaia
1884	Barbosa Rodrigues contacts Waimiri-Atroari on Jauaperi
1884	Karl von den Steinen's first descent of Xingu, contact with its tribes
1885	Ensign Duarte pacifies some Eastern Bororo
1885	Henri Coudreau travels from Rio Branco to upper Trombetas
1887	Steinen's second expedition to upper Xingu
1887	Col. Antonio Labre explores Acre to Madre de Dios; Col. F. A. Pimenta Bueno explores Brazil–Guiana frontiers
1889	Abdication of Emperor Pedro II, declaration of Republic
1890–2	Cândido Rondon among Eastern Bororo on Cuiabá–Goiás telegraph
1895–8 and 1902–present	Salesian missionaries run Bororo aldeias
1895	Col. Gregorio Thaumaturgo de Azevedo explores upper Juruá and Javari
1895–9	Henri Coudreau explores rivers of Pará
1896–7	Dominican Gil Vilanova contacts Kayapó, founds Conceição do Araguaia
1896, 1899	Hermann Meyer's Xingu expeditions
1899, 1902	Rebellions by seringueiros in Acre lead to

	Treaty of Petrópolis (17 Nov. 1903) whereby Brazil gains Acre
1900–3	Candido Rondon lays telegraph from Cuiabá south to Corumbá
1901	Rebellion by Guajajara (Tenetehara) near Barra do Corda, Maranhão
1903–5	Theodor Koch-Grünberg among tribes of Uaupés, Içana, Negro
1906	Rondon starts laying telegraph north-west from Cuiabá
1907–12	Americans under Percival Farquar build Madeira–Mamoré railway
1908–11	Reports on atrocities by Julio Arana's rubber company on the Putumayo lead to Roger Casement's enquiry of 1910
1908	Pro-Indian debate at Congress of Americanists in Vienna, anti-Indian article by Hermann von Ihering
1909	Indian supporters active at Brazilian Geographical Congress, enlist Minister Rodolfo da Rocha Miranda
1910	Rondon reaches Rio de Janeiro and agrees to lead new Indian Protection Service, inaugurated 7 September
1912–20	Collapse of Amazon rubber boom

Bibliography

ABBREVIATIONS

AA: *Archivo do Amazonas, Revisita destinada à vulgarisação de documentos geographicos e historicos do Estado do Amazonas*, ed. Bento de Figueiredo Tenreiro Aranha, 3 vols (Manaus, 1906–8).

ABAPP: *Anaes da Biblioteca e Arquivo Público do Pará* (Belém do Pará, 1901–).

ABNRJ: *Anaes da Biblioteca Nacional do Rio de Janeiro* (Rio de Janeiro, 1876–).

AMN: *Archivos do Museu Nacional* (Rio de Janeiro).

AN SSSR: Academy of Sciences of USSR.

ASBA: *Atas do Simpósio sôbre a Biota Amazônica*, Conselho Nacional de Pesquisas, 2 vols (Rio de Janeiro, 1967).

BMN: *Boletim do Museu Nacional (Antropologia)*.

BMPEG: *Boletim do Museu Paraense Emílio Goeldi* (Belém do Pará, 1895–1956; n.s., 1957–).

CAL: *Cahiers des Amériques Latines* (Institut des Hauts Études de l'Amérique Latine, Université de la Sorbonne Nouvelle–Paris III, 1970–).

CDSP: *Catálogo de documentos sôbre a história de São Paulo, existentes no Arquivo Histórico Ultramarino, de Lisboa*, 13 vols (Rio de Janeiro, 1956–9).

CNPI: Conselho Nacional de Proteção aos Índios.

DH: *Documentos Históricos da Biblioteca Nacional do Rio de Janeiro* (Rio de Janeiro, 1928–).

DI: *Documentos interessantes para a história e costumes de São Paulo*, ed. António de Toledo Piza, 86 vols (Archivo do Estado de São Paulo, 1894–1961).

GJ: *Geographical Journal* (The Royal Geographical Society, London, 1886–).

HAHR: *Hispanic–American Historical Review* (Baltimore, MD, and Durham, NC, 1918–).

HSAI: *Handbook of South American Indians*, ed. Julian H. Steward, Smithsonian Institution, Bureau of American Ethnology, Bulletin 143, 6 vols (Washington, DC, 1946–63).

IHGB: Instituto Histórico e Geográfico do Brasil.

JC: *Jornal do Commercio*, daily newspaper (Rio de Janeiro, 1827–).

JCET: *Jornal do Commercio, Edição da Tarde* (Rio de Janeiro, 1909–).
JRGS: *Journal of the Royal Geographical Society* (London, 1830–85).
JSAP: *Journal de la Société des Américanistes de Paris*, n.s. (Paris, 1903–).
RA: *Revista de Antropologia* (São Paulo, 1953–).
RAPM: *Revista do Archivo Público Mineiro* (Belo Horizonte, Minas Gerais).
RH: *Revista de História* (São Paulo, 1950–).
RHGB: *Revista do Instituto Histórico e Geographico Brasileiro* (Rio de Janeiro, 1839–). (Formerly *Revista trimensal de historia e geographia* and *Revista trimensal do Instituto Histórico, Geographico e Etnographico do Brasil*).
RMP: *Revista do Museu Paulista* (São Paulo: 1st series, 1895–1942; 2nd series, 1947–).

ABREU, JOÃO CAPISTRANO DE: *Capítulos de história colonial (1500–1800)* (Rio de Janeiro, 1907; 5th edn, Brasília, 1963).
ACCIOLI DE CERQUEIRA E SILVA, IGNÁCIO: *Corografia paraense, ou descripção física, historica, e politica, da Provincia do Gram-Pará* (Belém, 1833).
— *Memorias históricas e políticas da Província da Bahia*, ed. Bráz do Amaral, 6 vols (Bahia, 1919–40).
ADALBERT, PRINCE OF PRUSSIA: *Aus meinem Reisetagebuch, 1842–43* (Berlin, 1847), trans. Sir Robert H. Schomburgk and John Edward Taylor, *Travels of His Royal Highness Prince Adalbert of Prussia, in the south of Europe and in Brazil, with a voyage up the Amazon and Xingu, now first explored*, 2 vols (London, 1849).
— *Reise des Prinzen Adalbert von Preussen nach Brasilien*, ed. Kletke (Berlin, 1857).
AGASSIZ, JEAN LOUIS RODOLPHE AND MRS: *A Journey in Brazil* (Boston, Mass., and London, 1868); trans. Edgar Süssekind de Mendonça, Brasiliana **95**.
AGUIAR, FAUSTO AUGUSTO DE: *Relatório do Presidente da Provincia de Gram Pará* (Pará, 15 August 1851).
ALDEN, DAURIL: 'The Population of Brazil in the Late Eighteenth Century: a preliminary survey', HAHR **43** 173–205, May 1963.
— 'The Growth and Decline of Indigo Production in Colonial Brazil: a study of comparative economic history', *Journal of Economic History* **25**:1 35–60, March 1965.
— *Royal Government in Colonial Brazil* (Berkeley/Los Angeles, Calif., 1968).
— 'Black Robes versus White Settlers: the struggle for "freedom of the Indians" in colonial Brazil', in *Attitudes of Colonial Powers Toward the American Indians*, ed. Howard Peckham and Charles Gibson (Salt Lake City, Utah, 1969) 19–45.
— 'Economic Aspects of the Expulsion of the Jesuits from Brazil: a preliminary report', in *Conflict and Continuity in Brazilian History*, ed. Henry H. Keith and S. F. Edwards (Columbia, SC, 1969) 25–71.
— (ed.) *Colonial Roots of Modern Brazil* (Berkeley/Los Angeles, Calif., 1973).
— 'The Significance of Cacao Production in the Amazon in the Late Colonial Period: an essay in comparative economic history', *American Philosophical Society, Proceedings*, **120** 2: 103–35, April 1976.

— 'Late-Colonial Brazil, 1750–1807: demographic, economic, and political aspects', in Leslie Bethell (ed.), *The Cambridge History of Latin America* (Cambridge, 1984) **2** 601–53.

ALENCASTRE, JOSÉ MARTINS PEREIRA DE: *Memoria chronológica, histórica e corographica da Provincia do Piauhy*, RHGB **20** 5–164, 1857.

— *Annaes da Provincia do Piauhy*, (Rio de Janeiro, 1863), RHGB **27**:2 5–186, 229–349, and **28**:2 5–167, 1864–5.

ALINCOURT, LUIZ D': 'Reflexões sobre o systema de defesa que se deve adoptar na fronteira do Paraguai, em consequencia da revolta e dos insultos praticados ultimamente pela nação dos indios Guaicurus ou Cavalleiros' (Cuiabá, 1826), RHGB **20**, 1857.

ALMEIDA, EDUARDO DE CASTRO E: *Inventario dos documentos relativos ao Brasil existentes no Archivo da Marinha e Ultramar de Lisboa*, 5 vols (Rio de Janeiro, 1913–18).

ALMEIDA, FRANCISCO JOSÉ DE LACERDA E: *Diario da viagem pelas Capitanias do Pará, Rio Negro, Matto-Grosso, Cuyabá e S. Paulo, nos annos de 1780 a 1790* (São Paulo, 1841).

AMAZONAS: *Relatórios da Presidência da Provincia do Amazonas*, ed. S. J. Nery and A. C. Nery, 5 vols (Rio de Janeiro, 1906–8).

ANDERSON, ROBIN A.: 'A Cabanagem: uma interpretação da luta de raças e classes na Amazônia, 1835–1836', RHGB **307** 22-7, April–June 1975.

— 'Following Curupira: colonization and migration in Pará, 1758 to 1930, as a study in settlement of the humid tropics' (PhD dissertation, University of California, Davis, 1976).

ANDRADA E SILVA, JOSÉ BONIFÁCIO: *Apontamentos para a civilisação dos índios bravos do imperio do Brasil* (Rio de Janeiro, 1823).

ANDRADE, PEDRO CARRILHO DE: 'Memoria sobre os indios do Brasil', *Revista do Instituto Historico do Rio Grande do Norte* **7** (Natal, 1912).

ANON: 'Descripção geographica da Capitania de Matto Grosso. Anno de 1797', RHGB **20**, 1857.

— *Descripção geographica, topographica, historica e politica da Capitania de Minas Gerais* (1781), RHGB **71**:1 117–98, 1908.

— *Illustração necessaria e interessante relativa ao gentio da nação Mura* (1826), ed. Rodolpho Schuller, Documentos para a historia e ethnographia do Pará, Museu Goeldi ms. (Belém, 1912).

— 'Noticias da voluntaria reducção de paz e amizade da feroz nação do gentio Mura nos annos de 1784, 1785, e 1786', RHGB **36**:1 323–92, 1873.

— *Roteiro do Maranhão a Goiás pela capitania do Piauí*, RHGB **62**:1, 1899.

ARANHA, BENTO DE FIGUEIREDO TENREIRO: *Archivo do Amazonas (Revista destinada a vulgarisação de documentos geographicos e historicos do Estado do Amazonas)*, 3 vols (Manaus, 1906–8) = AA.

ARAUJO E AMAZONAS, LOURENÇO DA SILVA: *Diccionario topographico, historico, descriptivo da comarca do Alto-Amazonas* (Recife, 1852).

ARNAUD, EXPEDITO COELHO: 'Os índios Mirânia e a expansão luso-brasileira (Médio Solimões – Japurá, Amazonas)', BMPEG, n.s., Antropologia **81**, July 1981.

— 'O diritto indígena e a ocupação territorial: o caso dos índios Tembé do alto Guamá (Pará)', RMP, n.s., **28** 221–33, 1981–2.

'Os índios da Amazônia e a legislação pombalina', *Boletim Pesquisa CEDEAM* **3**:4 75–84, Manaus, Jan.–June 1984.

Avé-Lallement, Robert Christian Berthold: *Reise durch Süd-Brasilien im Jahre 1858*, 2 vols (Leipzig, 1859), trans. Eduardo de Lima Castro, 2 vols (Rio de Janeiro, 1953).

— *Reise durch Nord-Brasilien im Jahre 1859* (Leipzig, 1860), trans. Eduardo de Lima Castro, 2 vols (Rio de Janeiro, 1961).

— *Tabatinga am Amazonenstrom* (Hamburg, 1863).

Azara, Félix de: *Geografía física y esférica de las provincias del Paraguay y misiones guaraníes* (Asunción, 1790), ed. Rodolfo R. Schuller (Montevideo, 1904).

— *Voyages dans l'Amérique méridionale*, 4 vols (Paris, 1809), trans. (Madrid, 1923).

Azevedo, Gregório Thaumaturgo de: *Prefeitura do Alto Juruá. Relatório do primeiro semestre de 1906*; and *Segundo relatório* (Rio de Janeiro, 1906).

Baena, Antonio Ladislau Monteiro: 'Representação ao Conselho Geral da Provincia do Pará sobre a especial necessidade de um novo regulamento promotor da civilisação dos indios da mesma provincia', *Annaes da Bibliotheca e Archivo Público do Pará*, **2** 241–92, 1902.

Baena, Manoel: *Compendio das eras da provincia do Pará* (Pará, 1838).

— *Ensaio corographico sobre o Pará* (Pará, 1839).

Baldus, Herbert: *Bibliografia crítica da etnologia brasileira*, 3 vols (São Paulo, 1954; Hanover, 1968); vol. 3, ed. Thekla Hartmann, *Völkerkundliche Abhandlung* **9** (Berlin, 1984).

Barata, Francisco José Rodrigues: 'Memoria em que se mostram algumas providencias tendentes ao melhoramento da agricultura e commercio de Goyas' (1799), RHGB **4** 336–65, 1848, 2nd edn 1891.

Barata, Manoel: *Formação histórica do Pará* (Belém, 1973).

Barbosa, J. da C.: 'Qual seria hoje o melhor systema de colonizar os indios entranhados em nossos sertões', RHGB **2** 3–18, 1840.

Barman, Roderick J.: 'The Forgotten Journey: Georg Heinrich Langsdorff and the Russian Imperial Scientific Expedition to Brazil, 1821–1829', *Terrae Incognitae* **3** 67–96, Amsterdam, 1971.

Barreto, Domingos Alves Branco Moniz: 'Plano sobre a civilização dos índios do Brasil, e principalmente para a Capitania da Bahia' (1788), RHGB **19** 33–98, 1856.

Bastos, A. C. Tavares: *O valle do Amazonas: estudo sobre a livre navegação do Amazonas, estatistica, producções, commercio, questões fisicaes do valle do Amazonas* (Rio de Janeiro, 1866).

Bastos, Manoel José d'Oliveira: *Roteiro da Cidade de S. Maria de Belem do Gram-Pará pelo Rio Tocantins até o Porto Real do Pontal* (Rio de Janeiro, 1811).

Bates, Henry Walter: *The Naturalist on the River Amazons* (London, 1864, 1943).

Bauve, Adam de, and P. Ferré: 'Voyage dans l'intérieur de la Guyane',

Bulletin de la Société de Géographie, 1 ser., **20** 201–26 and 265–82; 2 ser., **1** 105–44 and 165–78, Paris, 1833–4.

BAYERN, THERESE, PRINZESSIN VON: *Meine Reise in den brasilienischen Tropen* (Berlin, 1897).

BECKER-DONNER, ETTA: *Brasiliens Indianer* (Museum für Völkerkunde, Vienna, n.d.).

BERTHELS, D. E., B. N. KOMISSAROV AND T. I. LYSENKO: *Materialen der Brasilien-Expedition 1821–1829 des Akademiemitgliedes Georg Heinrich Freiherr von Langsdorff (Grigorij Ivanovic Langsdorff)*, Völkerkundliche Abhandlungen **7** (Berlin, 1979).

BESCHOREN, MAX: 'Beiträge zur nähern Kenntnis der brasilianischen Provinz São Pedro do Rio Grande do Sul. Reisen und Beobachtungen während der Jahre 1875–1887', *Petermanns Mitteilungen* **96** 1–91, Gotha, 1889.

BIGORRE, FRANÇOIS: 'Quarante jours sur l'Araguaya (intérieur du Brésil) de Conceição à Leopoldina (Octobre–Novembre 1911)', *Les Missions Catholiques* **45** 475–7, 502–4, 513–15, 525–7, 537–40, 550–2, 561–3, 573–5, 585–7, 597–9, 607–10, Paris, 1913.

BOEHRER, GEORGE C. A.: 'Variant Versions of José Bonifácio's "Plan for the Civilization of the Brazilian Indians" ', *The Americas* **14**:3 301–11, January 1958.

— 'Some Brazilian Proposals to the Cortes Gerais, 1821–1823, on the Indian problem', in *Atas, III Colóquio Internacional de Estudos Luso-Brasileiros*, ed. Luis Lindley Cintra, 2 vols (Lisbon, 1959–60) **2** 201–9.

BOGGIANI, GUIDO: *Viaggi d'un artista nell'America Meridionale: I Caduvei (Mbaya o Guaycurú)* . . . (Rome 1896), trans. Amadeu Amaral Junior, ed. Herbert Baldus, *Os Caduveo* (São Paulo, 1945).

BRANDÃO, FREI CAETANO: *Memorias para a historia da vida do Veneravel Arcebispo de Braga D. Fr. Caetano Brandão*, ed. A. C. do Amaral (Lisbon, 1818); also in *Jornal de Coimbra*, **4–5**, 1815.

BRAUM, JOÃO VASCO MANOEL DE: *Descripção chorographica do Estado do Grão-Pará* (1789), RHGB **36**:1 269–322, 1873.

BRINTON, DANIEL G.: *The American Race* (Philadelphia, Pa, 1901).

BROWN, CHARLES BARRINGTON: *Canoe and camp life in British Guiana* (London, 1876).

— AND WILLIAM LIDSTONE: *Fifteen thousand miles on the Amazon and its tributaries* (London, 1878).

BUENO, JOÃO FERREIRA DE OLIVEIRA: 'Simples narração da viagem que fez ao rio Paraná' (1810), RHGB **1** 179–92, 1839.

BUENO, JOSÉ ANTONIO PIMENTA: 'Índios e população; extracto do discurso do Presidente da Provincia do Mato Grosso . . . 1 de março de 1837', RHGB **2** 172, 1840 or 1916.

BURMEISTER, HERMANN: *Reise nach Brasilien, durch die Provinzen von Rio de Janeiro und Minas Gerais* (Berlin, 1853), trans. Manoel Salvaterra and Hubert Schoenfeldt, *Viagem ao Brasil*, Editora Itatiaia (Universidade de São Paulo, 1980).

BURTON, RICHARD F.: *Explorations of the Highlands of Brazil* (London, 1869).

CALDAS, JOÃO AUGUSTO: *Memoria histórica sôbre os indígenas da Provincia de Mato Grosso* (Rio de Janeiro, 1887)

CAMPOS, LUIS THOMAS NAVARRO DE: *Relatorio da viagem por terra da Bahia athé Rio de Janeiro* (Rio de Janeiro, 1808; ms., Royal Geographical Society, London).

CANABRAVA, A. P.: 'Documentos sôbre os índios do Rio Juquiá', RMP, n.s., 3 391–404, 1949.

CARNAXIDE, ANTONIO DE SOUSA PEDROSO: *O Brasil na administração pombalina* (Rio de Janeiro, 1940).

CARNEIRO, JOÃO ROBERTO AYRES: 'Itinerario da viagem da expedição exploradora e colonizadora ao Tocantins em 1849,' ABAPP 7 1910.

CARNEIRO DE MENDONÇA, MARCOS: *A Amazônia na era pombalina: Correspondência inédita do . . . Francisco Xavier de Mendonça Furtado*, 3 vols (São Paulo, 1963).

CARVALHO, MARCOS JOSÉ MONTEIRO DE: *Instruções que regulam o método porque os Directores das povoações de indios das Capitanias do Grão Pará se devem conduzir . . .* (28 June 1776), IHGB, lata 107, doc. 12.

CASAL, MANUEL AIRES DO: *Corographia Brasílica* (1817), ed. Caio Prado Júnior, 2 vols (Rio de Janeiro, 1945).

— *Notice sur . . . Pará et le Solimoens*, Nouvelles Annales des Voyages 9 (Paris, 1821).

CASEMENT, ROGER: *Correspondence Respecting the Treatment of British Colonial Subjects and Native Indians Employed in the Collection of Rubber in the Putumayo District, Presented to Both Houses of Parliament by Command of His Majesty, July 1912* (London, 1912).

CASTELNAU, FRANCIS L. DE LAPORTE, COMTE DE: *Expédition dans les parties centrales de l'Amérique du Sud, de Rio de Janeiro à Lima, et de Lima au Pará*, pt 1: *Histoire du voyage*, 6 vols (Paris, 1850–1).

CASTRO, MIGUEL JOÃO DE, AND ANTÔNIO TOMÉ DE FRANÇA: 'Abertura de communicação commercial entre o districto de Cuyabá e a cidade do Pará por meio da navegação dos rios Arinos e Tapajós emprehendida em setembro de 1812', RHGB 31: 1 107–60, 1868.

CÉSAR, JOSÉ VICENTE: 'Todo o caminho percorrido para a formação do Estatuto do Índio', *Jornal de Brasília, JBr Cultura* 3–6, Brasília, 12 Aug. 1973.

CHAIM, MARIVONE MATOS: *Os aldeamentos indígenas na Capitania de Goiás* (Goiânia, 1974).

CHANDLESS, WILLIAM: 'Notes on the Rivers Arinos, Juruena, and Tapajós', JRGS 32 268–80, 1862.

— 'Ascent of the River Purûs', JRGS 36 86–118, 1866.

— 'Notes on the River Aquiry, the Principal affluent of the River Purûs', JRGS 36 119–28, 1866.

— 'Notes of a Journey up the River Juruá', JRGS 39 296–311, 1869.

— 'Notes on the rivers Maué-assú, Abacaxis, and Canumá, Amazonas', JRGS 40 419–32, 1870.

CHURCH, GEORGE EARL: 'Notes on the Visit of Dr. Bach to the Catuquinarú Indians of Amazonas', GJ **12** 63–7, 1898.

— *The Aborigenes of South America* (London, 1912).

COELHO, FELIPE JOSÉ NOGUEIRA: *Memórias cronológicas da capitania de Mato Grosso (1718–1779)*, RHGB **13** 137–99, 1850.

COELHO, Pe. JOSÉ MARIA: 'Duas memorias sobre a Capitania de São José do Rio Negro (1823)', RHGB **203** 109–134, 1949.

COLBACCHINI, ANTONIO: *I Bororos Orientali 'Orarimugudoge' del Matto Grosso (Brasile)* (Turin, 1926).

COLLIER, RICHARD: *The River that God Forgot* (London, 1968).

COOK, W. A.: 'The Bororo Indians of Matto Grosso, Brazil', *Smithsonian Miscellaneous Collections* **50** 48–62, Washington, DC, 1908.

COPPI, GIUSEPPE, OFM: 'La Provincia delle Amazzoni', ed. G. A. Colini, *Bolletino della Società Geografica Italiana*, anno 19, **22**, 2 ser., **10** 136–41, 193–204, Rome, 1885.

CORREA, FELIPE NERI: 'Direção com que interinamente se deve regular os indios das novas villas e lugares erectos nas aldeias da Capitania de Pernambuco e suas annexas' (1759, RHGB **46**: 1 121–71, 1883.

CORRÊA FILHO, VIRGÍLIO: 'Ricardo Franco de Almeida Serra', RHGB **243** 3–19, April–June 1959.

COSTA, ANTÔNIO DE MACEDO: *A Amazônia: meio de desenvolver sua civilização* (Rio de Janeiro, 1884).

COUDREAU, HENRI ANATOLE: *Voyage au Rio-Branco, aux Montagnes de la Lune, au Haut Trombettas* (Rouen, 1886).

— *La France Équinoxiale*, 2 vols and atlas (Paris, 1886–7), I: *Études sur les Guyanes et l'Amazonie*; II: *Voyage à travers les Guyanes et l'Amazonie*.

— *Les Français en Amazonie* (Paris, 1887)

— *Chez nos indiens. Quatre années dans la Guyane Française* (Paris, 1893).

— *Voyage au Xingu* (Paris, 1897).

— *Voyage au Tocantins–Araguaia* (Paris, 1897).

— *Voyage au Tapajoz* (Paris, 1897).

— *Voyage à Itaboca et à l'Itacayuna* (Paris, 1898).

— *Voyage entre Tocantins et Xingu* (Paris, 1899).

— *Voyage au Yamundá* (Paris, 1899).

COUDREAU, OLGA: *Voyage au Trombetas* (Paris, 1900).

— *Voyage au Cuminá* (Paris, 1901).

— *Voyage au Rio Curuá* (Paris, 1903).

— *Voyage à la Mapuera* (Paris, 1903).

— *Voyage au Canumã* (Paris, 1906).

COUTINHO, FRANCISCO DE SOUSA: 'Informação sobre o modo porque se effectua presentamente a navegação do Pará para Mato Grosso' (1797), RHGB **2** 283–306, 1840.

— 'Plano para a civilização dos indios na Capitania do Pará', IHGB Archive, 1, 1, 4 Conselho Ultramarino, 224–55, 2 August 1797.

CRAIG, NEVILLE B.: *Recollections of an Ill-fated Expedition to the Headwaters of the Madeira River in Brazil* (Philadelphia, Pa, and London, 1907).

CREVAUX, JULES: *Voyages dans L'Amérique du Sud*: 1. *Voyage dans l'intérieur des Guyanes (1876–1877) exploration du Maroni et du Yary*. 2. *De Cayenne aux Andes (1870–1879) exploration de l'Oyapock, du Parou, de l'Içá et du Yapurá* (Paris, 1883).

CUTWRIGHT, PAUL RUSSELL: *The Great Naturalists Explore South America* (New York, 1940).

DALTRO, LEOLINDA DE FIGUEIREDO: *Da catachese dos indios no Brasil: 1896–1911* (Rio de Janeiro, 1920).

DANIEL, JOÃO, SJ: *Thesouro descoberto no maximo rio Amazonas (c.* 1797), RHGB **2** 321–64, 447–512, **3** 39–51, 158–83, 282–9, **6** 422–41, **41**:1 33–142, 1840, 1841, 1878.

DEBRET, JEAN-BAPTISTE: *Voyage pittoresque et historique au Brésil*, 3 vols (Paris, 1834–9), trans. Sérgio Milliet, 2 vols (São Paulo, 1940).

DERBY, ORVILLE A.: 'O Rio Trombetas', *Boletim do Museu Paraense de Historia Natural e Ethnografia* **1**:3 366–81, Belém, 1897–8.

DIAS, MANUEL NUNES: 'Colonização da Amazônia (1755–1778)', RH **34** 471–90, 1967.

— *A Companhia Geral do Grão-Pará e Maranhão (1755–1778)* (São Paulo, 1971).

DOBRIZHOFFER, MARTIN: *Geschichte der Abiponer, einer berittenen und kriegerischen Nation in Paraguay*, 3 vols (Vienna, 1783–4), trans. Sara Coleridge, *An account of the Abipones, an equestrian people of Paraguay* 3 vols (London, 1822).

DODT, GUSTAVO LUIZ GUILHERME: *Descripção dos rios Parnahyba e Gurupy* (São Luis, Maranhão, 1873), Brasiliana, 5 ser., **138**, São Paulo, 1939.

DOUVILLE, JEAN-BAPTISTE: 'Voyage chez les sauvages du Brésil fait pendant les années 1833, 1834 et 1835', ed. Alfred Métraux, *Revista del Instituto de Etnología de la Universidad Nacional de Tucumán*, **1** 239–93, 1928.

DREYS, NICOLAU: *Noticia descritiva da provincia do Rio Grande de São Pedro do Sul* (1839) (Pôrto Alegre, 1961).

DRIVER, DAVID MILLER: *The Indian in Brazilian literature* Hispanic Institute in the United States (New York, 1942).

DURAND, ABBÉ: 'La Madeira et son bassin', *Bulletin de la Société de Géographie*, 6 ser., **10** 449–67, 587–605, Paris, 1875.

EDWARDS, WILLIAM H.: *A Voyage up the River Amazon, including a Residence at Pará* (London, 1847).

EHRENREICH, PAUL: 'Über die Botokuden der brasilianischen Provinz Espiritu Santo und Minas Gerais', *Zeitschrift für Ethnologie* **19**, Berlin, 1886.

— 'Viagem aos rios Amazonas e Purus' (1888) RMP **16**, 1929.

— 'Die Einteilung und Verbreitung der Völkerstämme Brasiliens nach dem gegenwärtigen Stande unsrer Kenntnisse', *Petermanns Mitteilungen* **37** 81–9, 114–24, Gotha, 1891, trans., 'Divisão e distribuição das tribus do Brasil segundo o estado actual dos nossos conhecimentos', *Revista da Sociedade de Geographia do Rio de Janeiro*, **8**:1 3–55, 1892.

— 'Beiträge zur Völkerkunde Brasiliens', *Veröffentlichungen aus dem König-*

lichen Museum für Völkerkunde, **2**:1–2, 1–80, Berlin, 1891, trans. Egon Schaden, 'Contribuições para a etnologia brasileira', RMP, n.s., **2** 7–135, 1948.

ELLIOTT, JOÃO HENRIQUE: 'Itinerário das viagens exploradoras . . . entre Antonina e o Baixo-Paraguay na provincia de Mato-Grosso' (1844–7), RHGB **10**, 1848 or 1870.

— 'Resume do itinerario de uma viagem exploradora pelos rios Verde, Itareré, Paranapanêma e seus affluentes pelo Paraná, Ivahy e sertões adjacentes . . .', RHGB **9** 17–42, 1847.

— 'A emigração dos Cayuaz', RHGB **19** 434–48,1856.

ESCHWEGE, BARON WILHELM LUDWIG VON: *Journal von Brasilien* or *Brasilien die neue Welt* (Weimar, 1818), trans. in Coleção Reconquista do Brasil **48** Editora Itatiaia (Belo Horizonte, 1978).

— *Pluto Brasiliensis*, 2 vols (Braunschweig, 1830); trans. Coleção Reconquista do Brasil **58–9** (Belo Horizonte, 1980), or Rodolfo Jacob, *Coletanea de cientistas estrangeiros* (Belo Horizonte, 1922).

FALCÃO, EDGARD DE CERQUEIRA: 'Alexandre Rodrigues Ferreira e a sua "viagem filosófica" às capitanias do Grão-Pará, Rio Negro, Mato Grosso e Cuiabá (1783–1792)', *Revista Medica Paulista* **76** 107–16, 1970.

— (ed.) Alexandre Rodrigues Ferreira, *Viagem filosófica às capitanias do Grão-Pará, Rio Negro, Mato Grosso e Cuiabá*, 2 vols (São Paulo, 1970).

FARABEE, WILLIAM CURTIS: 'The Amazon Expedition of the University Museum', *The Museum Journal*, University of Pennsylvania, **7** 210 ff., 1916.

— 'The Amazon Expedition of the University Museum. To the Head Waters of the Amazon', *The Museum Journal*, University of Pennsylvania, **8** 61–82, 1917.

— 'A Pioneer in Amazonia: the narrative of a journey from Manaos to Georgetown', *Bulletin of the Geographical Society of Philadelphia* **15** 57–103, Pennsylvania, Pa, Jan.–Oct. 1917.

— *The Central Caribs*, University of Pennsylvania Museum, Anthropological Publications **10** (Philadelphia, Pa, 1924).

FELDNER, WILHELM CHRISTIAN GOTTHELF: *Reisen durch mehrere Provinzen Brasiliens*, 2 vols (Liegnitz, 1828).

FERRAZ, LUIZ PEDREIRA DO COUTO: 'Apontamentos sôbre a vida do índio Guido Pocrane e sôbre o Francez Guido Marlière', RHGB **18** 426–34, 1855.

FERREIRA, ALEXANDRE RODRIGUES: *Diario da viagem philosophica pela Capitania de São-José do Rio Negro* (1786), RHGB **48**:1 1–234, **49**:1 123–288, **50**:2 11–142, **51**:1 5–104, 1885–8.

— *Viagem filosófica às capitanias do Grão-Pará, Rio Negro, Mato Grosso e Cuiabá*, ed. Edgard de Cerqueira Falcão, 2 vols (São Paulo, 1970). *Memória. Antropologia* (Rio de Janeiro, 1974).

— 'Memoria sobre o gentio Guaiacrus', (Paraguay River), 5 May 1791, in Thekla Hartmann, *A contribuição da iconografia para o conhecimento de índios brasileiros do século XIX* (São Paulo, 1975) 151–60.

— 'Roteiro das viagens, que fez pelas capitanias do Pará, Rio Negro, Mato Grosso, e Cuyabá' (1792), in Thekla Hartmann, *A contribuição da iconografia para o conhecimento de índios brasileiros do século XIX* (São Paulo, 1975) 133–42.

FERREIRA, MANOEL RODRIGUES: *A ferrovia do diabo, história de uma estrada de ferro na Amazônia* (São Paulo, 1959).

FLORENCE, HÉRCULES: *Esboço da viagem feito pelo Sr de Langsdorff no interior do Brasil, desde setembro de 1825 até março de 1829*, trans. Alfredo d'Escragnolle Taunay, RHGB **38**:1 338–469, 1875, and **38**:2 231–301, 1876.

FONSECA, BENTO DA: *Noticia do governo temporal dos indios do Maranhão* (1755), in Alexandre J. de Mello Moraes, *Corographia . . . do Imperio do Brasil*, 4 vols (Rio de Janeiro, 1858–60) **4** 122–86.

FONSECA, GONÇALVES DA: *Navegação feita da cidade do Gram Pará até a bocca do rio da Madeira*, Collecção Ultramarina, **4**:1 (Lisbon, 1826).

FONSECA, JOÃO SEVERIANO DA: *Viagem ao redor do Brasil, 1875–1878*, 2 vols (Rio de Janeiro, 1880–1).

FONSECA, JOSÉ PINTO DE: *Carta que escreveu ao Exmo. General de Goyazes, dandolhe conta do descobrimento de duas nações de indios, Santa Anna, 2 Aug. 1775*, RHGB **8** 376–90, 1846.

FOREIGN OFFICE: *Question de la Frontière entre La Guyane Britannique et le Brésil. Annexe au Mémoire Présenté par le Gouvernement de Sa Majesté Britannique*, 4 vols (London, 1903).

FOUNTAIN, PAUL: *The River Amazon, from its Sources to the Sea* (London, 1914).

FREIRE, JOSÉ RODRIGUES: *Relação da conquista do gentio Xavante* (1790), ed. Carlos Drummond (São Paulo, 1951).

FRESCAROLO, FR VITAL DE: 'Informações sobre os índios bárbaros dos sertões de Pernambuco' (1804), *Revista Trimensal do Instituto do Ceará* **27**, Fortaleza, 1913.

FREYRE, GILBERTO: *Casa-grande e senzala. Formação da familia brasileira sob o regime de economia patriarcal* (4th edn, Rio de Janeiro, 1943); trans. Samuel Putnam, *The Masters and the Slaves: a study in the development of Brazilian civilization* (New York, 1946; 2nd edn, 1956).

— *Sobrados e mucambos* (Rio de Janeiro, 1936), trans. Harriet de Onis, *The Mansions and the Shanties* (New York, 1963).

FREYREISS, GEORG WILHELM: *Beiträge zur näheren Kenntnis des Kaiserthums Brasilien* (Frankfurt am Main, 1824).

— *Reisen in Brasilien* (1825), ed. Stig Rydén (Stockholm, 1968), trans. Alberto Löfgren, *Revista do Instituto Histórico e Geográfico de São Paulo* **11** 158–252, 1907.

FRIČ, VOJTĚCH, AND PAUL RADIN: 'Contributions to the Study of the Bororo Indians', *Journal of the Anthropological Institute of Great Britain and Ireland* **36** 382–406, London, 1906.

— 'Sambaqui-Forschungen im Hafen von Antonina (Paraná)', *Globus* **91**:8 117–22, Brunswick, 27 Feb. 1907.

FURNEAUX, ROBIN: *The Amazon: the story of a great river* (London, 1969).

GALLAIS, ESTEVÃO-MARIA: *O apóstolo do Araguaia: Frei Gil de Vilanova, mission-*

ário Dominicano, trans. Fr Pedro Secondy and Soares de Azevedo (São Paulo, 1942).

— *Uma catequese entre os índios do Araguaia*, trans. Otaviano Esselin (Salvador, 1954).

GAMA LOBO DE ALMADA, MANOEL DA: *Descripção relativa ao rio Branco e seu territorio* (1787), RHGB **24** 617–83, 1861; trans. in Foreign Office, *Question de la Frontière entre La Guyane Britannique et le Brésil, Annexe* (London, 1903), **1** 182–95, and **4** 23–34.

GARDNER, GEORGE: *Travels in the interior of Brazil, principally through the northern provinces, and the gold and diamond districts, during the years 1836–1841* (London, 1846).

GENSCH, DR HUGO: *Die Erziehung eines Indianerkindes*, Annexe to *Verhandlungen des XVI. Internationalen Amerikanisten-Kongresses*, Vienna, 1908 (Vienna and Leipzig, 1910).

GOMES, VICENTE FERREIRA: *Itinerario da cidade da Palma, em Goyaz, à cidade de Belém no Pará, pelo rio Tocantins, e breve noticia do norte da Provincia de Goyaz* (1859), RHGB **25** 485–515, 1862.

GONÇALVES, MARIA DA CONCEIÇÃO OSORIO DIAS: 'O índio do Brasil na literatura portuguesa dos séculos XVI, XVII e XVIII', *Brasilia* **11** 97–209, Coimbra, 1961.

GRAHAM, MARIA: *Journal of a voyage to Brazil* (London, 1824).

GRAVIER, GABRIEL: *Étude sur le sauvage du Brésil* (Paris, 1881).

GRUPE Y THODE, G.: 'Über den Rio Blanco und die anwohnenden Indianer', *Globus* **16** 251–4, Braunschweig, 1890.

GUIMARÃES, CANON JOSÉ DA SILVA: 'Memoria sobre os usos, costumes e linguagem dos Appiacás . . .' RHGB **4**, 1854.

GURJÃO, MAJOR HILÁRIO MAXIMIANO ANTUNES: *Descripção da viagem feita desde a cidade da Barra do Rio Negro pelo rio do mesmo nome, até a serra do Cucui* (1854), RHGB **18** 183–96, 1855 or 1896; ed. Herculano Ferreira Penna, *Relatórios da Presidência da Provincia do Amazonas* **1** (Rio de Janeiro, 1906).

HARTMANN, THEKLA: *A contribuição da iconografia para o conhecimento de índios brasileiros do século XIX*, Coleção Museu Paulista, Série de Etnologia **1** (São Paulo, 1975).

— *Geology and physical geography of Brazil* (Boston, Mass., 1870).

HARTT, CHARLES FREDERICK: 'Contribuições para a etnologia do Valle do Amazonas', *Archivos do Museu Nacional* **6** 1–174, Rio de Janeiro, 1885.

HEMMING, JOHN HENRY: *Red Gold: the conquest of the Brazilian Indians* (London, 1978).

— *The Search for El Dorado* (London, 1978).

— 'Indians and the Frontier in Colonial Brazil', in *The Cambridge History of Latin America*, ed. Leslie Bethell (Cambridge, 1984) **2** 501–46.

— *Change in the Amazon Basin* 2 vols (Manchester, 1985).

HERNDON, WILLIAM LEWIS, AND LARDNER GIBBON: *Exploration of the Valley of the Amazon made under Direction of the Navy Department*, 2 vols (one by each author) (Washington, DC, 1854).

HUGO, VITOR: *Desbravadores*, 2 vols (Humaitá, Amazonas, 1959).

HUMBOLDT, ALEXANDER VON: *Relation historique du voyage aux régions équinoxiales du Nouveau Continent*, 3 vols (Paris, 1011 25), trans. Thomasina Ross, *Personal narrative of travels to Equinoctial Regions of America, during the years 1799–1804*, 3 vols (London, 1852–3).

HURLEY, JORGE: *A Cabanagem* (Belém, 1936).

JARDIM, JOAQUIM R. DE MORAES, AND ARISTIDES DE SOUZA SPINOLA: *O Rio Araguaya* (Rio de Janeiro, 1880).

JARDIM, RICARDO JOSÉ GOMES: *Creação da Directoria dos Indios na Provincia de Mato Grosso* (1846), RHGB **9** 548–59, 1847.

JOBIM, ANÍSIO: *O Amazonas, sua história (ensaio antropogeográfico e político)*, Brasiliana, 5 ser., **292** (São Paulo, 1957).

JORGE, NORBERTO JOÃO ANTUNES: *A catechese e civilisação dos índios no Brasil* (São Paulo, 1909).

JOSÉ, OILIAM: *Marlière, o civilizador* (Belo Horizonte, 1958).

KARASH, MARY: 'Damiana da Cunha: catechist and sertanista', in *Struggle and Survival in Colonial America*, ed. David G. Sweet and Gary B. Nash (Berkeley, Los Angeles, Calif., and London, 1981) 102–20.

KEITH, HENRY H., AND S. F. EDWARDS: (eds) *Conflict and Continuity in Brazilian Society* (Columbia, SC, 1969).

KELLER-LEUZINGER, FRANZ: 'Noções sobre os indígenas da Provincia do Paraná' (1867), in Lêda A. Lovato, 'A contribuição de Franz Keller à etnografia do Paraná', *Boletim do Museu do Índio. Antropologia* **1** 1–44, Rio de Janeiro, 1974.

— *Vom Amazonas und Madeira* (Munich, 1874), trans. *The Amazon and Madeira Rivers* (London, 1874).

KIDDER, REV. DANIEL P.: *Sketches of residence and travels in Brazil, embracing historical and geographical notices of the Empire and its several provinces*, 2 vols (Philadelphia, Pa, 1845).

— AND JAMES C. FLETCHER: *Brazil and the Brazilians, portrayed in historical and descriptive sketches* (9th edn, London, 1879).

KIETZMAN, DALE WALTER: 'Indian survival in Brazil' (doctoral dissertation, University of Southern California, 1972).

KOCH-GRÜNBERG, THEODOR: 'Die Guaikurustämme', *Globus* **81** 1–7, 39–46, 69–78, 105–12, Brunswick, 1902.

— *Reise in Matto Grosso (Brasilien). Expedition in das Quellgebiet des Schingú* (Vienna, 1902).

— 'Die Apiaká-Indianer (Rio Tapajós, Mato Grosso)', *Zeitschrift für Ethnologie* **34** 350–79, Berlin, 1902.

— 'Die Indianerstämme am oberen Rio Negro und Yapurá', *Zeitschrift für Ethnologie* **38** 166–205, Berlin, 1906.

— *Zwei Jahre unter den Indianern. Reisen in Nordwest-Brasilien 1903/1905*, 2 vols (Berlin, 1909–10).

— 'Die Miránya (Rio Yapurá, Amazonas)', *Zeitschrift für Ethnologie* **42** 896–914, Berlin, 1910.

— 'Meine Reise durch Nord-Brasilien zum Orinoco, 1911–1913', *Zeit-*

schrift der Gesellschaft für Erdkunde zu Berlin 665–94, Berlin, 1913.

— *Von Roroima zum Orinoco. Ergebnisse einer Reise in Nordbrasilien und Venezuela in den Jahren 1911–1913*, 5 vols (Berlin and Stuttgart, 1916, 1917, 1923 and 1928); vol. 2, trans. Henrique Roenick: 'Mitos e lendas dos índios Taulipáng e Areçuna', RMP, n.s., **7**, São Paulo, 1953.

KOENIGSWALD, GUSTAV VON: 'Die Botokuden in Südbrasilien', *Globus* **93** 37–43, Brunswick, 1908.

— 'Die Cayuás', *Globus* **93** 376–81, Brunswick, 1908.

— 'Die Corôados in südlichen Brasilien', *Globus* **94** 27–32, 45–9, Brunswick, 1908.

KOSLOWSKI, JÚLIO: 'Tres semanas entre los indios Guató', *Revista del Museo de la Plata*, **6**:2 221–50, La Plata, 1895.

— 'Algunos datos sobre los indios Bororós', *Revista del Museo de la Plata*, **6**:2 373–412, La Plata, 1895.

KOSTER, HENRY: *Travels in Brazil*, 2nd edn, 2 vols (London, 1817); trans. M. A. Jay, 2 vols (Paris, 1846).

KRAUSE, FRITZ: 'Bericht über eine ethnographische Forschungsreise in Zentralbrasilien', *Zeitschrift für Ethnologie* **61**, Berlin, 1908.

— 'Minha excursão investigadora à região central do Araguaya', RHGB **73**:1, 259–75, 1910.

— *In den Wildnissen Brasiliens* (Leipzig, 1911).

— 'Die Waurá-Indianer des Schingu-Quellgebietes, Zentral-Brasilien', *Mitteilungsblatt der Gesellschaft für Völkerkunde*, **7** 14–31, 25–40, Leipzig, 1936 and 1939.

— 'Beiträge zur Ethnographie des Araguaya–Xingugebietes', *XXI Congrès Internationale des Américanistes* (Göteborg, 1925).

KROEMER, GUNTER: *Cuxiuara. O Purus dos indígenas Conselho Indigenista Missionário* (São Paulo, 1985).

KUPFER, DR: 'Die Cayapó-Indianer in der Provinz Matto-Grosso' (1857), *Zeitschrift der Gesellschaft für Erdkunde* **5** 244–55, Berlin, 1870.

LABRE, ANTONIO: 'Colonel Labre's explorations in the region between the Beni and Madre de Dios Rivers and the Purus', *Proceedings of the Royal Geographical Society* **11** 496–502, 1889.

LACERDA, ADOLFO DE BARROS ALBUQUERQUE: *Relatorio apresentado à Assembléia Legislativa da Provincia do Amazonas* (Pernambuco, 1 October 1864).

LANGSDORFF, GEORG HEINRICH, BARON VON: *Bemerkungen über Brasilien* (Heidelberg, 1821).

LEAL, OSCAR: *Viagem ás terras goyanas (Brazil central)* (Lisbon, 1892).

— *Viagem a um paiz de selvagens* (Lisbon, 1895).

LE COINTE, PAUL: *L'Amazonie brésilienne*, 2 vols (Paris, 1922).

LEVERGER, AUGUSTO, BARÃO DE MELGAÇO: 'Roteiro da navegação do rio Paraguai desde a foz do São Lourenço até o Paraná', RHGB **25** 211–84, 1862.

— 'Apontamentos para o Diccionario chorographico da Provincia do Matto Grosso', RHGB **48**, 1884.

— 'Apontamentos cronológicos da Provincia de Mato Grosso', RHGB **205** 208–385, Oct–Dec. 1949.

LIMA, FRANCISCO DAS CHAGAS: 'Memoria sobre o descobrimento e colonia de Guarapuava', RIHGB **4** 43–64, 2nd edn 1863.
— 'Noticia da fundação e principios d'esta Aldêa de S. João de Queluz', RHGB **5** 72–6, 1843.

LISBOA, JOÃO FRANCISCO: *Jornal de Timon* (São Luis do Maranhão, 1854–9).
— Letters to Francisco Adolfo de Varnhagen, 1856–7, in Varnhagen, *Os indios bravos e o Sr Lisboa, Timon 3°* (Lima, 1867) 67–101.

LOPES, JOAQUIM FRANCISCO: *Itinerario . . . entre a provincia de São Paulo e a de Matto-Grosso pelo Baixo Paraguay* (1848–9), RHGB **13** 315–35, 1850 (2nd edn 1872).

MACLACHLAN, COLIN: 'The Indian Directorate: forced acculturation in Portuguese America, 1757–1799', *The Americas* **28**:4 357–87, April 1972.
— 'The Indian Labor Structure in the Portuguese Amazon, 1700–1800', in *Colonial Roots of Modern Brazil*, ed. Dauril Alden (Berkeley, Calif., 1973).

MAGALHÃES, D. J. G.: 'Os indigenas do Brasil perante a historia', RHGB **23** 3–66, 1860.

MAGALHÃES, JOSÉ VIEIRA COUTO DE: *Viagem ao Araguaya* (1862), Brasiliana **28** (São Paulo, 1934).
— 'Ensaio de anthropologia. Região e raças selvagens', RHGB **36**:2 359–516, 1873.
— *Região e raças selvagens do Brasil* (Rio de Janeiro, 1874).
— *Memoria sobre colonias militares nacionais e indigenas* (Rio de Janeiro, 1875).
— *O selvagem* (Rio de Janeiro, 1876).

MALHEIRO, AGOSTINHO MARQUES PERDIGÃO: *A escravidão no Brasil*, pt 2: *Indios* (Rio de Janeiro, 1867).

MARAJÓ, BARÃO DE: *As regiões amazônicas. Estudos chorographicos dos estados do Grão Pará e Amazonas* (Lisbon, 1895).

MARCOY, PAUL: *Voyage à travers l'Amérique du Sud, de l'Océan Pacifique à l'Océan Atlantique*, 2 vols (Paris, 1869).

MARLIÈRE, GUIDO THOMAS: 'Documentos', *Revista do Archivo Publico Mineiro*, **10** 383–668, Bello Horizonte, July–Dec. 1905.

MARTIUS, CARL FRIEDRICH PHILIP VON: *Von dem Rechtszustande unter den Urein-wohnern Brasiliens* (Munich, 1832).
— 'Como se deve escrever a história do Brazil', RHGB **6** 381–403, 1844.
— *Arztthum und die Heilmittel der Urbewohner Brasiliens* (Munich, 1844); trans. Pirajá da Silva, *Natureza, doenças, medicina e remedios dos índios brasileiros*, Brasiliana **154** (São Paulo and Rio de Janeiro, 1939).
— *Beiträge zur Ethnographie und Sprachenkunde Amerika's, zumal Brasiliens*, 2 vols (Erlangen and Leipzig, 1863, 1867).
— AND JOH. BAPT. VON SPIX (q.v.): *Reise in Brasilien . . .*, 3 vols (Munich, 1823– 31).

MATHEWS, EDWARD D.: *Up the Amazon and Madeira Rivers through Bolivia and Peru* (London, 1879).

MATTOS, JOÃO HENRIQUE WILKENS DE: 'Relatório sôbre o estado atual de decadência do Alto Amazônas' (1845), *Jornal do Commercio* 7–11 September 1950 (Rio de Janeiro); RHGB **325** 140–80, 1979.

— 'Alguns esclarescimentos sobre as missões da Provincia do Amazonas', RHGB **19** 124–31,1856.

MATTOS, RAYMUNDO JOSÉ DA CUNHA: *Chorographia historica da Provincia de Goyaz* (*c.*1825), RHGB **37**:1 213–398, 1874; **38**:1 5–150, 1875.

— *Itinerario do Rio de Janeiro ao Pará e Maranhão . . .*, 2 vols (Rio de Janeiro, 1836).

MAURO, FRÉDÉRIC: 'Le rôle des indiens et des noirs dans la conscience européisante des blancs: le cas du Brésil', CAL **9–10** 193–211, 1974.

MAURY, MATTHEW FONTAINE: *The Amazon, and the Atlantic Slopes of South America* (Washington, DC, 1853).

MAW, HENRY LISTER: *Journal of a Passage from the Pacific to the Atlantic, Crossing the Andes in the Northern Province of Peru, and Descending the River Marañon, or Amazon* (London, 1829).

MAWE, JOHN: *Travels in the Interior of Brazil, particularly in the Gold and Diamond Districts of that Country* (London, 1812).

MELLO FRANCO, AFRÂNIO A. DE: *Guido Marlière, o apóstolo das selvas mineiras* (Belo Horizonte, 1914).

MELLO-LEITÃO, C. DE: *História das expedições científicas no Brasil*, Brasiliana **209** (São Paulo and Rio de Janeiro, 1941).

MELLO MORAES, ALEXANDRE J. DE: *Corographia historica, chronographica, genealogica, nobiliaria e politica do Imperio do Brasil*, 4 vols (Rio de Janeiro, 1858–60).

— AND IGNACIO ACCIOLI DE CERQUEIRA E SILVA: *Ensaio corografico do Imperio do Brasil* (Rio de Janeiro, 1854).

MELLO MORAES FILHO, ALEXANDRE J. DE: *Revista da Exposição Anthropologica Brazileira* (Rio de Janeiro, 1882).

MENDES, FRANCISCANO: *Carta . . . sobre las costumbres, religión, terreno y tradiciones de los yndios Mbayás, Guanás y demas naciones que ocupan la región boreal del Rio Paraguay* (20 June 1772), in *Do Tratado de Madri à conquista dos Sete Povos (1750–1802)*, ed. Jaime Cortesão (Rio de Janeiro, 1969).

MERRICK,THOMAS W., AND DOUGLAS H. GRAHAM: *Population and Economic Development in Brazil, 1800 to the Present* (Baltimore, Md, 1979).

MÉTRAUX, ALFRED: 'Ethnography of the Chaco', HSAI **1** 197–370, 1946.

MEYER, HERMANN: *Tagebuch meiner Brasilienreise* (Berlin, 1897).

— Über seine Expedition nach Central-Brasilien', *Verhandlungen der Gesellschaft für Erdkunde zu Berlin* 172–98, 1897.

— 'Brief vom 16. VI. 1898', *Zeitschrift für Ethnographie* **30** Berlin, 1898.

— 'Bericht über seine zweite Xingú-Expedition', *Verhandlungen der Gesellschaft für Erdkunde zu Berlin* **27** 112–28, 1900.

MICHELENA Y RÓJAS, FRANCISCO: *Exploración oficial por la primera vez desde el norte de la América del Sur siempre por los ríos, entrando por las bocas del Orinóco, de los valles de este mismo y del Meta, Casiquiare, Rio-Negro ó Guaynia y Amazonas, hasta Nauta en el alto Marañon ó Amazónas, arriba de las bocas del Ucayali bajada del Amazonas hasta el Atlántico . . . en los años de 1855 hasta1859* (Brussels, 1867).

MOCHI, ALDOBRANDINO: 'I popoli dell'Uaupé e la famiglia etnica Miranhà',

Archivio per Antropologia e la Etnologia **32**, Florence, 1902.

MONZA, BARTOLOMEO DA: *Massacro di Alto Alegre* (Milan, 1908).

MOREIRA NETO, CARLOS DE ARAÚJO: 'Problemas de política indigenista brasileira', *V° Congresso Indigenista Interamericano* (Quito, 1964).

— 'Constante histórica do "indigenato" no Brasil', ASBA **2** (Antropologia) 175–85.

— 'A política indigenista brasileira durante o século XIX' (doctoral thesis, Rio Claro University, São Paulo, 1971).

— 'Some Data Concerning the Recent History of the Kaingáng Indians', in *The Situation of the Indian in South America*, ed. W. Dorstal, World Council of Churches (Geneva, 1972) 284–333.

MOTT, LUIZ R. B.: 'Descrição da capitania de São José do Piauí, 1772', RH **28**:56 543–74, 1977.

— 'Relação nominal dos índios de Sergipe del Rey, 1825', *Mensário do Arquivo Nacional*, **11**:10 3–13, Rio de Janeiro, 1980.

MOURA, IGNACIO BAPTISTA DE: *Viagem de Belém a São João do Araguaya* (1896) (Paris, 1910).

— 'Sur le progrès de l'Amazonie et sur les Indiens', *Verhandlungen des XVI internationalen Amerikanistenkongresses* (1908) (Vienna/Leipzig, 1910) 541–3.

MOURE, AMÉDÉE: 'Les indiens de la Province de Mato-Grosso (Brésil)', *Nouvelles Annales des Voyages, de la Géographie, de l'Histoire et de l'Archéologie*, **2** 5–19, 323–41, **3** 77–100, Paris, 1862.

MURPHY, ROBERT F.: *Headhunter's Heritage: social and economic change among the Mundurucú Indians* (Berkeley/Los Angeles, Calif., 1960).

NABUCO, JOAQUIM: *Frontières entre le Brésil et la Guyane Anglaise, question soumise à l'arbitrage de S. M. le Roi d'Italie*, 8 vols (Paris, 1903–4) (four vols contain three Mémoires: three vols have annexes to first and second Mémoires; one vol. of atlas for first Mémoire).

NASCIMENTO, JOSÉ FRANCISCO THOMAZ DO: 'Viagem pelos desconhecidos sertões de Guarapuava, Provincia do Paraná', RHGB **49**:2 267–81, 1886.

NAUD, LEDA MARIA CARDOSO: 'Índios e indigenismo: histórico e legislação', *Revista de Informação Legislativa*, **4**: 15–16 235–68, Brasília, July–Dec. 1967.

— 'O índio brasileiro. Apontamentos desde o descobrimento até a época do Império', *Boletim do Instituto Histórico, Geográfico e Etnográfico Paranaense* **12** 5–24, Curitiba, 1970.

— *Documentos sobre o índio brasileiro*, Arquivo Histórico, 2 pts (Brasília, 1971).

NEMBRO, METÓDIO DA: *Storia dell'atività missionaria dei Minori Cappucini nel Brasile (1538–1889)*. Institut. Historicum Ordinis Fr. Minor. Cappucin., in Francesco da Vicenza, ed., *I missioni cappuccini della Provincia Serafica* **9** (Città de Castello, 1931).

NIMUENDAJÚ, CURT (UNKEL): 'Os índios Parintintin do rio Madeira', JSAP, n.s., **16** 201–78, 1924.

— 'As tribus do alto Madeira', JSAP, n.s., **17** 137–47, 1925.

— 'The Social Structure of the Ramkokamekra (Canela)', *American Anthropologist*, **39** 565–82, 1937; **40** 51–74, 1938.

— *The Apinayé*, trans. Robert H. Lowie, Anthropological Series, Catholic University of America, **8** (Washington, DC, 1939).

— *The Šerente*, trans. Robert H. Lowie, Publications of the Frederick Webb Hodge Anniversary Publication Fund **4**, Southwest Museum (Los Angeles, Calif., 1942).

— *The Eastern Timbira*, trans. Robert H. Lowie, University of California Publications in American Archaeology and Ethnology **41** (Berkeley/Los Angeles, Calif., 1946).

— 'Tribes of the Lower and Middle Xingu River', HSAI **3** 213–43, 1948.

— *Mapa Etno-Histórico de Curt Nimuendajú* (1944), Fundação Instituto Brasileiro de Geografia e Estatística (Rio de Janeiro, 1981).

NORONHA, JOSÉ MONTEIRO DE: *Roteiro da viagem da cidade do Pará até as ultimas colonias do sertão da provincia* (Barcelos, 1768; Belém, 1862).

OLIVEIRA, JOSÉ JOAQUIM MACHADO DE: 'Noticia sobre as aldeias de indios da Provincia de São Paulo desde o seu começo até a atualidade', RHGB **8** 204–53, 1846.

— 'Noticia raciocinada sobre os indios da Provincia de São Paulo', RHGB **10**, 1848.

— 'Notas, apontamentos e noticias para a historia da provincia do Espirito Santo', RHGB **19** 161–335, 1856.

— 'Os Cayapós', RHGB **24** 491–524, 1861.

OLIVEIRA, L. HUMBERTO DE: *Coletânea de Leis, Atos e Memorias referentes ao indígena brasileiro*, CNPI **94** (Rio de Janeiro, 1947).

D'ORBIGNY, ALCIDE DESSALINES: *Voyage dans l'Amérique Méridionale exécuté pendant les années 1826, 1827, 1828, 1829, 1830, 1831, 1832 et 1833*, 11 vols (Paris, 1835–47).

— *L'homme américain considéré sous les rapports physiologiques et moraux (Part A of Voyage dans l'Amérique Méridionale . . .*, Strasbourg, 1840).

— *Fragment d'un voyage au centre de l'Amérique Méridionale* (Paris, 1845).

— *Voyage dans les deux Amériques* (Paris, 1853).

ORTON, JAMES: *The Andes and the Amazon* (New York, 1874).

OSCULATI, GAETANO: *Esplorazione delle regioni equatoriali lungo il Napo ed il fiume delle Amazzoni* (1846–8) (Milan, 1850).

OTÁVIO, RODRIGO: *Os selvagens americanos perante o direito*, Brasiliana **254** (São Paulo, 1946).

OTONI, TEÓFILO BENEDITO: *Noticia sobre os selvagens do Mucury* (1858), RHGB **21** 173–218, 1858.

OTTONI, JOSÉ ELOI: *Memória sôbre o estado actual da Capitania de Minas Gerais* (1798), ABNRJ **30**, 1912.

PALACIN, LUIZ: *Goiás 1722–1822: Estrutura e conjuntura numa capitania deminas* (Goiânia, 1976).

PALAZZOLO, JACINTO DE, OFM: *Nas selvas dos vales do Mucuri e do Rio Doce. Como surgiu a cidade de Itambacuri fundada por Frei Serafim de Gorízia, missionario*

Capuchino, 1873–1952. Brasiliana, 5 ser., **277** (São Paulo, 1952)

PAPAVERO, NELSON: *Essays on the history of neotropical dipterology*, 2 vols (São Paulo, 1973)

PAYER, RICHARD: 'Reisen im Jauapiry-Gebiet', *Petermanns Mitteilungen aus Justus Perthes' geographischer Anstalt* **52** 217–22, Gotha, 1906.

PEARSON, HENRY C.: *The Rubber Country of the Amazon* (New York, 1911).

PENNA, HERCULANO FERREIRA: *Relatórios da presidencia da Provincia do Amazonas*, 5 vols (Rio de Janeiro, 1906–8).

PINTO, OLIVÉRIO MÁRIO OLIVEIRA: 'Viajantes e naturalistas' in *História geral da civilização brasileira*, ed. Sérgio Buarque de Holanda (São Paulo, 1960; 4th edn, Rio de Janeiro/São Paulo, 1978), 5 (2:3) 444–66.

PIZARRO E ARAÚJO, JOSÉ DE SOUZA AZEVEDO: *Memórias históricas do Rio de Janeiro* (1820–2), 9 vols (Rio de Janeiro, 1945–8).

PLANE, AUGUSTE: *À travers l'Amérique Équatoriale. L'Amazonie* (Paris, 1903).

POEPPIG, EDUARD F.: *Reise in Chile, Peru und auf dem Amazonenstrome, während der Jahre 1827–1832*, 2 vols (Leipzig, 1835–6).

POHL, JOHANN EMANUEL: *Reise im Innern von Brasilien in den Jahren 1817–1821*, 2 vols (Vienna, 1832); trans. *Viagem no interior do Brasil empreendida nos anos de 1817 a 1821*, 2 vols (Rio de Janeiro, 1951).

PRADO, CAIO, JÚNIOR: *Formação do Brasil contemporâneo. Colônia*, 4th edn (São Paulo, 1963); trans. Suzette Macedo, *The Colonial Background of Modern Brazil* (Berkeley, Calif., 1967).

— *História econômica do Brasil*, 6th edn (São Paulo, 1965).

PRADO, FRANCISCO RODRIGUES DO: *Historia dos indios cavaleiros ou da nação Guaicuru* (1795), RHGB **1**, 1839.

QUADROS, FRANCISCO RAIMUNDO EWERTON: 'Memoria sobre os trabalhos de observação e exploração effectuada pela segunda secção da commissão militar encarregada da linha telegraphica de Uberaba a Cuiabá' (Feb.–June 1881), RHGB **55**:1 233–60, 1892.

RAIOL, DOMINGOS ANTÔNIO, BARÃO DE GUAJARÁ: *Motins políticos, ou História dos principais acontecimentos políticos da Provincia do Pará, desde o ano de 1821 até 1835*, 5 vols (Rio de Janeiro, 1865; São Luiz do Maranhão, 1868; Rio de Janeiro, 1883, 1884; Belém, 1891. Also, 3 vols, Belém, 1970).

— 'Catachese de índios no Pará' (1900), ABAPP **3** 117–83, 1903.

RAMOS PÉREZ, DEMETRIO: *El Tratado de Límites de 1750 y la Expedición de Iturriaga al Orinoco* (Madrid, 1946).

REGO, FRANCISCO RAPHAEL DE MELLO: 'O Forte de Coimbra', RHGB **67**:2 171–215, 1904.

REGO REIS, GUSTAVO MORAES: *A cabanagem – um episódio histórico de guerra insurrecional na Amazônia (1835–39)* (Manaus, 1965).

REINAULT, PEDRO VICTOR: *Relatorio da exposição dos rios Mucury e Todos os Santos* (1837), RHGB **8** 356–75, 1846 (2nd edn, 1867).

REIS, ARTHUR CÉZAR FERREIRA: *O processo histórico da economia amazonense* (Rio de Janeiro, 1944).

— *O seringal e o seringueiro* (Rio de Janeiro, 1953).

— *A Amazônia que os Portuguêses revelaram* (Rio de Janeiro, 1956).

— *A formação espiritual da Amazônia* (Rio de Janeiro, 1964).

— *Tempo e vida na Amazônia* (Manaus, 1965).

— 'O Amazonas nos primeiros tempos do Império', RHGB **316** 116–23, July–Sept. 1977.

REIS, PAULO PEREIRA DOS: 'Os Puri de Guapacaré e algumas achegas à história de Queluz', RH **30** 117–58, 1965.

RENDON, JOSÉ AROUCHE DE TOLEDO: *Memoria sôbre as aldeas de índios da provincia de São Paulo* (1798), RHGB **4** 295–317, 1842.

— *Oficio . . . para o Governador de São Paulo, Antonio Manuel de Melo Castro e Mendonça* (São Paulo, 10 Nov. 1802), CDSP **11** 184–91.

RIBEIRO, DARCY: *Os índios e a civilização* (Civilização Brasileira, Rio de Janeiro, 1970).

RIBEIRO, FRANCISCO DE PAULA: 'Memoria sobre as nações gentias que habitam o continente do Maranhão' (1819), RHGB **3** 184–96, 297–321, 442–56, 1841.

— 'Roteiro da viagem que fez ás fronteiras da Capitania do Maranhão e da de Goyaz no anno de 1815 . . .', RHGB **10** 5–80, 1848.

— 'Descripção do territorio dos Pastos Bons nos sertões do Maranhão', RHGB **12** 41–86, 1849.

RIVET, PAUL: 'Les Indiens Canoeiros', JSAP, n.s., **16** 169–81, 1924.

RIVIÈRE D'ARC, HÉLÈNE: 'La formation du lieu Amazonie au XIXe siècle', CAL **18** 183–213, 1978.

RODRIGUES, JOÃO BARBOSA: 'Os indios Tembé', 'Mundurucú', 'Yauaperis', 'A emancipação dos Mauhés', 'Tribu dos Ticunas', articles in Alexandre Mello Moraes Filho, *Revista da Exposição Anthropologica* (Rio de Janeiro, 1882).

— *Rio Jauapery: Pacificação dos Crichanás* (Rio de Janeiro, 1885).

ROHAN, HENRIQUE DE BEAUREPAIRE: *Viagem de Cuyabá ao Rio de Janeiro, pelo Paraguay, Corrientes, Rio Grande do Sul e Santa Catharina, em 1846*, RHGB **9** 376–97, 1847, 2nd edn 1869.

ROSCIO, FRANCISCO JOÃO: *Breve noticia da extensão de terreno que occupão os Sete Povos das Missões Guaranis, chamados communmente Tapés Orientaes ao Rio Uruguay, conquistados o anno passado a favor da Coroa de Portugal . . .* (1802), RHGB **21** 271–4, 1858, 2nd edn 1930.

ROSSI, BARTOLOMÉ: *Viage pintoresco por los rios Paraná, Paraguay, Sn Lorenzo, Cuyabá y el Arinos tributario del grande Amazonas, con la descripción de la Provincia de Mato Grosso . . .* (Paris, 1863).

RUGENDAS, JOHANN MORITZ: *Voyage pittoresque dans le Brésil* (Paris, 1835). *Malerische Reise in Brasilien* (Mühlhausen, 1835), trans. Sérgio Milliet (São Paulo, 1940).

— *Bilder und Skizzen aus Brasilien*, ed. G. H. Kletke (Augsburg, 1860), trans. D. Clemente da Silva Nigra, 'Imagens e notas do Brasil', *Revista do Patrimônio Histórico e Artístico Nacional* **13** (Rio de Janeiro, 1956).

SÁ, JESUINO MARCONDES DE OLIVEIRA: *Relatório apresentado pelo Ministro e Secretário de Estado da Agricultura à Assembléia Legislativa* (Rio de Janeiro, 1865).

SAIGNES, THIERRY: 'L'Indien, le Portugais et le Jésuite: alliances et rivalités aux confins du Chaco au XVIIIème siècle', CAL **9–10** 213–45, 1974.

SAINT ADOLPHE, J. C. R. MILLIET: *Diccionario geographico, historico e descriptivo do Imperio do Brazil* (Paris, 1845).

SAINT-HILAIRE, AUGUSTE DE: *Aperçu d'un voyage dans l'intérieur du Brésil, la Province Cisplatine et les missions dites du Paraguay* (Paris, 1823).

— *Voyage dans le district des diamans et sur le littoral du Brésil*, 2 vols (Paris, 1833).

— *Voyage aux sources du Rio de S. Francisco et dans la province de Goyaz*, 2 vols (Paris 1847).

— *Voyage dans les provinces de Rio de Janeiro et de Minas Gerais* (Paris, 1852).

— *Voyage dans l'intérieur du Brésil* (Paris, 1852).

SALESIANS: *Missões Salesianas em Matto Grosso* (Rio de Janeiro, 1912).

SAMPAIO, FRANCISCO XAVIER RIBEIRO DE: *Diario da viagem que em visita, e correição das povoações da Capitana de S. Joze do Rio Negro fez o Ouvidor e Intendente Geral da mesma . . . no anno de 1774 e 1775* (Lisbon, 1825); *Collecção de noticias para a Historia e Geografia das Nações Ultramarinas que vivem nos Dominios Portuguezes ou lhes são Visinhas*, Academia Real das Sciencias, Lisbon, **6** 3–102, 1856.

— 'Relação geographica historica do Rio Branco da America Portugueza', RHGB **13** 200–73, 1850, partly trans. in Foreign Office, *Question de la Frontière . . .*, **1** 127–33.

SAMPAIO, THEODORO: 'Considerações geographicas e economicas sobre o Valle do Rio Paranapanema', *Boletim da Commissão Geographica e Geologica do Estado de S. Paulo* **4** 87–156, São Paulo, 1890.

SÁNCHEZ LABRADOR, JOSEPH, SJ: *El Paraguay católico* (*c.*1772), 3 vols (Buenos Aires, 1910–17).

SANTA-ANNA NÉRY, F. J. BARON DE: *Le pays des Amazones* (Paris, 1885); trans. George Humphrey, *The Land of the Amazons* (London, 1901).

SANTOS, ROBERTO: *História econômica da Amazônia (1800–1920)* (São Paulo, 1980).

SÃO JOSÉ QUEIROZ, JOÃO DE: *Viagem e visita do sertão em o Bispado do Gram-Pará em 1762 e 1763*, RHGB **9** 43–106, 179–226, 328–75, 476–526, 1847 and 1869.

— *Visitas pastorais: memórias (1761 e 1762–1763)* (Rio de Janeiro, 1961).

SAWYER, ROGER: *Casement: The flawed hero* (London, 1984).

SCHADEN, EGON: 'O estudo do índio brasileiro ontem e hoje', *América Indígena* **14**:3 235–51, July 1954; also in RH **3**:12, São Paulo, Oct.–Dec. 1952.

— *Aculturação indígena* (São Paulo, 1969).

— AND JOÃO BORGES PEREIRA: 'Exploração antropológica', in *História geral da civilização brasileira*, ed. Sérgio Buarque de Holanda, 5 vols (São Paulo, 1963) **5** 425–43.

SCHADEN, FRANCISCO S. G.: 'Xokléng e Kaingáng', in *Homem, cultura e sociedade no Brasil*, ed. Egon Schaden, Coleção Estudos Brasileiros **1**, Editora Vozes (Petrópolis, 1972) 79–89.

SCHMIDT, MAX: *Indianerstudien in Zentralbrasilien. Erlebnisse und ethnologische Ergebnisse einer Reise in den Jahren 1900 bis 1901* (Berlin, 1905), trans. Catharina Baratz Cannabrava, Brasiliana Grande Formato **2**, Companhia Editôra Nacional (São Paulo, 1942).

— 'Die Paressi-Kabisi. Ethn. Ergebnisse der Expedition zu den Quellen des Jauru und Juruena im Jahre 1910', *Baessler-Archiv* **4** (Leipzig, 1914).

— 'Die Guató und ihr Gebiet. Ethnologische und archeologish Ergebniss der Expedition zum Caracará-Fluss in Matto Grosso', *Baessler-Archiv* **4**:6 (Leipzig, 1914).

— 'Ergebniss meiner zweijahrigen Forschungsreise in Matto Grosso, September 1926 bis August 1928', *Zeitschrift für Ethnologie* **40**, Berlin, 1929, trans. in BMN **14–17**, Rio de Janeiro, 1938–42, and RMP, n.s., **1** 11–60, 1947.

SCHOMBURGK, MORITZ RICHARD: *Reisen in Britisch-Guiana in den Jahren 1840–44*, 3 vols (Leipzig, 1847–8), trans. Walter Roth, *Travels in British Guiana, 1840–1844*, 2 vols (Georgetown, 1923).

SCHOMBURGK, SIR ROBERT HERMANN: 'Report of an Expedition into the Interior of British Guayana, in 1835–6', JRGS **6** 224–84, 1836.

— 'Report of the Third Expedition into the Interior of Guayana, comprising the Journey to the Sources of the Essequibo, to the Caruma Mountains, and to Fort San Joaquim on the Rio Branco, in 1837–38', JRGS **10** 159–90, 1840.

— 'Journey from Fort San Joaquim on the Rio Branco to Roraima, and thence by the rivers Parima and Merewari to Esmeralda on the Orinoco, in 1838–9', JRGS **10** 191–247, 1840.

— 'Journey from Esmeralda on the Orinoco to San Carlos and Moura on the Rio Negro, and thence by Fort San Joaquim to Demerara, in the spring of 1839', JRGS **10** 248–67, 1840.

— *Twelve Views in the Interior of Guiana* (illustrated by Charles Bentley) (London, 1841).

— 'Visit to the Sources of the Takutu in British Guiana, in the Year 1842', JRGS **13** 18–74, 1843.

— 'Journal of an Expedition from Pirara to the Upper Corentyne, and from thence to Demerara', JRGS **15** 1–104, 1845.

SCHÜTZ-HOLZHAUSEN, DAMIAN, FREIHERR VON: *Der Amazon* (Freiburg-in-Breisgau, 1883).

SEGURADO, RUFINO THEOTINO: *Viagem de Goyaz ao Pará em 1846 e 1847*, RHGB **10** 178–212, 1848, 2nd edn 1870.

SERRA, RICARDO FRANCO DE ALMEIDA: *Discripção geographica da Provincia de Matto Grosso* (1797), excerpt in RHGB **6** 156–96, 1844.

— *Navegação do rio Tapajos para o Pará* (1799), RHGB **9** 1–16, 1847 or 1869.

— *Memoria . . . sobre a Capitania de Mato-Grosso* (31 Jan. 1800), RHGB **2** 19–49, 1840.

— *Parecer sobre o aldêamento dos índios uaicurús e Guanás, com o descripção dos seus usos, estabilidade e costumes* (1803), RHGB **7** 196–204, 1845; **13** 348–95, 1850.

SHPRINTSIN, NOEMI G.: 'Materials of the Russian Expedition to South America Preserved in the Archive of the Academy of Sciences and in the Institute of Ethnography', *Sovetskaya Etnografiya* **2**, Leningrad, 1947.
— 'The Apiacá Indians (From the Materials of the First Russian Expedition to South America)', *Kratkiye Soobshcheniya Instituta Etnografii*, AN SSSR **10**, 1959.

SILVA, ANTONIO DELGADO DA: *Coleção da legislação portugueza desde a última compilação das ordenações* (Lisbon, 1825–30).

SILVA, ANTONIO JOSÉ PESTANA DA: *Meios de dirigir o governo temporal dos indios* (*c*.1788), in Alexandre J. de Mello Moraes, *Corographia historica . . . do Imperio do Brasil*, 4 vols (Rio de Janeiro, 1858–60) **4** 122–85.

SILVA, BERNARDO DA COSTA E: *Viagens no sertão do Amazonas* (Porto, 1891).

SILVA, JOAQUIM NORBERTO DE SOUZA E: 'Memoria historica e documentada das aldeias de indios da Provincia de Rio de Janeiro', RHGB **17** 71–532, 1854.

SILVA, JOSÉ BONIFÁCIO DE ANDRADE E: 'Apontamentos para a civilização dos índios bravos do Imperio do Brasil' (1822), in *Homenagem a José Bonifácio* (Rio de Janeiro, 1910), ed. George C. A. Boehrer (Lisbon, 1963).

SILVA, THOMAZ DA COSTA CORRÊA REBELLO E: *Memoria sobre a Provincia de Missões*, RHGB **2** 157–71, 1840.

SMITH, HERBERT HUNTINGTON: *Brazil: the Amazons and the coast* (New York, 1878; London, 1880).
— Newspaper articles in *Gazeta de Notícias* (Rio de Janeiro, July 1886–Oct. 1887), ed. João Capistrano de Abreu, *Do Rio de Janeiro a Cuiabá* (São Paulo, 1922).

SMITH, NIGEL J. H.: 'Destructive Exploitation of the South American River Turtle', *Yearbook, Association of Pacific Coast Geographers* **36** 85–102, Corvallis, Oreg., 1974.

SMITH, ROBERT C.: 'Requena and the Japurá: some eighteenth century watercolors of the Amazon and other rivers', *The Americas* **3**:1 31–65, July 1946.

SMYTH, LIEUT. WILLIAM, AND FREDERICK LOWE: *Narrative of a journey from Lima to Pará across the Andes and down the Amazon; undertaken with a view of ascertaining the practicability of a navigable communication with the Atlantic by the rivers Pachitea, Ucayali, and Amazon* (London, 1836).

SNETHLAGE, EMILIA: 'A travessia entre o Xingú e o Tapajoz', *Boletim do Museu Goeldi (Museu Paraense) de Historia Natural e Ethnographia* **7** 49–92, Belém, 1910.

SOUSA, ANDRÉ FERNANDES DE: *Noticias geographicas da Capitania do Rio Negro no grande Rio Amazonas* (*c*. 1820), RHGB **10** 411–504, 1848; partly trans. by Lieut. Smyth, JRGS **6** 14–23, 1836.

SOUSA, LUIZ ANTONIO DA SILVA E: *Memoria sobre o descobrimento, governo, população e cousas mais notaveis da Capitania de Goyaz* (Goiás, 1812), RHGB **12** 429–510, 1849.

SOUTHEY, ROBERT: *History of Brazil*, 3 vols (London, 1810–19).

Souza, Francisco Bernardino de: *Lembranças e curiosidades do Valle do Amazonas* (Pará, 1873).

— *Commissão do Madeira: Pará e Amazonas* (Rio de Janeiro, 1874).

Souza, Lincoln de: *Os Xavantes e a civilização* (Rio de Janeiro, 1953).

Spix, Johann Baptist von, and Carl Friedrich Philip von Martius: *Reise in Brasilien in den Jahren 1817 bis 1820*, 3 vols (Munich, 1823–31); vol.1 only trans. H. E. Lloyd, 2 vols (London, 1824); trans. Lucia Furquim Lahmeyer, 4 vols (Rio de Janeiro, 1938).

Spruce, Richard: 'On the River Purus, a tributary of the Amazon', in *Travels of Pedro de Cieza de Leon*, ed. Sir Clements Markham, Hakluyt Society, 1 ser., **33** (London, 1864).

— *Notes of a Botanist on the Amazon and Andes*, 2 vols (London, 1908).

Stauffer, David Hall: 'The origin and establishment of Brazil's Indian Service: 1889–1910' (thesis, University of Texas, Austin, 1955).

Steere, Joseph Beal: 'Narrative of a visit to Indian tribes of the Purus River, Brazil', in *Annual Report of . . . the Smithsonian Institution for the Year Ending June 30, 1901. Report of the U.S. National Museum* (Washington, DC, 1903) 359–93.

Steinen, Karl von den: *Durch Central-Brasilien. Expedition zur Erforschung des Schingú im Jahre 1884* (Leipzig, 1886); trans. Catarina Baratz Cannabrava, *O Brasil Central* (São Paulo and Rio de Janeiro, 1942).

— *Unter den Naturvölkern Zentral-Brasiliens. Reiseschilderung und Ergebnisse der zweiten Schingú-Expedition 1887–1888* (Berlin, 1894); trans. Egon Schaden, *Entre os aborígenes do Brasil Central* (São Paulo, 1940).

Stewart Clough, Rev. R.: *The Amazons, a Diary of a Twelvemonth's Journey on a Mission of Inquiry up the River Amazon, for the South American Missionary Society* (London, 1872).

Stradelli, Count Ermanno: 'Rio Branco. Note di viaggio', *Bolletino della Società Geografica Italiana*, 3 ser., **2**, anno 23, **26** 210–28, 251–66, Rome 1889.

— 'Dal Cucuhy a Manàos', *Bolletino della Società Geografica Italiana*, 3 ser., **2**, anno 23, **26** 6–26, Rome, 1889.

— 'L'Uaupés e gli Uaupés', *Bolletino della Società Geografica Italiana*, 3 ser., **3**, anno 24, **27** 425–53, Rome, 1890.

— 'Leggenda dell'Jurupary', *Bolletino della Società Geografica Italiana*, 3 ser., **3**, anno 24, **27** 659–89, 798–835, Rome, 1890.

Sweet, David G.: 'A Rich Realm of Nature Destroyed: the Middle Amazon Valley, 1640–1750' (doctoral thesis, University of Wisconsin, Madison, 1974).

Taggia, Frei Rafael de: 'Mappas dos indios Cherentes e Chavantes na nova povoação de Thereza Christina no rio Tocantins, e dos indios Charaós da aldêa de Pedro Affonso nas margens do mesmo rio . . .', RHGB **19** 119–24, 1856, 2nd edn 1898.

Tapajós, Torquato Xavier Monteiro: *Viagem ao Amazonas, Macapá, Tabatinga e São Joaquim* (Rio de Janeiro, 1893).

Taubaté, Modesto Rezende de, and F. M. de Primeiro: *Os missionários Capuchinos no Brasil* (São Paulo, 1929).

Taunay, Alfredo d'Escragnolle: 'Os indios Caingangs (Coroados de Guarapuava)', RHGB, supplement to **51** 251–310, 1888.
— 'A cidade de Matto-Grosso (antiga Villa-Bella) o rio Guaporé e a sua mais illustre victima', RHGB **54**:2 1–108, 1891.
— *Entre os nossos indios; Chanés, terenas, kinikinaus, guanás, laianas, guatós, guaycurus, caingangs* (São Paulo, 1913).

Teschauer, Carolos: 'Os naturalistas viajantes dos séculos XVIII e XIX no Brasil', in Teodoro Sampaio and Carlos Teschauer, *Os naturalistas viajantes e a etnografia indígena* (Salvador, Bahia, 1955) 191–305.

Thomas, Georg: 'Espírito Santo/Abrantes. Die Entwicklung einer Indianersiedlung des Brasilianischen Nordostens in Zeitalter Pombals', *Jahrbuch für Geschichte Lateinamerikas* **14** (Köln–Wien, 1977) 97–133.

Tocantins, Antonio Manoel Gonçalves: 'Estudos sobre a tribu Mundurucu', RHGB **40**:2 73–162, 1877.

Tschudi, Johann Jakob von: *Reisen durch Südamerika*, 6 vols (Leipzig, 1866), partly trans. Eduardo de Lima Castro, *Viagem às províncias do Rio de Janeiro e São Paulo*, Coleção Reconquista do Brasil, n.s., **14**, Editora Itatiaia (Belo Horizonte, 1980).

Ure, John: *Trespassers on the Amazon* (London, 1986).

Valladão, Manoel José, and others: 'Noticias da voluntaria reducção de paz e amizade da feroz nação do gentio Mura (1784–86)', RHGB **36**:1 323–92, 1873.

Varnhagen, Francisco Adolfo de, Visconde de Porto Seguro: *História geral do Brasil antes da sua separação e independência de Portugal*, 5 vols (São Paulo, n.d.; 3rd edn, São Paulo, 1927).
— *Os índios bravos e o Sr Lisboa, Timon 3º*. (Lima, 1867).

Vasconcellos e Souza, Luiz de: *Relação instructiva e circumstanciada para ser entregue ao seu successor* (1789), RHGB **4** or **23** 143–239, 1860.

Veríssimo, José: *Estudos Amazônicos* (Belém, 1970), includes works from *Primeiras páginas* (1878).
— *Cenas da vida amazônica* (Lisbon, 1886).
— 'As populações indigenas e mestiças da Amazonia', RHGB **50**:1, 295–390, 1887.
— *Estudos brasileiros (1877–1885)* (Pará, 1889).
— *A Amazônia, aspectos económicos* (Rio de Janeiro, 1892).

Vila Real, Tomas de Sousa: *Viagem pelos rios Tocantins, Araguaia e Vermelho* (1793), RHGB **9** 401–44, 1847.

Viotti, Helio Abranches, SJ: 'O pombalino império da Amazônia na Regência de Francisco Xavier de Mendonça Furtado', RH **25**:50 315–34, 1974.

Viveiros, Esther de: *Rondon conta sua vida* (Rio de Janeiro, 1958).

Waehneldt, Rodolpho: *Exploração da Provincia de Mato Grosso* (Petrópolis, 1863), RHGB **27**:1 193–230, 1864.

Wallace, Alfred Russell: *Narrative of Travels on the Amazon and Rio Negro, with an Account of the Native Tribes* (1853) (London, 1889), trans. Orlando Torres, Brasiliana **156** (São Paulo, 1939).

Walle, Paul: *Au pays de l'or noir: Pará, Amazonas, Mato Grosso* (Paris, c. 1910).

WALSH, ROBERT: *Notices of Brazil in 1828 and 1829*, 2 vols (London, 1830).

WATERTON, CHARLES: *Wanderings in South America, the North-West of the United States, and the Antilles, in the Years 1812, 1816, 1820, and 1824* (London, 1825).

WEINSTEIN, BARBARA: *The Amazon Rubber Boom, 1850–1920* (Stanford, Calif., 1984).

WELLS, JAMES W.: *Exploring and travelling three thousand miles through Brazil, from Rio de Janeiro to Maranhão*, 2 vols (London, 1886).

WICKHAM, HENRY ALEXANDER: *Rough notes of a journey through the wilderness, from Trinidad to Pará, Brazil by way of the great cataracts of the Orinoco, Atabapo and Rio Negro . . .* (London, 1872).

— *On the Plantation, Cultivation, and Curing of Pará Indian Rubber* (London, 1908).

WIED-NEUWIED, MAXIMILIAN, PRINZ ZU: *Reise nach Brasilien in den Jahren 1815 bis 1817*, 2 vols (Frankfurt, 1820–1); trans. J. B. B. Eyriès, 3 vols (Paris, 1821–2); trans. Edgar Süssekind de Mendonça and Flavio Poppe de Figueiredo, Brasiliana, 5 ser., 1 (São Paulo and Rio de Janeiro, 1940).

WILKENS, HENRIQUE JOÃO: *Muraída, ou a conversão e reconciliação do gentio* (c.1789) (Lisbon, 1819).

WILKES, CHARLES: *Exploring expedition during the years 1838–42, Madeira–Brazil* (New York, 1858).

WILLEKE, VENÂNCIO, OFM: *Missões Franciscanos no Brasil, 1500–1975* (Petrópolis, 1974).

— 'Os Franciscanos no Maranhão, 1600–1878', RHGB **318** 119–34, Jan.–March 1978.

WOLF, HOWARD AND RALPH: *Rubber: a story of glory and greed* (New York, 1936).

WOODROFFE, JOSEPH FROUDE, AND HAROLD HAMEL SMITH: *The Rubber Industry of the Amazon, and how its supremacy can be maintained* (London, 1915).

WRIGHT, ROBIN M.: 'The History and Religion of the Baniwa peoples of the Upper Rio Negro Valley' (doctoral dissertation, Stanford University, 1981).

Notes and References

Chapter 1   FALSE FREEDOM

1 *goods and commerce'. Ley porque V.
Magestade ha por bem restituir aos índios do
Grão-Pará e Maranhão a liberdade das suas
pessoas, e bens, e commercio, na forma que
nella se declara.* This famous law is in
the Pombaline Collection, Biblioteca
Nacional de Lisboa, cod. 457, fols
11−16v. It has been published in:
*Collecção chronologica de leis extravagantes
posteriores à nova compilação das Ordenações do Reino publicadas em 1603*, 6 vols
(Coimbra, 1819) **3** 421−34; Agostinho Marques Perdigão Malheiro, *A
escravidão no Brasil* (Rio de Janeiro,
1867) **2** 99, 102; L. Humberto de
Oliveira, *Coletânea de Leis . . .* (Rio de
Janeiro, 1847) 63−4; Mathias C.
Kieman, *The Indian Policy of Portugal in
the Amazon Region, 1614−1693* (Washington, DC, 1954) 452.

1 *in great misery.'* Ibid.

1 *to their forests]'.* Ibid.

1 *molested on them.'* Ibid. Friar Francisco
de Nossa Senhora dos Prazeres,
Poranduba Maranhense (1826), RHGB
54: 1 103, 1891.

2 *honour or dignity.'* Álvara of 4 April 1755,
Ley sobre os casamentos com as Indias.
Hemming, *Red Gold*, 476. It is worth
noting that this law foresaw marriages between white men and Indian
women − but not the reverse, for
whites jealously guarded the racial
superiority of their women.

2 *follow for them.'* Álvara com força de Ley,
porque V. Magestade ha por bem renovar a
inteira e inviolavel observancia da Ley de 12
de Setembro de 1653. Edict of 7 June
1755.

4 *regular missionary orders'.* Carneiro de
Mendonça, *A Amazônia*, **1** 28, Royal
instructions to Francisco Xavier de
Mendonça Furtado, Lisbon, 31 May
1751.

4 *pride and ambition'.* Mendonça Furtado
to Oeiras (Pombal), Pará, 21 Nov.
1751, Carneiro de Mendonça, *A
Amazônia*, **1** 66.

4 *of perpetual captivity'.* Ibid., 67.

4 *languages beyond count'.* João Daniel,
*Thesouro descoberto no maximo rio
Amazonas*, pt 2, ch. 15, RHGB **3** 50,
1841.

5 *ruined this state.'* Mendonça Furtado to
Pombal, Pará, 21 Nov. 1751, Carneiro de Mendonça, *A Amazônia*, **1** 76.

5 *or any age.'* João Gonçalves da Fonseca,
*Primeira exploraçao dos rios Madeira e
Guaporé em 1749*, in Candido Mendes
de Almeida, *Memorias para a historia do
extincto Estado do Maranhão* (Rio de
Janeiro, 1860) **2** 274.

5 *not escape captivity'.* Rodrigues Ferreira,
Diario da viagem philosophica, 30.

10 *like a yacht'.* Anon, *Diario da viagem que o
Illmo. e Exmo. Sr. Francisco Xavier de
Mendonça Furtado . . . fez para o rio Negro
a expedição das demarcações dos reais*

dominios de Sua Majestade, in Carneiro de Mendonça, *A Amazônia*, **2** 615. Mendonça Furtado never reached the frontier on the upper Negro, although he went up that river for a considerable distance; his Venezuelan counterpart never came anywhere near the meeting place.

10 *on the expedition.*' King to prelates of religious orders, Lisbon, 18 May 1753, Carneiro de Mendonça, *A Amazônia*, **1** 396. In his cortège, Mendonça Furtado took two surveyor-cartographers (then called 'astronomers' since land survey was based on star fixes), Miguel Antonio Viera and João Bruneli; three 'engineers', Antonio José Lande, Gaspar Gronfelts and Henrique Galucci; the first Vicar-General of the Rio Negro, José Monteiro de Noronha, who published an itinerary of his route; and two hundred soldiers with their officers.

10 *them by force.*' Ibid.

11 *constitute this State.*' Mendonça Furtado, Ofício, Belém do Pará, 21 May 1757, in João Lúcio de Azevedo, *Os Jesuítas no Grão-Pará*, 286. Hélio Abranches Viotti, 'O pombalino império da Amazônia', 322–3.

11 *title of director.*' Ibid.

11 *to the other*'. Ibid.

12 *rich and civilised.*' Mendonça Furtado to King, 21 May 1757, in João Capistrano de Abreu, *Capítulos de historia colonial* (1963 edn) 185, or in ABAPP **4** 184. The Directorate decree was called 'Diretorio que se deve observar nas povoações dos indios do Pará e Maranhão', 3 May 1757. This code was published in Lisbon in 1758 and subsequently in Antonio Delgado da Silva (ed.), *Collecção da legislação portuguesa desde a última compilação das ordenações* . . . (Lisbon, 1830) **1** 507ff. It is also in *Collecção chronologica de leis extravagantes posteriores à nova compilação das Ordenações do Reino publicadas em 1603*, **4** 25–68, and in Accioli de Cerqueira e Silva, *Corografia paraense* . . . (Belém, 1833) 78–112.

12 *the monastic orders.*' Mendonça Furtado to Pombal, 18 Feb. 1754, Carneiro de Mendonça, *A Amazônia*, **2** 503.

13 *of Indian women.*' Mendonça Furtado to Pombal, 2 Nov. 1752, ibid., **1** 259–60.

14 *and happy society*'. Diretório, art. 91. Other relevant articles of the legislation were: on education and language, 6–8; on separate family dwellings, 12, 74; on racial harmony, 88–91; on drunkenness, 13, 41. Good analysis of the Directorate legislation is in MacLachlan, 'The Indian Directorate', 360–73, and Anderson, 'Following Curupira', 109–10, 115–27.

14 *to the State*'. Diretório, arts 1–2.

14 *wild cacao.* The cacao trade started in the seventeenth century and had reached over a million pounds a year by the 1730s. In mid-century the price of cacao fell, partly because of competition from Venezuela and other American producers; but it rose again during the American War of Independence and Napoleonic wars. During the years of Pombal's Pará trading company, cacao exports ranged from 1.6 to 1.9 million pounds a year and they rose to an average of 5.5 million pounds in the early years of the nineteenth century. Most of this cacao was from the *furos*, the maze of channels between Belém and the main Amazon river, but some came from the lower Xingu, Tapajós and Amazon rivers and Marajó island. It is not clear what proportion of Brazilian cacao was wild or from plantations which were encouraged after the 1770s. Dauril Alden, 'The Significance of Cacao Production in the Amazon'; Anderson, 'Following Curupira', 6–7, 28, 46–8. Sarsaparilla was in great demand as a palliative for syphilis.

15 *by their labour* . . .' Diretório, para. 64. Correa, *Direção com que interinamente se deve regular os indios* . . ., Recife, 29 May 1759, RHGB **46**: 1 150, 1883.

16 *completely happy state*'. Diretório, para. 95. MacLachlan, 'The Indian Direct-

orate', 369. Other clauses of the Directorate were: para. 34 on the director's commission; para. 56 on the cabo's commission; para. 27 on the tithe; paras 56−8 on central marketing; paras 63, 68, 70 etc. on Indian labour for settlers.

17 *never to return.'* Law of 3 Sept. 1759 in Marcos Carneiro de Mendonça, *O Marquês de Pombal e o Brasil,* Brasiliana **299** (São Paulo, 1960) 59−63.

Chapter 2 OPENING AMAZONIA

19 *had good reason'* Daniel, *Thesouro descoberto,* pt 2, ch. 17, 166.

20 *losses upon them.'* Southey, *History of Brazil,* **3**, ch. 44, 724. Southey based his account of the Mura on Ribeiro de Sampaio's then unpublished *Diario da viagem.*

20 *without being assaulted.'* Anon, *Illustração necessaria, e interessante, relativa ao gentio da nação Mura,* ms. of 1826 in Biblioteca Nacional, Rio de Janeiro. André Fernandes de Sousa, *Noticias geographicas da Capitania do Rio Negro . . .,* RHGB **10** 431, 1848 (or second edn, 1870). Francisco Xavier Ribeiro de Sampaio wrote that in 1775 settlers living far up the Negro dared not cross the river to their cacao plantations: *Diario da viagem . . . Rio Negro* (Lisbon, 1825) 130. Accioli de Cerqueira e Silva, *Corografia paraense,* pt 1, 118−19. Ribeiro de Sampaio, *Roteiro da viagem,* 36, 38, 39, 130, 132.

20 *from their animosity.'* Anon, *Illustração.* This author described one evening attack on a Mura village in which the men escaped from the armed troops, but 300 women and children drowned when they tried to swim to safety. Ivelise Rodrigues, 'Alguns aspectos da ergologia Mura-Piranhã', *Antropologia* **65** (Belém, 1977) 3; Gunter Kroemer, *Cuxiuara. O Purus dos indígenas* (São Paulo, 1985) 38.

20 *and irreconcilable enmity'* Ribeiro de Sampaio quoted in Rodrigues Ferreira, *Diario da viagem philosophica,* RHGB **50**: 2 70, 1887. Also, Ribeiro de Sampaio, *Roteiro da viagem,* 33, 36, 130, 131.

20 *reduced to nothing'.* Ibid. A good picture of the upper Amazon and Rio Negro emerges from a series of descriptions by Portuguese and Brazilian officials: Governor Francisco Xavier de Mendonça Furtado wrote copious letters during his visits of 1754−5 and 1758; Bishop João de São José was on the lower Amazon in 1762−3; José Monteiro de Noronha published a fine report at Barcellos on the Negro in 1768; the chief magistrate Francisco Xavier Ribeiro de Sampaio wrote about visits to all its towns in 1774−5; the naturalist Alexandre Rodrigues Ferreira described his journeys on the Negro, Branco, Solimões and Madeira between 1783 and 1788; his fellow explorers Ricardo Franco de Almeida Serra, Antonio da Silva Pontes and Manoel da Gama Lobo d'Almada wrote reports on their expeditions; and João Vasco Manoel de Braum compiled a gazetteer of the region in 1789. In the early nineteenth century, the decline of Amazonia was recorded in a report by Father José Maria Coelho in 1823, by the German-British explorer Robert Schomburgk in 1830−9, and João Henrique de Matos in 1845; and there were histories of Amazonia by Ignacio Accioli de Cerqueira e Silva (1833) and Lourenço da Silva Araújo e Amazonas (1852).

20 *from settling there.'* Southey, *History of Brazil,* **3**, ch. 44, 725. Southey did not visit Brazil. For this part of his great history his sources were the reports of Ribeiro de Sampaio, and of Bishop Brandão published in the *Jornal de Coimbra* **4** 341−5, 1815.

21 *sex nor age'*. A. C. do Amaral, *Memorias para a historia da vida do veneravel Arcebispo de Braga D. Fr. Caetano Brandão* (Lisbon, 1818) 1 378.

21 *His Majesty's subjects'*. Rodrigues Ferreira, *Diario da viagem philosophica*, RHGB 50: 2 71, and cf. introduction by Edgard de Cerqueira Falcão to his edition of this work, 2 vols (São Paulo, 1970) 1 xiii–xiv. The attacks on this expedition were also mentioned by the geographer Lacerda e Almeida, *Diario da viagem* ... (1780–90) (São Paulo, 1841) 22, and by an anonymous account of this same voyage, *Viagem do Rio Negro até Villa Bella* (1781), RHGB 20 299, 1857. Rodrigues Ferreira to Governor Martinho de Sousa de Albuquerque, 15 March 1784, in *Diario da viagem philosophica*, 72–4.

21 *means of recognition.'* Araújo e Amazonas, *Diccionario topográphico*, 256. Henrique João Wilkens, a government surveyor-explorer, wrote a violently anti-Mura poem, *Muhraida. Conversão e reconciliação do gentio Mura*, at Ega in 1789. He rejoiced in the tribe's defeat and said that it surrendered to Mathias Fernandes (who was director of Indians at a village called Santo Antonio do Imaripy on the Japurá) because he had defeated them so often that he was 'the only white man they feared'. This poem is in the Archivo Histórico Ultramarino in Lisbon, with a copy in the Cedeam archive in Manaus. Kroemer, *Cuxiuara* 39.

21 *in our settlements'*. Rodrigues Ferreira, *Diario da viagem philosophica*, RHGB 50 pt 2, 74. Rodrigues Ferreira also wrote a report about the way in which he thought the Mura should be treated after their pacification: 'Memoria sobre os gentios Muras, que voluntariamento descerão para as povoações do Rio Negro, dos Solimõens, e da Madeira', unpublished ms. in Biblioteca Nacional, Rio de Janeiro, 21-2-43. Various reports about their pacification were published in RHGB 36: 1 323–92, 1873.

21 *them to flight.'* Southey, *History of Brazil*, 3, ch. 44, 725.

22 *friendship was sincere'*. Anon, 'Noticias da voluntaria reducção de paz e amizade da feroz nação do gentio Mura', RHGB 36: 1 325, 1873.

22 *to do this.'* João Pereira Caldas, Governor of Mato Grosso and Boundary Commissioner in Barcelos, ibid., 330.

22 *to the Mura.'* Ibid. Some Mura were baptised at Nogueira by Friar José de Santa Teresa Neves; some were settled on lake Amaná on the Japurá; others congregated on the labyrinthine Autazes Lakes near the mouth of the Madeira. Many Mura continued to surrender at the fishery called Caldeirão on the Solimões and the town of Manacapuru grew there with ten houses and three hundred Mura. Ibid., 337–8, 372–3.

22 *be completely exterminated.'* Johann Baptist von Spix and Carl Friedrich Philip von Martius, *Reise in Brasilien*, 3 vols (Munich, 1823–31) 3 bk 9, ch. 6, 1313, 1338, or in Portuguese translation of 1938, 3 409, 431. Directors' complaints of harassment by Mundurukú were recorded from Alter do Chão (former Iburari mission), Boim (former Santo Inacio) and Pinhel on the Tapajós, from Sousel (former Aricari) on the Xingu and from Portel (Aricará) and Oeiras (Bocas-Araticu) south of Marajó and close to Belém, between 1792 and 1795 in the 565-volume collection *Correspondencia de Diversos com o Governo* in the public archive (Biblioteca e Arquivo Público do Pará) in Belém. Anderson, 'Following Curupira', 54, 123.

24 *the white men.'* Robert F. Murphy, *Headhunter's Heritage* (Berkeley and Los Angeles, 1960) 27. The reference to rubber in the Mundurukú legend was premature, as it was only in the mid-nineteenth century that the tribe became (as it remains) rubber gatherers for the whites. Ricardo Franco de Almeida Serra, *Navegação do Rio Tapajóz para o Pará* (1799), RHGB 9 4–5, 1847. Fernandes de

Sousa, *Noticias geographicas*, 488–9. Accioli de Cerqueira e Silva, *Corografia paraense*, pt 1, 139.

24 *of white families.'* Fernandes de Sousa, *Noticias geographicas*, 425.

24 *of the Amazon'.* Almeida Serra, *Navegação do rio Tapajóz*, 5.

25 *by continued abuse.'* Araújo e Amazonas, *Diccionario topográphico*, 174, 247. Accioli Cerqueira e Silva, *Corografia paraense*, 285.

26 *the Rio Negro'* Southey, *History of Brazil*, 3 712.

26 *to the whites.'* Mendonça Furtado to Secretary of State, Barcellos, 4 July 1758, in [British] Foreign Office, *Question de la Frontière*, 1 67.

26 *and indispensable punishment.'* Ibid.

26 *of them were.'* Captain-General Manuel Bernardo de Melo e Castro, letter from Belém, 9 Aug. 1759. Henrique Jorge Hurley, *Belém do Pará sob o domínio português* (Belém, 1940) 214–15; Hélio Abranches Viotti, 'O pombalino império da Amazônia', 330.

27 *of San Carlos.'* Araújo e Amazonas, *Diccionario topográphico*, 248. For further comment on rivalries between the colonial powers on the Negro in this period, see: Agusto Gausto de Souza, *Fortificações do Brasil*, ms. of 1881 in archive of the Instituto Histórico e Geográphico, Rio de Janeiro (ms. 769, L-40) 50–1, 59–60; Arthur Cézar Ferreira Reis, *Limites e demarcações na Amazônia brasileira* (Rio de Janeiro, 1948) 1 65–6, 100; Hélio Viana, *História das fronteiras do Brasil* (Rio de Janeiro, 1949) 101–2; Annibal Barreto, *Fortificuçoes do Brasil: resumo histórico* (Rio de Janeiro, 1958) 46–74; Fernando Antonio Raja Gabaglia, *As fronteiras do Brasil* (Rio de Janeiro, 1916) 57; Antonio de Souza Júnior, *Fronteiras flutantes* (Rio de Janeiro, 1954) 36–8; Lewis A. Tambs, 'Geopolitics of the Amazon', in *Man in the Amazon*, ed. Charles Wagley (Gainesville, Florida, 1974) 68–70. On their side of the frontier, the Spaniards had been creating 'reductions' of Indians, often named after their chiefs. The first was San Fernando de Atabapo, established in 1758. By 1760 there were six reductions: Yavita (with the men of that chief, who had now joined the Spaniards), Cuseru, Macapu and Don Francisco Solano on the Casiquiare, and San Carlos where it flows into the Rio Negro. Chief Cucui and five other chiefs were settled at San Carlos, together with fugitives from the rebellion of 1757 farther down the Negro. In 1759 the Spaniards sent Sergeant Francisco Bobadilla down-river as far as the Corocubi rapids – the site of the later Portuguese fort of São Gabriel da Cachoeira (Uaupés). The Portuguese reacted by sending Captain José da Silva Delgado upstream from Barcelos in 1762 to occupy the lands of the Baré (around the Corocubi rapids) and the Marabitana north of them. Delgado ordered Bobadilla to leave this part of the river. The Baré and Marabitana were subjected to an oppressive director and in 1763 abruptly fled up-river into Spanish territory, leaving their lands empty. The vacuum was filled for a time with descents from the Uaupés and Içana. Mello de Castro to Mendonça Furtado, 12 March 1763, Belém do Pará, in Joaquim Nabuco, *Frontières entre le Brésil et la Guyane Anglaise* (Paris, 1903–4) *Limites* I, *Mémoire Brésilien Annexe* 2 87–8; José Monteiro de Noronha, *Roteiro da viagem* ... (1768) (Belém, Pará, 1862), and his *Synopse de algumas noticias geographicas* ... (22 Oct. 1764) ms. in Biblioteca Nacional, Rio de Janeiro; Robin Wright, 'History and religion of the Baniwa Peoples of the Upper Rio Negro Valley' (doctoral dissertation, Stanford University, 1981) 1 143–6.

27 *to man them.* Tinoco Valente was governor of Rio Negro from 1763 to 1779. His new forts successfully deterred a Spanish invasion. A Spanish spy called Don Nicolás Rodríguez went up the river in 1766 and report-

ed on the strength of the new forti-
fications and the canoes full of
Indians used for scouting and tran-
sport. A letter between two Spanish
governors reveals that they stopped a
Spanish attack on the upper Negro,
fearing that it would be repulsed.
Don José de Linares to Don Antonio
Barreto, Guayana, 25 April 1767, in
Joaquim Nabuco, *Frontières du Brésil et
de La Guyane Anglaise . . . Premier
Mémoire*, 94–5.

28 *country must be.'* J. C. Beaglehole (ed.),
*The Endeavour Journal of Joseph Banks,
1768–1771* (Sydney, 1963) **1** 191.

29 *supposed to do'.* Araújo e Amazonas,
Diccionario topográphico, 254.

29 *from the villages.'* Sousa Coutinho,
'Informação', 288.

29 *mortality among Indians'* Ibid., 285.

29 *settlements are exhausted.'* Ibid., 287.

29 *of our inhumanity.'* Amaral, *Memorias*, **1**
344.

29 *such a danger.'* Ibid., **1** 363.

30 *the compulsory service.'* Southey, *History
of Brazil*, **3** 715.

30 *of Dutch Guiana.* The early explorations of the Branco were carried out
by Captain Francisco Ferreira, who
was stationed at Caburis from 1700
to 1736 and often raided up the
Branco. A large slaving troop under
Christovão Ayres Botelho went up in
1736; and the 1748 raid was led by
José Miguel Ayres. Laurence Belfort
was accompanied by Francisco
Xavier de Andrade in 1740. There
had for many years been contact between the Manaus Indians of the
middle Negro and the Dutch of
Guiana: see references in Hemming,
Red Gold, 441, 639–40; Ribeiro de
Sampaio, *Roteiro da viagem*, 99;
Nabuco, *Frontières, Premier Mémoire*,
141–3; Foreign Office, *Question de la
Frontière*, **1** 69; Araújo e Amazonas,
Diccionario topográphico, 238. The governor of Rio Negro, Lourenço Pereira
da Costa, wrote to the Governor of
Grão Pará, Barcellos, 2 Sept. 1762,
recommending settlement of the
Branco; Mendonça Furtado wrote
from Lisbon, 21 June 1765, urging

that the Branco be fortified against
possible Spanish invasion; and in
1766 Governor Tinoco Valente sent
Lieutenant Diniz to investigate. A
Dutch document of 19 Nov. 1766
described the arrival of Diniz' expedition on the Tacutu, the eastern
headwater of the Branco: cited in the
British case in the Anglo-Venezuelan
boundary dispute, *Appendix to the Case
of the Government of Her Britannic
Majesty*, **3** 137.

30 *it is dangerous.'* Ribeiro de Sampaio to
the Governor of Grão Pará, Barcellos, 27 March 1775, in Foreign
Office, *Question de la Frontière*, **1** 92.
The stranger was called Gervase
Leclerc from Liège. He had gone up
the Essequibo and Rupununi before
crossing to the Tacutu and finding
the Spanish camp five days up the
Uraricoera. Sampaio, *Roteiro da
viagem*, 99; Nabuco, *Frontières, Premier
Mémoire*, 144, 165–6.

31 *a single plantation'.* Governor Tinoco
Valente to João Pereira Caldas,
Governor of Pará, Barcellos, 6 April
1775, in Foreign Office, *Question de la
Frontière*, 95, and Nabuco, *Frontières,
Premier Mémoire*, 166.

31 *of El Dorado.'* Sampaio, *Roteiro*, 101.

31 *dazzling the eyesight.'* Don Manuel Cen-
turión instructions for the expedition
to El Dorado and Lake Parima,
Guiana, 28 Dec. 1771, in Foreign
Office, *Question de la Frontière*, 89–91,
129–30, 250. The first expedition
was led by Lieutenant Nicolás
Martínez. It founded camps called
Santa Rosa and San Juan Bautista on
the Uraricoera. These were left in the
charge of a black sergeant called
Zapata. In 1775, a party under
Ensign Antonio López explored the
Tacutu eastwards towards the
Rupununi: the Portuguese under
Captain Sturm captured this group
as it returned downstream towards
the Branco. The Spanish authorities
protested about the capture of their
men, arguing that there was no sign
of any Portuguese presence on the
upper Branco. But article 8 of the

Treaty of Madrid had stated that the frontier here was the watershed. The Treaty of Madrid was annulled in 1761, but revived in the Treaty of San Ildefonso of 1 Oct. 1777. For a full account of the El Dorado legend, see John Hemming, *The Search for El Dorado* (London and New York, 1978).

32 *to receive it.'* Ribeiro de Sampaio, *Relação geographica historica do Rio Branco* (1778), in Foreign Office, *Question de la Frontière*, **1** 131.

32 *within their villages.'* Captain Felippe Sturm to Governor João Pereira Caldas, Fort São Joaquim, 20 Aug. 1781, Nabuco, *Frontières, Premier Mémoire*, 207.

32 *loath to abandon.'* Ibid.

33 *open before them.'* Ibid.

33 *fire and sword.'* João Pereira Caldas to Secretary of State Martinho de Mello e Castro, Barcellos, 19 Jan. 1782, Foreign Office, *Question de la Frontière*, **1** 142–3. The six short-lived villages were: Carmo, Santa Isabel and Santa Barbara on the Branco; Santo Antonio das Almas and Conceição on the Uraricoera; São Felippe on the Tacutu. The only one that did not desert was Carmo, in which a few Paraviana and Atroari remained 'in the royal service'.

33 *they can perform.'* Martinho de Mello e Castro to Governor-General of Pará, Queluz, 7 July 1783, Foreign Office, ibid., **1** 144.

34 *a continuous lake.'* Report by Captain Ricardo Franco de Almeida Serra and Dr Antonio Pires da Silva Pontes, Barcellos, 19 July 1781, in Foreign Office, ibid., **1** 138; Nabuco, *Frontières, Premier Mémoire*, 235.

34 *the Rio Branco'.* Foreign Office, *Question de la Frontière*, **1** 138.

34 *their bark canoes'.* Ibid., 140.

34 *track to follow.'* Rodrigues Ferreira, Report to João Pereira Caldas, Barcellos, 10 Aug. 1786, Foreign Office, ibid., **1** 170; Nabuco, *Frontières, Premier Mémoire*, 251. Rodrigues Ferreira also wrote about this journey in his *Tratado historico* on the Rio Branco, also of 1786.

35 *accord and motion.'* Foreign Office, *Question de la Frontière*, **1** 171. The artists who worked with Rodrigues Ferreira were José Joaquim Freire and Joaquim José Codina. They produced 912 drawings and prints to accompany his *Diario da viagem philosophica*. These, together with most of Rodrigues Ferreira's writings and collections, lay largely unpublished in libraries of Portugal and Brazil until recent times. Some were borrowed by French scientists, but were later returned to Portugal – a rumour that the French stole Rodrigues Ferreira's collections during the Napoleonic invasion of Portugal and then suppressed and plagiarised them is incorrect. The drawings have now been published, in editions in São Paulo in 1970 and Rio de Janeiro in 1974.

35 *and over them.'* Colonel Manoel da Gama Lobo d'Almada to Governor-General João Pereira Caldas, Uraricapara river, 1 April 1787, Foreign Office, *Question de la Frontière*, **1** 175.

35 *than among us.'* Gama Lobo d' Almada, Report on Rio Branco territory, 16 July 1787, in Nabuco, *Frontières, Premier Mémoire*, 275.

36 *law of liberty!'* Ibid., 276–7.

36 *in great esteem.'* Gama Lobo d'Almada, *Tratado descriptivo*, in Foreign Office, *Question de la Frontière*, **1** 188.

36 *of mountain salt.'* Ibid. **1** 188.

37 *not hate them.'* Gama Lobo d'Almada to directors of places receiving Branco Indians, Barcellos, 14 May 1790, in Nabuco, *Frontières, Premier Mémoire*, 227. This volume contains reports of the many expeditions to attract Indians to the Branco villages between 1784 and 1790: 210–15, 217, 219, 224–7. Also, Foreign Office, *Question de la Frontière*, **1** 200–2.

37 *on the Branco.* Araújo e Amazonas, *Diccionario topográphico*, 258–9.

38 *and lost there.* Ibid., 267. This author also said that Gama Lobo d'Almada sent the engineer Eusebio Antonio Ribeiro to explore the Cauaburis

further in 1791 but that he failed to do the job and was sent back to Belém under arrest. The Brazilian Foreign Ministry, Itamarati, has a number of fine maps from this period, but not the ones that Araújo e Amazonas described as missing. There is a good map of 1778 which was illustrated in Isa Adonias, *A cartografia da região amazonica. Catálogo descriptivo (1500–1961)*, 2 vols (Rio de Janeiro, 1963) 1 530. This book also mentions a map of 1781 based on that year's explorations of the Japurá, Negro and Branco, which is now in the Arquivo Militar (ibid., 1 536–7); and a map of 1793 showing

the work of Rodrigues Ferreira's *Diario da viagem philosophica*, in the Biblioteca Nacional (ibid., 1 537–8). A map of the voyages of the frontier commissions, drawn by Dr José Joaquim da Costa in 1797, was reproduced in Nabuco, *Frontières, Premier Mémoire*, 1 54 (atlas).

38 *a single patient.'* Quijano Otero, *Límites de la República de los Estados-Unidos de Colombia* (Seville, 1881) 195; Smith, 'Requena and the Japurá', *The Americas* 3: 1 43, 1946.

39 *Church calls charity.'* Araújo e Amazonas, *Diccionario topográphico*, 253.

Chapter 3   THE DIRECTORATE

40 *are being founded.'* Martinho de Mello e Castro, Secretary of State for Ultramar (Overseas), to José de Almeida e Vasconcellos, new Governor of Goiás, N. S. de Ajuda, 1 Oct. 1771, in Pereira de Alencastre, *Annaes da Provincia de Goyaz*, 246–7. The royal decree of 8 May 1758 extended the laws on freedom of Indians and abolition of missionaries' temporal powers to the rest of Brazil. The decree of 17 Aug. 1752 did the same for the Directorate legislation of 3 May 1757. Instructions about the new laws were issued in Pernambuco on 29 May 1759 (Felipe Neri Correa, *Direção com que . . .*, RHGB **46**: 1 121– 71, 1883; and for Bahia on 19 May 1759, published in Castro e Almeida, *Inventario dos documentos relativos ao Brasil*, 1 335–42.

40 *more important objective.'* Ibid.

40 *of those colonies.'* Ibid.

42 *and tend it.* Anderson, 'Following Curupira', 53. Return from Alemquer, 1781, in *Correspondencia de Diversos com o Governo* collection in Biblioteca e Arquivo Público do Pará in Belém, 207:11.

42 *Laurence Belfort.* This enterprising planter of Irish descent was also a

notorious slaver. He personally led 'ransom' or slaving expeditions to the upper Rio Negro in 1737–9 and in 1744–5. He also worked jointly with the slaver Estacio Rodrigues on the Uaupés and Içana rivers. Belfort established a slave depot at the mission of Dari (later Lamalonga) on the middle Negro and tried to prevent other slavers from operating above the rapids. However, one Pedro da Braga defied this embargo and even 'married' the niece of a chief called Aquipi from the upper river. Braga was soon slipping slaves past Belfort's post until the latter caught him and enlisted him to work for him on the Uaupés. Laurence Belfort told the Jesuit Father Ignacio Szentmartonyi that the Indians of the upper Uaupés had gold objects and that there was a lake full of gold near the source of that river. It was said that Belfort brought more than a thousand slaves from the Rio Branco to work on his plantations on the Mearim river in Maranhão. Arthur C. Ferreira Reis, *Apolítica de Portugal no vale do rio Amazonas* (Belém, 1940) 20; Sweet, 'A Rich Realm of Nature Destroyed', 604–5, 620–1, 670; Wright,

'History and Religion' 125–8.

43 *the Brazilian total.* Dauril Alden, 'The Significance of Cacao Production in the Late Colonial Period: an essay in comparative economic history', American Philosophical Society *Proceedings*, 120 n.s. 2 April 1976, 103–35.

43 *late eighteenth century.* Anderson, 'Following Curupira', 47, showed that out of 117 directors' reports, only six mentioned planting cacao in Indian villages. Cf. Roberto Santos, *História econômica da Amazônia (1800–1920)* (São Paulo, 1980) 17–18; Caia Prado Jr, *História econômica do Brasil* (São Paulo, 1965) 247. During the two decades of the Companhia Geral do Grão-Pará e Maranhão (1755–78), cacao accounted for an average of 61 per cent of the region's exports; but the quantity exported was no greater than it had been under the Jesuits. Plantation trees took five years to mature and in Amazonia they were always vulnerable to pests. The centre of Brazilian cacao planting therefore shifted southwards in the nineteenth century, to the area south of Bahia, which soon accounted for most of the country's exports; and the trees were, of course, exported to Ghana and West Africa.

45 *hopes and greed.'* Pestana da Silva, *Meios de dirigir o governo temporal dos indios* (1788), in A. J. de Mello Moraes, *Corografia historica ... do Imperio do Brasil*, 4 141.

45 *their poor Indians.'* Daniel, *Thesouro descoberto*, pt 2, ch. 14, 46–7.

45 *him falling asleep.'* Pestana da Silva, *Meios*, in Mello Moraes, *Corografia*, 150.

45 *than the military.'* Ibid., 165.

46 *earns per month!'* Ribeiro de Sampaio, *Roteiro da viagem*, 101.

46 *4 per cent.* Anderson, 'Following Curupira', 125.

47 *ruined the villages.'* João Pereira Caldas to Manoel Bernardo de Mello e Castro, Belém, 7 March 1773, quoted in ibid., 130.

47 *or other whites.'* Spix and Martius, *Reise*, 3 930–1.

47 *incessantly requires Indians.'* Rodrigues Ferreira, *Diario da viagem philosophica*, RHGB 49 pt 1, 196, 1886. Ribeiro de Sampaio made the same point, and included a table showing how many Indians from Barcellos were employed each year on the annual collecting expedition and other work for the state: *Roteiro da viagem*, 128–9.

48 *world and tireless'.* João de São José, *Viagem e visita do sertão . . .*, RHGB 9 90, 1847 or 1869.

48 *through the water.'* Smyth and Lowe, *Journey from Lima to Pará* (London, 1836) 273–4.

49 *bow and arrow.'* William Edwards, *A voyage up the River Amazon* (London, 1847) 81–2, 87, 90, 103, 135.

49 *chorus joined in.'* Adalbert of Prussia, *Aus meinem Reisetagebuch*, trans. Robert Schomburgk and John Taylor, 2 vols (London, 1849) 2 193.

49 *had been carried.'* João Barbosa Rodrigues' description of the Coatá rapids from 'O rio Yamundá' (1875), translated by Herbert Smith, *Brazil: the Amazons and the coast* (London, 1880) 252. The naturalist Richard Spruce described a similar ascent, *Notes of a botanist on the Amazon and Andes*, 2 vols (London, 1908) 1 89–90.

50 *his own eyes.'* Franz Keller, quoted in Neville Craig, *Recollections of an ill-fated expedition*, 34–5.

50 *of the passage.'* William Curtis Farabee, 'The Amazon Expedition of the University Museum. The Tapajos', *The Museum Journal*, University of Pennsylvania, 8 126, 1917.

50 *and all business.'* Pestana da Silva, *Meios*, in Mello Moraes, *Corografia*, 4 135.

51 *of the church!'* Ibid., 143.

51 *of the licence?'* Ibid., 149.

51 *on royal projects.'* Ibid., 150.

51 *Indians are valueless.'* Ibid., 150.

52 *my own distress.'* Ibid., 150.

52 *lives and sweat.'* Ibid., 156.

52 *the greatest inhumanity.'* Amaral,

Memorias, **1** 379. This incident was during the Bishop's fourth tour in 1788.

52 *know not why.'* Ibid.

52 *addicted to drink.'* Ibid., 363.

53 *pain and innocence.'* São José, *Viagem e visita,* 185–6.

53 *relapsed into barbarism.'* Saint-Hilaire, *Voyage dans le district des diamans,* **2** 6; also, Moritz Rugendas, *Viagem pitoresca,* 125.

53 *within these limits.'* Southey, *History of Brazil* **3** pt 3, ch. 44, 697.

53 *of such circumspection.'* Fernando da Costa Ataide Teive to Crown, Belém, 30 June 1768, Arquivo Nacional **99**, 2, 27, in Anderson, 'Following Curupira', 115.

53 *a ferocious tiger!'* Francisco de Sousa Coutinho, 'Plano para a civilização dos indios na Capitania do Pará', para. 3; MacLachlan, 'The Indian Labor Structure', 370.

54 *hope of them.'* Pestana da Silva, *Meios,* in Mello Moraes, *Corografia,* 164–5.

54 *with these excesses.'* Ibid., 165.

54 *by their directors.'* São José, *Viagem e visita,* 90–1.

54 *had high hopes.'* Pestana da Silva, *Meios,* in Mello Moraes, *Corografia,* 154.

54 *be pardoned lightly!'* São José, *Viagem e visita,* 339.

55 *endure nor prosper.'* Francisco de Sousa Coutinho, 'Informação sobre o modo porque se effectua presentamente a navegação do Pará para Mato Grosso', RHGB **2** 294–5, 1840, and his unpublished 'Plano para a civilização dos indios na Capitania do Pará' (2 Aug. 1797) in the archive of the Instituto Histórico e Geográfico do Brasil, para. 12. Pestana da Silva, *Meios,* in Mello Moraes, *Corografia,* **3** 150. Anderson, 'Following Curupira', 139. Magnus Mörner, *The Expulsion of the Jesuits from Latin America* (New York, 1965) 186. Mary Karasch, 'Damiana da Cunha: catechist and sertanista', 109.

55 *proclaimed for them.'* São José, *Viagem e visita,* 91.

55 *in 1794.* Anderson, 'Following Curupira', 130. The reports by directors are contained in the 565-volume collection of papers in the public archives in Belém (Biblioteca e Arquivo Público do Pará) entitled *Corespondencia de diversos com o governo.* Among these is a five-volume series called *Estatística da população* (BAPP 954–9) that contains documents about village populations during the Directorate period.

55 *has increased continuously.'* Ribeiro de Sampaio, *Roteiro da viagem,* 96, 134, 135.

55 *through the forests.'* Leonardo do Vale to Gonçalo Vaz de Melo, Bahia, 12 May 1563, in Serafim Leite (ed.), *Monumenta Brasiliae, Historica Societatis Iesu,* **87** (Rome, 1960) 4 12.

55 *pottery or fishery.'* Araújo e Amazonas, *Diccionario topográphico,* 261.

56 *at my expense.'* Manoel Bernardo de Mello e Castro to Francisco Xavier de Mendonça Furtado, 5 Nov. 1760, quoted in Anderson, 'Following Curupira', 132–3.

56 *them to come.'* Report from director of Santarém, 1796, *Correspondencia de Diversos com o Governo,* Belém Archive, **294**: 44, in Anderson, ibid., 131.

56 *children was greater.'* São José, *Viagem e visita,* 345.

56 *been sufficiently agile.'* Fernandes de Sousa, *Noticias geographicas,* 468.

57 *previous few years.* 'Relação dos índios silvestres que tem decidos dos matos no Estado do Grão Pará em o governo do Ilmo. e Exmo. Sr. José de Napoles Tello de Menezes, Governador e Capitão Geral do mesmo estado' (19 Nov. 1781), ms. in Biblioteca Nacional of Rio de Janeiro, cited in Anderson, 'Following Curupira', 129. Anderson also lists various directors' reports and letters from officials that mention descents.

57 *their own good.'* Ribeiro de Sampaio, *Roteiro da viagem,* 118–19, 42, 57.

57 *multiply far more.'* Ibid., 141.

57 *of descended Indians'.* Ibid., 99, 109, 111, 121.

57 *human misery.* Wright, 'History and Religion', 614–15.

57 *daily diminishing appallingly.'* Amaral,

Memorias, **1** 229.

58 *the next decades.* Francisco de Sousa Coutinho to Luis Pinto de Sousa, 1 Aug. 1706, in Anderson, 'Following Curupira', 127, together with her table of population statistics on p. 128.

58 *of this river.'* Ribeiro de Sampaio, *Roteiro da viagem,* 94.

58 *was done elsewhere'.* Ibid., 98.

58 *and Solimões rivers.'* André Prat, *Notas históricas sobre as missões carmelitanas no extremo norte do Brasil, séculos XVII e XVIII,* 2 vols (Recife, 1941−2) **2** 139; Eduardo Hoornaert, 'The Catholic Church in Colonial Brazil', in *The Cambridge History of Latin America,* ed. Leslie Bethell (Cambridge, 1984) **1** 550; Dauril Alden, 'Late Colonial Brazil, 1750−1808', in ibid., **2** 619, quoting letters in the Pará archive about the small numbers of missionaries left in Pará. For the wealth and decline of the Carmelite missions on the Negro, see David Sweet's thesis, 'A Rich Realm of Nature Destroyed'.

He lists deaths from the measles epidemic of 1749, taken from two missionary reports now in the Pará archives, in appendix K, **2** 734−8.

60 *satisfy his greed.'* Francisco de Sousa Coutinho, 'Plano para a civilização', trans. Anderson, 'Following Curupira', 139.

60 *rights and interests'.* Carta régia of 12 May 1798. Leda Maria Cardoso Naud, 'Índios e indigenismo: histórico e legislação', 238. Spix and Martius, *Reise,* **3** 931; Accioli de Cerqueira e Silva, *Corografia paraense,* pt 1, 141; Prazeres, *Poranduba Maranhense,* 117; Araújo e Amazonas, *Diccionario topográphico,* 261; Moreira Neto, *Política indigenista,* 335.

60 *them to react.'* Azevedo, *Os jesuítas no Grão-Pará, suas missões e a colonização,* trans. in Mörner, *The Expulsion of the Jesuits,* 188.

61 *from those districts.'* Governor Francisco de Sousa Coutinho, Circular letter, Pará, 9 Jan. 1799, RHGB **20** 448, 1857.

Chapter 4 MODEL VILLAGES

63 *satisfy their passion.'* João Pereira Caldas to King, Ociras de Piauí, 8 Aug. 1764, in Rodrigues Ferreira, *Diario da viagem philosophica,* RHGB **50**: 2 97, 1887.

63 *in their houses.'* Caldas to King, Oeiras do Piauí, 5 July 1765, ibid., 101.

63 *on the road.'* Caldas to King, Oeiras, 2 April 1766, ibid., 103.

63 *and scattered villages.'* Spix and Martius, *Reise,* **2** 804.

64 *of this captaincy.'* The ouvidor (judge) of Piauí, Antonio José de Morais Durão, wrote in 1772 that there were two Indian villages near Oeiras: Jaicós, now almost extinct with only sixty people; and Gueguês, eight leagues north of São João de Sende, with 252 people − half the number when the place had first been settled with Guenguen in about 1760. Luiz R. B. Mott, 'Descrição da capitania

de São José do Piauí − 1772', RH **28**:56 543−74 at 555, 1977. Ayres do Casal said that São Gonçalo was five leagues (thirty miles) from the mouth of the Canindé, and was founded in 1766 to house 900 Guenguen and 1600 Akroá from the headwaters of the Parnaíba and the hills further south: *Corografia Brasílica,* **2** 249. Spix and Martius, *Reise,* **2** 803−4, 806.

64 *way of life.'* Spix and Martius, *Reise,* **2** 805.

65 *Gonçalo d'Amarante.'* Ibid., 806.

65 *Akroá made peace.* Luiz Antonio da Silva e Sousa, *Memoria sobre o descobrimento, governo . . . de Goyaz,* RHGB **12** 450, 1849. These Goiás Akroá lived near the Tocantins' eastern tributary the Sono and on the Chapada das Mangabeiras hills. João de São José, *Viagem e visita,* 498−506. Raymundo

José da Cunha Mattos, *Chorographia historica*, RHGB **37**: 1 20, 1874; José de Souza Azevedo Pizarro e Araújo, *Memorias históricas do Rio de Janeiro*, 9 vols (Rio de Janeiro, 1945–8 edn) **9** 143. There is some confusion about the date of the surrender and settlement of these Goiás Akroá. Bishop São José, writing from Pará in 1763, said that the campaigns were in 1757–9; Pizarro e Araújo, writing in 1820, said the aldeias were founded in 1754; Father Silva e Sousa, writing in Goiás in 1812, said that the campaigns were in 1751. Southey, *History of Brazil*, **3** pt 3, ch. 41, 598–9.

65 *worst possible results.'* J. M. Pereira de Alencastre, *Annaes da Provincia de Goyaz*, RHGB **27**:2 130, 1864. He also quotes the Regimento for running Duro and Formiga, by Marcos de Noronha, São Felix, 13 June 1754, ibid., 130–2.

A charming map drawing from this period was bought by the Brazilian government in a sale at Sotheby's in November 1960. It shows the Tocantins and its tributaries, with the two aldeias formed of semi-circles of conical huts in the traditional manner of Gê tribes. The tile-roofed mission buildings of Duro are shown, and a Portuguese officer in blue tail-coated uniform and cocked hat, white breeches and sword is conversing with a naked Indian holding a bow and arrow. The map is illustrated in Adonias, *A cartografia da região amazônica*, **2** 640.

65 *the Jesuit missionaries. . . .'* Silva e Sousa, *Memoria*, 450–1.

65 *penalty after sentencing.'* Ibid., 458.

66 *wind or rain.'* George Gardner, *Travels in the interior of Brazil* (London, 1846) 315–16.

66 *of excellent water'.* Ibid., 316.

66 *state of starvation.'* Ibid.

66 *other iron tools.'* Ibid., 320. Gardner said that Formiga and another aldeia had been merged to form the single village of Duro. The Indians themselves called it Ropechedy, meaning

'beautiful location'. In Gardner's day its original population of a thousand was reduced to 250 persons, some of whom were runaway blacks. All the population spoke some Portuguese but only the two chiefs could read and write. There was no school or resident priest, and government aid to the village had ceased. The modern town of Dianôpolis, near Almas in northern Goiás, is on the location of Duro.

67 *great slaughter.'* Silva e Sousa, *Memoria*, 447.

67 *this town [Goiás].'* Ibid., 448.

68 *meant by captivity.'* José de Almeida Vasconcellos to the Governor of Goiás, Bananal island, 2 Aug. 1775, RHGB **8** 376, 1846, or also in Correspondence of Governors of Goiás, **84** 115, 1918. Affonso de Escragnolle Taunay, *Historia geral das bandeiras paulistas*, 11 vols (São Paulo, 1924–50) **11**: 1 263, 1950. In this letter, Vasconcellos said that the cruel raider had been Colonel Antonio Pires de Campos. But he had been killed in 1751, and Silva e Sousa blamed his successor João de Godois Pinto da Silveira for the raid to Bananal. Pereira de Alencastre, *Annaes*, 262. Fritz Krause, *In den Wildnissen Brasiliens* (Leipzig, 1911) 174.

68 *that overcame them.'* Pereira de Alencastre, *Annaes*, 271.

69 *from then onwards.'* Ibid.

69 *not fall ill.'* Chief Alve Nona to Governor of Goiás, Island of Santa Anna (Bananal), 3 Aug. 1775, in José Pinto da Fonseca, 'Carta que escreveu ao Exmo. General de Goyazes, dandolhe conta do descobrimento de suas nações de indios', RHGB **8** 389, 1846 or 1867.

69 *with the Portuguese.'* Declaration by Chief Alve Nona, Bananal, 31 Aug. 1775, in ibid., 389. Pereira de Alencastre, *Annaes*, 274.

70 *spent on it.* Pizarro e Araújo, *Memorias historicas*, **9** 184; Pereira de Alencastre, *Annaes*, 275–6; Silva e Sousa, *Memoria*, 457–8; Krause, *In den Wildnissen Brasiliens*, 174.

70 *settle in villages.'* Report by José de Almeida Vasconcellos to his successor, Goiás, May 1773, quoted in Pereira de Alencastre, *Annaes*, RHGB **27**: 2 306, 1864. This village was in fact built by the Ouvidor A.J. Cabral, but he named it Mossâmedes after the family barony of Governor Vasconcellos. It was originally created for the Akroá Indians after their rising at Duro and Formiga in 1777.

71 *and most success'.* Silva e Sousa, *Memoria*, 460. Johann Emanuel Pohl, *Reise im Innern von Brasilien* (Vienna, 1832), Portuguese translation *Viagem no interior* (Rio de Janeiro, 1951) **1** 360; Pizarro e Araújo, *Memorias históricas*, **9** 143; Machado d'Oliveira, 'Os Cayapós' (1860), RHGB **24** 509–17, 1861; Marivone Matos Chaim, *Os aldeamentos indígenas na Capitania de Goiás* (Goiânia, 1974); Karash, 'Damiana da Cunha: catechist and sertanista', 104–6.

71 *rate every year.'* Luiz da Cunha Menezes to Queen Maria I, Goiás, 10 Jan. 1782, in Pereira de Alencastre, *Annaes*, 319.

72 *and bloody heathen.'* José Rodrigues Freire, *Relação da conquista do gentio Xavante* (1790), ed. Carlos Drummond (São Paulo, 1951) 13.

73 *their meagre possessions.'* Ibid., 17.

73 *shouts and dances.'* Ibid., 18.

73 *of civilised society." '* Pereira de Alencastre, *Annaes*, 335. Lincoln de Souza, *Os Xavantes e a civilização* (Rio de Janeiro, 1953) 7–8. Governor Tristão da Cunha reported the arrival of the Chavante in a despatch dated 10 April 1788, and the Conselho Ultramarino replied on 17 October: DH **95** 99–101.

73 *by those barbarians'.* Conselho Ultramarino to Tristão da Cunha, Lisbon, 17 Oct. 1788, DH **95** 101.

73 *by those enemies'.* Conselho Ultramarino meeting of 17 Oct. 1788, DH **95** 103.

73 *our forces'.* Rodrigues Freire, *Relação da conquista*, 18.

73 *of no value.'* Conselho Ultramarino meeting of 22 Feb. 1780, DH **95** 89.

74 *their final transition.'* Rodrigues Freire, *Relação da conquista*, 19. On the introduction of the Javaé: Cunha Mattos, *Corographia historica*, 245–6.

75 *in many days.'* Rodrigues Freire, *Relação da conquista*, 19.

76 *with Indian women'.* Casal, *Corografia Brasílica*, **1** 337. Francisco de Assis Masacrenhas, 'Carta escripta no dia em que deu posse do governo da Capitania de Goyaz a Fernando Delgado Freire de Castilho' (1809), RHGB **5** 68, 1843 or 1885.

76 *with loaded muskets.'* Pohl, *Viagem no interior*, **1** 361.

76 *of the system.'* Ibid., 361.

77 *utility for themselves.'* Saint-Hilaire, *Voyage aux sources*, **2** 102–3.

77 *and chewing tobacco.'* Ibid., 111.

78 *open and spiritual.'* Ibid., 118–19.

78 *he makes sugar!'* Ibid., 114.

78 *as she wishes.'* Cunha Mattos, *Corographia historica*, 305. The story of Dona Damiana is also told by J. Norberto de Souza e Silva in RHGB **24** 525–38, 1861, and in Karash, 'Damiana da Cunha: catechist and sertanista', 102–20.

80 *half of it.'* Pohl, *Viagem no interior*, **2** 35.

80 *in the wilds.'* Ibid., 130.

80 *truly sad spectacle.'* Ibid.

80 *and carried off.'* Ibid.

80 *with their clubs.'* Ibid., 135.

Chapter 5   THE CENTRAL COAST

82 *from their work.'* Felipe Neri Correa, 'Direção com que interinamente se deve regular os indios das novas villas e lugares erectos nas aldeias da Capitania de Pernambuco e suas annexas', Recife, 29 May 1759, clause 19, RHGB **46**: 1 149, 1883. There was similar comment, generally quite intelligent, on the application of the Directorate legislation in

Bahia, in *Parecer do Conselho Ultra-marino da Bahia sobre os paragraphos do Diretorio para regimen dos indios das aldeias das capitanias do Pará e Maranhão* . . ., Bahia, 19 May 1759, in Eduardo de Castro e Almeida (ed.), *Inventário dos documentos relativos ao Brasil existentes no Archivo de Marinha e Ultramar de Lisboa*, 5 vols (Rio de Janeiro, 1913–18) **1** 335–42.

82 *the same settlers'.* Ibid., para. 74, 154.

82 *are generally indigent'.* Domingos Alves Branco Moniz Barreto, 'Plano sobre a civilização dos indios do Brazil' (1788), RHGB **19** 67–8, 1856.

83 *and spiritual welfare.'* Ibid., 69.

83 *bearded Capuchin fathers.'* Report by Sargento Mor de Artilheria of Pernambuco Jeronymo Mendes da Paz, 3 April 1761, enclosed with letter from Chancellor José Carvalho de Andrade to Count of Oeiras, Bahia, 1 Aug. 1761, in Castro e Almeida (ed.), *Inventário dos documentos relativos ao Brasil*, **1** 444–54.

83 *below the knees.'* Report by Mendes da Paz, ibid., 450. Reports by the *juiz de fora* João Ferreira Betencourt e Sá and others to the Conselho Ultra-marino in Bahia about Abrantes, are in the Archivo Histórico Ultra-marino, Lisbon, in a collection called *Sobre aldeias dos índios 1758/59*. These are analysed in Georg Thomas, 'Espírito Santo/Abrantes. Die Entwicklung einer Indianersiedlung des Brasilianischen Nordostens im Zeitalter Pombals', *Jahrbuch für Geschichte von Staat, Wirtschaft und Gesellschaft* **14** 97–133, Cologne–Vienna, 1977. There is a survey of Indian villages in Bahia and the São Francisco called 'Mapa curioso que contém não vulgares notícias de muitas aldeias de indios que, por ordem regia, são hoje vilas' in Luis dos Santos Vilhena, *Recopilação de notícias sotero-politanas e brasílicas* (or *A Bahia no século XVIII*), 3 vols (Bahia, 1969) **2** 460–1.

A number of missions ceased in 1761: Coripós, Pajeú, Pontal, Soro-babé and Unhunhum in Pernambuco and Santo Amaro in Alagoas. But other Franciscan missions continued to function. Friar Venâncio Willeke listed incumbents of missions in Bahia: Aricobé, from 1739 to 1860; Curral dos Bois, 1702–1843; Itapi-curu, 1689–1834; Jacobina, 1706–1843; Juazeiro, 1706–1843; Massa-cará, 1689–1854; Pambu; and Saí, 1697–1863. Willeke, 'Missões e mis-sionários da Província de Santo Antonio,' RH **38**:56 85–100, 1977.

84 *among the whites.'* José Xavier Machado Monteiro, ouvidor de Pôrto Seguro, to the Governor, April 1773, in Castro e Almeida (ed.), *Inventario dos documentos relativos ao Brasil*, **2** 272.

84 *of the whites'.* Ibid.

84 *land or sea.'* Instructions for directors in the Captaincy of Pôrto Seguro, José Xavier Machado Monteiro, 1777, in ibid., **2** 377.

84 *buy from them.'* Ibid., 378.

84 *city of Bahia'.* Governor Manuel da Cunha Menezes to Martinho de Mello e Castro, Bahia, 19 Jan. 1779, in ibid., **2** 421.

84 *this pernicious evil'.* Ibid.

85 *of their director.* Thomas José de Mello to officials of the town of Vila da Assumpção, Bahia, 13 March 1789, in Secretaria do Governo de Pernambuco, *Documentos do Arquivo*, 5 vols (Recife, 1942–50) **4** 66. Also other documents in this volume, pp. 32, 49 and 66–74.

85 *savage and fearsome'.* Casal, *Corografia Brasilica*, **2** 72–3.

85 *and aquiline noses.'* Maria Graham, *Journal of a voyage to Brazil* . . . (London, 1824) 294. The author went to see a group of Botocudo who visited Rio de Janeiro in 1823, presumably sent down by the French officer Guido Marlière.

86 *saliva running through.'* Ibid., 295.

86 *any other nation'.* Jacomé Monteiro, *Relação da provincia do Brasil*, in Serafim Leite (ed.), *Historia da Companhia de Jesus no Brasil* (1610), 10 vols (Lisbon–Rio de Janeiro, 1938–50) **8** 407.

86 *arrows to match.'* Pero de Magalhães

Gandavo, *Tratado da terra do Brasil* (1576), trans. John B. Stetson (New York, 1922) **2** 109.

86 *the forest floor).*' Monteiro, *Relação*, 407.

86 *hit by arrows.*' Fernão Guerreiro, *Relação annual dos padres da Companhia de Jesus* (Lisbon, 1605), in João Fernando de Almeida Prado, *Bahia e as capitanias do centro do Brasil*, 3 vols (São Paulo, 1945–50) **1** 199–200.

86 *those extensive forests'.* Anon, *Descripção geographica, topographica, historica e politica da Capitania de Minas Gerais* (1781), RHGB **71**: 1 178–9, 1908. On the smallpox epidemic: Antonio de Santa Maria Jaboatam, *Novo Orbe Serafico Brasilico. Parte primeiro, preambulo* (Lisbon, 1791) 20; Southey, *History of Brazil*, **2** 807.

86 *but not tamed.*' Anon, *Descripção geographica*, 178.

87 *an arrow comes.*' Vicar Roberto de Brito Granacho, *Descripção da Freguezia de São Boaventura de Poxim no Arcebispado da Bahia*, 20 Jan. 1756, in ibid., **1** 186.

87 *divided among them.*' Pizarro e Araújo, *Memorias históricas*, **8**: 2 39. Anon, *Descripção geographica*, 176–7. The Arrepiados hills are now called Serra do Caparaó, on the boundary between the modern states of Rio de Janeiro, Espírito Santo and Minas Gerais.

88 *of a lieutenant.*' Pizarro e Araújo, *Memorias históricas*, 43.

88 *and tame Indians'.* Capitão Mor João Gonçalves da Costa, *Memoria summaria e compendiosa da conquista do Rio Pardo* (1806–7), in Castro e Almeida, *Inventario dos documentos relativos ao Brasil*, 455–6.

88 *in their huts.*' Ibid., 456.

88 *our warlike drum'.* Ibid.

89 *calm and security.*' Wied-Neuwied, *Reise nach Brasilien* (1820), Portuguese translation (São Paulo and Rio de Janeiro, 1940) 410. This settlement has survived and grown into the modern town of Vitória da Conquista on the main road south from Salvador da Bahia.

89 *in the forest.*' Ibid., 413. Wied-Neuwied's meeting with the aged Colonel Gonçalves da Costa is in ibid., 429–30.

90 *well with shotguns.*' Ibid., 415.

90 *towards their oppressors.*' Ibid., 411. Casal, *Corografia Brasílica*, **1** 100 and **2** 100–1; Southey, *History of Brazil*, **2**, ch. 44, 804–5; Jean-Baptiste Debret, *Voyage pittoresque*, Brazilian translation, *Viagem pitoresco* (São Paulo, 1940) **1** 28–9. Southey based his description of the Camacans and Mongoios on Casal, with attribution; but Debret plagiarised from Wied-Neuwied's text and pictures without giving his source. The German artist Johann Moritz Rugendas painted some Camacans in the 1820s, but these were probably isolated members of the tribe whom he saw in towns of Minas Gerais.

90 *and died Catholics.*' Luis Navarro de Campos, *Relatorio da viagem por terra da Bahia athé Rio de Janeiro* (1 April 1808), ms. owned by Royal Geographical Society, London. Monteiro had the grandiose title Capitão Mor da Conquista, and he operated between Prado at the mouth of the Jucururú and the Mucuri. A few Maxakali survive, in an Indian Post of their name, near the town of Machacalis in the municipality of Aguas Belas in north-eastern Minas Gerais.

90 *two ferocious tribes'.* Ibid.

91 *of their women.*' Father José Pinho Salgado to the Archbishop of Bahia, Minas Novas, 24 Feb. 1794, in Castro e Almeida, *Inventário dos documentos relativos ao Brasil*, **3** 315.

91 *and agriculture?'* Campos, *Relatorio*.

91 *the settlers themselves.*' Ibid.

92 *have already done.*' Ibid., quoting Sargento Mor Francisco Alvarez Tourinho, Commandant of Caravelas, 5 May 1808.

92 *their sad remains.*' Carta régia to Governor of Minas Gerais from Prince Regent, Rio de Janeiro, 13 May 1808, text in *Revista do Archivo Publico Mineiro* 4 (Belo Horizonte, July–Dec. 1899) 783.

92 *in our society.*' Saint-Hilaire, *Aperçu d'un voyage*, 26.

92 *atrocities and anthropophagy.*' RAPM **4** 784. *This infamous decree has been published frequently, for instance in Perdigão Malheiro, A escravidão no Brasil,* **2** 123; Oliveira, *Coletânea de leis,* 66; Rodrigo Otávio, *Os selvagens americanos perante o direito* (São Paulo, 1946) 112–13.

93 *others farther distant.*' Saint-Hilaire, *Aperçu d'un voyage,* 14.

93 *if they were.*' Spix and Martius, *Reise,* **2** 806. The Pimenteiras originally lived between the sources of the Piauí and Corimatá rivers. They were peaceful for many years until the 1760s, when they started raiding fazendas who were invading their territory. Expensive campaigns were mounted against them and they were subdued; but the ouvidor Antonio José de Morais Durão wrote in 1772 that they were restless and ready to rebel again. Mott, 'Descrição de capitania de São José do Piauí', RH **28**:56 556, 1977.

93 *to the woods.*' Southey, *History of Brazil,* **3** pt 3, ch. 40, 543–4.

93 *the remaining inhabitants'*. Ibid., 544.

94 *placed in him.*' Spix and Martius, *Reise,* **2** 697.

94 *at his altar.*' Ibid.

94 *seeds of destruction.*' Ibid.

94 *they saw fit.*' Viceroy Luiz de Vasconcellos, *Relatório . . . ao entregar o governo ao seu sucessor o Conde de Resende* (20 Aug. 1789), RHGB **23** 184–5, 1860.

94 *of their race.*' Barreto, 'Plano', 69.

94 *José Carlos Barata!*' Thomas José de Mello to Bishop Alexandre Bernardino dos Reys, Bahia, 7 July 1796, in Secretaria do governo de Pernambuco, *Documentos do Arquivo,* 5 vols (Recife, 1942–50) **4** 79.

95 *of his family.*' Graham, *Journal of a voyage to Brazil,* 36.

95 *the Jesuit establishments.*' Ibid., 37.

95 *any apostolic capacity.*' Pereira de Alencastre, *Annaes,* 328; Curt Nimuendajú, *The Serente* (Los Angeles, 1942) 6–7.

95 *worse then useless.*' Koster, *Travels in Brazil* (London, 1817) **1** 272–3. During the Pombaline era, the other monastic and missionary orders were also emasculated or destroyed. The lay episcopacy was given complete control over the religious orders; and bishops were selected not only on the basis of piety, but also for being strongly anti-Jesuit and subservient to the secular government. The monastic orders were for a time forbidden to recruit novices. As a result their numbers declined and the few remaining friars or monks in Franciscan, Carmelite, Mercedarian or Oratorian monasteries became aged and inactive. Dauril Alden, 'Late-colonial Brazil 1750–1807: demographic, economic and political aspects', *Cambridge History of Latin America,* **2** 619; Eduardo Hoornaert, 'Historia da igreja no Brazil', ibid., **2** 550; Ebion de Lima, 'As missões oratorianas no Brasil', RHGB **323** 69–118, 1979. In the mid-1790s, the richest remaining order, the Mercedarians, who had large estates on Marajó island and the lower Amazon, were peremptorily recalled to Portugal and their properties confiscated. A few years later the other orders were required to surrender their lands in exchange for government bonds, and fined if they failed to do so. For a contemporary comment on this decline, see Luiz Antonio Oliveira Mendes, *Discurso preliminar . . . da Bahia* (c. 1789), ABNRJ **27** 286, 1905.

95 *in such activity.* Pestana da Silva, *Meios,* in Mello Moraes, *Corografia,* **4** 162, 172, 174.

96 *mind, or reflection.*' Spix and Martius, *Reise,* trans. H. E. Lloyd (London, 1824), **2** 261.

96 *religion with determination'*. Ibid., German original, **2** 494.

96 *please the whites.*' Moritz Rugendas, *Malerische Reise in Brasilien,* trans. Sergio Milliet, *Viagem pitoresca* (São Paulo, 1940), 126.

96 *had given them.*' Pizarro e Araújo, *Memorias históricas,* **3** 88.

97 *Indians' spiritual welfare'*. Ibid.

97 *than they were.*' Wied-Neuwied, *Reise,* **1** 131–2.

97 *their own villages'.* Pizarro e Araújo, *Memorias históricas*, **5** 253.

97 *in any way* 'Ibid., 254.

98 *the aldeia itself.'* Carta régia of 26 March 1819, in Moreira Neto, *Política indigenista*, 353. Saint-Hilaire, *Voyage aux sources*, **1** 36.

98 *neighbourhood with guards.'* John Mawe, *Travels in the Interior of Brazil* (London, 1812) 121.

98 *any regular employment.'* Ibid., 123–4.

98 *were truly surprising.'* Ibid., 124.

99 *and liking ornaments.'* Wied-Neuwied, *Reise*, **1** 130. Another German, Baron Eschwege, had visited the Coroado two years earlier, in 1813, and reported that they had a total population of 1900, scattered in 150 hamlets, for they tended to live isolated from one another. Eschwege, *Journal von Brasilien* (Weimar, 1818) **1** 120. Métraux, 'The Purí-Coroado Linguistic Family', HSAI **1** 523.

99 *were completely unclothed.'* Wied-Neuwied, *Reise*, **1** 136.

99 *avid for mirrors.'* Ibid., 141.

99 *gentleness and courtesy.'* Ibid., 144–5.

99 *encounter their huts."* 'Ibid., 162.

100 *at close range.'* Ibid., 210.

100 *into the jungles.'* Ibid., 215–16.

100 *lack good dogs.'* Rugendas, *Malerische Reise*, Portuguese translation (São Paulo, 1940) 122–3.

100 *men themselves — flee.'* Ibid., 123.

100 *of their bows.'* Ibid., 124.

101 *of public prosperity.'* Ibid., 124.

101 *of wild heathen'.* Sesmaria grant of 23 June 1787, in Paulo Pereira dos Reis, 'Os Puri de Guapacaré e algumas achegas à história de Queluz', RH **30** 126, 1965. *Documentos Interesantes para a Historia . . . de São Paulo*, 86 vols (São Paulo, 1894–1961) **33** 10, **84** 193, **87** 93–4. Lorena was called Nossa Senhora da Piedade before 1789, and is now on the road and railway between São Paulo and Rio de Janeiro. A path was cut through here to provide a route for the gold of Cuiabá to reach Rio de Janeiro instead of the port of Parati.

101 *and surrendered peacefully'.* Padre Francisco das Chagas Lima, *Noticia da*

fundação e principios desta aldeia de São João de Queluz, in Pereira dos Reis, 'Os Puri', 130.

101 *the very few'.* Captain-General Melo Castro e Mendonça to Secretary of State Rodrigo de Souza Coutinho, São Paulo, 27 June 1800, DI **29** 218. The land was awarded on 12 Feb. 1801.

101 *in the forests.'* Chagas Lima, *Noticia da fundação*, 146.

102 *on various occasions.'* Ibid.

102 *them to return'.* Ibid.

102 *and ardent charity'.* Entry by Francisco da Costa Moreira in the Livro do Tombo of Queluz, 20 Nov. 1803, in Pereira dos Reis, 'Os Puri', 149.

102 *among the colonists.'* Spix and Martius, *Reise*, English trans., **1** 293. This was a description of a village near Santa Anna das Arêas on the same road.

102 *many years ago'.* Report by Captain of Arêas, Gabriel Serafim da Silva, 6 May 1831, in Pereira dos Reis, 'Os Puri', 155–6.

103 *it to me.'* Captain-General Luiz Antonio de Souza Botelho Mourão to the Lieutenant of Cananéia, São Paulo, 30 Jan. 1767, DI **67** 69. The new aldeia for these nomadic Carijó was to be on the Sabaúna river. Other letters from this governor about administration of aldeias were to the director of the Aldeia da Escada, near Mogi das Cruces, and to the director of the aldeia of São José, ibid., 113, 134.

103 *over two centuries'.* Ofício by José Arouche de Toledo Rendon to Governor of São Paulo, Antonio Manuel de Melo Castro e Mendonça, São Paulo, 10 Nov. 1802, CDSP **11** 184. The remaining eleven aldeias with their populations in 1802 were: two original missions founded in 1560, São Miguel and Pinheiros (152 and many whites); five former Jesuit farms that still contained many Indians, Carapucuíba, Mboi, Itapecerica, Taquaqucetiba and São José (1316 white and Indian); three non-Jesuit missions, Barueri (580), Escada (282) and São João de Peroíbe;

and one former aldeia that had become a parish, Conceição de Guarulhos. Rendon's report of 1798, *Memoria sobre as aldeas de índios da provincia de São Paulo*, was published in RHGB **4**, 1842. The reward for Rendon's interest in this problem was his appointment in August 1798 as Director-General of the aldeias of São Paulo.

103 *female black slaves.*' CDSP **11** 185. Rendon's appointment by Governor Antonío Manuel de Melo Castro e Mendonça, São Paulo, 20 Aug. 1798, is published in CDSP **10** 329.

103 *nor stimulate them.*' CDSP **11** 185.

104 *church and priest.*' Ibid., 187. The

Governor who made this appalling ruling was Luis Antonio de Sousa Botelho Mourão.

104 *by their masters.*' Ibid.

104 *the [aldeia's] depopulation*'. Ofício by Rendon to Governor Antonio José da Franca e Horta, São Paulo, 7 July 1803, in ibid., 191.

104 *their complaints heard.*' Saint-Hilaire, *Voyage dans le district des diamans*, **2** 216 and 198, Pizarro e Araújo, *Memorias históricas*, **5** 99.

105 *are all Portuguese.*' Saint-Hilaire, *Voyage dans le district des diamans*, 217.

105 *himself empty-handed.*' Ibid.

105 *they are carefree.*' Ibid., 291.

Chapter 6   SOUTH BRAZIL

108 *was against veal.*' Casal, *Corografia Brasílica*, **1** 142.

108 *is terribly evident.*' Thomaz da Costa Correa Rebello e Silva, *Memoria sobre a Provincia de Missões*, RHGB **2** 160, 1840 (3rd edn 1916).

108 *for their families.*' Francisco João Róscio, *Breve noticia da extensão de terreno que occupão os Sete Povos das Missões Guaranis* (1802), RHGB **21** 273, 1858 (2nd edn 1930).

108 *with a beating.*' Ibid., 272.

109 *which they lived*'. Rebello e Silva, *Memoria*, 163. The lightning campaign was on the initiative of Captain Manoel dos Santos Pedroso and a dragoon soldier, José Borges do Canto, whose forty men were armed by the local Portuguese governor Lieutenant-Colonel Patrício José Correia da Câmara. See: Anon (but perhaps by Dr José de Saldanha), *Notícia abreviada dos principais sucesos da Guerra de 1801 . . .*, ed. Aurélio Pôrto, ABNRJ **51**, 1929 (Rio de Janeiro, 1938); Max Beschoren, *Beiträge zur nähern Kenntnis der brasilianischen Provinz São Pedro do Rio Grande do Sul*, 60.

109 *was to plunder.*' Rebello e Silva, *Memoria*, 163.

109 *the Guarani people.*' Ibid., 163–4.

109 *of those people.*' Ibid., 164.

109 *ideas to develop.*' Ibid., 166.

110 *beg for alms*'. Debret, *Viagem pitoresca*, **1** 60.

110 *Spaniards had done.*' Saint-Hilaire, *Aperçu d'un voyage*, 69.

111 *fresh, still bleeding.*' D'Orbigny, *Voyage dans l'Amérique Méridionale* (Paris, 1835) **1** 213.

111 *order and urbanity*'. Luis Antonio de Souza to Martinho de Mello e Castro, Secretary of State for Marinha e Ultramar, São Paulo, 20 Oct. :772. This same governor was also concerned to settle the Indians who were semi-nomads in the coastal forests near Cananéia: he suggested to his lieutenant in Cananéia, Afonso Botelho de S. Payo e Souza, that he create an aldeia for them on the Sabaúna river: letter from São Paulo, 30 Jan. 1767, DH **67** 68–9, 1943.

112 *and fierce dogs.*' Southey, *History of Brazil*, **2** 855. The Kaingáng were known in the early days of the conquest as Goyaná or Guayaná; and the settlers also called them by the insulting name Bugres or brutes. As well as being called Coroados (which

confuses them with the unrelated tribe also called by that name on the Paraíba do Sul), they were also sometimes called Botocudos, even though their lip discs were small in comparison with the Botocudos of Espírito Santo and Minas Gerais. The Botocudos of Paraná and Sànta Catarina were probably the Xokleng, a tribe related to the Kaingáng that also still survives in Santa Catarina state. Alfredo Taunay, who was President of Paraná in the 1880s, took credit for finding out that the tribe liked to be called Kaingáng: Taunay, 'Os indios Caingangs (Coroados de Guarapuava)', RHGB **51** 255, 1888.

112 *knife or club.'* Jules Henry, *Jungle People: A Kaingáng Tribe of the Highlands of Brazil* (1941; New York, 1964) 3.

112 *towards the west.'* Casal, *Corografia Brasílica,* **1** 222.

113 *these barbarian Indians.'* Carta régia to Governor Antonio José da Franca Horta, Rio de Janeiro, 5 Nov. 1808, in Oliveira, *Coletânea de leis,* 67; Moreira Neto, *Política indigenista,* 338.

113 *for fifteen years.'* Ibid.

113 *imprisoning many'.* Chagas Lima, *Memoria sobre 'o descobrimento e colonia de Guarapuava,* RHGB **4** 60, 1863.

113 *of their language.'* Ibid., 46.

114 *difficult to instruct.'* Ibid., 49.

114 *dancing and fishing.'* Ibid.

114 *signs of religion.'* Ibid., 52.

114 *in these obscenities!'* Ibid., 55.

115 *of their enemies.'* Ibid., 56.

115 *and final sacraments.'* Ibid., 58.

115 *consumed many people.'* Ibid., 59.

115 *from their homelands.'* Ibid., 61.

115 *of this life.'* Ibid., 61.

116 *of these people.'* Deed of foundation of Nossa Senhora de Belém in Guarapuava, Atalaia, 9 Dec. 1819, in Taunay, 'Os indios Caingangs', 282–3.

116 *expense, to disappear.'* Instruction to Colonel Luciano Carneiro Lobo for Guarapuava attack, São Paulo, 1829, in Pereira dos Reis, 'Os Puri', 155.

116 *rather than benefits.'* Ibid.

117 *horses and sheep.'* Francisco Rodrigues do Prado, *Historia dos indios Cavalleiros ou da nação Guaycuru* (1795), RHGB **1** 05, 1000.

117 *eight thousand horses.'* Almeida Serra, *Parecer sobre o aldêamento dos indios Uaicurus e Guanás* (1803), RHGB **7** 202, 1845 (or 1931 edn).

117 *to cure it.'* José Sánchez Labrador, *El Paraguay católico* (1770) **1** 298.

117 *to regroup them.'* Ibid., 245.

118 *no other purpose.'* Casal, *Corografia Brasílica,* **1** 279.

118 *choose for war.'* Almeida Serra, *Parecer,* 368.

118 *like a halter.'* Casal, *Corografia Brasílica,* **1** 279.

118 *all their glory'.* Mendes, *Carta . . . sobre las costumbres . . . de los yndios Mbayás . . .* (1772), in Jaime Cortesão (ed.), *Do Tratado de Madri à conquista dos Sete Povos* (Rio de Janeiro, 1969) 61.

119 *in their path.'* Prado, *Historia,* 20.

119 *women and children.'* Almeida Serra, *Parecer,* 368–9.

119 *Portuguese in Cuiabá.'* Félix de Azara, *Viajes por la América Meridional* (Madrid, 1923) 65.

119 *succeed in doing.'* Almeida Serra, *Parecer,* 357.

120 *emerges more easily.'* Azara, *Viajes,* 66–7.

120 *freer to divorce.'* Mendes, *Carta,* 61; Almeida Serra, *Parecer,* 357.

120 *own loved ones.'* Labrador, *Paraguay,* **2** 31; Herbert Baldus' introduction to Guido Boggiana, *Os Caduveo* (São Paulo, 1945) 22.

120 *will soon cease.'* Prado, *Historia,* 26.

120 *backs and arms.'* Rodrigues Ferreira, 'Memoria sobre o gentio Guaiacurus', in Thekla Hartmann, *A contribuição da iconografia para o conhecimento de índios brasileiros do século XIX,* 155.

120 *and sustained effort.'* Prado, *Historia,* 33; Labrador, *Paraguay,* **1** 244–5; Kalervo Oberg, *The Terena and the Caduveo of Southern Mato Grosso, Brazil* (Washington, DC, 1949) 5.

121 *do it together.'* Almeida Serra, *Parecer,* 353–4.

121 *not very docile.'* Mendes, *Carta,* 64.

121 *all these operations.'* Prado, *Historia*, 24.

121 *sleeping and eating'.* Amédée Moure, 'Les indiens de la Province de Mato-Grosso (Brésil)', *Nouvelles Annales des Voyages* **3** 87, Paris, 1862. For a full discussion of the evolution of Guaikurú body painting, see Hartmann, *A contribuição da iconografia*, 124–6; Alfred Métraux, 'Ethnography of the Chaco', HSAI **1** 280–4. There are striking photographs and drawings of facial tattooing by the Kadiwéu subtribe of the Guaikurú in Claude Lévi-Strauss, *Tristes tropiques* (Paris, 1955 and later editions).

121 *diet to recover.'* Moure, 'Indiens', 86.

122 *bout or festival.'* Mendes, *Carta*, 63.

122 *carousing and festivities.'* Almeida Serra, *Parecer*, 354.

122 *by the river.'* Ibid., 354–5, 357.

122 *be brave men.'* Southey, *History of Brazil*, **3** 621.

122 *some other woman.'* Almeida Serra, *Parecer*, 356.

123 *of their jalatas.'* Ibid., 358. I have seen a man in the modern Bororo village on the São Lourenço, not far from Guaikurú territory, who always dressed as a woman and was accepted as such by the rest of the villages.

123 *them in this.'* Mendes, *Carta*, 62.

123 *Spanish and Portuguese.'* Almeida Serra, *Parecer*, 196.

123 *even carnal pleasures.'* Azara, *Viajes*, **2** 96–7; Roberto Cardoso de Oliveira, *O processo de assimilação dos Terena* (Rio de Janeiro, 1960) 30–7; Baldus' introduction to Boggiani, *Os Caduveo*, 26. The Alsatian Ulrich Schmidel, who ascended the Paraguay with the first explorers in the mid-sixteenth century, first recorded the relationship between the two tribes in his *Warhaftige Historie einer wunderbaren Schiffart* (Frankfurt, 1567), trans. Luis Dominguez, Hakluyt Society **81**, 1889.

123 *used to suffer.'* Almeida Serra, *Parecer*, 199.

123 *emphasis and arrogance.'* Mendes, *Carta*, 62; Rodrigues Ferreira, 'Memoria', 158.

123 *good and evil.'* Mendes, *Carta*, 67.

124 *the [Guaikurús'] shamans.'* Ibid., 67–8.

124 *are so abundant,'* Ibid.

124 *veritable Delilahs'.* Francisco Raphael de Mello Rego, *O Forte de Coimbra*, RHGB **67**: 2 182, 1904; Almeida Serra, *Parecer*, 369; Francisco José de Lacerda e Almeida, *Diario da viagem pelas capitanias do Pará* (1790) (São Paulo, 1841) 69; Rodrigues Ferreira, 'Memoria', 153; Augusto Leverger, Barão de Melgaço, 'Apontamentos cronológicos da provincia de Mato Grosso', RHGB **205** 278, 1949; Francisco Rodrigues do Prado, in Pizarro e Araújo, *Memorias históricas*, **9** 38. Some authors date this attack in 1781, but Serra and Ferreira, who both visited the Guaikurú shortly afterwards, gave the date 1778.

125 *of the Portuguese'.* Almeida Serra, *Parecer*, 382.

125 *My friend Queimá.'* Rodrigues Ferreira, 'Memoria', 153.

125 *and ordinary people.'* Leverger, 'Apontamentos cronológicos', 291.

125 *of his Majesty'.* Text of treaty between Guaikurú and Governor João de Albuquerque de Mello Pereira e Cáceres, Vila Bela, 30 July 1791, in Casal, *Corografia Brasílica*, **1** 283–4; Rodrigues Ferreira, 'Memoria', 151–2, 160. The interpreter Victoria had been the slave of a woman in Cuiabá. She and other black slaves escaped and fled down the Paraguay. They fell into the hands of the Guaikurú, who killed all the men but raised Victoria and her sister for many years as part of their tribe.

126 *located anywhere else.'* Leverger, 'Apontamentos cronológicos', 297. Chief Tacadauana of the Kadiwéu group of Guaikurú submitted at this time and was settled at Miranda. His name survives in the modern town of Aquidauana, and the Kadiwéu still live in a reserve in the nearby Serra da Bodoquena. João Augusto Caldas, *Memoria historica sobre os indigenas da Provincia de Matto Grosso* (Rio de Janeiro, 1887) 12.

126 *and in consternation'.* Almeida Serra, *Parecer*, 386; Leverger, 'Apontamentos cronológicos', 297–8. The

new Governor of Mato Grosso was
Caetano Pinto de Miranda Montenegro. Almeida Serra, *Memoria . . .
de sobre Mato Grosso* (1800), RHGB ?

36, 1840.
127 *these until death.*' Almeida Serra,
Parecer, 349.
127 *not contemplate this.*' Ibid., 349–50.

Chapter 7   ATTITUDES TO INDIANS

132 *among other nations.*' Pero de
Magalhães Gandavo, *Tratado da terra
do Brasil* (1576), trans. John B.
Stetson, 2 vols (New York, 1922) 1
90–1.
132 *without further cares.*' Jean de Léry,
Voyage au Brésil (La Rochelle, 1578;
ed. Charly Clerc, Paris, 1927) 172–3.
132 *laws of nature.*' Gandavo, *Tratado*,
trans. Stetson, 92.
133 *of this realm.*' *Gazeta da Colonia*, Belém,
2 July 1800, in Nelson Papavero,
*Essays on the History of Neotropical Dipter-
ology*, 1 38.
135 *but timid look'.* Wied-Neuwied, *Reise*,
1 130, 136. A number of books give
summaries of the foreign visitors and
scientific expeditions to Brazil,
although none gives a full list of all
observers of Indians. These reviews
include: Santa-Anna Néry, *The land of
the Amazons* (1885), 287–308; Paul
Ehrenreich, *Beiträge zur Völkerkunde
Brasiliens*, 1891; Rodolfo Jacob,
Coletanea de cientistas estrangeiros (Belo
Horizonte, 1922); Rodolfo Garcia,
Historia das explorações scientificas, in
Instituto Histórico e Geográfico
Brasileiro, *Diccionario histórico, geográphico e ethnográphico do Brasil* (Rio de
Janeiro, 1922) 1 856–910; C. de
Mello-Leitão, *Historia das expedições
cientificas no Brasil* (São Paulo and Rio
de Janeiro, 1941); Egon Schaden, *O
estudo do índio brasileiro ontem e hoje*
(1952), and his chapter with João
Borges Pereira in vol. 5 of Sérgio
Buarque de Holanda, *Historia geral da
civilização brasileira* (1963); Teodoro
Sampaio and Carlos Teschauer, *Os
naturalistas viajantes e a etnografia indígena*
(1955); Olivério M. Oliveira Pinto,
Viajantes e naturalistas, also in Buarque
Holanda's *Historia geral*; Victor W.
Von Hagen, *South America Called Them*
(New York, 1945); Edward J. Good-

man, *The Explorers of South America*
(1972); Papavero, *Essays on the History
of Neotropical Dipterology* (1973);
Thekla Hartmann, *A contribuição da
iconografia* (1975).
135 *length of time.*' Koster, *Travels in Brazil*,
1 185–6.
135 *or great evil.*' Ibid., 189.
135 *are imperiously treated'.* Ibid., 185.
136 *themselves their superiors.*' Ibid., 190.
136 *a wealthy Indian.*' Ibid.
136 *arouses their appetite.*' Casal, *Corografia
Brasílica*, 1 59.
136 *the starry firmament.*' Spix and Martius, *Reise*, English trans., *Travels*, 2
242–3.
136 *their childish folly.*' Ibid., German edn,
2 494.
137 *almost never awake.*' Ibid., 495.
137 *race of red-skins.*' Ibid., 3 934–5; or
Portuguese trans., 3 49.
137 *fruits of humanity.*' Ibid., *Reise*, 3 935.
138 *of the American.*' Ibid., *Travels*, 1 320.
138 *and physical degeneracy.*' Ibid., *Travels*, 1
320; 2 219.
139 *their chief occupations.*' Ibid., 2 241;
also 2 261, 3 1207–8, or Portuguese
edn 3 358–9. The Bavarian scientists' ugly picture of Indians was
echoed by the French artist Debret,
Viagem pitoresca, 1 18, 22–3.
139 *and tripping gait.*' Spix and Martius,
Reise, German edn, 2 480.
139 *legs and breasts.*' Ibid.
139 *is otherwise beautiful.*' Wied-Neuwied
diary, quoted in Hartmann, *A contribuição da iconografia*, 10.
140 *scene in hell.*' Spix and Martius, *Reise*,
English trans., 2 820.
140 *vessel is empty.*' Wied-Neuwied, *Reise*,
Portuguese trans., 2 417.
140 *gives them presents.*' Saint-Hilaire,
Aperçu d'un voyage, 3.
140 *would be capable.*' Ibid., 4.
141 *are ferocious beasts.*' Saint-Hilaire,
Voyage dans le district des diamans, 2 370.

141 *parts of America.'* Ibid., **2** 22.

141 *state of starvation.'* Gardner, *Travels in the interior of Brazil*, 317.

142 *overdose of food.'* Ibid., 318.

142 *your metal axes!'* Steinen, *Unter den Naturvölkern*, Brazilian trans. (São Paulo, 1940) 98; Julio Cézar Melatti, *Índios do Brasil* (Brasília, 1970) 179—80.

143 *destroying their culture.'* Ibid.

143 *similar ridiculous things.'* Barreto, 'Plano', 86, 89.

143 *as auxiliary soldiers.'* Debret, *Viagem pitoresca*, **1** 7. On the Kayapó, see Silva e Sousa, *Memoria*, 460; On the Pataxó: Balthasar da Silva Lisboa, *Memoria*, 12; Saint-Hilaire, *Aperçu d'un voyage*, 3, on Coroados of Rio Bonito; Accioli de Cerqueira e Silva, *Corografia paraense* 139; Marlière, *Documents, Revista do Archivo Público Mineiro*, **10** 1905: letter of 26 Oct. 1824 to President of Minas Gerais, 503, letter of 12 Nov. 1824 to the same, 520; José, *Marlière*, 131; Francisco das Chagas Lima, *Memoria*, 58, re attraction of Votorões Kaingáng; Moritz Rugendas, *Viagem pitoresca*, 108; José Francisco Thomaz do Nascimento, *Viagem pelos . . . sertões de Guarapuava* (1886), RHGB **49** pt 2, 273, 1886, on attraction of Kaingáng; Richard Payer, *Reisen im Jauapiry-Gebiet*, **220**, on tools for uncontacted Waimiri; Graham, *Journal of a voyage to Brazil*, 294—5, on a Botocudo visit to Rio de Janeiro.

143 *the working population. . . .'* Prado, *Historia*, **9** 112—13.

144 *by their efforts.'* Report by Frei Luiz de Cemitille on the Kaingáng, in Taunay, 'Os indios Caingangs', RHGB **51** suppt. 267—8, 1888.

144 *and of order!'* Couto de Magalhães, *Viagem ao Araguaya* (1862), 1934 edn, 207—8.

144 *dies, I die!"'* Bartolomé Rossi, *Viage pintoresco por los ríos Paraná, Paraguay . . . y Arinos* (Paris, 1863) 115—16.

145 *or enchanting drink'.* São José, *Viagem e visita*, 187.

145 *their incorrigible vices.'* Caetano Brandão, *Memorias*, in *Jornal de Coimbra* **4** 122; Southey, *History of Brazil*, **3** 699. Correa, 'Direção', 145.

145 *accustomed to insubordination.'* Balthasar da Silva Lisboa, *Memoria*, in Castro e Almeida, *Inventario dos documentos relativos ao Brasil*, **5** 11.

145 *them only good.'* Moritz Rugendas, *Viagem pitoresca*, 126.

145 *amid intoxicating drink.'* Chagas Lima, *Memoria*, 55.

145 *those of Africa.'* Koster, *Travels in Brazil*, 187; Florence, *Esboço da viagem*, 243, 247.

146 *to distil it.'* Wied-Neuwied, *Reise*, **1** 144; Saint-Hilaire, *Voyage dans le district des diamans*, **2** 22, about Waitaká of São Pedro dos Indios; Spix and Martius, *Reise*, **2** 805, about acculturated Piauí tribes; Saint-Hilaire, *Voyage aux sources*, **2** 112, 117.

146 *for the colonists.'* Moritz Rugendas, *Viagem pitoresca*, 126.

146 *in the street.'* Guido Marlière to Colonel João J. Lopes Mendes Ribeiro, 11 July 1825, *Revista do Archivo Público Mineiro*, Belo Horizonte, **10** 611, **11** 81, 83; José, *Marlière*, 206—7.

146 *suckled their babies.* Bishop of Mariana, 1826, quoted in José Vicente César, *Todo o caminho percorrido . . ., Jornal de Brasília Cultura*, 12 Aug. 1973, 5. São João Batista do Presídio is now called Visconde do Rio Branco.

146 *abandoned to drunkenness.'* Castelnau, *Expédition*, **2** 42.

147 *he for this. . . .'* Ibid.

147 *ready for work.'* Ibid., 272.

Chapter 8   WHAT SHOULD BE DONE ABOUT INDIANS?

148 *this vast land.'* Almeida Serra, 'Discripção', 177.

148 *chance as savages'.* Southey, *History of Brazil*, **3**, ch. 42, 616.

149 *in the forests.*' Rodrigues Ferreira, *Diario da viagem philosophica*, RHGB **48** pt 1, 98−9, 148, also 57, 1885. The evil reputation of colonial society was also stressed by Prazeres, *Poranduba Maranhense*, 104.

149 *delights of freedom.*' Debret, *Viagem pitoresca*, 28.

149 *over the centuries.*' Ibid. Also, Spix and Martius, *Reise*, English trans., **1** 320 (about the Puri of the Aldeia da Esacada); German edn, **2** 805 (about tribes of Piauí).

149 *them successively disappeared.*' Spix and Martius, *Reise*, English trans., **2** 219.

149 *family never failed.*' Friar Luiz de Cemitille, quoted in Taunay, 'Os índios Caingángs', 267.

149 *and other vices.*' Couto de Magalhães, *O selvagem*, 118.

149 *to simple men.*' Henrique de Beaurepaire Rohan, *Viagem de Cuyabá ao Rio de Janeiro . . .* (1846), RHGB **9** 377−8, 1847 or 1869.

150 *live in peace.*' Barreto, 'Plano', 91.

150 *to the State.*' Guido Marlière, Memorandum about Indian education, 7 Jan. 1825, *Revista do Archivo Público Mineiro*, **10** 543; José, *Marlière*, 86.

151 *Indians and settlers.*' Regulations of 28 Jan. 1824 about creation of three aldeias for Botocudo on the Rio Doce in Espírito Santo, José Joaquim Machado de Oliveira, 'Notas, apontamentos e noticias para a historia da provincia de Espírito Santo', RHGB **19** 222, 1856 or 1898.

151 *had large populations.*' José Rodrigues Barata, 'Memoria em que se mostram . . . Goyaz' (1799), RHGB **4** 348, 1848 or 1891.

151 *under twelve families'.* Caetano Pinto de Miranda Montenegro to Visconde de Anadia, Recife, 22 July 1805, in *Documentos do Arquivo de Pernambuco*, 5 vols (Recife, 1942−50) **4** f284. He was describing the Villa de Santa Maria on an island upstream of the Villa de Assumpção in the Moxotó district of the lower São Francisco.

151 *close to decadence.*' Pohl, *Viagem no interior*, 367. Pizarro e Araújo,

Memorias históricas, **9** 218.

152 *wanted to know.*' Francisco de Paula Ribeiro, *Roteiro da viagem* (1815), RHGB **10** 63, 1848 or 1870.

152 *of hopeless labour'.* Southey, *History of Brazil*, **2** 762.

152 *only disastrous results.*' Moritz Rugendas, *Viagem pitoresca*, 102.

152 *danger of punishment.*' Ibid., 126.

152 *was never considerable.*' Spix and Martius, *Reise*, English trans., **2** 88.

152 *the female sex.*' Ibid., 126−7.

153 *pitiful hybrid existence'.* Ibid., German edn, **2** 805. Also, pp. 806 on the robust Pimenteiras, 819−20 on the Timbira of Piauí, and 845 on the pathetic Tupinamba of Maranhão island.

153 *possess almost nothing'.* Florence, *Esboço da viagem*, 462; Prazeres, *Poranduba Maranhense*, 135; Wied-Neuwied, *Reise*, Portuguese trans. of 1940, **2** 410−11.

153 *to anyone else'.* Kidder, *Sketches of residence*, **2** 224; Castelnau, *Expédition*, **2** 42.

153 *and good faith.*' Leal, *Viagem a um paiz de selvagens*, 127; Gomes, *Itinerario*, 495.

153 *points of view'.* Coudreau, *Voyage au Tapajós*, 144.

153 *intermingled with us.*' Almeida Serra, *Parecer*, 205−6; Barreto, 'Plano', 78−9; Instructions by the Secretary of State for Colonies, Martinho de Mello e Castro to the Governor of Goiás, 1 Oct. 1771, in Pereira de Alencastre, *Annaes*, 247.

153 *of public prosperity'.* Moritz Rugendas, *Viagem pitoresca*, 124.

154 *despair and idleness.*' Luiz de Vasconcellos e Souza to King, Rio de Janeiro, 2 Oct. 1784, RHGB **4** 159, 2nd edn 1863.

154 *vagrancy and idleness'.* José Xavier Machado Monteiro, Ouvidor of Porto Seguro, to the Governor, April 1773, in Castro e Almeida, *Inventario dos documentos relativos ao Brasil*, **2** 272.

154 *houses of whites'.* Ibid.

154 *father to son.*' Ibid.

154 *can be civilised.*' Debret, *Viagem pitoresca*, **1** 54.

154 *masters on journeys.'* Ibid., 57.

155 *and exciting beauty.'* Ibid., 58.

155 *become useful citizens.'* Father Manoel Ferraz de Sampaio's plans, described in a letter by Miguel Antonio de Azevedo Veiga to the Conde de Palma, Governor of São Paulo, Sorocaba, 11 Dec. 1815, DI **2** 136; also his letter to Palma, Itú, 13 Jan. 1817, and Father Ferraz' report, Itú, 3 March 1822, ibid., 151–2, 156–7.

155 *leave their tutelage'.* Ibid.

155 *without suffering hardship.'* Order by the President of São Paulo, Francisco Antonio de Souza Queiroz, São Paulo, 12 Sept. 1835, about Indians removed from the Juquiá in what is now Paraná, in A. P. Canabrava, 'Documentos sôbre os índios do Rio Juquiá', RMP n.s. **3** 391, São Paulo, 1949.

156 *an uncertain future.'* Saint-Hilaire, *Voyage aux sources*, **2** 270, 254. Cf. Eschwege, *Brasilien die neue Welt*, **1** 86.

156 *are mostly naked.'* Pohl, *Viagem no interior*, **1** 363.

156 *but attractive breasts.'* Dr Kupfer, 'Die Cayapó-Indianer in der Provinz Matto-Grosso', *Zeitschrift der Gesellschaft für Erdkunde zu Berlin*, **5** 247, 1870. Gardner, *Travels in the interior of Brazil*, 316–17, on the nudity of the Indians of northern Goiás in 1838.

156 *clothing, beads, etc.'* J. H. Elliott, 'Resume do itinerario de uma viagem exploradora . . .' (1845), RHGB **9** 18, 1847 or 1869.

157 *active and industrious.'* Gomes, *Itinerario*, 511.

157 *crafty and vicious.'* Coudreau, *Voyage au Tocantins–Araguaya*, 108.

157 *cheap trade goods.'* Koenigswald, 'Die Corôados im südlichen Brasilien', 28.

157 *who are nomadic.'* Proposal by Francisco Moniz Tavares, 4 Oct. 1821 and 1 April 1822, *Diario do Governo*, 1821, no. 235, 517; 1822, no. 78, 539; *Diario das Cortes*, V Session, 1 April 1822, 683; *Correio do Porto*, 117, Porto, 18 May 1822, 1. George Boehrer, 'Some Brazilian Proposals to the Cortes

Gerais, 1821–1823, on the Indian Problem', *III Colóquio Internacional de Estudos Luso-Brasileiros* (Lisbon, 1959–60), *Actas* **2** 204–6.

157 *worse than useless.'* Gardner, *Travels in the interior of Brazil*, **1** 272–3.

158 *to the sword.'* Letter from the Bishop of Pernambuco, Dom José Joaquim da Cunha de Azeredo Coutinho, to the Prince Regent, 1804, in Mello Moraes, *Corografia*, **2** 458.

158 *in our society.'* Cunha Mattos, *Chorographia historica*, 25; speech by Dr José Antonio Pimenta Bueno, President of Mato Grosso, to Legislative Assembly, Cuyabá, 1 March 1837, RHGB **2** 172–3, 1840 or 1918.

158 *enrich his subjects.'* Pohl, *Viagem no interior*, **2** 90.

159 *sick with arrows!'* Spix and Martius, *Reise*, **2** 823; Koster, *Travels in Brazil*, **1** 272.

159 *of the colony.'* Moritz Rugendas, *Viagem pitoresca*, 125.

159 *paid their salaries.'* Antonio José da Franca e Horta to Colonel Arouche Rendon, São Paulo, 13 Aug. 1803, DI **44** 114, 1915.

159 *for their families'.* Roscio, *Breve noticia . . . das missões Guaranis* (1802), RHGB **21** 273, 1858 or 1930. Almeida Serra, *Parecer*, 206.

159 *for the King'.* Pohl, *Viagem no interior*, **2** 36; Saint-Hilaire, *Voyage dans le district des diamans*, **2** 217, 288; Wied-Neuwied, *Reise*, **1** 176, or Portuguese trans. **1** 133, 411. Debret, *Viagem pitoresca*, **1** 33.

160 *live and die.'* Southey, *History of Brazil*, **2** 729.

160 *live or die.'* Sousa Coutinho, 'Informação', 287. José Monteiro, Instructions for directors of Indians in Porto Seguro (1777), in Castro e Almeida, *Inventario dos documentos relativos ao Brasil*, **2** 378.

160 *for the colonists.'* Moritz Rugendas, *Viagem pitoresca*, 126; Pohl, *Viagem no interior*, **2** 36; José, *Marlière*, 124, 208; Avé-Lallement, *Viagem pelo norte do Brasil*, **1** 240.

160 *among the Portuguese.'* Eschwege,

Brasilien die neue Welt, **1** 94.
160 *lost to them.* Saint-Hilaire, *Voyage dans*

le district des diamans, **2** 14–18, *Voyage aux sources,* **2** 283.

Chapter 9   IDEALISTS' SOLUTIONS

163 *restored to them'.* Order of 16 March 1813. This was published among almost three hundred pages of documents about Guido Thomas Marlière in the *Revista do Archivo Público Mineiro* **10** 392 Belo Horizonte, July–Dec. 1905. A biography of Marlière was largely based on this collection of documents: Oiliam José, *Marlière, o civilizador* (Belo Horizonte, 1958) 35.

163 *decide their fate.'* Conde de Palma to Marlière, Vila Rica, 12 April 1813, *RAPM,* **10** 394.

163 *only of Coroado.'* Marlière letter of 28 March 1827, RAPM **12** 576.

164 *most were Puri.* Marlière to the Vice-President of Minas Gerais, 1824, RAPM **12** 499; José, *Marlière,* 54–5. The aldeias in this report were: São João Batista do Presidio, 700 Coroado; São Manuel da Pomba, 300 Coropó; Rio Pardo and Paraíba, 500 Puri; Santa Rita da Meia Pataca, 400 Puri; São Paulo do Manuel Burgo, 1000 Puri; São Pedro do Rio Preto, 600 Puri; Sant'Ana de Abre-Campo, 800 Puri.

164 *the virgin forests.'* Pedro Maria Xavier de Ataíde e Mello, Vila Rica, RAPM **11** 314; José, *Marlière,* 128.

164 *nearly a thousand.'* Graham, *Journal of a voyage to Brazil,* 53.

165 *reduce the heathen'.* Dom João appointment of Marlière, Rio de Janeiro, 15 Nov. 1820, RAPM **10** 415–16, 1905.

165 *with the Indians.'* Marlière to King, Vila Rica (Ouro Prêto), 24 April 1822, RAPM **10** 425.

165 *be a problem.'* Marlière to Sen. Marechal, Onça Pequena Barracks, 9 Sept. 1824, RAPM **10** 483.

165 *nor punish crimes.'* Marlière to Gonçalo Gomes Barreto, RAPM **11** 153.

166 *than the primitive.'* Guy Marlière, Memorandum on Indian education, 7 Jan. 1825, RAPM **10** 542, 1905; Saint-Hilaire, *Voyage dans le district des diamans,* **2** 339; José, *Marlière,* 93–4.

166 *and 200 knives.'* Marlière to Padre José Pereira Lidoro, 1824, RAPM **10** 72.

166 *not by guns.'* Marlière letter, 1821, RAPM **10** 419; José, *Marlière,* 92.

166 *leaving that habitat.'* Marlière to Colonel J. J. Lopes Mendes Ribeiro, 11 July 1825, RAPM **10** 613.

167 *other philanthropic benefits.'* RAPM **10** 573.

167 *shoemaking and tailoring.'* Marlière to Colonel Lopes Mendes Ribeiro, 11 July 1825, RAPM **10** 612.

167 *to enjoy work.'* Marlière to Saint-Hilaire, 6 Dec. 1824, RAPM **10** 521. Saint-Hilaire, *Voyage dans le district des diamans,* **2** 340.

167 *exhausted my philanthropies.'* Marlière to Antonio José Coelho, 14 Dec. 1824, RAPM **10** 527.

168 *paid to protect.'* Marlière to Sargeant Francisco José Luiz, commandant of Petersdorff aldeia, 20 April 1826, José, *Marlière,* 124.

168 *the public peace.'* Marlière to the President of Minas Gerais, 14 Dec. 1824, RAPM **10** 524.

168 *was no use.'* Marlière article in *Abelha,* 5 Jan. 1825, RAPM **10** 541.

168 *they also died.'* Ibid.

169 *infect an army.'* Marlière to President, 27 Aug. 1825, RAPM **10** 628.

169 *the nineteenth century!'* Marlière to King, Vila Rica, 24 April 1822, RAPM **10** 425.

169 *in the Constitution?'* Marlière to President of Minas Gerais, 12 Nov. 1824, RAPM **10** 510.

169 *love and liberty.'* Marlière to Colonel J. J. Lopes Mendes Ribeiro, 11 July

1825, RAPM **10** 613.

170 *new to them'.* Spix and Martius, *Reise,* English trans., **2** 217.

170 *as free citizens.'* Ibid., 218. Other Germans and Swiss visited Marlière at this time — before he had become more famous for his years of work among Indians: Wilhelm Freyreiss (with Eschwege), *Reisen in Brasilien* (Stockholm, 1968 edn) 55, 57; Moritz Rugendas, *Viagem pitoresca,* 125. On Marlière's reconciliation between the Coroado and Puri: report of 1817 by Frei Tomaz de Città di Cadello, in Jacinto de Palazzolo, *Nas selvas dos vales do Mucuri e do Rio Doce* (São Paulo, 1952) 72–3.

170 *for military service.'* Spix and Martius, *Reise,* English trans., **2** 219.

170 *the neighbouring stream.'* Ibid., 225.

170 *has been hanged!'* Marlière to Colonel João J. Lopes Mendes Ribeiro, 11 July 1825, RAPM **10** 609.

170 *in their midst.'* Saint-Hilaire, *Voyage dans le district des diamans,* **2** 340.

171 *wanted to ensure.'* Ibid. The Prussian Prince Adalbert and Count Bismarck visited the Puri and Coroado fifteen years after Marlière's retirement. The Coroado were at the Aldeia da Pedra on the south bank of the Paraíba, and the Puri were on the north bank confronting the Botocudo. Their priest, Friar Florido, had been at the Aldeia da Pedra for sixteen years and said that he had baptised 650 Coroado and 150 Puri, as well as 20 families of Coropó. The Germans found the tribes apathetic and semi-acculturated: they preferred to go naked, but quickly dressed when they saw Europeans; they had some huts built in the traditional manner and they could still put on a tribal dance; but they tended to prefer money and alcohol to glass beads. Adalbert of Prussia, *Travels* **1**, 49–60.

171 *loved the Indians.'* Marlière's memo about educating Indians, 7 Jan. 1825, RAPM **10** 544.

171 *are [legally] free.'* José Bonifácio de Andrada e Silva and Martim Francisco Ribeiro de Andrada, *Viagem mineralogica na Provincia de São Paulo* (1820), published in French translation by A. de Menezes Drummond, in *Journal des Voyages, Découvertes et Navigations Modernes* **36** (Paris, 1827) and in Nereo Boubée, *Geologia elementar aplicada à agricultura e indústria* (Rio de Janeiro, 1846). Octávio Tarquínio de Sousa, *José Bonifácio* (Rio de Janeiro, 1972) 74.

172 *men into activity.'* José Bonifácio de Andrada e Silva, *Apontamentos para a civilização dos índios bravos do Império do Brasil:* first version, Cortes Gerais, 7 March 1822, *Diário das Cortes,* **5** 395; second version, *Annaes do Parlamento Brazileiro. Assembléa Constituinte,* sessions of 12 May and 18 June 1823 (Rio de Janeiro, 1874) **1** 47 and **2** 74. There are many later published versions of the essay, including *O Patriarcha da Independencia,* Brasiliana **166** (São Paulo and Rio de Janeiro, 1939) 275–88. Maria da Conceição Osorio Dias Gonçalves, 'O índio do Brasil na literatura portuguesa dos séculos XVI, XVII e XVIII', *Brasilia* **11** 160–1, Coimbra, 1961.

172 *the wild animals.'* Ibid., *Brasilia* edn, 259.

172 *usurpers and Christians.'* Ibid. George Boehrer, 'Some Brazilian Proposals to the Cortes Gerais, 1821–1823, on the Indian problem', in Luis Felipe Lindley Cintra (ed.), *III Colóquio Internacional de Estudos Luso-Brasileiros. Actas,* 2 vols (Lisbon, 1959–60) **2** 207. Dr Boehrer also discusses the various published versions of José Bonifacio's *Apontamentos* in 'Variant versions of José Bonifácio's "Plan for the Civilization of the Brazilian Indians" ', *The Americas,* **14**: 3 301–12, Jan. 1958.

172 *laws of Christianity.'* Ibid.

172 *and good conduct.'* Ibid. Boehrer, 'Some Brazilian Proposals', 208.

173 *of the nation.'* Constituent Assembly, session of 18 June 1823, *Annaes do Parlamento Brazileiro. Assembléa Constituinte,* **2** 74. Other plans about Indians were also submitted: by

Francisco Moniz Tavares, a priest and deputy from Pernambuco, session of 3 Oct. 1821; by Domingos Borges de Barros from Bahia, session of 18 March 1822, recommending that Moravian Brethren rather than Catholic missionaries be used to contact Indians; José Caetano Ribeiro da Cunha, whose Memoria was dated Belém, 20 May 1821, and complained of the difficulties in obtaining Indian labour in Pará; and Francisco Ricardo Zany, a plantation-owner who employed many Indians near Manaus and who became a friend of Spix and Martius when they were on the Amazon. Zany wanted newly contacted Indians to be placed for seven years in repartições under the care and instruction of lay directors. These were to make the Indians receive religious and civil instruction, and apply them to 'useful work'. Zany's was the only plan to be approved by the Portuguese Comissão do Ultramar and published in the *Diário das Cortes*, 7, Session of 26 Aug. 1822, 241. Spix and Martius, *Reise*, **3**, bk 9, ch. 1, 1116, 1215, 1220. Boehrer, 'Some Brazilian Proposals', 202–6, 'Variant Versions', 305.

173 *with civilised colonists.'* Decree of 28 Jan. 1824, in Moreira Neto, *Política indigenista*, 357.

173 *efforts to achieve'.* Ministério do Império resolution of 18 Oct. 1825 to Espírito Santo, in ibid., 358. Similar letters went to other provinces: 3 Dec. 1824 to Minas Gerais about kindness to its Indians; 25 May 1825 to São Pedro do Sul (now Rio Grande do Sul); 8 Nov. 1825 to Rio Negro, Oliveira, *Coletânea de leis*, 70.

174 *labourers for agriculture.'* Barão de Congonhas do Campo to Senate, 1 April 1826, in José Vicente César, 'Todo o caminho percorrido para a formação do Estatuto do Índio', *JB Cultura*, 12 Aug. 1973, 3.

174 *be totally forbidden.'* Caetano Maria Lopes Gama response to Senate, 30 Aug. 1826, Leda Maria Cardoso

Naud, *Documentos sobre o índio brasileiro* (Arquivo Histórica, Brasília, 1971) 83.

174 *of the evangel'.* Ibid.

174 *their ancient woods.'* Dom Tomás Manuel de Noronha e Brito, Bishop of Olinda, to Governor Francisco de Paulo Cavalcanti e Albuquerque, 16 Sept. 1826, in ibid., 114.

174 *have treated them.'* Colonel José da Cunha Lustosa to Ministro do Império, Quartel de Parnagoá, Piauí, 6 Feb. 1827, in ibid., 117.

175 *peace and harmony.'* Bishop of Mariana, Minas Gerais, to Ministro do Império, in ibid., 103. São João Batista do Presídio, home of the Coroado and Coropó, is now Visconde do Rio Branco, a hundred kilometres south-east of Ouro Prêto in south-eastern Minas Gerais.

175 *Indians and Brazilians.'* Antônio Eustáquio da Silva Oliveira to Ministro do Império, Uberaba, 2 Oct. 1826, in ibid., 89.

175 *and prior provocation?'* Guido Marlière to President José Teixeira da Fonseca Vasconcellos, Barão de Caeté, 14 Dec. 1825, César, 'Todo o caminho', 3; Marlière to Council of Minas Gerais, 7 March 1826, in ibid., 96.

175 *status of orphans.* Law of 27 Oct. 1831 issued by the Regency in the name of Pedro II (acting on a Senate resolution of 3 Nov. 1830). The provisions about the orphan status of Indians were in the Decree of 3 June 1833 and in ch. 4, art. 5, of the Regulamento of 15 March 1842: Oliveira, *Coletânea de leis*, 71; Moreira Neto, *Política indigenista*, 360–1; Debret, *Viagem pitoresca*, 1 52.

176 *Brazil in 1500.* For the population of pre-Conquest Brazil, see John Hemming, *Red Gold*, 487–501, and 'The Indians of Brazil in 1500', *The Cambridge History of Latin America*, **1** 119–43. Dauril Alden has analysed the population of late-eighteenth- and early-nineteenth-century Brazil in his 'Late Colonial Brazil, 1750–1808', ibid., **2** 602–10. He relied on a

letter from the British minister Lord Strangford to Sir Arthur Wellesley (later Duke of Wellington), Rio de Janeiro, 20 May 1810 (PRO, RO 63/84/ERD/2255), and supplemented this for missing provinces from earlier censuses. There were obvious discrepancies in census criteria in different provinces — for instance, the numbers of Indians recorded for Maranhão, Goiás and Mato Grosso seem far too low, whereas those for Piauí and Rio Grande do Sul may be too high even though the latter contained remnants of the Jesuits' missionised Guarani as well as newly contacted Kaingáng. Alden's table, in geographical order from north to south and in round figures, is:

Province	Population	Indians	Percentage
Pará	80,000	16,000	20.0
Maranhão	78,900	3,900	5.0
Piauí	59,000	13,900	23.6
Goiás	55,400	2,900	5.2
Mato Grosso	26,800	1,000	3.8
Pernambuco	392,000	12,500	3.2
Bahia	359,400	5,400	1.5
Rio de Janeiro	229,600	4,600	2.0
Minas Gerais	494,800	8,900	1.8
São Paulo	208,800	6,300	3.0
Rio Grande do Sul	66,400	22,600	34.0
Total	2,051,100	98,000	4.7

177 *Regimento das Missões.* Provincial law of 2 Oct. 1840, Pará; Relatórios by President Bernardo de Souza Franco, Pará, April 1841, 14, and April 1842, 11; Aviso of Regent Pedro de Araújo Lima (later Marquis of Olinda) of 15 May 1840; Decreto 285, 21 June 1843 and Decreto 373 of 30 July 1844 about import of Capuchins; Decreto 426, 24 July 1845. Oliveira, *Coletânea*, 71–2; Moreira Neto, *Política indigenista*, 365–70; Naud, *Índios e indigenismo*, 238–9; Antonio Domingos Raiol, 'Catachese de indios no Pará', ABAPP 1903, 163.

178 *by the Indians'.* Decreto 426, 24 July 1845, art. 1, paras 2, 3, 4, 12, 13. Perdigão Malheiro, *A escravidão no Brasil,* **2** 141–4.

179 *from the capital.'* Colonel Ricardo José Gomes Jardim, *Creação da directoria dos indios na Provincia de Mato Grosso,* RHGB **9** 553, 1847 or 1869.

179 *had traditionally occupied.'* Moreira Nato, *Política indigenista,* 71, 76.

179 *of many aldeias.'* J. Marcelino de Brito, Ministro do Império, report of 1847, 33, in ibid., 72.

179 *in the aldeias.'* Ibid.

180 *of their neighbours.'* Otávio, *Os selvagens americanos perante o direito,* 151–2. Law no. 601, 18 Sept. 1850, and Decree no. 1318, 30 Jan. 1854, which regulated it.

180 *the civilised population.'* Decision of 21 Oct. 1850 by Ministro do Império, in Moreira Neto, *Política indigenista,* 374. The Financial Tribunal of Ceará put this into effect on 18 Dec. 1852, selling off Indian aldeias as unoccupied land.

180 *resolve them judicially.'* Report by Ministro do Império, L. P. Couto Ferraz, 1856, 36, in Moreira Neto, ibid., 72.

180 *the other inhabitants'.* Ibid.

Chapter 10   THE TOCANTINS–ARAGUAIA FRONTIER

181 *a powerful patron.'* Koster, *Travels in Brazil,* **1** 184–5.

183 *of the disaster.'* Francisco de Paula Ribeiro, 'Descripção', 70, or

'Roteiro', 27.

184 *ceremony next day.'* Ribeiro, 'Roteiro', 45–6.

185 *forget this affair.'* Ibid., 78–9.

185 *best of monarchs.'* Ibid., 78–9.

185 *an inviolable alliance'.* Ibid., 41–2.

185 *suffered appalling hunger.'* Ibid., 42.

185 *hatred of us'.* Ibid., 42.

186 *done to them.'* Ibid., 44.

186 *of the disease.'* Ibid., 44–5. Prazeres, *Poranduba Maranhense*, 137.

186 *the same fate.'* Ribeiro, 'Roteiro', 46. Nimuendajú, *Eastern Timbira*, 35, discusses the known references to this tribe with his usual erudition. They were said to have attacked Pinto de Magalhães' Krahó a few years later: Cándido Mendes de Almeida, *A Carolina* (Rio de Janeiro, 1851) 52. In 1851 they were located on the Grajaú river: Cézar Augusto Marques, *Apontamentos para o Diccionario Histórico . . . do Maranhão* (São Luis, 1864), entry for 'Índios'. Their survivors may have merged with the Canela of Ponto. The Nyurukwaye are even more elusive. Pinto de Magalhães located them west of the Tocantins and Raymundo da Cunha Mattos said that they attacked his settlement of Cherente in 1824. Cunha Mattos, *Chorographia historica*, 357; J. C. R. Milliet Saint-Adolphe, *Diccionario geographico . . . do Imperio do Brasil* (Paris, 1845), entry for 'Norogagés'; Pohl, *Reise*, 2 682; Marques, *Apontamentos*, entry for Tocantins; Nimuendajú, *Eastern Timbira*, 36.

187 *a battle order.'* Antonio Luiz Tavares Lisboa, 'Roteiro da viagem que descendendo pello rio Tocantins mandou fazer o illmo Governador da capitania de Goyaz Jozé de Almeida Vasconcellos' (1774), in Luiz dos Santos Vilhena, *Cartas de Vilhena* (Bahia, 1922), and Curt Nimuendajú, *The Apinayé* (trans. Robert H. Lowie, Washington, DC, 1939) 2.

187 *Karajá and Apinagé.'* Report by Governor of Pará, 1804, in Julio Paternostro, *Viagem ao Tocantins* (São Paulo/Rio de Janeiro, 1945) 137.

187 *enemies of ours.'* Ribeiro, 'Roteiro', 34.

188 *attention in Europe.'* Pohl, *Reise*, 2 168; *Viagem no interior*, 2 151. The two women wanted to leave with Pohl, but the sensible Indian benefactor Placido Moreira de Carvalho put a stop to the idea.

188 *live completely naked!'* Gomes, 'Itinerario', 492–3.

188 *das Duas Barras.'* Pohl, *Viagem no interior*, 2 135.

188 *they were devastated.'* Silva e Sousa, *Memoria*, 495; Pizarro e Araújo, *Memorias históricas*, 9 217.

188 *they are causing.'* Carta régia of 5 Sept. 1811, *Leis do Brasil*, 102–3; Moreira Neto, *Política indigenista*, 341.

189 *only through war.'* Paternostro, *Viagem ao Tocantins*, 137.

189 *on the Araguaia.* Silva e Sousa, *Memoria*, 470; Cunha Mattos, *Chorographia historica*, RHGB 37: 1 362, 1874, and 38: 1 18, 1875; Lincoln de Souza, *Os Xavantes e a civilização*, 8–10.

189 *very few champions.* Nimuendajú, *The Apinayé* (Washington, DC, 1939) 4; Paternostro, *Viagem ao Tocantins*, 170.

189 *north of Carolina.* Cunha Mattos, *Chorographia historica*, 21.

189 *against the Kamekran.'* Accioli de Cerqueira e Silva, *Corografia paraense*, 130.

190 *losing their lives.'* Ribeiro, 'Roteiro', 47. The destroyed fazendas were Sacco in 1808 and Vargem de Pasco in 1809.

190 *against enemy attack.'* Pohl, *Viagem no interior*, 2 148.

190 *of his men.'* Ibid., 149. Nimuendajú, *Eastern Timbira*, 27.

191 *his own captives'.* Saint-Adolphe, *Diccionario*, entry for 'São Pedro de Alcántara'; Nimuendajú, *Eastern Timbira*, 24; Paternostro, *Viagem ao Tocantins*, 169–70.

191 *receive a handful.'* Ribeiro, 'Roteiro', 14.

191 *of the seducers!'* Ibid., 75–6.

191 *Indians to sell.'* Ibid., 76.

192 *were left disfigured.'* Pohl, *Viagem no interior*, 2 155.

192 *at us now.'* Wakuke Cherente talking to David Maybury-Lewis, *The Savage*

and the Innocent (London, 1965) 100. Also, Maybury-Lewis, 'Some Crucial Distinctions in Central Brazilian Ethnology', *Anthropos* **60** 353, St Agustin, Germany, 1965.

193 *and collar shackles.*' Speech by President A. A. Pereira da Cunha, Goiás, 1865, 15.

193 *in the fighting.*' Silva e Sousa, *Memoria*, 463; Cunha Mattos, *Chorographia historica*, RHGB **38**: 1 19, 1875. The expedition of 1789 was led by Sargento José Luiz, who was wounded in the fighting. There were many more subsequent bandeiras against the Canoeiros. Cunha Mattos wrote that they lived in the forested hills between the Maranhão river (the old name for the upper Tocantins), Santa Teresa and Amaro Leite rivers. Silva e Sousa said that they were also on the Manoel Alves and Palmas rivers.

193 *death in combats.*' Silva e Sousa, *Memoria*, 495.

193 *they are causing.*' Carta régia of 5 Sept. 1811, *Leis do Brasil*, 102−3.

194 *led to fighting.*' Pohl, *Viagem no interior*, **2** 91.

194 *inflamed disappeared completely.*' Ibid., 91.

194 *in the future.*' Ibid., 93. Castelnau mentioned another early nineteenth-century expedition to destroy the Canoeiro, led by Miguel de Arruda e Sá: *Expédition*, **2** 110.

195 *of our courage.*' Presidential address by Luiz de Gonzaga Camargo Fleury, Goiás, 1838, 12−13.

195 *evils they suffer.*' Ibid., Moreira Neto, *Política indigenista*, 192.

195 *dispossessed or enslaved.*' Pohl, *Viagem no interior*, **2** 91.

195 *peace with us.*' Presidential address by

Vice-President F. F. dos Santos Azevedo, Goiás, 1842, 11, 13. There was familiar talk of winning over tribes through missionaries, or even of reviving the moribund aldeia of Carretão, north of Goiás.

196 *an immense rapier.*' Castelnau, *Expédition*, **1** 351, 334.

196 *made them tremble.*' Ibid., 445.

197 *abandoned to drunkenness.*' Castelnau, *Expédition*, **2** 42. Castelnau saw only two Krahó villages of 140 and 150 people respectively: there were probably other Krahó villages further inland from the Tocantins. Cunha Mattos, *Chorographia historica*, RHGB **38** pt 1, 20, 286, 1875; Nimuendajú, *Eastern Timbira*, 25.

197 *the savages' clubs.*' Castelnau, *Expédition*, **2** 48−9.

197 *of Our Lady!*' Speech by Vice-President F. F. dos Santos Azevedo, Goiás, 1842, 13; Couto de Magalhães, *Viagem ao Araguaia*, 1934 edn, 109. Castelnau, *Expédition*, **2** 69, 77−9, 81−2, 116.

197 *the civilised classes.*' Presidential speech by J. Ignacio Ramalho, Goiás, 1846, 13−14.

198 *customs are different.*' Ibid., 15.

198 *satisfy these needs.*' Presidential speech by J. I. Ramalho, Goiás, 1847, 13.

198 *society by terror.*' Ibid.

198 *territory they inhabit.*' Presidential speech by A. M. de Aragão e Mello, Goiás, 1861, 14.

198 *give no quarter.*' J. V. Couto de Magalhães, *Viagem ao Araguaya* (1934 edn) 104.

199 *which were decimated*'. Ibid., 105, 107.

199 *of Akwe-Chavante.* Paul Ehrenreich, 'Die Einteilung und Verbreitung der Völkerstämme Brasiliens', *Petermanns Mitteilungen* **37** 40, 1891.

Chapter 11   THE BORORO

201 *despite his presents.*' Almeida Serra, *Discripção geographica*, 163, 178; Leverger, 'Apontamentos cronologicos', 280, 281, 283, 296.

203 *mainly tending cattle.*' Florence, *Esboço*

da viagem, 247.

203 *the feminine sex.*' Julio Koslowski, 'Algunos datos sobre los indios Bororos', *Revista del Museo de La Plata* **6** 381, Buenos Aires, 1895.

203 *taken his tribute.'* Ibid.
204 *side, and decorations.'* Florence, *Esboço da viagem*, 274. Various modern authors have described the Langsdorff expedition: Alfredo d'Escragnolle Taunay, in his introduction to his translation of Hércules Florence's journal and in his essay 'A cidade de Matto Grosso (antiga Villa Bella) ... ', RHGB **54**: 2 12–15, 1892; C. de Mello-Leitão, *Historia das expedições científicas no Brasil*, 232; Sampaio and Teschauer, *Os naturalistas viajantes e a etnografia indígena*, 200–2; Edward Goodman, *The Explorers of South America*, 300–1; B. N. Komissarov, *Brazil in the Accounts of the Participants of the Russian Expedition*; N. G. Shprintsin, *The Apiacá Indians* and *Materials of the Russian Expeditions to South America*; Roderick J. Barman, 'The Forgotten Journey: Georg Heinrich Langsdorff and the Russian Imperial Scientific Expedition to Brazil, 1821–1829'; Thekla Hartmann, *A contribuição da iconografia*, 108–112; Berthels, Komissarov and Lysenko, *Materialen der Brasilien-Expedition 1821–1829 des Akademiemitgliedes Georg Heinrich Freiherr von Langsdorff*.
204 *on the people.'* Langsdorff's journal for 11 April 1828, in Shprintsin, 'The Apiacá Indians', 87, 89. Barman, 'The Forgotten Journey', 95.
204 *and grotesque fury.'* Taunay, 'A cidade de Matto Grosso', 14–15.
204 *from southern Europe.'* Florence, *Esboço da viagem*, 276.
205 *terrible Apiaká tribe.'* Almeida Serra, *Navegação do rio Tapajós*, 4, 11. The first descent was by Sargento-mór João de Sousa Azevedo in 1746. There was a brief gold rush at Santa Isabel on the east bank of the Arinos, but this was abandoned by 1749.
205 *bows and arrows.'* Captain Miguel João de Castro and Antonio Thomé de França, 'Abertura de communicação commercial entre . . . Cuyabá e . . . Pará . . .' (1812), RHGB **31**: 1 116, 150–3, 1868; Casal, *Corografia Brasílica*, **1** 308–9; Santa-Anna Nery,

The land of the Amazons, 340; Spix and Martius, *Reise*, **3** 105; Southey, *History of Brazil*, **2** ch. 44, 843–4.
205 *afflict civilised men.'* Florence, *Esboço da viagem*, 283.
205 *have infected them.'* Ibid., 281–2.
206 *what I did.'* Shprintsin, 'The Apiacá Indians', 188; Barman, 'The Forgotten Journey', 89.
206 *would endure yesterday.'* Ibid.
206 *that I live.'* Shprintsin, 'The Apiacá Indians', 95–6; Barman, 'The Forgotten Journey', 89.
206 *of his associates.'* Kidder, *Sketches of residence*, **2** 332.
207 *as the Apiaká.* The first inspector of the Apiaká found a settlement called São Francisco at the Salto Augusto in 1832, but it was abandoned in the following year. The next inspector, João Soares Muniz, went to the Apiaká in 1834. The final attempt of 1841–5 was made by an inspector called Amazonas. Leverger, 'Apontamentos cronologicos', 344, 348, 354, 359–61, 367.
207 *the commander's orders.'* Leverger, ibid., 342, 341. The 1830 raid was led by Lieutenant José Teodoro de Araujo.
207 *most horrific scenes.'* João Augusto Caldas, *Memorias históricas sobre os indigenas da Provincia de Matto Grosso* (Rio de Janeiro, 1887) 19. Leverger, 'Apontamentos cronologicos', 357.
207 *of its settlers.'* Ibid.
208 *of their villages.'* Ibid.
208 *them to parley.'* Speech by President Herculano Ferreira Pena, Cuiabá, 1862, 118–19. Also speeches by Augusto Leverger, 1852, 8; by Antonio Pedro de Alencastro, 1860, 14; by Herculano Ferreira Pena, 1863, 13, 62.
208 *travellers and settlers'.* Speech by President Francisco José Cardoso Junior, Cuiabá, 1872, 62. Moreira Neto, *Política indigenista*, 146–7, 150, 151, 153, 158, 164.
208 *the Campanha Bororo'.* Speech by Vice-President M. Alves Ribeiro, Cuiabá, 1848, 8–9.
208 *pity or mercy'.* Moure, 'Indiens', **3** 78.

208 *the Cabaçal Bororo'.* Castelnau, *Expédition,* **3** 45.

208 *respected the missionary'.* Moure, 'Indiens', **3** 78.

209 *urucum [anatto] dye.'* Castelnau, *Expédition,* **3** 46.

209 *become useful labourers.'* Moure, 'Indiens', **3** 79. Speech by President Ricardo José Gomes Jardim, Cuiabá, 1846, 33, in which he planned more mission villages on the Jauru and on the São Lourenço for the eastern Bororo.

209 *in name only.'* Ibid., 47, 49.

209 *short time ago'.* Rodolpho Waehneldt, 'Exploração da provincia de Mato Grosso', RHGB **27** pt 1, 226, 1864.

209 *them be killed.'* Ibid.

209 *sex or age.'* Report by the Diretor Geral dos Indios de Mato Grosso, annexed to the 1872 report by President Francisco José Cardoso Junior. Census statistics from this report of 1872 and that of 1848 in the archive of the Diretoria dos Indios in Cuiabá show that the Campanha (Plains) Bororo declined less violently than the Cabaçaes living to their north:

the Campanha from 200 to 180, but the Cabaçaes from 100 to 40. Also, Report on the Indian population of Mato Grosso attached to the annual report of President Joaquim José de Oliveira, 1849. Antonio Colbacchini, *I Bororos Orientali,* Moreira Neto, *Política indigenista,* 169.

210 *a profound melancholy.'* Waehneldt, 'Exploração', 226.

210 *more civilised nations.'* Ibid., 215.

210 *take just revenge.'* Ibid., 224.

210 *indolent, inoffensive tribe'.* Chandless, 'Notes on the Rivers Arinos, Juruena and Tapajós, JRGS **32**, 270–1, 278, 1862. Moure, 'Indiens', 339–40; Leverger, 'Apontamentos cronologicos', 354 (on the 1836 raid); speech by Herculano Ferreira Penna, Cuiabá, 1863, 62, 65–6; report by Director-General of Mato Grosso Indians attached to that of President Francisco José Cardoso Junior, 1872, Moreira Neto, *Política indigenista,* 154–5, 171, 182–4. The Cabixi tribe, closely akin to the Parecis, was blamed for most of the aggressions that provoked these reprisals.

Chapter 12   *THE CABANAGEM REBELLION*

212 *region very surely'.* Araújo e Amazonas, *Diccionario topográphico,* 257. On the economic affairs of Amazonia in the late eighteenth century, see: Manuel Nunes Dias' essays in praise of the Companhia Geral; but Dauril Alden showed that the average output of cacao during the Company period was actually less than it had been under the missionaries, 'The Significance of Cacao Production in the Amazon in the Late Colonial Period'; Arthur Cézar Ferreira Reis, *O processo histórico da economia amazonense,* 40–6; Santos, *História econômica da Amazônia,* 17–20.

212 *the royal treasury.* Manoel da Gama Lobo d'Almada to Sousa Coutinho, 10 March 1798, *Biblioteca e Arquivo Público do Pará,* cod. 703, 81; Mac-

Lachlan, 'The Indian Labor Structure', 219–20.

213 *and uninterrupted crisis'.* Luiz Cordeiro, *O Estado do Pará, seu commercio e industrias, de 1719 a 1920* (Belém, 1920) 20; Ferreira Reis, *O processo histórico da economia amazonense,* 45–6; Santos, *História econômica da Amazônia,* 27–8; MacLachlan, 'The Indian Labor Structure', 227–8.

214 *of our society.'* Araújo e Amazonas, *Diccionario topográphico,* 153.

214 *in name alone.'* Ibid., 153–4. This was confirmed in an official report by Major José de Brito Inglês, who was sent by the government to examine conditions in the province. His report was presented in 1819 and described the primitive way of life and determined efforts to subdue the

tropical Amazonian environment. Towns were stagnant and most development occurred on large estates — tracts of river and forest that were partly cleared as ranches or plantations. The authorities were trying to suppress revolutionary ideas that might undermine Portuguese authority in this backwater. Wherever he went, Major Brito Inglês reported exploitation of native labour that amounted to slavery. Brito Inglez, *Memoria sobre a Capitania do Pará*, RGHB **203**, 1949.

215 *and public charity.*' Fernandes de Sousa, *Noticias geographicas*, 474.

215 *should derive profit.*' Ibid., 474.

215 *for their work.*' Ibid., 475.

215 *cloth mills, etc.*' Araújo e Amazonas, *Diccionario topográphico*, 264; Accioli de Cerqueira e Silva, *Corografia paraense*, 279. Spix and Martius also visited a large plantation that Governor Victorio da Costa had at the mouth of Lake Ega (Tefé) on the Solimões, using Indians 'in forced labour or for trifling pay', *Reise*, **3** 1165; Portuguese trans., **3** 263.

215 *province] currently languishes.*' Fernandes de Sousa, *Noticias geographicas*, 478. Father José Maria Coelho, ecclesiastical visitor of the province, visited the Negro and Branco in 1823 and gave precise reports of the catastrophic depopulation. He listed the number of dwellings in twenty-seven riverside settlements and found a total of only 246 hearths still occupied. By contrast, Father Coelho listed the number of hearths in each settlement when it was flourishing under the missionaries in mid-eighteenth century. He arrived at the extraordinary total of 25,110 dwellings in those same twenty-seven settlements. There had thus been depopulation of 99 per cent! José Maria Coelho, *Duas memorias sobre a Capitania de São José do Rio Negro*, RHGB **203** 125–8, 1949. Two decades later, João Henrique Mattos reported that the Rio Negro had only eighteen settlements where

it had once had thirty-two, 'and these heavily depopulated and ruined'. Mattos, *Relatorio do estado de decadencia em que se acha o Alto Amazonas (1845)* RHGB **325** 146–7, 1979. According to Coelho, the only town that had grown was Barra (Manaus); but Mattos said that by 1845 Barra was also very reduced.

215 *already almost inanimate.*' Ibid., 479.

216 *of another species.*' Ibid.

216 *their customary idleness.*' Francisco Ricardo Zany memorial to the Emperor, in Arthur Cézar Ferreira Reis, 'O Amazonas nos primeiros tempos do Império', RHGB **316** 119–20, July–Sept. 1977. Colonel Zany went from strength to strength. When the militia was abolished after the Cabanagem rebellion, he became a colonel in the regular army. He also became a Comendador of the Order of Christ, Inspector of all state factories of the Rio Negro, and 'Director of Natural Produce'. He used his position as inspector of government factories to slaughter the cattle of the Rio Branco. But, according to João Henrique de Mattos in 1845, Zany 'disliked the new system of government' after the Cabanagem and returned to his native Italy, where he died. Mattos, *Relatório*, 160.

216 *in the forests.*' Spix and Martius, *Reise*, **3**, bk 9, ch. 1, 1116, Portuguese trans., **3** 222. Although they all came from the Japurá–Caquetá tributary of the Solimões, the three tribes spoke different languages: Pasé spoke Aruak, Yurí their own isolated tongue, and Makuna spoke Tukano.

217 *almost bestial manner.*' Ibid., **3**, bk 8, ch. 4, 1071; Portuguese trans., **3** 182.

217 *any other tribe.*' Ibid., 1073.

217 *themselves good houses.*' Anon, 'Illustração necessaria e interessante, relativa ao gentio da nação Mura', ms. quoted in Moreira Neto, *Política indigenista*, 11.

218 *rather than fear.*' Marcoy, *Voyage*, **2** 397.

218 *by other natives.*' Spix and Martius, *Reise*, **3**, bk 8, ch. 3, 1051.

218 *with unparalleled cruelty.'* Ibid., **3**, bk 8, ch. 4, 1069—70; Portuguese trans., **3** 181.

218 *some already Christians.'* Casal, *Corografia Brasílica*, **2** 319—20.

218 *and even poorer'.* Captain Miguel de Castro and Antonio de França, *Abertura de communicação commercial . . . por meio da navegação dos rios Arinos e Tapajós*, RHGB **31**: 1 126—7, 1868.

219 *their free condition.'* Spix and Martius, *Reise*, **3**, bk 9, ch. 6, 1310. At the time of the Germans' visit in 1819, the Mundurukú were being resettled in new villages of former Jesuit missions: a thousand warriors (or a total population of some five thousand people) in each of the villages of Santa Cruz (founded 1803, seven days' journey above Santarém), Boim (former Santo Inácio), and nearby Pinhel on the Tapajós; 1600 warriors at the big Maué mission (Uasituba) run by the 'fine old' Carmelite missionary José Alves das Chagas; a thousand at the mission of Novo-Monte-Carmelo on the Canumã; and a total population of a thousand at Jurutí, all west of Santarém on small southern tributaries of the Amazon. Ibid., 1317 and 1338.

219 *civilised community life.'* Ibid.

219 *towards his charges.'* Ibid., **3**, bk 9, ch. 4, 1219—20; Portuguese trans., 323.

220 *the white judge.'* Ibid., 1221.

220 *not buy them.'* Ibid., 1230.

220 *in racial mixing.'* Ibid., 1237.

220 *all other Indians.'* Ibid., 1242.

221 *are too sour.'* Ibid., 1249—50.

221 *better than blood.'* Ibid., 1250.

221 *died without attention.'* Ibid., 1264—5. Martius wrote that twenty thousand Indian slaves had been brought down from the Japurá during the previous eighty years. The first reference to the Miranya was by Monteiro de Noronha, who went up the Solimões in 1768: he spoke of the tribe's anthropophagy, its tapir- and cayman-hide shields, its poisoned arrows, and the distinctive black line

that its warriors painted between their ears and noses. Rodrigues Ferreira said in 1788 that the Miranya were one of the most populous tribes of the north bank of the Solimões and were constantly at war with neighbouring tribes from whom they took prisoners. Alexandre Rodrigues Ferreira, *Viagem filosófica . . . Memoria antropologia* (1788) (Rio de Janeiro, 1974), 91; Expedito Arnaud, 'Os índios mirânia e a expansão luso-brasileira (médio Solimões—Japurá, Amazonas)', BMPEG *Antropologia*, Nova série, **81** 2, Belém, July 1981.

221 *liver and dropsy.'* Ibid., 1277.

222 *and other circumstances.'* Ibid., 1277.

222 *down by disease.'* Silva e Sousa, *Noticias geographicas*, 489.

222 *they usually own.'* Ibid., 489—90.

222 *and immoral men!'* Ibid., 490.

223 *out for remedy.'* Ibid., 501.

223 *to continue unheard.'* Ibid., 501.

223 *God and men.'* Ibid., 502—3.

223 *in deep sleep.'* Ibid.

224 *use of Indians.'* Henry Lister Maw, *Journal of a passage from the Pacific to the Atlantic* (London, 1829), 267.

224 *boats or canoes.'* Ibid., 270.

224 *Indians at work'.* Ibid., 308.

224 *all three combined'.* Ibid., 319.

224 *the absolute authority?'* Ibid., 434.

224 *found and captured.'* Ibid., 435.

224 *esteem or humanity.'* Ibid., 432.

225 *uninhabitable for Indians'.* Governor Sousa Coutinho to Rodrigo da Sousa Coutinho, Belém, 2 Aug. 1797, in MacLachlan, 'The Indian Labor Struggle', 227.

226 *in the city.'* H. Smith, *Brazil: The Amazons and the coast*, 71. Domingos Raiol, *Motins políticos . . . da provincia do Pará*, 5 vols (Rio de Janeiro and Belém, 1865—91) **1** 60. Accioli de Cerqueira e Silva, *Corografia paraense*, 223.

226 *or six years.'* Adalbert of Prussia, *Aus meinem Reisetagebuch*, trans. Robert Schomburgk and John Taylor, *Travels of His Royal Highness Prince Adalbert of Prussia* **2** 153—4. Accioli de Cerqueira

e Silva, *Corografia paraense*, 223—4.

226 *full of tumults.'* H. Smith, *Brazil*, 73—4.

227 *to anything white.'* Francisco Soares d'Andrea in Moreira Neto, *Política indigenista*, 15.

227 *abyss of revolts!'* Bernardo Lobo de Souza, President of Pará, to the Ministro do Império, Chichorro da Gama, Belém, 13 May 1834, in ibid., 16.

229 *lost their lives.'* Charles Jenks Smith to John Forsyth, Belém, 20 Jan. 1835, quoted in Herndon and Gibbon, *Exploration*, 1 341.

230 *length of time.'* Moraes Rego Reis, *A Cabanagem* (Manaus, 1965) 41. The main historian of these turbulent events was Domingos Raiol, Baron of Guajará, who published a five-volume history between 1865 and 1891: *Motins políticos . . . da Provincia do Pará*. Also Jorge Hurley, *A Cabanagem* (Belém, 1936) and Ernesto Cruz, *Historia do Pará* (Belém, 1963).

230 *horror and anarchy'*. Adalbert of Prussia, *Travels*, 154.

230 *more than here.'* Ibid., 154—5.

230 *classes of society.'* Sérgio Buarque de Holanda, *História geral da civilização brasileira*, II, *O Brasil monárquico* (4th edn, Rio de Janeiro and São Paulo, 1978) 2 116—17; João Capistrano de Abreu, *Capítulos de história colonial* (5th edn, Brasília, 1963) 190; Basílio de Magalhães, *Estudos de História do Brasil*, Brasiliana 171 (Rio de Janeiro and São Paulo, 1942) 213; Leslie Bethell and José Murilo de Carvalho, 'Brazil from the Middle of the Nineteenth Century to the Paraguayan War', in L. Bethell (ed.), *The Cambridge History of Latin America* (Cambridge, 1985) 3 702—4.

231 *superior white Brazilians.'* Eduard Poeppig, *Reise in Chile, Peru and auf dem Amazonenstrome*, 2 439.

231 *white man alive.'* President Francisco Jozé de Souza Soares d'Andrea, *Falla dirigida . . . à Assemblea Provincal*, Belém, 2 March 1838, 4; Moreira Neto, *Política indigenista*, 19.

231 *is very general.'* William H. Edwards, *A voyage up the River Amazon* (London, 1847) 10.

231 *suffered from it.'* Bernardino de Souza, *Lembranças e curiosidades do valle do Amazonas* (Pará, 1873) 113—14.

231 *their own faces.'* Richard Spruce, *Notes of a botanist on the Amazon and Andes*, 2 vols (London, 1908) 1 61.

231 *all the Europeans.'* Smyth and Lowe, *Journey from Lima to Pará*, 300.

232 *numbers of Portuguese.'* Ibid.

232 *of the fort*. Angelim told this story to Domingos Raiol, who recorded the incident in *Motins políticos*, 5 39.

233 *of the day.'* Kidder, *Sketches of residence*, 2 318.

234 *by sure methods!'* Soares d'Andrea, *Falla*, Belém, 2 March 1838, 5; Moreira Neto, *Política indigenista*, 19—20.

234 *the despised Indians.'* Kidder, *Sketches of residence*, 2 318—19.

234 *their bestial instincts'*. Bento de Figueiredo Tenreiro Aranha, *Archivo do Amazonas*, 2 vols (Manaus, 1906, 1908), 1 20. Captain João Henrique de Mattos, who wrote a report on the state of the upper Amazon in 1845, said that Bararoá claimed to be of German descent. He had been exiled to the Rio Negro for political crimes. Bararoá claimed repayment from the government for the costs of his private army and President Manoel Jorge Rodrigues agreed. Bararoá demanded from the authorities in Manaus that he be rewarded by cattle from the upper Rio Branco (modern Roraima) and Captain Mattos saw his men ship jerked meat from 391 animals down to Belém. João Henrique de Mattos, *Relatório sôbre o estado de decadência em que se acha o Alto Amazonas*, RHGB 325 159, 1979.

In July 1838 the Schomburgk brothers were entertained at Fort São Joaquim on the upper Rio Branco by Bararoá's brother Pedro Ayres. Schomburgk described Captain Ambrosio Ayres as 'commander of the military and civil affairs of the

Upper Amazons' and wrote how impressed he was by the reception he received from a government fully engaged in suppressing a five-year-old insurrection. Robert Schomburgk, 'Journey to the sources of the Essequibo', JRGS **10** 179–80, 1841.

235 *them in cruelty.'* H. Smith, *Brazil*, 75–6. Mattos, *Relatório*, 145–6.

235 *a horrifying interpretation.'* Araújo e Amazonas, *Diccionario topográphico*, 67.

235 *of this victim.'* President Soares d'Andrea to Minister of War, Belém, 23 Oct. 1838, quoted in Moreira Neto, *Política indigenista*, 21. Bernardino de Souza, *Lembranças*, 21. Lucas Alexandre Boiteux, *Marinha imperial versus Cabanagem*, 63. Robert Schomburgk wrote that Ambrosio Ayres 'Bararoá' was killed by the Cabanos while trying to dislodge them from an island from which they had been harassing shipping on the lower Madeira and Amazon rivers. Schomburgk, 'Journey from Fort San Joaquim on the Rio Branco to Roraima . . .', JRGS **10** 192–3, 1841.

235 *that devours everything.'* Soares d'Andrea to Ministro do Império, Belém, 8 Nov. 1836, in Moreira Neto, *Política indigenista*, 18.

235 *of noble sentiments'.* Soares d'Andrea to his successor Bernardo de Souza Franco, Belém, 8 April 1839, in ibid., 22.

236 *by his conduct.'* Soares d'Andrea, 8 April 1839, paras 5 and 6, in ibid., 25.

236 *who deserve it'.* Ibid., 25.

236 *commanded by terror.'* Bernardo de Souza Franco, Oficio, 25 Dec. 1839, ms. in Arquivo Nacional quoted in ibid., 27.

236 *and civil wars.'* Ibid.

236 *and received them.'* Annual report to Legislative Assembly by the new President of Pará, João Antonio de Miranda, Belém, 1840, 7. Luzéia was the former mission of Maués. In 1798 it had been formed into a town (surrounded by the huts of the Mawé Indians) by Captains Luiz Pereira da Cruz and José Rodrigues Pinto, and its name Luzeia was a contraction of their first names. Lourenço Araújo e Amazonas wrote that in 1852 it contained 3400 Mawé and Mundurukú living in four hundred huts: *Diccionario topográphico*, 178–9.

236 *that never fled?'* Maugin de Lincourt report quoted in Herndon and Gibbon, *Exploration of the Valley of the Amazon*, **1** 315. The English naturalist Henry Walter Bates was reminded of Mundurukú alliance with the whites: *The Naturalist on the River Amazons*, 1943 edn, 243. Chief Joaquim was given a commission in the Brazilian army. But he was denied greater rewards from the Emperor because of an adverse report about the Mundurukú by a Brazilian colonel. Robert Murphy, *Headhunter's Heritage*, 33. João Henrique de Mattos, an officer in the government forces during the Cabanagem, said that its last battle was in Mundurukú territory on the upper Abacaxis river. He praised the tribe as being half civilised, of great utility to the state, 'skilled in all labour, docile to civil education and religion.' But the Mundurukú had been neglected and had not progressed because of the rebellion. Mattos, *Relatório*, 172, 174.

236 *befits his position.'* H. Smith, *Brazil*, 133.

Chapter 13 TREATMENT OF INDIANS IN AMAZONIA

238 *and negro immigrants.'* Bates, *Naturalist*, 41.

238 *with the family.'* Ibid., 41–2.

238 *their base ingratitude.'* Ibid., 42.

239 *with great dignity.'* Ibid., 42.

239 *most complete immobility.'* Osculati, *Esplorazione delle regioni equatoriali lungo . . . il fiume delle Amazzoni* (Milan, 1850) 167.

239 *form of work.'* Avé-Lallement, *Reise*

durch Nord-Brasilien, trans. Lima Castro (Rio de Janeiro, 1961) **2** 87.

239 *in Vila Bela.'* Ibid.

239 *easy to grow.* Humboldt, *Political essays* (London, 1822) bk 4, ch. 9, 380.

239 *regular easterly breezes.* Professor Agassiz in *Jornal do Commercio*, Rio de Janeiro, 18 May 1865. A. C. Tavares Bastos, *O valle do Amazonas* (Rio de Janeiro, 1866) 303.

240 *that attracts imports.'* Tavares Bastos, *Amazonas*, 293.

240 *and Indian blood.'* Bates, *Naturalist*, 83–4.

240 *insolence and insubordination'.* Spruce, *Notes of a botanist*, **1** 271.

240 *caused by glaciation.* Prof. Agassiz, *Jornal do Commercio*, Rio de Janeiro, 18 May 1865; E. Reclus, *Revue des Deux Mondes*, Paris, 13 June 1862; Gonçalves Dias letter from Manaus, 1861, in Tavares Bastos, *Amazonas*, 300; Chandless, 'Notes on the rivers Maué-assú', 424; Mathews, *Up the Amazon*, 59. Olga Coudreau described malaria forcing back explorers of the Cuminá (a tributary of the northern Curuá river) in 1877 and 1891. She lost her explorer husband to the disease on the Trombetas in 1899, and suffered from it on the Curuá in 1901 and Mapuera later that year: Coudreau, *Voyage au Trombetas*, 122–3, *Voyage au Cuminá*, 142; *Voyage au Rio Curuá*, 80; *Voyage à la Mapuera*, 16.

240 *the Indian energy.'* Louis Agassiz quoted in Santa-Anna Néry, *The land of the Amazons*, 146–7.

240 *of the Indian'.* Ibid., 146.

240 *but very indolent'.* Ibid.

240 *any disagreeable odor.'* Professor and Mrs Louis Agassiz, *A journey in Brazil* (London, 1868) 263.

241 *suspicious and resentful.'* Araújo e Amazonas, *Diccionario topográphico*, 154 and 147.

241 *standing of slaves.'* Ibid., 156.

241 *of the region.'* Ibid.

241 *gift of patience.'* H. Smith, *Brazil*, 388–9.

242 *are mutually rewarded.'* Spix and Martius, *Reise*, **3**, bk 9, ch. 6, 1363.

242 *be carefully examined.'* Humboldt quoted in Santa-Anna Néry, *The land of the Amazons*, 288.

242 *and La Plata.'* Herndon and Gibbon report to Congress, February 1853, in ibid., 293–4.

243 *an incalculable prosperity.'* Abbé Durand, 'La Madeira et son bassin', *Bulletin de la Société de Géographie*, 461, Paris, 1875.

243 *take their rise.'* Richard Spruce, 'On the River Purus, a Tributary of the Amazon', in Clements Markham (ed.), *Travels of Pedro de Cieza de León*, Hakluyt Society, 1 ser., **33** (London, 1864) 1.

243 *if we must'.* Maury, *The Amazon, and the Atlantic Slopes of South America* (Washington, DC, 1853), in Hélène Rivière d'Arc, 'La formation du lieu Amazonie au XIXe. siècle', CAL **18** 196, 1978.

243 *no more recognisable.'* Mawe, *Journal of a passage*, 45.

243 *history of nature.'* Spix and Martius, *Reise*, **3** 935, 1208.

243 *the Amazon region.'* Bates, *Naturalist*, 42.

243 *things fast approaching'.* Keller, *The Amazon and Madeira Rivers* (London, 1874) 115.

244 *from these regions.'* Ibid.

244 *to this result.'* Coudreau, *Voyage entre Tocantins et Xingu* (Paris, 1899) 122.

244 *or are extinguished.'* Coudreau, *Voyage au Tapajóz* (Paris, 1897) 25.

244 *repast of friendship.'* Ibid., 145–6.

244 *them by assimilation.'* José Verissimo, 'As populações indigenas e mestiças da Amazonia' (Pará, 1878), RHGB **50**: 1 388–9, 1007.

244 *men of goodwill.'* Coudreau, *Voyage au Tapajóz*, 146.

245 *against the weaker.'* Raiol, 'Catachese de índios no Pará', 145.

245 *fatal to them.'* Ibid., 175.

245 *of our money.'* Couto de Magalhães, *O selvagem*, 190.

246 *ceased to exist.'* Koch-Grünberg, *Festschrift Eduard Seler* (Stuttgart, 1922) 241, trans. by Kenneth Grubb, *From Pacific to Atlantic: South American Studies* (London, 1933) 230.

246 *powerless to assist.'* Grubb, *Amazon to Andes*, 27.

246 *even in Europe.'* Spix and Martius, *Reise*, **3**, bk. 9, ch. 4, 1205. Martius had separated from Spix during this journey up the Japurá in January 1820.

246 *whites have passed.'* Stradelli, 'L'Uaupés e gli Uaupés', *Bolletino della Società Geografica Italiana*, 3 ser., **3** 434, 1890.

246 *of uambé liana.'* Ibid., 435.

247 *dull and shy.'* Chandless, 'Notes on the rivers Maué-assú, Abacaxis, and Canumá', JRGS **40** 425, 1870.

247 *as a pendant.'* Araújo e Amazonas, *Diccionario topográphica*, 155.

247 *covers the breast'.* Ibid.

247 *to support them.'* Avé-Lallement, *Viagem pelo norte do Brasil*, **2** 117.

247 *rapidly with age.'* Ibid.

247 *in that wilderness.'* Araújo e Amazonas, *Diccionario topográphico*, 35.

248 *fish and hammocks.'* Edwards, *A voyage up the River Amazon*, 156. Accioli de Cerqueira e Silva, *Corografia paraense*, **1** 274.

248 *the desirable effect.'* Edwards, *A voyage up the River Amazon*, 156.

248 *a valuable product'.* Ibid., 157. Copaíba is *Copaifera officinalis*; quinine comes from the bitter bark of the quina shrub, *Cinchona*.

248 *injure the system.'* Ibid. Herndon and Gibbon, *Exploration*, **2** 307. For more information on guaraná, see: Ghillean T. Prance, 'The Increased Importance of Ethnobotany and Underexploited Plants in a Changing Amazon', in John Hemming (ed.), *Change in the Amazon Basin*, vol. 1, *Man's Impact on Forests and Rivers* (Manchester, 1985) 130–1; Marcoy, *Voyage*, **2** 446.

249 *the civilised world.'* Edwards, *A voyage up the River Amazon*, 157.

249 *the wet months.'* Bates, *Naturalist*, **2** 212. Rodrigues Ferreira, 'Memoria sobre a jurararreté' (1786) and 'Memoria sobre as variedades de tartarugas que hão no Estado do Grão Pará e do emprego que lhe dão'

(undated), both unpublished manuscripts in the Seção de Manuscritos of the Biblioteca Nacional in Rio de Janeiro. Robin Anderson, 'Following Curupira', 16–18. General surveys of turtle fishing include: J. Coutinho, 'Sur les tortues de l'Amazone', *Bulletin de la Société de Zoologie d'Acclimatation*, 2 ser., **5**, Paris, 1868; J. Mallinson, 'The River Turtles of the Amazon', *Oryx* **8**:4, 1966; Nigel J. H. Smith, 'Destructive Exploitation of the South American River Turtle', *Yearbook: Association of Pacific Coast Geographers* **36** 85–102, Corvallis, Oregon, 1974; R. Mittermeier, 'A Turtle in Every Pot', *Animal Kingdom*, 9–14, April–May 1975.

250 *he is secured.'* Edwards, *A voyage up the River Amazon*, 152; Laurent Saint-Cricq, *Voyage à travers l'Amérique du Sud de l'Océan Pacifique à l'Océan Atlantique* (Paris, 1853), trans. (London 1873) **2**:1 40 (about the Conibo). Henry Bates and Jules Crevaux both include drawings of turtle hunts in their books.

250 *of the product.'* Manoel da Gama Lobo d'Almada, *Descriptive account of the Rio Branco* (1788), in Foreign Office, *Question de la Frontière, Annexe*, **1** 189.

250 *such as piranha'.* Rodrigues Ferreira, 'Memoria sobre a jurarareté', in Anderson, 'Following Curupira', 16. Jurarareté is the Indian name for the podocnemis turtle.

251 *to the other.'* Herndon and Gibbon, *Exploration*, **2** 304. On the use of turtle-egg oil for lighting lamps, see Major José de Brito Inglez, *Memoria sobre a Capitania do Pará* (Rio de Janeiro, 1819), in RHGB **203** 142, 1949.

251 *for turtle rising.'* Chandless, 'Ascent of the River Purûs', JRGS **36** 93, 99, 1866.

251 *deposited their eggs.'* Coudreau, *Voyage au Yamundá* (Paris, 1899) 71.

251 *have collected together.'* Edward Mathews, *Up the Amazon*; N. Smith, 'Destructive Exploitation', 93–4. J. Coutinho, 'Sur les tortues de

l'Amazone', 160. Humboldt, *Personal narrative of travels in the equinoctial regions of America* (London, 1852) **2** 189; Spix and Martius, *Reise 3*, bk 9, ch. 2, 1118 Nigel Smith gives a table of annual quantities of turtle oil in 'Destructive Exploitation', 93. His màin sources for these statistics are: José Verissimo, *A pesca na Amazônia* (Belém, 1895); Luis Gonçalves, *The Amazon: historical, chorographical and statistical outline up to the year 1903* (New York, 1904); Santa-Anna Néry, *The land of the Amazons*.

252 *goods they exchange.'* Jerónimo Francisco Coelho, Relatório to provincial assembly, 1849, in Moreira Neto, *Política indigenista*, 44—5.

252 *of the Indians.'* Avé-Lallement, *Viagem*, **2**, 129.

252 *do not commit.'* Bishop Dom Antonio de Macedo Costa to the Ministro do Império, Belém, 21 Dec. 1865, in Tavares Bastos, *Amazonas*, 285; Arthur Cézar Ferreira Reis, *O seringal e o seringueiro*, 125.

253 *debt to him.'* Francisco Carlos de Araújo Brusque, Relatório, 1 Sept. 1862, in Moreira Neto, *Política indigenista*, 49—50.

253 *on his service.'* Ibid., 50.

253 *among his accomplices.'* Ibid.

253 *[and] horrible iniquities.'* Araújo e Amazonas, *Diccionario topográphico*, 42.

254 *for the regatao.'* Speech of President A. B. C. de Albuquerque de Lacerda, Manaus, 1864, 135.

254 *their designs upset.'* President B. A. de Magalhães Taques, São Luis do Maranhão, 1857, in Moreira Neto, *Política indigenista*, 108. Tavares Bastos, *Amazonas*, 283, 286; Araújo e Amazonas, *Diccionario topográphico*, 43; José Verissimo, *As populações indígenas* (Belém, 1878), RHGB **50**: 1 311, 1887.

254 *objects of curiosity.'* Raiol, 'Catachese de indios', 164; Antonio Henrique Leal, *Locubrações*, 49.

255 *of their Indians.'* President Sebastião do Rego Barros, Fala, Belém, 26 Oct. 1855, 36—7, in Moreira Neto, *Política*

indigenista, 46—7.

255 *whites usually are.'* Bates, *Naturalist*, 270.

255 *'those official persecutors'* President A. B. C. de Albuquerque de Lacerda, Relatório, Manaus, 1864, 135, in Moreira Neto, *Política indigenista*, 86; Barão de Jaguarary, Report on Indians of Pará, Annexo 28 to Relatório of President Manoel Frias e Vasconcellos, Belém, 1 Oct. 1859, in Raiol, 'Catachese de indios', 165. This report named the ten Indian aldeias in Pará as: Acará, Capim, Bragança, Cametá, Oeiras, Xingú, Souzel, Paru and Jari, Trombetas, Tapajós.

255 *witnessed these facts.'* Dom António, Bishop of Pará, to Ministro do Império, Belém, 21 Dec. 1865, in Tavares Bastos, *Amazonas*, 289—90.

256 *they were treated.'* President A. M. de Campos Mello, Relatório, São Luis, 1862, 10. The colónia of São Pedro do Pindaré (now the town of Pindaré Mearim) had 120 Indians of various tribes in 1849 but had shrunk to fifty adults and eighteen children by the time of the 1862 report. In 1864 it was down to a total of forty-four: César Augusto Marques, *Diccionário histórico-geographico da Provincia do Maranhão*, 142–3. Charles Wagley and Eduardo Galvão, *Os índios tenetehara* (Rio de Janeiro, 1961) 25.

256 *and disastrous conflict.'* President Olimpio Machado, Relatório, São Luis, 1854, 31. Moreira Neto, *Política indigenista*, 100. Nimuendajú, *Eastern Timbira*, 15.

257 *they are accustomed.'* President Olimpio Machado, Relatório, São Luis, 1854, 31.

257 *determine its origin.'* Ibid., 61.

257 *to become extinct'.* President B. A. de Magalhães Taques, Relatório, São Luis, 1857, 18. Moreira Neto, *Política indigenista*, 108. Marques, *Apontamentos*, entry for 'Colonização'. Nimuendajú, *Eastern Timbira*, 15.

257 *for social life'.* Report on Maranhão Indians, probably by the Diretor

Geral de Indios, 1855, in Moreira Neto, *Política indigenista*, 104.

257 *hospitable and faithful.'* President Magalhães Taques, Relatório, 1857, 19. The colonia of Januária was founded in 1854 near an old Jesuit mission called São Francisco Xavier that still had eighty Guajajara (Tenetehara). A further 128 Indians were attracted to it.

258 *more cultivated life'.* Ibid.

258 *daily declining'.* President João Silveira de Souza, Relatório, São Luis, 1860, 20. By 1864 Januária had 121 Indians (compared to 779 under the Jesuits a century earlier): Marques, *Diccionário*, 143. Wagley and Galvão, *Os índios tenetehara*, 25. By the end of the nineteenth century this area was invaded by settlers who founded the towns of Santa Cruz and Sapucaia. Both towns were abandoned in 1913 because of attack by Urubu Indians and the collapse of the rubber boom.

258 *rather harsh behaviour'.* Relatório of Diretor Geral de Indios of Maranhão, annexed to annual report of President Campos Mello, 1862, 11.

258 *among the Indians'.* Ibid. Moreira Neto, *Política indigenista*, 114. Nimuendajú, *Eastern Timbira*, 33.

259 *our civilised people.'* Vice-President M. Jansen Ferreira, Relatório, São Luis, 1867, 7; Moreira Neto, *Política indigenista*, 118.

259 *white and intelligent'.* President Manoel Freitas, Relatório, São Luis, 1883, 22. The 1872 report was by S. E. Carneiro da Cunha.

259 *fazendeiros and farmers.'* Ibid. Moreira Neto, *Política indigenista*, 122−3.

260 *considered primitive.'* João Barbosa Rodrigues, 'Tribo dos Tembés: índole, casamento e morte', in Mello Moraes Filho, *Revista da Exposição de Anthropologia Brasileira* (Rio de Janeiro, 1882) 25. Gustavo Dodt, *Descrição dos rios Parnahyba e Gurupy* (1872) (Brasiliana, 5 ser. **138**, São Paulo, 1939) 172. Expedito Arnaud, 'O direito indígena e a ocupação territorial: o caso dos índios Tembé do alto Guamá (Pará)', RMP n.s. **28** 223, 1981/2.

260 *the martyred missionaries.* Mercio Gomes, 'Porque índios brigam com posseiros: o caso dos índios Guajajara', in Dalmo de Abreu Dallari, Manuela Carneiro da Cunha and Lux Vidal (eds), *A questão da terra*, Cadernos da Comissão Pró-Índio **2** (São Paulo, 1981) 54−5; Nimuendajú, *Eastern Timbira*, 33; Charles Wagley, 'Cultural Influences on Population: a comparison of two Tupi tribes', in Daniel R. Gross (ed.), *Peoples and Cultures of Native South America* (New York, 1973) 146−7; S. Fróes Abreu, *Na terra das palmeiras* (Rio de Janeiro, 1931) 215−27; Charles Wagley and Eduardo Galvão, *Os índios tenetehara* (Rio de Janeiro, 1961) 27.

261 *in his behalf.'* Edwards, *A voyage up the Amazon*, 20.

261 *of apathetic indifference.'* Ibid. Also, Kidder, *Sketches of residence*, **2** 268.

261 *with these blunderbusses.'* Richard Schomburgk, *Reisen in Britisch-Guiana*, trans. Walter Roth (Georgetown, 1923) **2** 235. The Schomburgks were the second foreign expedition to describe Fort São Joaquim. In 1816 Charles Waterton, the eccentric squire of Walton Hall near Wakefield in Yorkshire, ventured into northern Brazil in search of the poison curare. Stricken by malaria, the commander of the Fort took pity on him and nursed Waterton back to health. Waterton described the fort as much neglected, with its gate and parts of its walls destroyed by flood waters. It was being repaired by the present commander. Charles Waterton, *Wanderings in South America* (1826), ed. L. Harrison Matthews (London, 1973) 29. After unpaid and mutinous troops killed the fort's commander, it was rebuilt in 1842. Despite this, João Henrique de Mattos described it a few years later as 'all fairly ruined'. Mattos, *Relatório do estado de decadencia*, RHGB **325** 153, 1979.

262 *upon their drivers.'* M: Richard Schomburgk, *Reisen,* 2 235.

262 *for the navy'.* Robert Schomburgk, 'Report of the Third Expedition into the interior . . .', JRGS 10 183, 1841.

262 *to his allies'.* Robert Schomburgk to T. F. Buxton, Fort São Joaquim, 25 April 1838, in Foreign Office, *Question de la Frontière, Annexe,* 2 8.

262 *to their backs.'* Schomburgk, 'Report', 189.

262 *loaded and primed.'* Ibid.

262 *the darker ages.'* Schomburgk to T. F. Buxton, São Joaquim, 25 Aug. 1838, in Foreign Office, *Question de la Frontière, Annexe,* 2 9.

263 *would be returned.'* Schomburgk, 'Report', 190. This Ambrosio Ayres was 'Bararoá', the notorious hunter of Cabanagem rebels.

263 *only by women.'* Ibid., 253.

263 *the slaving expedition'.* Ibid., 255. Also, Robert Schomburgk, *Twelve Views in the Interior of Guiana,* 23–4.

263 *the next day.'* Schomburgk, 'Report', 263.

263 *in the forests.'* Spruce letter to George Bentham, São Gabriel, 15 April 1852, in *Notes of a botanist,* 1 271.

263 *of civil war.'* Herndon and Gibbon, *Exploration,* 1 (by Herndon) 264–5. The Guarda Policial took the place of the Guarda Nacional, disbanded during the Cabanagem in 1836.

264 *disposition to resist.'* Franz Keller, *The Amazon and Madeira Rivers* (London, 1874) 38.

264 *questions are asked.'* Agassiz, *A journey in Brazil,* 269, also 258 and 290.

264 *them especially victims.'* Ibid., 290–1.

264 *a Tapuyo Indian.'* Paul Marcoy, *Voyage à travers l'Amérique du Sud,* 2 vols (Paris, 1869) 2 409, 336.

264 *of their birth.'* Wickham, *Rough notes of a journey through the wilderness* (London, 1872) 135–6.

264 *the Brazilian army'.* Ibid., 140, 293.

264 *the Paraguayan War'.* Brown and Lidstone, *Fifteen thousand miles on the Amazon* (London, 1878) 356.

265 *entire Indian population'.* Castelnau, *Expédition,* 5 143.

265 *before the door'.* Robert Schomburgk, *Twelve Views in the Interior of Guiana,* 24.

265 *of the Indians.'* Ibid.

265 *without any recompense.'* Richard Schomburgk, *Travels in British Guiana,* 2 315.

265 *and private gain.'* President Jerónimo Francisco Coelho address to provincial assembly, Belém, 1 Oct. 1849, quoted in Herndon and Gibbon, *Exploration,* 1 276–7.

265 *speculation by abuse!'* Ibid., 277.

265 *more than three-quarters'.* Ibid.

266 *in his employ'.* Edwards, *A voyage up the River Amazon,* 81.

266 *it has done.'* Ibid.

266 *serve the State'.* Herndon and Gibbon, *Exploration,* 1 256.

266 *and manioc flour).'* Castelnau, *Expédition,* 5 143.

266 *or regular labour.'* Report by President Herculano Ferreira Pena, Manaus, 1853, 217, in Moreira Neto, *Política indigenista,* 72.

267 *and domestic service.'* Ibid.

Chapter 14   THE RUBBER BOOM

272 *called seringa milk'.* Rodrigues Ferreira, 'Memoria sobre os gentios Cambebas' (ms. in Biblioteca Nacional, Rio de Janeiro, 1783), quoted in Ferreira Reis, *O seringal e o seringueiro,* 50. Charles Marie de la Condamine, *Relation abrégée d'un voyage fait dans l'intérieur de l'Amérique Méridionale* (Paris, 1745) 78–9. Condamine wrote about rubber in a letter from Quito which was read to the Academy of Sciences by Buffon on 24 June 1736; Condamine then lectured about it to the Academy on 28 April 1745. Fresnau's lecture was in 1751. Other chroniclers who mentioned

seeing rubber were: Pedro Martyr d'Anghiera, Bernardo de Sahagun, Antonio de Herrera Tordesillas and Francisco Javier de Torquemada in his *Monarquía Indiana* of 1615. For the early history of rubber, see: Fordyce Jones, 'Early History to 1826', in P. Schidrowitz and T. R. Dawson (eds), *History of the Rubber Industry* (Cambridge, 1952); René Bouvier, *Le Caoutchouc* (Paris, 1947) 11, 28–9. There are summaries of the early history of the rubber industry in: Caio Prado Júnior, *História econômica do Brasil* (6th edn, Brasiliense) 242–3; Ferreira Reis, *O seringal e o seringueiro*, 50–6; Richard Collier, *The River that God Forgot* (London, 1968) 41–2; Santos, *História econômica da Amazônia*, 29, 43–50.

272 *impermeable by water'.* Rodrigues Ferreira, 'Memoria sobre os gentios Cambebas', 50.

272 *even gonorrheal materials'.* Manoel Barata, 'Apontamentos para as Ephemérides Paraenses', RHGB **99** 52–3, 1924.

272 *not always decent.'* Spix and Martius, *Viagem pelo Brasil*, **3** 30–1.

273 *found most suitable.'* Dunlop's patent, in Robin Furneaux, *The Amazon* (London, 1969) 148.

274 *in sufficient quantity.'* Spruce, *Notes of a botanist*, **1** 507; Adalbert of Prussia, *Travels*, **2** 219; Marcoy, *Voyage*, 422, 488; Santos, *História econômica da Amazônia*, 29; Ferreira Reis, *O seringal e o seringueiro*, 60; Joseph Woodroffe and Harold Smith, *The Rubber Industry of the Amazon* (London, 1915) 27.

274 *times the value.* Although the tendency of rubber prices and production was upwards during these decades, there were some wild fluctuations in the price of rubber. There was a drop in 1893 owing to a panic in the United States. In 1907 the price of rubber hit $2 per pound and then fell in a few months to half that price; but it rose again steadily, to reach $3 per pound by 1910. For discussions of these prices and output, see: Henry Pearson, *The Rubber Country of the Amazon* (New York, 1911); Paul Le Cointe, *L'Amazonie brésilienne* (Paris, 1922); Caio Prado Júnior, *História econômica do Brasil*; Woodroffe and Smith, *The Rubber Industry of the Amazon*; John Melby, 'Rubber River . . .', HAHR **22**, 1942; Furneaux, *The Amazon* 151; Santos, *História econômica da Amazônia*.

275 *horse on champagne.'* Furneaux, *The Amazon*, 153.

276 *his murderers belonged.'* Pearson, *The Rubber Country*, 148–9. The English photographer Cecil Beaton wrote a charming book about his aunt who married one of the Suárez rubber millionaires: *My Bolivian Aunt* (London, 1971).

276 *insult or treachery.'* Charles Domville-Fife, *Among Wild Tribes of the Amazons* (London, 1924) 101–2.

276 *an Indian tribe.'* Coudreau, *Voyage au Tapajóz* (Paris, 1897) 60–1.

276 *quest for rubber'.* Craig, *Recollections of an Ill-fated Expedition*, 257.

276 *not hurt Indians'.* Ibid., 258.

276 *from their presence.'* Mr Dalton, assistant to the resident engineer of the Madeira & Mamoré Railway Company, quoted in Julio Pinkas, *Relatório apresentado a . . . João Ferreira de Moura, Ministro de . . . Agricultura, Commércio e Obras Públicas* (Rio de Janeiro, 1885) 113.

277 *fall to pieces'.* Ibid.

277 *in the forest.'* Ibid., 112. On Bolivian Indians, 110–11.

278 *build the road.'* Petition in Chancery by Public Works Construction Company, London, 1873, in Craig, *Recollections of an Ill-fated Expedition*, 57. The first idea for a railway came from the Bolivian General Quentin Quevedo; and Brazilian engineer João Martins da Silva made the same proposal in the year 1861. Franz Keller was commissioned, with his father, to make the survey and described his findings in his book *The Amazon and Madeira Rivers*. His estimates of cost ranged from US $450,000 for ship ramps, to

$4,250,000 for a railroad and over $10 million for canals. Craig, *Recollections of an Ill-fated Expedition*, 37−57; Kenneth Grubb, *Amazon and Andes*, 19−20; Collier, *The River that God Forgot*, 81−2, 219−25; Santos, *História econômica da Amazônia*, 93−4.

278 *of terrible fevers'*. Barrington Brown and Lidstone, *Fifteen thousand miles*, 343.

279 *those distant forests*. For the history of the Acre dispute see: Leandro Tocantins, *Formação histórica do Acre* (Rio de Janeiro, 1961); Lewis A. Tambs, 'Rubber, Rebels and Rio Branco: the contest for the Acre', HAHR **46** no. 3, 254−73, Aug. 1966; Hélène Rivière d'Arc, 'La formation du lieu Amazonie au XIXe siècle', *Cahiers des Amériques Latines*, 18 183−213, Paris, 1978; Pearson, *The Rubber Country*, 161−5; Arthur César Ferreira Reis, *Límites e demarcações da Amazônia brasileira* (Rio de Janeiro, 1948). The mameluco explorer Manuel Urbano da Encarnação went up the Purus every year in the 1830s and 1840s to gather forest drugs. Major João Henrique de Mattos praised him for having 'snatched from the forests fourteen Indian tribes, bringing them down to the river banks, making them settle and farm plantations of manioc and other crops' (Mattos, *Relatório*, 171). Mattos recommended that Manuel Urbano be appointed Director of these tribes of the Purus, because they respected and worked for him. The next Director was the woodsman João Rodrigues Cametá, who reached the mouth of the Ituxi in 1847 and who worked among the Mura near the lower Purus. His successor was Joaquim Bruno de Souza, who told the passing French traveller the Count of Castelnau about all the tribes of the middle Purus in 1847. Francisco Manoel da Cruz also told Castelnau about the tribes of the Juruá. Castelnau, *Expédition dans les parties centrales de l'Amérique du Sud 5*

86−7. José Castelo Branco, 'Caminhos do Acre', RHGB **195** 107−8; Gunter Kroemer, *Cuxiuara* 46−7.

279 *no medical help*. Spix and Martius, *Reise*, **3**, bk 9, ch. 2, 1152, or Brazilian edn of 1938, **3** 253.

279 *of pernicious fever.'* Ibid., bk 9, ch. 5, **3** 1292; also **3** 1220, 1230, 1237, 1250, 1265.

279 *by disease, etc.'* President João Antonio de Miranda, Relatório á Assembleia Provincial, Belém, August 1840, 61. Raiol, 'Catachese de indios', ABAP 1903, 134.

279 *sleep at night'*. Herndon and Gibbon, *Exploration*, **2** 303, 305; Edwards, *A voyage up the Amazon*, 130. But both Herndon and Edwards also commented that malaria was rare in Manaus and on the Amazon itself: *Exploration*, **1** 322, and *Voyage*, 157.

280 *probably in consumption.'* Bates, *Naturalist*, 279. Spruce, *Notes of a botanist*, **1** 116−17. Bates himself caught malaria at Tefé, which was considered a particularly unhealthy place. The Venezuelan investigator Francisco Michelena y Rojas was also there in the late 1850s and said that even soldiers posted to Tefé died rapidly: *Exploración oficial . . .* (Brussels, 1867) 511.

280 *victims to it.'* Spruce, *Notes of a botanist*, **1** 117.

280 *even feed himself.'* Ibid., 267.

280 *little quiet repose.'* Wallace, *Narrative of Travels*, in Paul Russell Cutwright, *The Great Naturalists Explore South America* (New York, 1940) 290.

281 *this terrible scourge.'* Agassiz, *A journey in Brazil*, 226.

281 *price be offered.'* Chandless, 'Ascent of the River Purûs', 96, also 92 and 110.

281 *for the remainder*. Le Cointe, *L'Amazonie brésilienne*, **1** 214.

282 *the tropical sun'*. Spruce, *Notes of a botanist*, **1** 117.

283 *up into pills.'* Pearson, *The Rubber Country*, 125−6. Beriberi was caused by deficiency of the thiamine vitamin found in cereals and brown rice.

283 *week is run.'* Grubb, *Amazon and Andes*, 20. The wood-burning railway was closed in 1971, although part of the track has been reopened for tourist excursions.

283 *lots of fish.'* Pearson, *The Rubber Country*, 128.

284 *every 1,000 seeds.'* Collier, *The River that God Forgot*, 31. Collier's book is an excellent and highly readable account of the rubber boom. Wickham's book about his Negro trip was *Rough notes of a journey through the wilderness*, 134, on rubber trees. The idea of smuggling rubber out of Amazonia had been mooted as early as 1791 by James Anderson in the magazine *The Bee*, Edinburgh, 23 March 1791; and later by James Collins, Curator of the Museum of the London Pharmaceutical Society, in a paper in 1872.

Bouvier, *Le Caoutchouc*, 61; Ferreira Reis, *O seringal e o seringueiro*, 67; Melby, 'Rubber river', 464; John Ure, *Trespassers on the Amazon* (London, 1986) 48−56.

284 *bring it off?'* Wickham, *On the Plantation, Cultivation, and Curing of Pará Indian Rubber* (London, 1908) 47.

284 *the Alto-Amazonas direct'.* Ibid., 47.

284 *voyage to Liverpool.'* Ibid., 48.

285 *to insure ventilation.'* Ibid., 51.

285 *of the Tapajós.'* Ibid., 52.

286 *dinghy hauled aboard.'* Ibid., 54.

286 *odd of them.'* Ibid., 55.

286 *the river mouth.'* Ibid., 55−6. The Royal Botanic Gardens, Kew, claim that they had permission to export rubber seeds and that Wickham's account of smuggling them out was an exaggeration.

Chapter 15   INDIANS AND RUBBER

288 *boss could know." '* Antonio Gonçalves Tocantins, 'Estudos sobre a tribu Mundurucu', RHGB **40**: 2 148, 1877; Bates, *Naturalist*, 1863 edn, 233; Chandless, 'Notes on the rivers Arinos, Juruena, and Tapajós', JRGS **32** 275, 1862; Murphy, *Headhunter's Heritage*, 38−41.

289 *jury absolved her'.* Tocantins, 'Estudos', 158.

289 *and attractive appearance'.* Ibid., 158.

289 *from their hearts?'* Frei Pelino de Castrovalva to President of Pará, 14 Aug. 1876, in Tocantins, ibid., 107.

290 *and some lives!'* Complaint by traders of Itaituba to Legislative Assembly of Pará, 1 March 1874, in ibid., 135−6.

290 *the Indian workman.'* H. Smith, *Brazil*, 254.

290 *den of vice.'* Frei Pelino de Castrovalva to President of Pará, 20 Jan. 1876, in Tocantins, 'Estudos', 137−8.

290 *receive for it'.* Chandless, 'Ascent of the River Purûs', 93.

290 *for a trader'.* Chandless, 'Notes of a

journey up the River Juruá', JRGS **39** 299, 1869.

291 *of the Puru-Purus" '.* Barrington Brown and Lidstone, *Fifteen thousand miles*, 435.

291 *as a result.'* Woodroffe and Smith, *The Rubber Industry*, 28.

291 *were completely extinguished.'* Ibid., 27.

291 *the following day.'* President Sebastião do Rego Barros, Relatório, Belém do Pará, 15 Aug. 1854; Manoel Barata, *A antiga produção e exportação do Pará* (Belém, 1915) 320; Santos, *História econômica da Amazônia*, 70.

291 *annihilating all others'.* Ibid.

292 *and blind class.'* President Francisco Carlos de Araújo Brusque, Relatório, Belém, 1 Sept. 1862, in Santos, *História econômica da Amazônia*, 164.

292 *someone else's profit.'* M. A. Pimenta Bueno, *A borracha* (Rio de Janeiro, 1882) 15.

293 *to enslave himself!'* Euclides da Cunha, *À margem da história* (new edn, São Paulo, 1976) 27. On seringueiro debt bondage, see also: Barrington Brown

and Lidstone, *Fifteen thousand miles*, 463; H. Smith, *Brazil*, 254; Grubb, *From Pacific to Atlantic*, 105, and *Amazon and Andes*, 4; Wickham, *Rough notes of a journey through the wilderness*, 297–8; Woodroffe and Smith, *The Rubber Industry*, 28; Paul Walle, *Au pays de l'or noir*, 169–72; Theodor Koch-Grünberg, *Zwei Jahre unter den Indianern*, 1 33, 266, 279.

293 *in complete independence'*. João Maria de Moraes, Discurso, Belém, 15 Aug. 1846, 4–5.

294 *are clamoured for.'* James de Vismes Drummond Hay, 'Report on the Industrial Classes in the Provinces of Pará and Amazonas, Brazil', Belém, 1870, in Wickham, *Rough notes of a journey through the wilderness*, 292.

294 *the national service'*. Ibid., 293.

294 *seek employment elsewhere.'* Ibid.

294 *the rubber-tree . . . returns.'* Ibid., 294.

295 *gaiola [cage] launch.'* Cunha, *À margem da história*, in Ferreira Reis, *O seringal e o seringueiro*, 95. Grubb, *Amazon and Andes*, 3–4.

295 *Nothing more.'* Cunha, in Ferreira Reis, *O seringal e o seringueiro*, 95.

295 *of the region.'* Dr Oswaldo Gonçalves Cruz, *Considerações gerais sobre as condições sanitárias do Rio Madeira* (Rio de Janeiro, 1910) 11.

295 *die of hunger.'* Ibid.

296 *to flow out.'* Grubb, *Amazon and Andes*, 5.

296 *of his task.'* Ibid., 7.

296 *abuses and wrongs.'* Grubb, *From Pacific to Atlantic*, 104.

296 *and sordid lust.'* Ibid.

296 *were making yearly.'* Barrington Brown and Lidstone, *Fifteen thousand miles*, 438.

297 *they will perish.'* José Eustacio Rivera, *La voragine*, quoted in Grubb, *From Pacific to Atlantic*, 105.

297 *fled from civilisation.'* Therese, Prinzessin von Bayern, *Meine Reise in den brazilianischen Tropen* (Berlin, 1897) 80. Annual reports by governors Jeronymo Ferreira Correa, 1849; Tenreiro Aranha, 1852; Ferreira Pena, 1853. Alípio Bandeira, *A cruz*

indígena (Pôrto Alegre, 1926) 47.

298 *the Madeira River'*. Mathews, *Up the Amazon and Madeira Rivers* (London, 1879) 30. For the early history of the Parintintin, see Curt Nimuendajú, 'Os índios Parintintin do rio Madeira', JSAP n.s. 16 205–8, 1924; and his 'As tribus do Alto Madeira', JSAP n.s. 17 138, 1925. He cites Martius, *Beiträge zur Ethnographie*, 202; Casal, *Corografia Brasílica*, 256; José da Silva Guimarães, *Memoria sobre . . . Appiacás*, RHGB 4, 309, 1854; and Castelnau for evidence that the Parintintin had migrated away from the Mundurukú on the Tapajós–Juruena. Reports by Presidents Herculano Ferreira Pena, 1853, 178–80; Gustavo Ramos Ferreira, 1866; João Wilkens de Mattos, 1870; Domingos Monteiro Peixoto, 1873; Domingos Jacy Monteiro, 1877. Moreira Neto, *Política indigenista*, 71, 88, 91. Alípio Bandeira, *A cruz indígena*, 49–50. For persecution of the Parintintin by the Mundurukú, see: Araújo e Amazonas, *Diccionario topográphico*, 219; Tocantins, 'Estudos', 83, 94–5, 140–3. Alípio Bandeira, *A cruz indigena*, 49–50, gives a full list of all Parintintin attacks between 1852 and 1874. Also João Severiano da Fonseca, *Viagem ao redor do Brasil* (Rio de Janeiro, 1881) 2 316.

299 *and its tributaries.'* Mathews, *Up the Amazon*, 20–1.

299 *brush with savages'*. Ibid., 35. Julio Pinkas, *Relatório apresentada a . . . João Ferreira de Moura . . .* (Rio de Janeiro, 1885) 111–12. Pinkas made an official report on the Madeira railway plan in 1884. He acknowledged that the Parintintin prevented settlement of the Machado river, but suspected that many stories of their ferocity were exaggerated.

299 *with the "barbaros"'*. Mathews, *Up the Amazon*, 35.

299 *of their forests'*. Keller, *The Amazon and Madeira Rivers*, 40.

299 *off many victims.'* Barrington Brown

and Lidstone, *Fifteen thousand miles*, 346, 340.

299 *with superstitious awe.'* Craig, *Recollections of an Ill-fated Expedition*, 364–5. Plane, *L'Amazonie*, 103.

300 *on the Machado.'* Coudreau, *Voyage au Tapajóz*, 39–40. Plane, *L'Amazonie*, 117. Nimuendajú says that the Jarú spoke the same language as the Tora. He calls the Parintintin (whom he helped to pacify) by their correct name Kawahiwa (often rendered as Tupi-Kawahib), rather than the Mundurukú word Parintintin.

300 *almost completely destroyed'.* Plane, *L'Amazonie*, 103.

300 *suitable as earrings.'* Spix and Martius, *Reise*, **3**, bk 9, ch. 3, 1188. (Spix went alone to Tabatinga, but he drew a vivid picture of the Tukuna dance.) The best picture of the ceremony was by Henry Walter Bates, who was there in 1857–8: *Naturalist*, 397–401. José Monteiro de Noronha and Francisco Xavier Ribeiro de Sampaio both described Tukuna masks, seen on their journeys in 1768 and 1774 respectively. Other descriptions were by Castelnau in 1846 (*Expédition*, **5** 41–6); Herndon and Gibbon, *Exploration*, 234–48; Barboza Rodrigues, 'Ticuna', in A. J. de Mello Moraes Filho, *Revista da Exposição Anthropologica*, 52–3, 152; Marcoy, *Voyage*, 336, 147–8; Curt Nimuendajú, *The Tukuna* (Berkeley and Los Angeles, 1952) 9–10; Avé-Lallement, *Viagem pelo norte do Brasil*, 186–7; Maw, *Journal*, 218–27.

301 *ill-educated Brazilian women.'* Bates, *Naturalist*, 278.

301 *to his forests.'* Crevaux, *Voyages dans l'Amérique du Sud*, 338.

302 *of human flesh.'* Ibid., 375.

302 *and abused Indians.* Tavares Bastos, *Amazonas*, 366; Antonio Epaminondas de Mello, *Relatório a administração da Provincia do Amazonas* (1866), in *Amazonas: Relatórios da presidência* (Rio de Janeiro, 1907) **3** 351; Expedito Arnaud, 'Os índios Mirânia e a expansão luso-brasileira', BMPEG

n.s. Antropologia **81** 8–9, July 1981.

302 *examples of it!'* J. Barbosa Rodrigues, 'Miranhas', in Moraes Filho, *Revista da Exposição*, 124. Theodor Koch-Grünberg saw Miranya enslaved on the Apaporis at the beginning of the twentieth century: 'Die Miranya (Rio Yapurá, Amazonas)', *Zeitschrift für Ethnologie* **42** 900, Berlin, 1910.

303 *of indomitable natives.'* Captain Antonio Luis Von Hoonholdtz, in *Revista da Sociedade de Geografia do Rio de Janeiro* **4** 182, 1888. Anísio Jobim, *O Amazonas, sua historia*, 188–9. The 1866 expedition was led by Captain José da Costa Azevedo (later Barão de Larário) and by the great geographer Manuel Ruan y Paz Soldán for the Peruvians. The man killed by Indians was Soares Pinto. The 1874 expedition was led by Von Hoonholdtz, later Barão de Tefé. This expedition reached the source of the river, but its surveys were inaccurate and had to be recalculated by another demarcation expedition led by Captain Cunha Gomes in 1897. By that date, the river was infested by seringueiros and caucheros. José Moreira Brandão Castello Branco, 'Caminhos do Acre', RHGB **196** 74–222, 1950; Julio César Melatti, *Javari* (Centro Ecumênico de Documentação e Informação, *Povos indígenas no Brasil* **5**, São Paulo, 1981) 17–18.

303 *be no compromise.'* Ferreira Reis, *O seringal e o seringueiro*, 128. Henri Coudreau, *Voyage au Xingu*, 32, 87–8, 134. The Asurini mentioned by Coudreau were finally contacted only in 1972: this author had the privilege of seeing them immediately after their contact. The Suyá were contacted only in the early 1960s and now live in the Xingu National Park close to the remaining Juruna near Diauarum.

304 *heads with bullets.'* Alfredo Lustosa Cabral, *Dez anos no Amazonas* (João Pessoa, 1949) 63–4. The Purus river

filled with seringueiros because of its abundance of hevea trees and easy, rapid-free access. One of its greatest explorers and exploiters was Colonel António Rodrigues Pereira Labre. He first saw the Purus in 1869 and returned in 1871 with men and merchandise to trade in rubber. He learned from Manoel Urbano da Encarnaçao how to attract and use Indian labour. Labre founded the future city of Lábrea in Paumari territory and traded for food with the Catauixi. He described some of his explorations, during which he saw or contacted many tribes, in a lecture to the Sociedade de Geografia do Rio de Janeiro in 1888 (translated in *Proceedings of the Royal Geographical Society*, n.s. **11**, 1889). He reckoned that on the Ituxi river alone there were eight thousand tribal Indians – but there were already a thousand seringueiros. By the time of the Brazilian Republic in 1889 there were 120,000 civilisado inhabitants on the Purus: the town of Lábrea had a population of some 22,000, Canutama had over 15,000 and Entemari had 13,500. Antonio C. R. Bittencourt, *Municipio de Lábrea. Noticias sobre o seu desenvolvimento e sobre o rio Purus* (Manaus, 1918); Paulo Ehrenreich, 'Viagem aos rios Amazonas e Purus' (1888); Joseph Beal Steere, 'Narrative of a visit to Indian tribes of the Purus River, Brazil', *Annual Report, US National Museum* 1901, 359–93; Kroemer, *Cuxiuara* 79–84. Ferreira Reis, *O seringal e o seringueiro*, 129.

304 *women and children.*' James W. Wells, *3000 Miles through Brazil*, 224.

304 *away unheard of.*' Ibid., 225.

304 *the Jauaperi Indians*'. Report to Legislative Assembly of Amazonas, Governor Pires Ferreira, Manaus, Jan. 1898. Moreira Neto, *Política indigenista*, 96.

304 *this abnormal situation.*' Ibid.

304 *Indians without exception.*' Grubb, *Amazon and Andes*, 30.

304 *the Winchester constitution.*' Ibid., 12.

305 *managed to escape.*' Tastevin, 'Le Haut Tarauacá', *La Géographie* **45** nos 1–2, 54, Paris, Jan.–Feb. 1926.

305 *of rubber stores.*' Ibid. 50, 49, Paul Rivet and C. Tastevin, 'Les tribus indiennes des bassins du Purús, du Juruá et des régions limitrophes', *La Géographie* **35**: 5 463, May 1921, mentions Katukina fleeing westwards across the Tarauacá to escape persecution by rubber men. Tastevin also talks of Chief Teskon and the extermination of Indians, in 'Le "Riozinho da Liberdade" ', *La Géographie*, **49**: 3–4, 211, 1929. Kenneth Grubb, *The lowland Indians of Amazonia*, 100. Harald Schultz and Vilma Chiara, 'Informações sôbre os índios do alto rio Purus', *Revista do Museu Paulista*, n.s. **9** 182, São Paulo, 1950–1.

305 *they encountered them.*' Report of Amazonas Indian inspectorate, 1906, in Darcy Ribeiro, *Os índios e a civilização* (Rio de Janeiro, 1970) 45.

306 *reached the camp.*' Report by inspectors of Serviço de Proteção aos Indios, 1911, ibid., 44. Thaumaturgo de Azevedo issued a circular dated 12 Dec. 1905 to all civilisado inhabitants of Acre forbidding them from raiding Indians or invading Indian reserves. The circular then itemised all Indian territories in the Department of the Upper Juruá. He later ordered rubber bosses to pay a tax of 5 milreis for every Indian under ten in their employ and 10 milreis for Indian adolescents. This levy on child labour was to be used to pay missionaries or for a protective agency. Gregorio Thaumaturgo de Azevedo, *Prefeitura do Alto Juruá. Relatorio do primeiro semestre de 1906* . . . (Rio de Janeiro, 1906) 68–9; and *Prefeitura do Alto Juruá. Segundo relatorio* . . . (Rio de Janeiro, 1906) 48.

306 *all their possessions.*' Another SPI report about incidents in June 1913, ibid., 46.

306 *in complete misery.*' Report by SPI

Inspetoria do Amazonas, 1912, ibid., 46.

306 *limits of navigation.'* Pearson, *The Rubber Country*, 137. William Curtis Farabee, 'The Amazon Expedition of the University Museum', *The Museum Journal* 7, 212, Philadelphia, 1916. Koch-Grünberg, *Zwei Jahre unter den Indianern* 1 340.

307 *men have seen.'* Algot Lange, *In the Amazon Jungle* (New York and London, 1912) 371—2.

307 *of these savages'.* Ibid., 372.

307 *and imposing array'.* Ibid., 133.

307 *of a Napoleon.'* Ibid., 377—8.

308 *pointed Jaguar teeth.'* Ibid., 382—3.

308 *Spaniard's head off.'* Ibid., 383.

308 *at my feet.'* Ibid., 384.

309 *by slow degrees.'* J. C. Arana's testimony, Appendix 3, *Report and Special Report from the Select Committee on Putumayo, Proceedings, Minutes of Evidence* (House of Commons paper 148, XIV, London, 1913). Roger Sawyer, 'Origins and Career of Roger Casement, with particular reference to the development of his interest in the rights of dependent ethnic groups' (dissertation, Bembridge, Isle of Wight, 1979).

311 *their desperate agony.'* *Truth*, London, 22 Sept. 1909. Furneaux, *The Amazon*, 171.

312 *better than yourself.'* Telegram from Julio Arana to Sir Roger Casement, 14 June 1916, Public Record Office, London, FO 371 2798. This was first published by Robin Furneaux, *The Amazon*, 198. This book, and John Ure's *Trespassers on the Amazon*, 69—90, provide thorough accounts of the entire Putumayo affair. Roger Sawyer gives the sources of the Putu-

mayo affair in his excellent 'Origins and Career of Roger Casement' and *Casement: the flawed hero*. The Iquitos newssheet that first published the atrocities in July 1907 was *La Sanción*, renamed *La Felpa* later that year and suspended in January 1908. The story was carried in *O Jornal do Commercio*, Manaus, 2 June 1908, and *Provincia do Pará*, Belém, 4 June 1908. Walter Hardenburg's narrative was published in *Truth*, London, from 22 Sept. 1909, and as a book, *The Putumayo*, ed. Reginald Enock, London, 1912. The Parliamentary enquiry was published as *Minutes of Evidence, Report and Special Report from Select Committee on Putumayo*. The *Blue Book on the Putumayo* was published in July 1912. A British consul was appointed at Iquitos, and the first incumbent George B. Michell wrote *Report by His Majesty's Consul at Iquitos on his Tour in the Putumayo District*, Miscellaneous no. 6, 1913, Cmd 6678.

312 *tame Mundurukú Indians'.* Raymundo Pereira Brazil, *O rio Tapajóz* (Belém, 1914) 33.

312 *belong to them'.* Coudreau, *Voyage au Tapajóz*, 57.

313 *part been lost'.* Hartt, 'Contribuições para a etnologia do Valle do Amazonas', AMN 6, 117, 1885.

313 *as in tribe-life'.* Chandless, 'Notes on the rivers Maué-assú', 424. Murphy, *Headhunter's Heritage*, 34.

313 *to the region'.* Farabee, 'The Amazon Expedition of the University Museum' 8, 139.

313 *with the whites'.* Ibid.

313 *last human head.'* Coudreau, *Voyage au Tapajós*, 144.

Chapter 16   MESSIANIC MOVEMENTS

315 *entire 260 leagues'.* Francisco Michelena y Rojas to Venezuelan Minister, Belém, 12 Feb. 1856, in Michelena y Rojas, *Exploración oficial*

... (Brussels, 1867) 391.

315 *of the earth.'* Spruce, *Notes of a botanist*, 1 268; Hilário Gurjão, *Descripção da viagem* ... (1854), RHGB 18 190,

1855 or 1896; Araújo e Amazonas, *Diccionario topográphico*, 198, 263; Wickham, *Rough notes of a journey through the wilderness*, 135 (to 1000); Captain Joaquim Firmino Xavier (1858), in Avé-Lallement, *Viagem pelo norte do Brasil*, 2 134, 139, 141; and particularly, João Henrique de Mattos, 'Relatório sobre o estado atual de decadencia do Alto Amazonas', of 1849 in the *Jornal do Commercio*, 7–11 September 1950. Wallace, *Narrative of Travels*, 136.

316 *the Rio Negro.'* Friar José dos Santos Inocentes to Canon de Azevedo, 6 March 1852, *Archivo do Amazonas* 1: 2 27, 1907; Robin Wright, 'History and Religion of the Baniwa People of the Upper Rio Negro Valley' (Stanford University, California, 1981), 255.

316 *during the day!'* Wallace, *Narrative of Travels*, 157.

317 *and private security.'* President J. B. F. Tenreiro Aranha, Relatório, Manaus, 1852, in Moreira Neto, *Política indigenista*, 68–9.

317 *Commandant of Marabitanas.'* Friar Gregorio José Maria de Bene report, 1854, AA 1: 2 37, 1907; Wright, 'History and Religion', 234; Koch-Grünberg, *Zwei Jahre unter den Indianern*, 2 8; Foreign Office, *Question de la Frontière, Annexe*, 1 84; J. H. Wilkens de Mattos, RIHCB 19 127, 1856.

317 *show any kindness'.* Lieutenant Jesuino Cordeiro to President of Amazonas, 7 Jan. 1853, AA 1 no. 3, 70.

318 *take them down-river.'* Ibid., 60; Wright, 'History and religion', 237.

318 *to Barra [Manaus]'.* Wallace, *Narrative of Travels*, 251. The Kobewa were called Cubeo by Wallace. Robin Wright identified the Carapaná (a lingua geral word meaning 'mosquitoes') as being the Hohodene group of Baniwa of the Ayari tributary of the Içana, with whom he himself worked in 1976–7.

318 *the great house.'* Ibid., 252.

318 *authorises the practice.'* Ibid., 206.

318 *at the business'.* Ibid., 206.

318 *at times ill-treated'.* Ibid., 206.

319 *taken very young'.* Ibid., 207. Wallace was at São Jeronimo on the lower Uaupés with Richard Spruce in mid-1851, then returned and went farther up the river in March–April 1852, while Spruce returned after August 1852. Spruce later wrote to Wallace that the Tariana chief Bernardo was still raiding for Indian captives on the Papuri river, and Lieutenant Cordeiro reported to the provincial president that this chief had brought back ten children. Spruce, *Notes of a botanist* 1 329–30; Cordeiro to President, 5 July and 28 Aug. 1853, AA 1:3 66; Wright, 'History and Religion', 252.

319 *expected of captives.'* Spruce, *Notes of a botanist*, 1 344.

319 *outraged by them.'* Ibid., 325–6. João Henrique de Mattos described Chief Callistro six years earlier as being very useful to traders and in helping people pass the rapids on the Uaupés. The Tariana were already trading much farinha that they grew and forest produce that they gathered. Mattos, *Relatório*, 168.

319 *in these expeditions.'* Ibid., 355.

319 *them almost gratuitously.'* Friar Gregorio J. M. de Bene to President of Amazonas, 24 April 1852, AA 1: 3, 37–8; Wright, 'History and Religion', 254.

319 *lances and clubs.'* Lieutenant Cordeiro to President of Amazonas, 1 July 1853, AA 1: 3, 59, 1907. Wright, 'History and Religion', 248.

319 *place last year.'* Wright, ibid., 248.

320 *the drum: tuu-tuu-tuu.'* Account by several Hohodene Baniwa of the Aiari river to Robin Wright, 1976, in ibid., 243.

320 *is what happens.'* Captain Joaquim Firmino Xavier to President Amaral, 27 Oct. 1857, *Correspondência dos Ministérios da Guerra: Amazonas*, relatório 10, 1858, in ibid., 264. The recommendation to build a fort at Cucui was made by Major Hilário Gurjão, who was sent up the Negro by the provincial

government in 1854 and wrote a report on his journey.

321 *and forced labour.'* Michelena y Rojas, *Exploración*, 394, 399. There were two official reports on the Rio Negro by Brazilian officials in 1855: by the civil engineer João Manuel Júnior to the President of Amazonas, 8 Feb. 1855, quoted in ibid., 394; and by Artillery Major Hilário Maximiano Antunes Gurjão, Manaus, 12 Feb. 1855, quoted in ibid., 394–8, and published in RHGB **18** 183–96, 1855 or 1896. Neither report was as thorough as that of João Henrique de Mattos of 1845.

322 *threatened with ruin.'* Captain J. F. Xavier report on his expedition to the Içana, 1857, in Avé-Lallement, *Viagem pelo norte do Brasil*, **2** 123. In 1823 Father José Maria Coelho had said about the appalling condition of Fort Marabitanas: 'If the fort of São Gabriel da Cachoeira is in such a state that a dozen men could sieze it, this fort is so bad that four or six could do the same to it!' Coelho, *Duas memorias sobre . . . Rio Negro*, RHGB **203**, 1949, 128.

322 *he asked for.'* Captain J. F. Xavier to the Diretor dos Indios, 1 Jan. 1858, AA **1**: 4, 116. Wright, 'History and Religion', 279.

322 *lack of food.'* Report of Municipal Justice Marcos de Sousa, section 3, 8 Sept. 1858, in ibid., 281.

323 *foreign missionary'.* Friar Manuel Salgado to President Furtado, 10 Feb. 1858, AA **2**: 5 14.

323 *one called Christ.'* Ibid.

323 *reduced to ashes'.* Captain Joaquim Firmino Xavier report to Provincial President, AA **1**: 4, 115. Robin Wright gives the fullest account of Venancio Christo's crusade, in his thesis, 'History and Religion', 265– 88. He used some two hundred pages of official reports collected by a Juiz Municipal who was sent to investigate the affair, many of which were published in AA **1**: 3 62–3, **1**: 4 111– 25, 1907; **2**: 5, 11–15, **2**: 7, 82–90,

1908. Captain Xavier and Friar Manuel da Santa Ana Salgado hated each other and wrote damning, slanderous accusations about one another. Captain Xavier accused Friar Manuel of immoral acts with women on the Içana and at Barcellos, of selling cachaça and charitable items, of lending money at exorbitant interest to the soldiers, and demanding high payments for religious and other services. President Francisco José Furtado, Relatório, Manaus, 1859, 218–19. The military commander and Indian director at Marabitanas, Captain Mathias Vieira de Aguiar, was formally accused in June 1858 of having committed violence and abuse of his authority. One of the four accusations against him was that he sent the expedition that sacked villages of the lower Içana in November 1857. He was also accused of having his soldiers man a large canoe for trading activities, of selling goods at exorbitant prices, of cheating customers, and of beating and abusing people who did not obey him. Captain Aguiar was relieved of his command, but acquitted of the accusations for lack of evidence: AA **2**: 7 82–3, 1908.

323 *children as slaves.'* Captain Xavier report, AA **1**: 4, 122.

324 *to deceive them.'* Captain Pinheiro to Juiz Municipal, 3 Aug. 1858, Wright, 'History and Religion', 271. Captain Xavier's report from Cucui, 31 Dec. 1858, was published by the German traveller Avé-Lallement, *Viagem pelo norte do Brasil*, **2** 120–35. In it, Captain Xavier described his journey up the Içana in November– December 1857. He found deserted settlements everywhere: S. Lourenço at the mouth of the Xié (formerly eleven houses and a chapel); Nossa Senhora de Guia at the mouth of the Içana; the military post of São Marcellino on the lower Xié. He found a few Indians farther up the

Içana: Nazaré village with thirty Mutum Indians; Tunuí, above the river's main rapids, with Acaiaca Indians, Santa Ana de Cuari at the mouth of the Cuari river, with Siusi Indians; and less contacted Baniwa tribes near the headwaters (Iandu near the Iandu rapids; Quati; Ipeca; Suaçu; Tatu, taller and darker than the others, naked and newly emerged from the forest; Tapiíra near the Apuí rapids – the forty-third and last rapids on the Içana; Acari near the source).

324 *and savage dances.'* Captain Xavier report of 31 Dec. 1858, in Avé-Lallement, *Viagem pelo norte do Brasil,* **2** 126–30.

324 *the Christ Venancio.'* Antonio Gonçalves Dias, 'Diario da viagem ao Rio Negro, 15 agosto – 15 outubro de 1861', ms. in Biblioteca Nacional, Rio de Janeiro, in Wright, 'History and Religion', 287. Sacred objects brought back by Gonçalves Dias are now in the Museu Nacional, Rio de Janeiro: Marechal Boanegres Lopes de Sousa, *Do Rio Negro ao Orenoco. A terra – o homem,* Conselho Nacional de Proteção aos Indios, publication 111 (Rio de Janeiro, 1959) xvii.

325 *can do justice.'* Wallace, *Narrative of Travels,* 193.

325 *have governed them '* Report of Juiz Municipal Marcos Antonio Rodrigues de Sousa, 3 July 1858, in Wright, 'History and Religion', 297.

325 *all civilised people'.* Friar Romualdo Gonçalves de Azevedo to President Furtado, 1858, AA **2**: 7, 89.

325 *'multitudes'.* Friar Romualdo Gonçalves de Azevedo, in Report of the Juiz Municipal, 1858, f. 37, Wright, 'History and Religion', 307.

326 *enter the temple.'* Ibid., 307.

326 *the next day.'* *Estrella do Amazonas,* Manaus, 25 Dec. 1858, in ibid., 310. Lieutenant Jesuino Cordeiro continued to live on the upper Negro for many years. The Italian traveller Count Ermanno Stradelli met him in 1881, shortly before his death. He described the lieutenant as 'little more civilised than the people he was civilising', and was shocked when he entered Lieutenant Cordeiro's house one day and found him and his family naked. The lieutenant calmly explained that wearing clothes all the time consumed too much soap. Stradelli, 'L'Uaupés e gli Uaupés', 433.

326 *without any violence.'* President Francisco José Furtado, Relatório, Manaus, 1859, 218–19, in Moreira Neto, *Política indigenista,* 82.

327 *in fact arduous.'* Avé-Lallement, *Viagem pelo norte do Brasil,* **2** 129.

327 *want to labour.'* Ibid., **2** 131.

327 *governed by anyone.'* Ibid., 130.

327 *of the forest'.* Bernardino de Souza, *Lembranças e curiosidades do Valle do Amazonas,* 82.

327 *of a tyrant.'* Ibid., 122. Villa Bella da Rainha was renamed Villa Nova da Imperatriz in honour of the Empress; it was often called Tupinambaranas, because it was at the eastern end of that vast riverine island; in 1880 it became a city and acquired its present name Parintins – not to be confused with the Parintintin tribe, far away to the south-west on the middle Madeira river.

328 *go amongst them.'* Bates, *Naturalist,* 246. Friar Pedro de Ciriana had built a church and school at Andirá and attracted some two thousand people – Mawé Indians and settlers – to his mission. It was thus one of the rare instances of Indians being shown the 'benefits' of mixing with 'civilised' people. Metódio da Nembro, who wrote a eulogistic account of the Capuchin Franciscan missions in Brazil, said that Friar Pedro left Andirá because he 'considered the work of catechism and civilising to be concluded'. Nembro, *Storia dell'attività missionaria dei minori cappuccini nel Brasile* 436.

The President of Amazonas freely admitted that he sent Friar Pedro de Ciriana to the Purus in order to assemble its numerous tribes into settlements and 'make that great river more frequented'. (Herculano Ferreira Penna, *Relatório*, Manaus, 1 Aug. 1854, in Ferreira Penna, ed., *Relatorios da presidencia da Provincia do Amazonas* 1 (Rio de Janeiro, 1906) 321.) The new mission was on lake Uamurá, 150 km from the mouth of the Purus, and was called São Luís Gonzaga. Once again, Friar Pedro's successful trading of Indian produce aroused the fury of the regatão traders who were cut out of this lucrative source of exploitation. Another campaign of vilification led to his expulsion on 21 April 1856, less than two years after the foundation of the Purus mission. Friar Pedro (Pier Paolo) returned to Italy and became a missionary at Patna in India, where he died in 1888 aged 75. President João Pedro Dias Vieira dismissed him because he had 'lost his moral authority' (Vieria, *Relatório*, Manaus, 8 June 1856, in Penna ed., *Relatorios da presidencia* 1 482–3). Kroemer, *Cuxiuara* 51–2.

328 *a lay vila.* Friar Pedro de Ciriana was at Andirá from 1848 to 1855. Reports of João Baptista de Figueiredo Tenreiro Aranha, Manaus, 30 April 1852, 32; Jeronymo Francisco Coelho, Belém, 1 Oct. 1849, 784; Manuel Gomes Correa de Miranda, Manaus, 5 Sept. 1852, 128; João Henrique Wilkens de Mattos, 'Alguns esclarecimentos sobre as missões da Provincia do Amazonas', 128; Nimuendajú, 'The Maué and Arapium', HSAI 3, 246. The other missions in Amazonas were Pôrto Alegre on the upper Rio Branco near Fort São Joaquim (but about to collapse, with the departure of Friar José dos Santos Inocentes); and the mission of the Japurá and Içá on the north bank of the Solimões. On guaraná (*paullinia cupana*) see Ghillean T. Prance, 'Increased Importance of Ethnobotany in Amazonia' in Hemming (ed.), *Change*

in the Amazon Basin, 1 130–2.

328 *them in villages'.* Friar Giuseppe Coppi, 'La Provincia delle Amazzoni', ed. G. A. Collini, *Bolletino della Società Geografica Italiana,* anno 19, 2 ser., **22**:10 136, Rome, 1885. The mission of São Pedro on the middle Madeira was founded in 1854: it had ninety-three Mura Indians by 1864; seventy-five by 1874; and ninety in 1876 when the missionary withdrew. (Presidents' annual reports; Nimuendajú, 'Os indios Parintintin do rio Madeira', 211.) The nearby mission of Crato was formed in 1856 with Mundurukú and Mura; in 1857 it had Mura and Karipuna; and in 1864 Mura and Tora – but its missionary fell ill soon after arriving there, and achieved nothing (ibid.). São Francisco, the third mission on the Madeira, was founded in 1871 above the mouth of the Machado, and lasted until 1882. The early exploration of the Purus was by the local director of Indians João da Cuna Correia (also known as João Cametá) in 1848; by Serafim da Silva Salgado in 1852 (a five-month expedition guided by Chief Mamurite: report attached to annual address of President Herculano Ferreira Pena, Manaus, 1853, translated by Richard Spruce, in Clements Markham (ed.), *The Travels of Pedro Cieza de Leon,* Hakluyt Society, 1 ser. **33** (London, 1864) 4–10); in 1861 and 1863 the mameluco Manuel Urbano da Encarnação, a remarkable natural geographer and explorer, went far up the Purus to the Aquiri river (report attached to annual presidential address of 1865, trans. by Henry Bates, JRGS **36** 126–8, 1866); by the brilliant and modest English explorer William Chandless from June 1864 to February 1865 – reported only in JRGS **36** 86–112 and 119–23, 1866. The Juruá was investigated by its Director of Indians, Romão José de Oliveira; in 1857 by João da Cunha Correia; 1867

by William Chandless, who went up as far as the Liberdade, JRGS **39** 296–311, 1869. Meanwhile, the rivers were opened up to colonisation –a settlement on the Purus in 1852 by Manoel Nicolau de Melo, others by João Gabriel de Carvalho e Melo from 1857 onwards; a regular steamer service on the Purus from 1869; in 1871 Colonel Antonio R. Pereira Labre founded the town of Lábrea, which still flourishes on the Purus, and in January 1875 the government of Amazonas made a contract with him to catechise the Indians of the Purus and teach their adults and children. Also, G. E. Church, *Aborigenes of South America* (London, 1912) 136–50; Ferreira Reis, *O seringal e o seringueiro*, 31–5; Anisio Jobim, *O Amazonas*, 190–2. The first six Italian Capuchins reached Manaus in 1870 and were warmly welcomed. It was hoped to return to missionary contact of forest tribes, after the abolition in 1866 of the failed system of 'partial directors' set up in the 1845 legislation. Three missions were planned on the Purus. Friar Venâncio Zilocchi made several unsuccessful attempts to establish a mission and finally went in 1878 to the south-eastern tributary the Mucuím; but he was soon forced to leave because of malaria. Friar Mathieu Canioni tried to create a mission on the large southern tributary, the Ituxi. In 1876 Friars Samuel Mancini and Venâncio Zilocchi had gone upriver by steamer (steamers had been plying the rapid-free Purus since the 1850s) and canoe to try to convert the Ipurinã of the Acre river. These efforts failed, and in 1877 Canioni and Zilocchi made various attempts to settle Ipurinã or Jamamadi in a mission on either the Sapatini or Mamoriá rivers. There followed an expedition in 1879 up the Ituxi river and the descent of some Ipurinã Indians. But this group was struck by influenza and the tiny mission was already clashing with rubber traders. Some potential converts were already addicted to cachaça and 'all the vices acquired from the enchanting civilisation of the itinerant traders'. By 1881 the friars withdrew, having failed to establish any mission on the Purus. Gunter Kroemer gives a detailed account of these attempts, based on the archive *Curia Generale dei Franciscani Minori. Missio Manaus (M1, M2)* in his *Cuxiuara* 70–5. Also, Venâncio Willeke, *Missões franciscanos no Brasil* (Petrópolis, 1974).

English Protestant missionaries were also active on the Purus at this time – one of the first Protestant missions permitted in Brazil. Missionaries called McCaul, Duke and Resuek-Polak founded a school for Indian children, mostly Ipurinã and Jamamadi, at Hyutanahã on the middle Purus in 1870. For a while they succeeded in teaching bright and 'enchanting' children, but their mission failed in the early 1880s because of disease and the alienation of the Apurinã by seringueiros. The worst exploiter of these tribes was Brás Gil da Encarnação, son of the explorer and rubber-boss Manoel Urbano. *South American Missionary Magazine*, London, 1880; Paul Ehrenreich, 'Viagem aos rios Amazonas e Purus' (1888), RMP **16**, 1929; Kroemer, *Cuxiuara* 75–7.

329 *and moral precepts.'* Coppi, 'La Provincia', 137. The mission of São Francisco had been established under Friar Teodoro Portararo. The worst trader was called Jerónimo Cunha Vieira.

329 *hunter or fisherman.'* Koch-Grünberg, *Zwei Jahre unter den Indianern*, 1 33.

329 *'stern but fatherly'.* Ibid.

330 *in balata [rubber].'* Gordon Mac-Creigh, *White Waters and Black* (New York, 1926) 313, 314.

330 *vagabond and hermaphrodite.'* Koch-Grünberg, *Zwei Jahre unter den Indianern*, 1 39, 203.

330 *festival after festival.'* Ibid. Wright, 'History and Religion', 328.

330 *first human being.'* Koch-Grünberg, *Zwei Jahre unter den Indianern* 1 200. Wright, 'History and Religion', 329.

330 *and transform everything.'* Ibid., 329–30.

331 *as a result.'* Coudreau, *La France Equinoxiale*, 2 199; Stradelli, 'L'Uaupés e gli Uaupés', 430; Koch-Grünberg, *Zwei Jahre unter den Indianern*, 1 40.

331 *regular disciplined life.'* Friar Giuseppe Coppi, 'La Provincia', 140.

331 *the highest degree.'* Ibid., 139.

332 *'bizarre'.* Coudreau, *La France Equinoxiale*, 2 148.

332 *and authoritarian missionary'.* Ibid., 150.

332 *and best ordered'.* Coppi, 'La Provincia', 195. The various villages over which the Capuchins claimed control in 1883 were as follows. On the Uaupés river, Taraquá (and its subsidiary villages Jurapecuma, Micurapecuma and Ananapecuma), with 483 Tukano; Panoré, with 336 Tariana; Iviturapecuma, with 78 Arapaso; Juquira, with 164 Pira-Tapuiá; Iauareté (now on the frontier with Colombia, and still a large Salesian mission) with 402 Tariana; Umar, with 86 Tukano; Carurú and Jutica, with 252 Wanana. The Uaupés itself thus had 1800 Indians in eleven villages. On the Tiquié river, Tucano, Uiraposo, Maracayú and Turí villages, with 920 largely Tukano. On the Papuri, Turigarapé, with 162 Tukano. The total on the three rivers was 2882 Indians, all Tukana-speaking, in sixteen villages. These villages also had saints' names: Taraquá was São Francisco, Ananapecuma (or Nanarapecuma) was São Bernardino, Panoré (or Ipanoré) was São Jerónimo-Jesus-Maria-José, Juquirapecuma was São Miguel, Iauareté was São António, Carurú was São Leonardo. On the Tiquié, Tucano was Santa Izabel, Uiraposo was Nazareth, Maracayú was São José, Turí was São Pedro do Tiquié.n the Papuri, Turí-Igarapé

was Santa Lucia.

332 *and private order'.* Ibid., 195.

332 *of the missionary'.* Ibid., 195.

332 *Baniwa and Kobewa.'* Ibid., 198. Coppi also hoped to convert many other tribes: 686 Baniwa on the Querari; 590 Kobewa on the Cudiari; 460 Maku on the Papuri; 288 Carapaná (Hohodene), 306 Tatú-Mira (both Baniwa tribes) and 566 Tukana-speaking Desana on the Içana.

332 *'ferocious and terrible'.* Ibid., 198.

333 *the Rio Negro.'* Stradelli, 'L'Uaupés e gli Uaupés', 439.

333 *resemble burn marks.'* Koch-Grünberg, *Zwei Jahre unter den Indianern*, 1 84. Many other authors described this disease, which was also common on the Purus river south of the Solimões. It may have been a form of Leishmaniasis, carried by forest rodents and transmitted by insects. Spix and Martius, *Reise*, 3, bk 9, ch. 2, 1147; Barrington Brown and Lidstone, *Fifteen thousand miles*, 433–4; Oswaldo Cruz, *Relatório sobre as condições medico-sanitárias do vale do Amazonas* (Ministerio da Agricultura, Rio de Janeiro, 1913); A. Hirsch, *Handbuch der historisch-geographischen Pathologie* (Berlin, 1886); J. B. Montoya y Flores, *Recherches sur le caratés de Colombie* (Paris, 1893); E. Roquette-Pinto, *Rondonia*, Brasiliana, 5 ser. 39 (São Paulo, 1935) 183–5; Carlos da Silva Lacaz, Roberto Baruzzi and Waldomiro Siqueira, *Introdução à geografia médica do Brasil* (São Paulo, 1972) 281–6.

333 *of these Indians.'* Koch-Grünberg, *Zwei Jahre unter den Indianern*, 51.

333 *for your blessing.'* Stradelli, 'L'Uaupés e gli Uaupés', 441.

333 *do this most.'* Ibid.

334 *fancy takes them.'* Coudreau, *La France Equinoxiale*, 2 224, 221–2.

334 *stop them paddling'.* Ibid., 243.

334 *of the voyage.'* Ibid., 148.

334 *in the forest.'* Ibid., 150.

334 *dishevelled like bacchantes.'* Ibid., 212.

335 *with their amulets.'* Coppi, 'La Provincia', 200.

335 *prepare the dance.'* Ibid., 43–4. For a discussion of the significance of the

sloth and howler monkey among modern Barasana Indians of the upper Uaupés, see Stephen Hugh-Jones, 'Male Initiation and Cosmology Among the Barasana Indians' of the Vaupés area of Colombia' (doctoral thesis, Cambridge, 1974) 183–4; Wright, 'History and Religion', 339–40. The Jurupari cult was described by Coppi, 'La Provincia', 199–200; Coudreau, *La France Equinoxiale*, **2** 185–94; Stradelli, 'Leggenda dell' Jurupary', *Bolletino della Società Geografica Italiana* **3** ser., 3, anno 24, **27** 659–89, 798–835; Aldobrandino Mochi, 'I popoli dell'Uaupé e la famiglia etnica Miranhà', *Archivio per Antropologia e la Etnologia* **32** 445ff., Florence, 1902. On the history of the Uaupés missions, in addition to the above sources, see documents in AA **1–2** (Manaus, 1906–7) nos 2–6; Friar Venâncio Willeke, *Missões Franciscanas no Brasil (1500/1975)* (São Paulo, 1976) 163ff.; Gerardo Reichel-Dolmatoff, *Amazonian Cosmos: sexual and religious symbolism of the Tukano Indians* (Chicago, 1971). On early use of the word Jurupari, Hemming, *Red Gold*, 58–9.

336 *has various ornaments.'* Coudreau, *La France Equinoxiale*, **2** 187.

336 *pain of death.'* Coppi, 'La Provincia', 199.

336 *surrounding these objects'.* Ibid., 202.

336 *and touched it.'* Ibid., 202.

336 *of the izi.'* Ibid., 202–3.

337 *in his hands.'* Ibid., 203.

337 *angry with you.'* Coudreau, *La France Equinoxiale*, **2** 200–1. Coudreau heard the Jurupari cult from Friar Guiseppe Coppi and thus wrongly equated it with the Christian Devil. The Italian traveller Count Stradelli interrogated an Indian with a mother from the Uaupés, and obtained a correct version from him. The Catholic Bishop of Amazonas, Dom Frederico da Costa, in 1908 confirmed that it was wrong to identify Jurupari with the demon (*Carta pastoral de D. Frederico Costa a seus amados diocesanos*, Fortaleza, 1908, 53). Cf. Wright, 'History and Religion', 344.

337 *emblem of Jurupari'.* Coudreau, *La France Equinoxiale*, **2** 138.

338 *of their pastors.'* Koch-Grünberg, *Zwei Jahre unter den Indianern*, **2** 10.

Chapter 17   RIO BRANCO–NORTH AMAZON

339 *a large number.'* Adalbert of Prussia, *Travels*, **2** 247, 215. Report by President João Maria de Moraes, Belém, 1846, 9.

340 *profit of humanity.'* João Wilkens de Mattos to Dr Bernardo Augusto Nascentes d'Azambuja, Manaus, 7 Aug. 1855, in Foreign Office, *Question de la Frontière, Annexe*, **2** 84. Rev. Youd had been sent by the Church Missionary Society to set up a mission among the Makuxi and Wapixana at their village Pirara on the upper Rupununi in 1838. By 1839 the Brazilians had sent a small military detachment to occupy and claim Pirara. They later withdrew, but there was much diplomatic protest and uncertainty about the exact location of the frontier. Pirara village lay on the Brazilian side of the watershed; but its Makuxi claimed to prefer British rule. Major João Henrique Wilkens de Mattos met British boundary commissioners on the Rupununi in 1842 (*Relatório*, 158) and was impressed by Pôrto Alegre mission. He reported that by 1843 Friar José dos Santos Inocentes was too old and ill to make expeditions to attract more Indians, but that Chief Cosme of the Wapixana (who had been given a rich uniform and other presents) was 'an Indian friendly to the whites and respected by other tribes'. Mattos also visited a short-lived mission called Serra do Baricó that Friar José had started on the

south bank of the Uraricoera. *Relatório*, 150.

340 *the two Governments.'* Rev. Thomas Youd's Journal for 5 Feb. 1840, in Foreign Office, ibid., 21.

341 *theirs, they lie." '* Youd to Governor Henry Light, Urwa Rapids, Rupununi river, March 1840, in ibid., 19.

341 *of their territory.'* Ibid., 20.

341 *them for observation.'* Report by William Crichton to Governor Light, 10 April 1841, ibid., 33.

341 *of the enemy?'* Richard Schomburgk, *Travels*, **2** 85, 97. Leverger, 'Apontamentos cronológicos', 346. Ferreira Reis, *A Amazônia que os Portuguêses revelaram*, 75.

341 *out the responses.'* Schomburgk, *Travels*, 133.

342 *the purpose intended.'* Ibid.

342 *forced its way.'* Schomburgk, 'Journal of an expedition from Pirara to the Upper Corentyne, and from thence to Demarara', JRGS **15** 6, 1845; Foreign Office, *Question de la Frontière, Annexe*, **1** 148.

342 *adjacent forest trees.'* Schomburgk, 'Journal', 6.

343 *waistlap was suspended.'* Ibid., 77–8.

343 *thread is conducted.'* Ibid., 84.

343 *gradually withdrew themselves.'* João Wilkens de Mattos to Dr Bernardo Augusto Nascentes d'Azambuja, Manaus, 7 Aug. 1855, in Foreign Office, *Question de la Frontière, Annexe*, **1** 84.

343 *with those Indians.'* President Francisco Coelho, Relatório, Belém, 1849, in Moreira Neto, *Política indigenista*, 42.

343 *from this appointment.'* Ibid. The new missionary was Friar Gregorio José Maria de Bene.

344 *treated most shamefully.'* Declaration of Chief George P. Wishrop of the Atorai, 12 Nov. 1857, in Foreign Office, *Question de la Frontière, Annexe*, **1** 85.

344 *or punish them.'* Lieutenant-Governor W. Walker to Mr Labouchère, Demerara, 24 Nov. 1857, ibid., 85.

344 *impeded by rapids.* Report by I. C. Dawson of a Journey to the Rio Rupununi, sent by Lieutenant-Governor Walker to Lord Stanley, Demerara, 8 May 1858, ibid., 86.

344 *forcibly carried off.'* Ibid.

344 *incredible cruelty.'* Georg Hübner and Theodor Koch-Grünberg, 'Die Yauapery', *Zeitschrift für Ethnologie* **39** 220, Berlin, 1907; João Barbosa Rodrigues, *Rio Jauapery. Pacificação dos Crichanás* (Rio de Janeiro, 1885); Verenilde Santos Pereira, Egydio Schwade and others, *Resistência Waimiri/Atroari* (MAREWA, Itacoatiara, 1983) 12.

345 *incessantly and implacably.'* Marcel Monnier, *Des Andes au Pará* (Paris, 1890) 423. Report by President José de Miranda da Silva Reis, Manaus, 1870, listing hostilities by the Atroari (then also known as Crichaná or Crixaná, or Jauapery) during the 1860s; report by President Domingos Monteiro Peixoto, 1873; report by President Domingos Jacy Monteiro, 1877. Moreira Neto, *Política indigenista*, 88, 91, 93.

345 *into their territory.'* Brown and Lidstone, *Fifteen thousand miles*, 363. We know of at least one punitive, slaving raid up the Jauaperi, in 1712. This was led by Domingos de Sá and was in pursuit of Aruak Indians who had killed the Mercedarian missionary Friar João das Neves. Francisco Xavier Ribeiro de Sampaio, *Diario da viagem . . . do Rio Negro* (1774–5) (Lisbon, 1856 edn) 65; David Sweet, 'A Rich Realm of Nature Destroyed: the middle Amazon valley, 1640–1750' (doctoral dissertation, University of Wisconsin, Madison, 1974) **1** 312. On the events at Pedreira and Moura in 1873, see also: João Barbosa Rodrigues, *Rio Jauapery: pacificação dos crichanás* (Rio de Janeiro, 1885) and his article in Mello Moraes Filho, *Revista da Exposição Anthropologica*, 47; Ermanno Stradelli, 'Rio Branco: note di viaggio dal Cucuhy a Manaos', *Bolletino della Società Geografica*

Italiana 3 ser., 2, anno 23, **26** 215–16, Rome, 1889. The Italian mission was that of Friar Antonio Tunaré at Tauaguera in 1855. The various military expeditions were: that of Manoel Pereira de Vasconcellos in 1856; Colonel Rego Barros Falcão in 1873; Lieutenant Horta in 1874; and a bloody attack at Catingueira in 1905. Bandeira, *A cruz indigena*, 6–7.

345 *from the woodwork.'* Brown and Lidstone, *Fifteen thousand miles*, 363.

345 *'many were killed.'* Stradelli, 'Rio Branco', 216. Bandeira, *A cruz indigena*.

346 *Jauaperi.'* Barbosa Rodrigues, *Rio Jauapery*, 40; Pereira, Schwade *et al.*, *Resistência Waimiri/Atroari* 12–13. The campaigns against the Atroari-Waimiri in 1873 had been led by Colonel João Rego Falcão and later by Lieutenant Pastana.

346 *on a branch.'* Barbosa Rodrigues, *Rio Jauapery*, 41. The punitive expeditions of 1875 and 1876 were also sent by the provincial government. The latter was led by Lieutenant Malaquias José Netto.

346 *with the civilisados.'* Barbosa Rodrigues, in Mello Moraes Filho, *Revista da Exposição Anthropologica*, 47.

346 *whites are bad.'* Ibid., 47.

347 *end of you!'* Ibid., 48.

347 *and machine guns.'* Ibid., 48.

347 *sword, and sacrificed.'* Ibid., 48.

347 *knives and mirrors.'* Monnier, *Des Andes au Pará*, 424.

347 *forget you."'* Barbosa Rodrigues, *Rio Jauapery*, 55. Stradelli, 'Rio Branco', 216–21; Koch-Grünberg, *Zwei Jahre unter den Indianern*, 1 19; Arthur Johim, *O Amazonas, sua história* (São Paulo, 1957) 196.

347 *not forget you.'* Monnier, *Des Andes au Pará*, 424.

347 *will be respected.'* Barbosa Rodrigues, *Rio Jauapery*, 56–7. Raiol, 'Catachese de índios', 172.

348 *obliged to flee.'* Coudreau, *La France Equinoxiale*, **2** 414. Coudreau was a boastful, disagreeable explorer, always ready to disparage the work of other travellers and to despise Indians. Count Stradelli was on the Rio Branco in 1886, a year after Coudreau's visit, and remarked how unpopular the Frenchman had made himself with local people. He also exposed some of Coudreau's many inaccuracies.

348 *have just massacred.'* Ibid., 113. Fifteen years later, in 1899, Coudreau was on the Nhamundá river to the east of Atroari-Waimiri territory and was sure that he had a fleeting contact with this tribe, now considered dangerous despite the pacification of 1884–5. Coudreau, *Voyage au Yamundá*, 54.

348 *were the same.'* Richard Payer, 'Reisen im Jauapiry-Gebiet', *Petermanns Mitteilungen* **52** 220, Gotha, 1906.

348 *and all ages'.* Koch-Grünberg, *Vom Roroima zum Orinoco* (Berlin, 1917) **1** 5; G. Hübner and Koch-Grünberg, 'Die Yauapery', *Zeitschrift für Ethnologie*, 225, Berlin, 1907.

349 *and one woman.'* Alípio Bandeira, *Jauapery* (Manaus, 1926) 6.

351 *grim and lonely.'* Barrington Brown, *Canoe and Camp Life* (London, 1876), 296.

351 *and private ranches.* Schomburgk wrote that the first cattle were farmed by Antonio Amorini and Évora in 1796 with fifty head of cattle near the fort. The cattle multiplied, but the ranchers went bankrupt and their ranches were taken over by the government. In 1838, the national fazendas of São Marcos, São José and São Bento were said to consist of 3000 head penned and 5000 wild, plus 500 horses; but Schomburgk thought these figures exaggerated. Twenty-two local Indians tended these herds. Schomburgk, 'Journey', 180. Coudreau, *La France Equinoxiale*, **2** 407.

351 *and harder journey.'* Grupe y Thode, 'Ueber den Rio Blanco', *Globus* **57** 253, 1890. João Henrique de Mattos gave interesting information about the cattle herds of the upper Rio Branco in his *Relatório* of 1845. Gama

Lobo d'Almada had brought the first thirteen animals to the region in 1787, after which cattle were introduced from all parts of Portuguese Amazonia. Someone called Évora founded São José ranch and Sarmento founded São Marcos, but when they died the state took over all three ranches. By 1838 they still had three thousand cattle and two thousand horses, but these were reduced to 500−600 cattle and 150 horses by 1843. The decline was due to depredations during the Cabanagem: Ambrosio Pedro Aires ('Bararoá') was rewarded for his military exploits with almost 400 cattle; and the Italian Colonel Francisco Ricardo Zany 'ordered as much slaughter as he wanted on the ranches of the Rio Branco' on the pretext of feeding government factories (*Relatório*, 160). Subsequent administrators, two of whom were criminals exiled from Brazil's north-east, continued the annihilation for their personal profit. Another exiled killer, Ignácio Lopes de Magalhães, started to revive the herds, particularly at Caracaraí, in the 1840s.

351 *love of order'.* Schomburgk, in William Curtis Farabee, *The Central Caribs* (Philadelphia, 1924) 14.

351 *they are young.'* Stradelli, 'Rio Branco', 264.

352 *thousand of them.'* Coudreau, *La France Equinoxiale,* **2** 400−1. Gustavo Suckow, 'Carta do Sr. Gustavo Suckow ao *Jornal do Commercio'*, *Revista de Geographia do Rio de Janeiro* **7** 278, 1891.

352 *whom he spoke.'* Barrington Brown, *Canoe and Camp Life*, 158.

352 *Yes, truly," etc.'* Ibid., 158−9.

353 *an unpleasant one.'* Ibid., 285−6.

353 *each other incessantly.'* Ibid., 165.

353 *a man drunk.'* Ibid.

353 *fun of vomiting.'* Ibid.

354 *gentle and fearful.'* Coudreau, *La France Equinoxiale,* **2** 378.

354 *for white men.'* Ibid., 376.

354 *learned about us.'* Farabee, *The Central Caribs*, 156; Farabee, 'A Pioneer in Amazonia', 21. Apart from Schom-

burgk in 1837 and Coudreau in 1884, the only other person to describe a visit to the Wai-Wai was John Ogilvie of Harvard University who saw them in 1910. Charles Barrington Brown approached but did not reach Wai-Wai territory in 1870.

355 *roll of tobacco'.* Coudreau, *La France Equinoxiale,* **2** 357.

355 *the others combined.'* Farabee, *The Central Caribs*, 166.

355 *down their bows.'* Ibid., 188.

356 *in our direction.'* Farabee, 'A Pioneer in Amazonia', 31.

356 *a defenseless man.'* Ibid. Farabee spells the tribe's name Parikutu in this paper of 1917, but Parukutu in his book of 1924. Parikotó is the spelling used by Nimuendajú. This tribe should not be confused with another Carib tribe called Purukotó which lives north of Maracá island on the Uraricuera headwater of the Rio Branco.

356 *each other perfectly.'* Ibid., 36.

356 *must drink it.'* Ibid., 37.

356 *we understood perfectly.'* Ibid., 37−8.

356 *other like mad.'* Ibid., 38.

356 *of the sexes.'* Ibid., 33.

357 *about to collapse.'* Crevaux, *Voyages dans l'Amérique du Sud*, 249−50.

357 *of chili pepper.'* Ibid., 99. Crevaux and other French writers call the Wayana Roucouyennes because they paint themselves with red urucum dye.

357 *to the ground.'* Ibid., 100.

358 *eau de cologne.'* Olga Coudreau, *Voyage au Cuminá*, 155−6.

359 *with hideous barbarism.'* Ibid., 118. The report of 1862 was by President Araújo Brusque of Pará (pp. 56−7 about Thomas Antonio d'Aquino's journey up the Trombetas). On the failed expeditions: Henri Coudreau, *La France Equinoxiale,* **2** 363, and Olga Coudreau, *Voyage au Cuminá*, 141−2. On hostilities between blacks and Indians: Orville A. Derby, 'O rio Trombetas', *Boletim do Museu Paraense de Historia Natural e Ethnographia* **1**: 3 369−70, Belém, 1897−8; Braz Dias de Aguiar, *Nas fronteiras da Venezuela e Guianas Britânica e Neerlandesa* (Rio de Janeiro, 1943) 89, 116; Frikel,

Hirama and Matchuhuaya, 'Tradições histórico-lendárias dos Kachúyana e Káhyana', RMP n.s. Antropologia 9 226, 1955; Frikel, *Os Kaxúyana: notas etno-históricas*, Publicações Avulsas do Museu Goeldi, 14 (Belém, 1970) 40–1.

359 *for the vultures.*' Coudreau, *Voyage au Cuminá*, 119.

359 *not human beings.*' Ibid., 132.

359 *unable to carry.*' Adam de Bauve and P. Ferré, 'Voyage dans l'intérieur de la Guyane', *Bulletin de la Société de Géographie* 20: 127 267, Paris, Nov. 1833.

359 *be their tomb.*' Ibid., 268. The Wayapí are also spelled Oyampi or Oyampik. Their own tribal tradition said that they originated among the many Tupi-speaking tribes south of the Amazon. During the eighteenth century they acted as mercenaries and slave-raiders for the Portuguese, who armed them with guns and sent them into what is now Amapá. (Claude Tony, 'Voyage dans l'intérieur du continent de la Guyane', *Nouvelles Annales des Voyages*, 4 ser., 97 232–3, 1843; Henri Froidevaux, 'Explorations françaises à l'intérieur de la Guyane pendant le second quart du XVIIIe siècle (1720–1742)', *Bulletin de la Géographie et Histoire des Descouvertes* 47, 1897; Henri Coudreau, *Chez nos indiens* (Paris, 1893) 279; Alfred Métraux, 'Migrations historiques des Tupi-Guarani', *Journal de la Société des Américanistes de Paris*, n.s. 19 31, 1927; Expedito Arnaud, 'Os índios Oyampik e Emerilon (rio Oiapoque)', BMPEG Antropologia, n.s., 47 3, 2 Feb. 1971. By the early nineteenth century, the Wayapí (Oyampi) were established on the Oiapoque river. The French traveller Leprieur visited them in 1832 and saw villages with twelve hundred people, whereas the engineer Bodin had reckoned there were six thousand of them 'predominantly nomadic' in 1824. (M. Leprieur, 'Voyage dans la Guyane Centrale', *Bulletin de la Société de Géographie*, 2 ser., 1 208, Paris, 1834; Coudreau, *La France Equinoxiale*, 2 43; Arnaud, 'Os índios', 4.) By 1835 Governor Legrange of French Guiana said that they were still quite numerous even though nine-tenths of them had died of disease. In 1839 Bernardino de Souza said that the Wayapí had a village on the Jari and they were known to have fought the Boni blacks of Guiana until the latter were massacred by French troops in 1842. By the end of the nineteenth century, their numbers were much diminished but the Wayapí had at least made peace with their old Carib enemies the Wayana (Roucouyennes). J. Hurault, 'Les indiens Oyampi de la Guyane Française', *Journal de la Société des Américanistes*, n.s., 51 66, Paris, 1962.

360 *have completely disappeared.*' Crevaux, *Voyages dans l'Amérique du Sud*, 217.

360 *within our reach.*' Schomburgk, 'Report', 171. Nicholas Guppy, *Wai-Wai* (London, 1958) 32.

360 *to our camp.*' Schomburgk, 'Journal of an Expedition from Pirara to the Upper Corentyne', *JRGS* 15 31, 1845; Guppy, *Wai-Wai*, 33–4.

361 *to his mouth.*' Bauve, *Voyage dans l'intérieur*, 275.

361 *thirst, or sweat.*' Crevaux, *Voyages dans l'Amérique du Sud*, 251.

361 *all the people.*' Farabee, 'A Pioneer in Amazonia', 29.

361 *was through fighting.*' Frikel, Hirama and Matchuhuaya, 'Tradições histórico-lendárias dos Kachúyana e Kahyána', 226; Frikel, *Os Kaxúyana*, 41.

361 *than a memory.*' Coudreau, *Voyage à la Mapuera*, 88.

362 *into civilised people.*' Coudreau, *Voyage au Cuminá*, 171.

362 *bring them tears?*' Ibid., 170.

362 *are not abolished.*' Coudreau, *Voyage à la Mapuera*, 91.

362 *died in time.*' Koch-Grünberg diary, Vista Alegre, 1924 (shortly before he died of malaria) in Egon Schaden, 'A obra cientifica de Koch-Grünberg', *Revista de Antropologia* 1–2, Rio de Janeiro, 1953; Veríssimo de Melo, 'Koch-Grünberg', *Revista de Atualidade Indígena* 2:8 31–2, Brasília, Jan.–Feb. 1978.

Chapter 18   BOTOCUDO

365 *a single assailant.*' Theóphilo Bene-
dicto Otoni, 'Noticia sobre os
selvagens do Mucury', RHGB **21**
178−9, 1858 or 1930.
366 *a thousand ways.*' Ibid., 180.
366 *extract those riches.*' Pedro Victor
Reinault, *Relatório da exposição dos rios
Mucury e Todos os Santos* (1837), RHGB
8 357, 1846 or 1867.
366 *unknown to them.*' Ibid., 370.
367 *so many years.*' Ibid., 371.
367 *of Minas Novas.*' Ibid., 373.
367 *river] to entrepreneurs.*' Ibid., 373.
367 *in Espírito Santo.*' Ibid., 179.
367 *Rio de Janeiro.*' Ibid., 213. Otoni
spelled the tribal name Machacali;
Nimuendajú spelled their name
Mašakarí and the Indian service
Funai spells it Maxacali. The tribe
still occupies the reserve on the
Ribeirão dos Prates, just inside
Minas Gerais and now called Posto
Indígena Maxacali. The tribe's language is isolated.
367 *conqueror and victor.*' Ibid., 214.
368 *peace and friendship.*' Hermenegildo
Antonio Barbosa d'Almeida,
'Viagem as villas de Caravellas,
Viçosa, Porto-Alegre, de Mucury e
aos rios Mucury e Peruype', RHGB **8**
443, 1846 or 1867.
368 *and other places'.* Ibid.
368 *which deformed them.*' Ibid., 444.
369 *Museum of Paris.*' Ibid., 181. Avé-
Lallement, *Viagem pelo norte do Brasil*, **1**
171: he called the family Vidal.
369 *by hideous passion.*' Reinault, *Relatório*,
184.
369 *winning their friendship.*' Otoni to
President of Minas Gerais, 27 Jan.
1853, in Otoni, 'Noticia', 186.
370 *with [Poton's] people.*' Ibid., 190.
370 *large plantation there.*' Ibid., 190.
371 *tribes between themselves.*' Ibid., 191.
371 *amid excruciating suffering.*' Jacinto de
Palazzolo, *Nas selvas dos vales do Mucuri
e do Rio Doce . . .* (São Paulo, 1952) 67.
371 *can use them.*' Ch. Fred. Hartt, *Geology
and physical geography of Brazil* (Boston

and London, 1870) 591.
371 *which facilitates bleeding.*' Ibid., 591.
371 *destroyed the race.*' Ibid., 601.
372 *the murdered savages.*' Otoni, 'Noticia',
179.
372 *these poor creatures!*' Hartt, *Geology*,
601.
372 *from the disease.*' Otoni, 'Noticia',
185.
372 *given insufficient food.*' Ibid., 198.
373 *Urucu to beg.*' Hartt, *Geology*, 602.
373 *were seriously wounded.*' Ibid., 202. The
settlement of Philadelphia (Fila-
délfia in modern Brazilian spelling)
was renamed Teófilo Otoni in
honour of its founder. It is now a
sizable town on the main road
between Rio de Janeiro and Salvador
da Bahia, roughly midway between
the two cities.
373 *was called Pojichá.*' Ibid., 203−4.
374 *with the Portuguese.*' Ibid., 206. J. J.
von Tschudi, *Reisen durch Südamerika*,
6 vols (Leipzig, 1866) **2** 226ff.
Tschudi gave a breakdown of the
various Botocudo tribes at the time
of his visit: Naknyanuk in small
family groups on the upper Mucuri
and Todos os Santos rivers; Aranau
lower on the Mucuri; Bakué between
the Pampan and Santa Clara rivers;
Urufu below or west of the latter and
almost on the coast. On the Riberão
de Saudade, a southern tributary of
the Mucuri, lived the Pojichá; east of
the Riberão das Lages lived the
Mekmek, Jiporok and Potik (the
Jiporok, who were visited by Prince
Maximilian of Wied-Neuwied, were
on the Urucú tributary of the
Mucuri); Porokun, Batata and other
groups lived on the headwaters of the
São Mateus. Alfred Métraux, 'The
Botocudo', HSAI **1** 531−2. Hartt,
Geology, 592−5.
374 *his liberal politics.* Avé-Lallement,
Viagem pelo norte do Brasil, **1** 176−7,
197; Palazzolo, *Nas selvas*, 74−5; José
Cândido Gomes, *Relatório da Comissão*

Liquidadora da Companhia do Mucuri (Rio de Janeiro, 1862); Américo Brazelino, 'A emprêsa do Mucuri', *Revista Popular* 1;3 163—75, Rio de Janeiro, July 1859; Godofredo Ferreira, *Os bandeirantes modernos — Desbravamento e colonização das matas do vale do rio Mucuri, em Minas Gerais* (Teófilo Otoni, 1934); Basilio de Magalhães, *Teófilo Otoni* (Rio de Janeiro, 1945) 26, 56.

374 *Philadelphia were built.*' Hartt, *Geology*, 131.

374 *proved a failure.*' Ibid., 132.

375 *in that horde!*' Avé-Lallement, *Viagem pelo norte do Brasil*, 231.

375 *of perfect idiocy.*' Ibid., 231.

375 *a civilised man*'. Ibid., 231.

375 *truly hideous shape!*' Ibid., 236.

375 *truly horrible impression.*' Ibid., 241.

376 *life with them.*' Tschudi, *Reisen durch Südamerika*, 2 222.

376 *blacks and mulattoes.*' Hermann Burmeister, *Reise nach Brasilien*, trans. Hubert Schoenfeldt, *Viagem ao Brasil* (São Paulo, 1980) 164.

376 *attracts the blacks.*' Ibid., 166.

376 *with bare walls.*' Ibid., 166.

376 *during this task.*' Ibid., 168—9.

376 *civilised Indian owns.*' Ibid., 169.

377 *than the blacks.*' Ibid., 166.

377 *themselves far superior.*' Ibid., 167.

377 *in this particular.*' Ibid.

378 *then considered "tamed".*' Report by Antonio Luiz de Magalhães Mosqueira, Diretor Geral dos Indios of Minas Gerais, to Minister of Agriculture, Commerce and Public Works, 1873, in Palazzolo, *Nas selvas*, 77.

378 *nervous and exhausted.*' Friar Serafim de Gorízia, 'Oficios e relatórios', by directors of the Aldeamento indígena de Itambacurí, three volumes of manuscripts in the archive of the Convento de São Sebastião, Rio de Janeiro: 2 13, in Palazzolo, ibid., 90. Itambacurí is now a village on the main road just south of Teófilo Otoni. Its river flows into the upper Doce.

378 *already badly diminished.*' Ibid., 90.

379 *of both races.*' Friar Ângelo de Sassoferato, 'Sinópse da Missão Catequese dos selvícolas do Mucuri, Estado de Minas Gerais', manuscript in Convento de São Sebastião, Rio de Janeiro, in ibid., 93.

378 *of that settlement.*' Farmers and settlers of Philadelphia to Emperor Dom Pedro II, 1 Jan. 1885, in ibid., 196.

380 *the provincial coffers.*' Ibid., 105. The mission for the Araná Botocudo on the Doce was run by Friar Virgilio de Amblar, who called it Aldeia da Imaculad Conceição. His Indians were angry because two of their girls had run off to Nossa Senhora dos Anjos de Itambacurí and the Capuchins there refused to make them go home.

380 *and copious cachaça*'. Serafim de Gorízia to Diretor Geral dos Indios Brigadeiro Antonio Luiz de Magalhães Mosqueira, early 1875, ibid., 108.

380 *day as slaves*'. Friar Serafim to the same, 8 Dec. 1877, ibid., 115.

380 *labour, or eliminate.*' Report by Diretor Geral dos Indios to Minister of Agriculture, Ouro Prêto, 1879, in ibid., 139.

381 *return half-roasted monkey.*' Friar Ângelo de Sassoferato report, 30 June 1884, in ibid., 186—7.

382 *like dangerous beasts.*' Friar Serafim de Gorízia to Diretor Geral dos Indios in Ouro Prêto, Itambacurí, 1885, Archive of the Convento de São Sebastião, Rio de Janeiro, *Correspondência, oficios e relatórios*, 2, ibid., 207. The great German ethnologist Paul Ehrenreich visited the area and reckoned that there were five thousand Botocudo in all. Of these, 886 were settled at the mission of Itambacurí and 241 at Immaculada Conceição on the Rio Doce. Paul Ehrenreich, 'Über die Botokudens der brasilianischen Provinzen Espíritu Santo und Minas Gerais', *Zeitschrift für Ethnologie* 19 8—11, Berlin, 1887.

382 *in cotton spinning.'* Friar Serafim report of 30 June 1888, Palazzolo, *Nas selvas*, 215.

383 *who visited it.'* Friar Ângelo de Sassoferato report, 1893, ibid., 252.

383 *will die later.'* Ibid., 261.

384 *a pure specimen.'* Mello Moraes Filho, *Revista da Exposição Anthropologica*, 2.

384 *and feel happy.'* Ibid., 30.

384 *or dawn breaks!'* Ibid.

Chapter 19   MISSIONARY ZEAL

385 *the civilised classes.'* President J. Ignácio Ramalho, Relatório, Goiás, 1846, 13–14.

385 *gradually and imperceptibly.'* Ibid., 15–16.

386 *society by terror.'* Ramalho, report for 1847, 13.

386 *and given presents.'* Ibid., 15.

386 *for two milreis.'* Report of President Padua Fleury, Goiás, 1848, 27. This aldeia of Salinas was inland from the east bank of the Araguaia, some 120 kilometres south of Bananal island. It was the site of an earlier aldeia created in 1785 for the Chavante, who soon disliked it and left. Taggia is on the Ligurian coast of Italy near Sanremo and the French border.

386 *of Pedro Afonso.'* Frei Rafael Tuggia, 'Mappas dos indios Cherentes e Chavantes na nova povoação de Thereza Christina no rio Tocantins, e dos indios Charaós da aldea de Pedro Affonso nas margens do mesmo rio . . .', RHGB **19** 122, 1856 or 1898.

386 *it is healthy.'* President Padua Fleury, Relatório, Goiás, 1848, 27. Nimuendajú, *Eastern Timbira*, 25; Júlio Cezar Melatti, *Índios e criadores: a situação dos Krahó na área pastoril do Tocantins* (Rio de Janeiro, 1967); Manuela Carneiro da Cunha, *Os mortos e os outros* (São Paulo, 1978) 5.

387 *live without religion.'* Rafael de Tuggia, *Mappas*, 122.

387 *and good hunters.'* Ibid., 123.

387 *die without treatment.'* Ibid.

387 *love of him.'* Ibid.

387 *where none exists.'* James Wells, *Three thousand miles through Brazil* (London,

1886) **2** 218–19.

388 *Manoel Alves Pequeno.'* Ibid., 219.

388 *the new settlers'.* President F. J. da Gama Cerqueira, Relatório, Goiás, 1859, 50–1. Another later missionary, the Dominican Father Etienne-Marie Gallais, wrote in 1906 that the Krahó remained pagan after Friar Rafael's death: Gallais, *O apóstolo do Araguaia, Frei Gil Vilanova* (Conceição do Araguaia, 1942) 130. Friar Rafael himself wrote that the Krahó were reduced to 620 after violent epidemics of 1849 and 1850 (*Mappas*, 122), and a traveller reported that in 1859 they were in three villages near Pedro Afonso (Gomes, 'Itinerario', 490). Nimuendajú, *Eastern Timbira*, 25.

388 *beyond his capacity.'* Ibid.

388 *as a white box.'* Wells, *Three thousand miles*, **2** 219.

388 *is a madman.'* Ibid., 224.

389 *children as captives.'* Ibid., 224.

389 *afford to pay.'* Ibid., 225.

389 *for their support.'* Rafael de Taggia, *Mappas*, 120. By 1857 President A. A. Pereira da Cunha reported that Teresa Cristina had 3800 Cherente and Chavante; but Pedro Afonso had declined to two hundred Krahó and had been invaded by three hundred colonists from Bahia and Piauí. Pereira da Cunha, Relatório, Goiás, 1857, 19. On the history of the Cherente move in 1850: J. M. Pereira de Alencastre, Relatório, 1862, 45. Moreira Neto, *Política indigenista*, 220, 235.

389 *loaded with presents.'* Wells, *Three thousand miles*, 219.

389 *affection and respect.*' Ibid.

389 *establish their domicile.*' President Antonio Joaquim da Silva Gomes, Relatório, Goiás, 1851, 40−1,

390 *purely animal instincts.*' J. M. Pereira de Alencastre, Relatório, Goiás, 1862, 48−9.

390 *of those savages*'. F. J. da Gama Cerqueira, Relatório, Goiás, 1859, 52.

390 *punishments and tortures].*' A. A. Pereira da Cunha, Relatório, Goiás, 1856, 15−16.

391 *to replenish themselves.*' Eduardo Olympio Machado, Relatório, Goiás, 1850, 26; Padua Fleury, Relatório, 1848, 28; Silva Gomes, Relatório, 1851, 45; Pereira da Cunha, 1857, 19.

391 *'horrible slaughter'*. F. J. da Gama Cerqueira, Relatório, Goiás, 1859, 52. Castelnau described the Italian missionary as a fine modest man who had reached Boa Vista in 1841: *Expédition*, 2 24−5.

391 *to be baptised*'. Ibid.

391 *takes in them.*' F. J. da Gama Cerqueira, Relatório, Goiás, 1859, 52.

391 *to escape reprisals.* Nimuendajú, *Eastern Timbira*, 16; Marques, *Apontaentos*, entry for 'Santa Thereza'; Gomes, *Itinerario*, 194−5; Luiz Guilherme Dodt, *Descripção dos rios Parnahyba e Gurupy* (Maranhão, 1873) 121.

392 *of this mission.* Jeronimo Francisco Coelho, Falla, Belém, 1848, 76; Fausto Augusto d'Aguiar, Relatório, Belém, 1851, 53; José Joaquim da Cunha, Falla, Belém, 1852, 82; Sebastião do Rego Barros, Falla, 1854, Annexo, 56. Castelnau had noted the danger from the Gaviões in 1844: *Expédition*, 2, 11, 17, 18. Nimuendajú, *Eastern Timbira*, 17.

392 *and farming ranches*'. Jesuino Marcondes de Oliveira Sá, *Relatório apresentado . . . à Assembléia Legislativa* (Rio de Janeiro, 1865) 157. Expedito Arnaud, 'O comportamento dos índios Gaviões do Oeste face a sociedade nacional', BMPEG Série antropologia 1:1 11, June 1984.

392 *in extreme misery.*' Oliveira Sá, *Relatório*, 157. That visit was in 1859. The director went on with an Indian interpreter to visit some uncontacted Gaviões, three days' march away, and these agreed to move their huts closer to the village of pacified Indians.

392 *confidence in us.*' Rufino Theatino Segurado, *Viagem de Goyaz ao Pará*, RHGB 10 191, 1848 or 1870.

392 *"Presidio [fort], no."* ' Ibid., 194−5.

393 *near these villages.*' Ibid.

393 *defend the presidio.*' A. M. de Aragão e Mello, Relatório, Goiás, 1861, 14. São João do Araguaia (formerly São João das Duas Barras − 'St John of the Two Bars') is forty kilometres east of the modern town of Marabá, on the left bank of the Araguaia immediately opposite the entry of the Tocantins. Santa Maria was ninety kilometres upstream of Conceição do Araguaia, some four hundred kilometres south of São João as the crow flies and about twice that distance up the river.

393 *men to flight.*' Ibid.

393 *territory they inhabit.*' Ibid.

393 *from Santa Maria.* Bigorre, 'Quarante jours', 513; Gallais, *O apóstolo do Araguaya*, 148. By 1911, Bigorre wrote that Santa Maria had eight hundred people. It was ninety kilometres upriver from Conceição, near modern Araguacema; the hamlet of Santa Maria Velha opposite Conceição is an older location of this mission/fort.

394 *centre of evangelisation*'. Bigorre, 'Quarante jours', 607. J. Couto de Magalhães, *Viagem ao Araguaya* (Brasiliana edn, São Paulo, 1934) 134−5, 139.

394 *sentiment and education*'. Couto de Magalhães, quoted in President Aristedes de Souza Spinola, Relatório, Goiás, 1879, 24.

394 *to be useful.*' Ibid. Moreira Neto, *Política indigenista*, 254.

395 *a savage life.*' Gallais, *O apóstolo do Araguaya*, 177. Annual reports by President Antero Cicero de Assis, Goiás, 1872, 30; the same president, 1875, 39; Aristedes de Souza Spinola,

1879, 24. Colegio Isabel was founded in 1871 at a settlement called Dumbasinho, two leagues below Leopoldina but on the opposite or west bank. Various travellers left accounts of the Araguaia during the years of the steamship service: an army engineer Major Joaquim de Moraes Jardim, who went with the President of Goiás, Dr Aristides de Souza Spinola, in 1879 and published jointly *O Rio Araguaya* (Rio de Janeiro, 1880); Dr Paul Ehrenreich, who went down by steamer in 1888; Dr A. Cavalcanti (after seeking a site for the future capital of Brazil: he chose the location of modern Brasília) in 1896; Henri Coudreau in 1896−7; Friar Gil Vilanova and other missionaries, 1891−1905; Fritz Krause, 1908.

The President of Goiás visited Colegio Isabel in 1871 and found twenty-one Karajá, Kayapó and Gorotire children of both sexes learning reading and writing in Portuguese (President Antero Cicero de Assis, Relatório, Goiás, 1872, 30). This President's report for 1875 said that the school had thirty boys and nine girls, from a greater number of tribes. The children were good at reading and writing but bad at mechanics: two had tried to run away. By 1879 the school had fifty-two pupils from five tribes (including Chavante, Tapirapé and Guajajara).

395 *for colonising efforts'*. President Aristedes de Souza Spinola, Goiás, 1880, 32. Leopoldina was founded in 1850 as Santa Leopoldina, but its garrison and those of other Araguaia presidios was moved east to the Tocantins in 1853. Refounded in 1855 on the left bank of the Vermelho river, it was then moved in 1856 to the site of the modern town Aruanã. Santa Maria had been revived in 1851 but its men moved to the Tocantins two years later. It was refounded in 1858 for the third time, near modern Araguacema.

395 *of the river.'* Ibid.

395 *we esteem them.'* President José Boni-

fácio Gomes de Siqueira to Captain commanding presidio of Santa Maria do Araguaia, Goiás, 21 May 1867, in Moreira Neto, *Política indigenista*, 241.

396 *persons to slavery'*. Ibid.

396 *forests and rivers.'* President Joaquim de Almeida Leite de Morais, Goiás, 1881, 79, 98. Moreira Neto, *Política indigenista*, 268−9.

396 *civilise, but corrupt'.* President Leite de Morais, Goiás, 1881, 98.

396 *symbol of peace.'* Ibid.

396 *of their chief.'* Modesto Rezende de Taubaté and F. M. de Primeiro, *Os missionários capuchinos no Brasil* (São Paulo, 1929), quoted in Moreira Neto, *Política indigenista*, 249.

397 *on the Araguaia!'* Ibid.

397 *any plausible motive.'* President J. M. Pereira de Alencastre, Relatório, Goiás, 1862, 45. The attacks were on the Rivers Claro, Bonito, Caiapó Grande and Pequeno, tributaries of the Maranhão (upper Tocantins) north-west of modern Brasília. This president sought government funds to settle these Kayapó in aldeias. Other southern Kayapó still lived in reduced numbers in villages on the Piquiri and Parnaíba rivers, south of modern Brasília on the road between Goiás and São Paulo: Amédée Moure, 3 79−80.

397 *and vice versa.'* Aristedes de Souza Spinola, Relatório, Goiás, 1880, II, 17. Moreira Neto, *Política indigenista*, 262−3.

397 *hatred of them.'* Ibid., 18.

398 *Kayapó Indian nation'.* Gallais, *O apóstolo do Araguaia*, 83. The Bonito river rises in the Serra do Caiapó and flows into the Caiapó tributary of the upper Araguaia between the modern towns of Barra do Garças and Goiânia.

398 *a bad beast.'* Ibid., 85.

398 *an immense raid.'* Ibid., 101.

398 *all pitilessly massacred.'* Ibid., 101.

398 *these dangerous savages.'* Ibid., 77.

399 *with those Indians.'* President José Bonifácio Gomes de Siqueira to commander of presídio of Santa Maria do Araguaia, 21 May 1867, in his report for 1867, 6. Castelnau had reported

in 1844 that one group of Kayapó lived opposite Salinas (he presumably meant the Chavante on the Mortes) and the Gradaú tribe to the north, between the Araguaia and Xingu with a territory stretching northwards towards the major rapids on the Araguaia (*Expédition*, 2 114). Dr Rufino Theotino Seguardo wrote that in 1847 the Gradaú lived three days' march west of the Araguaia; and Joaquim de Moraes Jardim confirmed this location in 1880. The first mention of these Gradaú Kayapó was by Raymundo da Cunha Mattos in 1825: RHGB **37** 361, 393; **38** 18. The presídio of Santa Maria was opposite modern Conceição do Araguaia. Krause, *In den Wildnissen Brasiliens*, 368. The name Kayapó has variant spellings: Cayapó, Caiapó, Kaiapó. It is not a Gê word and means nothing to the Kayapó tribes themselves. Terence Turner reckons that it comes from Tupi words *kaya* (monkey) and *po* (resembling), i.e. 'people who look like monkeys': Turner, 'Social Structure and Political Organisation Among the Northern Kayapó' (thesis, Harvard University, 1965). Gustaaf Verswijver, 'Enquête ethnographique chez les Kayapó-Mekragnoti', (thesis, Ecole des Hautes Etudes en Sciences Sociales, Paris, 1978) 1. The Gradaú who lived near the Araguaia called themselves Iran-Amranire.

399 *dead or prisoners.'* Antero Cícero de Assis, Relatório, Goiás, 1876, 31–2.

399 *a deep scar.'* Aristedes de Souza Spinola, Goiás, 1880, 34.

400 *of national colonists'.* Souza Spinola, Goiás, 1880, II, 18.

400 *bosom of civilisation'.* Paul Ehrenreich, 'Die Einteilung und Verbreitung der Völkerstämme Brasiliens', *Petermanns Mitteilungen* **37** 37, 1891. Krause, *In den Wildnissen Brasiliens*, 368.

400 *wished to win'.* Bigorre, 'Quarante jours', 514. In January 1891, Gil Vilanova had walked westwards from Pedro Afonso on the Tocantins, along a 200 kilometre trail through the Serra do Estrondo to Santa Maria

on the Araguaia. The settlers of Santa Maria urged him to try to convert the Kayapó on the west bank, but he failed to make contact after a tough expedition. He then had himself paddled upstream past Bananal island, hoping to contact the Chavante of the Rio das Mortes; but his paddlers refused to enter that dangerous river. Friar Gil walked back to the Tocantins in March 1891 and went to spend two years as a missionary in the town of Uberaba.

400 *to live well'.* Gallais, *O apóstolo*, 183.

401 *a Christian education.'* Gallais, *O apóstolo do Araguaia*, 237. It was the French explorer Henri Coudreau who told Vilanova about the bluff on which he built Conceição do Araguaia. Coudreau had been hired by the government of Pará to explore the rivers flowing into the lower Amazon. He met his compatriot Vilanova in April 1897 and they became good friends. Coudreau quoted a letter to him from Vilanova, 28 July 1897: *Voyage à Itaboca et à l'Itacayuna* (Paris, 1898) 44–7; *Voyage au Tocantins–Araguaya* (Paris, 1897) 108. Fritz Krause, 'Minha excursão investigadora á região central do Araguaya' (1908), RHGB **73**:1 270, 1910.

401 *grace of baptism.'* Gil Vilanova, during a fund-raising trip to the Dominicans in Toulouse, in Gallais, *O apóstolo do Araguaia*, 241–2.

401 *read and write.'* Vilanova, in ibid., 241.

401 *in their territory.'* Ibid., 242.

402 *them in Conceição.'* Ibid., 252.

402 *to their aldeia.'* Ibid., 215.

402 *susceptible and vengeful.'* Ibid., 190.

402 *like animated children.'* Ibid.

404 *big white beads'.* Gustaaf Verswijver, 'The Intertribal Relations Between the Juruna and the Kayapó Indians (1850–1920)', *Jahrbuch des Museums für Völkerkunde zu Leipzig* **34** 310, Berlin, 1982; Verswijver, 'Séparations et migrations des Mekrãgnoti, groupe Kayapo du Brésil Central', *Bulletin de la Société Suisse des Américanistes* **42** 47–8, 1978. Curt Nimuendajú, 'Os Gorotire', RMP n.s. **6** 428, 1952.

Coudreau, *Voyage à Itaboca*, 46, 79. Orlando and Cláudio Villas Boas, 'Os Juruna no Alto Xingu', *Reflexão* (Revista do Instituto de Ciências Humanas e Letras da Universidade

Federal de Goiás) 1:1 61−2, 1975.
404 *to use them.*' Cícero Cavalcante, '12 anos convivendo com os Kaiapó', *Atualidade Indigena* 12 18, Brasília, July−Aug. 1981.

Chapter 20   BORORO SURRENDER

405 *who wanted rum.*' Koslowski, *Algunos datos sobre . . . Bororos*, 383.
405 *syphilis and cachaça.*' Karl von den Steinen, *Unter den Naturvölkern Zentral-Brasiliens*, 442, trans. Egon Schaden, *Entre os aborígenes do Brasil Central* (São Paulo, 1940) 568.
406 *Mato Grosso itself.*' Severino da Fonseca, on the Parecis and Cabixis, in Mello Moraes Filho, *Revista da Exposição Anthropologica*, 139−40. A report of 1848 in the Indian directorate of Cuiabá said that there were two hundred to two hundred and fifty Paresi living near Diamantino and Mato Grosso. They sometimes appeared in the towns to trade manioc sieves, baskets, hammocks, feather-work, guinea pigs, or tobacco laced with the hallucinogenic urumbamba 'which is much sought-after by smokers'. There were also four hundred Maimbaré and five hundred hostile Kabishi. In 1888 a Captain Antonio Annibal da Motta visited three villages of Paresi on the upper Sepotuba, Formoso and Juba rivers: they traded rubber and ipecac at São Luis de Cáceres and fought warlike Nambikwara and hostile elements of Kabishi. There were also four villages of tame Kabishi on the Cabaçal river, and they were similar to the Paresi in language and customs. Steinen visited some Paresi near Diamantino at this time and wrote an ethnographic study of them. He also noted that 'the women removed their Brazilian clothing without much ado and wore beneath it tight red girdles thirty centimetres wide.' Steinen, *Unter den Naturvölkern*, 430.

406 *capture of settlers.*' Ibid., 140.
406 *this capital [Cuiabá].*' Report of President João José Pedrosa, Cuiabá, 1878, 35. He condemned the raid organised by his predecessor F. J. Cardoso Júnior.
406 *"Expeller of Indians" '.* Ibid.
406 *a large role.*' Steinen, *Unter den Naturvölkern*, 445.
407 *resistance is offered.*' Report of President J. J. Pedrosa, Cuiabá, 1879, 10.
407 *and well paid.*' Ibid., 10 and 22−3.
407 *crushed his body.*' Colbacchini, *I Bororos Orientali*, VIII.
407 *to offer them.*' João Augusto Caldas, *Memoria histórica sobre os indígenas da Provincia de Matto Grosso* (Rio de Janeiro, 1887) 21.
407 *with considerable strength.*' Report by Alferes Antonio José Duarte, Cuiabá, 16 June 1886, in Caldas, *Memoria histórica*, 24. Caldas himself was on the expedition, as a cadet.
408 *are conveniently lodged.*' *Situação*, no. 1040, Cuiabá, 20 June 1886.
408 *29 June 1886.*' Caldas, *Memoria histórica*, 36−7.
408 *naturally genial gentleman.*' Steinen, *Unter den Naturvölkern*, 446.
408 *to the parade.*' *Provincia de Matto-Grosso*, Cuiabá, 22 Aug. 1886. Everyone agreed that this pacification was the achievement of President Pimentel: Estavão de Mendonça, *Quadro Chorographico de Matto Grosso* (Escolas Profissionaes Salesianos, Cuiabá, 1906); Colbacchini, *I Bororos Orientali*, X; Vojtěch Frič and Paul Radin, 'Contributions to the Study of the Bororo Indians', *Journal of the Anthropological Institute* 36 382, London, 1906. Steinen, *Unter den Naturvölkern*,

446, or *Entre os aborígenes*, 572.
408 *that of civilisation'*. Caldas, *Memoria histórica*, 39.
408 *'frightening grunts'*. Ibid
408 *expansive merriment everywhere!'* Steinen, *Unter den Naturvölkern*, 452, or *Entre os aborígenes*, 583.
409 *cost him much.'* Ibid., 447.
409 *or the huts.'* Ibid., 452.
409 *false and treacherous.'* Viveiros, *Rondon conta sua vida*, 334. Rosa Bororo's story was recorded by the wife of General Mello Rego, a later president of Matto Grosso. It was a favourite parable of Cândido Rondon, who told it in his famous lecture of 15 Oct. 1915. Lieutenant Pyrineus, a fellow officer of Rondon, met Rosa Bororo in the village of the Bakairi on the Teles Pires river where her son José Coroado was chief. Rondon, *Conferencias de 1915*, Commissão de Linhas Telegraphicas Estrategicas de Matto-Grosso ao Amazonas, no. 43 (Rio de Janeiro, 1916), trans. R. G. Reidy and Ed Murray (Rio de Janeiro, 1916) 291−4. Rondon, *Índios do Brasil*, 2: *Das cabeceiras do rio Xingu, dos rios Araguaia e Oiapóque*, Conselho Nacional de Proteção aos Índios (Rio de Janeiro, 1953) 44.
410 *not being Christian.'* Frič and Radin, 'Contributions to the Study of the Bororo', 383; Friar Antonio Malan, 'Da Cuiabá alle rive del vorticoso Araguaya', *Bolletino Salesiano*, 198−9, Oct. 1902; Colbacchini, *I Bororos Orientali*, 128.
410 *cattle suffered hunger.'* Ibid., 128.
411 *to frighten them.'* Viveiros, *Rondon conta sua vida*, 67. Travelling in this region with some Bororo almost ninety years after the building of the telegraph line, the author saw a line of decayed poles and found their heavy ceramic insulators.
411 *have been victims."'* Ibid., 78−9.
411 *presence is disagreeable.'* Ibid., 93. Gomes Carneiro died a hero's death fighting in the battle of Lapa in 1893 against a revolution launched by José de Melho and Saldanha da Gama

against the new republic. Rondon worked from 1890 to 1898 on the new telegraph line and building a road along its route between Cuaibá and Goiás.
412 *of pinga [rum].'* Ibid., 140.
412 *of using them.'* Report by Friar Giovanni Balzola, *Bolletino Salesiano*, 125, May 1896; Colbacchini, *I Bororos Orientali*, 143.
412 *the daily thunderstorms.'* W. A. Cook, 'The Bororo Indians of Matto Grosso, Brazil', *Smithsonian Miscellaneous Collections* 50 48, Washington, DC, 1908.
413 *bows and arrows.'* Ibid., 49.
413 *in the water.'* Ibid., 56.
413 *search of food.'* Ibid., 60.
413 *mounted on it.'* Ibid., 58.
413 *and foul smelling.'* Ibid., 51.
414 *fire preparing food.'* Ibid., 51. There are, of course, many more expert ethnographic accounts of the Bororo, notably by Antonio Colbacchini, Herbert Baldus, Claude Lévi-Strauss, Robert H. Lowie, Arthur Ramos and Vincent M. Petrullo.
414 *to shapeless masses.'* Colbacchini, *I Bororos Orientali*, 132; Frič and Radin, 'Contributions to the Study of the Bororo', 383.
414 *did domestic work.'* Friar Giovanni Balzola, 'Una fortunata escursione', *Bolletino Salesiano*, Oct. 1908, and 'Da Cuiabá alle sponde del Rio Vermelho', *Bolletino Salesiano*, Nov. 1908−Jan. 1909; Colbacchini, *I Bororos Orientali*, 133−4.
415 *for the Fathers.'* A. Henry Savage-Landor, *Across Unknown South America*, 2 vols (London, New York, Toronto, 1913) 1 281. The great Cândido Rondon also visited some of these missions in that same year, and was less impressed: Amílcar A. Botelho de Magalhães, *Impressões da Comissão Rondon* (São Paulo, 1942) 118−19. By this time, the Salesians had various missions, all well to the east of Cuiabá: Sagrado Coração de Jesus (or Tachos) on the Barreiro; Imaculada Conceição on the Garças;

Sangradouro on the river of that name; and Palmeiras. They reckoned that they had five hundred Indians living in these missions, and that there were a further 1037 Eastern Bororo living beyond missionary control (Colbacchini, *I Bororos Orientali*, 168). The Eastern Bororo called themselves Orarimugu, meaning '*pintado* fish'; or Orarimugu-dogue — dogue is a plural suffix. Sangradouro is still a Salesian mission, although the majority of its inhabitants are now Chavante who fled there from across the Rio das Mortes when their territories were invaded in the 1960s. When I visited Sangradouro in 1972, its Bororo were still distressed that the linear plan of their village violated tribal custom: they badly wanted a men's house in the centre.

415 *basin with impunity.*' Colbacchini, *I Bororos Orientali*, 133.

Chapter 21　XINGU

416 *of its course.*' Karl von den Steinen, *Durch Central-Brasilien* (Leipzig, 1886) 2, or Portuguese translation by Catarina Baratz Cannabrava (São Paulo and Rio de Janeiro, 1942) 24. The English explorer William Chandless described the western Bakairi in 1862 as 'a small and very timid tribe' ('Notes on the Rivers Arinos, Juruena and Tapajós', *JRGS* **32** 270, 1862) and this was confirmed in presidential reports of Mato Grosso: by Herculano Ferreira Pena, 1862, 120; by A. M. Albino de Carvalho, 1864; and by a report attached to the annual address by Francisco José Cardoso Junior, 1872. This last report said that there were about two hundred Bakairi on the upper Arinos and upper Teles Pires (then called Paranatinga) and that they welcomed acculturation.

417 *is a clearing.*' Steinen, *Durch Central-Brasilien*, 157; trans., 187.

417 *one behind him.*' Ibid., 158; trans., 187.

418 *feeling of relief.*' Ibid.; trans., 188.

419 *shoot them dead.*' Ibid., 159–60; trans., 189–90.

419 *and refuse tobacco.*' Ibid., 165; trans., 195.

419 *me with animation.*' Ibid., 181; trans., 217.

420 *broad, straight avenue.*' Ibid., 188; trans., 223.

420 *of the tropics.*' Ibid., 187; trans., 221.

420 *from our beach.*' Ibid., 191–2; trans., 226.

420 *beat our chests.*' Ibid., 192; trans. (inaccurate here, as in other places), 227.

420 *to our camp.*' Ibid., 193; trans., 229.

420 *of the river.*' Ibid., 193; trans., 229.

421 *space of time.*' Ibid., 194; trans., 229.

421 *a similar fate.*' Ibid., 196; trans., 233.

421 *their huts overland.*' Ibid., 200; trans., 237.

422 *fixed on us.*' Ibid., 201; trans., 239.

422 *with these redskins.*' Ibid., 201–2; trans., 239–40.

422 *was in progress.*' Ibid., 202; trans., 240.

423 *the Medici Venus.*' Ibid., 204; trans., 242.

423 *in their decay.*' Steinen, *Unter den Naturvölkern Zentral-Brasiliens* (Berlin, 1894) 64.

424 *to cause it.*' Ibid., 58.

424 *and natural openness.*' Ibid., 190–1.

424 *might upset me.*' Ibid., 64.

424 *and curious wrappings.*' Ibid.; *Durch Central-Brasilien*, 160.

425 *be well received.*' Steinen, *Unter den Naturvölkern*, 69–70. A few weeks later, Steinen asked the Suyá to draw their map, which was even more accurate.

426 *than one woman!*' Steinen, *Durch Central-Brasilien*, 220; trans., 261. This proposition to attack the Trumai was made far down the Xingu, north of the mouth of the Manitsaua-miçu

and close to the Von Martius Rapids. The few survivors of the Trumai now live alongside Pôsto Leonardo, hundreds of kilometres up-river from there.

426 *luck to you!*' Ibid., 202; trans., 240.

426 *research and exploration.*' Ibid., 224; trans., 266. Martius had passed the mouth of the Xingu when he and Spix went up the Amazon in 1819. The German expedition of Prince Adalbert of Prussia and Count von Bismarck had explored up the Xingu, almost as far up-river as the Von Martius Rapids, in 1845. The rapids are still called Cachoeira Von Martius.

427 *of our race.*' Coudreau, *Voyage au Xingu* (Paris, 1897) 81. Nimuendajú, 'Tribes of the Lower and Middle Xingu', HSAI 3 218−19, 222−3.

429 *from the Culiseiu.*' Hermann Meyer, 'Bericht über seine zweite Xingu-Expedition', *Verhandlungen der Gesell-* *schaft für Erdkunde zu Berlin* **27** 126−7, 1900.

429 *so many canoes.*' Meyer, 'Über seine Expedition nach Central-Brasilien', 187.

430 *endless flute concert.*' Ibid., 192.

430 *the wrong time.*' Max Schmidt, *Indianerstudien in Zentralbrasilien* (Berlin, 1905) 49. On the various other ill-fated expeditions, see: ibid., 23−4 and 37; Schmidt, 'Os Bakairi', 19; Eduardo Galvão and Mário F. Simões, 'Mudança e sobrevivencia no alto Xingu', *Revista de Antropologia* (São Paulo, 1966) **14** 38. Colonel Paula Castro had been the lieutenant in charge of the soldiers on Steinen's second expedition of 1887.

430 *than a visit.*' Schmidt, *Indianerstudien*, 74.

431 *ready to fire.*' Ibid., 86.

431 *for two days*'. Ibid., 87.

431 *one of these.*' Ibid., 108.

Chapter 22 **THE PARAGUAY RIVER**

432 *sun and wind.*' Georg Langsdorff diary entry for 26 Dec. 1826, in Barman, 'The Forgotten Journey', 84−5; Florence, *Esboço da viagem*, 428−31.

433 *of all tribes*'. Florence, *Esboço da viagem*, 248.

433 *poorer than I.*"' Henrique de Beaurepaire Rohan, 'Viagem de Cuyabá ao Rio de Janeiro ...', RHGB **9** 378, 1847 or 1869. Castelnau, *Expédition*, **3** 10 19. Bartolomé Rossi, *Viage pintoresco por los ríos Paraná, Paraguay* ... (Paris, 1863) 49. Joaquim Alves Ferreira, Director of Indians of Mato Grosso, Report to Ministro de Negócios do Império, Cuiabá, 2 Dec. 1848, in Max Schmidt, 'Resultados de mi tercera expedición a los Guatós, efectuada en el año de 1928', *Revista de la Sociedad Científica del Paraguay* **5**:6 72, Asunción, 1942.

433 *to simple men.*' Rohan, 'Viagem', 377.

Moure, 'Indiens', 81−3.

434 *over flooded land.*' Augusto Leverger, Barão de Melgaço, 'Guatós', in Mello Moraes Filho, *Revista da Exposição Anthropologica*, 122−3.

434 *way of life.*' Leverger, Report as Vice-President of Mato Grosso, Cuiabá, 1863, 13.

434 *the dead man*'. Julio Koslowski, 'Tres semanas entre los indios Guatós', *Revista del Museo de La Plata* **6** 247, 1895.

434 *of this disease.*' Ibid., 234−5.

435 *a short time.*' Koslowski, 'Tres semanas', 235. Mello Moraes confirmed this decimation, but he reported angrily that the Guató, who had appeared so friendly to the settlers, had revealed their hatred by killing some of the defeated garrisons of Coimbra and Corumbá and refusing to help others by ferrying them to Cuiabá in their canoes. Mello

Moraes Filho, *Revista da Exposição Anthropologica*, 99.

435 *woes they felt.'* Koslowski, 'Tres semanas', 237—8.

436 *be treated leniently.* Florence, *Esboço da viagem*, 413—15. For an account of the fighting between Mbayá (Kadiwéu) and Paraguayans, see J. R. Rengger, *Reise nach Paraguay in den Jahren 1818 bis 1826* (Aarau, 1835) 335—40.

436 *reptiles and insects.'* Castelnau, *Expédition*, 2 394. Castelnau's figure of two thousand for the population of Albuquerque may have been exaggerated. Henrique Rohan was there the following year (1846) and gave 1600 as its native population (*Viagem de Cuyabá ao Rio de Janeiro*, 381). An official report by President Ricardo José Gomes Jardim of the same year gave 1300: *Creacão da directoria dos indios na Provincia de Mato Grosso*, RHGB 9 549, 1847 or 1869.

436 *one with horror!'* Castelnau, *Expédition*, 2 404.

436 *pieces of cloth.'* Florence, *Esboço da viagem*, 425.

438 *whom they massacred.'* Castelnau, *Expédition*, 2 469. Kalervo Oberg, 'The Terena and the Caduveo of Southern Mato Grosso, Brazil', *Smithsonian Institution, Institute of Social Anthropology* 9 3—4, Washington, DC, 1949. Joaquim Francisco Lopes, 'Itinerario... entre S. Paulo e Matto-Grosso', RHGB 13 322, 327, 1850 or 1872, on Terena raiding in 1848.

438 *for their subsistence.'* Report by President Augusto Leverger, Cuiabá, 1856, 17—18, and reports by this same president, 1851, 44—5, and 1854, 33. The Kinikinao aldeia thirty kilometres from Albuquerque was called Matto Grande and had seven hundred people in 1851; by 1856 it as known as Bom Conselho. The missionaries also attempted to convert a small group of Chamakoko, a Zamuko-speaking tribe of the Chaco, who had settled near Albuquerque: these sent a delegation to Cuiabá in 1854 to ask for protection against the

Caduvéo. Moreira Neto, *Política indigenista*, 145, 147, 149—50.

438 *capital city [Cuiabá].'* Report by Herculano Ferreira Pena, Cuiabá, 1862, 117. Moreira Neto, *Política indigenista*, 151.

438 *of our population.'* Report by Vice-President Augusto Leverger, Cuiabá, 1863, 13. Moreira Neto, ibid., 158. In 1864 the Capuchin missionary who had been running the Kinikinao aldeia, Friar Angelo de Caramonico, was transferred to try to convert the newly settled Kaiwá and Kaingáng near Dourados. There had been disturbances and serious allegations against Friar Angelo, which was why he was removed from the Kinikinao aldeia do Bom Conselho. Friar Mariano de Bagnaia was in charge of the Terena aldeias near Miranda in 1863. He was removed by President José Cardoso Junior in 1872, on the recommendation of the provincial Diretor Geral de Indios, and replaced by a cavalry major.

439 *they decorate themselves.'* Survey by Diretor Geral dos Indios de Matto Grosso, annexed to presidential report by Francisco José Cardoso Junior, Cuiabá, 1872, in Moreira Neto, *Política indigenista*, 166—7.

439 *air of superiority.'* João Enrique Elliott, 'Itinerario das viagens exploradoras...', RHGB 10 169—70, 1848 or 1870. Elliott was the son of an American father and an English mother, who served in the United States and then the Brazilian navies. He settled in Curitiba in 1840, when he was thirty-one, and served on various expeditions organised by the Baron of Antonina.

440 *rank of Captain. . . .'* Bartolomé Rossi, *Viage pintoresco por los ríos Paraná . . .* (Paris, 1863) 28. Couto de Magalhães, *O selvagem*, 165.

441 *they gave us.'* Francisco Raphael de Mello Rego, 'O Forte de Coimbra' (1892), RHGB 67:2, 184, 1904. Roberto Cardoso de Oliveira, *O processo de assimilação dos Terêna* (Rio de

Janeiro, 1960) 65—6.
441 *shoot their game.'* George Thompson, *The War in Paraguay* (London, 1869) 203. Alfredo d'Escragnolle Taunay, *A retirada de Laguna* (14th edn, São Paulo, 1957).
441 *on the Bonito.'* Alfredo d'E. Taunay, *Memórias do Visconde de Taunay* (edn São Paulo, 1948) 268.
442 *to the usurer.'* Missão Rondon, *Relatório dos trabalhos realizados de 1900—1906* (Rio de Janeiro, 1949) 83. Cardoso de Oliveira, *O processo de assimilação*, 69.
442 *police chief, orders.'* Rondon, *Relatório*, 83. Viveiros, *Rondon conta sua vida*, 179—80.
443 *notice two alike.'* Lévi-Strauss, *Tristes tropiques*, 192, or trans. by John and Doreen Weightman (London, 1973) 187. Guido Boggiani, *Viaggi d'un artista nell'America Meridionale. I Caduvei*

(Mbayá o Guaycurú) (Rome, 1895) figs 43, 74, 90, etc., also trans. Amadeu Amaral Júnior, *Os Caduveo* (São Paulo, 1945). Herbert Baldus, in an important introduction to this translation, wrote of the Caduveo shaman and the visiting Czech anthropologist Vojtěch Frič, pp. 36—8. The story about the visit of the Brazilian warship *Maracanã* is in Claudio Soido, 'Guaicurus', in Mello Moraes Filho, *Revista da Exposição Anthropologica*, 92. Thekla Hartmann, *A contribuição da iconografia*, 124—9. Alfred Métraux, 'Ethnography of the Chaco', HSAI 1 217—18, 280—4.
443 *to their village.'* Viveiros, *Rondon conta sua vida*, 180. Fernando Altenfelder Silva, 'Mudança cultural dos Terena', RMP n.s. 3 285, 1949; Oliveira, *O processo*, 67, 84. Rondon, *Relatório*, 81.

Chapter 23   *KAINGÁNG DEFIANCE*

444 *etc. among them.'* João Enrique Elliott, 'Resume do itinerario de uma viagem exploradora pelos rios Verde, Itarere, Parapanema . . .', RHGB 9 18, 1847 or 1869. The village of Chief Manal was called São João Baptista and was on the Verde river 110 kilometres from the Baron Antonina's fazenda Perituva near modern Curitiba.
445 *dead beside it.'* Ibid., 35.
445 *and other trinkets.'* Ibid., 36. Elliott called this group by the pejorative word bugres and said that the expedition judged them to be 'Botocudos' or Xokleng. But he noted that the men wore amber-coloured stone plugs in their lower lips, which was a favourite ornament of the Kaiwá and other Tupi-speaking tribes. The men of the tribe asked for cigarettes in bad Spanish — a further indication that they were

Kaiwá who had migrated from former Jesuit missions farther to the west.
445 *of great beauty.'* Ibid.
446 *before their departure.'* João Enrique Elliott, 'A emigração dos Cayuaz', RHGB 19 438, 1856. On slave raids against the Kaiwá by neighbouring tribes: Debret, *Viagem pitoresca*, 1 17; Florence, *Esboço da viagem*, 414; Castelnau, *Expédition*, 2 395—6.
446 *body leaning backwards.'* Lopes, *Itinerario*, 318—19.
446 *them very well'*. Ibid., 334.
446 *entrusted to him.'* Ibid., 438—9.
447 *in their necessities.'* Ibid., 441. For a summary of these expeditions, see Plínio M. da Silva, 'As entradas de Joaquim Francisco Lopes e João Enrique Elliott', *Revista do Instituto Histórico* 28, São Paulo, 1930.
447 *from their chiefs'*. Lopes, *Itinerario*, 444.
447 *delighted the Indians.'* Ibid., 446.

447 *into the trees.'* Ibid. John Henry Elliot planned to publish a Descriptive Corography of the Province of Paraná and did a number of water-colours for this. His drawings of Indians are stiff and naïve, but accurate in detail. The manuscript of his unpublished work is in the Mapoteca of the Brazilian Ministry of External Relations, Itamarati. Another artist who painted the Kaiwá was the German engineer Franz Keller, who was commissioned with his father to explore the Ivaí, Paranapanema and Tibagi rivers during the Paraguayan War in 1863. See Thekla Hartmann, *A contribuição da iconografia*, 117–20.

448 *arrogance and force.'* Franz Keller, *Noções sobre os indígenas da Provincia do Paraná* (1866), in Lêda A. Lovato, 'A contribuição de Franz Keller à etnografia do Paraná', *Boletim do Museu do Índio. Antropologia* 3 12, Rio de Janeiro, November 1974.

448 *in the aldeia.'* Ibid., 15. Telêmaco Borba, who was in charge of São Pedro de Alcantara from 1863 to 1873, wrote that it had originally had 400–600 Kaiwá in 1854. Telêmaco Morosini Borba, *Actualidade indígena* (Curitiba, 1908) 51.

448 *navigating the Paranapanema.'* Colonel Francisco Raimundo Ewerton Quadros, 'Memoria sobre os trabalhos de observação e exploração . . . da linha telegraphica de Uberaba a Cuiabá' (Feb.–June 1881), RHGB 55:1 250–1, 1892.

448 *the government's discretion.'* Annual report by A. M. Albino de Carvalho, Cuiabá, 1865, 88–9. Moreira Neto, *Política indigenista*, 161. Dr Amédée Moure had predicted that the Kaiwá would soon be peacefully incorporated into the Brazilian Empire, in 1862. He described them as 10,000–12,000 sedentary farmers, living on the Iguatemi and upper Paraná rivers. Moure, 'Indiens', 331–2.

448 *quality among savages'.* Survey by Diretor Geral dos Indios de Mato Grosso, attached to annual report by President Francisco José Cardoso Junior, Cuiabá, 1872, in Moreira Neto, *Política indigenista*, 165. It was known by this time that Friar Angelo de Caramonico had been captured and killed by the Paraguayans during the war.

449 *they look machine-made.'* Keller, *Noções*, 15–16.

449 *Indians] to work. . . .'* President Francisco Antonio de Souza Queiroz, Ofício, São Paulo, 12 Sept. 1835, in A. P. Canabrava, 'Documentos sôbre os índios do rio Juquiá', RMP n.s. 3 391, São Paulo, 1949. Thirty-three Indians were named in this document, with their ages and the families to which they were assigned.

450 *their rightful property.'* Speech to provincial assembly by Marshal Manoel da Fonseca Lima e Silva, São Paulo, 7 Jan. 1847, 101. Carlos Moreira Neto, 'Some data concerning . . . the Kaingáng Indians', 292.

450 *of the earth.'* Speech by President Dr Domiciano Leite Ribeiro, São Paulo, 25 June 1848, 14, in ibid., 292–3.

450 *few poor Indians.'* Ibid. The four aldeias to be revived were: Carapucuyba, Baruery, Itaquaquecetuba and São Miguel.

451 *granted to them.'* Speech by Dr José Thomaz Nabuco d'Araújo, São Paulo, 1 May 1852, 31, in ibid., 294.

451 *has happened there'.* Ibid., 294.

452 *any active resistance.'* Report by President of São Paulo, Manuel Felisardo de Souza e Mello, São Paulo, 7 Jan. 1844, 50, in ibid., 297.

452 *attacked his shelter.'* Telemaco Borba, *Actualidade indígena* (Curitiba, 1908) 5 28; Silvio Coelho dos Santos, *A integração do índio na sociedade regional: A função dos postos indigenas em Santa Catarina* (Florianópolis, Santa Catarina, 1970) 35.

452 *Condá and Viry'.* Ibid.

453 *devastation among them.'* Reinhold Hensel, 'Die Coroados der brasilianischen Provinz Rio Grande do Sul', *Zeitschrift für Ethnologie* 1 124–

35, Berlin, 1869, or translated in *Revista do Museu e Archivo Público do Rio Grande do Sul* **20** 65, 1928.

453 *with their intrigues.'* Report by President João Lins Vieira Cansansao Sinimbú, Pôrto Alegre, 2 Oct. 1854, 30−1, Moreira Neto, 'Some data', 308. The Indians moved to Nonoái in 1849 were those of Portela in Passo Fundo: report by President João Capistrano de Miranda Castro, Pôrto Alegre, 4 March 1848, 20−1.

454 *more accessible places.'* Report by President Francisco José da Rocha, Florianópolis, 1887 (published Rio de Janeiro, 1888) 346, in ibid., 305.

454 *and eventual extermination.'* Ibid., 308.

454 *the province's settlements'.* Report by President Joaquim Antão Fernandes Leão transferring the presidency of Rio Grande do Sul to his successor, Pôrto Alegre, 1861, 19; and similar reports by the Baron of Curitiba, 28 April 1856; Patricio Corrêa da Camara, 1857; and by Angelo Moniz da Silva Ferras and Patricio Corrêa da Camara, 1859. A detailed account of the movements of the Kaingáng during these years is in ibid., 308−10.

454 *mean their death.'* Ibid.

454 *to their ravages.'* Hensel, 'Die Coroados ... Rio Grande do Sul', *Zeitschrift für Ethnologie* **1** 129, Berlin, 1869.

455 *thus became friends.'* Beschoren, 'Beiträge zur nähern Kenntnis', 24.

456 *and Ivaí valleys.'* Borba, *Actualidade indígena*, 51; Lovato, 'A contribuição de Franz Keller', 36.

456 *the Palmas plains.'* Keller, *Noções*, 20; Lovato, 'A contribuição de Franz Keller', 20.

456 *the former enemies.'* Ibid.

457 *adopting our customs.'* Report by President Dr Venâncio José de Oliveira Lisboa, Curitiba, 15 Feb. 1872, 67, Moreira Neto, 'Some data', 300.

457 *pure European blood'.* Report of President José Pedrosa, Curitiba, 1881, in ibid., 301.

457 *these to peace.'* Luís Bueno Horta Barboza, *O Serviço de Protecção aos Índios e a historia da colonização do Brasil* (Rio de Janeiro, 1919) 24. Beschoren, 'Beiträge zur nähern Kenntnis', 15. Bandeira, *A cruz indígena*, 83. The Capuchins in 1868 were Virgilio de Amplar at Lages and Estevam de Vicenza at Itajaí.

458 *a sarcastic farewell.'* Luis de Cemetille quoted by Alfredo d'Escragnolle Taunay, 'Os indios Caingangs (Coroados de Guarapuava)', RHGB supplement to **51** 267, 1888. The historian Taunay was President of Paraná in 1885−6.

458 *'vigilant guards'.* Report by President Carlos de Carvalho, Curitiba, 1883, 89, in ibid., 302. The Sete Quedas ('Seven Waterfalls') on the Paraná were some of the world's most spectacular falls, but are now lost beneath the gigantic Itaipú hydroelectric dam.

458 *his intrepid companions.'* Ibid.

458 *as many claim.'* José Francisco Thomaz do Nascimento, 'Viagem pelos desconhecidos sertões de Guarapuava, Provincia do Paraná', RHGB **49**:2 273, 1886.

459 *women's sexual organs.'* Hugo Gensch, *Die Erziehung eines Indianerkindes*, in Bandeira, *A cruz indígena*, 87.

459 *terrified by surprise.'* Eduardo de Lima e Silva Hoerhan, Report of 1910 to SPI, in Darcy Ribeiro, *Os indios e a civilização*, 109−10.

459 *inhabitants of Brazil.'* Report by Marques de Olinda, Rio de Janeiro, 1858, 56.

459 *the civilised inhabitants.'* Report by J. A. Pereira Filho, Ministro do Imperio, Rio de Janeiro, 1860, in Moreira Neto, *Política indigenista*, 89.

460 *their parents' barbarity.'* Manoel Felizardo de Sousa e Mello, Minister of Agriculture (this ministry had taken over Indian affairs from the Ministro do Imperio in 1861), Rio de Janeiro, 1861, 74, in ibid., 90.

460 *emigration to Brazil.'* Barros Barreto, Minister of Agriculture, Rio de Janeiro, 1872, 21, in ibid., 91.

460 *these barbarians' children.'* President of Santa Catarina, Dr João Coutinho, speech to provincial assembly, 1856, in Sílvio Coelho dos Santos, *A integração do índio na sociedade regional: a função dos Postos Indigenas em Santa Catarina* (Florianópolis, 1970) 32.

460 *assailants to flight'.* J. Antonio Saraiva, Minister of Agriculture, Rio de Janeiro, 1882, 103–4, in Moreira Neto, *Política indigenista*, 91.

460 *of our civilisation.'* Colonel Francisco Raimundo Ewerton Quadros, *Memoria sobre os trabalhos*, 253.

460 *of their assaults.'* José Deeke, *Das Munizip Blumenau und seine Entwicklungsgeschichte* (São Leopoldo, 1917) 3 71–2; Francisco S. G. Schaden, 'Xokléng e Kaingáng', in Egon Schaden (ed.), *Homem, cultura e sociedade no Brasil*, 86. José Ferreira da Silva, *Blumenau em cadernos* (Blumenau, 1967) 104.

461 *their daily food.'* Report by President Galdino Pimentel, Pôrto Alegre, 1889, 34. The report by President Carlos Thompson Flores of 1880 had revealed the following distribution of Kaingáng in Rio Grande do Sul: Fongui's people, 250 at Nhacorá, 100 at Guarita, 140 at Pinheiro Ralo; Nonoái, 285 people; Doble's tribe, 200 at Pontão; Captain Chico, 140 at Cazeros; Campo do Meio, 90; Campos of José Bueno, 50. Moreira Neto, 'Some data', 310.

461 *stop such attacks.'* A. F. de Souza Pitanga, 'O indio brasileiro perante o direito', RHGB 58:1, 24, 1901.

461 *and blood-curdling laughter'.* Report by President Francisco José da Rocha, Florianópolis, 1887 (printed Rio de Janeiro, 1888) 344, in Moreira Neto, 'Some data', 304.

461 *'barbarous revenge'.* Ibid., 344.

461 *and kills them.'* Ibid.

462 *could for you."'* An incident in 1919 described by Eduardo Hoerhan to Darcy Ribeiro, in his *Os índios e a civilisação*, 400. Another German colonist, Krause, also tried to educate a thirteen-year-old Xokleng girl: Dr Wettstein, *Brasilien und die*

deutsch-brasilienische Kolonie Blumenau (Leipzig, 1907) 57.

463 *into the forests.'* Gustav von Koenigswald, 'Die Coroados im südlichen Brasilien', *Globus* 94:2, 27, Braunschweig, July 1908. On the westward movement of the frontier in São Paulo: Bruno Giovanetti, *Esboço histórico da Alta Soro-cabana* (São Paulo, n.d.) 168; Amador Coimbra, *Recanto do sertão paulista* (São Paulo, 1943) 268; Edgard Lage de Andrade, *Sertões do noroeste, 1850–1945* (São Paulo, 1946) 169–80; Fausto Ribeiro de Barros, 'Um ciclo pastoril nos campos de Avanhandava', *Anais do IX Congresso Brasileiro de Geografia* 5 631–44, Rio de Janeiro, 1944; Pierre Monbeig, *Pionniers et planteurs de São Paulo* (Paris, 1952) 84–6, 114–16.

463 *who remained unpunished.'* João C. Gomes Ribeiro, *Suum cuique tribuere – Esboço de um projeto de lei sôbre os índios do Brasil* (Rio de Janeiro, 1912) 8; Herbert Baldus, *Bibliografia crítica da etnologia brasileira* (São Paulo, 1954) 1 582–3.

464 *men were massacred.'* Clovis de Gusmão, *Rondon: a conquista do deserto brasileiro* (Rio de Janeiro, 1942) 123–4; Amílcar A. Botelho de Magalhães, *Rondon, uma relíquia da patria* (Curitiba, 1942) 69.

464 *ransack the encampment.'* *Correio da Manhã*, Rio de Janeiro, 16 Oct. 1908; David Hall Stauffer, *The Origin and Establishment of Brazil's Indian Service* (Austin, Texas, 1955) 12.

464 *that awaited them.'* Report by bugreiro João Pedro to Commission of Enquiry into conflicts in the zone of the Estado de Ferro Noroeste, 1911 (ms. in archive of Serviço de Proteção aos Índios, now FUNAI) 17–18. Darcy Ribeiro, *Os índios e a civilização*, 105.

464 *arose from this.'* Darcy Ribeiro, *Os índios e a civilização*, 105.

464 *real people, Lieutenant.'* Ibid., 105.

465 *that spared nobody.'* Ibid., 106.

465 *from their victims.'* Ibid. Also, Bandeira, *A cruz indígena*, 75–7.

465 *states of Brazil!'* Vojtěch Frič,

'Sambaqui-Forschungen im Hafen von Antonina (Paraná)', *Globus* **91**:8, 121, Braunschweig, 28 Feb. 1907. Also, Alberto Frič, 'Völkerwanderungen, Ethnographie und Geschichte der Konquista in Südbrasilien',

Verhandlungen des XVI. Internationalen Amerikanisten-Kongresses (Vienna and Leipzig, 1910) **1** 65–6.
465 *on the ground."* ' Ibid.
465 *of the forest.* Ibid.

Chapter 24 EXTERMINATION OR PROTECTION?

466 *of the Empire?'* F. A. de Varnhagen, *Memorial organico* (Madrid, 1849, amended in 1850 and republished in the literary review *Guanabara*, Rio de Janeiro, 1851), quoted in Varnhagen, *Os indios bravos e o Sr. Lisboa, Timon 3°* (Lima, 1867) 40.
466 *of the nation.'* Ibid., 41.
466 *freedom of communications'*. Ibid., 60.
467 *when treated kindly.'* Ibid., 61.
467 *Christians of them.'* Ibid., 42.
467 *in an asylum.'* Ibid., 61.
467 *are our convictions.'* Varnhagen, *Memorial organico*, in J. F. Lisboa, *Obras* (Lisbon, 1901) 2. Carlos Moreira Neto, 'Constante histórica do "indigenato" no Brasil', ASBA Antropologia) **2** 178–9, 1967.
467 *civilisation of nations.'* Moreira Neto, 'Constante histórica', 179. The bishop whom Varnhagen quoted was Azeredo Coutinho.
467 *of their forests.'* Ibid.
468 *people, now extinct.'* Gonçalves Dias, *Os Timbiras* (1857). Fernando de Azevedo, *Cultura brasileira*, trans. William Rex Crawford, *Brazilian culture* (New York, 1950) 207; Paul Teyssier, 'Le mythe indianiste dans la littérature brésilienne', *Annales du Faculté des Lettres de Toulouse* **7**:1–2, *Littérature* **6** 108–9, 1958; Frédéric Mauro, 'Le rôle des Indiens et des noirs dans la conscience européisante des blancs: le cas du Brésil', *Cahiers des Amériques Latines* **9–10** 202–4, Paris, 1974; Antônio Cândido de Mello e Souza, 'A literatura durante o Império', in Sérgio Buarque de Holanda (ed.), *História geral da civilização brasileira*, II: *O Brasil monárquico* (São Paulo, 1982) **3** 346–7; L. S.

Rebelo, 'Brazilian literature', in S. Collier, H. Blakemore and T. E. Skidmore (eds), *The Cambridge Encyclopedia of Latin America and the Caribbean* (Cambridge, 1985) 370.
468 *shame! oh ruin!'* Gonçalves Dias, *Canção do Tamoio*, in Viveiros, *Rondon conta sua vida*, 330. Claudio Soido, 'Guaicurus', 115. The most thorough description in English of the Indianist literary movement is David Miller Driver, *The Indian in Brazilian Literature* (New York, 1942), 42–143.
470 *about the Republic'*. Rodrigo Otávio, *Os selvagens americanos perante o direito* (São Paulo, 1946) 154; Leda Maria Cardoso Naud, 'Índios e indigenismo: histórico e legislação', 239. Laws about Indians during the last decades of the Empire were: 2 Jan. 1854, Aviso to use forced labour by Indians in Maranhão; 25 April 1857, instructions for Indian colónias in Paraná and Mato Grosso, stressing use of missionaries; Law of 27 Sept. 1860 provided funds for religious conversion of Indians, but ordered the sale of abandoned old mission lands; 1861, Indian affairs were transferred from the Ministerio do Imperio to the Ministerio da Agricultura; 7 Dec. 1866, Amazon river basin opened to foreign shipping; 19 May 1862, Aviso abolishing various aldeias in São Paulo, Pernambuco, Paraíba and Sergipe; 30 Aug. 1865, Aviso giving habeas corpus rights to Indians imprisoned for more than six days; 21 Sept. 1870, Aviso creating Couto de Magalhães' Colegio for educating Indian children of the Araguaia river; Jan. 1875, contract

with Colonel Antonio Rodrigues Pereira Labre for protection and conversion of Indians of upper Purus river; 27 March 1872, abolition of aldeias in Pernambuco; 20 Oct. 1875, Law no. 2.672 removing lands of extinct aldeias; 8 March 1878, Decision about selling off mission lands; 20 Oct. 1887, Lei Orçamentária no. 3.348 awards unclaimed lands of extinct aldeias to local municipalities.

470 *and sympathetic nations'.* Ibid.

470 *of their lands.'* Oliveira, *Coletânea de leis,* 82; Otávio, *Os selvagens,* 155; Naud, 'Indios', 239; José Vicente César in *Jornal do Brasilia Cultura,* 12 Aug. 1973, 5; José Maria de Paula, 'Terra dos índios', *Boletim do Serviço de Proteção aos Índios* 1 65, Rio de Janeiro, 1944; Expedito Arnaud, 'O direito indígena e a ocupação territorial', RMP n.s. 28 222, 1981/2; Joe Foweraker, *The Struggle for Land* (Cambridge, 1981) 84–5.

473 *since colonial times.'* Rondon, 'O extermínio dos índios', *Jornal do Comércio,* Rio de Janeiro, 11 Feb. 1909; Stauffer, *Origin and Establishment,* 149.

474 *to exterminate them.'* Hermann von Ihering, *The Anthropology of the State of São Paulo* (São Paulo, 1906; trans. RMP, 1907); Sílvio de Almeida article, *Estado de São Paulo,* 12 Oct. 1908; Stauffer, *Origin and Establishment,* 66–7. For Alberto Frič's impassioned speech to the Congress in Vienna, see his 'Völkerwanderungen, Ethnographie und Geschichte der Konquista in Südbrasilien', 1 65–7.

474 *our best instincts'.* Luis Bueno Horta Barbosa, 'Em defesa dos indigenas brasileiros', *Jornal do Comércio,* Rio de Janeiro, 11 Nov. 1908, in Stauffer, *Origin and Establishment,* 70.

474 *will gradually disappear.'* Article by Ihering, *Estado de São Paulo,* 20 Oct. 1908. Stauffer, *Origin and Establishment,* 87.

475 *the same consideration.'* Ihering speech to Instituto Histórico e Geográfico de São Paulo, 20 Oct. 1908, in Stauffer, *Origin and Establishment,* 95.

475 *land of Brazil.'* Sílvio de Almeida in *Estado de São Paulo,* 26 Oct. 1908; Stauffer, *Origin and Establishment,* 105.

475 *of innocent persons.'* R. Teixeira Mendes to President of Brazil, published in *Jornal do Comércio,* 11 Nov. 1908; Stauffer, *Origin and Establishment,* 109.

475 *this criminal idea.'* Statement by Museu Nacional, *Jornal do Comércio,* 6 Dec. 1908, and *Archivos do Museu Nacional* 15 256ff. 1909; Stauffer, *Origin and Establishment,* 116.

475 *their manual labour.'* Leolinda Daltro lecture to Associação de Proteção aos Selvícolas do Brasil, in her *Da catechese dos índios no Brasil* (Rio de Janeiro, 1920) 623–4; Stauffer, *Origin and Establishment,* 119–20.

476 *uncivilised forest Indians.'* Hermann von Ihering, 'Extermínio dos indígenas ou dos sertanejos?', *Jornal do Comércio,* Rio de Janeiro, 15 Dec. 1908. Stauffer, *Origin and Establishment,* 126.

476 *exist or not.'* Ihering, 'Extermínio'; Stauffer, *Origin and Establishment,* 131.

477 *ignorance and poverty.'* Antonio Carlos Simoens da Silva, 'Protecção aos índios', *Anais do Primeiro Congresso Brasileiro de Geografia* 9 26, Rio de Janeiro, 1910; Stauffer, *Origin and Establishment,* 179; Nelson Coelho de Senna, 'Os índios do Brasil: memória ethnográphica' (Belo Horizonte, 1908) or *Trabajos del Cuarto Congresso Científico . . . Santiago de Chile* 17:3, 374–450, 1909. The Campinas Commission was called Comissão Promotora da Defesa dos Indios and was created on 27 March 1909. Its pamphlet was *A questão indígena: appello dirigida à opinião pública do Brasil* (Campinas, 1909).

478 *of its constitution.'* Leolinda Daltro, *Anais do Primeiro Congresso,* 1 236. Stauffer, *Origin and Establishment,* 184.

480 *lofty national aspiration'.* Circular by

Minister Rocha Miranda, 5 March 1910, in *Relatório do Ministério da Agricultura*, 1910, II, 13; *Jornal do Comércio*, 6 March 1910; Stauffer, *Origin and Establishment*, 234.

480 *as helpless rustics'*. Circular by Minister Rocha Miranda, 5 March 1910, in *Relatório*, 13, in Stauffer, *Origin and Establishment*, 235.

Index

A grid reference is given locating places and tribes on the five maps in this book (pp. xvi–xxi). References in brackets give locations for places not entered on the maps. 'Off maps' indicates that a place lies outside the area covered by the maps.

Picture Acknowledgements

The British Library: 1, 10, 12, 22. John Hemming: 2, 3, 13, 16, 17, 18, 19, 23, 24, 28, 29, 30, 32, 33, 34, 38, 39, 40, 41, 50, 51, 53. Museu Nacional de Arte Antiga, Lisbon: 20. Museum F. Völkerkunde, Vienna: 11. Royal Geographical Society: 4, 5, 6, 7, 8, 9, 14, 15, 21, 22, 25, 26, 27, 31, 35, 36, 37, 42, 43, 44, 45, 46, 47, 48, 49, 52, 54, 55, 56, 57, 58, 59, 60.